C447798400

NEWCASTLE UPON TYNE
CITY LIBRARIES

D0715112

920
LLO

LOYD GEORGE & CHURCHILL

RICHARD TOYE is a senior lecturer in the
department of history at the University of Exeter.
He lives in Exeter with his wife and son.

NEWCASTLE UPON TYNE CITY LIBRARIES	
Bertrams	27/10/2008
920 LLO	£8.99

RICHARD TOYE

LLOYD GEORGE
&
CHURCHILL

Rivals for Greatness

PAN BOOKS

First published 2007 by Macmillan

First published in paperback 2008 by Pan Books
an imprint of Pan Macmillan Ltd
Pan Macmillan, 20 New Wharf Road, London N1 9RR
Basingstoke and Oxford
Associated companies throughout the world
www.panmacmillan.com

ISBN 978-0-330-43472-0

Copyright © Richard Toye 2007

The right of Richard Toye to be identified as the
author of this work has been asserted by him in accordance
with the Copyright, Designs and Patents Act 1988.

Photographic Acknowledgements
Centre for the Study of Cartoons and Caricature, University of
Kent – 19, 24 (David Low, Evening Standard 1929 / Solo Syndication),
36 (David Low, Evening Standard 1945 / Solo Syndication). Empics – 21, 35.
Getty Images – 1, 2, 4, 7, 8, 9, 11, 12, 13, 14, 15, 17, 18, 20, 25, 26, 28, 30, 33, 37, 38, 39.
ITN / British Pathé – 27, 34. National Portrait Gallery, London – 16, 22, 23, 29, 31.
Pall Mall Gazette – 6. Punch Cartoon Library – 5, 10.

All rights reserved. No part of this publication may be
reproduced, stored in or introduced into a retrieval system, or
transmitted, in any form, or by any means (electronic, mechanical,
photocopying, recording or otherwise) without the prior written
permission of the publisher. Any person who does any unauthorized
act in relation to this publication may be liable to criminal
prosecution and civil claims for damages.

1 3 5 7 9 8 6 4 2

A CIP catalogue record for this book is available from
the British Library.

Typeset by SetSystems Ltd, Saffron Walden, Essex
Printed and bound in Great Britain by
Mackays of Chatham plc, Chatham, Kent

This book is sold subject to the condition that it shall not,
by way of trade or otherwise, be lent, re-sold, hired out,
or otherwise circulated without the publisher's prior consent
in any form of binding or cover other than that in which
it is published and without a similar condition including this
condition being imposed on the subsequent purchaser.

Visit **www.panmacmillan.com** to read more about all our books
and to buy them. You will also find features, author interviews and
news of any author events, and you can sign up for e-newsletters
so that you're always first to hear about our new releases.

Contents

Acknowledgements vii

Introduction – A Relationship and its Reputation 1

One – PATHS TO POWER, 1863–1905 11

Two – SUPPORTERS RAMPANT 38

Three – ALLIANCE UNDER STRAIN 72

Four – TOUT EST FINI 121

Five – DON'T GET TORPEDOED 159

Six – MASTER AND SERVANT 195

Seven – TWO WAYS OF LIBERALISM 238

Eight – POLITICS AND MEMORY 272

Nine – THESE TWO PIRATES 300

Ten – I SHALL WAIT UNTIL WINSTON IS BUST 336

Eleven – Epilogue 391

Notes 411

Bibliography 475

Index 489

Acknowledgements

This book could not have been written without the help and support of numerous people and institutions. Homerton College, Cambridge, provided a marvellous working environment. I am grateful to all the libraries and archives I have used in my research, which are listed in the bibliography; but special mention must go to the Churchill Archives Centre and its Director, Allen Packwood. He and his staff have been unfailingly helpful, efficient and supportive. I am also much indebted to my agent, Natasha Fairweather of A. P. Watt Ltd., who provided help and encouragement at all stages. My thanks go out, too, to my editor, Georgina Morley, and everyone else at Macmillan, who have collectively made the publishing process a very smooth one. Paul Corthorn, Julie Gottlieb, Ben Griffin and David Reynolds all read drafts of the book and were unfailingly insightful in their comments and suggestions. Such errors that remain are, of course, my own responsibility. My wife, Kristine, also read the entire manuscript, and her input was wonderfully helpful. It is to her, and our son Sven, that I dedicate this book.

I am grateful to the following individuals and organizations for granting their kind permission to reproduce copyright material: The Master, Fellows and Scholars of Churchill College, Cambridge (Clementine Churchill, Maurice Hankey, Eric Phipps); The Trustees of the Liddell Hart Centre for Military Archives (Basil Liddell Hart); Neville C. Masterman (Lucy Masterman); Lady Avon (Anthony Eden); Special Collections, Information Services, University of Birmingham (Neville Chamberlain, Austen Chamberlain, Francis Brett Young); The Viscount Addison (Christopher Addison); Mrs Jennifer Longford (for her own writings and those of Frances Stevenson); the National Library of Wales (David Lloyd George, Thomas Jones, A. J. Sylvester); Christopher Osborn (Margot Asquith); the Bodleian Library, on behalf of both the Bonham Carter family trustees and of Nuffield College (H. H. Asquith,

Stafford Cripps); the Parliamentary Archives (David Lloyd George, Lord Beaverbrook); Her Majesty Queen Elizabeth II (Royal Archives); The Viscount Tenby (Gwilym Lloyd George); and Curtis Brown Ltd., on behalf of the Estate of Sir Winston Churchill, Copyright Winston S. Churchill. Extracts from the diary of Wilfrid Scawen Blunt are reproduced by permission of the Syndics of the Fitzwilliam Museum to whom rights in this publication are assigned. Strenuous efforts have been made to contact copyright holders; anyone whose copyright has been inadvertently infringed should contact the publishers, who will be pleased to make the necessary arrangements.

Introduction

A Relationship and its Reputation

David Lloyd George and Winston Churchill were the two most
important figures in twentieth-century British politics. Not only were
both renowned wartime Prime Ministers, but they both also established impressive track records in terms of domestic reform. During
the inter-war years they both spent long periods out of office, yet
their exclusion from power helped cement their respective reputations
as far-sighted visionaries: Lloyd George put forward ambitious plans
to deal with mass unemployment, and Churchill warned against the
dangers of Nazism. The link between them spanned more than four
decades. The connection was not always as warm or comfortable as
they themselves at various times suggested. But it was undoubtedly,
for both, their most important single political relationship. Their
association – and intermittent alliance – was a factor in the widespread distrust that these two 'great contemporaries' attracted. They
were often spoken of in the same breath, frequently in harsh terms.
Talking privately in 1937, Stanley Baldwin, the Conservative Prime
Minister, repeated with approval a saying he had heard: 'L.G. was
born a cad and never forgot it; Winston was born a gentleman and
never remembered it'.[1]

There were significant contrasts between the two men's characters. Lloyd George was a notorious philanderer and virtual bigamist
(known as 'the Goat'), who sold honours to raise money for party
funds; but he was also a wonderful listener, speaker and organizer.
Churchill was irreproachable in his private life, but, for all his
qualities, lacked Lloyd George's gift of empathy and his interest in
others. Lord Hankey, the most influential civil servant of the age,
summarized the difference between them as follows: 'Imagine the
subject of balloons crops up. Winston, without a blink, will give you
a brilliant hour-long lecture on balloons. L.G., even if he has never

seen you before, will spend an hour finding out anything you know or think about them.'[2] There were also, of course, significant similarities between the two. Neither was a straightforward party man. Lloyd George, making coalition with the Conservatives his vehicle, destroyed the Liberals as a political force. Churchill 'ratted' from the Conservatives to the Liberals in 1904, and then 're-ratted' in the 1920s. Both were supreme egotists. Each was a non-Christian who, somewhat paradoxically, thought that Providence was preserving him for greatness. This seemed appropriate for an age in which politics was increasingly concerned with secular rather than religious issues, and yet at the same time seemed to place growing value on 'charisma', a quality previously associated with spiritual rather than worldly leaders.[3]

The two men lived during a period of fantastically rapid change. For example it was only in 1865, two years after Lloyd George's birth, that Joseph Lister first used carbolic acid as an antiseptic during surgery. Lloyd George died, eighty years later, mere months before the explosion of the first atomic bomb. Similarly, it was only in 1876, two years after Churchill was born, that Alexander Graham Bell made the world's first telephone call. Churchill died in the space age, eight years after the 1957 launch of the first Sputnik satellite. Technical change and social progress did not, by any means, always go hand in hand. Undoubtedly, though, the relationship between new technology and societal change influenced the landscape across which Lloyd George and Churchill moved as political actors.

It was a landscape they also helped shape. During World War I they each showed a strong interest in mechanized warfare, perhaps most notably in the development of the tank. Mechanization was an important aspect of the new era of 'total war', which in turn necessitated the planning of resources to meet the unprecedented demands placed upon the economy. It was in this field, in his role as Minister of Munitions (1915–16), that Lloyd George showed himself most startlingly inventive. (Churchill, who served in the same post in 1917–18, was not quite such an innovator, but still deserves considerable credit for helping to ensure that Britain had the weapons it required.) Although Lloyd George was not solely responsible for the bureaucratic revolution over which he presided, it is fair to say that the practice of British government has not been the same since.

Furthermore, the dramatic changes in technology and in the

nature of government were paralleled by the transformation of the conduct of politics. This was the age when Britain made its transition to mass democracy. There were major extensions of the franchise in 1867 and 1884, but it was only in 1918 that the vote was granted to all adult men. Some groups of women received the vote then too, but it was extended to all of them only in 1928. The process of democratization was viewed with trepidation by significant sections of the political classes. Some thought that the masses were so ignorant – and women so hysterical – that to give them the vote would be a step towards the end of civilization. (Although historians debate the electoral impact of the expansion of the electorate, it is a clear irony that it was accompanied not only by the rise of the Labour Party – which might have been expected – but also by the growing dominance of the Conservative Party, which had generally been inclined to resist the changes.) Even the most pessimistic politicians had to adjust to the demands of the new mass politics whilst others, Lloyd George and Churchill included, seized the opportunities it presented with positive enthusiasm. New policies became necessary, and the two men helped provide these, not least in their roles as Edwardian pioneers of the modern welfare state. Equally important was the grasp of a new political style. Lloyd George – like Gladstone before him – was a master of the mass meeting. (Churchill was not quite so brilliant in this regard, although even some of his critics conceded he was entertaining, if not moving. Edwin Montagu, a detractor from within the Liberal Party, wrote in 1909: 'He delights and he tickles, he even enthuses the audience he addresses – but when he has gone, so also has the memory of what he has said.'[4] Later on, though, Churchill's World War II broadcasts demonstrated an effectiveness on radio that Lloyd George never achieved.) But the willingness to reach out to the people was not without its costs, and led both men, in the pre-1914 era, to be labelled as demagogues who were ready to pander to the basest instincts of their audiences in the quest for popularity and votes. The distrust they aroused – which, it must be said, was not always wholly unjustified – does much to explain the course of their respective careers.

The relationship between Lloyd George and Churchill is thus not only interesting on its own terms; it also can be used as a lens through which to view some fundamental shifts in British society and politics, many of the consequences of which can still be felt today. That relationship was not only long but was frequently intense as well. They first met in February 1901, and they were in touch until a few weeks before Lloyd George's death in March 1945. Moreover, the links between them were politically significant for the great bulk of that period. For, although Lloyd George left office in 1922 and never returned, he was still a very significant figure. Dingle Foot MP wrote in 1967 that, 'Even after his fall Lloyd George remained until the last two years of his life, with the possible exception of Churchill, the most fascinating and dynamic figure in British politics.'[5] This may have been a slight exaggeration, but Churchill's strenuous efforts to persuade Lloyd George to join his War Cabinet in 1940 pay ample testament to the latter's continuing mesmeric capacity. Furthermore, a powerful mythology surrounded the relationship, and has largely been maintained since.

In the same way that they romanticized other aspects of their lives, the men themselves made an active contribution to this. Their version of the story was encapsulated – to give but one example – in speeches they made at a dinner in 1936, in celebration of the completion of Lloyd George's *War Memoirs*. Churchill said of Lloyd George: 'I personally have a feeling of gratitude towards him no matter how often I am riled at the line he takes and the things he does and the differences of opinion, I can never alter my foundation based on the affection and regard I have for him.' Lloyd George reciprocated in kind: 'in spite of the fact that we have fought against each other on many occasions there has never been an occasion when I could not call Mr. Winston Churchill my friend and I think that he could do the same'.[6]

In later years, many who had known them echoed this tale. For example, Lloyd George's eldest son, Richard (who was in many respects a hostile critic of his father), wrote of their 'link of true friendship . . . which was to sustain every pressure'.[7] Churchill's son Randolph, whilst not denying an element of rivalry between the two politicians, likewise wrote of a friendship 'which had its ups and downs: but with many disagreements on public affairs it remained firm until the end.'[8] It would not be fair to say that historians have always accepted this picture in its entirety. Many writers, including leading biographers of both men, have written sensitively and with some degree of scepticism about the relationship. Nonetheless, the image that Lloyd George and Churchill established has proved very influential, and few scholars have resisted making some kind of nod in its direction. Tellingly, of the two existing book-length studies of the pair (by Marvin Rintala and Robert Lloyd George respectively) one is subtitled *How Friendship Changed Politics* and the other *How a Friendship Changed History*.[9] They emerge from such treatment as joint men of destiny, sometimes kept down by the jealousy of others, but personally inseparable even when trading harsh words in the rough and tumble of political life.

This master-narrative of personal constancy spiced by manly disagreements over matters of state is, superficially, very attractive. It acknowledges the men's many wrangles, but removes their bitter taste. It cannot, however, be accepted at face value. As this book will demonstrate, Lloyd George and Churchill did not always feel affection towards one another, and at crucial moments the relationship broke down. At times they were brutally frank about each other's failings, and about the underlying realities of the connection between them. Lloyd George once said of Churchill: 'He would make a drum out of the skin of his own mother in order to sound his own praises.'[10] Another telling comment was made by Churchill in January 1916, when he was serving on the Western Front, having temporarily withdrawn from politics following a crisis in his career but hoping to make a comeback. He wrote to his wife that, although Lloyd George would not be sorry if he, Churchill, were killed, he would find it politically inconvenient. Therefore, even though her own severe criticisms of Lloyd George's personal disloyalty had much merit, she should stay in touch with him all the same – because he stood to be useful in the future.[11] Yet at other moments the claim that political conflict had never descended into personal acrimony was politically convenient for both Lloyd George and Churchill; hence, in part, their displays of comradeship and protestations of mutual devotion. This is not to say that their personal connection, and the things they said about it, should be viewed in a purely cynical way. If their joint myth was in many respects misleading, they derived emotional as well as political benefits from its creation. The process of building and manipulating the image of the relationship was, in fact, central to the relationship itself.

This book provides the most detailed and systematic account to date of that relationship. It is also a book about the image, myth and *reputation* of the relationship. This may seem an unusual concept. We usually think of individuals or institutions, rather than relationships, as having reputations. But the way these two men were perceived as individuals was for a long time wrapped up in the way that they were perceived jointly. Just as they often sought to portray themselves as matching up to an ideal of political friendship, so their detractors depicted them as a malign pairing. Lloyd George and Churchill acted as 'memory entrepreneurs' who actively and often consciously sought to embed their (individual and joint) actions within the historical record and to influence popular perceptions of the past.[12] But they were not the only such entrepreneurs – diarists, journalists, biographers, historians, lovers, wives, family members, and hangers-on contributed to their legend. Meanwhile, those who, like Baldwin, were hostile to Lloyd George and Churchill put their own negative spin on it, but in so doing reinforced its symbolic importance. The process by which the reputation of the relationship was established and contested, then, should be central to our understanding of the men themselves.

There are many questions to answer. At the end of the Great War Lloyd George was held in very high esteem by the public, just as Churchill was during World War II. He was thought to have made a decisive contribution to victory; and, unlike Churchill in 1945, he succeeded in winning the general election that came at the war's end. 'We must never let the little man go,' said Andrew Bonar Law, the leader of the Conservative Party, on the day of the Armistice;[13] yet four difficult post-war years later Law himself would play a key role in destroying Lloyd George's coalition, and personally replaced him as Prime Minister. Lloyd George's reputation has never since stood as high as it did in 1918; indeed, anecdotal evidence would suggest that today there is little popular awareness of Lloyd George's significance as a political figure and as a war leader. Even in his native Wales there are fewer streets and buildings named after him than after Churchill.[14] He did not receive the customary memorial in Westminster Abbey until 1970, and there is still no outdoor statue of him in London (although plans are afoot to erect one in Parliament Square).

Churchill, by contrast, retains an iconic status that is much more powerful. During his lifetime he was seen by many contemporaries as hot-headed, irresponsible, and wildly opportunistic. Yet in the decades since his retirement and death, political leaders ranging from John F. Kennedy and Lyndon B. Johnson to Margaret Thatcher and Ronald Reagan have invoked him as a symbol of courage, constancy and determination. His style was even copied by Saddam Hussein who, prior to the invasion of Iraq in 2003, promised to 'fight them [the coalition forces] on the streets, from the rooftops, from house to house. We will never surrender.'[15] Churchill's reputation has not, of course, gone uncontested by either historians or politicians. Whereas George W. Bush has praised Churchill for his 'conscience and unshakeable determination',[16] President Thabo Mbeki of South Africa has criticized him as an imperialist and a racist.[17] Yet it seems indisputable that, whether he is approved of or not, he has eclipsed Lloyd George in the public memory.

Part of the purpose of this book is to explain why this should be so, and, in order to do this, it addresses a number of key questions. Was Lloyd George more effective than Churchill in terms of domestic policy prior to 1914, and to what extent did they share a common approach to issues such as social welfare, women's suffrage, and constitutional reform? Why did Churchill's career all-but implode during the Great War, whilst that of Lloyd George (who was ostensibly the less military-minded of the two men) went from strength to strength? Was Lloyd George's leadership during that terrible time equal to (or even greater than) that of Churchill in 1940–5? Which man showed better judgement during the crucial 1918–22 period over such issues as Ireland, the Middle East, and the Russian civil war? After Lloyd George fell from office, and Churchill returned to the Conservatives, they clashed over issues such as unemployment: was the former's bold interventionism or the latter's pragmatic caution the right approach? Later, when they were both in the political wilderness during the 1930s, could they, if they had coordinated their actions better, have done more to counter the National Government's policy of appeasement of Hitler and Mussolini? Why, after Churchill at last achieved the premiership in 1940, did Lloyd George refuse his repeated invitations to join the War Cabinet? Was it, as Lloyd George appeared to suggest to members of his entourage, because he wanted to avoid political entanglement in the hope of replacing Churchill in 10 Downing Street himself and making a compromise peace with Germany? And finally, why, after

1945, did Churchill go to such lengths to play up his friendship with Lloyd George at a time that the Lloyd George name was a declining political currency?

There is already, of course, an enormous literature on both men. What, then, is the justification for adding to it? Contrary to the common perception, not all the significant facts about them have already been published. For example a careful combing of the archives brought to light a report of a speech made by Lloyd George in April 1900, retained in his own private papers and long forgotten, which contains his first known (and unflattering) public reference to Churchill, made some months before the two men met. Furthermore, Lloyd George's letters to his brother – which have become generally available to researchers in full only in the fairly recent past – contain some pithy comments about Churchill, but also demonstrate Lloyd George's inconsistencies in his attitude towards him. Sometimes, moreover, original manuscript or typescript diaries turn out to be considerably more revealing than the 'official' published versions. For example Lucy Masterman, an astute observer of the Edwardian political scene, recorded the pair's attempts to interfere in a scandalous divorce case involving two fellow MPs. Likewise, the unexpurgated diary of Christopher Addison MP turns out not only to be much ruder about Churchill than the libel laws would have permitted when it was first published in book form, but also contains details about Lloyd George's manoeuvres over conscription during World War I that Addison suppressed. There are many further examples of valuable manuscript sources, including the file from the Royal Archives concerning the granting of war medals to Lloyd George in 1919. As will be seen, Churchill, as Secretary of State for War, worked hard to bring this about, and only overcame the resistance of King George V with considerable difficulty. Some such documents have the status of intriguing curiosities; the contents of others, such as Churchill's 1937 article on the Jews (which was never published, in part because Lloyd George had recently produced an article on the same topic) are explosive.

Ultimately, though, new facts are significant only if they lead to new interpretation, which is what this book aims to provide. It seeks to challenge the predominant, excessively sentimental view of the Lloyd George–Churchill relationship – what we might call the 'myth of David and Winston', the supposedly inseparable friends who never felt personal bitterness no matter how much they might differ on policy. It takes on the myth not for the dirty thrill of iconoclasm, but to extract the lessons that a more realistic appraisal of this important story can yield. If the two men frequently deployed the rhetoric of political friendship in order to present an idealized picture of their own conduct, they were not alone in this habit. During and after World War II, for example, Churchill created a similar mythology about his relationship with President Franklin D. Roosevelt. This is not to say that he was insincere, merely that he – like Lloyd George and many others – harnessed his emotions for political ends. This is something to remember when we hear modern politicians declare that their domestic or international political partnerships rest on a solid foundation of personal friendship.

To observe that Lloyd George and Churchill engaged in a strategic romanticization of their relationship is not cynicism; nor does the fact of it diminish their joint significance. But the avoidance of the romantic view does allow us to examine them in proper perspective. Upon the death of Lloyd George the Labour MP Aneurin Bevan, one of the few people in twentieth-century British politics who could rival him as an orator, paid tribute in the House of Commons. Almost inevitably, he compared him to Churchill. Bevan reminded his listeners of the period after 1922: 'When Lloyd George was denied office towards the end of his life by a concurrence of hostile political currents, I thought, as I watched him during those years, and at the same time watched the Prime Minister [i.e. Churchill], who also for some time was out of office, that it must cause some of us to feel extremely humble, because there were two of the most eminent and brilliant Parliamentarians of this era denied employment by the State.' The moral of this, he argued, was 'that even the most superabundant personal qualities are irrelevant if not associated with great mass machines', in other words the political parties.[18] As this book will demonstrate, the ultimate trajectories of the two men's careers – and also of their respective reputations – suggest that this was a truth that Churchill painfully learned, and Lloyd George carelessly forgot.

Chapter One

PATHS TO POWER, 1863–1905

DAVID LLOYD GEORGE, probably the most famous Welshman of the twentieth century, was in fact born in Manchester, England, on 17 January 1863. The end-of-terrace house at 5 New York Place, Chorlton-upon-Medlock, was in stark contrast to the residence near Oxford where Winston Churchill entered the world eleven years later. This was not because Lloyd George's background was nearly so humble as, for political purposes, he later liked to make out, but because Blenheim Palace makes a remarkable contrast with pretty much anywhere. David's father, William George, was a schoolteacher from Wales who had met his wife-to-be, Elizabeth Lloyd, when he was in charge of a school in her native Caernarfonshire. After their marriage the Georges moved briefly to Lancashire, where Mary, their first surviving daughter, was born, before William took up a temporary headship in Manchester. (Their firstborn daughter had died before being christened.)[1] Shortly after David's birth William George abandoned teaching, and the family returned to his native Pembrokeshire, taking the tenancy of a smallholding near Haverfordwest. But William's health had been weak for a long time, and in June 1864 he contracted a severe chill and died at the age of 41. His second son, also named William, was born the following February. The brief connection with Manchester later had its political uses for David. As the younger William recalled: 'In later years my brother visited Manchester on many occasions, and whilst there he never failed to acclaim himself as a Manchester boy.'[2] Campaigning for Churchill at the Manchester North-West by-election of 1908 he was greeted by a friendly, if somewhat ironical, call of 'Three Cheers for the Manchester Welshman'.[3]

William George's death left his wife and family in a precarious position. Elizabeth's brother, Richard Lloyd, came to the rescue. He helped them sell up and move to North Wales, where he welcomed them into his home, in Llanystumdwy, near Criccieth, at the base of the Lleyn peninsula. Lloyd George was always keen to stress the humbleness of his background. At the dawn of the democratic era, his claim to be a 'cottage-bred man' – true in strictly literal terms – had clear political advantages. Yet, as modern writers have been keen to stress, 'Uncle Lloyd' (who was a shoemaker, and also a lay pastor at a local Baptist chapel) was a well-respected community figure and, as befitted a master craftsman, by no means impoverished.[4] The relative lack of material advantage aside, the young Lloyd George was in many ways luckier in his upbringing than the aristocratic young Churchill. The latter's parents deputed his care to servants and boarding schools, their neglect being by no means totally benign. ('Please do do do do do do come down to see me', he wrote to his mother from school when he was 16. 'Please do come. I have been disappointed so many times about your coming.'[5] To his own son he claimed not to have had more than a few hours' continuous conversation with his father in his whole life.)[6] For Lloyd George, though, Uncle Lloyd proved a more than adequate father substitute, doting on the boy and providing him with encouragement. He was no saint, as his rather cruel refusal to allow his other nephew to style himself William *Lloyd* George demonstrates. (He remained plain William George.) Nevertheless, his household provided the atmosphere, and the books, that allowed Lloyd George to become very well read at a young age. Churchill, for his part, was nearly 22 before 'the desire for learning came upon me', and, as a late-starting autodidact, set about supplementing his earlier and rather indifferent experience of private education.[7]

At the age of three and a half, David entered Llanystumdwy school, there being no local Nonconformist alternative to this Anglican establishment. He stayed there nearly twelve years, proving an apt, but not always obedient, student. In a famous episode that took place when he was 12 or 13, he rebelled against the school's requirement that even the Nonconformist majority of its pupils learn the Anglican catechism. On the day of the annual inspection by the diocesan representatives, he organized a conspiracy of silence, so that when the headmaster asked the children for a recital of the Creed, he was met only with a blank stare. His brother, who was also a pupil, was finally moved out of pity for the headmaster to end the protest. It had, however, the desired effect. As William George recalled: 'After this I never remember the children being marched to church on festival days, nor being called upon to make a public recital of the Creed of a Church of which neither they nor their parents were members.'[8] Although Lloyd George was soon to lose his religious faith, he retained throughout his life a strong Nonconformist sensibility, relishing singing the hymns he heard in Chapel and recounting anecdotes about Welsh preachers. Furthermore, rather like Churchill, he developed in time an inchoate belief in a Fate or Providence that, he thought, was preserving him in order that he might perform some great service to humanity.[9] After his first visit to the House of Commons, on a Saturday in 1881 when the House was not sitting, he noted in his diary: 'I will not say but that I eyed the assembly in a spirit similar to that in which William the Conqueror eyed England on his visit to Edward the Confessor, as the region of his future domain. Oh, vanity!'[10]

Churchill was born on 30 November 1874, only seven and a half months after his parents' wedding. Whether or not his birth was a genuine case of prematurity is unclear. His father, Lord Randolph Churchill, had married Jennie Jerome, an American heiress, only after protracted financial negotiations between the families, and it is not impossible that the young couple had rather jumped the gun. Lord Randolph's father, the seventh Duke of Marlborough (who was the owner of Blenheim) had opposed the match. Years later, at the time of the controversy over Lloyd George's notorious 1909 Budget, King Edward VII was irritated by a 'vulgar and "American"' speech by Churchill in its favour. He claimed privately, with more than a hint of regret, that his own actions when he had been Prince of Wales had in some measure been responsible for this rhetorical excess. 'If it had not been for me and the Queen, that young man would never have been in existence . . . The Duke and the Duchess both objected to Randolph's marriage, and it was entirely owing to us that they gave way.'[11] This may have been an exaggeration, although the royal efforts doubtless played some part in the decision. What the story demonstrates for our purposes is that, for all the unhappiness experienced in his childhood, Winston Churchill had at least one potential advantage that David Lloyd George lacked: an impressive set of establishment connections.

Unfortunately, the mercurial and impetuous and unprincipled

Lord Randolph, who had been elected to the House of Commons in the Conservative landslide of February 1874, quickly managed to turn himself into a social pariah. He achieved this by trying (as it was perceived) to blackmail the Prince of Wales in an attempt to save his own brother, the Marquess of Blandford, from scandal. Lord Aylesford, a friend of the Prince, was planning to divorce his wife, citing the Marquess as co-respondent. Lord Randolph wrote to the Prince to try to get him to prevent this and the attendant publicity. Furthermore, he threatened to publish the Prince's own intimate letters to Lady Aylesford if he did not comply. The plan worked insofar as the divorce case was dropped, but the Prince was understandably outraged. The Queen, the Prime Minister and the Leader of the Opposition all learnt of the matter. Not only was Lord Randolph forced to apologize, but the Prince also ensured that he and his family were subjected to a comprehensive social boycott.

The Duke of Marlborough now accepted Prime Minister Benjamin Disraeli's offer of the Lord Lieutenancy of Ireland, and Lord Randolph accompanied his father to Dublin as an unpaid private secretary. Hence Winston Churchill's first memories were of that island. 'My nurse, Mrs. Everest, was nervous about the Fenians. I gathered these were wicked people and there was no end to what they would do if they had their way.'[12] (The horrific murder of the Chief Secretary of Ireland in 1882 showed these fears were not unreasonable.) Irish issues would be an important theme throughout both Churchill's career and Lloyd George's, from the Edwardian period to the early 1920s.

After the Tory defeat of 1880 Lord Randolph came back to London and embarked upon a parliamentary career that was as technically accomplished as it was opportunistic. As his successes mounted, the social ostracism eased. As a member of the so-called 'Fourth Party', a tiny group of brilliant rebels, he was as effective at goading his own party's leaders as he was at scoring off the Liberal front bench. On 28 April 1884, the 21-year-old Lloyd George, in London to take the final exams that would qualify him as a solicitor, witnessed him in action from the gallery.[13] Lord Randolph tackled the Prime Minister, William Gladstone, to considerable effect. The business at hand was the Reform Bill, a measure that would bring about a major extension of the franchise and hence, it was expected, benefit the Liberals in future elections. An allied question was redistribution – that is the adjustment of the constituencies, which also had potentially important repercussions for the parties and in which the Tories had a deep interest. Gladstone, for sound tactical reasons, was determined to postpone discussion of redistribution until the current Bill was out of the way. Lord Randolph ridiculed his suggestion that the question would be dealt with the following year, suggesting that the government might not survive long enough to tackle it. 'Where will the Prime Minister and his government be next year?' he asked. 'He would be a very bold man, indeed, who would hazard a conjecture.'[14] 'It was a clever piece of comedy,' Lloyd George recalled much later. 'I thought Churchill an impudent puppy, as every Liberal was bound to do – but I thoroughly enjoyed his speech.'[15] (As regards the issues at hand, the parties in the end struck a deal whereby the Conservatives allowed the Reform Bill to pass the Lords in exchange for a redistribution measure out of which they did well.)

Lord Randolph cannot be credited with a particularly important role in provoking Lloyd George's interest in politics (although he seems to have influenced his speaking style to some degree). The young Welshman had made his first political speech at the Portmadoc debating society in the autumn of 1878. He had been involved in electioneering in Caernarfonshire at the 1880 general election and at a subsequent by-election. And, as we have seen, he had been much stimulated by his 1881 Commons visit, quite some time before he saw Lord Randolph in action.

For the meantime, though, a political career remained a mere aspiration. Lloyd George's years as an apprentice solicitor, the start of which coincided with his family's move to Criccieth, were hard ones. Although qualified and with his own practice, he achieved financial security only after his brother, who had followed him into the profession, joined him in 1887. At this time Winston Churchill was still a schoolboy. Dispatched to a preparatory school at Ascot at the age of seven, he experienced his fair share of the masters' brutality. He recalled in his autobiography that flogging with the birch was 'a great feature' of the school's curriculum, and claimed that the beatings 'exceeded in severity anything that would be tolerated in any of the Reformatories under the Home Office'.[16]

The impact of this brutality on Churchill's character is difficult to quantify. One day at the Paris Peace Conference in 1919 he, Lloyd

George and Andrew Bonar Law (the Conservative leader) were sitting together at a restaurant. The talk turned to corporal punishment. Lloyd George claimed (quite inaccurately, according to his wife) to have led a campaign against flogging at his own school. Someone then put a question to Churchill. He responded: 'Thrashed? I have been misunderstood from my childhood up. Of course I was thrashed.' There was a moment's pause before Bonar Law turned to the Prime Minister and said, 'Ll.G, what *would* Winston have been like if he hadn't been thrashed?'[17]

The schoolboy Churchill's misery lasted two years until, in 1883, he was transferred to a school at Brighton run by two kindly and sympathetic ladies. Here, in a faint echo of Lloyd George's earlier revolt, he staged an abortive religious rebellion. In this he was influenced by his nurse's Low Church principles. The school often attended services at the town's Chapel Royal, and was accommodated in pews that ran north–south. 'In consequence, when the Apostles' Creed was recited, everyone turned to the East', he remembered. 'I was sure Mrs. Everest would have considered this practice popish, and I conceived it my duty to testify against it.' He thus remained in place without moving, but to his surprise, no one punished him for his demonstration, which did not even receive comment. However, on the next occasion, the school was shown into pews facing east. It seemed to him excessive to turn *away* from the east: 'I therefore became willy-nilly a passive conformist.'[18] Unlike Lloyd George, Churchill never did quite get the hang of religious politics.

The next staging post on his road of education was Harrow, which he entered in April 1888. His parents continued to show an almost total lack of interest in him. By this point Lord Randolph's political career had already imploded. After the Conservatives had triumphed over Gladstone at the Irish Home Rule election of July 1886, Lord Salisbury, the new Prime Minister, reluctantly appointed him as Chancellor of the Exchequer. That December Lord Randolph threatened to resign over army and navy 'estimates' (spending proposals) he thought excessive: 'If the foreign policy of this country is conducted with skill and judgement our present huge and increasing armaments are quite unnecessary and the taxation which they involve perfectly unjustifiable.'[19] Salisbury, irritated with his Chancellor's erratic behaviour, accepted his resignation, to the latter's shock. Lord

Randolph never held office again, his efforts to make a comeback thwarted by the disease, possibly syphilis, that destroyed him mentally before killing him in 1895. He was not quite 46.[20]

Winston Churchill, a strong partisan of his father, was too young at the time to understand the events surrounding his fall. Later, having himself switched to the Liberals, he re-imagined Lord Randolph's failed power-seeking manoeuvres as an exercise in principle.[21] This reading of a demagogic and inconsistent Tory career was reflected in the *Manchester Guardian*'s review of Churchill's biography of his father, which was published during the 1906 general election. A. F. Pollard, a noted historian, gave his readers a classic statement of the traditional Liberal case. He explained that international peace and the retrenchment of public expenditure that accompanied it implied a reduction of armaments, of the national debt, and consequently of the rate of interest. This in turn reduced the incomes of the richer classes who lived off investments, whilst cuts in armaments limited the naval and military posts upon which the younger sons of the aristocracy were so often quartered. That, he argued, was why lavish public expenditure was popular with the upper classes. 'For this reason Lord Randolph's attempt to convert his party into an instrument for economical administration was foredoomed to failure; and it is the hopelessness of this attempt which has driven his son to cross the floor of the House of Commons and take part in a Liberal Government.'[22] However, as will be seen in Chapter 3, when Churchill and Lloyd George fell out in early 1914 over the size of the Royal Navy, the latter pointedly and publicly recalled that Lord Randolph had resigned rather than agree to 'bloated' spending on armaments. If Churchill's father's supposed legacy was exploitable for political purposes, it was by no means single-edged.

Lloyd George himself entered parliament when Lord Randolph was still on the scene ('His glory has departed, his nerves are shattered, and his powers impaired', noted the newcomer).[23] A few years earlier he had warned Margaret Owen, his future wife: 'My supreme idea is to get on ... I am prepared to thrust even love itself under the wheels of my Juggernaut, if it obstructs the way'.[24] Appointed Secretary of the Anti-Tithe League for South Caernarfonshire in 1886, he carved out something of a niche for himself in Welsh radicalism, and soon sought to be nominated as the Liberal candidate for the constituency of Caernarfon Boroughs. The nomination was brought firmly within his grasp by his triumph in the 1888 Llan-frothen burial case. The rector of Llanfrothen had denied a family the right to bury one of their number in his churchyard with Noncon-formist rites, as they were legally entitled to do. On Lloyd George's advice they broke into the churchyard and buried the man them-selves. The small-minded rector took them to court, the case hingeing on the precise legal status of the part of the churchyard where the body now lay. The prejudiced judge, amazingly enough, misrecorded the jury's verdict, which was favourable to the family. Conveniently for Lloyd George, his subsequent victory at the Court of Appeal came a mere two weeks before the Caernarfon Boroughs Liberal Associa-tion met to select a candidate. He was duly chosen. Somewhat more than a year later, in March 1890, the sitting Tory MP died of heart failure. After a hard-fought campaign, Lloyd George won the result-ant by-election by a majority of 18.

In June he made his Commons maiden speech, on the subject of the licensing laws. At this time drink was seen as a major social problem, 'a gigantic evil' linked to crime, disorder, prostitution and poverty. It was, moreover, a party political issue. Temperance was one of the great Nonconformist causes, and many radical Liberals urged popular control of the drink trade in the interest of the public good. Conservatives, for their part, tended to portray attempts at state regulation as part of a 'collectivist' or 'socialistic' assault on traditional British freedom; which in turn brought allegations that they were in the pay of the brewers and publicans. In 1889 Lord Randolph Churchill had described the trade as 'destructive and devilish' and had gone on to introduce his own licensing Bill.[25] This was a short-lived and somewhat opportunistic crusade, and Lloyd George used part of his speech to poke fun at it. Lord Randolph's previous temperance ardour had, the new MP claimed, evaporated. 'Like many another temperance advocate the holidays seem to have affected his temperance principles. His, at the best, was a kind of mushroom teetotalism, which grew no one knew why, or when, and which has disappeared, how, no one exactly knows'; although it seemed 'the constant communications of the noble Lord with the licensed victuallers' were to blame. He went on to describe both Lord Randolph and Joseph Chamberlain (the Conservative government's Liberal Unionist ally) as 'political contortionists . . . who can set their feet in one direction and their face in another'.[26]

This kind of raillery was Lloyd George's stock-in-trade through-out his career. During his first years in parliament he used his rhetorical skills and his remorseless energy to considerable effect, but not, as far as the Liberal leadership was concerned, to a con-structive one. He was determined to ensure that disestablishment of the Welsh Church took a prominent place in his party's agenda – although this was, by definition, an issue not likely to inspire the English voters whose support it needed. His rebelliousness was blamed – unfairly – by some for the eventual collapse of the con-genitally weak Liberal government of 1892–5. If he were to achieve the commanding position in Welsh politics he desired – and he would not manage it without setbacks – it was necessary for him to champion such issues. But if he were to progress from this, and achieve a position of national leadership in the United Kingdom as a whole, he also needed, in due course, to move beyond them. His opposition to the Boer War helped him do this. The war also brought Winston Churchill great public prominence – as a hero for the other side.

After leaving Harrow, where he had not distinguished himself greatly, Churchill had gained entry to the Royal Military Academy at Sandhurst at the third attempt. His time there, in 1893–4, ended very shortly before his father's death in January 1895. The month after that he joined the Fourth Hussars, a cavalry regiment. In the autumn of the same year he gained his first experiences of both war and journalism. Taking advantage of an extended spell of leave, he travelled via the USA to Cuba, where the Spanish rulers were trying to put down a local rebellion. His reports to the newspapers earned him much-needed income: Lord Randolph had not left a great deal, and Churchill's salary was insufficient to meet his expenses. Later, after he and his regiment had been sent to India, restlessness, financial necessity, and a willingness to pull strings led him to the adventure on the North-West Frontier that resulted in his first book. This, *The Story of the Malakand Field Force* (1898), brought him the friendly attention of Lord Salisbury. The Prime Minister's support in turn helped Churchill join Sir Herbert Kitchener's Sudan campaign, over the latter's strenuous objections. Churchill participated in the September 1898 Battle of Omdurman, and was very critical of the conduct of Kitchener – with whom he and Lloyd George would clash during World War I. Churchill determined to reiterate the charge that the general had allowed the killing of enemy wounded: 'This will be very unpopular and I shall expect perfect scorn.'[27] However, the criticisms of Kitchener contained in the first edition of *The River War* (1899) were excised from the one-volume edition that came out after Churchill became an MP.[28] In the spring of 1899 he left the army, and that summer stood as a Conservative at a by-election at Oldham, losing narrowly. In October he left for South Africa as a correspondent of the right-wing *Morning Post*. As he sailed, no shots had yet been fired, but it was clear that war between the British Empire and the Boers was imminent.

The Boers were South African Calvinists of mainly Dutch descent. The Transvaal (which, like the Orange Free State, was an independent Boer republic) had been annexed by the British in 1877. A surprise British defeat at the time of the first Boer War four years later led to the restoration of its autonomy, and an uneasy peace. Further conflict at last came about over the – ostensible – issue of the 'Uitlanders'. These were (predominantly British) non-Boers who, attracted to the Transvaal in vast numbers largely by the discovery of vast mineral riches, were denied political rights by the Boers. Alfred Milner, the British High Commissioner in South Africa, and Joseph Chamberlain, Lord Salisbury's powerful Colonial Secretary, determined on a tough line. Their demands for the extension of the franchise to the Uitlanders were finally rejected by the Transvaal government, which then issued an impossible ultimatum, making war inevitable. The British were now involved in a war that was either a bid to extend the Empire's protection to fellow-countrymen in distress (Churchill's opinion) or an outrage perpetuated in the name of human freedom (Lloyd George's). Lloyd George later claimed that he had been considered 'a little Englander and a traitor' by Churchill for his views, although the latter denied this.[29]

The Boers scored early victories over the poorly led British forces. Learning of the disasters upon landing in South Africa, Churchill travelled to Estcourt, forty miles from Ladysmith, in Natal, which was under siege by Boer forces. On 15 November 1899, he joined a reconnaissance mission aboard an armoured train. When the train came under fire, and was then partially derailed by the Boers, Churchill, refusing to take his civilian status seriously, bravely took charge. Having helped get the engine with a cargo of wounded out of danger, he himself dismounted in order to track down the stragglers – and was promptly captured, as indeed those for whom he was looking had been. He languished for a few weeks in captivity in Pretoria before making a brilliant and daring escape, arriving safely at Durban on 23 December. 'I was received as if I had won a great victory', he recalled in his memoirs, adding: 'Youth seeks Adventure. Journalism requires Advertisement. Certainly I had found both. I became for the time quite famous.'[30] This fame helped ensure his victory at Oldham at the 'Khaki' general election – so-called because of the successful Tory appeal to patriotic and militarist sentiment – in the autumn of the following year. Churchill's result was but one part of a wider Conservative triumph, at a point when it seemed that the war (which in fact dragged on until May 1902) was as good as won.

The Tory victory had a hollow ring. Even before the war broke out, Lloyd George had predicted that the coming conflict would be the government's downfall. 'If they go on the war will be so costly in blood and treasure as to sicken the land', he told his wife.[31] In fact, the immediate effect was to split the Liberal Party into pro-war 'Liberal Imperialist' and anti-war 'pro-Boer' factions. Yet the war exposed too the poor health of many of the would-be recruits, which promoted a cross-party concern. Widespread poverty, it was believed, was behind the physical deterioration of the working classes, which in turn threatened to weaken the nation as a whole. Revelations about social conditions not only took the shine off the military victories in South Africa, which at any rate were too long in coming, but also created an atmosphere from which the Liberals in due course benefited. The post-1905 welfare reforms, with which both Lloyd George and Churchill were to be closely associated, were in part the product of this quest for 'national efficiency' – a catchphrase that incorporated the idea that it was necessary to improve social conditions in order to create an imperial people.

Lloyd George's opposition to the war was not founded on anti-imperialism any more than it was on pacifism. Rather, he saw it as unnecessary, having come about because the government had sought redress of Uitlander grievances in such in such a way as to forestall compromise. It was conducted, also, in a cruel and blundering fashion. It was horribly expensive to boot, wasting money that could have been spent on social reform at home. As will be seen, these oft-repeated views made him on occasion the target of popular violence. They also provided the context for his first known reference to Churchill, made in a speech at Penrhyn Hall in Bangor on 13 April 1900 (i.e. some months in advance of the general election and thus before Churchill became an MP). It should be noted that this was only a passing remark made during a long speech. It should also be noted that it was not favourable. Here is how the *North Wales Observer* reported his words, and the response of the crowd: 'There were only forty thousand of the Boers; ten thousand had been wiped out. Mr. Winston Churchill had written that the only way to conquer the Boers was to grind them down, to kill them one by one, dozen by dozen, commando by commando ("Shame").'[32]

The two men met for the first time on 18 February the following year. This was the day that Churchill made his maiden Commons speech, following directly a speech by Lloyd George. The background to the day's events was as follows: Lloyd George had put down an amendment proposing that 'subject to the overlordship of the British crown' the Boers would receive 'full local autonomy' when hostilities came to an end. If this were to be put to a Commons vote, though, it risked splitting the Liberal Party yet again: the Liberal Imperialists might well vote against it. Accordingly, Sir Henry Campbell-Bannerman, the party's leader and himself an opponent of the war, pressed his Chief Whip to discourage Lloyd George from moving it. In this he was successful.[33] Nevertheless, Lloyd George did not tone down the language of his speech: 'It is difficult within the bounds of Parliamentary propriety to describe what one thinks about all this infamy which is perpetuated in the name of Great Britain in Africa.'[34] He knew in advance that Churchill was to reply to him, and that other members were expecting a 'cockfight'. 'He is the new Tory bully', Lloyd George wrote to his brother. 'Bydded. [So be it.] Quite prepared.'[35]

Churchill listened to Lloyd George's speech with mounting anxiety. As he recalled in his memoirs, he had earlier learned that 'a rising young Welshman, a pro-Boer, and one of our most important bugbears, named Lloyd George' would probably be called at about nine o'clock that evening; and that he, Churchill, could follow him if he wished. Churchill had committed his own speech to memory, never having mastered the art of speaking off the cuff. Yet he was going to need to make some kind of link with what the previous speaker had said. In Churchill's words:

Mr. Lloyd George spoke from the third bench below the gang-way on the opposition side, surrounded by a handful of Welsh-men and Radicals, and backed by the Irish Nationalist party . . . Encouraged by the cheers of the 'Celtic fringes' he soon became animated and even violent. I constructed in succession sentence after sentence to hook on with after he should sit down. Each of these poor couplings became in turn obsolete. A sense of alarm and even despair crept across me.

Happily, though, Thomas Gibson Bowles, an experienced MP sitting beside him, suggested a phrase just in time. According to Churchill's memory, Lloyd George then said that he 'would curtail his remarks as he was sure the House wished to hear a new member' – although these words are not recorded in Hansard – and suddenly resumed his seat.[36] Picking up on Bowles's suggestion, Churchill began his speech by noting that Lloyd George's intended amendment had been mild and moderate in tone, yet his speech had been very bitter. It seemed likely, therefore, that the moderation was that of Lloyd George's political friends and leaders, but the bitterness was that of the man himself. 'It has been suggested to me that it might perhaps have been better, upon the whole, if the hon. Member, instead of making his speech without moving his Amendment, had moved his Amendment without making his speech.'[37] This remark received a cheer, and Churchill made it through the rest of his speech without either entirely suppressing his nerves or letting them cause him to come unstuck.

Much of the press coverage of Churchill's effort made compari-sons, favourable and otherwise, with the speaking style of his famous father. Some of it, though, commented on his 'duel' with Lloyd George. Whereas the Unionist *Daily Telegraph* said that Churchill had summarized the latter's 'rhetorical outburst in a cluster of happy phrases', the Liberal *Daily News* praised both men to differing degrees. Its article, written by the anti-war journalist H. W. Massingham, noted that 'The personal contrast was as striking as that of the treatment and method.' Massingham harped on about the 'pleasing face', 'natural refinement' and 'true parliamentary style' of Lloyd George. By comparison, Churchill's address, accent and appearance did not help him. 'But he has one quality – intellect.' Remarks such as his comment on the impossibility of the ex-Boer republics returning to prosperity under military government 'showed that this young man has kept his critical faculty through the glamour of association with our arms'.[38] The fulsome remarks about Lloyd George were hardly surprising: the man himself had recently engineered a takeover of the paper by a moderate pro-Boer syndicate, and now sat on the paper's board.[39] But Massingham's (qualified) willingness to compliment Churchill's views could also be seen as a sign that the member for Oldham was already recognized in Lloyd George's circle as a pleasingly unconventional Tory. Given Lloyd George's remark to his brother, though, it would be a mistake to push this idea too far. We may also note that in some other quarters of the Liberal Party Churchill's speech was better received than Lloyd George's. The former Home Secretary H. H. Asquith reported to his wife: 'Lloyd George made a long rather offensive attack on the army, & Winston made his début wh. was quite a success. It was not over elaborate or assured and was well received.'[40]

Lloyd George and Churchill's first meeting took place immediately after the debate. They were introduced at the bar of the House of Commons. In *My Early Life*, published in 1930, Churchill wrote: 'After compliments, he said "Judging from your sentiments, you are standing against the Light." I replied "You take a singularly detached view of the British Empire". Thus began an association which has persisted through many vicissitudes.'[41] In 1932 Lloyd George remembered the conversation in markedly similar terms. (It is, of course, by no means impossible that he was influenced in this by Churchill's own account.) In 1938, though, he claimed that they 'first met in 1890, and throughout all the vicissitudes and quarrels between them their friendship had survived all these forty-eight years'. This seems to have been a fabrication, although doubtless not a deliberate one. In 1890 Churchill had been only 16, and there is no other evidence to suggest such an early meeting.[42] It was, however, an example of the way in which both men at various times romanticized their friendship by exaggerating its intensity, and in this case even its length. Their reasons for so doing were partly sentimental, but often, too, the myth of their unbroken amity had a certain political convenience.

It was by no means the case that the two men, upon their first meeting, immediately fell upon one another 'with the fervour of two long-separated kindred lizards' (to use a phrase coined by Churchill

in another context).[43] The start of their friendship, as opposed to
their acquaintanceship, would have to wait until political circumstances were more propitious. Within months of their first encounter,
though, Lloyd George was exploiting that acquaintanceship publicly,
as a means of hurting the government. At a peace meeting in Llanelli
on 7 October, he tried to wound his opponent and future ally by the
best means to hand: praising him. He observed:

> Last week there was a very interesting speech delivered by a
> brilliant young Tory member, Mr. Winston Churchill. There is
> no greater admirer of his talents, I assure you, than the individual
> who is now addressing you, and many a chat have we had about
> the situation. We do not always agree, but at the same time we
> do not black each other's eyes.

Churchill, Lloyd George went on, had observed that the war
situation was 'serious and disquieting', and that 'the position is as
momentous to-day as it was two years [ago] before the first shot was
fired'. This, he reminded his listeners, was the statement of a strong
supporter of the war. Joseph Chamberlain had alleged that the
speeches of the pro-Boers were bringing comfort to the enemy. If
the Boers did indeed have the leisure to sit around reading speeches,
he suggested, they would also read Churchill's. 'They will say, "We
know him: that is the young fellow we caught in the armoured train;
a bright, intelligent young lad, he is."' They would see that the
Unionists were saying that the British position was as bad as it had
been two years earlier. Lloyd George continued: 'I ask . . . whether
a statement like that of Mr. Winston Churchill is not much more
likely to encourage the Boers than any poor speech that I can
deliver.'[44]

The comment about the two men's private talks is interesting
evidence of the potential that already existed for a close relationship.
But if, for the time being, Churchill was less hostile to Lloyd George
than many Tories were, this was merely a measure of the extremity
of the hatred the Welshman aroused. This found its most violent
manifestation at the end of the year, when Lloyd George tried to
deliver a speech in Birmingham, Chamberlain's home city. Birmingham had some history of political disorder. In 1884 Lord Randolph
Churchill and his colleague Sir Stafford Northcote were severely
hustled when a Conservative meeting ended in riot. The disruption

received arms-length encouragement from Chamberlain, who at that point was still a Liberal.[45] When he arrived in the city on 18 December 1901, Lloyd George encountered a ferocious reception. Chamberlain had not generated the hostile atmosphere – the local press had done that – but nor had he sought to calm it down. A crowd of 30,000, many of them armed with an array of fearsome weaponry, surrounded the Town Hall, where Lloyd George was to speak. The hall itself had been infiltrated by protesters, and when he opened his mouth he was drowned out. According to *The Times*, there was no violence for a while, although stones were thrown through the windows by the crowd outside. 'Suddenly a rush was made for the platform and a number of men gained the raised structure placed in front for the reporters. The police . . . with considerable difficulty drove back the storming party.'[46] Lloyd George retired from the platform, and in the end made good his escape from the building disguised as a policeman.

The risk to Lloyd George's person had been genuine. Churchill's disgust at the events was intensified by a sense that the violence had been inexpedient as well as immoral. He wrote to J. Moore Bayley, a Birmingham Tory politician and an admirer of Lord Randolph, that the episode was a blot upon the good name of the city. 'I shudder to think of the harm that would have been done to the Imperial cause in South Africa if Mr Lloyd George had been mauled or massacred by the mob', he added. 'Personally, I think Lloyd George a vulgar, chattering little cad, but he will have gained a hundred thousand sympathisers in England by the late proceedings.'[47]

Certainly, the episode heightened Lloyd George's national prominence. Moreover, once the war came to an end in May 1902, when the Boers acknowledged British rule, a key source of the animosity towards him was removed, as was a cause of Liberal division. In addition, shortly before this, the government handed the Liberals another stick to beat it with. This, a long overdue Education Bill, was the brainchild of Arthur Balfour, who in July succeeded his uncle, Lord Salisbury, as Prime Minister. The Balfour Act was an intelligent attempt at reform, but it was politically explosive. It brought voluntary schools, including Church of England schools, under local government control. Nonconformists objected strenuously to subsidizing Anglican establishments through local taxation. Lloyd George rode the wave of protest, leading a high-profile and sophisticated campaign against the legislation; although he was considerably more willing than many of his supporters to reach a compromise. Under these conditions it was hardly surprising that Churchill found the idea of having to make a speech on the Bill – of which he was a strong advocate – 'a somewhat depressing prospect'.[48]

In 1903, there was a further shift in the political landscape. This was over the issue of trade. Britain had for decades been a free trade country. The 1846 abolition of the Corn Laws (which restricted imports in order to protect British farmers) had been a crucial moment in the transition to a laissez-faire system under which consumers had benefited from cheap imports. This system formed the bedrock of late-Victorian prosperity, but it was increasingly called into question as the USA and Germany, which protected their own industries through the use of tariffs, threatened to outstrip Britain economically. Such fears of decline lay behind Joseph Chamberlain's public announcement, on 15 May 1903, of his conversion to a new scheme of tariffs, including a system of imperial preference whereby countries within the Empire would treat each other's products more favourably than goods that came from outside. This plan for 'tariff reform' would, crucially, have raised tariffs on foodstuffs. For the Liberals, free trade was an article of faith. Seizing their opportunity, they attacked Chamberlain's proposed 'food taxes' as an imposition on the working classes.

The Tories were divided. Churchill quickly came out against Chamberlain's proposals. The issue provided the occasion for, if not necessarily the cause of, Churchill's transition to the Liberals in 1904. (Balfour, for one, always believed that he left the Tories because he was not given high office.)[49] It was thus the precondition for his subsequent alliance with Lloyd George. It is worth asking, therefore, where Churchill's ideas on the subject of trade came from. Certainly, he was influenced by his reading of Adam Smith (whom he had read when in India), John Stuart Mill and the French economist Claude Frederic Bastiat; and also received informal briefings from Sir Francis Mowat, the Permanent Secretary of the Treasury.[50] By his own account, though, his most important initial grounding in free trade arguments came from a source hitherto unsuspected by historians: the work of Leo Chiozza Money.

Although now almost completely forgotten, Chiozza Money achieved some renown in the first decades of the twentieth century

as a politician and economic thinker. Born in Genoa in 1870, his
original name was Leone Giorgio Chiozza. By the 1890s (but exactly
when is not clear) he had moved to England. He was an expert
statistician and was managing editor of *Commercial Intelligence* from
1898 to 1903. He was a Liberal MP from 1906 to 1918 (with a short
break in 1910), and rendered Lloyd George 'magnificent service' with
regard to the 1911 National Insurance scheme.[51] He won the
admiration of Churchill, who told him: 'You are a master of efficient
statistics and no one states a case with more originality and force.'[52]
He was parliamentary private secretary to Lloyd George at the
Ministry of Munitions during the Great War, and then served as a
junior minister. He was knighted in 1915. At the end of the war
Chiozza Money switched to the Labour Party, for whom he unsuccessfully contested a seat in 1918; he never sat in parliament again.
In 1928 he was acquitted of committing an indecent offence with a
young lady in Hyde Park, in a case that became a cause célèbre
because of the defects it revealed in police procedures; but five years
later he was convicted of indecency with a woman in a railway
carriage. In the 1930s he drifted towards sympathy for the European
dictators. He died in 1944.[53]

His particular impact on Churchill derived from his book *British
Trade and the Zollverein Issue*, published in July 1902. This work sought
to expose the weaknesses of the various tariff proposals that were, by
this time, already in the air. Chiozza Money noted that nobody was
proposing a true 'British Zollverein or Imperial Customs Union',
i.e. a system of complete free trade between members of the Empire
and a common external tariff. Rather, he observed, what was urged
was a system whereby all Empire countries would levy such duties as
they saw fit, but would, nonetheless, charge lower, or 'preferential',
rates on each other's products than on those of 'foreign' countries.
Although this idea was superficially appealing, it was impractical, he
argued: 'If we are to make the most of our national existence we
must lay under contribution every known source of the commodities
we require ... In but few cases are the best and cheapest supplies
procurable in our colonies. It follows, therefore, that an industrial
nation like ours cannot afford to benefit the colonies by giving a tariff
preference to their products, for, while they have little besides raw
materials and food to sell, they cannot supply them in sufficient
quantities to support our industries and people.'[54]

At the time the book was published, Churchill had not made up his mind on the issue. 'My instinct is profoundly against the Zollverein', he wrote in May 1902, 'but I should like to see the case for it set out in black and white; for after all it is primarily a matter of profit and loss, and it might be worth our while – though I do not think it likely – to pay something by this means to the Colonies (for this is what it comes to) in return for some substantial accession of military strength – such as is undoubtedly in their power to confer.'[55] Chiozza Money's arguments had the effect of confirming his instincts. As Churchill wrote to the author in 1914: 'I well remember in 1904 travelling to London with Sir Michael Hicks Beach [Chancellor of the Exchequer 1885–6 and 1895–1902] & hearing him praise your destructive analysis of Chamberlain[']s Preferential tariff. From this work I learned my first and soundest lessons on that wide question.'[56]

It must be said that Churchill's recollections at this point were clearly somewhat loose. To begin with, he was wrong about the date. He himself recommended the book to a correspondent – '[It] puts some direct practical considerations forward with a force difficult to ignore' – as early as July 1903.[57] What we do not know, therefore, is whether Churchill had read it *before* Chamberlain's démarche, or even as early as October 1902, when he first hinted to Lord Rosebery that the tariff issue, should it arise, might provide the cue for them to work together in a Tory–Liberal 'central coalition'.[58] Equally, we must not forget that Churchill may have been trying to flatter Chiozza Money by playing up the influence the book had had on him. As will be seen in a later chapter, at the point when he wrote this letter he was trying to recruit his help in a crucial political battle with Lloyd George. Still, there seems no reason to doubt his central contention: that Chiozza Money had an early and important impact on his thinking about trade.

Churchill remained flexible, however. Balfour announced his conversion to the idea of tariffs for the purposes of retaliation against other countries' trade barriers, this moderate idea falling well short of Chamberlain's grander scheme. Churchill favoured that principle, and also wanted 'a scientific, disinterested and impartial inquiry . . . to see how that principle can be applied'.[59] Although he subsequently denounced Balfour's policy, he did so only after concluding that it was merely 'an embroidered curtain to conceal the preparation of the Chamberlain battering rams'.[60] He later noted that Chamberlain benefited from keeping his proposals vague and uncertain, as 'Very few people would pay for lottery tickets after the result has been declared.'[61]

It must be emphasized, though, that although Churchill came down firmly on the side of free trade, he was not immediately disposed to make a straightforward transfer of allegiance to the Liberals. Rather, he continued to assert (in private) that 'With a little care we might very easily set up a great Central government neither Protectionist nor Pro boer'.[62] That is to say, he hoped for a coalition government incorporating the moderate elements in both parties. He hoped this would be headed by Lord Rosebery, who, although a total failure as Liberal Prime Minister in 1894–5, continued to inspire his would-be supporters with occasional and eloquent disquisitions. The idea that Rosebery would again take an active part in politics was, though, little more than a pipe dream.

Even had it been otherwise, Lloyd George was not the most obvious candidate for inclusion in such an administration. Churchill, indeed, was alert to the dangers of being publicly associated with him. In October he wrote to Alfred Harmsworth (later Lord Northcliffe), the owner of the *Daily Mail*, protesting at the heading the paper had placed above some extracts from a letter written by Churchill to his constituents. 'The heading seems to attribute to me the use of a somewhat crude joke that Mr. Lloyd George made at Oldham on Saturday, and it looked at first sight to others – (though not I confess to me) as if it were intended to create prejudice against me.'[63] All the same, Churchill recognized by this time that 'if Lord R lets the opportunity pass, it may never return'.[64] Rosebery's continued refusal to take a leadership role foreclosed Churchill's already narrowing options. He needed new comrades.

Churchill's denunciations of Chamberlain and his criticisms of Balfour had lost him the confidence of his constituency party. Over the turn of the year he contemplated entering the Liberal fold. Moreover, on New Year's Eve 1903 he lunched privately with Lloyd George 'and had a very interesting and not altogether unsatisfactory conversation with him'. This is the first substantive conversation between the two men of which there exists a record (in the form both of a letter from Churchill to his friend and fellow Tory MP Lord Hugh Cecil, and of one from Lloyd George to William

George). Much of their talk focused on the education question, over which Lloyd George was struggling to reach a compromise. 'I do not pretend to understand the passions of the Education controversy,' Churchill told Cecil, who was a dedicated Anglican, 'and it seemed to me, talking to Lloyd George yesterday, that some of the differences were astonishingly small and petty.' For instance, according to Lloyd George, 'his people will rather die than give "facilities for inside control"', i.e. denominational religious instruction within school hours. But they did not object to such teaching outside school hours ('outside facilities') and were prepared to shorten school hours accordingly! Churchill observed: 'the difference between inside facilities which Nonconformists resist as tyranny and outside facilities which no reasonable man could refuse appear to me simply to be whether the School hours officially begin at nine o'clock on the days that denominational teaching is appointed or at nine thirty.' Yet even though the differences between the Nonconformists and the Anglicans seemed trivial to him, the controversy would rumble on and bedevil the first years of the next Liberal government.

Churchill also wrote that 'Lloyd George spoke to me at length about a positive programme. He said unless we have something to promise as against Mr. Chamberlain's promises where are we with the working men?' This was a significant remark: there has been much debate about the degree to which the 1905 Liberal government's programme was motivated by electoral expediency. But none of the three main promises Lloyd George wanted to make to the voters comprised the kind of welfare reform with which he and Churchill would soon become associated. The first two – fixity of tenure for tenant farmers and taxation of site values (the latter was an alternative to the taxation of buildings and improvements) – concerned the land. The third was a Trades Disputes Bill, designed to loosen legal restrictions on the trade unions, a move that might be expected to appeal to many working-class voters. Churchill told Cecil:

> I was very careful not to commit myself on any of these points and I chaffed him as being as big a plunderer as Joe [Chamberlain]. But *entre nous* I cannot pretend to have been shocked. Altogether it was a very pleasant and instructive talk and after all Lloyd George represents three things: – Wales, English

Radicalism and Nonconformists, and they are not three things which politicians can overlook.[65]

Lloyd George, who two years before had been a 'vulgar, chattering little cad', was now being sized up as a potential brother-in-arms. Indeed, according to Lloyd George's account, Churchill committed himself rather more than he had indicated to Cecil:

Met Churchill by appointment today. He is willing to come over to our side and thinks 30 other Unionists will accompany him. I told him that on Education and Temperance we were inexorable. He is willing to meet us on these. In fact he is willing to play the Progressive game all round, but thinks that Cecil and I had better meet to settle upon Education as the situation on both sides is in our hands more than any other two men. He thinks Cecil will do much to thwart Joe Chamberlain.[66]

In fact, Churchill's hope of brokering a compromise on education between Cecil and Lloyd George was as unrealistic as his belief that thirty MPs would follow him if he switched parties.

Although the Conservative whip was withdrawn from him in January 1904, Churchill's decision had yet to be cemented. But on 29 March, when Churchill rose to speak in the Commons (following Lloyd George) during a debate on the adjournment for Easter, the bulk of Tory members walked out. This looked like an orchestrated insult. At the end of April he accepted an invitation from the Liberals of North-West Manchester to contest the seat at the next election. On 31 May, when parliament reassembled, he made the final symbolic break, crossing the floor of the House. He sat down next to Lloyd George, in the seat from which he believed – in fact wrongly – that his father had operated in the days of the 'Fourth Party'.[67]

There were, of course, a few awkward things about his switch to be explained away. A few days earlier Lloyd George had told a meeting in Wales that Churchill and other Tory turncoats had supported the Education Bill only under duress from their party's whips.[68] There were those who, understandably, were suspicious of Churchill, but on the whole he received a warm welcome. On 4 June Churchill joined Lloyd George and about forty other Liberal MPs on the platform at a great free trade demonstration at Alexandra Palace (a large London venue), over which Sir Henry Campbell-Bannerman presided.[69] Lloyd George was clearly eager to strengthen relations with the new convert. In July he reported to his brother on an all-night sitting of the Commons that, he said, had delayed the progress of the government's Licensing Bill. This was a measure designed to ensure that, save in cases of misconduct, publicans could not be deprived of their licences without financial compensation. 'It was a great fight and we beat them – [Reginald] McKenna, Churchill & I', Lloyd George wrote.[70] (This was, however, only a short-term tactical success and the Bill passed after the government curtailed debate on it.) At around the same time Churchill referred, in a letter that does not appear to have survived, to a proposal for collaboration that Lloyd George had put to him. The reply to this letter from Churchill's uncle, the Liberal peer Lord Tweedmouth, makes clear that some kind of ginger group was suggested. 'I am very interested in what you say about LG's proposition', Tweedmouth wrote. 'I should say go into it – but warily and under conditions – make your party one of young Liberals and avoid the old hacks . . . be vigorous but avoid much bitterness or sarcasm at the expense of your own molluscs on the front bench, be a cheering voice and a spur to them rather than a whip.'[71]

Nothing like an organized group seems to have emerged, but there are some signs that Lloyd George and Churchill now started working in concert. In October 1904, they both spoke at a meeting in Caernarfon. Churchill's statement that 'Mr. Lloyd-George was the best fighting general in the Liberal ranks' was greeted by loud cheers. Lloyd George in turn 'congratulated Mr. Churchill upon having come to Carnarvon to strengthen his infant steps as a Liberal.' He welcomed the defection of 'young, bold, daring men like Mr. Churchill' from the Unionist ranks.[72] Churchill appears also, on at least one occasion, to have consulted his new colleague about his speeches, as Lloyd George counselled him against making commitments that might prove inconvenient in the future.[73] A degree of closeness between the two is indicated by the fact that, after one dinner party, they stayed up talking until after midnight.[74] And they appear to have coordinated their parliamentary antics. In his unpublished autobiography, Lloyd George's son Gwilym recounted a (possibly exaggerated) story that must date to this period. It referred to Austen Chamberlain, who became Chancellor at the time of his father Joseph's resignation in 1903. The younger Lloyd George recalled:

I remember . . . my father's account of a little enterprise he and
Winston Churchill engaged in . . . In the course of one of his
speeches on the Finance Bill [Austen] Chamberlain irritated
them by looking and sounding pompous; they resolved therefore
to keep him up all night as a penalty for this offence. The matter
under discussion was highly technical and they knew nothing
about it; happily, however, three elderly and notoriously boring
members who knew everything about it were known to intend
to speak. Churchill and my father diligently wrote down everything they said and repeated it with oratorical elaborations until
the morning; the Chancellor must have found the experience
chastening.[75]

Yet Lloyd George also appeared to experience a touch of
schadenfreude when things went wrong for Churchill (to whom,
significantly, he now referred by his Christian name). 'Winston
delivered a very elaborately prepared phillipic [sic] today', he wrote
on one occasion. 'Fell very flat. He is sick about it. Calls it a misfire.'[76]

Inevitably, their names began to be coupled in the public prints.
In the spring of 1905 Lord Rosebery remarked sarcastically that the
men who could hope to be appointed to 'high positions' in government were not those who had given proof of administrative ability,
but those who could make the most speeches and come up with the
most stinging epigrams. The Pall Mall Gazette on 18 April published a
cartoon that showed Lloyd George and Churchill justifying their
'mud throwing' on the grounds that they were qualifying themselves
for 'high positions' in the next Liberal government. Churchill sent a
copy to Rosebery, asking him to observe that 'your sportive arrows
are deflected into the bosoms of your friends!' The former premier
wrote back rejecting 'the poisonous insinuation that I was thinking
of you or Lloyd George when I made my last speech'. Churchill, in
an emollient reply, said that he had only sent the cartoon in order
to make Rosebery laugh. Indeed, he wrote, 'There is a good deal of
truth in it.'[77]

A previous cartoon, published in Punch in January, had shown a
lethargic Balfour wishing that he could find a doppelgänger to perform his duties in the House of Commons. Lloyd George and
Churchill, standing nearby, were both saying to themselves: 'Ought
not to be any difficulty about that!'[78] There was truth here too. Not

only were they both ambitious, but there was, indeed, also a rivalry inherent in the relationship between them, notwithstanding the fact that Lloyd George was obviously the senior partner. It was true too that the government, riven by divisions that Balfour could not overcome, was not far from giving up. It staggered on, though, until 4 December, when Balfour handed in its resignation to King Edward VII. Balfour's hope was that the attempt to form an administration would expose Liberal splits, allowing the Tories to return. In fact Campbell-Bannerman proved equal to the task. Three key 'Liberal Imperialists' – H. H. Asquith, Sir Edward Grey and R. B. Haldane – had agreed among themselves in September that they would not accept office under him unless he agreed to conduct his premiership from the House of Lords and allocate posts according to their wishes. This was known as the 'Relugas Compact' after the Scottish fishing lodge where the deal was hatched. However, when it came to the point, Grey and Haldane found that Asquith had, in November, already wrecked the compact, by accepting Campbell-Bannerman's promise of the Exchequer. The new Prime Minister was thus able to remain in the Commons and dispense appointments as he saw fit.

Ministerial hopefuls waited in trepidation to find out if they would be asked to serve and if so in what capacity. The day after Balfour's resignation, which happened to be a Tuesday, Lloyd George sent a telegram to Churchill asking him to join him for lunch at the Reform Club. Two other MPs, Reginald McKenna and Thomas Shaw, were also to be there.[79] Lloyd George and Churchill appear to have stayed in close touch throughout the week. Lloyd George later recalled that he and Churchill dined at the Café Royal several nights running, together with other aspirants for office.[80] One can imagine that the atmosphere was rather tense. 'Poor Winston is very excited', he noted. 'He is afraid he won't be in the Cabinet.'[81] Churchill's agony must have increased when Lloyd George received a summons to see the Prime Minister on the Friday. He told his brother: 'Winston and McKenna [have] not yet heard, which shows they have not been reached even as names. It also means Cabinet I think [i.e. for Lloyd George himself] for that is the first thing they settle.'[82] The outcome of the interview was Lloyd George's appointment as President of the Board of Trade with a seat in the Cabinet. He reported: 'Winston and McKenna think I have the most important post in the Ministry at this juncture.'[83] This was a fawning exaggeration: but Lloyd George was never averse to flattery.

Churchill had to wait until the next day for his invitation to serve, in a junior role outside the Cabinet. Boldly he turned down the offer of the post of Financial Secretary to the Treasury (which eventually went to McKenna). Judging, presumably, that his talents were indispensable, he held out instead for the post of Undersecretary for the Colonies. This was, on the face of it, a less senior position than the one he had rejected. The *Manchester Guardian* wrote, 'It is interesting to note that as the Colonial Secretary (Lord Elgin) is in the other House Mr. Churchill will, in the House of Commons, practically fill the official position formerly held by Mr. Chamberlain and lately by Mr. Alfred Lyttelton.' (Chamberlain had stepped down as Colonial Secretary in September 1903 to pursue his tariff reform campaign in the country.) This may have been Churchill's calculation; but there was no realistic hope that even an activist junior minister could rival the dominance Chamberlain had achieved. As yet, moreover, he was still a long way from reaching a position of equality with Lloyd George.

In later years, this inequality was obscured from the two men's memories. In February 1933 Churchill and Lloyd George dined together at a restaurant in Charlotte Street, London. According to Lloyd George's private secretary, their talk was of brilliant quality. 'Winston said that at the very commencement of the Liberal Government in 1905 they [i.e. the ministers] had almost decided to throw up their hands.' Grey, Haldane and McKenna had all said they did not see how the government could go on, he claimed. 'Winston then passed a note over to L.G. saying: "If you are going to speak, now is the time, otherwise it will be too late." L.G. spoke, with the result that they stayed in for eight years.'[84] This was sheer invention. Campbell-Bannerman's government had been safe from the moment he secured the services of Asquith, Grey and Haldane. But the fantasy – which held the false implication that Churchill (and McKenna) had been in the Cabinet at the time, passing notes over the Cabinet table – was an agreeable one to both men, not least during the 1930s when they were trapped in the political wilderness. If Churchill was retrospectively elevating his own importance, he was, in effect, doing the same thing for Lloyd George, by painting him as the saviour of the Liberal government. This was an important aspect of the mythology of their partnership: that they were inseparable comrades, constantly stiffening the backbones of their more pusillanimous colleagues. In reality, the relationship was much more vexed than this; and, by 1905, had by no means reached its full intensity.

Chapter Two

SUPPORTERS RAMPANT

VIOLET ASQUITH, the daughter of H. H. Asquith, who became Chancellor of Exchequer when the Liberal government was formed, recalled in later life that the alliance that developed between Lloyd George and Churchill was the closest that existed within that government, yet in some ways also the most incongruous. From Lloyd George, she wrote, Churchill learnt the language of radicalism: 'It was Lloyd George's native tongue, but it was not his own, and despite his efforts he spoke it "with a difference".' Whilst squires, landowners and parsons were Lloyd George's 'hereditary enemies', Churchill had no strong feelings about parsons, and counted squires and landowners among his friends and relations. 'Lloyd George was saturated with class-consciousness. Winston accepted class distinction without thought.'[1] This was not the only explanation for the differing emphases of their respective 1906 election campaigns. In their political priorities, Nonconformist Wales and free-trade Manchester overlapped in some ways, but were by no means identical, and this the candidates were bound to reflect. But certainly, Lloyd George and Churchill's differing backgrounds had an impact on their use of the language of radicalism; and this helped explain the tensions within their relationship as well as its effectiveness as a political axis.

In his satire *The New Machiavelli*, H. G. Wells wrote that although the 1906 election would doubtless figure in history as a momentous conflict, 'there was scarcely a sign that a great empire was revising its destinies. Now and then one saw a canvasser on a doorstep. For the most part people went about their business with an entirely irresponsible confidence in the stability of the universe.'[2] Yet, for those caught up in the political maelstrom the atmosphere was heady – especially, of course, for those who sensed they were on the winning side. If anything, the excitement was increased by the fact that (as was always the case until 1918) polling took place over an extended period, from 12 January to 7 February during this election. Therefore, results in some parts of the country were known before others. Churchill's result came early, on 13 January, and Lloyd George's a week later.

Unlike Churchill, who was contending with a previous Tory majority, Lloyd George was not facing a serious opponent in his constituency. He was able to boast that R. A. Naylor, a businessman who was unknown locally, had been put up against him only to prevent him going off and speaking for other Liberals elsewhere; and at any rate he was sufficiently confident to make a tour in support of free-trade candidates in England.[3] Lloyd George told his constituents that 'The first thing we are going to do is to remedy the wrongs of the Education Act.'[4] (In fact, the failure to solve the problem was to profoundly weaken the new government.) Decrying the 'greedy, selfish' policy of the Church of England and the Catholic Church, he declared that Liberals and Nonconformists 'simply asked for fair play'.[5] He also predicted that the other great question before the next parliament would be free trade.[6] (In fact, because the Liberals merely wanted to maintain the status quo, parliament would not be required to pass any new legislation.) Britain's trade 'had fastened on the rocks of freedom, and the commercial storms that had swept over her over during the past 60 years had failed to injure her.' Protection was an 'empty folly' that would wreak devastation.[7]

As the campaign went on, he continued to stress these issues, and raised other points too, such as Welsh disestablishment and the Cabinet's plans to bring in a Bill to improve the legal position of the trade unions. In London he spoke on the question of the workers from China who had been imported into the Transvaal. This issue ('Chinese Slavery', as others dubbed it) appealed at once to the humanitarian instincts of those who opposed the poor pay and treatment of these indentured labourers and to the racist ones of those who thought that they were taking jobs that properly belonged to white men. Lloyd George went to neither extreme, but accused the former government of having, just before it fell, signed 16,000 new contracts that could not be broken save at great expense. This, he claimed, amounted to a trick by the Tories to ensure that the current system was maintained even though they themselves were no longer in office.[8] Just before polling in his constituency, he mentioned old age pensions, rather as an afterthought. Chamberlain, he said, was perfectly sincere in his advocacy of pensions, but the South African war had swallowed up the money. It would be impossible at the present time, Lloyd George argued, to get the British people to face up to the cost of a new scheme. 'Therefore, the matter, when taken up, must be taken up gradually. They must, first of all, put the national finances in spick and span order, and then see that every man too old to pursue his ordinary avocation should be saved from the humiliation of the workhouse or parish charity.'[9] The caution he expressed seems to have been, if anything, more significant than the noble aspiration to which it attached.

In Manchester North-West, it was left to Churchill's Conservative opponent, William Joynson-Hicks, to discuss unemployment relief – 'the present system of our workhouses should be entirely changed' – and to advocate pensions (for 'the veteran of labour – he did not mean the scallywags').[10] This did not necessarily mean that Churchill was insensible to the sufferings of the poor, but, showing even greater caution than Lloyd George, he argued that it 'was not possible by any mechanical state system to adequately deal with this question. The Lifeboat Service of the world was manned by the arms of men, and rescue work was voluntary.'[11] Joynson-Hicks also tried to make play of the alleged Liberal threat to the Church, claiming in his election address that Lloyd George had said that every member of the Cabinet was in favour of disestablishment.[12] It was difficult for him, though, to move debate away from trade. The Liberal slogans on the hoardings included 'Churchill and Free Trade', 'Cheap Food', and 'A United Empire'.[13]

Churchill was seen by the *Daily Mail* as the star of the campaign: he not only gave ju-jitsu demonstrations but he also wore interesting hats.[14] Another rather novel feature was the disruption of his meetings by Votes for Women campaigners, although this had happened to him even in advance of the fall of the old government. In 1904, on the only occasion he had had a chance to vote on the question in the Commons, he had in fact supported the enfranchisement of women, but he was clear that if he was 'subjected to any further annoyances, I shall say plainly that I do not intend to vote for Female Suffrage in the next Parliament'.[15] When the prominent suffragette Sylvia Pankhurst interrupted one of his election meetings, he did make such a statement, but then withdrew the remark; and his attitude to the question continued to be ambiguous.[16] On the issue of Chinese labour, Churchill's biographers tend to claim he was relatively circumspect. After the election, he made a remark that has become famous: that to describe paid contracts entered into voluntarily for a brief period as 'slavery' was to run 'some risk of terminological inexactitude'.[17] Nevertheless, during the election itself he referred to 'the battle of white labour against the whole force of the capitalist interest in South Africa', and two years later he spoke of 'how the yellow plague had been stayed and the coolies sent home' by the Liberal government.[18]

Thus, neither Lloyd George nor Churchill campaigned to any significant degree in favour of the great social reforms with which their names are now associated. They would be driven to these measures, at least in part, by political necessity, as well as, in Churchill's case and possibly in Lloyd George's too, by changing ideology. In the meantime the largely negative tone of their respective campaigns did them no harm. Churchill defeated Joynson-Hicks by a majority of 1,241, which was fairly comfortable in those days. This brought him a congratulatory telegram from Lloyd George: 'Glorious even Welsh language fails to express delight'.[19] Lloyd George's own victory was by a margin of 1,224, which, like Churchill's win, was part of a wider Liberal landslide. The voters returned 400 Liberals, 83 Irish Nationalists, and (in a significant breakthrough) 30 Labour members against 157 Conservatives. The Tories would not be so badly beaten for another ninety-one years.

In spite of its majority, though, the government faced difficulties. Most significant was the inbuilt Conservative dominance in the House of Lords, which freely exercised its capacity to veto legislation, and in particular 'faddist' measures which Tories claimed did not command the support of the electorate as a whole. Although possessed of the gift of stolidity, Campbell-Bannerman was unable, in the face of this, to give a clear direction to his administration. And although Lloyd George's work at the Board of Trade did his reputation great favours, he and Churchill did not yet have the opportunity to dynamize and/ or antagonize their colleagues in the way that they would do from 1908. J. H. Lewis, the MP for Flintshire and an ally of Lloyd George, noted in that year that his friend's initial major alliance had been with John Burns, the popular but ineffectual President of the Local Government Board: 'L.G. supported J.B. in matters relating to London, J.B. supported L.G. in questions relating to Wales and

Nonconformity. As L.G. shot ahead the alliance seems to have cooled off.' It was only after this that Lloyd George and Churchill became 'great pals'.[20] Before Asquith's accession to the premiership, and in particular before 1907, contacts between them were relatively limited. There were, however, some significant episodes and connections.

The first of these derived from the Colonial Conference that was held in the spring of the year after the election. The British faced demands from the representatives of the colonies, and particularly from the Australians, that the trade preferences they granted Britain should be reciprocated. The Liberal government, which had, after all, been elected on a free-trade ticket, could hardly concede this. In their speeches to the conference, Asquith, Churchill and Lloyd George all made this clear. Lloyd George, however, differed markedly from his colleagues in his manner of doing so. Churchill, using stronger language even than Asquith, told the delegates that a preference system would be 'vicious in itself and dangerous for the concord of the British Empire'.[21] (Lloyd George described this in private as 'a rasping & injudicious speech full of highsounding phrases'.)[22] Churchill later said that the government would not 'give a farthing's preference on a single peppercorn'.[23]

Lloyd George couched his refusal more delicately. The government, he said, heartily agreed 'that the Empire would be a great gainer if much that was now bought from foreign countries could be produced and purchased within the Empire'. He differed from the proponents of imperial preference 'only on ways and means'.[24] Thus, the pro-tariff-reform *Times* noted that although neither Lloyd George nor Churchill had yet 'found salvation', the former's tone was 'refreshingly sympathetic when compared with that of his colleagues'.[25] The colonial representatives probably shared this view. Nevertheless, the difference between the two men was, on this occasion, mainly, if not wholly, presentational. Certainly, Lloyd George was no free-trade dogmatist, but, as one of his early biographers noted in relation to this episode, he possessed 'perhaps more than any of his colleagues, the ability to say things not in themselves welcome to those he addressed so pleasantly that they sounded conciliatory and attractive'.[26] By contrast, no one ever accused Churchill of an excess of tact.

The Colonial Conference had an interesting and neglected sequel. If imperial preference were to be refused, the delegates could not be sent away completely empty-handed. Sir Wilfrid Laurier, the Canadian Prime Minister, raised the issue of imperial communications. The steamship service between Britain and Canada was slow, and Australia and New Zealand lacked an effective transport connection with the mother country. Laurier proposed a steamship service between Britain and Canada equal in speed to the best that ran between the UK and the USA, and to link this service by means of the Canadian railways to a fast steamship route from Vancouver to New Zealand and Australia.[27] This All-British (or 'All-Red') Route provided, it might be thought, an ideal way of expanding imperial trade without offending laissez-faire principles – as Lloyd George had suggested was desirable. A resolution in favour of the project was passed unanimously. The trouble was that such a service would require a hefty subsidy, and even though Canada was prepared to contribute, this offended against Liberal orthodoxy almost as much as tariffs did. Churchill noted that the plan put the government in some difficulty: if it went ahead, it would be reproached with inconsistency, but if it failed to live up to its promise to the colonies, it would court criticism from those quarters. Nevertheless, he wrote, 'it may be doubted that the best way to resist a Protectionist movement under an Imperialist guise, is by an attitude of uniform and unrelieved negation on every path'. Therefore, if a workable proposal could be devised, it should be supported.[28] Lloyd George helped to push the scheme forward. He and Churchill both served on the committee set up to deal with the issue. As Churchill observed in 1908, after having replaced him at the Board of Trade, 'Hitherto Lloyd-George has been the "motor-muscle".'[29] Although Lloyd George's new role as Chancellor put him in the position of 'devil's advocate' – being virtually obliged to object, given his office, on grounds of expense – the scheme in the end went ahead, without the political controversy that had been feared.[30]

Another aspect of the Empire gave rise to a further episode that connected the two men, although in this case the consequences were somewhat delayed. Churchill made a tour of Africa during the parliamentary recess. In total, he spent five months abroad, returning in January 1908. On his outward journey he stopped in Cyprus, which was a British protectorate. He became disquieted at the 'violent & widespread' movement for unity with Greece.[31] Hoping, it seems, to calm such sentiment, he made a speech to Cyprus's Legislative

Council in which he promised that the British grant-in-aid to the island would be continued at the current level. 'Winston's warm-hearted indiscretion' had repercussions in 1910, when Lloyd George was Chancellor.[32] The Treasury now wanted to cut the grant-in-aid, in the light of Cypriot prosperity. Churchill saw himself as being 'committed upon this question in a special and personal sense', and put up resistance.[33] In Cabinet 'a long wrangle occurred between George & Churchill', and the matter was referred to a committee of ministers.[34] Charles Hobhouse, the Financial Secretary to the Treasury and an advocate of economy, wrote: 'On the facts the Committee agreed with me, but Ll.G. *spontaneously* said that as Winston Churchill's word was involved he could not but give way. Finance he took no account of.'[35] If this account is to be taken at face value, this was one of the rare occasions when Lloyd George, in his relations with Churchill, put personal considerations ahead of practical and political ones. It is quite possible, though, that he had some ulterior motive for courting Churchill's favour at this particular time.

Often, indeed, when he spoke of Churchill to others in private, there was a note of disparagement, albeit mixed with admiration. We see this in some of his earliest comments, in his letters to his brother. In May 1907 he wrote: 'Dined with Churchill last night alone. Very ambitious – very clever – very unscrupulous.'[36] Two months later, after Churchill had had a rough time in the Commons, Lloyd George wrote: 'Poor Winston had a very heavy House and he felt it keenly, as the applause of the House is the very breath of his nostrils. He is just like an actor. He likes the limelight and the approbation of the pit.'[37] There was more than a touch of schadenfreude here, as well as hypocrisy; Lloyd George was hardly loath to accept applause himself. There is also some indication, though, that Lloyd George did on occasion derive emotional sustenance from Churchill's friendship and advice. In November 1907, Mair Lloyd George, the second of his five children, died of appendicitis at the age of 17. This personal catastrophe damaged his relationship with his wife. He later spoke of how 'after Mair's death they had drifted apart', as they 'each had their poignant grief but could not go to each other for sympathy and understanding'.[38] In the summer of 1913 William George's baby boy also died after contracting throat trouble. Lloyd George advised his brother not to look backwards: 'Another maxim I found comfort in was given me by Winston, "Never press the spear to your breast", which means, don't brood unnecessarily and dwell incessantly on the details of the catastrophe and travel over its burning surface again and again.'[39] In 1921, Churchill was to suffer a similar tragedy when his fourth child, Marigold, died at the age of two.

Although Lloyd George's connections with Churchill prior to 1908 had some significance for the future, the relationship was, as yet, not an intense one. Nevertheless, Lloyd George's activities as President of the Board of Trade helped set the parameters for the man who would succeed him in that year. His legislative achievements were significant. One of these was the Merchant Shipping Act (1906), which aimed to improve conditions for crews of cargo ships without blunting the British Merchant Navy's competitive edge. Another was the Patents and Designs Act (1907), which clarified and closed gaps in the existing law. In a bold and imaginative move he also established a national census of production.[40] Moreover, he drew up a Bill, the purpose of which was to establish a Port of London Authority, to improve the capital's docks. When he moved to 11 Downing Street he bequeathed the proposal to Churchill. During 1908 the two men steered the Bill through the Commons together, amid mutual compliments. ('It has been from the first the guiding principle of my right hon. Friend the Chancellor of the Exchequer to prefer the general interests to the sectional interests'; 'I am glad that my right hon. Friend the President of the Board of Trade has decided to stand by this Clause'; etcetera.)[41] If the Board of Trade had not been a greatly important department when Lloyd George took control, he certainly turned it into one. In fact, he did so much at the Board that Churchill feared, on taking it over, that he was faced with 'A gleaned field'.[42] Nevertheless, he too was to achieve much there.

The change in offices was occasioned by Campbell-Bannerman's retirement. By January 1908 the Prime Minister, who had suffered several heart attacks, was mortally ill. However, he continued in office for some weeks. At the end of January Lord Esher, a confidant of the king, recorded in his diary a discussion with Churchill. 'We discussed a successor to C.B.', he wrote. 'He thinks Asquith has higher claims than Grey', the Foreign Secretary. Esher mentioned as a possible candidate the veteran John Morley, the Secretary of State for India, who was also the biographer of Gladstone. This was a silly thought, because although Morley was a talented writer he was more

notable in the political field for his habitual threats of resignation
than for his concrete achievements. But Churchill, according to
Esher, leapt at the idea 'like a salmon. He was carried off his feet
by the very notion. He is going to talk it out with Lloyd George and
his radical friends, and also speak to Morley.'[43] Of course, nothing
came of this. At the beginning of March Edward VII indicated to
H. H. Asquith that he would call on him in the event of Campbell-
Bannerman's death or resignation – and then departed for the South
of France. Campbell-Bannerman at last resigned at the start of April,
and Asquith travelled to Biarritz, where he kissed hands. The king
had not cared to return to London merely in order to appoint a new
Prime Minister.

Once it had been made clear to Asquith that he was the heir
apparent, he felt free to begin discussing ministerial appointments.
And so did everyone else. Esher's diary reported some of the gossip:

> It seems that Haldane [Secretary of State for War] wants the
> Exchequer, and Asquith wants him to go there. But the Radicals
> in the Cabinet want Lloyd George, who is poor, and wants it
> himself. Winston would like the Local Government Board. He
> does *not* want to succeed Lloyd George – who has been a success
> – at the Board of Trade.[44]

The reference to Lloyd George's poverty is explained by the fact
that the Chancellor received a higher salary than the President of the
Board of Trade. If Esher's account was correct, then Churchill
quickly changed his mind; for, after a discussion with Asquith during
which the Colonial Office, the Admiralty and the Local Government
Board were mentioned as possibilities, he wrote the premier-in-
waiting a letter expressing a preference for the first.[45] This does not
necessarily mean, though, that Esher's sources of information were
not good, for on 20 March he went on to predict correctly the final
disposition of offices.

> Lloyd George will go to the Exchequer. There is no further
> question of Haldane, as Asquith sees that it would break up the
> Cabinet. Winston, who wanted the Local Government Board,
> now apparently, does *not* want it. He will, I expect, *have* to go to
> the Board of Trade, whether he likes it or not. There is no other
> place vacant.[46]

On the day of his appointment, Asquith wrote to Lloyd George and Churchill from Biarritz offering them the posts in question. It might not have been something he did with unmitigated enthusiasm; he was aware that some within the Liberal ranks regarded both men as a danger.[47] Reportedly, he remarked to Lord Crewe at around this time, 'Lloyd George has no principles and Winston no convictions.'[48] Perhaps, though, he also recognized that such flaws in character were not without their potential advantages to the government.

Even before Asquith returned to Britain, a list of the chief Cabinet changes appeared in the *Daily Chronicle*, in advance of the official announcement. The Prime Minister's wife, Margot, was outraged at the leak, and determined that it could only have come from 'Winston himself, whom I was sure it was not, or Lloyd George *whom* I was sure it *was*'. Churchill, to whom she imparted this suspicion, stood up for Lloyd George, and advised her against interfering in politics. Tact was never one of Margot's strong points, however, and she went about collecting evidence of the Chancellor's guilt, before informing her husband.[49] On 10 April, the day that Asquith arrived back, she wrote to Churchill. 'I'm told Lloyd George dines with you tonight. I *wish* you wd speak to him & tell him quite plainly that the staff of *Daily Chronicle* have given him away to 3 independent people.' She added: 'Lloyd George's best chance if he *is* a good fellow, wh I take yr word for, is *not* to lie about it when H [Asquith] speaks heavily to him but to give up his whole Press Campaign'. Moreover, 'I've just driven H from the station & he said to me "he hoped to God Winston would give it him".'[50] Churchill broached the matter with Lloyd George as requested, but, unsurprisingly, the latter flatly denied the accusation, affecting an air of injured innocence.[51] He wrote to Asquith the next day: 'Winston told me last night that some of my colleagues had rushed to you immediately on your arrival with the amiable suggestion that I had been responsible ... there is not a shadow of truth in the insinuation and I am ashamed to think that it should be even necessary to say so.'[52] As Violet Asquith later recalled: 'I am sure that Winston believed in his innocence, and equally sure that no one else did.'[53]

Churchill's staunch defence of Lloyd George casts some doubt on another story connected with the Cabinet changes. This is attributed to Sir Francis Hopwood, Permanent Undersecretary of State at the Colonial Office. Hopwood alleged that on the day when it became known who the new Chancellor was to be, 'Churchill walked into his (Hopwood's) room; took up his position with his back to the fire; smiled broadly, and with an air of great satisfaction said, "Hopwood, I have great news for you. Lloyd George has accepted the Chancellorship, which means that he will never be in another Government."' Hopwood's interpretation of this was that 'Winston thought that his great rival, Lloyd George, the man who, in his opinion, might stand in his way for the Premiership – would act so incompetently as Chancellor that he would kill himself politically, and have no great political future.'[54] Although Hopwood's tale cannot be entirely discounted, it must be noted that he himself may have had something of a grudge against Churchill. Moreover, were Lloyd George, the man with whom Churchill was now increasingly associated, to have fallen flat on his face, the benefits to his younger rival might actually have been mixed.

Indeed, most of the evidence suggests that Churchill clearly saw the benefits of a strong working partnership with a Chancellor who, though his working methods were erratic and his detailed knowledge of finance suspect, was to prove a huge success. Lloyd George, for his part, went a little out of his way to help his colleague. At this time new appointees to the Cabinet were obliged to resubmit themselves to the voters. Churchill, therefore, had a by-election to fight in Manchester. Lloyd George travelled to the city to make his first speech since becoming Chancellor in support of his candidature. This went against convention, but 'In his opening sentences Mr. Lloyd George made light of the fuss that has been raised about a Cabinet Minister taking part in a by-election'. There was no reason, he said, 'for the much talked-of "rule", and so he was very pleased to break it, in order to help "a colleague assailed by every monopoly and privilege which stands in the path of progress"'. He went on to offer a romanticized picture of how he had become acquainted with Churchill: 'when I first saw him, five years ago [sic], in Parliament, at the outset of a career which I knew was going to be a great one, ready to put the whole of his great and brilliant powers at the service of the people, I welcomed his comradeship with a glad heart, and, if you will allow me to say so, I believe that he and I, working together, can do something – something, at any rate, to remove this degradation upon the social condition of England.' Late that night, after he had addressed three further meetings, he and Churchill returned to their hotel. They had a slightly stagy conversation, for the benefit of the reporters, about how well the campaign was going.[55] Unfortunately, though, the Chancellor's best oratorical efforts were not quite good enough to secure victory. On 23 April Joynson-Hicks, who was standing again, defeated Churchill by a margin of 429 votes. In May, though, the new President of the Board of Trade successfully contested Dundee, thus gaining, he mistakenly believed, a seat for life. 'Winston has made a bad choice in going to Dundee', Lloyd George wrote to William George. 'If every English Liberal statesman, the moment his own countrymen scowl at him, ran away to the bosom of the Celt to be coddled, England will think Liberalism a purely Celtic party'.[56]

That August Churchill became engaged to Clementine Hozier, an attractive but not wealthy woman ten years his junior. 'Your luck has followed you into the most important transaction of your life', Lloyd George told him.[57] Leo Amery, who had been a near contemporary of Churchill's at Harrow, and who within a few years was to be elected a Conservative MP, commented on the forthcoming nuptials in a private letter. He contrasted Churchill's behaviour with the rumour and scandal surrounding Lloyd George and Asquith at this time. Amery noted: 'The talk is that L.G. may have private trouble . . . in the shape of divorce proceedings raised by C. S. Henry M.P.' (Charles Henry had been elected as a Liberal in 1906, and Lloyd George was indeed close to Julia, his American wife, but the rumours cannot be fully substantiated. There were no divorce proceedings.) Meanwhile, he wrote, the Asquiths were shocking 'the world', and Nonconformist opinion in particular, on account of their friendship with Maud Allan, the dancer who had recently taken London by storm with her powerful interpretation of *The Vision of Salome*. This was not a role that called for modest attire; her risqué performances made her into a sex symbol, not at all the sort of person with whom Prime Ministers were expected to associate. According to Amery, the Asquiths 'have Maud Allan almost living in their house with them, and send her into lunch with amazed ambassadors. As a counterblast Churchill is marrying for love, or at any rate for beauty unadorned with shekels & habitually to be seen in opaque garments.'[58]

Churchill's wedding took place at St Margaret's, Westminster, on 12 September. Lloyd George was present – most other Cabinet members invited were unable to make it at short notice – and he was asked to sign the register.[59] (Churchill had thanked him, in advance, for his present of a silver fruit basket, writing, 'It will always be preserved in my family as the gift of a remarkable man & as the symbol of a memorable political association' – but in fact it later went missing.)[60] The following month the Chancellor reported to one of his chief confidants, the newspaper proprietor George Riddell, 'that he had never met anyone with such a passion for politics as Winston Churchill. He said that after his marriage he commenced talking politics to him in the vestry and was quite oblivious of the fact that he had to take out the bride.'[61]

Churchill's activities at the Board of Trade can be understood only in relation to of those of Lloyd George as Chancellor, which in turn can be understood only in terms of the constraints set down by Asquith, the previous holder of that office. The most important of these was the decision to introduce a system of non-contributory old age pensions. There is no reason to doubt that this expensive commitment was made for reasons of conviction. At the same time it would be foolish to deny that it was politically expedient to put belief into practice. As Edwin Montagu, Asquith's parliamentary private secretary, wrote to his boss in January 1907:

> So far as the last General Election turned upon Free Trade, we frightened the people into a panic of any change; and, if you cannot provide them with the material for their Social reforms by Free Trade methods, you will rivet together the quacks and the dupes into a concerted effort to raise money by other means: you will drive the Labour Party into the arms of Chamberlain's successors ... And all this leads up to an urgent request for a popular Budget this year.[62]

Asquith himself later echoed this argument: 'I have realized from the first that if it could not be proved that Social Reform (not socialism) can be financed on Free Trade lines, a return to Protection is a virtual certainty.' He added: 'Old age pensions were inevitable.'[63] His 1907 Budget made financial provision for the scheme introduced the following year. This allowed him to blanket the Conservatives, keep the Liberals' Labour allies on side, and steal a march on his own party's left wing (including Lloyd George). All of this helped put some backbone in a government that was frustrated by the actions of the Lords and was staggering under a series of by-election defeats. But Asquith had underestimated the cost of pensions, which was to spiral in future years. This meant that, in order to meet it, the new Chancellor, as Lloyd George himself was to put it, needed to find a hen-roost to rob. The problem was compounded by a cut in sugar duties – which was a boon to working-class consumers but which meant a loss of revenue – in the May 1908 Budget. (Asquith, rather than Lloyd George, introduced that Budget, as he had been the one who had prepared it.) In addition, the burgeoning naval race with Germany created a new dimension to the problem.

Therefore, while Lloyd George welcomed the pension scheme – 'it will, I think, help to stop the electoral rot' – he had a keen appreciation of the difficulties it created for him.[64] His first instinct, though, was to meet these through economy rather than by increased taxation. As he commented privately the day after the Budget: 'You see the position in which I am placed. Asquith has taken 3 millions off sugar. He has put the burden of finding 4 millions next year for Old Age Pensions. A large increase on Education, and possibly, a large amount, 3 or 4 millions, for the Navy. Where is it to come from? I will not put on taxes. What can come out of the Army?'[65]

He pursued this quest for cuts in spending in alliance with Churchill. Asquith appointed both men, together with Lewis 'Lulu' Harcourt, the First Commissioner of Works, to a Cabinet committee to review the War Office estimates. In mid-May Haldane reported to his sister on his problems as Secretary of State for War: 'Ll.G. has opened fire – wants to cut down the Army. My reply has been a point blank refusal.'[66] ('Clearly his [Haldane's] *bête noire* is Lloyd George, and after him Winston Churchill', noted Beatrice Webb, 'the young generation knocking at the door.')[67] A month later Churchill circulated a memorandum claiming that Haldane's proposed expeditionary force of 166,000 men was excessive. When Haldane responded by highlighting the potential demands the army might face in different theatres at the same time, he argued that the conjunction of dangers could be avoided by skilful diplomacy.[68] In July the row became public when *The Times* published an attack on the unnamed 'mischievous busybodies of the Radical party', who 'intent upon wild-cat schemes of social revolution, for which they cannot find the money without robbing somebody or something',

had 'selected the Army as their preliminary prey'.[69] This was published against Haldane's own urging, as he suspected it would be
counter-productive; and indeed the Liberal papers retaliated with
demands for economy.[70] Ten days later, though, he reported victory:
'Yesterday I had a fight in the Cabinet for money, but I had prepared
the ground, & successfully beat off a determined attack'.[71] Shortly
afterwards Charles Hobhouse, the recently appointed Financial Secretary to the Treasury, noted in his diary:

> Winston Churchill's introduction to the Cabinet has been fol-
> lowed by the disappearance of that harmony which its members
> all tell me has been its marked feature. He and Lloyd George
> have embarked on a crusade against expenditure and are fight-
> ing Asquith, Grey and Haldane. I cannot help suspecting that
> Winston Churchill is deliberately urging Lloyd George to ride
> for a fall. Lloyd George and Churchill have a good case, but
> personal discourtesy will not help them, and that is C's chief
> weapon.[72]

What, though, if increased armaments could be rendered
unnecessary through an easing of international tension? This was
what Lloyd George and Churchill now set out to achieve, in a way
that was foolhardy, if not downright irresponsible. That summer the
Chancellor made a trip to Germany, ostensibly for the purpose of
investigating the country's social insurance system. On 12 August the
Vienna *Neue Freie Presse* published an interview in which he called for
an Anglo-German entente 'in order that we may be able to devote
ourselves wholly to the tasks of peace, of progress, and of social
reform'.[73] Two days later the President of the Board of Trade stated
in a speech in Swansea that 'there is no real reason for any quarrel
between England and Germany'.[74] Writing from Hamburg, in the
same letter in which he congratulated him on his engagement, Lloyd
George told him: 'Your Swansea speech was tiptop and pleased the
Germans immensely.'[75]

Lloyd George and Churchill were, however, straying outside their
respective areas of responsibility, without prior consultation with the
Foreign Secretary. The periodical *Justice* felt the interview and the
speech confirmed its view of them as 'Two Cabinet Bounders'.[76]
They were also criticized by *The Times*[77] and, equally predictably, by
the King. 'I cannot conceive how the Prime Minister allows them

ever to make speeches on foreign affairs concerning which they know nothing', he fulminated.[78] On 23 August Esher wrote in his diary that Haldane was convinced that the two men aimed at the capture of the Prime Minister. 'They think that by destroying Haldane, and even Grey, they can carry on the Government, with Asquith as a respectable figure-head.'[79] But Lloyd George had already received a telegram slapping him down, and had agreed not to make further foreign policy interventions.[80] A couple of months later Haldane was saying that 'Winston and L. George have quite collapsed, and are perfectly amenable.'[81]

The two men's own relationship was tinged with ambiguity. In April 1908 J. H. Lewis noted their closeness. He wrote of Lloyd George's attitude to Churchill: 'He trusts him and believes him to be perfectly loyal.' However, he added, 'I believe that there will some day be a desperate fight between these two desperate natures.'[82] A few months later, he recorded a conversation with Lloyd George: 'Speaking about Winston Churchill I asked whether he trusted him. "I'm afraid I don't," he said. "I would not trust him a yard."' Lewis replied, 'if he saw a chance to pass you he would not hesitate a moment'. To this the Chancellor answered, 'I know he would not. It is his nature to go ahead, but I have not the least doubt that he would be willing enough to pick me up afterwards.'[83] For the time being, they stuck together. In October 1908 there were rumours in some quarters that they were intriguing for a dissolution of parliament the following spring, but Asquith, sensibly, chose to ignore these.[84] The Prime Minister's patience, however, was often tested. J. A. Pease, the Liberal Chief Whip, recorded: 'Asquith growling at [House of Commons] Questions at Lloyd George's absences – Winston stuck up for him on my other side & said everyman must not be judged by the same rules.'[85] They faced some barriers to smooth social relations, though. When Lloyd George spent one Sunday with Churchill at Blenheim, the Duke of Marlborough taunted him, and the visit was not repeated.[86]

At the end of November the House of Lords vetoed the Licensing Bill, a government measure that constituted a modest attack on the drink trade. (It cannot be emphasized too strongly that the Lords' power of veto posed a genuine threat to the government's legislative programme as a whole.) Although the evidence on the point conflicts slightly, it seems probable on balance that Lloyd George and

Churchill stood firm against the idea of dissolving parliament and calling an election.[87] Churchill's unconvincing story, mentioned in the previous chapter, about them propping up the government in 1905 may have been a misremembered account of this episode. On 11 December Asquith made clear in public that there would be no dissolution, and said that the Liberal Party should 'treat the veto of the House of Lords as the dominating issue in politics'.[88] This firm declaration against the power of the Lords gave the government new vigour, but at the same time set the stage for the ensuing constitutional crisis.

Equally, the Cabinet's internal divisions had not been resolved. Lloyd George and Churchill, having failed to cut down the army, now turned their joint attention to the navy. Their antagonist was Reginald McKenna, now the First Lord of the Admiralty. Already, in September, they had provoked his suspicions by straying into his area of responsibility. Both men, worried about unemployment in the engineering and ship-building trades, had urged McKenna to start building ships from the next year's programme in order to ensure a more even amount of work available; they did not anticipate this would involve extra cost. He in turn had declared that everything that could be done was already being done.[89] Now Lloyd George feared the expense of McKenna's proposed naval building programme, and Churchill backed up the Chancellor's protests strongly. McKenna wanted to lay down six of the revolutionary new Dreadnought class of battleship. Lloyd George and Churchill were prepared to countenance only four. Just before Christmas Lloyd George had a premature scent of victory in the economy campaign, thanking Churchill 'for the assistance you rendered me in smashing McKenna's fatuous estimates'.[90] But the conflict rolled over into the New Year.

All this was taking place against the background of a popular campaign for more Dreadnoughts. The slogan ran: 'We want eight and we won't wait'. But, as Asquith wrote to his wife on 21 February, 'The economists are in a state of wild alarm, and Winston & Ll. George by their combined machinations have got the bulk of the Liberal press – such as it is – into the same camp.' (The term 'economist' referred to an advocate of economy, rather than one who studied economics.) 'They (the two) go about darkly hinting at resignation (which is bluff) ... I am able to keep a fairly cool head amidst it all, but there are moments when I am disposed summarily to cashier them both.'[91] A few days later accommodation was reached on the basis of a compromise that Lloyd George played a considerable part in promoting. Four Dreadnoughts were to be laid down at once, and preparations were to be made so that four more could be built quickly were it to prove necessary – as indeed it was soon judged to be.

In *The World Crisis*, published after World War I, Churchill conceded that on this occasion, 'although the Chancellor of the Exchequer and I were right in the narrow sense' – because the Admiralty's short-term predictions of how many ships the Germans would build were in fact exaggerated – 'we were absolutely wrong in relation to the deep tides of destiny'.[92] This candid admission creates a problem for those who argue that Churchill's dramatic changes of view on naval policy can be explained in terms of a statesmanlike reaction to changed circumstances.[93] It also, though, obscures the complexities of Lloyd George's position. In 1914 Churchill, as First Lord himself, would come into conflict with him over the same question, the Chancellor still being, as it were, on the 'wrong side'. (But, as will be seen in the next chapter, Lloyd George again relented at the last minute, having done as much as he could to protect his radical credentials without actually resigning.) In the aftermath of this 1908–9 naval crisis Lloyd George made considerable attempts to butter up Lord Fisher, the First Sea Lord, who was one of the primary advocates of the 'Big Navy'.[94] As Grey commented, very perceptively, in September 1908, 'the Germans were inclined to think the radicals would weaken. "George will not weaken, because he will never face a navy scare!"'[95] In other words, although Lloyd George had to pay lip service to economy, his overriding concern was public opinion. The 'four plus four' compromise allowed him to maintain his pose as an economist whilst at the same time appeasing the popular agitation for more ships. And at the same time he gained a rhetorical weapon to use in the government's forthcoming battle with the House of Lords over the Budget. Whereas working men patriotically dropped in their coppers to help pay for Dreadnoughts, he was to argue, a request for a contribution from the rich produced only a howl of protest.

There was, therefore, a strong link between foreign and domestic issues, although the latter were not Churchill's primary interest.

'There is nothing to do here', he complained of his posting at the Board of Trade. 'Lloyd George has taken all the plums.'[96] Nevertheless, during his period in office (which straddled the crisis surrounding the People's Budget) he worked in harness with the Chancellor (although not always in harmony with him) to produce a substantial amount of further constructive legislation. There is room for debate about how revolutionary these efforts really were, but at the time they were perceived as marking a significant break with the past. The Fabian Socialist Beatrice Webb noted in 1911: 'neither party has really tackled the problem of poverty until the Lloyd George–Winston schemes of expenditure'.[97]

Contrary to what some of his more cynical colleagues said, Churchill's discovery of the problem of poverty was not new, although perhaps his fervour was.[98] As has been seen, he was, as late as the 1906 election, unconvinced of the merits of state action in order to solve it. However, a speech he gave in October of that year marked an important shift in his thinking. 'The cause of the Liberal Party is the cause of the left-out millions', he declared. He went on to add: 'I should like to see the State embark on various novel and interesting experiments', concerning itself increasingly, among other things, with the care of children, the sick and the aged. Churchill was open to a wide array of influences, but it is interesting to note that this landmark oration, with its references to competitive selection as the mainspring of society, and to 'the vision of a fair [i.e. beautiful] Utopia', came very shortly after he had read H. G. Wells's *A Modern Utopia* (1905).[99] (He was a great admirer of Wells, whose impact on Churchill's thinking has been overlooked.[100] Similarly, Lloyd George said of Wells that 'He is the only writer whose opinions on politics interests [*sic*] me in the least'.)[101] Shortly before his move from the Colonial Office he developed his ideas further in a seminal article entitled 'The Untrodden Field in Politics'. In it he argued for the establishment of a 'Minimum Standard' of living 'below which competition cannot be allowed, but above which it may continue healthy and free, to vivify and fertilise the world'.[102]

Although, at the Board of Trade, Churchill to a considerable extent followed in Lloyd George's reforming footsteps, he did not do so slavishly. In April 1908 the new Chancellor was asked what had been the most important feature of his time in his previous post. 'The largest question', he replied, 'was undoubtedly that of the railways', and he spoke tentatively in favour of nationalizing them.[103] He had set up a departmental committee to consider the industry's problems, but his successor took little interest. 'Churchill seemed to care nothing about these railway problems and the Committee was not his child', noted one of its members. As a consequence it produced no significant results.[104] Moreover, Churchill lacked Lloyd George's brilliant skill as an industrial conciliator, thanks to which a crippling railway strike had been averted in 1907. As one civil servant observed, 'He talks too much himself.'[105] He did make important reforms, including the introduction of Labour Exchanges (to match unemployed workers to jobs) and of minimum wages in low-paid industries (the 'sweated trades'). In terms of the influences upon them, these owed little to Lloyd George and a good deal to the Board of Trade civil servants. The question of compulsory state insurance against sickness and unemployment did, however, involve the two men in close collaboration.

Lloyd George's 1908 trip to Germany, foreign policy excursions aside, had been a fact-finding mission. He discovered useful information about continental schemes of invalidity and sickness insurance, but not about unemployment insurance.[106] After his return in August he discussed the question with Churchill, and they agreed to divide responsibility, the Board of Trade dealing with unemployment and the Treasury with health.[107] They faced opposition from colleagues, however, in part because of the reputation of their relationship. Lucy Masterman, wife of the junior minister Charles Masterman, wrote in her diary that 'the distrust of the Ll.G.-Churchill combination is so profound in the Cabinet they distrust everything they advance.'[108] In December Churchill advised Asquith that he and Lloyd George had agreed on delay: 'I don't think I could press my Unemployment Insurance plan until Lloyd-George has found a way of dealing with Infirmity or (wh is possible) has found that there is no way.'[109] The National Insurance Bill was not, therefore, ready until after Churchill had moved to the Home Office. In April 1911, shortly before introducing the Bill in the Commons, Lloyd George wrote a long letter to Alexander Murray, who had recently become Chief Whip. (Murray, the heir to a Scottish peerage, bore the title 'Master of Elibank'.) In the letter Lloyd George denounced Churchill's part in drawing up the scheme. He reviewed what he claimed was the history of the Bill:

In a weak moment I revealed my plans to Winston. He walked
off with them to the Board of Trade; got the Prime Minister's
consent to introduce a Bill on those lines himself ... when I
found it necessary to examine the Bill a few weeks ago I found it
a hopeless, indefensible muddle ... Winston had not even read
the Bill which he had circulated to the Cabinet ... as far as I
can see Winston had confined his labours in the matter to
delivering an elaborate speech in the House of Commons laying
down vague general principles which had been given to him
months before on my return from Germany.[110]

Exactly what provoked this diatribe is unclear. Lloyd George
must have realized he had been unfair, because he immediately
followed it up with another letter, asking that his criticisms not be
mentioned to Churchill. 'Perhaps I have taken in it too gloomy a
view of the work done by him on the Bill', he admitted. 'It is just
possible he left the Board of Trade before he had time to consider
how he could translate the excellent sentiments he gave expression to
in his speech into the prosaic words of an act of Parliament.'[111] Only
days later Churchill complained to his wife: 'Lloyd George has
practically taken Unemployment Insurance to his own bosom, & I
am I think effectively elbowed out of this large field in wh I consumed
so much thought and effort.' But he added: 'Never mind! There are
many good fish in the sea.'[112] These petty jealousies tell us more
about the stresses of high office than they do about the history of
national insurance. In spite of considerable opposition from vested
interests, the Bill, which was to form one of the foundation blocks of
the British welfare state, passed into law later in the year.

This, however, is to anticipate. The dominating feature of politics
in 1909–11 was the government's struggle with the House of Lords
over the constitution, foreshadowed by Asquith's reaction to the
rejection of the Licensing Bill and directly provoked by Lloyd
George's 'People's Budget'. He and Churchill had reacted to the
rejection of the Licensing Bill in differing ways. Neither of them was
greatly attached to the measure in and of itself, but the Lords' action
was a symbol of the hereditary chamber's contempt for the elected
one. Dining at the Commons, Churchill stabbed at his bread,
murmuring: 'We shall send them up such a Budget in June as shall
terrify them, they have started the class war, they had better be

careful.'[113] Lloyd George, by contrast, was more phlegmatic in his response, realizing that the death of the Bill gave him the opportunity of taxing the drink trade. He wrote to his brother on 9 December 1908: 'The Prime Minister has approved of my plans as they are now ... "Budget Sensational".'[114] Edwin Montagu reported to Asquith around this time that the Chancellor's 'plan of finance varies from day to day, and varies also by millions as though they were half-pence'.[115] But even if he had not yet hit on a cut-and-dried scheme, in terms of overall strategy, Lloyd George, Churchill and Asquith were all in harmony.

Churchill was eager to take joint credit for the Budget. He claimed that Asquith had lost influence with the radicals because of his addiction to hobnobbing with fine society. 'But,' he said, 'Lloyd George and I have re-established his credit with our Budget.' Because it was so unpopular with the upper ranks, it had put a stop to the Prime Minister's 'social career'.[116] Lloyd George later ridiculed the idea that Churchill had made any significant contribution to the Budget's design. 'Winston', he said, 'is opposed to pretty nearly every item in the Budget except the "Brat", and that was because he was expecting soon to be a father himself.'[117] (The 'Brat' was an income tax allowance for people with children; Churchill's daughter Diana was born in July 1909.) This comment was malicious and inaccurate. At the time, Lloyd George had written to his brother that Churchill was very pleased with the draft of the Budget speech: 'Thinks it will put life into the old Radical horse once more'.[118] Indeed, Churchill fully appreciated that the government's attack on the Lords 'must be backed by some substantial political or social demand which the majority of the nation mean to have and which the Lords cannot or will not give'.[119] Lloyd George's derisive remark can perhaps best be explained in relation to another of his sayings that Lucy Masterman recorded: 'Sometimes when I see Winston making these speeches I get a flash of jealousy and I have to say to myself, "Don't be a fool. What's the use of getting jealous of Winston?"'[120]

Thus, if they were in agreement on issues of substance, the personal tensions between them were significant. Yet in order to understand their respective roles during this crucial period, we have to understand not only their connection with one another, but also how they, as partners and rivals, related to Asquith. Some contemporaries portrayed him as being unable to rein in their disruptive influence. In October 1908, St. Loe Strachey, editor of *The Spectator*, wrote to John Burns: 'I am afraid L.G. and W-C, with a weak foreman of the works over them, who, though he means well, cannot keep order, will destroy the efficiency of the Cabinet and demoralise the whole gang of workers.'[121] In a similar vein, at the end of 1909, *Punch* published a cartoon entitled ' "Supporters" Rampant'. It showed the Prime Minister staggering under the weight of his two troublesome lieutenants, the subtitle being 'An Heraldic Inversion'.[122] Yet although Asquith was sometimes embarrassed by the excesses of their public rhetoric, the idea that he was often railroaded into major policy decisions by his more radical ministers was a misapprehension. In regard to the People's Budget, at least, he was in firm control of the direction of his government.[123] Lloyd George's success in getting his Budget proposals through the Cabinet was ultimately dependent on his support, helpful though Churchill was too. Churchill and Asquith's relative importance is shown by a comment made by Lloyd George to a friend not long after: 'I should say that I have Winston Churchill with me in the Cabinet, and above all the Prime Minister has backed me up through thick and thin with splendid loyalty.'[124]

Lloyd George introduced the Budget in the Commons on 29 April 1909, in an immensely long and virtually inaudible speech. The most important points were as follows. The scale of death duties – that is, the tax on inheritance – was to be increased. Income tax went up, but only on unearned income. A super-tax of sixpence ($2\frac{1}{2}$p) in the pound was to be introduced on incomes over £5,000 per year. There were to be new taxes on motor vehicles. Duties on liquor licences were to go up, as were duties on alcohol and tobacco. Most controversial, however, were the new land taxes; or rather, as the immediate yield of these was to be rather small, the land valuation that was to accompany them. The taxes themselves, indeed, were really a blind for the valuation scheme, which Lloyd George hoped would help him to extract greater revenue in the future. The stratagem was necessary because he could not have hoped to get a land valuation Bill through the Lords in its own right; but he had a reasonable expectation of getting his scheme passed if it was attached to a financial instrument. This was because, by convention, the Lords did not interfere with the Budget.

This raises the hoary question of whether or not the Budget was framed deliberately to provoke the Lords into rejecting it, in order to justify an assault by the Commons on their power. The answer would seem to be 'not in the first instance', but, as the agitation against the proposals grew, Lloyd George increasingly courted rejection, in part by using inflammatory public rhetoric. This was on the grounds that it might be better to go down to posterity as one who had defeated the peers – the rejection of the Budget having provided the excuse for action – than as the author of a successful financial scheme.[125] Churchill, for his part, was criticized as early as January by the Nonconformist *British Weekly* for courting disaster through his apparent public admission that the Lords might be able to force a dissolution on the Budget.[126] (He had said that the upper house had 'the power, though not, I think, the constitutional right' to do this, adding 'If they want a speedy dissolution they know where to find one.')[127] If he did not in fact expect the Lords to walk into the trap, he was not sorry when they chose to do so. In October, he remarked privately 'that his hope and prayer was that they would throw out the Bill';[128] although he bet his cousin, the Duke of Marlborough, £25 that they would in fact pass it. When he was in due course obliged to pay up, he wrote a note on the cheque (which the Duke did not cash, and is preserved in his papers at the Library of Congress). It read 'cheap at the price'.[129]

This, however, was still in the future. In the meantime there lay ahead a long battle to get the Finance Bill through the Commons. The Cabinet was divided on tactics. When Lloyd George proposed, in June, to guillotine the Bill – i.e. curtail debate on it – only Churchill supported him.[130] At the same time, agitation for and against the Budget was carried on outside parliament. Churchill became President of the Budget League, an organization designed to counter the Conservatives' Budget Protest League. A flavour of its activities can be gained from the printed programme for one of its meetings. The words for a number of songs were given, including 'Hurrah for the Budget', which was to be sung to the tune of 'Bonnie Dundee':

> Hip Hurrah for the Budget, the taxes are good!
> Let them run on the Landlords, and not on the food;
> If beer, and the baccy, must share in the stress,
> Then perhaps we can do with a little the less.[131]

Readers might gain an inkling from this of why the Liberals and their plans were not universally popular.

In the 1830s the Conservative statesman Robert Peel had followed a strategy of 'government in opposition'; Lloyd George and Churchill now pursued 'opposition in government'. At the end of July 1909 Lloyd George's oration at Limehouse, in the East End of London, shocked many Liberals, as well as Conservatives, for the violence of its language. The great landlords' day of reckoning was at hand, he suggested; such remarks were interpreted as socialist in spirit and as a menace to the rights of property ownership. In October he followed it up with a speech in Newcastle in which he mocked and denounced the peers. A 'fully equipped duke costs as much to keep up as two "dreadnoughts" and they are just as great a terror', he mocked. He went on to describe the House of Lords as 'five hundred men, ordinary men chosen accidentally from among the unemployed'; they were, he said, forcing a revolution, which, however, would be directed not by them but by the people.[132] Even Churchill could not compete with such brilliant invective, although he too used strong language. At Leicester in September he asserted that 'if they [the Lords] lose we will smash to pieces their veto'.[133]

Such language courted the displeasure of many. At around this time the Duke of Beaufort expressed his wish 'to see Winston Churchill and Lloyd George in the middle of twenty couple of dog hounds'.[134] Edward VII was more restrained. Esher noted: 'I don't think that the king objects to the Budget, but he dislikes intensely the tone of certain speeches. L. George's and Winston's.'[135] Sir Almeric Fitzroy, clerk to the Privy Council, put part of the blame on Asquith's sometimes ill-concealed fondness for alcohol. This is made clear in a passage excluded from Fitzroy's published diaries. 'It is a disagreeable task to have to emphasize in a Prime Minister a failing which would be fatal to a footman,' he noted haughtily, 'but there is no doubt of his frequent incapacity from so humiliating a disease as drink.' He added: 'With a Chief subject to periods of occultation [concealment, i.e. because he was drunk], it is unnecessary to seek far for the source which gives Winston Churchill & Lloyd George such uncontrolled liberty of speech.'[136]

However, just as the Prime Minister's drink problem (which did exist) was often exaggerated by hostile commentators, so too was the degree of licence he allowed Lloyd George and Churchill.

When it suited him, he delivered hints that he disapproved of the more intemperate of their remarks. In the Commons (shortly before Churchill's Leicester speech), Asquith, replying to a jibe from Balfour, said that the two men 'had added enormously to the picturesque resources of the English tongue in the course of the last few years, and they had done this with a *minimum* of indiscretion'.[137] This tactful rebuke had no immediate effect on Churchill,[138] who also came under pressure from other quarters. Ivor Guest MP, his cousin and near contemporary, had, like him, defected from the Tories over free trade. Guest now warned that Churchill and the Chancellor 'seem started on a path which leads into the unknown and which it seems to me must separate you from many of your colleagues and friends'.[139]

Perhaps it was the combination of such warnings that in due course led Churchill to distance himself, ever so slightly, from Lloyd George. On 2 November he wrote to his wife: 'I have seen Lloyd George on business repeatedly, & have made him feel a sensible difference in my attitude – without emphasis of any kind'.[140] He wrote again on the 3rd: 'We had an exciting cabinet this morning on the question of what we should do if the Lords reject – as is now assumed. I took a vy clear line, & was almost alone at first, but gradually they all came round to my view, and that in the face of Lloyd George's and the Lord Chancellor [Lord Loreburn]'s (a queer combination) dissent. I am in quite friendly relations with Ll.G: but more formal & independent than before.'[141] The Bill finally passed the Commons the next day. On 30 November, the Lords voted down the Budget by 350 to 75. This made a general election inevitable, and parliament was prorogued on 3 December.

The precise nature of Churchill's variance with Lloyd George over strategy is unclear. Crucially, though, in spite of what may have been agreed by the Cabinet, the government's position remained uncertain. This was Asquith's fault. In December the King made it clear that he would not countenance the creation of new peers for the purpose of forcing through legislation to deal with the Lords' veto until after the electorate had had yet a further chance to give its verdict on the idea in a *second* general election. But the Prime Minister did not convey this fact to the outside world or even to his own colleagues. Therefore, the election was fought, not least by Lloyd George and Churchill, on the basis that, if the Liberals won, the powers of the Lords would be dealt with. In fact, the crisis was to be prolonged.

Polling took place between 14 January and 19 February 1910. Lloyd George and Churchill were returned comfortably, but nationally the Liberals met with substantial losses. ('What is the use', Churchill later recalled Lloyd George as saying, 'of having a large army if you cannot afford to face heavy casualties?')[142] They secured 275 seats to the Conservatives' 273. The balance was held by 40 Labour MPs and 82 Irish Nationalists, and this ensured that Liberal government would continue. Some people were sure they knew how to apportion the blame for the losses. 'Lulu' Harcourt told Asquith: 'I found all over the country that all Ll.G.'s speeches and Winston's earlier ones . . . had done so much harm even with advanced men of the *lower* middle class: they excited alarm in some minds and disgust in others, and probably account for the heavy losses in the South.'[143] According to Margot Asquith, though, both her husband and Edward Grey were pleased with Churchill's speeches, which she, for one, considered to be more moderate than those of the Chancellor. She recorded in her diary how she summoned him after the election in order to praise him for his temperate line and cajole him into keeping it up:

> *Margot:* 'I don't want to balk at you, Winston, now. It's pretty
> obvious that now you see character pays more than
> anything in English politics. You've got a lovely wife and
> nice little child, why alienate *every* one – why not turn over a
> completely new leaf and make everyone love you and
> respect you? You think it's dull, but it's much duller to talk
> to journalists and to be always bracketed with Lloyd
> George. Why not walk with Edward Grey for a change?
> Didn't you mind Lloyd George's violent speeches? Do you
> realize, whether truly or not, at least 30 seats are attributed
> by our defeated men to Lloyd George?'
> *Winston:* 'Well, I'm not sure that he didn't win as many as he
> lost, but he certainly said a good many cheap things.'
> Putting tea in his sugar, '*I* at any rate was not going to
> compete in the same line of business.' Before we parted he
> shook me warmly by the hand and held one of my hands in
> his and said I was the truest of women and that he would
> never forget what I had said.[144]

As if this wasn't enough, once she learnt that Churchill was to become Home Secretary (Lloyd George remained at the Exchequer), she followed up her lecture with a letter. Urging him to 'keep up that moderation of language wh had struck so many in this election', she again did her best to split him off from Lloyd George: 'Believe me cheap scores, hen-roost phrases & oratorical want of dignity is out of date.'[145]

The distinctly lukewarm nature of Churchill's defence of Lloyd George, as recounted by Margot, by no means constitutes evidence that the men's partnership, which had many years still to run, was at an end. But, if her account forms anything to go by, it would seem that Churchill's later claims to have stuck by him through thick and thin were considerably exaggerated. It would also suggest that even if, as may well be imagined, he did not take Margot's interventions terribly seriously, he was happy to pretend that he did, perhaps on the off-chance that winning her support by disclaiming Lloyd George's methods would improve his position with the Prime Minister.

Neither, it should be added, was Lloyd George a great defender of Churchill in private. He mocked his vanity, ambition and lack of humour, although this was undoubtedly more for the pleasure of it than for any obviously political motive. Their rivalry came through in their occasional private bickering. Shortly after the election both men were guests of the Mastermans in Folkestone. 'You see,' Churchill remarked to Lloyd George one evening, 'in spite of your trying to keep me out of the Budget, I made a show after all.' (This was because he resented not having been asked to speak on the Third Reading of the Finance Bill.) 'I like that,' replied Lloyd George, 'I offered to hand you over the whole of Part II, the income tax.' 'Oh, that's detail!' came Churchill's response, 'I'm not going to do detail.'[146]

The government was by now at an impasse. The election had put its fate into the hands of the Irish. The Budget needed to pass the House of Commons once more, and they were in a position to prevent this. There were some things about it, such as the whiskey taxes, that they disliked in themselves. More importantly they wanted the veto dealt with in order to clear the way for the passage of Home Rule – i.e. substantial autonomy for Ireland from Britain, something the Lords would inevitably oppose – and were prepared to use their leverage to achieve this. But, on 21 February, Asquith confessed in the House of Commons that he had not secured from the King the guarantees that would allow the veto to be tackled. In the wake of this bombshell, the government almost collapsed. On 25 February, Lloyd George told J. H. Lewis 'that but for him and Winston Churchill the Cabinet would have resigned this afternoon. He said they were thinking too much of their own feelings, forgetting that they were the Trustees of a great cause.'[147] Lloyd George toyed with the idea of dropping the whiskey duties as the price of Irish support – Churchill was the only member of the Cabinet to agree[148] – but only the promise of action on the veto would satisfy. The problem was solved in mid-April when Asquith made clear that the requisite guarantees would be sought from the King in advance of a second general election.

One of Churchill's (rather archaic) duties as Home Secretary was to send regular letters to the King informing him of proceedings in the House of Commons. In early April a speech by Lloyd George on the question of the veto provoked a comment in one of these missives that is worth quoting at length. Writing about himself in the third person, Churchill told King Edward:

> What struck Mr. Churchill as curious was that the speaker was more successful in stirring Conservative consciences than in rousing Liberal enthusiasm. There are some vy deep and strong points of resemblance between the present Chancellor of the Exchequer and Mr. [Joseph] Chamberlain. Mr. Churchill has often been powerfully struck with them. They appear in manner, in view, in mood and expression. Mr. Churchill has seen a photograph of Mr. Lloyd George taken about ten years ago without his moustache, which really presented an extraordinary resemblance in type to the Chamberlain of the early eighties. And certain it is that both, though strong radicals by temperament have possessed in a peculiar degree the power of pressing the springs which actuate the ordinary Conservative mind.[149]

In emphasizing Lloyd George's similarity to Chamberlain, a one-time firebrand who had moved towards Conservatism, Churchill may have had a political motive. But the passage is also indicative, surely, of the fascination that his colleague held for him. Violet Asquith later recalled that 'the most curious and surprising feature' of the two men's partnership during these years 'was that while it exercised no influence whatsoever on Lloyd George, politically or otherwise, it directed, shaped and coloured Winston Churchill's mental attitude and his political course'. Indeed, 'His was the only personal leadership I have ever known Winston to accept unquestioningly in his whole political career.'[150]

This verdict is, to a considerable extent, borne out by other testimony. At the end of April 1910 Charles Hobhouse came across the two men debating the whiskey tax. 'The noticeable feature was Winston suggested, Ll.G. accepted or refuted suggestions, and Winston caved in, with a biting phrase or two, *but* caved in.'[151] Similarly, Churchill now favoured replacement of the House of Lords by an elected second chamber with restricted powers. Lloyd George, by contrast, was prepared to countenance total abolition but realized this was unrealistic, and therefore supported mere modification of the Lords' veto. Lucy Masterman recorded Churchill as saying 'No, no, no; I *won't* follow George if he goes back to that d—d Veto'. But she noted that, three weeks later, Churchill was making passionate speeches in favour of the veto policy. Lloyd George, she wrote, said that 'for three weeks while he is at a thing, he [Churchill] is very persistent, but he always comes to heel in the end'.[152]

At the end of April the Budget was finally approved by the Commons and the Lords in turn, but the powers of the upper house still had to be dealt with. The situation was complicated on 6 May by the death of Edward VII at the age of 68. A few weeks later Churchill sent a letter to Alexander Murray in which he described electoral planning in military terms. 'I do trust you are driving steadily ahead with your preparations for war', he wrote. 'George will no doubt have told you he is aiming at September', i.e. as the month for a general election. Churchill went on: 'The struggle will be a hard one; but I am sure if the constituencies are properly manned we shall win decisively.' He added: 'I put no faith in any hope of peaceful settlements . . . If any settlement is to be reached, it will only be by marching straight on to war.'[153] Murray, though, favoured an initiative by the new king, George V, to bring about a compromise between the parties. This 'truce of God' idea had been mooted publicly by J. L. Garvin, the editor of the *Observer*. He argued that Edward, on his deathbed, would have wanted his people to lay party passions aside. The Cabinet approved the idea of a

constitutional conference to thrash out an agreement, and in June
Arthur Balfour, as Tory leader, accepted Asquith's invitation to
participate. Lloyd George was one of the four government representatives; Churchill was not.

There was in fact no realistic prospect of agreement with the
Tories over curtailing the powers of the House of Lords. Lloyd
George tried to break the deadlock with an ambitious but improbable
plan for a coalition of Liberals and Conservatives. In a memorandum
of 17 August, he wrote: 'I cannot help thinking that the time has
arrived for a truce, for bringing the resources of the two Parties into
joint stock in order to liquidate arrears which, if much longer
neglected, may end in national impoverishment, if not insolvency.'
He proposed joint action on a wide range of social problems,
although his statements about how these might be tackled were rather
vague. On 29 October, after the Conservative leaders had sought
clarification, he followed up this memorandum with a more detailed
explanation that made clear, in particular, that he was prepared to
compromise on the tariff issue.[154] He assumed that 'as a condition
precedent' to any understanding with the Tories, 'a compact on the
Constitutional issue was essential', and that agreement on education
and Welsh Church questions were a necessary preliminary to
coalition.[155] Compromise over Ireland would also be needed.

At the end of September Lloyd George invited Churchill and his
wife to stay with him and Margaret in Criccieth. (Margaret was
probably not very pleased. Lucy Masterman noted the following
year that 'Winston is one of Mrs. George's fixed aversions' and that
she would squint 'portentously', rubbing her hands together and
'making a sound between a coo and a sneer', whenever his name
was mentioned.)[156] He advised Churchill to bring his golf clubs, and
described the other attractions of the area, but also said that he
hoped 'to squeeze in some serious talk about the future'. The
government, he feared, risked drifting along without policy or purpose. 'This aimlessness, if persevered in, means utter disaster. It is not
too late to pull ourselves together: on the contrary I think it is just
the time when we ought to be thinking out our next step (a) if
Conference succeeds, (b) if it fails. I have some ideas and I think they
are winning ones.'[157] Churchill enjoyed his visit. While out on a walk
he fell into a mountain stream, but when he got up said cheerfully,
'As I am wet through I may as well have some fun out of it,' and

stayed for half an hour in the stream damming the flow with stones
while Lloyd George looked on with amusement.[158] The men also
talked politics. It is clear that Lloyd George told Churchill of his
coalition plan – even before he had shown his first memorandum to
the Prime Minister. According to Lloyd George's later account, the
crucial exchange took place on the golf course, leading Churchill to
forget all about the game:

> I said to Winston, 'I have two alternatives to propose – the first
> to form a coalition, settle the old outstanding questions, including
> Home Rule, and govern the country on middle lines which will
> be acceptable to both parties but providing measures of moder-
> ate social reform. The other, to formulate and carry through an
> advanced land and social reform policy.' Mrs Winston, who was
> there, said, 'I am for the second.' Winston replied, 'I am for the
> first!'[159]

Writing to Lloyd George afterwards, however, Churchill gave the
coalition plan only a tentative welcome. 'It is not for me to take the
lead', he emphasized. 'I cannot tell how such an arrangement might
ultimately affect democratic political organizations. But if we stood
together we ought to be strong enough either to impart a progressive
character to policy, or by withdrawal to terminate an administration
[i.e. a coalition one] which had failed in its purpose.'[160] He was eager
to be part of such a government should it come into being, but did
not want to go out on a limb in order to bring it into existence. His
emphasis on 'standing together' with Lloyd George reflected a
perhaps legitimate fear that his colleague might abandon him. Lucy
Masterman recorded that Churchill lost interest in the scheme when
he found out that Lloyd George did not intend that he should be
included in the new Cabinet: 'he worked himself up into an astonishing state of indignation, pouring forth rhetorical denunciation of the
whole affair'.[161]

Of course, the success of the coalition idea depended on Conservative assent, but at the beginning of November the Tory leaders
rejected it. A few days later the constitutional conference broke down.
The government succeeded in extracting from a reluctant George V
the guarantees they needed on Lords reform. If the Liberals won
another general election, he would create sufficient peers to pass a
Parliament Bill, removing the upper chamber's powers over money

bills and replacing its capacity to veto other legislation with a mere delaying power.

In spite of his conversation with Margot Asquith earlier in the year, Churchill's election speeches were not excessively moderate. Lloyd George, for his part, was liberal with the hyperbole and deployed facts with his customary casualness. In one of his addresses he referred to the case of David Davies, 'the Dartmoor Shepherd', whom he and Churchill had come across during a recent joint visit to Dartmoor prison: 'On that bleak, mist-sodden upland I saw an old man of 65, in a convict garb, who had been sentenced to 13 years penal servitude because, under the influence of drink, he had broken into a church poor-box and stolen 2s.' Lloyd George used this example to draw a contrast with the Lords, the descendants of the 'plunderers of the poor', as he put it, who criticized him for taxing the wealthy and sparing the poor.[162] This was good electioneering material; Davies had indeed been treated harshly, but Lloyd George failed to mention that he was an habitual petty criminal (albeit one whose offences were always trivial) who had been in and out of jail for years. And Davies's sentence was not quite as claimed. He had, in fact, been sentenced to three years' penal servitude plus ten years' 'preventive detention', the latter made possible under an act passed in 1908 by the Liberal government itself. Churchill used his powers as Home Secretary to remit the additional ten years, and Davies was released at the close of 1910, after the election. Unfortunately, although he was found a job, he absconded the next day, and was subsequently convicted for housebreaking and sentenced to another nine months. The newspapers, of course, had a field day. 'The Tory press have behaved like cads', Lloyd George complained privately. 'In their eagerness to malign Winston and myself they have persecuted this wretched old man who has been so grievously punished for his peccadilloes.'[163] According to Clementine Churchill's much later account, her husband was 'very angry' about the episode, 'and complained bitterly to Lloyd George who had first interested him in the case of the Dartmoor Shepherd, because he had not taken more care of the man when he emerged from prison'.[164]

Polling in the election took place between 2 and 9 December 1910. As to the result, Lloyd George wrote to his wife on the 14th, 'It looks like our ending "as we were".'[165] The Liberal and Conservative parties won an equal number of seats – 272 – whilst Labour gained two, as did the Irish Nationalists. The government was able to continue, therefore, and the solution to its worst immediate problem was in hand. During the remaining years of peace it was, however, to face continuing serious difficulties.

Shortly before the election Beatrice Webb wrote in her diary that 'The big thing that has happened in the last two years is that Lloyd George and Winston Churchill have practically taken the *limelight*, not merely from their own colleagues but from the Labour Party.'[166] During this period, moreover, the relationship between Lloyd George and Churchill had reached its greatest warmth and intensity, squabbles, disagreements and jealousies notwithstanding. The two men were, as Margot Asquith noted, bracketed together with enormous frequency. In September 1908 Edward Grey made a private comparison between the two: 'His view of Lloyd George is that he has not risen to the occasion; that he behaves in office as if he were in opposition; that he "has not grown" . . . Winston, on the other hand, he thinks a genius. His fault, that phrases master him, rather than he them. But his faults and mistakes will be forgotten in his achievements.'[167]

This remark, of course, showed considerable insight as regards Churchill. But it was also unfair to Lloyd George; or rather, it showed insufficient appreciation of the new style of government that Lloyd George pioneered and Churchill emulated. For the relationship between the two men was not yet one of equals. Churchill was Lloyd George's partner, but a junior one, and he was often a supplicant for advice. This is not to say that Lloyd George did not respect his powers, or even sometimes envy them. The tone of the relationship, though, was encapsulated in a remark the Chancellor made to George Riddell in 1911. Commenting on Churchill he said, 'Very often I hear him come stalking down the hall at Downing Street, and then I see him put his head inside the door and look round the room. I know from his face that something has happened, and I always say, "What's wrong now?" '[168]

Chapter Three

ALLIANCE UNDER STRAIN

HISTORY IS EXPERIENCED not only as 'one damned thing after another', as the saying goes, but also, frequently, as several damned things at exactly the same time. In the years from 1911 to 1914 the Liberal administration dealt with welfare reform, industrial unrest, votes for women, changes to the powers of the House of Lords, defence and foreign policy, as well as with the threat of civil war in Ireland. For much of the summer of 1914 the last of these problems appeared more serious to ministers than the crisis in the Balkans that led to the outbreak of World War I. Lloyd George and Churchill were closely involved with all these matters, as well as contending (in the case of the former) with personal scandal. Understandably, their partnership suffered under the pressure of events.

This was in part the inevitable product of their differing political perspectives, but perhaps of opportunism too. In March 1912, at a point when Lloyd George's popularity had waned temporarily, J. H. Lewis noted: 'There are signs that the Lloyd George–Churchill alliance is weakening. So long as the L.G. chip was on the crest of a wave the Churchill chip was there too, but now that the L.G. chip is in the trough the Churchill chip seems to be sheering off.'[1] The relationship reached its pre-war low point early in 1914, when the two were the chief contenders in a bitter and semi-public row over the cost of the navy. Some of the differences between them, though, were more apparent than real. And in spite of the harsh words spoken by each about the other, there was never a total breakdown of relations. This is to be explained less by the sentimental ties of friendship than by the continuing political utility of the connection between them.

Before considering these developments, it is worth pausing to reflect on the way they were viewed by those who knew them.

Opinions, of course, were often contradictory, and said as much about their authors as they did about Lloyd George and Churchill. Not surprisingly – before events damaged their credibility in this regard – they found favour with the Irish Nationalists. John Redmond, the party's leader, favoured them because he believed that they, unlike Asquith, Grey and Haldane, were sincere about Home Rule. Likewise, John Dillon, another prominent nationalist MP, thought them both men of genius and incredible eloquence. He believed Lloyd George, as a Celt, was 'entirely in sympathy with Ireland and all the causes Irishmen care for'. Churchill was 'less one of themselves, but he [Dillon] admires and believes in both.'[2] Equally predictable was the hostility they generated in some quarters of the Establishment, where Celtic (or American) blood was considered a disadvantage. Take, for example, John Spencer Ewart, Director of Military Operations and Intelligence at the War Office, whom Churchill (when President of the Board of Trade) was eager to help with regard to economic intelligence on Germany. In 1909 Ewart wrote in his private diary: 'It is dreadful to think that we have such men in the Cabinet as Winston Churchill and Lloyd George. The one a half-bred American politician, the other a silly sentimental Celt'. He saw them as demagogues, pouring out upon the country 'Torrents of scurrilous and socialist oratory'.[3] Similarly, it was not unnatural that some of their Cabinet colleagues, perhaps envious of their talents, expressed a degree of scorn. John Burns described them as 'the two Romeos', presumably on the basis that they viewed themselves as romantic heroes.[4] A remark in his diary about 'Castor and Pollux' – the mutually devoted Roman twin deities – also seems to refer to them.[5] In addition, they were nicknamed – it is not known by whom – as 'the Heavenly Twins', in reference to an 1894 novel of that title by Sarah Grand.[6]

Some contemporaries, however, developed opinions of the two men that were more nuanced than those quoted above. The former Liberal MP Lord Rendel concluded that 'at bottom there is more loyalty and straightforwardness in Lloyd George than in Winston Churchill'. Rendel, admittedly, was a good friend of Lloyd George (as well as the man who coined one of his favourite sayings: 'there are no friendships at the top'). Given that, it is interesting that he added: 'in any case, I suppose, Winston Churchill will outstrip him. He has far more varied resources.'[7] R. B. Haldane – who, it will be recalled, had clashed with the pair over expenditure on the army – was another person who found Lloyd George in some ways superior to his colleague and ally. In his memoirs he wrote that in Cabinet 'Churchill was as long-winded as he was persistent . . . Lloyd George however was very good.'[8] Beatrice Webb, who had some admiration for both, demonstrated her impartiality by changing her mind. Just after Churchill's switch to the Liberals 1904 she noted that 'Lloyd George is altogether superior both in character and in intellect to Winston Churchill'.[9] Four years later, she wrote that 'He [Lloyd George] is a clever fellow, but has less intellect than Winston, and not such an attractive personality – more of the preacher, less of the statesman.'[10]

It was natural enough that these two complex characters should have provoked such divergent responses. Although they had many aims and objectives in common, there were significant contrasts in their political styles. In the public sphere, this manifested itself most obviously in their speech making. Lloyd George's genius was for spontaneity – or rather, for making his carefully prepared declamations appear spontaneous. His major speeches received several hours of advance preparation. He would dictate the fruits of his thought to a shorthand writer and commit the results to memory. He would distribute copies to the press in advance: on occasion, in a thoughtful gesture to hard-pressed journalists, the word 'cheers' was inserted at appropriate points.[11] He made sure that each speech had a simple theme, which he would drive home repeatedly. Churchill recalled in the 1950s that 'Lloyd George used to say that oratory is the art of successful dilution.'[12] He relied not merely on words, but was also a master of the subtle art of gesture. The cumulative effect could be to bring the audience to their feet, as one, with tears in their eyes.

Churchill certainly followed Lloyd George's prescription of a single theme per speech, and was not afraid of the repetition this necessitated. But spontaneity, apparent or real, was not his strong suit. In April 1904, three-quarters of an hour into a Commons speech on trade union reform, which he was making without notes, his mind went blank. He faltered and sat down and put his head in his hands, leading members to wonder if he was experiencing the same mental decline that had afflicted his father. After that, he almost always spoke from very detailed notes.[13] He was, of course, a master of language, and, as the events of 1940 were to prove, his dramatic, if slightly old-fashioned, manner of delivery could be highly effective. But whereas Lloyd George used language as a tool to persuade people of his proposition of the moment, Churchill tended to adapt his ideas to coincide with the happy phrases upon which he so often lit. As J. A. Spender recalled, Churchill was not unprincipled, but 'his real inclination was to conclude that a thing was right and true if it could be stated in a rhetorically effective manner'.[14] This tendency explains a remark by Lloyd George to Joachim von Ribbentrop, a leading Nazi, during the former's visit to Germany in 1936: 'Ribbentrop asked L.G. about Winston. L.G. replied that he was a rhetorician and not an orator. He thought only of how a phrase sounded and not how it might influence crowds.'[15]

There were also contrasts in their habits of conversation – a matter of political importance, not least with regard to Lloyd George's superior skill with delegations. Conversations with Churchill were often found to be rather one-sided affairs, with the other party being treated to rehearsals of phrases that later turned up in speeches. People found the experience fascinating, but disconcerting. When battling verbally with colleagues he preferred the blunderbuss to the rapier. In the 1930s Lloyd George joshed him about this lack of subtlety. 'Whenever you were going to be particularly truculent in Cabinet, you always prefaced your remarks by saying: "Of course, I am only a humble person." We knew then what was coming.' Churchill, on the same occasion, observed that Lloyd George's own forte was persuasion, not exposition: 'L.G. was at his best when trying to persuade ten or a dozen people.' Lloyd George's great skill lay in the fact that he – as he himself put it – 'simply talked the stuff that he knew was in the other fellows' minds'.[16] It was not that Lloyd George was less egotistical than Churchill – he was quite ruthless and would drop friends and colleagues when he had exhausted their use to him – but he did have one capacity the other man lacked. He knew how to appear interested in people, and how to listen. It has often been said that one left an encounter with Churchill convinced that one had just met the most interesting man in the world, but one left a meeting with Lloyd George believing that one was *oneself* the most interesting person alive.[17]

In July 1912, Elizabeth Asquith, the Prime Minister's youngest daughter, observed to Lloyd George that his colleague Reginald McKenna's faults were on the surface: 'You don't have to dig them

up.' She continued: 'Winston digs his faults up for you. He saves you
the trouble.' She then remarked to Lloyd George of his own faults
that 'I think you would have to dig pretty deep to discover yours.'[18]
This comment, if read in terms of political rather than personal
morality, was astute. It was a tribute less to the Chancellor's superior
virtue than to his relative lack of transparency. Many politicians
distrusted Lloyd George and Churchill equally, but were much more
easily able to grasp what the latter was *up to* at any given moment.
This was perhaps related to the fact that, as Elizabeth's half-sister
Violet later put it, 'Winston knew when he was being unscrupulous,
whereas Lloyd George did not.'[19] Lloyd George's subtlety in comparison to Churchill's transparent manoeuvrings and brazen ambition
can be seen in their respective handling of a number of pre-war
issues. One of the most intractable of these – although it had many
rivals on this score – was the question of women's suffrage.

Male as well as female suffrage campaigners had been pressing
for female enfranchisement since the 1860s. In 1897 a variety of
groups had formed the National Union of Women's Suffrage Societies (NUWSS), an organization led by Millicent Fawcett. Fawcett's
moderate, peaceful tactics did not, however, lead to immediate,
concrete achievements. In 1903 Emmeline Pankhurst formed the
Women's Social and Political Union (WSPU), a body in which her
daughters were also to become prominent. The WSPU adopted the
militant tactics for which it was to become famous – and which
distinguished the 'suffragettes' from moderate 'suffragists' – in 1905.
In October of that year Christabel Pankhurst and her devoted friend
Annie Kenney interrupted one of Sir Edward Grey's public meetings
(in the Free Trade Hall in Manchester), demanding to know whether
the anticipated Liberal government would give votes to women. Grey
actually favoured doing so, but he nonetheless refused to commit
himself, and, after considerable perseverance, the two women succeeded in their aim of getting arrested. Afterwards, Christabel
expressed her satisfaction that she had managed to assault a policeman.[20] The campaign of suffragette violence, sustained over the next
few years, gave the vote question a prominence in public life that it
would not otherwise have had, although it could also be argued that
it played into the hands of the anti-suffragists by confirming their
stereotype of women as hysterical and incapable of exercising political
responsibility.

However, the key reason that women did not get the vote before 1918 was determined by the structure of party politics. The Conservatives as well as the Liberals were divided on the issue. Balfour, for example, was in favour of votes for women, whereas Asquith was opposed. After 1906 a majority of MPs favoured some measure of female enfranchisement. What could not be agreed upon was the *extent* of any such measure – that is to say, which groups of women should be included. As Lloyd George and Churchill both came to appreciate, any decision was likely to have an impact on future elections, to the benefit of one major political party or the other. A narrow measure, bringing propertied women onto the electoral register, was likely to benefit the Tories; a wider one was likely to bring female working-class votes to the Liberals. As will be seen, these considerations of party advantage stymied any change, which was made possible in due course only by the altered conditions of coalition government during the Great War.

When Churchill became Home Secretary after the general election that took place at the beginning of 1910, there seemed to be some prospect of a solution. The radical journalist and suffragist Henry Noel Brailsford was proposing a Conciliation Committee – an all-party group to devise a Bill that would command general favour. Fawcett's NUWSS supported the initiative. The WSPU, perhaps worried that its stunts were losing their freshness, reluctantly went along with it, agreeing to suspend militant tactics for the time being. In April 1910 Brailsford secured the support of Churchill, among other politicians, albeit in general terms and without any specific commitment to back any solution at which the committee might arrive.[21] He did not, though, get the backing of Lloyd George. This may seem strange, given that Lloyd George was in fact more committed to the principle of votes for women than Churchill was. But the Chancellor appreciated, more clearly than his colleague, the problems that any likely Bill would produce for the Liberal Party. To understand this, it is necessary to recall that there was not yet full suffrage in Britain even for men. Being the head of a household was the main way that the right to vote was acquired. (There were also other qualification mechanisms, including the ownership of property, hence the possibility of having more than one vote. It should also be noted that women ratepayers, for example widows or spinsters who owned property, were already allowed to vote in local government elections and to be councillors.) If, therefore, the vote were now given to women on the basis of a household franchise, as the Conciliation Committee in due course proposed, there would be created a limited number of mainly prosperous new electors. The Liberal Whips did not like this;[22] nor did Lloyd George. As Brailsford wrote to Churchill in July, just before the debate on the Conciliation Bill, 'I had hoped that Lloyd George would have consented to be neutral, but he is quite determined to do his best to smash us . . . because it is not adult suffrage.'[23] When he had given it some thought, Churchill realized he did not like the proposal either. Lucy Masterman recorded that he had originally intended to vote for the Bill, but was reminded by her husband of Lloyd George's opposition, and the reasons for it. Taking this as his cue 'Winston began to see the opportunity for a speech on these lines, and as he paced up and down the room, began to roll off long phrases. By the end of the morning he was convinced that he had always been hostile to the Bill and that he had already thought of all these points himself.'[24]

During the Commons debate, therefore, both he and Lloyd George denounced the Bill as 'anti-democratic'.[25] Brailsford concluded, perhaps unfairly given that he had received no formal pledge, that Churchill's behaviour was treacherous, and told him so explicitly.[26] He was not the only one who was upset. A few days later, W. Llewelyn Williams, MP for Carmarthen Boroughs, recounted how his wife and her sister, both convinced suffragists, had observed the proceedings from the Ladies' gallery:

> They were very anxious about Lloyd George's attitude, and surrounded Mrs Lloyd George in the refreshment room begging her to use her influence with her husband and asking whether they should send a letter signed by them all. In the midst of the vehement suffragists she sat quietly eating her cold tongue and drinking her tea. All she did was to placidly remark that they might send him a letter if they liked. Mrs Winston Churchill was very angry and disappointed in her husband's attitude [as] she understood from him until 2 or 3 days previously that he was going to vote for the Bill.[27]

The Bill in fact passed its Second Reading by a majority of over one hundred, but the government was not prepared to grant the parliamentary time necessary for it to pass its remaining stages. It was referred at once, by an even greater majority, to a committee of the whole House, a polite way of indicating that nothing was going to happen for the time being.[28] (A Bill had to pass all its stages in one parliamentary session were it to become law.) 'Women's Suffrage killed for this year – killed altogether as far as yesterday's Bill is concerned', Lloyd George wrote to his brother. 'The Suffragettes are for the moment concentrating their hate on Winston – although annoyed with me also'.[29]

The annoyance with Lloyd George was soon demonstrated. On one occasion in October 1910 two male suffragists approached the Chancellor and berated and insulted him; one grabbed hold of his coat. Afterwards Churchill, who as Home Secretary oversaw the Metropolitan Police, demanded 'an explanation of the circumstances in which the Chancellor of the Exchequer was assaulted last night by a gang of male suffragists'. He proclaimed himself at a loss to understand how it was that his colleague had not received proper protection. When the police commissioner pointed out that there had been no gang and no assault, Churchill noted that 'The fact remains that an assassination with a knife could easily have taken place.' He suspected that the men were 'paid ruffians', which turned out not to be true.[30] Churchill can be forgiven his overexcited imagination – it is by no means impossible that Lloyd George had talked the incident up – because his concern with his colleague's security was wholly legitimate. On later occasions Lloyd George was attacked with considerably more vigour. And in February 1912 suffragettes exploded a bomb at a house being built for Lloyd George at Walton Heath in Surrey. The fact that it was deliberately timed to go off when he wasn't there can have provided only limited reassurance to those concerned for his well-being.

The WSPU's truce held for the time being – it would do so, with a short interruption, until November 1911. Shortly before the election of December 1910 Asquith announced that the government would give parliamentary time to allow a revived Conciliation Bill to pass the House of Commons. The Pankhursts found this promise inadequate, and there followed a temporary resumption of militancy. The following May, with the truce again in place, the Bill again passed a Second Reading by 255 to 88. This time Lloyd George voted in favour, and Churchill abstained.[31] Again the government said it would not offer enough time during that session for it to become law.

However, it was announced that a week would be granted during 1912, and Grey subsequently made clear that this would be an 'elastic' week, in other words enough to get the Bill through all its stages.[32] Lloyd George was sceptical. In June he told C. P. Scott, the editor of the *Manchester Guardian*, that 'he did not think that even the extended week indicated by Grey wd suffice to get the Bill through in the face of the formidable opposition it wd encounter led by men like Churchill' and others. 'As for himself if his amendment admitting women to the register on their husbands' qualification were rejected he inclined to think he shd have to vote against the Bill'.[33] There was little chance that such an amendment would be accepted by the Speaker of the Commons as being in order. In September Lloyd George laid out frankly his objections to the Bill in a letter to The Master of Elibank:

> The Conciliation Bill would on balance add hundreds of thousands of votes throughout the country to the strength of the Tory Party . . . We have never really faced the situation manfully and courageously. I think the Liberal Party ought to make up its mind as a whole that it will either have an extended franchise which would put the working-men's wives on to the register as well as spinsters and widows, or that it will have no female franchise at all.

He thought that 'through sheer drifting, vacillation and something which looks like cowardice', the Bill was likely to get through. 'Say what you will, that spells disaster to Liberalism.'[34]

His next stroke, therefore, was to persuade Asquith to make a surprise announcement that the government would introduce its own Bill, extending the franchise to men who were currently excluded. This measure would be open to amendment so that, if MPs wanted, women could be included too. 'It is entirely my doing,' Lloyd George boasted to his brother, 'The Pankhursts are furious'.[35] This was because the effect of the announcement was to undermine the narrower measure, which Liberal suffragists would now be less inclined to support. Although the suffragette leaders might have been expected to be pleased at the possibility of a wider female franchise, they doubted the government's good faith. From now on they would settle for nothing less than a government-backed measure of full sex equality. However, Lloyd George secured the partial cooperation of the more moderate Brailsford, with whom he met on more than one occasion around the time of Asquith's crucial 7 November announcement. Brailsford found him slippery.[36] 'I told you then that you could never come near carrying your democratic plan unless you got a nearly solid Irish vote', Brailsford wrote to the Chancellor some months later. 'You replied that you would do a deal with the party . . . Also I have a note that both you and Elibank assured me that you could secure Winston's help. You did not of course pledge him but you said that you could get him.'[37] Churchill, however, was much opposed to the new plan. Just before Christmas 1911, George Riddell noted in his diary: 'I met Winston. He was evidently much perturbed. He was on his way to see L.G. He said "what has made him take up this attitude on the suffrage question. He will smash the Government; it is most serious." '[38]

Riddell subsequently recorded that 'L.G. says Winston is bitter against the suffragettes because they spoil his perorations, they might just as well cut Diana's throat (Diana is Winston's charming little daughter).'[39] The interruptions to his speeches may indeed have played a part in determining his attitude. To C. P. Scott, he 'practically admitted that his present wrecking tactics are the outcome of resentment at the treatment he has received from the W.S.P.U.'. But he did still declare himself a suffragist, albeit, in Scott's words, 'a quite impracticable one', who would admit only up to a hundred thousand women to the register. This would be done by categories: graduates, doctors, Poor Law Guardians and members of town councils would be eligible.[40] One of his major objections to Lloyd George's viewpoint was that to press ahead with something approaching full adult suffrage would divide staid and traditional Liberals from the party's more radical wing.

'I cannot help feeling anxious about the women', Churchill wrote to Lloyd George on 16 December. 'If you and Grey go working yourselves up into a state of mawkish frenzy on the "are they not our flesh and blood" cry, all sorts of grave difficulties of a personal character will be added to the many wh on this topic already loom before us: & this strong Government on wh your life's work depends may easily come to grief.' He went on to argue that he and Lloyd George had worked together for so long, and with such significant achievements, 'that I feel I have some right to ask you to be considerate of personal feelings as well as of the general interest'.

However, he then indicated that his own personal loyalty to Lloyd George would not stretch to supporting him on this issue. He would, he said, 'refrain from sharp decisions' as long as possible. 'But', he emphasized, 'if you were to get yourself into the sort of state where the enfranchisement of 6,000,000 women, *without a fresh appeal to the country* [i.e. another election], became the most important political object in your mind, I cd not find any good foothold for common action.'[41] There was, therefore, some truth in the rumours that developed in Tory circles that Churchill greatly resented Lloyd George's attitude, and had 'told LG not to rely on him' in any quarrel that might develop over the Bill.[42]

After writing to Lloyd George, Churchill sent letters, over the next few days, to Grey, Elibank and Asquith. A Franchise Bill amended to add 8 million women to the electorate would be rejected by the Lords, he argued. How then, he asked, could the Prime Minister honourably use the provisions of the new Parliament Act to force it onto the statute book when he himself had declared the enfranchisement of women to be a disastrous mistake? Dissolution of parliament followed by defeat at the polls was the likely outcome, he thought. In a letter to Elibank of 18 December, he wrote that 'I do not understand LG at all . . . He is exactly like Joe [Chamberlain] in 1903.' He also suggested that 'If LG & Grey go on working themselves up, they will have to go', if female suffrage were not incorporated into the Bill. On the other hand, Asquith's position would become impossible were it put in.[43] By the time of his letter to Asquith three days later, though, he was claiming to have patched up a compromise. This was that Lloyd George and Grey would agree, if a clause enfranchising women were carried, to a referendum in which the women concerned would be asked if they did indeed want the vote. In return, Churchill would support the main thrust of the Bill. The men did not, however, commit themselves definitely to this idea.[44] This plan, in fact, went nowhere, as Asquith was not keen on the referendum idea, and Lloyd George subsequently promised Brailsford (who considered it a damaging obstacle to the achievement of the suffrage) not to support it.[45] The episode implies, though, that the relationship between Lloyd George and Churchill may not have been in quite the dire condition that the latter's remarks in his letter to Elibank seemed to suggest.

Indeed, not long after, Lloyd George went to some lengths to defend Churchill in private – and this was not something of which he usually made a habit. In March 1912, with a new vote on the Conciliation Bill looming, Brailsford wrote to Lloyd George denouncing Churchill, who, he claimed, was intriguing to persuade the Irish to vote against it. Brailsford also accused the Chancellor himself of failing to live up to his promises. He said: 'the moment has come when everything turns on your moving the Irish ... The whole mischief, so far as I can trace it, is Winston's doing. He has thoroughly scared them into believing that not only Loreburn but Asquith himself will resign if our Bill, or suffrage in any form is carried.'

The significance of this was that, had Asquith resigned, it would have raised doubts over the future of Home Rule. Brailsford also claimed, as mentioned earlier, that Lloyd George had said in November he could win Churchill to the cause. He went on: 'Now I doubt if you have even managed to keep Elibank. Surely the first step is now to make the Irish understand that Winston has misled them – that there can be no question of any resignations over our Bill or of Asquith's at any point.'[46]

Lloyd George responded robustly, saying that he had indeed been full of hope at the time in question that votes for women could be achieved; 'but I have repeatedly reminded you that I also told you on that occasion that the realization of those hopes depended entirely upon the tactics which would be pursued by the militants.' Their tactics had in fact 'exasperated those upon whose support I had relied' and 'roused the active hostility of others upon whose apathy I had depended'. Churchill had recently courted controversy by speaking in favour of Home Rule in Belfast. Brailsford, Lloyd George pointed out, had 'overlooked the fact that both at Belfast and at Glasgow both he [Churchill] and Mrs. Churchill were much more annoyed and persecuted by the Suffragettes than by all the Orange mob of Ulster put together. He is not the kind of man to overlook that.' Lloyd George concluded: 'Grey and I will still do our best, but we are by no means hopeful, whilst the Anti-Suffragists are exultant.'[47] At the end of March the Commons rejected the Conciliation Bill by 222 to 208. The Irish divided 35 to 3 against it, having supported it the previous time by 31 to 9.[48] Lloyd George was pleased it was out of the way, even though he had been personally pledged to vote in favour (which he did). 'I always hated it', he told his brother.[49]

Churchill and Lloyd George had each made a significant contribution to the defeat of the Bill, and thus to postponing even the
limited female suffrage it envisaged. Others – and not only anti-
suffragists – shared the responsibility. Through their acts of militancy,
the suffragettes were indeed engaged in a kind of self-sabotage, as
Lloyd George alleged. The defeat of the Conciliation Bill would not
have mattered if a solution along the lines of Asquith's announcement had been forthcoming. But in January 1913 the Speaker of
the Commons ruled that any amendment to the Franchise Bill to
incorporate women would be out of order. The government then
withdrew the Bill. Ministers had not foreseen explicitly the possibility
of the Speaker acting in this way; but they had nonetheless acted in
doubtful faith. Lloyd George, Churchill and their colleagues were in
a position to appreciate that, in Brailsford's words, 'Adult suffrage
means Greek Calends' – that is to say, it would never come.[50] In the
Edwardian era, some obstacle to it could be relied upon to turn up.
By promoting adult suffrage, Lloyd George effectively subverted the
Conciliation Bill, the only measure of female enfranchisement that
stood a realistic chance of getting onto the statute book in advance of
the Great War. Churchill's intervention with the Irish MPs (as alleged
by Brailsford) seems to have helped seal the Bill's fate.

What Lloyd George and Churchill had in common on the issue
was a concern for the health of the Liberal Party. What divided
them – only briefly, albeit with strong words on Churchill's side –
was less the principle surrounding votes for women than how Liberal
interests should best be promoted. Indeed, during the 1920s they
were both opposed to extending the vote beyond the limited number
of women enfranchised in 1918. The diary of the Conservative MP
Victor Cazalet records that Churchill was 'very strong against' the
equalization of the franchise, and that he was eager to know Lloyd
George's opinion of the proposal. Lloyd George, Cazalet informed
him, 'thought it criminal, suicidal, and disastrous to the British
Empire'.[51]

Churchill's denunciation of Lloyd George's supposed recklessness
over franchise reform, at the end of 1911, should be seen as a
squabble rather than a rift. It was, though, a sign of his increasing
desire to establish his independence of the older man, with a view,
perhaps, to usurping his commanding position. If not immensely
serious in itself, it was an episode in the decline of the two men's

political intimacy. This decline can be traced to Churchill's transition from the Home Office to the Admiralty earlier that autumn. The background to that move, and Lloyd George's part in it, therefore need to be traced.

At the start of 1911 their relationship was in good health. This was symbolized by their participation in the launch of the Other Club, a cross-party society. The credit for the Club's formation is often given to Churchill and F. E. Smith. (Smith was a Conservative MP whose brilliantly witty 1906 maiden speech, breaking the convention that such efforts should be short and uncontroversial, had included pot-shots at Lloyd George and Churchill among others. His friendship was to prove important to both men.) But Lloyd George was undoubtedly a prime mover. This can be seen from a letter Churchill wrote to Lord Northcliffe in May 1911, which does not mention Smith: 'The Chancellor of the Exchequer and I are getting up a small club for the purpose of pleasant fortnightly dinners. It is to be non-political, twelve members on each side of the House of Commons have joined, and we are asking a few distinguished outsiders to come in.'[52]

The rules of the club stated that 'Nothing in the rules or intercourse of the Club shall interfere with the rancour or asperity of party politics.'[53] 'We attempted to form a non-party Club; but it was a time of very deep fierce personal and political rancours', Lloyd George recalled at its 'coming of age banquet' in 1933. 'The things that were said about Winston on some occasions I could not repeat in this highly respectable Club,' he joked. 'We can hardly realize it in these days when no one is hated outside his own party!'[54] The Club's activities lapsed in 1913, perhaps as a consequence of the Marconi scandal (see pp. 93–8), but sprang to life again upon the outbreak of war. It was to remain an important point of social contact for Lloyd George and Churchill as late as the 1930s.

Political cooperation paralleled the jollity. In November 1910 a miners' strike in the Rhondda Valley erupted into violence. Churchill, as Home Secretary, appealed to Lloyd George to use his good offices to bring the strike to an end. 'I am satisfied that your influence in Wales and your knowledge of the Welsh language fully justify the departure from ordinary departmental practice', he wrote.[55] In the event, Churchill himself sent troops to restore order (contrary to myth, this did not result in loss of life). In March the following year he again appealed to the Chancellor, this time in order to help win the miners' confidence. Accidents in the mines were causing an appalling death toll. 'Levy a special surcharge of 3d upon mining royalties earmarked for the express purpose of the prevention of accidents, and give me the resulting £80,000 a year to spend upon experiment and inspection', Churchill requested, urging that the matter should not be left to civil servants to sort out. 'This is not a matter for Departmental correspondence but between ourselves.'[56] Soon after, he was able to report to the King that he had secured from Lloyd George the 'substantial financial assistance' needed to make his safety proposals effective.[57] Such support for his own schemes contributed to Churchill's willingness to describe Lloyd George as 'the greatest political genius of the day'.[58] Lloyd George for his part valued Churchill's goodwill, albeit apparently more for reasons of utility rather than sentiment. This can be seen from a letter he wrote to his brother in April. He was, he said, due to play golf the next day with Churchill, F. E. Smith, and Andrew Bonar Law (who was soon to succeed Balfour as Unionist leader). He was in the process of finalizing the National Insurance plan. 'It will make it so much easier to get it through to be on pleasant terms with these men', he wrote. 'I shall have to fight vested interests & there is not too much time to spare this Session. So I must do a good deal of "smoothio".'[59]

Moreover, Lloyd George seems to have become increasingly worried, as the year drew on, about Churchill's handling of industrial unrest. In August, a railway strike broke out. This was at the time of the Agadir crisis – discussed in detail below – and the threat of war with Germany made the strike's potential consequences that much more serious. Lloyd George felt great anxiety, but Churchill seemed to relish the fight. Looking back on events from the perspective of October 1914, Lloyd George was heard to recall:

> Winston then had a plan to shut the Welsh miners into their valleys by a military cordon and to starve them out. A mad plan. He had all the country planned out for a military campaign. I shall never forget the remarkable scene which I witnessed at the Home Office. Winston with his generals, and his plan of campaign. He is an extraordinary fellow. Too wild and impulsive. He makes me very uneasy.[60]

These memories and observations were, of course, coloured by subsequent events, but they are borne out to some degree by other evidence. Lloyd George was able to end the strike quickly, partly by appealing to the railwaymen's patriotism. According to Lucy Masterman, Churchill telephoned him as soon as the news came through. 'I'm very sorry to hear it', Churchill said. 'It would have been better to have gone on and given these men a good thrashing.'[61] A contrasting account can be found in the diary of John Burns, who clearly felt that the settlement was unsatisfactory. He found Churchill at the Home Office in a velvet lounge suit, 'unduly elated at end of dispute that leaves R[ailwa]y Directors discredited, men defeated[,] Government as they were and the police[,] soldiers and public resigned.'[62]

In spite of the tensions, the collaboration continued, in the sphere of foreign and defence policy. Together, early in 1911, Lloyd George and Churchill had continued the quest for naval economy – a reprise of their previous battle with McKenna. However, both men's attitudes then changed dramatically as a consequence of German aggression. Churchill's conversion was the deeper of the two; Lloyd George's, in terms of public perceptions, the more dramatic. (Churchill's attitude had been prefigured when, at a dinner in 1908, he appeared to give credence to fears of German invasion. Lloyd George, according to Esher, 'was rather shocked' by this.)[63] In July an international crisis developed, provoked by the German decision to send a gunboat, the *Panther*, to the port of Agadir in Morocco. Morocco was effectively under French control, and Kaiser Wilhelm II clearly intended to challenge France in an attempt to extract from her territorial concessions in Africa. Sir Edward Grey met the German ambassador and demanded that Britain be consulted in the drawing up of any new arrangements. For two weeks he waited for an official response, which was not forthcoming.

The question for Britain was, should she get involved in this dispute between the continental rivals? As Churchill recalled in his memoirs, the Liberal Imperialist section of the government had usually been kept in check by the radical element, 'on whose side the Chancellor of the Exchequer and I had usually leaned'. This 'equipoise' between the militaristic and the peaceable might make it impossible for the nation to speak with one voice. 'In these circumstances the attitude of the Chancellor of the Exchequer became of peculiar importance.' Churchill himself seems to have adopted a bellicose stance without much hesitation, but Lloyd George, he recorded, equivocated for a long time. Then, on 21 July, Churchill visited him before Cabinet. 'I found a different man', he wrote. 'His mind was made up. He saw quite clearly the course to take.' That evening, Lloyd George, having consulted Grey, made his annual speech to a City audience at the Mansion House. He stated that, were Britain 'to be treated where her interests were vitally affected as if she were of no account in the Cabinet of nations, then I say emphatically that peace at that price would be a humiliation intolerable for a great country like ours to endure.' This statement, coming from whom it did, was 'a thunder-clap to the German Government', Churchill recalled. Their ambassador had not foreseen it. But, Churchill noted, until only a few hours before, even Lloyd George's colleagues had not known. 'Working with him in close association, I did not know. No one knew. Until his mind was definitely made up, he did not know himself.'[64] Lloyd George and Churchill spent part of the next morning trying to win over C. P. Scott. Lloyd George placed much importance on the attitude of Scott's Liberal and pacific *Manchester Guardian*. On the basis of this discussion, Scott concluded that the Chancellor was 'not immune from the microbe of Germanophobia'. Churchill's contribution, Scott noted, was largely restricted to 'highly rhetorical denunciations repeated at intervals of the insolence of Germany and the need of asserting ourselves and teaching her a lesson'.[65]

Lloyd George's dramatic intervention did not put an immediate end to the Moroccan crisis.[66] It did, though, bring the issue of military preparedness sharply to mind, and on this he and Churchill were again in accord. There was a pronounced division of opinion between the different branches of the armed forces. This came to a head at a meeting of the Committee of Imperial Defence (CID) on 23 August. The Prime Minister and a select group of his colleagues – Churchill, Lloyd George, Grey, Haldane and McKenna – were present. The army, represented by Brigadier Henry Wilson (the Director of Military Operations), thought that a major British deployment would be crucial to holding off the Germans should they attack France. In other words, if war broke out Britain would have to become involved in order to prevent a German triumph. The Royal

Navy, represented by Sir Arthur Wilson (the First Sea Lord), had no such plan in mind, and was largely content in the event of hostilities simply to maintain naval supremacy. In this view, Britain need not get embroiled in a continental land war. After Henry Wilson made his lengthy presentation there was, as he recorded, 'Much questioning, especially by Winston and Lloyd George.'[67] By contrast, Arthur Wilson's inept performance won him few favours with them, although he was firmly backed by McKenna. As Maurice Hankey, one of the officials present, noted, Lloyd George and Churchill were 'more or less converts to the military [i.e. army] view'.[68] 'I am inclined to think the chances of war are multiplying', Lloyd George wrote to Churchill two days later. ' "Be ye therefore ready." '[69] The two agreed with Henry Wilson's proposal that should the French mobilize, Britain should do so at the same time, and should send the maximum possible force of men across the Channel.[70] At the same time Lloyd George and Churchill corresponded about their concerns over the current direction of the Admiralty, which they thought lacking in leadership and direction.[71] Haldane also pressed for a change.

There was, therefore, a strong 'pull factor' behind Asquith's decision to appoint Churchill First Lord of the Admiralty in McKenna's stead (with McKenna going to the Home Office), and behind Lloyd George's apparent promotion of this idea. The existing state of affairs seemed unsatisfactory, and Churchill was an evidently dynamic figure who might be expected to put things right. To appoint Haldane, the rival candidate, who had already reorganized the army, might appear too tactless a symbol of criticism of the current regime; and there was also the argument that the First Lord needed to be in the Commons, not the Lords. But there may also have been a 'push factor': the sense that Churchill was underperforming at the Home Office. One cannot, however, be certain, as the accounts of several of the main participants differ.

What is clear is that in late September Churchill went to stay with Asquith at Archerfield, the latter's house in Scotland. 'The day after I arrived there, on our way home from the links, he asked me quite abruptly whether I would like to go to the Admiralty', Churchill wrote in his account of the period. 'I accepted with alacrity.'[72] Haldane, who lived at nearby Cloan, told a different story, in private conversation in the 1920s:

Winston's account of his appointment to the Admiralty in 'The
World Crisis' was not very close to the facts. Asquith had
arranged that Haldane should go to the Admiralty to build up a
Naval General Staff, as he had done at the War Office. When
he got there [i.e. to Archerfield] he found Winston had arrived
before him. 'He is an importunate widow,' said Asquith, 'begging
to be given the Admiralty'. Asquith shut both of them up in a
room together to fight it out. Haldane gave in on condition that
Winston would undertake to create a General Staff.[73]

Haldane later gave a variant of this story (with the criticism of
Churchill somewhat toned down) in his autobiography.[74] It corre-
sponds in certain essentials with his more tactful contemporary
account, in a letter to Grey.[75]

Lloyd George, however, gave yet another explanation. In November 1911 Riddell wrote in his diary that dealing with the problems
of industrial discontent had weighed heavily with Churchill: 'It was
obvious that he was gradually setting his teeth and that being a soldier
he would be likely to act in a thorough and drastic manner in the
event of further labour troubles.' Furthermore, the situation 'was
obviously causing anxiety to the Prime Minister and Lloyd George'.
Once the Cabinet changes had been made, Lloyd George told Riddell:
'I think I am entitled to the credit. I went to Archerfield in August
and I told the Prime Minister that we must make the change.'[76] There
is also some other evidence that backs up the suggestion that domestic
political calculations played a part in the switch.[77] But whether Lloyd
George made the suggestion to Asquith, or whether he made it to
Churchill, who then pressed it upon the Prime Minister himself, there
is no doubt that the decision pleased Churchill as much as it angered
McKenna. Lloyd George wrote to his wife on 10 October that he had
lunched with Churchill, who 'is so happy about his transfer to the
Admiralty & so gratefully [sic] – at least for the moment – to me for
fighting his cause.'[78]

McKenna, sulking, resisted his own removal to Churchill's old
place at the Home Office. He told Asquith that the army's plan for
the use of British troops in France increased the danger of war, as it
would encourage the French to provoke Germany. The implication
was that McKenna needed to stay at the Admiralty in order to
withstand the pressure from the War Office. The Prime Minister

protested that the assumption of McKenna's argument was that he himself was 'a mere figurehead pushed along against his will and without his knowledge by some energetic colleagues'. This was a clear reference to Lloyd George and Churchill. 'Such a thing might be possible in cases like that of the Insurance Bill but not in the case of peace or war', Asquith claimed.[79] McKenna failed to postpone the change of offices.

At the end of October John Burns noted that Lloyd George was cheerful but worn down by hard work, whereas Churchill, in his new task, was 'as merry as a Sand Boy'.[80] It seems that, for the time being, the Churchill–Lloyd George alliance remained strong. Soon after Churchill took up his new position, Haldane recorded 'a very useful talk' with him and Lloyd George. 'This is now a very harmonious Cabinet. It is odd to think that three years ago I had to fight those two for every penny for my army reforms.' (Lloyd George, Haldane noted, had used to call him 'the Minister for Slaughter'.)[81] Riddell wrote of Churchill: 'Many people think that he and Lloyd George are only veiled friends, but this is not the case. They act in the closest co-operation and are obviously impressed with each other's powers.'[82]

Tensions in the relationship were soon to emerge, however. The two men's harmony on defence issues had been encouraged and facilitated by the risk of imminent war. But at the beginning of November, France and Germany reached agreement over Morocco, Germany receiving French territory in the Congo. As the crisis subsided, the more pacifically minded ministers were angered to learn of the August CID meeting, and demanded that the Cabinet be informed of any future plans for military cooperation with France. The Chancellor was also criticized in the press for his Mansion House speech.[83] In these circumstances, Lloyd George was willing to make at least rhetorical gestures in the direction of his former position in order to preserve his radical credentials. Churchill, absorbed in his new job, maintained a more bellicose stance, failing, as his colleague saw it, to take the round view. In February 1912 Churchill stated in public that the German navy was a 'luxury'. 'Winston's Navy speech most mischievous at this juncture', Lloyd George wrote. 'He would sacrifice anything & anybody for a sensation.'[84] 'Winston is Navy mad', he complained a few months later. 'As usual he regards the office which he presides over for the time being as the pivot upon which the Universe attends.'[85]

At the same time, Lloyd George's popularity with the electorate, and his influence over his colleagues, seemed to be waning. The introduction of National Insurance was not popular with the workers who were part of the scheme, as it involved a weekly deduction from their pay packets. This would, of course, win them entitlement to future benefits in the event of illness or unemployment, but the pain was more immediate than the gain. The Conservatives started to do well in by-elections. This may have disinclined the Chancellor's colleagues to listen to him on other issues. On 1 March the best part of a million coal miners went on strike in support of the Miners Federation's demand for a national minimum wage in the industry: five shillings a week for men, two shillings for boys. Two weeks later Asquith declared his willingness to introduce minimum wage legislation, but not to specify a figure in the statute. When the Cabinet discussed this, Lloyd George spoke up firmly in favour of including the five- and two-shilling minimum in the Bill (and even in favour of nationalizing the mines, if the owners did not comply with state regulation). Churchill took the opposite view, and described the idea as a 'surrender to menace'. According to J. A. Pease, President of the Board of Education, 'He & George had evidently differed before they came into the cabinet, & their eyes & teeth were flashing & set respectively.'[86] Lloyd George was overruled, the Bill passed in its more limited form, and the men returned to work. The following month Charles Masterman told Riddell: 'The alliance between LG and Winston has broken up. They are still as friendly as ever, but are not concerting joint plans of action as formerly.'[87] It might have been truer to say that they were a little less friendly than before, but that the alliance between them was suffering tension rather than collapse. Lucy Masterman observed in June, 'I think the alliance shows distinct signs of strain, as indeed I always thought it would.'[88]

Even while their rivalry grew, neither could fully dispense with the other's support, or at least neither dared risk the other's active hostility. For example, in the summer of 1912, Lloyd George was planning to launch a Land Campaign. This was his scheme to revive Liberal fortunes, although the precise means by which he hoped to solve the evils of landlordism remained hazy and the launch of the campaign was to be delayed for this reason. He claimed, in a letter to his brother, that the leading Liberals were supportive, 'Winston alone being doubtful – but he has become very reactionary of late.

However Winston is not going to give trouble provided I give him money for his navy. If he keeps quiet he is worth a million or two.'[89] Although he did at times praise Churchill highly in private, he also criticized what he claimed were his increasingly reactionary tendencies. He alleged (in July) that Churchill had meditated upon, and then abandoned, the idea of rejoining the Tories. Although the two men still had long talks, Riddell recorded that Lloyd George 'seemed uneasy about Winston, and it is obvious that their relations are not quite what they were'.[90] Although much of the chaffing was good natured, at least on the surface, things could turn sharp. In November Asquith and his wife hosted an impromptu dinner for a few key ministers to discuss the political outlook. Margot's diary shows that Lloyd George expressed concern about cleavages in the Liberal Party over Lords reform. Churchill, in response, said that Lloyd George was too 'easily down-hearted' and called him, according to Margot, 'everything but a funk'. 'What do you know about the situation!' came the retort. 'You've spent the last two months down a submarine!'[91]

Churchill, for his part, was at this time very anxious about the navy. The men were underpaid and dissatisfied. He feared 'a great mutiny'.[92] There followed, by his own account, a terrible fight between ministers – though it was by no means as fierce as the one that would break out over the estimates of military expenditure in 1914. His original demand for £750,000 in order to solve the problems was cut down to £350,000 by the Treasury and Cabinet. This latter figure, he complained, was £26,000 below what would have enabled him to give the men enough to satisfy them (although in fact no mutiny followed). 'I have held out as long as I could,' he observed after this defeat, adding, 'I cannot understand Lloyd George.'[93] He even wondered whether his colleague was using 'this paltry question' as a means to get rid of him.[94] A few days later, at the start of December, Lloyd George reported that Churchill 'is not quite so annoyed with me as he was. He drove me home last night which is always a good sign.' Again, the Chancellor complained about his colleague's excessive concentration on his own affairs. 'He has not got the art of playing in cooperation with others . . . When we refuse him anything he talks of resigning.'[95]

Lloyd George soon had reason to be grateful that this particular squabble had been patched up. At the close of 1912 it became clear to him that he was facing a scandal that had the potential to destroy his career. This was the notorious Marconi affair. In order to withstand it, he needed all the allies he could secure. In the past, he had engaged in some doubtful financial dealings. (These included, in the 1890s, his promotion to investors of a Patagonian gold mining syndicate that can only be described as dubious, and which eventually failed. The episode showed a lack of both competence and scruples on his part.)[96] More recently – and it must be emphasized that this was not an uncommon practice and that he did not profit personally – he had engaged in the sale of honours. When, in 1909, his colleague J. A. Pease denounced him to his face for doing so (in order to raise funds for the Budget League), Churchill rebuked Pease, saying that his comments should be reserved for another occasion.[97] In other words, Churchill was not squeamish about such matters, or overly obsessed about financial propriety himself.

This is not to say that Lloyd George's actions over Marconi were corrupt, though they were certainly misjudged. The story is a compli-cated one. In March 1912 the government accepted a tender from the (British) Marconi Wireless Telegraph Company to build an eighteen-station wireless network spanning the Empire. (As a project to improve imperial communications, this had a similar impulse to the 'All Red' transport route scheme discussed in Chapter 2.) This information was made public. The managing director of the British company, Godfrey Isaacs, was the brother of Rufus Isaacs, the Attorney General and a friend of Lloyd George. Godfrey Isaacs was also a director of the American Marconi Company, which was, however, a legally separate entity that did not stand to make a profit from the British company's new government contract. On 14 April the American company signed a lucrative – and for the time being secret – contract with Western Union and the Great Northwestern Telegraph Company of Canada. Knowing this, Rufus Isaacs bought 10,000 shares in the American company from his brother, and the same day (17 April) sold 1,000 shares each to Lloyd George and the Master of Elibank. By early May the bulk of Lloyd George's shares had been sold at a healthy profit, but later in the month he and Elibank bought more shares. The price then fell, and the upshot was that both men ended up losing money. Given that the British and American companies were independent of one another, the ministers had not done anything wrong.

Their real error of judgement came later, in the face of rumours of corruption in relation to the British company's imperial telegraphy contract. It would have been wise to make clear the exact nature of the dealings they had made. Instead, in October, Rufus Isaacs denied in the Commons having had transactions in the shares of 'that company' (i.e. the British one), and said that this went for Lloyd George too. This denial was at once correct and unnecessarily evasive. The failure to mention the American share purchases at this point was bound to lead to trouble later. In late December or early January something – presumably a belief that word was about to leak out – prompted Lloyd George and Isaacs to make a confession to Asquith. Asquith rejected their proffered resignations.[98] Lloyd George was also at pains to shore up his support elsewhere. He was never a great writer of letters, but on 8 January 1913 he took the trouble to send Clementine Churchill a note thanking her for the gift of some apples. He added a postscript: 'I was so encouraged to hear from Winston that you took his view of my little worry. I am almost ill with worry over it.'[99] She responded reassuringly: 'I am so very sorry for your anxiety. Winston and I have been thinking much about it – we feel so certain that it is a passing one & that a few months from now you will wonder that it ever existed.' She added: 'Anyhow if the whole truth is known I don't see how even one dog could bark.'[100] Over the ensuing months, one person close to Lloyd George later attested, Churchill's loyalty and affection towards him were as strong as a rock.[101]

However, Lloyd George did not, as yet, choose to make a public disclosure. The heat was turned up in February, when Leo Maxse, whose right-wing journal the *National Review* had run numerous insinuating articles on the issue, testified to the Parliamentary Select Committee that was examining the original Marconi contract.[102] Maxse pointed out that Lloyd George had never explicitly denied owning Marconi shares. In Paris, *Le Matin* reported Maxse's testimony, but did so inaccurately. This gave Isaacs and Herbert Samuel (who as Postmaster General had been responsible for the Marconi contract, but who had owned shares in neither Marconi company) the opportunity to sue for libel. In the course of the case their lawyers – Edward Carson and F. E. Smith – were able to bring out the facts about the American shares without causing too much of a storm. (Churchill had persuaded Smith and Carson to appear. Aside from

their legal eminence, this had the advantage of preventing these two
prominent Unionists from making political capital out of the affair.)[103]
The lack of a newspaper frenzy at this point can partly be accounted
for by the fact that, at some stage, Churchill had gone to see Lord
Northcliffe, owner of *The Times* and the *Daily Mail*. He had asked
him 'to treat the Marconi matter on non-Party lines', at the same
time offering assurances that there was not much to the scandal.[104]
Northcliffe complied. In April, however, he warned Churchill that
'Your Marconi friends' were mismanaging their media strategy. As
he put it, 'the system of making mysteries of pieces of evidence in the
enquiry, and doling them out like a serial story, has a bad effect on
the public'.[105] Churchill promised to pass on his advice.[106] He
rendered Lloyd George further service by a vigorous performance
in front of the Select Committee at the end of the same month.
Churchill had been called in order to give him the opportunity to
deny in public the wholly false rumour that he too had traded in
Marconi shares. He gave the committee a dressing down, for having
summoned him urgently 'upon the merest unsupported tittle-tattle
. . . to give an answer as to whether or no he has sat still while his
friends and colleagues came forward and voluntarily disclosed their
position'.[107] Although this had little to do with the main issue, it may
have acted as a morale booster for his embattled colleagues. The
affair seemed to be dying down.

On 5 June 1913, though, there was another bombshell. It was
revealed that Elibank, in addition to the shares he had bought for
himself, had purchased others on behalf of the Liberal Party. (Lord
Elibank, as he had become when he had stood down as Chief Whip
in 1912, was at this point away on a business trip to South America.)
Churchill swiftly moved to assure Northcliffe that neither he nor
Lloyd George, nor anyone else in the government, had known about
this.[108] Lord Esher dined with Lloyd George and Churchill a few
days later: 'They seemed quite unconscious of the gravity of their
situation or their peril.'[109] On 13 June the Liberal-dominated Select
Committee published a majority report completely exonerating ministers. This, though, simply looked like a cover-up. Lloyd George's
fate hinged on the debate on the report, held on the 18th and 19th.
His speech on the first day fell short of an expression of 'regret' for
what he had done. He had, he admitted, been thoughtless, careless
and even mistaken, but he had acted innocently, openly and hon-

estly.[110] In her diary, Lucy Masterman described the impact of his words:

> He has an extremely winning voice on these occasions, and the whole House was soon crying. Winston had two large tears rolling down his face. Rufus was sitting with his head bent so that no one could see his face and his hands dropped upon his knees. Charlie [Masterman] was crying. The P.M. was crying. An old member, named Holt, who had been suffering a particularly militant set of scruples boo-hooed in a very vocal manner. George had them all in the hollow of his hands.[111]

Churchill thought the Tories could have used the scandal to bring the government down, but 'Some of them were too stupid and, frankly, some of them were too nice.'[112] The Chancellor's survival, though, was substantially attributable to Asquith, whose sterling support in his own speech the next day was essential to the defeat of the hostile motion at hand by a majority of 78. By putting his personal authority at stake he brought those Liberals who were doubtful about Lloyd George back into the fold, and thus retained a talented minister, whose wings were at the same time conveniently clipped.

Churchill's help, significant though it was, was nothing to this, but in the aftermath of these events he further spoke up for the Chancellor. In a speech at the National Liberal Club he claimed that 'no stain of any kind' rested upon the integrity of Lloyd George or Isaacs. They had, he said, been subject to 'a campaign of calumny and slander' that, he further suggested, was motivated by unworthy political concerns.

> My right hon. friend the Chancellor of the Exchequer is more bitterly hated in certain powerful classes, certain great organized confederated groupings of public opinion, he is more bitterly hated and more relentlessly pursued than even Mr. Gladstone was in the great days of 1886. I do not know how one can measure the degree of hatred with which he has been pursued in certain quarters. I do not believe my right hon. friend the Attorney-General would ever have been attacked in the way he has been but that they wanted to strike at Mr. Lloyd George.[113]

The Marconi events gave Churchill a good claim to be regarded as a foul-weather friend of Lloyd George. There is little reason to think that, in defending his colleague, he had any ulterior motive. Although, after his appointment to the Admiralty, relations between the two had cooled rather, the attacks on a man whom Churchill genuinely liked and respected stimulated the chivalrous element in his nature. This was much to his credit. But it should not be allowed to disguise the fact that, throughout their long association, Churchill's loyalty to Lloyd George was episodic – Marconi being a particular high point – rather than continuous, as at certain moments he liked to suggest. Moreover, the fact that he had on this occasion sprung to Lloyd George's side merely heightened his own sense of betrayal, when, as he felt, his good faith was not reciprocated during the crisis of May 1915. His attempts to vindicate his colleague were not wholly selfless – few things are – but something for which in due course he expected to be paid back. Lloyd George, for his part, was happy to accept Churchill's aid, but without accepting a sense of obligation in return.

Their relationship, important as it still was to both of them, was thus unbalanced, as well as fitful. As the rest of this book will demonstrate, it was, almost until the last, somewhat one-sided, and was punctuated by repeated rows, which were followed in turn by reconciliation, reassurance and protestations of devotion. To this extent it was similar to that between Lloyd George and his mistress-cum-confidential secretary, Frances Stevenson.[114] She requires introduction here for three reasons. First, she was an important witness to much that passed between Lloyd George and Churchill until the former's death. Second, in later life she was one of those who promoted the myth that the political conflicts of interest between the two men never interfered with their friendship. This view, which she presented in her memoirs, was strongly contradicted by many of the stories she recorded in her contemporary diary. (Unsurprisingly, her diary reveals her as a strong Lloyd George partisan, at the expense of Churchill.) Third, the question of what Churchill knew about Lloyd George's virtual bigamy with Stevenson, and when, is of intrinsic interest. It is difficult to answer with precision, but the evidence does seem to indicate, as with some other discreditable aspects of Lloyd George's behaviour, amused toleration on Churchill's behalf of his colleague's peccadilloes.

It must be remembered that exposure of the truth about Lloyd George's infidelities would have ended his political career. This must have been driven home to him by the case of Eliot Crawshay-Williams, which developed while the Marconi affair was unfolding. After unsuccessfully contesting a seat for the Liberals in 1906, Crawshay-Williams had been appointed assistant private secretary to Churchill at the Colonial Office. He married in 1908, won a seat at Leicester in 1910 and was subsequently appointed parliamentary private secretary to Lloyd George. He looked set for a bright political future, but in 1913 he was named in a divorce case launched by Hubert Carr-Gomm, a fellow Liberal MP. 'What made the case a bad one', according to Lucy Masterman, was not only that Crawshay-Williams was married with several children, but that he was also Carr-Gomm's 'most intimate friend at school, college and in politics'. She also recorded that Lloyd George had made fruitless efforts to bring the Carr-Gomm couple back together, and that Churchill had been involved in an attempt 'to frighten Carr-Gomm out of bringing the case, a proceeding which naturally made him angry'.[115] When the case eventually came to court, Carr-Gomm's wife Kathleen and Crawshay-Williams did not deny adultery, and the divorce was granted. Crawshay-Williams felt he had no alternative but to resign from the Commons, although Lloyd George and Churchill urged him to continue in politics. (They were also involved in efforts to persuade Carr-Gomm to fulfil his promise to pay an allowance to his ex-wife.) Following his own divorce he married Kathleen – although the marriage did not last – and went on to achieve literary success with works of poetry, fiction and memoir. But his political talents were never put to further use.[116] Lucy Masterman wrote that whereas Lloyd George regarded 'an irregular love affair as a very trifling matter – even in a married woman', Rufus Isaacs, by contrast, took the episode 'rather grimly'. One day at lunch Isaacs denounced Crawshay-Williams's seduction of his friend's wife as 'unpardonable, absolutely unpardonable behaviour'. In response to this, Lloyd George bent down to his plate 'feeling vaguely that he was being scolded, and said in a very meek voice – "I suppose it *was* rather wrong!" '[117]

Awareness of the risks does not seem to have deterred Lloyd George in the slightest. Where it survives, documentation on his sexual affairs prior to the point he met Frances Stevenson is ambiguous.

However, it seems quite likely that he was serial adulterer.[118] In fairness, his marriage was not an ideal one. Margaret disliked London, and stayed for long periods in Wales away from her husband, who reproached her with neglecting him. 'I have scores of times come home in the dead of night to a cold, dark & comfortless flat with out a soul to greet me', he complained in 1897. 'I am not of the nature either physically or morally that I ought to have been left like this.'[119] He did not cease to feel affection for her, but the death of their daughter Mair drove a wedge between them. None of this excuses his behaviour, although he had his own rationalization for it: 'the greater the man the greater the weakness'.[120] Margaret stuck loyally to him in the face of public rumours. In 1909 the *People* newspaper hinted that Lloyd George was to have been named as the co-respondent in a divorce case, and that £20,000 hush money had been paid to avoid this. He sued for libel; Margaret accompanied him to court; he testified to his innocence; the paper retracted and paid substantial damages.[121] Asquith, the Chancellor noted, had 'been a brick throughout'; Churchill too had been 'a true friend'.[122]

Lloyd George's partnership with Frances Stevenson was far more significant than any of his previous infidelities. The two first met in July 1911, when she was 22 and he was 48. She had graduated from Royal Holloway College, London, the previous year, after which she took a job at a boarding school. Lloyd George was looking for a tutor for his daughter Megan and a series of coincidences led Stevenson to be interviewed by him for the post at 11 Downing Street. She recalled in her memoirs the warmth of his voice, the kindliness of his manner, and his eyes, 'grave and gay almost simultaneously', that conveyed a sympathetic understanding of all one's feelings and difficulties. Under the influence of his profound and exciting magnetism, 'I left Downing Street under the impression that I was a free and independent person: in truth I was enslaved for life.' She spent the summer at Criccieth, and afterwards remained in close contact with him. They did not immediately become lovers. Lloyd George in due course made it clear that he would like her to become his Secretary at the Treasury. This, she realized, 'would be on his own terms, which were in conflict with my essentially Victorian upbringing'. At the end of 1912, she visited friends in Scotland, intending to think things over carefully. She soon received an urgent letter from

Lloyd George, saying something terrible was about to happen and that he needed her. Returning to London she found him in a panic over the Marconi affair. Feeling that she was necessary to his well-being, she accepted the terms of his bargain, i.e. that she must not hope for marriage to him, but that if he were ever in a position to wed her he would do so.[123] From then on, until Margaret's death in 1941, he maintained the façade of being a conventionally married man, but in reality led what was almost a double life.

How much did Churchill – who was devoted to his own wife – know of this? On the one hand, he much preferred to talk about himself than about other people, and this was hardly the most effective way to pick up gossip. On the other hand, surely, at some point between 1913 and Lloyd George's marriage to Stevenson thirty years later, he must have developed some inkling of what was going on. Notwithstanding his capacity for crass insensitivity, it would make a complete mockery of his claims to friendship with Lloyd George had he contrived to remain oblivious of this central fact of his life. Moreover, as time went on, Lloyd George and Stevenson took greater risks, and their affair seems, within a limited circle, to have been an open secret. George Riddell (who could be trusted with a confidence) appears to have known; and Nancy Astor[124] (who could not) either knew or suspected. And when, during the 1919 Peace Conference, Churchill and his wife and others picnicked with Stevenson and Lloyd George in the woods near Fontainebleau, were they really under the illusion that she was merely his secretary?[125]

There is an intriguing reference in a letter Lloyd George wrote to Stevenson from Criccieth in May 1923, some months after he had lost office. He was at this point, it seems, anticipating a political crisis consequent on the resignation of Bonar Law as Prime Minister. He had, he told his lover, hoped to find some excuse attendant on this for coming to see her. 'But Winston didn't play up', he wrote. 'He always was a disappointing colleague!'[126] What is unclear is whether Churchill knew that it was hoped that he would provide some sort of alibi; whether his failure to do so was witting or unwitting; and whether, if it was witting, this was because in fact he disapproved. Stevenson's granddaughter and biographer tells us that 'neither Winston Churchill or his wife could be bothered to be polite to LG's secretary' and that 'later when they took over Frances' London flat, they were extraordinarily abrupt'.[127] If so – and it is possible that

Stevenson was a little paranoid – it is hard to know for certain what lay behind the rudeness. One may hazard that Churchill was taking a cue from his wife, who may have felt some sympathetic resentment on Margaret Lloyd George's behalf. If he did develop a negative attitude towards Stevenson, it seems unlikely that it derived purely from censoriousness, although perhaps double standards were involved. In 1909, he heard that H. G. Wells was 'behaving very badly with a young Girton girl of the new emancipated school'. (Wells's ideas, incidentally, were a great influence on Stevenson.) Although, in a letter to Clementine, he noted that very serious consequences had followed, his concluding remark on the matter was 'These literary gents!!'[128] This was hardly a harsh condemnation, and his friendship with Wells does not seem to have been affected. It is possible to speculate, therefore, that Churchill viewed Lloyd George's well-known reputation for womanizing in a similar light, whether or not he was closely informed of the actual facts. It is equally possible that he combined this with a rather less broad-minded attitude towards Stevenson, as a 'girl of the new emancipated school', with whom his colleague was misbehaving – a kind of hypocrisy that would not have been uncommon at the time.

This, though, cannot be said with any degree of certainty. The conflict between Churchill and Lloyd George over the naval estimates in 1914 offers a return to firmer ground, and also illustrates the unresolved tensions in the two men's relations. The prehistory of this dispute relates to the land issue. As Ian Packer explains in his book *Lloyd George, Liberalism and the Land*, British Radicals saw land reform as the potential solution to a variety of social evils, urban as well as rural, including housing shortages and unemployment. However, having settled on the idea of a land campaign in 1912, Lloyd George repeatedly delayed its public launch because the expert group that he convened to devise a policy did not get its proposals ready on time. In the meantime he kept Churchill and other key colleagues up to date with the progress of the land enquiry's work.[129] In spite of his tendency to criticize Churchill as a reactionary, Lloyd George appears to have made fair progress in converting him. In March 1913 the Duke of Marlborough published a series of articles in the *Daily Mail*, in the form of an open letter to Churchill, his cousin. They seemed to suggest that the Liberals should accept military conscription in exchange for Tory support for better agricultural wages and housing.[130] It seems that these were inspired, if not actually written, by Churchill himself. Lloyd George, in turn, appears to have been aware of this, and to have approved.[131]

Although this particular idea did not come off – there was no chance that the Liberal Party would be converted to National Service in peacetime – Lloyd George secured Churchill's support. 'I had quite a useful discussion with him at Criccieth, but he hates inflicting any hurt upon the aristocracy', the Chancellor wrote to Charles Masterman in September 1913. However, he claimed, 'The drama of the situation appeals so much to him that for the moment he was prepared for human sacrifice.'[132] Accordingly, Churchill backed Lloyd George when he brought his proposals to Cabinet in October. His plan was for a new Land Ministry, which would fix agricultural wages as well as dealing with tenancy, rents, and land acquisition. Having manoeuvred skilfully to secure his colleagues' backing, he launched his programme with major speeches in Bedford and Swindon. The assault on landlordism was to form the backdrop to the general election that was expected to follow soon. It also offered Lloyd George personally the chance to bounce back after the tribulations of Marconi. Churchill, together with other ministers, backed the campaign publicly.[133] After he spoke on the minimum wage proposal, the Chancellor wrote to Clementine: 'Winston's Manchester speech was first rate. How well he put the labourer's case. I want him so much to help in this great struggle. No living man can present an issue as brilliantly as he can'.[134]

Churchill was a vigorous, but perhaps not a wildly enthusiastic, exponent of land reform. As was typical, Lloyd George gave different accounts to different people of what his colleague's view really was. After his own Bedford speech, he wrote to his brother: 'It has quite converted Winston'.[135] The explanation he gave to Riddell, though, did not attribute the conversion to the power of oratory:

> Most people have a price of some sort. Very often the price is the support of some policy in which they are very much interested. For example: *I have made a bargain with Winston. He has agreed to support my land policy with which he is not in sympathy, and I have agreed to give him more money for the Navy. You may call this a bribe, but I have nothing to gain personally. I am only endeavouring to carry out my scheme of social reform, which I believe is for the good of the people.*

> *I am not at all sure that the bargain will meet with the approval of some of*
> *our party. Indeed I already see signs that it will not.*[136]

It seems quite likely that there was indeed such a deal; and Lloyd George's comments about its impact on the Liberal Party were prescient. The next entry in Riddell's diary records a conversation with Rufus Isaacs, who said: 'It is quite obvious that he [Lloyd George] has made a bargain with Winston. Our people are beginning to see it. It will be very unpopular.'[137] Again, Margot Asquith sought to interfere, writing to Lloyd George on 17 November: 'Don't let Winston have too much money – it will hurt our party in every way – Labour & even Liberals. If one can't be a little economical when all foreign countries are peaceful I don't know *when* we can.'[138]

Things came to a head in Cabinet meetings on 8, 15 and 16 December. There was, as Lloyd George told his brother, 'real genuine revolt against Naval expenditure'.[139] Churchill presented a naval estimate for 1914–15 of £50,694,800, an increase of nearly £3 million over the previous year. Churchill had already enraged much Liberal opinion by a speech at the Guildhall in London in which he referred to the 'measured and unbroken development of the German Navy' and called for increased British naval spending.[140] Ministers hostile to his proposals included McKenna, Hobhouse, Samuel, Pease and Walter Runciman. Lloyd George had described the Guildhall speech as 'a piece of madness' on the grounds that 'The public will not stand provocative speeches of that sort.'[141] But in terms of substance he was initially supportive of Churchill. The two men presented to the Cabinet an agreement, reached between them in private, to trim £728,000 from the estimates. This may well have been an artificial concession designed to appease the 'economists'. Moreover, between the first and second Cabinet meetings, Lloyd George stressed in private that he would 'be no party to driving Winston out of the Cabinet' and that it was 'better to have him with us than against us'.[142] But in the final meeting he shifted his position, as the strength of feeling became clear. Hobhouse noted: 'An interesting feature of these discussions was Ll.G's repudiation of the bargain, which had evidently been come to between Churchill and himself, as soon as he saw others were prepared to fight Churchill.'[143]

Although the 'economists' were unable to bring down the headline figure for 1914–15, they had better luck in pressing for a cutback in the shipbuilding programme a year over the horizon, in 1915–16. Lloyd George's support for the latter idea provoked a bitter note, passed across the Cabinet table by Churchill. It read, 'I consider that you are going back on your word: in trying to drive me out after we had settled, & you promised to support the estimates.' This drew a rejoinder from the Chancellor. He had, he said, agreed to the figure for the current year and had stood by it '& carried it' much to the disappointment of his 'economical friends'. But, he claimed, 'I told you distinctly I would press for a reduction of a new programme with a view to 1915 & I think quite respectfully you are unnecessarily stubborn.' In response, another note came back from Churchill: 'No. You said you would support the Estimates.'[144] Churchill left the meeting in a huff. Lloyd George, who just a few days earlier had been saying that he would never forget Churchill's support over Marconi, now observed that 'Winston has been a loyal friend to me, but there comes a time when one cannot allow oneself to be influenced by personal considerations of that sort.'[145]

Further discussion of the issue was postponed until after Christmas, but with Asquith coming under severe pressure from Liberal MPs opposed to the estimates, Lloyd George appeared to throw in his lot more firmly with the economizers. He drew up a memorandum suggesting that two Dreadnoughts could safely be cut from the 1914–15 programme. Then he fanned the flames further by going public on the row. In an interview with the Daily Chronicle, published on 1 January 1914, he did his best to personalize the issue at stake. In an obvious dig at Churchill, he contrasted current rates of expenditure on arms with the much lower levels that had obtained in 1887; Lord Randolph Churchill, he pointed out, had considered even those levels to be 'bloated and profligate'. He further argued that relations with Germany had improved of late, and that continental countries were increasingly concentrating on land forces, so Britain's naval power was unlikely to be challenged.[146]

Churchill was at this point in France. When he learnt of Lloyd George's words he was predictably wrathful. 'The Chancellor of the Exchequer's interview in the Daily Chronicle is a fine illustration of his methods', he wrote, 'and I should imagine that it would deeply vex the Prime Minister.'[147] Asquith, in a letter to Venetia Stanley, the young confidante to whom he had begun to pour out a stream of indiscreet and increasingly impassioned letters, did indeed contrast

Lloyd George's 'heedless folly' with Churchill's 'dignified and moody' public silence.[148] But he made no decisive intervention.

The Lloyd George–Churchill split was now the subject of extensive public comment. Churchill made a show of not responding directly to the *Chronicle* article. On 5 January the *Daily Mail* reported that Churchill had declined an interview with its representative in Paris on the grounds that he made it a rule not to give interviews to newspapers on important questions while they were under the consideration of the Cabinet. In an incisive article, the *Mail* commented sarcastically that 'It must not, of course, be assumed that by this pointed refusal to grant an interview ... Mr. Churchill desired to reflect upon his colleague, Mr. Lloyd George, who has just granted an interview in identical circumstances.' It summarized contrasts between Lloyd George's interview and Churchill's November Guildhall speech. 'On fundamental issues the two Ministers are in complete antagonism', the paper observed. Churchill wanted more money for the navy; Lloyd George said that too much was being spent on it already. Churchill said that Germany's attitude rendered any idea of disarmament out of the question; Lloyd George declared that the strain with Germany had relaxed. The article continued: 'The conflict between the two Ministers is causing uneasiness in the party, where it is being regarded by some as the first sign of a struggle between them for the Liberal leadership should Mr. Asquith carry out an intention, at which he has not infrequently hinted, of resigning after Home Rule and Welsh Disestablishment have been carried into law.'[149] Churchill himself admitted privately that 'The situation is serious & may prove fatal to the government, unless it shd turn out that the Chancellor is only "trying it on".'[150] Asquith noted that Churchill 'is of course angry with Ll.G. and determined to beat him in the Cabinet, which he is confident he will be able to do'.[151]

As the *Mail* implied, Churchill's failure to speak out openly was something of a pose. He too was trying to manipulate the media, albeit in a less ostentatious manner than Lloyd George was. His correspondence with Leo Chiozza Money reveals this hitherto unknown aspect of the crisis. Although he had established himself as a devoted adherent of the Chancellor, Chiozza Money had written to the Liberal press, arguing that the German naval spending had twice been increased at a time when Great Britain was reducing its expenditure.[152] By now Churchill had returned to London. On 13

January he sent Chiozza Money a flattering private letter – referred to in a different context in Chapter 1 – in which he claimed to have been heavily influenced by his thinking on trade ten years earlier. He also praised the 'political courage' of his statements in the present crisis. 'Now it is a real encouragement to me to find that an independent study of the facts of the Naval situation shd have led you to confirm the conclusions of the responsible experts. Come & see me one day here [i.e. at the Admiralty] and let us have a talk – there is an arsenal of figures available for future engagements.'[153] It seems certain that some such meeting took place. On 23 January, James Masterton-Smith, Churchill's private secretary, wrote to Chiozza Money enclosing a table of naval statistics that had been prepared at the latter's request. 'It contains only such information as you can use and is based on data that are accessible to the "man on the omnibus" if he reads his British and German newspapers', Masterton-Smith wrote. 'On the other hand it should *not* be stated that the information is contained in a printed Admiralty table.'[154] It is clear the information was intended to be deployed in the public prints, whilst the actual source was kept secret; and the following day Churchill thanked Chiozza Money for the 'admirable' articles he had already received from him. He added: 'I am keeping the proof to encourage the Chancellor of the Exchequer.'[155]

By this point, the argument between the First Lord and the Chancellor had undergone some further rapid twists. Churchill's position had been complicated by the news that the Canadian government would not revive its plans, previously rejected by the Senate, to construct three Super-Dreadnoughts as a contribution to the defence of the Empire. This meant yet more money might be required for the British estimates, and Churchill started to talk about a total figure of £53–4 million. In mid-January Lloyd George reported to C. P. Scott that he had had two hours of discussion with Churchill, 'friendly in tone but fruitless'. During these talks, he claimed to have learnt information about which he had previously been kept in the dark: 'It had emerged that there was actually due, or wd be by the end of the financial year, to contractors 3 millions in addition to the amount authorised by Parliament.'[156] Lloyd George told Riddell (correctly) that he himself had been late entering into the whole estimates controversy but also (falsely, as it turned out) that having done so he would not back down. 'The PM must choose between Winston and me', he said. 'Winston has acted disgracefully', he continued, alleging that Churchill was guilty of 'gross negligence and extravagance'. He alleged, not for the first time, that Churchill wanted 'to get back to the Tory party again'.[157] Asquith wrote to his wife on the 20th that 'Ll.G. and Winston are still poles apart over the Navy, and it looks as if it might eventually come to breaking point.' He told her further that 'If this were plainly inevitable[,] sooner than have a smash-up and resignation, I should probably dissolve Parliament and run the risk of the election.'[158] Lloyd George's long interviews with Churchill alone and with him and the Prime Minister together were 'polite but deadly'.[159]

By this point, the difference between Lloyd George and Churchill was no longer about the 1914–15 estimates, but about the ones for 1915–16. The Chancellor was prepared to find the money to meet all the Admiralty's existing obligations, including its planned building programme, in exchange for a guarantee that the following year's estimates would be brought down to between £46 and £47 million, the level of 1913–14. Churchill was obdurate. His argument was that none of his predecessors had ever been required to forecast spending so far in advance. Lloyd George seemed eager to twist the knife. He claimed to C. P. Scott that he had said that, whatever was settled, he would require guarantees regarding 1915–16 directly from Asquith rather than Churchill himself. When Churchill asked why, he replied, 'Because I do not trust you.'[160]

Yet on the 22nd, two days after this spat, Lloyd George told his brother that he was 'on the best of terms' with Churchill: 'No quarrel. I hope to get things through.'[161] An awareness of the likely consequences of pushing things too far probably explains this. In another letter four days later he emphasized that although the Cabinet economists were out to get Churchill, 'I am not out for blood – but for an honourable peace'.[162] Two days after that he commented on his difficulties, 'not the least being the strong personal antipathy to Winston felt by several of his colleagues. Yesterday my worry was with Winston now it is with those who wish to hound him out of the Cabinet under the guise of economy'.[163] Lloyd George did his best to disguise this desire to reach a compromise with Churchill from those very colleagues, albeit without complete success. This is the light in which to read his continuing denunciations, or mock denunciations, of Churchill. How much Churchill actually understood this is open to question. He seems to have sensed that Lloyd George, potentially, was an ally rather an antagonist on the estimates question. 'LG will not make up his mind to go with me', he told Riddell. 'If he would, we could win easily.' But after a further private talk with the Chancellor he confided: 'I am nearly at the end of my tether. I can't make David (LG) out'.[164]

Thus, in the bitter exchanges over the coming days, Lloyd George was shadow-boxing, but Churchill may well have been genuinely angry. The latter briefly appeared to agree that the 1915–16 estimates should see a reduction; but he almost immediately followed this up with a letter in which he said that he could not be bound to the figures he had mentioned 'in any extraordinary or improper sense'. He added: 'I recognise your friendship, but I ask no favours & I shall enter into no irregular obligations.'[165]

At around noon on 27 January Lloyd George showed Churchill's letter to a group of the ministerial economizers who had been called to the Treasury to meet him. 'This', he said, 'justifies all your doubts of Winston's sincerity.'[166] He also sent a copy to Asquith, to whom he wrote: 'I have laboured in vain to effect an arrangement between Churchill & the critics of his Estimates . . . I have utterly failed. I have my own opinion as to where the blame lies but you will judge for yourself.'[167] He also sent a denunciatory missive direct to Churchill, having taken care to show it to his 'economist' colleagues first. 'I have repeatedly been told that I was being made a fool of; I declined to believe it', he wrote. 'Your candour now forces me to acknowledge the justice of the taunt.' He warned that the ship of Liberalism was about to be wrecked: 'the responsibility is yours and yours alone'.[168]

Given that each man wrote at least one letter to the other on 27 January, and that the letters were received (via government messenger) on the day they were sent, there is clear potential for confusion about the sequence. Accordingly, two of these letters are printed in the documentary companion volume to the official biography of Churchill in what appears from internal evidence to be the wrong order. This is made the more understandable by the fact that what (I would argue) is Churchill's reply to Lloyd George's letter quoted above appears, on the face of it, to be a complete *non sequitur*. 'My dear David', it begins. 'Only a line to thank you for the warmth and kindness of your letter. It is a comfort to me that if the worst happens, personal ill-will between us will not be added to the many other causes for regret.'[169] As Lloyd George's letter had been neither warm nor kind, the official biographers posit the existence of another letter, now lost; but this is unconvincing and is not corroborated by Charles Hobhouse's diary description of the exchange of letters.[170] An alternative hypothesis is that Churchill was being profoundly sarcastic.

Churchill might not have understood what Lloyd George was really up to, but the 'economists' were already more than a little suspicious. (A few days earlier Riddell had observed to McKenna that Lloyd George always tended to favour compromise. 'Yes,' the Home Secretary replied, 'the sort of compromise in which Winston will get all his own way.')[171] Hobhouse recorded that he and the other ministers parted from the Chancellor 'in the hope but not the fixed belief, that Ll.G. had decided finally to walk the path of economy'. At Cabinet, however, 'it soon became evident that a reconciliation had been effected'. Although Lloyd George gave a lecture on the desirability of economy, to which Churchill responded with a disquisition on national security, there was no attempt on either side to deliver a knock-out blow. Nothing was decided. Next morning a group of ministers met at McKenna's house and 'found no new reason to trust Winston's ability to reduce estimates, nor Ll.G.'s sincerity in asking for reduction'. There were further Cabinets that day and the next. At the latter meeting, Hobhouse wrote, Lloyd George gave the 'economists' no help. Moreover, 'both he and Churchill endeavoured to get the cabinet to assume that £52½ millions were the estimates agreed to'.[172] Hobhouse, McKenna, Simon, Runciman and Lord Beauchamp (the First Commissioner of Works) were alarmed, and wrote to Asquith. They questioned whether Churchill's figures, and Lloyd George's plan that they should be matched with a guarantee of economy for 1915–16, were 'best calculated to make more certain the happy issue of the legislative programme to which you and we stand committed'. They feared an arms race with the Germans and a split in the Liberal Party.[173] A few days later McKenna told C. P. Scott that Lloyd George had given up the fight for economy: 'he is now Churchill's man'. Scott noted that the only explanation McKenna could suggest 'was that Lloyd George was acting as bell-wether to bring the stalwarts into the Churchill fold'.[174] That was not far from the truth.

At the end of January Lady Randolph wrote to her son: 'I am

glad to see by the papers . . . that you have your own way with L.G. – it was bound to be'.[175] But it was not until 11 February that agreement on the estimates was finally reached. The Estimates were to be £51,580,000 – which was £1,613,200 more than Churchill had agreed with Lloyd George in their attempted stitch-up of December. In return for this, Churchill was induced to promise 'under proper reserves' a £2 million reduction the following year. (As he commented wryly in his memoirs, 'when the time came, I was not pressed to redeem this undertaking'.)[176] An anecdote told by Megan Lloyd George to Randolph Churchill in 1962, confirming a story his father had previously recounted to him, runs as follows.

There were many Cabinets about the Estimates, but the matter was not resolved and Asquith said Lloyd George and WSC [i.e. Churchill] must decide between themselves one way or the other. The point had been reached where both were determined to resign rather than yield. Lloyd George said to WSC, 'Come to breakfast tomorrow at No 11 and we shall settle the matter.' WSC arrived next morning fully expecting that he would have to resign. Lloyd George greeted him and said, 'Oddly enough, my wife spoke to me last night about this Dreadnought business. She said, "You know, my dear, I never interfere in politics; but they say you are having an argument with that nice Mr. Churchill about building dreadnoughts. Of course I don't understand these things, but I should have thought it would be better to have too many rather than too few." So I have decided to let you build them. Let's go in to breakfast.'

The tale had obviously improved somewhat in the telling, but it is quite possible that Lloyd George did make some such folksy quip. Randolph Churchill, rightly doubtful about how seriously the story should be taken, wrote that 'It is possible that Lloyd George involved his wife in the story to sweeten and cover his own retreat.'[177] To the outside world the outcome of the estimates battle did look like a retreat by Lloyd George. And of course, for a politician even the appearance of defeat can be a serious business. However, Lloyd George had throughout the last part of January tried to present himself as being *forced* to retreat, that is to say, driven from the position that he had in fact been obliged to adopt when the strength of Cabinet feeling against Churchill's plans became apparent. In practice, he was happy to concede the substance of what Churchill wanted, provided that he could achieve in return some symbolic concessions for the sake of honour. This was what he eventually got, and one suspects agreement might have been reached sooner had not Churchill been so obtuse. This explains why at times during the crisis Lloyd George became genuinely infuriated with him, even though the two were not far apart on principles. How many of Lloyd George's calculations took place at the conscious rather than the subconscious level is hard to say. But certainly, in a rather perverse way, he fulfilled his bargain with Churchill over the Land Campaign. For, as it turned out, he could give effective support to the estimates only by putting himself at the head of the opposition to them, and then emasculating it.

If Churchill did not recognize the charade, or play his part with maximum skill, Lloyd George perhaps did not appreciate Churchill's problems sufficiently. The latter's intransigence was not just a product of mule-headedness. Towards the end of January he explained privately why he could make no more concessions. The Admiralty Board, he said, would not agree. 'It is useless to put political arguments to them', he pointed out. 'The Liberal Party is nothing to them. Indeed they would not be sorry to see us out.'[178] In other words, he might have preferred to play a more sophisticated political game. But he was hamstrung by his officials (many of whom, it might be added, he had alienated by his capricious style of management). This was ironic, as he faced persistent allegations that his attitude in the crisis was determined by personal ambition. Sir Francis Hopwood perpetuated the rumour that, at the crucial Cabinet, 'Winston solemnly announced, to the consternation of his colleagues, that if Ulster was not excluded from the operation of the Home Rule Bill, he would immediately resign! The idea of Winston stumping the country against the coercion of Ulster was more than they could face; and the opposition to the Estimates ended in abject surrender.'[179] This story was untrue; but Lloyd George had at one point in January accused Churchill to his face of *intending* to perform some such manoeuvre. According to C. P. Scott, to whom Lloyd George told the story:

In the presence of the Prime Minister he stated there was a strong impression among important people, and those not merely Churchill's opponents on the question of naval armaments, that

if he did not resign on that he would resign on the Irish question
and that therefore it was useless to make concessions to him,
and Lloyd George challenged him to say if this were so or not.
Churchill greatly confused and taken aback. Had no such
intention but could not commit himself in advance etc. Asquith
expressed his full confidence in him and so the matter ended,
but the effect will be to make it far more difficult for Churchill
to take the course which had been foretold.[180]

Of course, Lloyd George's story of Churchill's incomplete denial
cannot be considered hard evidence. It has the same status as his
repeated but unsubstantiated claims that his younger colleague was
planning to rejoin the Tories. In fact, in the aftermath of the estimates
controversy, he sought to work with Churchill over Ireland.

The general elections of 1910 had left the Liberals in the
Commons dependent on Irish Nationalist vote. This brought the
largely dormant issue of Home Rule back towards the centre of
the British political stage. The passing of the Parliament Act in
1911 ensured that the House of Lords could only delay, rather than
veto, the passage of a measure to bring it into law. In April 1912
the third Home Rule Bill was introduced. (Gladstone's two failed
ones had been introduced in 1886 and 1893.) Lloyd George and
Churchill, although obliged to speak up for Home Rule in public,
had reservations about it. These concerned the Northern Irish province of Ulster, the population of which was predominantly Protestant.
Protestant Unionists opposed 'Rome Rule' not only because they
feared subjugation by the Catholic majority in Ireland as a whole;
but also because they thought it might damage the prosperity of
Ulster, which was the wealthiest and most industrialized part of the
island. Furthermore, the Unionists in Ireland had important political
allies on the British mainland. Both Lloyd George and Churchill
served on the Cabinet committee established in January 1911 to deal
with Home Rule. Both devised (separate) proposals that tried to
remove the issue's sting by including some measure of devolution for
other parts of the United Kingdom too. But both plans were rejected
in favour of the formula that Gladstone had used, whereby there
would be an all-Ireland parliament in Dublin, but Westminster would
maintain control of trade, defence and foreign policy.[181] The two
men tried to persuade the Cabinet that Ulster should be excluded

from the operation of the Bill, but, as Churchill later reminded Asquith, Lord Loreburn 'repulsed us in the most blood thirsty manner'.[182] Of course, even a permanent exclusion for Ulster would not have suited the significant Unionist minority in the South of Ireland, and many Unionists opposed such an arrangement, which they considered would be a betrayal of this group.

In July 1912, a speech by Andrew Bonar Law, the new, hard-line Tory leader, showed that the opponents of Home Rule were prepared to countenance the use of force. Bonar Law had been born in Canada to Presbyterian immigrant parents (his father was from Ulster, although of Scottish ancestry). He now stated: 'I can imagine no length of resistance to which Ulster will go in which I shall not be ready to support them'.[183] This was tantamount to a threat of civil war. Churchill wrote to John Redmond that 'I do not believe there is any real feeling against Home Rule in the Tory Party apart from the Ulster question, but they hate the Government, are bitterly desirous of turning it out, and see in the resistance of Ulster an extra parliamentary force which they will not hesitate to use to the full.'[184] The possibility of violence was a real one. After the Home Rule Bill passed its Third Reading in January 1913, the Ulster Volunteer Force (UVF) was created. The formation of this paramilitary organization, designed to resist the imposition of Home Rule by force, was countered in November by the birth of the nationalist Irish Volunteers. Both sides set about arming themselves.

In spite of the growing tensions, and the opposition of the House of Lords, the Bill surmounted all parliamentary obstacles, and was set to become law in 1914. In October 1913, however, Churchill – who was increasingly alarmed about the prospect of civil war – sought to defuse the tense situation by reassuring the Unionists. With Asquith's agreement, he did his best to negotiate directly with the Conservative leaders. And in a speech in Dundee he said that Ulster's claim for special treatment could not be ignored and that major changes to the Bill might be possible – but that this could be achieved only through agreement and goodwill rather than by violence.[185] (He told Austen Chamberlain, a leading Conservative, that 'Both sides had to make speeches full of party claptrap & no surrender & then insert a few sentences at the end for wise & discerning people on the other side to see & ponder.')[186] The Prime Minister was under much pressure from the King, who strongly opposed putting Ulster under the control of a Dublin parliament. In the spring of 1914 Lloyd George and Augustine Birrell, the Chief Secretary for Ireland, helped Asquith's efforts to persuade the Nationalists to accept a temporary exclusion for Ulster. At the beginning of March John Redmond, their leader, gave his reluctant consent to a six-year opt-out – enough time for the British public, if they wished, to elect a Tory government to amend or reverse the legislation. However, Edward Carson MP, spokesman for die-hard unionism, memorably dismissed this substantial concession as a 'sentence of death with a stay of execution for six years'.[187]

Lloyd George, at this point, was eager to patch up relations with Churchill after the spat over the naval estimates. If that conflict had been somewhat artificial, it had nonetheless been bruising. Lloyd George saw an opportunity to massage his colleague's ego, by persuading him that he was uniquely placed to 'sell' the exclusion plan to the recalcitrant Irish Unionists. On 14 March 1914 he told Riddell that Churchill was going to make a major speech on the Ulster question that afternoon (in Bradford). He explained:

> I got him to do it. I said to him this is your opportunity. Providence has arranged it for you. You can make a speech which will ring down the corridors of history. I could not do it. The P.M. could not do it: You are the only member of the Cabinet who can make such a speech. You are known to have been in favour of Conciliation for Ulster. Now you can say that having found a compromise the Ulstermen will either have to accept it or take the consequences.

A further argument he employed was that the speech would help Churchill get the estimates through the Commons – presumably because it would put him in good odour with Liberal opinion.[188] (The strategy appears to have worked. 'Churchill introduces his naval estimates and the Radicals, instead of cursing, coo softly', noted Leo Amery. 'Unionists wonder if, by chance, this was the sole meaning and object of the Bradford speech.')[189] This rather confirms that Lloyd George's own opposition to the estimates had been a sham; and indeed, during Churchill's 17 March statement on them he was an ostentatious and implicitly supportive presence on the front bench.[190] It also reinforces the point that not only did ministers have to contend with many different issues at the same time, but those issues were frequently interlinked, increasing the complexity of political calculations. At any rate, it seems that Churchill responded enthusiastically to the combination of flattery and argument, and that Lloyd George then secured Asquith's agreement to the speech being made.[191]

Churchill's speech emphasized the sincerity of the government's offer to Ulster, arguing at the same time that it removed the slightest excuse for unconstitutional opposition to Home Rule. Furthermore, he said, there was no lawful measure from which the government would shrink in order to enforce its will. Indeed, 'there are things worse than bloodshed, even on extreme scale'. Such things included the trampling down of law and order, and the abdication of responsibility by the Executive.[192] Lloyd George thought this statement 'the right word at the right moment', adding, 'I am glad that I am largely responsible for it'.[193] (He followed it up with a speech of his own at Huddersfield on 21 March in which he referred to Ulster as a 'spoilt child'.)[194] Unfortunately, Churchill's words helped to exacerbate the government's problems rather than solve them. They created an atmosphere in which it was widely believed that the government was about to use force to coerce Ulster into accepting Home Rule.

In fact, the measures that the government took, including Churchill's dispatch of the Third Battle Squadron to within a short distance of Belfast, were purely precautionary. But, on 20–21 March there followed the notorious 'Curragh mutiny'. Brigadier General Hubert Gough, of the Third Cavalry Brigade (which was based at the Curragh, in County Kildare) declared that he and fifty-seven junior officers would rather be dismissed than engage in 'active military operations against Ulster'. Jack Seely, the Secretary of State for War, in a cack-handed attempt to smooth away dissent, responded with written guarantees that the army would not be employed 'to crush political opposition' to the Home Rule Bill. Asquith, a few days later, disavowed this pledge, asserting the principle of civilian control of the army, and Seely resigned.[195] John Burns wrote in his diary on 31 March that the crisis was over, Asquith's 'decisive action' having quelled the storm, and Lloyd George and Churchill's respective utterances having 'shewn this is a collective and not a sectional move'.[196] But the damage had been done. The government, having set out to establish its authority, now appeared to lack the will, and even the capacity, to do so.

In certain quarters, these events became known as 'the plot that failed'. Exactly what had been plotted, and by whom, varied according to taste. The Conservative MP W. A. S. Hewins, for example, thought that the Tory front bench had been in on the plan. The idea, in his view, had been to *provoke* resistance, rather than crush it, in order to shock the English electorate into supporting exclusion for Ulster. 'But', he wrote, 'it seems to have been forgotten that Winston is a criminal lunatic and Seely a fool.'[197] Sir Francis Hopwood, the Admiralty official who had a habit of bad-mouthing Churchill, had his own theory. He told Gerald Balfour, the former Prime Minister's brother, that Churchill's 'pique and annoyance' at the Unionists' rejection of the proposal regarding the exclusion of Ulster 'were vented in the "plot that failed"'. Furthermore, 'Lloyd George's violent speech at Huddersfield ... simply meant that he thought Winston's *coup* was going to succeed, and therefore wanted to be "in it".'[198] According to John Morley, who might have been expected to have been more sympathetic, the effects of Churchill's speech 'had been aggravated a thousandfold by Lloyd George's lurid oratory'.[199] In other words, the episode served to reinforce yet further the suspicions about the two men that many fairly influential people held; by now, virtually anything they did or said was likely to be taken by some as evidence of conspiracy.

Lloyd George now favoured permanent, rather than temporary, exclusion for Ulster from the term of the Bill. Over the next few months, although the government moved towards acceptance of this position, it proved impossible to reach a solution acceptable to all sides. In July, in an attempt to break the impasse, there was an inter-party conference at Buckingham Palace. Carson and Redmond were unable to find a compromise, and after three days the talks collapsed. On 24 July the Cabinet had an inconclusive discussion about what to do next. The threat of civil war loomed large. At the end of the meeting Sir Edward Grey moved to another subject: the situation in the Balkans. He told ministers that Austria had issued an ultimatum to Serbia, consequent on the assassination of the Archduke Franz Ferdinand in Sarajevo on 28 June. He said there was a possibility of 'a European Armageddon'.[200] Churchill recalled, in typical style, that 'The parishes of Fermanagh and Tyrone faded back into the mists and squalls of Ireland, and a strange light began immediately, but by perceptible gradations, to fall and grow upon the map of Europe.'[201]

The ultimatum, of course, was to trigger the outbreak of the Great War. This had the effect of suppressing the problems of Ireland – for the time being. It was also to form a watershed in the relationship between Churchill and Lloyd George.

Their respective roles in Britain's entry into that war will be examined in the next chapter. Here, though, it is appropriate to reflect on the state of their relations in the months and years immediately preceding it. Different writers have reached radically differing conclusions on this. Churchill's son Randolph wrote in his official biography that the Marconi scandal was of crucial importance: 'it was probably that at this time their lifelong friendship was cemented'.[202] But, whatever affection they might have felt for one another, there were major limits to its practical consequences. As has been seen, although Lloyd George acknowledged Churchill's loyalty, he emphasized that he would not allow himself to be influenced in political matters by personal considerations. Churchill likewise recognized his colleague's friendship, but declared that he would ask no favours and enter into no 'irregular obligations'. (Earlier, as seen for example in relation to the 1910 Rhondda strike, he had been more than happy to exploit the personal connection in 'departure from ordinary departmental practice' when it suited him to do so.) Arthur Marder, the pioneering naval historian of this period, has for his part claimed that the Churchill–Lloyd George alliance, previously under severe strain, 'collapsed when Churchill presented the 1914–15 estimates to the cabinet' in December 1913.[203] If Randolph Churchill's view is over-romantic, Marder exaggerates the differences between the two men. The harsh words that flew back and forth cannot always be taken exactly at face value (although Churchill probably took things to heart rather more than Lloyd George did). Lloyd George may have complained that Churchill did not 'understand the method which made the Welsh footballers so successful. The passing of the ball from 1 player to the other.'[204] But he still wanted him on the team, to the success of which, perhaps, the departure of either man would have been fatal.

To portray their supposed friendship purely as a politically convenient façade would be over-simplistic. When, in 1912, Churchill invited Lloyd George for a cruise on the Admiralty yacht *Enchantress*, he might, of course, have had some idea of interesting him in the problems of the navy.[205] But when, for example, Lloyd George went to the theatre in the company of the Churchills, it seems reasonable to assume that he did so in large part for the pleasure of their company.[206] The fact that Churchill called Lloyd George by his Christian name – in which he was unique outside the latter's family – is oft-cited and important evidence of their social familiarity. (Roy Jenkins notes that he did not start to address him as 'David' in letters until 1910, two years after Lloyd George had started to write 'My dear Winston'.)[207] All the same, political calculation was never far away.

Churchill liked to boast of his closeness to the Chancellor, emphasizing, by implication, his own importance. In 1914 he claimed that for ten years barely a day had gone by when the two had not had half an hour's conversation together. Augustine Birrell responded: 'How bored you must both be'.[208] (Another version of the story has Birrell saying 'In that case neither of you can be easily bored.')[209] And there is evidence that, on occasion at least, Lloyd George *was* bored by Churchill. In November 1910 he wrote to his brother that he had begun a letter to him the previous day 'but Winston came in & once he starts talking it is all over for at least an hour'.[210] The following year, after Churchill's transfer to the Admiralty, he complained that the new First Lord 'was really a perfect terror to his colleagues'. Churchill would bear down, saying, 'Look here, David, I want to talk to you,' and, Lloyd George lamented, 'he declaimed for the rest of the morning about his blasted ships'.[211] Lloyd George, who was never afraid to cut a colleague who had ceased to be useful to him, was perhaps to some extent guilty of politically motivated forbearance.

We cannot, therefore, ignore the evidence of a genuine attachment between the two, but at the same we should not overstate it or the role it played in affairs. Asquith might have put his finger on it during the estimates crisis when he wrote: 'Neither of them wants to go and in an odd sort of way they are really fond of one another.'[212] The oddness of the connection was as significant as the fondness, and one may speculate that either would have jettisoned the link had so doing been essential to retain office. In fact, avoiding a decisive break was essential protection for the careers of both. Hence Lloyd George's bid to reassure his colleague, after the naval fracas, that he, Churchill, was 'the only member of the Cabinet' who could carry off the government's Ulster policy. The dynamic between them, and within the Cabinet as a whole, was well captured in a 1912 diary entry by Charles Hobhouse: 'Ll. George has humour – great quickness of thought, and a wonderful power of managing men for a short time. He knows no meaning in the words *truth* or *gratitude*. Asquith is afraid of him, he knows it, but likes and respects Asquith. He is a little afraid of Grey – and of no one else, and treats Winston Churchill like he would a favourite and spoilt naughty boy.' (Churchill himself, Hobhouse added, with more than a hint of paradox, was 'ill mannered, boastful, unprincipled, without any redeeming qualities except his amazing ability and industry.')[213] Treating Churchill as a juvenile allowed Lloyd George to indulge him when it was convenient to do so, but was also a way of trying to keep him in his place. The coming of war was to confirm Lloyd George's ascendancy in the relationship, showing that, at least for the time being, he could do without Churchill, whereas Churchill, no matter what he thought at times, could not do without Lloyd George.

Chapter Four

TOUT EST FINI

JOHN MORLEY, the veteran Cabinet minister, had imagined that 'if there is a war, Winston will beat L.G. hollow'.[1] Given Churchill's penchant for all things military, the idea that he would thrive politically in wartime was not a surprising one, but Morley's prediction was to be confounded. Lloyd George, whose career had been faltering, went from strength to strength in the new conditions. Churchill, for his part, soon found himself desperately humiliated, and was driven, not for the last time, into the political wilderness. A nadir in the men's relationship followed. Churchill even declared that it was finished. He cursed Lloyd George for not defending him sufficiently when he came under attack during the political crisis of 1915. Having discovered that his colleague did not value old alliances above current necessities, he declared the friendship at an end. But his resolution did not last long. The grudge was not a convenient one for him to bear, because the key to his political resurrection remained in Lloyd George's hands.

During the crisis leading to Britain's involvement in the Great War, the firmness of Churchill's stance was never in question. He did not want war for its own sake, but supported it once he reached the conclusion that to enter it was vital to Britain's interests. Lloyd George was cast, at first, on the opposite side of the Cabinet divide, as a potential leader of a peace party. When Germany violated Belgian neutrality his attitude changed, and this played an important part in ensuring that the government entered the war largely united. During the tense discussions Churchill made emotively worded appeals to Lloyd George for his support. But to view the issue mainly in the light of their personal relations would be misleading – except, that is, insofar as their personal connection continued to be conditioned by wider political forces. Churchill deployed the rhetoric of personal sentiment to secure an objective to which he was emphatically committed. Lloyd George fell in with this object because, fundamentally, he was predisposed to do so, at least if certain conditions were met, and not because he had suddenly started to put friendship before politics.

Historians have long recognized that Lloyd George's attitude to European developments in the summer of 1914 was not that of an instinctive pacifist. That much should be clear from his approach to the Agadir episode three years earlier, when he had thought the moment ripe for hostilities against Germany, as indeed had Churchill.[2] (According to the latter, during that crisis the Chancellor had 'electrified' the King and Queen 'by observing that he thought it wd be a great pity if war did not come now'.)[3] On the other hand, it would be wrong to view him purely as a Machiavellian realist. He blended an overwhelming concern with the power and prestige of the British Empire with a rather naive view of the likely course of Anglo-German relations. This was his explanation, made in private, in January 1912:

> There were two things, he said, that Germany had to learn[:] firstly that we intended to maintain the supremacy of our Navy at whatever cost, and secondly that we did not propose to allow her to 'bully' whomsoever she pleased on the continent of Europe. After she had thoroughly realised these two things, then was the time to come to terms and ask her: 'is there any part of the world, which is not ours, that you would like?'[4]

On this analysis, it was quite logical to follow the firm British stance over Agadir with an attempt to reach an understanding. The pressures of military spending on the national finances were, of course, an additional consideration. Therefore, Lloyd George was supportive of the Cabinet's February 1912 decision to send Haldane as an emissary to Berlin; and hence his particular anger with Churchill's speech (mentioned in Chapter 3) referring to the German navy as a 'luxury'. He told Churchill this was 'most imprudent and calculated to ruin Haldane's mission to Germany, which was on a fair way to success'.[5] The mission failed, in fact, because the British were unwilling to give an unconditional guarantee of neutrality in the event of a European war.[6] It might be added that as late as May 1914, Churchill himself proposed talks with Germany aimed at slowing down the naval race. The plan was scotched by Grey.[7]

Lloyd George's habitual error was not, then, that he was fundamentally negligent of British interests. Rather, he was prone to wishful thinking about the prospect of Britain's rivals accommodating them. ('It is no use reproaching me', Churchill once wrote to him when updating him on Austria's naval building plans. 'I can no more control these facts than you can.')[8] Churchill, for his part, too often allowed the serious and statesmanlike aspect of his approach to foreign affairs to be overshadowed by his exuberance and ambition. This led many who knew him – including some relatively friendly observers – to view him as irresponsible. Part of the problem was that he was prone to share his military fantasies with others. Ralph Hawtrey, who was briefly Lloyd George's private secretary, recalled making a car journey with both men to Brighton in 1910–11. 'Churchill began to talk about the next war', Hawtrey wrote. 'He described how, at the climax, he himself, in command of the army, would win the decisive triumph in the Middle East, and would return to England in triumph. Lloyd George quietly interposed, "And where do I come in?"'[9]

Lloyd George sometimes suggested that Churchill took an excessively narrow and egotistic view of foreign affairs. The First Balkan War (1912–13) saw Montenegro, Bulgaria, Greece and Serbia fight Turkey, with considerable success. The Chancellor, by his own account, 'urged Winston to take up the pro-Balkan line in the Cabinet and press for some kind of definitely sympathetic action'. But Churchill, he claimed, was uninterested in the war. The First Lord 'gave his reasons perfectly frankly. "I don't see where the navy comes in," he said'.[10] In fact, Churchill was both strongly anti-Turk and alive to the significance of the Balkan situation for the future peace of Europe. 'It only needs a little ill will or bad faith on the part of a great power to precipitate a far greater conflict', he wrote.[11] As usual, though, Churchill's self-absorption and his other eccentricities gave Lloyd George plenty of opportunities to denigrate him through mockery.

The greater conflict that Churchill feared was triggered by the assassination of Archduke Franz Ferdinand on 28 June 1914; or rather, by the 23 July ultimatum to the Serbian government, whom the Austrians suspected of involvement in the killing. (In the interim

Lloyd George had spoken more than once of his confidence that war could be avoided.) Finding the emollient reply to its note insufficient, Austria-Hungary declared war on Serbia on 28 July. Russia, Serbia's ally, mobilized her forces in response. Germany, which had given her Austro-Hungarian allies carte blanche to deal with Serbia, mobilized in turn. By the end of the first day of August Germany was at war with Russia. On 3 August she declared war on France, which had by that point mobilized as well. This was because the German war plan involved dealing with the French before turning on France's Russian allies. The assault on France was to be made via Belgium – the neutrality of which was guaranteed by a treaty to which both Germany and Great Britain were signatories. Britain had no formal obligation to support France, but Sir Edward Grey warned his colleagues that if an uncompromising non-interventionist policy were adopted he would resign. Yet there was also a strong, if inchoate, body of non-interventionist opinion within both the government and wider Liberal circles.

In a diary entry written after Britain's involvement in the war had been determined, Charles Hobhouse gave a jaundiced view of Lloyd George and Churchill's respective roles in the Cabinet debates. 'At first Ll.G. was very strongly anti-German', he wrote, '. . . but as the Liberal papers were very anti-war, he veered round and became peaceful. Churchill was of course for any enterprise which gave him a chance of displaying the Navy as his instrument of destruction.'[12] Asquith put things in a slightly different perspective in a letter of 1 August. The Prime Minister found the Chancellor 'all for peace' but 'more sensible and statesmanlike' than anti-war colleagues such as Morley. He was 'for keeping the position still open'. Asquith by contrast, thought 'Winston very bellicose & demanding imme-diate mobilization.'[13] (These comments masked the fact that, in practice, Asquith himself was quite close to Churchill's position.)[14] At the emotional level, Churchill and Lloyd George's reactions to the situation were indeed quite different. Lloyd George, even as he moved towards support for the war, was filled with horror at the prospect of it. As he wrote to Margaret on 3 August, 'I am moving through a nightmare world these days.'[15] Churchill, by contrast, had written to Clementine a few days before: 'Everything tends towards catastrophe and collapse. I am interested, geared up & happy. Is it not horrible to be built like that?'[16] At the substantive level, though, the difference between their positions was by no means unbridgeable.

This can be seen from their exchange of notes in Cabinet on 1 August. Ministers had been made aware, on 27 July, of the possibility that the Germans would violate Belgian neutrality. In the aftermath of Agadir, Lloyd George had been clear that 'to bring the British public to fighting point it would be requisite that Germany should have passed into Belgium for the purpose of attacking France or should have crossed the French frontier'.[17] (Churchill, similarly, later explained in private that Belgium turned the issue into 'one the country would understand, and especially our own party . . . although there was really nothing in the treaties obliging us to fight'.)[18] This provided the context for the question Lloyd George now asked Churchill: did he intend to commit himself in public to war if Belgium was invaded 'whether Belgium asks for our protection or not'? Churchill gave the answer 'No.' This answer was pleasing to Lloyd George, who wrote back: 'If patience prevails & you do not press us too hard tonight we [personally] might come together.' From this it may be deduced that Lloyd George could have been persuaded to agree to a commitment to the defence of Belgium were she to ask for it.

Nevertheless, in his oral contributions to the Cabinet meeting, he seems to have *appeared* to continue to side with the non-intervention-ists. Otherwise it is difficult to account for the hysterical tone of Churchill's subsequent scribbled appeals. To begin with: 'Please God – It is our whole future – comrades – or opponents.' And later: 'I am most profoundly anxious that our long cooperation may not be severed. Remember your part at Agadir. I implore you to come and bring your mighty aid to the discharge of our duty.' Then: 'All the rest of our lives we shall be opposed. I am deeply attached to you & have followed your instinct & guidance for nearly 10 years.' Churchill's final note suggested that if the two men stuck together 'we can carry a wide social policy'. It also appealed to the Chancel-lor's economical instincts: 'The naval war will be cheap – not more than 25 millions a year.' It concluded as follows: 'You *alone* can take the measures wh will assure food being kept abundant and cheap to the people.'[19] He also sought to use further means of pressure. General Wilson, who had been in close touch with both men at the time of Agadir, noted in his diary that Major Alfred Ollivant, also of the War Office, had been asked by Churchill 'to lecture Lloyd George on [the] European military situation!' Ollivant sent the Chancellor a memorandum arguing that the fate of France hinged on a British expeditionary force being sent to the continent at once.[20]

It seems that Churchill's appeals were largely superfluous, being based on a misunderstanding of Lloyd George's position, which seems already to have moved towards intervention. The latter continued, however, to camouflage his intentions. In the evening of 1 August, the news came through of Germany's declaration of war on Russia. In response, Churchill quickly ordered the navy to be mobilized. He did this with Asquith's acquiescence, but contrary to the Cabinet's decision taken earlier that day. On 2 August, at 10.15 a.m., Lloyd George met with Lewis Harcourt, Earl Beauchamp, John Simon, J. A. Pease, and Walter Runciman. According to Pease, these ministers 'all agreed we were not prepared to go into war now, but that in certain events we might reconsider [the] position, such as the invasion wholesale of Belgium'.[21] The Cabinet then met. Asquith concluded that 'we are on the brink of a split.' He placed Lloyd George amongst those 'who are against any kind of intervention in any event.'[22] This categorization was inaccurate; and at Cabinet the next day Lloyd George made 'a strong appeal' to Simon, Morley, Beauchamp and Burns not to resign.[23] A powerful speech by Grey in the House of Commons on 3 August helped damp down anti-war sentiment.

The definitive news that the Germans had invaded Belgium came through the following day. 'This simplifies matters', Asquith noted.[24] It gave Lloyd George the means necessary to justify his 'conversion' to intervention, as well as facilitating the shift of other ministers towards support for war. Morley and Burns were to be the only two of his Cabinet colleagues to actually resign. An informed guess about the Chancellor's intentions throughout was offered by Frances Stevenson in her memoirs: 'My own opinion is that L.G.'s mind was made up from the first, that he knew we would have to go in, and that the invasion of Belgium was, to be cynical, a heaven-sent excuse for supporting a declaration of war.'[25] In fairness, Lloyd George's claims to have experienced emotional distress over his decision were probably genuine, and he may have reached it as much through intuition as through explicit calculation. Nonetheless, it seems to have been a choice little influenced by the heartfelt tone of Churchill's appeals to their common personal history.

The British ultimatum to the Germans, requesting an assurance of respect for Belgian neutrality, was to expire at 11 p.m. on 4 August. Half an hour beforehand, Asquith sent a message to Lloyd George, asking him to join him in the Cabinet room. The Chancellor found the Prime Minister sitting anxiously with Grey and McKenna. He later told Margot Asquith how 'Big Ben struck eleven, very slowly came the Boom – Boom – Boom – we sat in complete silence, I should say for 10 minutes after the last Boom.' Then, the solemn atmosphere was shattered: 'Winston dashed into the room radiant, his face bright, his manner keen and he told us – one word pouring out on the other – how he was going to send telegrams to the Mediterranean, the North Sea and God knows where!' Lloyd George added: 'You could see he was really a happy man. I wondered if this was the state of mind to be in at the opening of such a fearful war as this.'[26] Nor was Lloyd George the only person who testified to this attitude of Churchill's. Some years later Margot herself reminded Churchill that he had said 'Oh! this *delicious* war!'[27] And Violet Asquith recorded him saying, in February 1915, 'I think a curse should rest on me – because I *love* this war. I know it's smashing & shattering the lives of thousands every moment – & yet – I *can't* help it – I enjoy every second of it'.[28] It is not difficult to see why many of his colleagues regarded him with unease.

Churchill, in his memoirs, wrote that he did not see Lloyd George, other than at Cabinet, between 2 and 24 August. (Riddell, however, recorded a meeting of the Other Club on 6 August, 'the first dinner we have had since Marconi days', at which Churchill proposed a toast to the success of the British army.)[29] In the interim, the Chancellor was much occupied trying to stave off financial crisis. The slogan 'business as usual' provided him with a cloak for huge confidence-restoring interventions in the insurance and financial markets.[30] He also indulged his habit of private ridicule of Churchill. 'L.G. said he thought Winston was sorry he was not at the War Office, where there was so much doing instead of at the Admiralty. He added laughing Winston is like a dog sitting on the Dogger Bank, with his tail between his legs looking at the pal who is just poking his nose out of the hole on the opposite side of the water.'[31] There was an element of truth in this remark. The navy's overall strategic role was, of necessity, undramatic. Keeping command of the seas, deterring the Germans from venturing out of port, and restricting their trade, were of great importance but did not offer the prospect of dramatic symbolic victories. The First Lord started to involve himself – some might say interfere – with matters outside his field of responsibility.

It would, of course, have been unnatural for him to disclaim all interest in the land war. This was not progressing well. The Germans, in spite of resistance that was stiffer than they expected, advanced rapidly through much of Belgium. As they did so, they committed major atrocities, often in response to the supposed activities of Belgian *francs-tireurs* (i.e. 'free shooters' or, as George W. Bush might have it, 'illegal combatants'). Contrary to later mythology, these German crimes were not the invention of allied propaganda or of the *Daily Mail*. Mass executions of civilians began as early as 5 August. According to an authoritative recent study, a total of 5,521 citizens were killed in Belgium during the invasion. (By the end of the year, around 900 civilians were also killed in atrocities in France.) For instance, at Melen on 8 August German soldiers took seventy-two villagers – including eight women and four pre-teenage girls – to a field and executed them in a group. One witness claimed that the soldiers forced children to dance before the corpses singing a nursery rhyme. During a massacre at Andennes-Seilles later in the month, during which 262 civilians died, a 10-year-old child was bayoneted in the back, a family of seven were executed in their cellar, and men were killed in front of their wives by soldiers impatient to start the executions.[32] Such atrocities (the examples given represent merely the tip of the iceberg) accompanied continued German military success. All resistance at Liège ended on 16 August. Brussels fell four days later.

At 7 a.m. on 24 August Churchill was sitting in bed in Admiralty House working, when Lord Kitchener, the new Secretary of State for War, brought him the news of the fall of Namur in Belgium. The Channel ports were now threatened. Churchill later recalled how, not having seen Lloyd George alone over the previous three weeks, 'with this fateful news, I felt intensely the need of contact with him, and I wanted to know how it would strike him and how he would face it'. Later in the morning he crossed Horse Guards Parade and found the Chancellor in the Treasury Board Room, engaged in one of his intense meetings with bankers and businessmen, aimed at shoring up the British financial system. The room was crowded, Churchill remembered.

> He saw me at once: I beckoned with my little finger and he came out. We went into a little room scarcely bigger than a cupboard which adjoined, and I told him what had happened. I was relieved and overjoyed at his response. He was once again the Lloyd George of Agadir. Not since the morning of the Mansion House speech, three years before, had I seen him so strong and resolute for our country or so sure of its might.[33]

Lloyd George, indeed, was in the process of transforming his reputation. In the last period of peace he had met with damaging setbacks. He had been tainted by Marconi, and had suffered the appearance – if not the full reality – of defeat in his battle with Churchill over the estimates. Then, his 1914 Budget, prepared too hastily, had turned into something of a fiasco: he had been forced by a combination of procedural problems and internal party opposition to drop from the Finance Bill a scheme for amending the system of local government taxation. But he now put these difficulties behind him. The former pro-Boer and veteran of Limehouse was to emerge from the war as a symbol of national leadership, transcending party and factional boundaries.

His speech at the Queen's Hall in the West End of London on 19 September 1914 was a landmark. It ranks, in its impact on the public, with Churchill's famous speeches of 1940. Admittedly, the military context, from the British point of view, was not as dire. (At the beginning of the month, Paris had been threatened – the French government left the city on 2 September – but subsequent Allied successes had stabilized the situation.) But the oratory was as powerful. Lloyd George sought to show that the war could not have been avoided 'without national dishonour'. He focused, predictably, on the violation of Belgian neutrality, although he refused to wallow in the details of the atrocities. He savaged the German view of treaties as mere scraps of paper that could readily be violated. 'Have you any of those neat little Treasury £1 notes?' he asked his audience. 'If you have, burn them; they are only scraps of paper. What are they made of? Rags. What are they worth? The whole credit of the British Empire.' He went on to enjoin determination and sacrifice.

They think we cannot beat them. It will not be easy. It will be a long job; it will be a terrible war; but in the end we shall march through terror to triumph. We shall need all our qualities – every quality that Britain and its people possess – prudence in counsel, daring in action, tenacity and purpose, courage in defeat, moderation in victory; in all things faith!

His peroration centred on a metaphor from his Welsh boyhood. He had, he said, known a beautiful valley between the mountains and the sea, 'sheltered by the mountains from all the bitter blasts' of the wind, and therefore snug and comfortable, but 'very enervating'. The British people had, he said, been living in a sheltered valley for generations.

We have been too comfortable and too indulgent, many, perhaps, too selfish, and the stern hand of fate has scourged us to an elevation where we can see the everlasting things that matter for a nation – the great peaks we had forgotten, of Honour, Duty, Patriotism, and, clad in glittering white, the towering pinnacle of Sacrifice pointing like a rugged finger to Heaven. We shall descend into the valleys again; but as long as the men and women of this generation last, they will carry in their hearts the image of those mighty peaks whose foundations are not shaken, though Europe rock and sway in the convulsions of a great war.[34]

Although Lloyd George's own first instinct was that the speech had been unsuccessful, it was received with great enthusiasm by the press, by politicians of all parties, and, as far as can be gauged, by the public at large. It was printed and circulated widely. It was not, however, a speech without false notes. As Grigg has pointed out, Lloyd George's claim that he envied young people their 'opportunity' to fight sat uncomfortably with his private desire to keep his own sons out of harm's way. He used his influence to get them positions as aides-de-camp to generals, although they both later undertook more dangerous service.[35] Churchill, it seems, helped smooth their path. A few days before the Queen's Hall speech he sent Richard and Gwilym a telegram: 'Please forward your applications direct to Colonel Fitzgerald War Office stating units in which you wish to serve'.[36]

Churchill, for his own part, could not resist rushing to action. Lloyd George remarked, two days after Queen's Hall, that 'he cannot trust Winston – never knows what he may be up to, and [is] afraid to leave town for long for fear Winston may bring forward some dangerous plan'.[37] In early October, after travelling to the continent, Churchill took personal charge of the defence of Antwerp. Braving the shellfire with apparent unconcern, he succeeded in delaying its fall for a few days. The military advantages of doing so were debatable. The time bought may have been valuable, but a large number of men who might otherwise have escaped were lost or captured. Moreover, although many of Churchill's colleagues recognized the heroic aspect of his activities, he also courted their ridicule. On 5 October Asquith wrote to his confidante, Venetia Stanley, that 'Winston succeeded in bucking up the Belges, who gave up their panicky idea of retreating to Ostend'. But he also reported 'a real bit of tragic-comedy'. He had received from Churchill a telegram in which he proposed 'to resign his Office, in order to take command in the field' of the force being sent to the rescue of the Belgians. The Prime Minister rejected the offer at once. When he read out the telegram in Cabinet it was greeted 'with a Homeric laugh. W. is an ex-Lieutenant of Hussars, and would if his proposal had been accepted, have been in command of 2 distinguished Major Generals, not to mention Brigadiers, Colonels &c'.[38]

Lloyd George was among those who criticized Churchill over the episode behind his back. On 6 October, according to Riddell's diary, 'L.G. said that we had made a mistake to send our men to Antwerp, and that this was Winston's doing.'[39] However, a day later (the same day, incidentally, that Churchill learnt he had become a father for the third time), he wrote: 'Congratulations on your brilliant effort to rescue Antwerp. What are the prospects?'[40] Even if, as seems unlikely, this was a genuine change of heart, it was short lived. On 10 October he made some acerbic remarks to a company that included not only Riddell, Masterman, Isaacs, and McKenna and his wife, but also Robert Donald, editor of the *Daily Chronicle*, and the publisher Hedley Le Bas. When McKenna poured scorn on the Antwerp expedition, Lloyd George concurred. 'He is an extraordinary fellow', he said, speaking of Churchill. 'Too wild and impulsive. He makes me very uneasy.' He criticized his habit of interfering with land and naval operations, and added: 'Winston is like a torpedo. The first you hear of his doings is when you hear the swish of the torpedo dashing through the water.'[41] Frances Stevenson had recently started keeping a diary, in which she referred to Lloyd George as 'C.', i.e. 'Chancellor'. On 23 October she recorded, 'C. is rather disgusted with Winston still about Antwerp, and thinks that the P.M. is too. Having taken untrained men over there, he left them in the lurch. He behaved in rather a swaggering way when over there, standing with shells bursting near him, & actually promoting his pals on the field of action.'[42] Some of the more colourful details here would seem to be embellishments, although they did not necessarily originate with Lloyd George himself. Piling on the criticism, the latter said to Riddell two days later: 'Winston is really dangerous. The PM should speak to him.'[43] To C. P. Scott, at the end of November, he again criticized the Antwerp expedition, at some length. He further said that Churchill was partly to blame for Turkey's recent entry into the war on Germany's side. (Churchill had pressed strongly for British action against the Turks, and the Cabinet had been little consulted by him and Grey before hostilities were launched at the start of the month.) Scott thought it obvious that Lloyd George had 'a strong personal antagonism to Churchill'.[44]

It is unclear to what extent Churchill was aware of this hostility. He continued to make efforts to keep Lloyd George friendly. In October he invited the latter's daughter Olwen to launch the *Carysfort*, a light cruiser, from Pembroke. In the same letter he congratulated the Chancellor, who had recently paid his first visit to the front, on his 'baptism of fire', adding 'The taste forms if not cloyed by surfeit.'[45] Lloyd George, for his part, had not ceased to value Churchill's support in Cabinet. When Kitchener opposed the idea of a Welsh-speaking Army Corps, partly on the grounds that the Welsh were inherently wild and insubordinate, Churchill backed his colleague's heated protest. Lloyd George therefore wrote him a letter of thanks. 'I feel deeply grateful to you for the way you stood up for fair play to my little nationality this morning,' it read.[46] But not long afterwards they clashed over the question of press censorship. Lloyd George thought that Churchill and Kitchener were trying to arrange matters so that only things that suited them would be published.[47] According to Hobhouse's account, 'W.S.C. became white (or green) with anger, denounced Ll.G's "insolence", which he would not tolerate from anyone. Ll.G. responded equally hotly, and the P.M. intervened.'[48] Shortly before Christmas Lloyd George claimed to Frances Stevenson that Churchill was trying to interfere with the French military campaign. She wrote that he had sent a note to Lloyd George across the Cabinet table: 'The French are behaving odiously.' 'Which means', Lloyd George observed, 'that they refuse to alter the whole of their plans in order to add to Winston's personal glory.'[49]

His attitude to Churchill in the first months of war can therefore be described as one of severe and sustained irritation. His differences with Kitchener, however, were of greater substance. The Secretary of State for War was a military legend, but, although he had strong conservative instincts, he was no politician. He was a popular hero of the Battle of Omdurman (Churchill, having criticized him at the time as a war criminal, had by this point patched up his differences with him) and of the Boer War. He also served as Commander-in-Chief in India (1902–9), and then as British Agent and Consul General in Egypt (1911–14). He had spent his adult life outside Britain, and now found himself a stranger in his own country. Since his appointment, made on the outbreak of war, his iconic status, as the face of the famous recruiting poster, had been confirmed. He could not be criticized in public, as the *Daily Mail* discovered to its cost when it published an attack on him in May the following year. Circulation and advertising dropped radically and copies were burned in the street and on the floor of the Stock Exchange.[50] Kitchener was by no means unintelligent – he realized very early on that the war was likely to last at least three years and that this necessitated a massive expansion of the army. Yet he loathed having his military judgement challenged, and his Cabinet colleagues found it very hard to work with him.

Lloyd George conceded that Kitchener had moments of greatness. 'He was like one of those revolving lighthouses which radiate momentary gleams of revealing light far out into the surrounding gloom and then suddenly relapse into complete darkness', he recalled.[51] But from September onwards the Chancellor became increasingly alarmed at what he saw as the likelihood of a severe shortage of munitions. Kitchener would barely acknowledge the problem, and was deeply reluctant to share information on the matter with the Cabinet. He thought that the issue should be dealt with by the War Office exclusively. On the last day of the year, Lloyd George wrote to Asquith, 'I am uneasy about the prospects of the War unless the Government take some decisive measures to grip the situation. I can see no signs anywhere that our military leaders and guides are considering any plans for extracting us from our present unsatisfactory position . . . You remember the guns and ammunition incident. When I raised the question in the Cabinet the War Office had only ordered 600 guns in all – those were to be delivered by next September.'[52] The developing munitions crisis was to prove a major cause of the fall of the government.

Churchill shared Lloyd George's broad concern about the direction of the war, which had settled down to the stalemate of trench warfare. On 1 January Asquith noted that he had received two long memoranda, 'one from Winston, the other from Lloyd George (quite good, the latter) as to the public conduct of the war. They are both keen on a new objective & theatre, as soon as our new troops are ready.'[53] The solutions they proposed were different. Lloyd George argued 'that any attempt to force the carefully prepared German lines in the west would end in failure and appalling loss of life'. Inasmuch as a 'clear definite victory' could not be achieved on the Western Front, he suggested a scheme involving two independent operations 'which would have the purpose of bringing Germany down by the process of knocking the props [from] under her'. The first of these involved using British forces to attack Austria, in collaboration with Serbia, Romania, and Greece. (It was a major object of British foreign policy to make allies of these latter two neutral states, together with Bulgaria.) The troops would be landed at Salonika or on the Dalmatian coast. The second operation involved attacking Turkey, by landing 100,000 men in Syria, thus cutting off the Turkish forces that were at this time threatening the Suez Canal. 'Unless we are prepared for some project of this character I frankly despair of our achieving any success in this War', he wrote.[54] Churchill's proposal, by contrast, involved an attack in the North. He argued that the allies should capture the German island of Borkum as a means of excluding the German fleet from the North Sea; and follow this with an attack on the Kiel Canal via Schleswig-Holstein. The British fleet would secure command of the Baltic, facilitating a Russian landing on its shore 'less than 100 miles from Berlin'.[55]

There was also a third memorandum, by Lieutenant Colonel Maurice Hankey, Secretary to both the Committee of Imperial Defence and the recently formed War Council. Like Lloyd George and Churchill, he wanted to break the impasse. He asked: 'Is it impossible now to weave a web around Turkey which shall end her career as a European power?' He believed that if Bulgaria and Greece could be induced to cooperate, Constantinople, the Dardanelles and the Bosphorus could be occupied; and that a simultaneous attack by Russia on Hungary with the help of Serbia and Romania would help bring about the downfall of the Austrians.[56] It was the idea of an attack on the Dardanelles – the 28-mile straits that separate Europe from Asia – that was in time to be enacted, in preference to Lloyd George and Churchill's respective plans.

The series of decisions that brought this about were much influenced by the severe Russian anxiety about the ongoing Turkish offensive in the Caucasus. News of these fears, at the start of the New Year, prompted concern that Russia would drop out of the war. 'The only place that a demonstration might have some effect in stopping reinforcements going East would be the Dardanelles', Kitchener told Churchill on 2 January 1915.[57] He was not, however, offering troops, and Churchill at this stage did not believe that a purely naval action could be effective. However, on 3 January he sent a telegram to Vice-Admiral Carden, Commander-in-Chief in the Mediterranean, asking whether he considered the forcing of the Dardanelles by ships alone to be a practical proposition.[58] On 13 January he reported to the War Council Carden's encouraging (and surprising) response – that although it was impossible to 'rush' the straits, 'it might be possible to demolish the forts one by one'. Carden's proposal commanded general assent, including from Lloyd George, who 'liked the plan' (which he did not see as incompatible with his own idea of a Salonika expedition).[59] Although the attack on the Dardanelles had not originated with Churchill, its failure was to be indelibly associated with his name.

It was not military failure alone, though, that led to the personal and political catastrophe that, within months, was to overwhelm him. His vexed relationship with his First Sea Lord, Admiral Lord Fisher, was in large part to blame. In October 1914 he had personally insisted on Fisher's appointment (or reappointment: he had served in the same post from 1904 to 1910). Although he was 73 at the time, Fisher still had a great deal of vigour, as his prolific and eccentric correspondence makes clear. (After his resignation he wrote to the erstwhile German Minister of Marine, Admiral Von Tirpitz, with whom he felt a kind of kinship, with the salutation 'Dear Old Tirps' and signing off, as he often did, 'Yours till hell freezes'.)[60] He now grew increasingly erratic, in both behaviour and views. His opinions on the merits of the Dardanelles attack oscillated wildly, and he seems to have been consistent only in his determination to secure, by hook or by crook, a veto over Admiralty policy.

The Churchill–Fisher relationship has been subjected to minute examination by historians. However, the fact that Lloyd George was one of the (several) people being fed information by Fisher that was derogatory of Churchill has tended to escape comment. On 25 January Lloyd George defended Fisher to Margot Asquith ('He is not at all gaga'), and, in the course of the same conversation, attacked Churchill. 'McKenna's judgement is 1,000 times better than Winston's!' he said. 'Really if it wasn't for Winston's affectionate quality and good temper I sometimes think I can hardly do with him!' he continued: 'Winston, like all really self-centred people ends by boring people. He's as you say, such a child!'[61] It is unclear to what extent, in making these remarks, Lloyd George was influenced by the letters from Fisher that he had now been receiving for at least a fortnight. (Of those that survive, none earlier than 29 January could be considered an explicit attack on Churchill, but some may have been lost or destroyed.)[62] But J. H. Lewis's diary for 12 February records a significant remark by the Chancellor: 'Fisher writes me every day or two to let me know how things are going. He has a great deal of trouble with his chief, who is always wanting to do something big and striking.'[63] Whether or not Fisher's intelligence made a material difference to Lloyd George's view of Churchill, the important point is that he had early warnings of trouble at the Admiralty. His instinct, it is clear, was by no means to leap to Churchill's defence.

What, specifically, was Lloyd George told? Although Fisher had initially seemed happy to go along with Carden's plan, he soon developed the conviction that the transfer of ships from the North Sea, which he saw as the decisive theatre, would be dangerous. He now deprecated the Dardanelles operation, unless the army were to be deployed on the Gallipoli peninsula (on the European side of the Straits) in order to assist the naval action. Towards the end of January he sent a protest to Churchill, who, in an emollient reply, denied that the dominance of the North Sea fleet would be weakened. Asquith refused to allow the exchange to be circulated to the members of the War Council. On 29 January Fisher nevertheless sent a copy of his

1. *Above.* Even as a teenager, Lloyd George dreamed of dominating Parliament.

2. *Right.* Churchill's daring escape from a Boer prison brought him worldwide fame.

3. *Below.* Lloyd George circa 1905: a marked contrast with his rather more genial image in later years.

4. Margaret Lloyd George (centre) with her children in 1905. From left to right: Gwilym, Mair, Richard, Olwen and Megan.

READY TO OBLIGE

Right Hon. Arth-r J. B-lf-r (medititively, aloud). 'I wish
I could find a double to take my place in the house!'

Mr. Winston Churchill
(aside to himself)   } 'Ought not to be any
Mr. Ll-yd-G-rge   difficulty about that!'
(aside to himself)

[John Chilcote, M.P. in Mrs Thurston's novel (about to be drama-
tised) has a double who acts as his substitute in Parliament]

5. *Punch*'s view in 1905.
Balfour resigned later that year.

The Prime Minister (to Messrs. Lloyd-George and Churchill): 'I'm afraid, gentlemen, that in this persistent mud-throwing you only waste your time!'

Messrs. Lloyd-George and Churchill: 'Not a bit of it, we're qualifying for 'high positions' in the next Liberal Government.'

['The man who may hope most to be appointed to a high position (in the Government) is not the man who has given proof of the qualities of administration; it is the man who can make the most stinging epigrams to the tender places of a decadent government.' — Lord Rosebery at the Liberal League Meeting.]

6. From the *Pall Mall Gazette*, April 1905.

7. The Colonial Conference of 1907. Churchill stands behind Asquith on the far left. Lloyd George is on the far right.

8. Family man – ostensibly. Margaret and David Lloyd George, with Megan in 1910.

9. Churchill in 1909. As President of the Board of Trade he complained: 'Lloyd George has taken all the plums.'

10. *Punch*'s view in December 1909. Asquith was sometimes embarrassed by the behaviour of these two men, but they were also a source of strength to his government.

"SUPPORTERS" RAMPANT.

AN HERALDIC INVERSION.

11. *Right*. The Constitutional
Conference of 1910 failed
to break the impasse
between the party leaders.
Lloyd George and Asquith
are in the foreground.

12. *Below*. Budget day, 1910.
Lloyd George and Churchill
are flanked by Margaret
Lloyd George and William
Clark, one of Lloyd George's
private secretaries.

THE DAWN OF HOPE.

Mr. LLOYD GEORGE'S National Health Insurance Bill provides for the insurance of the Worker in case of Sickness.

Support the Liberal Government
in their policy of
SOCIAL REFORM.

13. *Left*. Liberal Party poster, 1911.

14. *Below*. Man of the past: Asquith leaves the Reform Club, a few weeks after resigning as Prime Minister.

15. Lloyd George as Prime Minister in 1917, not long before he asked Churchill to join his government.

16. Frances Stevenson in 1917. How much did Churchill know of her relationship with Lloyd George?

17. Churchill with munitions workers on a ministerial visit in 1918. Lloyd George had taken a political risk in appointing him.

18. Churchill and Lloyd George in Downing Street in July 1919.

19. This cartoon of August 1920 was inspired by a remark made by Lloyd George: 'Lenin, I believe, is an aristocrat, and Trotsky is a journalist. My Right Hon. Friend the Secretary for War is an embodiment of both.'

paper to Lloyd George. He wrote, 'The reason I am sending it to you is that I find myself *invariably* in agreement with all you say.'[64] Lloyd George replied that he found the memo 'very impressive' but disquieting. 'I wish I could disagree with it but I find myself unable to do so.' He piled on the flattery: 'We poor ignorant civilians must necessarily depend in these matters on the guidance of experts like yourself.'[65] On 10 February Fisher wrote to him again: '*to bombard Dardanelles without military cooperation on the Gallipoli Peninsula is most deplorable*'.[66]

Although, in approaching Lloyd George, Fisher was guilty of improper behaviour, and although his overall approach was riddled with inconsistencies, this specific argument had merits. Hankey was among those who believed the naval operation should be supported by a strong military force. Churchill himself believed it essential that 50,000 men should be within three days of the Dardanelles, in case they were needed in order to capitalize on a successful naval attack. In the War Council on 19 February, Lloyd George argued that, 'If we had some troops in the East, as proposed by Mr. Churchill, they would be available either for Constantinople or, if that operation failed, to support the Serbians.'[67] Kitchener, however, proved the stumbling block. He successfully resisted Churchill's heartfelt request, which was backed by Lloyd George, Asquith and Hankey, to send out the army's well-trained 29th Division. (The 29th had at one stage been earmarked for the abortive Salonika expedition, as proposed by Lloyd George, the offer of which had been turned down by the Greek government.) Churchill undoubtedly valued Lloyd George's support. He wrote to his brother Jack that 'LG has more true insight & courage than anyone else. He really sticks at nothing – no measure is too far reaching, no expedient too novel.'[68] But the failure to get sufficient men, and to deploy them effectively in combination with the navy at an early stage, had a serious outcome. As Martin Gilbert has written, Churchill 'so believed in the need for victory that he was prepared to go ahead with the plans for an entirely naval attack. However much he continued to argue that these plans might fail, by agreeing to go ahead with them, he made himself responsible for the very disaster that he forecast.'[69]

The initial bombardment of the outer forts of the Dardanelles took place on 19 February. There was then a few days' delay owing to bad weather. In the meantime, at the War Council on the

24th, there was a significant exchange between Lloyd George and Churchill:

> MR. LLOYD GEORGE agreed that a force ought to be sent to the Levant, which could, if necessary, be used after the Navy had cleared the Dardanelles, to occupy the Gallipoli Peninsula or Constantinople. He wished to know, however, whether, in the event of the naval attack failing (and it was something of an experiment), it was proposed that the Army should be used to undertake an operation in which the Navy had failed.
>
> MR. CHURCHILL said this was not the intention. He could, however, conceive a case where the Navy had almost succeeded, but where a military force would just make the difference between failure and success.
>
> MR. LLOYD GEORGE hoped that the Army would not be required or expected to pull the chestnuts out of the fire for the Navy. If we failed at the Dardanelles we ought to be immediately ready to try something else. In his opinion, we were committed by this operation to some action in the Near East, but not necessarily to a siege of the Dardanelles.[70]

Lloyd George's intelligent caution was swamped by the euphoria that attended the further, successful bombardment that took place on the 25th and 29th. Ministers started making plans for the future disposition of Turkish territory, rather like a team of robbers arguing about what to do with the property of a victim they have not yet succeeded in dispossessing. Further progress was slow, and on 16 March Admiral Carden, unable to face the continuing strain, gave up his command. On 18 March Carden's successor, John de Robeck, launched the main assault in an attempt to force the Narrows and break through to the Sea of Marmara and onwards to Constantinople.

The attack began at 10.45 a.m. At first, things went well, as the Turkish forts were subjected to a rain of explosives. But just before 2 p.m. the *Bouvet*, a French battleship, suffered an explosion and sank with the loss of 600 hands. It was unclear whether a Turkish shell or a mine was to blame. The attack continued. At 4.11 p.m. the *Inflexible* hit a mine, and a few minutes later the *Irresistible* started to list. De Robeck called an immediate end to operations. Moreover, during the attempt to rescue the men of the *Irresistible*, the *Ocean* hit a mine, and both ships later sank. In addition, the *Gaulois* became beached during the withdrawal. Although these setbacks did not lead to despair in London, their consequence was the suspension of the naval assault. On 23 March de Robeck informed Churchill that he thought it inadvisable to relaunch it before the army was ready to carry out a coordinated land assault. (On 10 March Kitchener had suddenly announced that he was prepared to send out the 29th Division after all.) This would not be before mid-April. Although one of the original attractions of the Dardanelles plan was that it could be called off altogether if it went wrong, no one now considered doing this. The army would now have to pull the navy's chestnuts out of the fire, rather as Lloyd George had warned.

Thus there was a lull in the action at the Dardanelles while the army prepared. Lloyd George was at this time experiencing continued frustrations with regard to munitions, the shortage of which was hampering the army in France. His bugbear was the War Office, and, especially, Major-General Sir Stanley Von Donop, Master General of the Ordnance, who in his view stood in the way of efficiency. On 22 March Lloyd George, Churchill and Asquith held a meeting on the subject, together with Edwin Montagu and Arthur Balfour. Balfour, although a Tory, had joined the War Council on the Prime Minister's invitation. As a result of these talks, Asquith informed Kitchener that there would be a new Cabinet committee. In the interests of speeding up production, this committee would have the right to place munitions contracts on its own authority. But then Kitchener submitted a list of conditions that were clearly intended to preserve the War Office's control.[71] 'If he adheres to this position, I cannot undertake this work; nor can Balfour', Lloyd George wrote to Churchill. 'We should simply be obstructed by Von Donop the whole way through.'[72] The committee received from Asquith the authority the Chancellor wanted, but it still failed to function properly owing to the War Office obstruction the latter had feared. Lloyd George began to conclude that more radical measures were needed to solve the munitions problem.[73]

His worries on this issue were a symptom of burgeoning discontent within and without the government over the running of the war. One manifestation of this was a series of rumours of intrigue against Asquith. These – perhaps partly as a consequence of their and Balfour's joint concern with the munitions question – attached themselves to Lloyd George and Churchill. Asquith reported to Venetia Stanley that Montagu was 'a good deal exercised by the hypnotic ascendancy wh. he thinks A.J.B. [Balfour] is gaining over Ll.G. as well as Winston.' Montagu thought Balfour was secretly hostile to Asquith, and that he was 'a dangerous confidant, when these impulsive rhetoricians pour all their grievances against K. [Kitchener] & the rest of their colleagues into his ears.'[74] A few days later, on 24 March, H. W. Massingham, editor of the *Nation*, told Margot Asquith 'a horrible tale' that 'Winston is "intriguing hard" to supplant E. Grey at the Foreign Office & to put A.J.B. in his place.' She wrote to Lloyd George asking him to warn Churchill to be careful what he said to Balfour; so it might not have been too great a shock to the Chancellor when the Prime Minister asked him the next day what he thought of the story. To Asquith's surprise 'he said he believed it was substantially true. He thinks that Winston has for the time at any rate allowed himself to be "swallowed whole" by A.J.B., on whom he, L.G., after working with him for a week or two, is now disposed to be very severe.'[75]

A few days later, McKenna told Asquith that Lord Northcliffe – whose papers had been praising Lloyd George for a number of weeks – was conspiring to replace him with his Chancellor. 'McK is of course quite certain that Ll.G, & perhaps Winston are "in it".'[76] Asquith claimed not to believe the rumour, but confronted Lloyd George with it nonetheless. The latter 'made a most bitter onslaught on McKenna whom he believes, thro' his animosity against Winston, to be the villain of the piece and the principal mischief-maker'.[77] It will be recalled that two months earlier he had described McKenna's judgement as '1,000 times better' than Churchill's. When Asquith brought Lloyd George and McKenna together the next day, 30 March, the meeting was stormy. (Churchill felt confident that Asquith would absolve him of wrongdoing and did not attend.) 'Ll. G. proceeded to accuse McK of always seeing imaginary plots: e.g. in this very matter, Winston's supposed campaign against Grey.'[78] Yet four days earlier he had said that he believed the tale of this 'supposed campaign' to be 'substantially true'. He defended Churchill only once he himself had been put in the frame with him. It is improbable, in fact, that either Lloyd George or Churchill was actually involved in any plot. Asquith himself seems to have reached the same conclusion, and let the matter drop. The episode shows the Chancellor as disloyal not to the Prime Minister but – in a small though significant way – to the First Lord of the Admiralty.

Given the febrile atmosphere, it was scarcely surprising that Lloyd George and Churchill sometimes fell to squabbling. A question close to both men's hearts, for very different reasons, was that of alcohol. Lloyd George, a near teetotaller, was concerned about the impact of excess drinking by munitions workers on their productivity. There was some evidence to suggest that this was a genuine problem, although proposals for the strict control of the drink trade also represented an opportunity to shore up his Nonconformist support. As an initial step in his campaign he secured a pledge from George V not to touch alcohol for the duration of the war. This was meant to set an example, although the King was understandably irritated when no minister save Kitchener followed suit. Churchill, for his part, was a fairly heavy drinker, although more so in later life than at this time. (During a train journey in 1941, he estimated that for the past forty-eight years he had drunk, on average, half a bottle of champagne a day. He asked F. A. Lindemann, his friend and scientific adviser, to calculate the volume of this, and was 'v. disappointed to find it wouldn't fill half the dining saloon'.)[79] He had paid lip service to the cause of temperance in pre-war days, and was now prepared to support a limitation of the opening hours of pubs – which he did not himself frequent anyway.[80] But he thought that Lloyd George's obsession was unreasonable. On 5 April, the two men discussed the drink question, in the presence of Edwin Montagu and Herbert Samuel. According to Frances Stevenson:

> Churchill put on the grand air, and announced that he was not going to be influenced by the King, and refused to give up his liquor – he thought the whole thing was absurd. C. was annoyed, but went on to explain a point that had been brought up. The next minute Churchill interrupted again, 'I don't see –' he was beginning, but C. broke in sharply: 'You will see the point', he rapped out, 'when you begin to understand that conversation is not a monologue!'

At this, Churchill 'went very red' but did not answer. Stevenson recorded that Lloyd George 'soon felt rather ashamed of having taken him up so sharply, especially in front of the other two'.[81] Later that day, therefore, he sent a letter of apology, regretting that 'I got angry & said what I ought not to have allowed myself to say.' He said, by way of explanation, that he had been 'very rattled' after a disappointing discussion with Kitchener, and was worried about the conduct of the war.[82] Churchill at once responded in kind: 'It was *I* who was churlish and difficult.' He emphasized his admiration for Lloyd George's 'energy courage & resolve'. He added: 'I share your anxieties, & am not at all removed in thought from your main policy.'[83]

After this episode Stevenson noted: 'The two are very fond of each other I believe.'[84] Her remark must of course be taken seriously. The quarrel was not of great significance in its own right, and, given the strain both men were under, the loss of temper was quite understandable. However, it also fell into their established pattern of recrimination followed by reconciliation. That, in itself, can be taken as an indication of the enduring nature of the tie between them, even if it was also a sign of the somewhat dysfunctional nature of the relationship. Their brief burst of acrimony in April was merely a foretaste of the harsh words that would pass between them in May.

A few days after the spat over the King's Pledge, Lloyd George remarked to Riddell over dinner that 'Winston has acted too impetuously regarding the Dardanelles, and that things out there are not going well.' He added: 'He is an able fellow, but very dangerous. He will not look at the arguments on the other side.'[85] His strictures on Churchill were par for the course – in conversation with Margot Asquith, for example, he did not hesitate to reinforce her negative view of him[86] – but he was right to be concerned about the Dardanelles. Early in the morning of 25 April, two weeks after these comments, the army's assault on the Gallipoli peninsula began. The landings were botched. Although Allied forces (which included the Australian and New Zealand Army Corps) outnumbered the Turks, poor communications led to confusion, and the superior force failed to capitalize on such successes as it had. By the end of the day the army had not achieved any of its main objectives, and had only established a toehold on the edges of the promontory. Nor, in spite of some minor advances, was there any big breakthrough in subsequent days and weeks. The men – those who avoided serious injury or death – were to be trapped in their grim conditions until the end of the year. Churchill did not have direct responsibility for the operations – the navy's main role at this stage was simply to get the men on to the shore – and even though his name was to be long associated with the Gallipoli disaster, it was not in fact the direct and immediate cause of his political downfall.

In his memoirs Lloyd George rightly argued that the downfall of the Liberal government and its replacement with a cross-party coalition could not be ascribed to a sole specific cause. There were, rather, a number of contributing factors, which included disappointment at the results in the Dardanelles (a feeling deepened by Churchill's arguments with Fisher), as well as at the failure of the Allied offensive in France, in addition to public revelations about the army's shortage of shells. Underlying all such anxieties was a general sense that the war was not being conducted 'either with sufficient seriousness or adequate energy'.[87]

When the storm clouds finally broke events moved rapidly. On 20 April, in a speech at Newcastle, Asquith had given a categorical assurance that there was no truth in allegations that the army was being hampered by a lack of ammunition. On 9 May the British attack at Aubers Ridge was repulsed with heavy losses. General Sir John French, Commander-in-Chief of the British Expeditionary Force in France, blamed the failure on a shortage of shells. (He had been pressing Kitchener for more for a considerable time, but had assured him he had enough for this particular battle, and the War Secretary had passed on this assurance to Asquith, who had extrapolated it into the inflated claims of his Newcastle speech.) Arguably, he was looking for a scapegoat. Accordingly, he briefed Repington of *The Times*, whose famous dispatch on the shell crisis was published on 14 May. Its message was that 'The want of an unlimited supply of high explosive was a fatal bar to our success'.[88] In the early hours of the next day – for reasons unconnected with these events – Fisher resigned as First Sea Lord. The combination of these developments made a coalition inevitable. It was the only way to forestall a breach of the shaky truce between the parties. And it was equally inevitable that if the Tories were to participate in a coalition, then Churchill could not continue at the Admiralty. He was so unpopular with them that they would insist on his being moved. Lloyd George appreciated this much sooner than Churchill did.

Fisher's resignation was on the flimsiest of grounds. Having agreed with Churchill a series of proposals as to what reinforcements were to be sent to the Dardanelles, he suddenly took umbrage at the other man's afterthought, put to him for comment, that two additional submarines could also be spared. Fisher had, in fact, become more or less unhinged. But that fact did not avert the consequences of his departure. During the morning of 15 May, a Saturday, Lloyd George encountered him in the lobby of 10 Downing Street, 'and was struck by a dour change in his attitude'. 'I have resigned!' Fisher greeted him. 'I can stand it no longer!' He was, he said, on his way to see the Prime Minister, having determined to have no further part in the Dardanelles 'foolishness', and was leaving for Scotland that night. The Chancellor remonstrated – would the old man not stay until Monday, when he could put his case before the War Council? But Fisher would not hear of it. Lloyd George therefore sent a message to Asquith, who was at a wedding, requesting that he see Fisher. Yet neither the Prime Minister, nor subsequently McKenna, was able to persuade him to stay in London.[89] Frances Stevenson wrote in her diary that day that Lloyd George was 'very disturbed' about the situation, as well he might be.

> He says that if Fisher's resignation is accepted, Churchill will have to go. He will be a ruined man. 'It is the Nemesis', said C. to me, 'of the man who has fought for this war for years. When the war came he saw in it the chance of glory for himself, & has accordingly entered on a risky campaign without caring a straw for the misery and hardship it would bring to thousands, in the hope that he would prove to be the outstanding man in this war.'[90]

The crisis now widened, because Fisher tipped off the Conservatives that he had thrown in the towel. 'W.C. is a bigger danger than the Germans by a long way', he wrote to Bonar Law.[91] On Monday the 17th the Tory leader went to see Lloyd George at the Treasury, and asked him 'point-blank' if Fisher really had resigned. When told that he had, Bonar Law made it clear that matters had gone so far that he would not be able to prevent his followers from attacking the government, although he recognized that this posed a threat to national unity. 'He was specially emphatic as to the impossibility of allowing Mr. Churchill to remain at the Admiralty', Lloyd George recalled. After further discussion, the two men agreed that the formation of a coalition was the only sure way to secure a united front. Lloyd George asked Bonar Law to wait whilst he went to see

Asquith at No. 10, 'and put the circumstances quite plainly before him'. The Prime Minister quickly agreed to reconstruct the Cabinet and bring in some of the Tory leaders. Lloyd George recollected: 'This decision took an incredibly short time.'[92]

Historians have long pondered over Asquith's decision, which brought to an end the last exclusively Liberal government that Britain has known. Was it a tactical master stroke aimed at self-preservation, or was he, with his mind dominated by personal matters, merely suffering from weak will? (Venetia Stanley, the young woman whom he had been bombarding with passionate letters, had told him a few days before that she was marrying his colleague Edwin Montagu.) Or did Lloyd George force him into it? Churchill stated in his memoirs that the Chancellor had told him, on the same day the decision was made, that he 'had informed the Prime Minister that he would resign' unless a coalition 'were formed at once'.[93] Churchill certainly seems to have believed at the time that this was what had happened, and appears to have told his wife this version of events. If it was true, the speed of Asquith's action is easily explained, as the government could not have withstood such a blow. At the time, Lloyd George was emphatic that he had not threatened to resign, and in later years, said that Churchill's memoirs were wrong on the point.[94] But even if he had never made an explicit threat of resignation, it is nonetheless clear that he was a believer in the necessity of coalition, knowing full well that it would mean Churchill leaving his beloved Admiralty.

Margot Asquith's first instinct, though, was to blame Churchill rather than Lloyd George for the government's downfall, maybe because she believed the false rumour that he had played a part in inspiring the revelations about the munitions shortage. She wrote:

> My dear Mr Ll George,
>   *How* tragic! Our great Cabinet that has stormed crisis after crisis Veto – Welsh church, Home Rule etc – all crumpled up like a scrap of paper! I said years ago to Henry I like Winston but he is the man who will do for yr Cabinet he or LGeorge. If he doesn't get fond of you well there you *are*.
>   Every one devoted to you & you quite passionately loyal & devoted to me & Henry.[95]

It took some time for the consequences of coalition to dawn on Churchill. In the afternoon of 17th May he arrived at the House of

Commons fully expecting to make a statement on Fisher's resignation and the reconstituted Admiralty Board. But when he got there, Lloyd George told him what had happened and said that action to form the new government must be immediate. Churchill then saw Asquith, who declined to let him make his statement and made it clear to him that he was to be moved from the Admiralty. Would Churchill take a different office in the new government, he asked, or would he prefer a command in France? At this point Lloyd George entered the room and suggested to the Prime Minister that Churchill be sent to the Colonial Office. Churchill did not accept the suggestion, but before the discussion could continue he was called away to deal with urgent Admiralty business. He clearly still did not appreciate the gravity of his position, because that evening he wrote to Asquith declining any other than a military department. He also offered counsel on the idea that Lloyd George should replace Kitchener at the War Office: 'I am sure LG will not do for WO. Balfour with LG doing Munitions as well as Treasury will be a far sounder arrangement.'[96]

The idea that Asquith was likely to take notice of his advice at this stage showed a poor grasp of reality. 'I know I am hurt, but as yet I cannot tell how badly', Churchill told Lloyd George the following day. On the 19th – new offices not having yet been allocated – he seemed inclined to put up a fight to remain as First Lord. According to Frances Stevenson, he completely lost his temper when he perceived that both Lloyd George and Grey assumed he would be moving. 'You don't care', he said to Lloyd George, 'what becomes of me. You don't care whether I am trampled under foot by enemies. You don't care for my personal reputation . . .' 'No', came the devastating reply. 'I don't care for my own at the present moment. The only thing I care about now is that we win this war.'[97] Lloyd George persuaded Churchill – whom he later described as having an expression 'like the faces we used to see on old mugs' – not to make a statement to the Commons, on the grounds that it would have a bad effect on opinion abroad. 'I read his statement', he told Riddell. 'When I came to the part in which he referred to his own services, I could see his eyes filling with sympathy for himself.'[98]

After increasingly pathetic appeals to Asquith, Churchill finally conceded, on 21 May: 'I will accept any office – the lowest if you like – that you care to offer me'.[99] He was at last given the Chancellorship

of the Duchy of Lancaster. Lloyd George wrote later that this was a
post 'generally reserved either for beginners in the Cabinet or for
distinguished politicians who had just reached the first stages of
unmistakable decrepitude. It was a cruel and unjust degradation.' He
claimed in his memoirs that, 'When I learned the office finally offered
to Mr. Churchill, it came to me as an unpleasant surprise.'[100] At the
time, he told Riddell that he 'had fought to get Winston high office
– the Colonies, the India Office, the Viceroyalty of India'. This was
in spite of the fact that, as he put it, 'Winston had acted foolishly'
and 'written some very wild and silly things to the PM'.[101] There
seems no particular reason to doubt this account. Indeed, we have
Churchill's own word that Lloyd George had suggested the Colonial
Office idea to Asquith. But Lloyd George had not put friendship
above reasons of state, and had not hesitated to see Churchill moved
as the price of coalition. He was disarmingly candid about his
motives. When Churchill said to him that, as a return for past
favours, Lloyd George might have said the word that would have
kept him at the Admiralty, he was quite frank. 'But my dear
Churchill', he said, 'I have said all along that I did not think you
ought to stay there, that the Dardanelles campaign was a great
mistake, and that someone else ought to be put into your place.'[102]
He cannot be fairly said to have stabbed Churchill in the back.

Churchill believed otherwise. 'Whatever you thought,' he told his
colleague, 'I always thought you would stand by me when it came to
the point.'[103] The depths of his bitterness were made clear in a
conversation he had with Riddell on 26 May. He said:

> Lloyd George is responsible for the coalition government. He
> has treated me disgracefully. He has no sense of honour. Not-
> withstanding our former relations, notwithstanding how I stood
> by him in Marconi days, he did nothing to help me. He never
> put out a hand. He acted just as if they had been killing a rat. I
> will never work with him again. He never hesitates to sacrifice a
> friend if he stands in the way of his game.

After describing Fisher as 'a treacherous devil', he continued:
'remember what I say regarding LG. Whatever your friendship or
relations with him may have been, he will never scruple to sacrifice
you without compunction if you stand in the way of his plans.'[104]
The unpublished diary of Lord Reading (formerly Rufus Isaacs,

who had been appointed Lord Chief Justice in 1913) demonstrates that Churchill's allies felt that his animus against Lloyd George was likely to rebound on him. On 27 May Reading saw Frederick Guest MP, a cousin and an ardent supporter of Churchill. Guest reported that 'Winston [was] desperately annoyed & angry with L.G. who has left him in the lurch. We agree this state of feeling ought to be stopped if it possibly can be. Freddy very anxious about it because Winston vows vengeance agst L.G.' Guest wanted Reading to calm Churchill down. Having seen Lloyd George, who swore he had 'done all he possibly could', Reading went to see Churchill at Admiralty House. 'Winston makes very strong case against Fisher . . . but as regards L.G. is very sore. Says can never be friends again and will never break bread with him again . . . W. says [he] has always supported L.G. through thick & thin but L.G. has now made his dispositions in such a way as to bring Winston down – perhaps subconsciously only but it is there.' Reading tried to get him to agree to see Lloyd George, but Churchill was clearly afraid that if he did so he would be won over against his will. 'You know him', he said, 'at an interview he will smooth everything.'[105] It appears that the next day, Churchill rebuffed Lloyd George when they met at Cabinet '& L.G. made to speak to him in a friendly way.'[106]

Churchill's harsh strictures on Lloyd George were not merely words that tumbled out in the heat of the moment. In the coming weeks he frequently gave vent to his grievance. In June, he wrote to his young friend Archibald Sinclair, who was serving in France. He attributed the formation of the coalition in part to Lloyd George's 'striking out for power in alliance with Northcliffe'. (Northcliffe's *Times* had not only published Repington's crucial dispatch but had attacked Churchill in an editorial at the height of the Cabinet crisis.) He told Sinclair: 'Between me & Ll G tout est fini.'[107] The day he sent this letter, 9 June, Clementine Churchill visited Margot Asquith, who had invited her to tea as a good-will gesture. The pleasantries quickly descended into a blazing row. Clementine alleged that Lloyd George had 'blackmailed' the Prime Minister into forming the coalition. She alternated denunciations of Lloyd George with attacks on Asquith. According to Margot, she accused the latter of having thrown Churchill to the wolves, 'and harangued me in fish-wife style on Henry's defects'. In the evening, rather remarkably, they managed to sit through a dinner party together at No. 10, at which not only their respective husbands but also Kitchener and Lloyd George were present. The latter left early, and Margot accompanied him downstairs and quizzed him about his relations with Churchill. Lloyd George said Churchill thought he had blackmailed Asquith by threatening to resign, but claimed the story was nonsense. While they were talking, Churchill came downstairs, which created an awkward moment. Margot tried to smooth things over by praising one of Churchill's recent speeches, an overture to which he proved responsive. But when Lloyd George spoke to Churchill, he directed his answer to Margot, to the other man's visible discomfort. After Churchill went out of the door, Lloyd George turned to Margot and observed that Churchill was very sulky. 'I'm afraid he'll never forgive me', he said to her.[108]

It should be noted that the resentment was mainly on one side. Although, during the crisis, Lloyd George criticized Churchill to his face as well as to others, his scathing comments did not go much beyond his habitual forms of belittlement. He himself was more politically secure than ever, whereas Churchill had lost out and was looking for people to blame. However, a relationship cannot be maintained unilaterally. Churchill's repeated declarations that the friendship and working partnership were at an end make nonsense of his later claims to have stuck with Lloyd George through thick and thin. The latter was perfectly well aware how his colleague felt. He told Riddell that 'Winston is angry and hurt'.[109] Later, though, he would go along with the fiction that in four decades the two men had never had a personal rift.

Churchill's fall from grace plunged him into anguish and despair. 'When he left the Admiralty he thought he was finished', his wife remembered. 'I thought he would die of grief.'[110] Lloyd George, by contrast, went from strength to strength. On 19 May, in the midst of the Cabinet turmoil, he had sent Asquith a letter protesting that the War Office was withholding vital information from the recently formed Munitions Committee. His previous warnings had been ignored, he said, and 'all the horrible loss of life which has occurred in consequence of the lack of high explosive shell is the result'.[111] The Prime Minister responded to the pressure by appointing him the head of a new Ministry of Munitions.

In abandoning the Exchequer Lloyd George was taking a huge political risk, but he took to his task with enthusiasm. The Ministry found premises in a house at 6 Whitehall Gardens. The only items of furniture were two tables and a chair. Lloyd George's secretaries put in an urgent order for a more adequate supply; but before it arrived men came from the Office of Works to remove what little furniture there was on the grounds that it did not belong to the new department! (Happily, they showed mercy.) From these farcical beginnings the new minister built up an enormous establishment manned by thousands that was to revolutionize the country's production of armaments. He brought in 'men of push and go' from private industry to help, and, in a spirit of brilliant improvisation, not only got the maximum out of his experts, but also showed his own best qualities of dynamism and sheer mental endurance.

A typical anecdote was told by Eric Geddes, a former managing director of the North Eastern Railway, brought in to help step up production. In July 1915 Geddes tried to calculate how many machine guns the army required. After some difficulty he established from Kitchener that two per battalion was the minimum requirement; four was the usual maximum; and anything above four could be counted as 'a luxury'. Geddes took this information to Lloyd George, who told him: 'Take Kitchener's maximum (four per battalion); square it; multiply that result by two; and when you are within sight of that, double it again for good luck.'[112] During Lloyd George's thirteen and a half months at the ministry, production of medium-calibre guns increased to 380 per cent, and of heavy guns to 1200 per cent, of the May 1915 level.[113] There is some room for debate about how much this success was due to him personally, and how far it in fact depended on the War Office's own earlier efforts. But revisionism should not be allowed to go too far. Churchill later served as Minister of Munitions himself. In his memoirs he granted that the credit for the achievements of his own tenure belonged 'in the first instance to Mr. Lloyd George', who had gathered the majority of the ministry's able staff and 'whose foresight in creating the national factories laid the foundations for subsequent production'.[114]

Lloyd George took centre stage, as Churchill looked on from the sidelines. 'You see how much this man dominates the Cabinet', the latter observed to Walter Long, a Conservative Minister.[115] At this time the armed forces were still relying on voluntary recruitment. In a speech on 3 June Lloyd George hinted that conscription, although it should be a last resort, might yet become necessary. He also suggested that, in order to make production more efficient, the state should have greater powers to direct labour.[116] These issues were highly controversial within his party, as compulsion cut across the tenets of liberalism, and it was also likely to upset the unions. Two days later, in a speech in his constituency, Churchill gave his own views. He said he would support conscription if it became necessary, but he did not think this likely; and that in the meantime it would be an error to throw away the 'great moral advantage' of having a volunteer army.[117] (This was the speech that Margot Asquith praised, when trying to escape the awkward moment caused when Churchill found her talking to Lloyd George.) This may have been a mere difference in emphasis, or it may have been, as one author has suggested, a clear rejection of conscription and thus a deliberate sideswipe at Lloyd George.[118]

In private, Churchill did not hesitate to suggest that personal ambition was a factor in Lloyd George's stance. On 3 June he told J. A. Pease, who had lost his ministerial position (as president of the Board of Education) when the coalition was formed, that he 'thought George meant to be War Minister – & by bringing in Tories he would gain his end'.[119] A few days after that conversation, Churchill sent a letter to Jack Seely, the former Secretary of State for War, who was now in the army. 'LG is making a strong gas attack on GHQ supported by the Northcliffe batteries heavy & light, & hopes to capture the position in the course of the summer,' he wrote. 'His successive failures in the Marconi, Anti-Navy, Anti-War and Prohibition operations do not seem at all to have affected his prestige or morale.' He added that he himself occupied 'a detached position *en potence* covering GHQ' – which presumably symbolized 10 Downing Street – whilst maintaining communications with the left wing.[120] In August Wilfrid Scawen Blunt visited him at Hoe Farm, Hascombe, Surrey, which the Churchills had taken for the summer months. Blunt witnessed one of Churchill's early attempts at his new hobby of painting, and listened as he opened his mind. Churchill bemoaned 'his colleagues who had failed to support him in the crisis, a blow which had fallen on him absolutely without warning, all had deserted him, even his intimates in the Cabinet, Lloyd George and Edward Grey, who had given him cold sympathy'. He also speculated that Lloyd George would lead the Liberal Party after the war.[121]

By the time of Blunt's visit Churchill's resentment of Lloyd George had diminished from its earlier intensity. A dinner in mid-July appears to have been the key to this. Churchill, Lloyd George, F. E. Smith and Reading were present. The talk eventually came round to the formation of the coalition. According to Reading's diary, 'Winston says [this had been a] masterstroke of L.G. but it has failed – he L.G. more isolated than ever before.' Reading found this embarrassing and slightly ridiculous: 'device a little too obvious – object seemed to be to prove to L.G. how he had miscalculated the effect of his groupings & had left out those best able to help him.' After Churchill had got this off his chest, the talk continued until 12.45 a.m. Reading noted: 'Even then there was much to say – & by common consent dinner to be renewed – I am not so sure – my object of reconciling L.G. and W. has already been achieved.'[122]

Lloyd George's ability to 'smooth everything' doubtless played its part in this (partial) reconciliation. At the same time, Churchill realized that there was little profit in setting himself against the powerful Minister of Munitions, however much he might resent his earlier conduct. He wrote to Archie Sinclair at the end of July: 'LG is necessary to the State. He has the war making quality. I do not intend to allow any personal feelings to prevent me working with him. But distrust based on experience is a terrible barrier.'[123] Therefore, Churchill broke his earlier vow that the relationship was over. Perhaps he could not help himself. In September Frances Stevenson noted that, although Churchill had been 'sore' with Lloyd George, he 'soon came round – he could not keep away'.[124] This was due to a combination of Lloyd George's magnetism and Churchill's sense of the opportune.

A degree of collaboration between them was restored, although the situation remained uneasy. By mid-August both men were in accord with Lord Curzon, former Viceroy of India and now a Tory minister, on the need for National Service. Asquith was aware of this, writing to Margot that Kitchener was 'sound & strong against Conscription, for wh. there is a real intrigue brewing, engineered largely by Geo. Curzon, but I can see that both Ll. George & Winston are up to the shoulders in it'.[125] In mid-September the three last-named dined together. Curzon told the other two that the Conservatives were ready to approach Asquith to demand not only conscription but also the removal of Kitchener from the War Office.

Churchill and Lloyd George agreed to throw in their lot with him. Frances Stevenson recorded this, but also noted Lloyd George's doubts. (Now that he had ceased to be Chancellor she referred to him in her diary as 'D.', for 'David', rather than 'C.')

> D. says he cannot possibly be a party any longer to the shameful mis-management and slackness ... however, he hates going against his party, & he fears that the Liberals will hate him violently if he goes against them now. He fears Churchill too. He is not sure whether Churchill will come too, or whether he will remain & get the P.M. to put him into D.'s shoes at the Munitions Office. D. says that Churchill is the only man in the Cabinet who has the power to do him harm, and he does not trust him when it comes to a matter of personal interest.[126]

Matters might not have been helped by Churchill's meddling in the affairs of the Ministry of Munitions. A member of the Ministry's Trench Warfare Supply Department tipped him off that 'nothing had been done' about the production of the Stokes gun, a form of light mortar, of which Lloyd George had ordered a thousand. Churchill took the matter up, perpetrating what Christopher Addison MP, one of Lloyd George's key subordinates in the Ministry, considered to be 'astonishing libels' against officials. Addison recorded in his diary that 'L.G. roared with delight at Winston's discomfort' when he was shown to have got his facts wrong. (Addison also noted that Churchill had 'a good deal more influence with L.G. than is good'.)[127] There was 'another of Winston's amazing performances' on similar lines the following month, when he 'made all sorts of wild charges to L.G.', without, it appeared, 'any investigation whatever of the facts'. This led Addison to conclude that Churchill had no sense of truth or honour, and suffered from the kind of moral deficiency that can sometimes accompany genius.[128]

More problematic than these episodes were Lloyd George and Churchill's differences over military strategy. On some aspects of this they were united. At the start of October, C. P. Scott had lunch with them. 'Both very hostile to the policy of attack now being carried out on the Western Front, any considerable success from which they regarded as impossible', he wrote. 'Both Lloyd George and Churchill insisted on the far greater possibilities of the Eastern front.'[129] But they disagreed about the details of what should be done there.

Churchill suspected Lloyd George wanted to abandon the Dardanelles, something to which he himself refused to be a party. Lloyd
George still wanted an expedition to Salonika, and was 'sick with
Churchill, who will not acknowledge the futility of the Dardanelles
campaign'. According to Frances Stevenson, he blamed him for
preventing Asquith from facing the facts, 'by reminding him that he
too is implicated in the campaign, & tells him that if the thing is
acknowledged to be a failure, he (the P.M.) as well as Churchill will
be blamed'.[130]

The differences between our two principals at this time should
not be overemphasized. Churchill thought Lloyd George should be
appointed to the War Office (although, in a rare moment of self-
restraint he held back from giving Asquith the benefit of this advice).
Furthermore, he told the Prime Minister that he thought Lloyd
George was 'seeking the truth' on the Gallipoli question, '& although
we approach it from different poles, I think we could together thrash
it out thoroughly'.[131] And, with the situation deteriorating in the
Balkans, Churchill and Lloyd George jointly 'swooped down' on
Kitchener, with the idea of sending telegrams to Romania and
Greece, offering to send 150,000 men to Salonika if the countries in
question would join the Allies. They obtained his reluctant sanction,
and that of Asquith, and the telegrams were sent, but the offer was
refused.[132] A smaller allied force was sent to Salonika nonetheless,
where, although subsequently beefed up, it spent much of the rest of
the war in apparent futility, before at last achieving significant success
in 1918.

There were important limitations to their joint effectiveness nonetheless. Towards the end of October 1915 J. H. Lewis noted in his
diary that 'During the last few weeks a struggle has been going on in
the Cabinet between the conscriptionists and the anti-conscriptionists.'
Northcliffe, he wrote, wanted to get rid of Asquith and Grey and the
Liberal anti-conscriptionist Ministers and to install 'a Tory Government including Churchill and Lloyd George, the latter as Prime
Minister'.[133] The crisis had come to a head at the middle of the
month, Margot Asquith writing that 'It is clear as day that Ll.G.
Curzon & Winston are going to try and wreck the Gov.'[134] She also
wrote to warn Kitchener that Curzon was to bring the conscription
question before the Cabinet. He would be backed by Lloyd George
and Churchill, and, in the country, by a press campaign run by

Northcliffe. 'If the Cabinet go against them they threaten to resign.'[135] According to Frances Stevenson, Lloyd George, Churchill and six Tories had indeed made up their minds to resign if Asquith would not consent to some form of conscription. She also claimed that Lloyd George did not want to displace Asquith as Prime Minister, even though the Conservatives were 'very anxious' to achieve this outcome.[136]

The conscriptionists were frustrated, in part, by a typical Asquith manoeuvre. This was the promulgation in mid-October of the so-called 'Derby scheme'. The Earl of Derby had just been appointed Director General of Recruiting. His plan was that eligible men between 18 and 41 years of age should be asked to 'attest' their willingness to join up in due course. If enough did so, it was argued, conscription would be proved unnecessary. It seemed impossible for the conscriptionists to resign before the Derby scheme had been given a trial – unless they had the support of Kitchener. But Asquith acted to prevent Kitchener lending weight to their side by telling him that the conscriptionists' real object was to oust him from the War Office. (What Kitchener didn't know was that Asquith wanted him out too.) There was also another element to the story. Lloyd George appears to have switched sides abruptly. According to Addison's unpublished diary, Lloyd George said on 20 October that 'after a considerable fight' he had brought his pro-conscription colleagues 'to a reasonable frame of mind' – that is to say, he persuaded them to give Derby's scheme a chance before pressing for further legislative power. Addison recorded that 'Churchill and Curzon, and Curzon particularly, in their usual hotheaded manner, wanted to plunge in for a demand for legislation now; but L.G. managed to carry most of the rest against them.'[137] When Addison published his diary in 1934, he disguised the truth of the episode by omitting part of this entry.[138] Whether or not Lloyd George's apparent change of heart was in fact decisive in delaying conscription remains unclear, as do the reasons for it. Perhaps he simply saw the way the wind was blowing and abandoned his alliance with Churchill and Curzon for that reason.

At the start of November the Prime Minister sidelined Kitchener by sending him abroad on a long fact-finding mission, taking day-to-day charge of the War Office himself. Getting rid of Kitchener in practice but not in name in turn mollified Lloyd George, whilst avoiding a negative public reaction. Asquith also made other concessions to Lloyd George's point of view. The result was the institution of a streamlined War Committee to replace the existing Dardanelles Committee (as the War Council had for some time been known). Lloyd George was of course to serve on it. Asquith initially intended to include Churchill too. But when its composition was finally announced, he was excluded. To heap insult onto injury, and to Lloyd George's great annoyance, McKenna (now Chancellor) was added to the membership. Having first offered to stand down at the end of October, Churchill sent Asquith a definitive letter of resignation on 11 November. He was in agreement with the decision to form the new committee, he wrote, but he 'could not accept a position of general responsibility for war policy without any effective share in its guidance & control'.[139] He had determined to join the army instead. On 15 November he made a resignation speech in the House of Commons, defending his record at the Admiralty. He won some praise for it, although his defence of the Dardanelles expedition as 'a legitimate war gamble' disturbed many.[140] 'One's general impression is that Winston was more anxious to defend himself than to assist the country', Addison noted.[141] The next day Lloyd George sent Churchill a letter.

> Dear Winston
>   I am so sorry that I have to leave for France this afternoon so that I cannot see you to say 'au revoir'.
>   Your speech yesterday was amazingly clever both in substance & tone.
>   Under the circumstances you are right to go. All the same it is a blunder – a stupid blunder – to let you off. Here your special knowledge & gifts would be invaluable. I cannot help thinking that you must soon return
>   In a hurry. Good luck to you
>   Yours sincerely
> D Lloyd George[142]

On 18 November, Churchill crossed the Channel. When he reported for duty 'Nobody seemed madly enthusiastic', as one soldier reported in a letter. 'He has hit about as hard a push as can be met with in the service, and they are going to put him through it good and proper.' However, Churchill impressed his new comrades with his uncomplaining acceptance of the discomfort of army life.[143] After a few weeks in which he accustomed himself to trench warfare, he was appointed to the command of a battalion which in January 1916 moved into the line at Ploegsteert, aka 'Plug Street', in Belgium.

Lloyd George's sorrow at Churchill's departure appears to have been genuine enough. He seems to have felt a kind of nagging discomfort at the absence of his erstwhile colleague. 'Like a political Mrs. Gummidge, he still hankers after Winston', noted Riddell, not long after Churchill's departure.[144] (This was a reference to the fretful sailor's widow in *David Copperfield*, whose irritating behaviour is always excused by other characters on the grounds that she is pining for her late husband.) He had regarded Churchill's removal from the Admiralty with equanimity, and was probably not entirely sorry to see him put in his place. But things had gone too far, with first the crushing demotion to the Duchy of Lancaster and then the War Committee debacle. Churchill was not the most reliable of allies at the best of times, and the rapprochement of the summer and autumn had only been partial. Yet he was an ally nonetheless, and Lloyd George may have regretted his leaving for this reason, not least at a time when he himself was becoming yet further alienated from the radicals. Equally, the Minister of Munitions now had fewer opportunities to enjoy his habit of Churchill-baiting. The bully was deprived of his victim.

On 1 December 1915, at St Omer, Lord Esher met Churchill fresh out of the trenches: 'he looks extraordinarily well, and is supremely happy. He called himself the "escaped scapegoat". The idea of evacuating Gallipoli infuriates him, and he declares that if this is decided upon, he will go back to the House of Commons and denounce his colleagues. Of these, without exception, he has no great opinion.'[145] (The evacuation had in fact already been decided upon, and was later carried out successfully.) In criticizing his ex-colleagues, Churchill made no caveat in favour of Lloyd George. He knew, however, that if he himself were ever to make a political comeback, cooperation with him would be essential. At the very end of 1915 Clementine Churchill wrote to her husband describing Lloyd George as 'the direct descendant of Judas Iscariot'.[146] He responded: 'Ll.G. is no doubt all you say: but his interests are not divorced from mine and in those circumstances we can work together – if occasion arises.'[147] Churchill and Lloyd George, it is clear, continued to have very strong, very mixed feelings about each other. It is equally clear they both viewed their relationship in a light that was instrumental more than sentimental. This was to be seen yet again when Lloyd George became Prime Minister, only to dash Churchill's initial hopes of inclusion in his government.

Chapter Five

DON'T GET TORPEDOED

AT CHRISTMAS 1915 Churchill returned to London for a few days' leave. 'He thinks there is going to be a political crisis on compulsion', noted Louis Spiers, a young army friend of Churchill's whom he saw just after his return to France. 'He saw Lloyd George who is going to try & smash the Government when either Bonar Law or LG wd be PM & Churchill get Munitions or Admiralty the remaining one getting the W[ar] O[ffice].'[1] Writing from Dover on 27 December, Churchill urged Lloyd George to keep in touch, adding: 'Don't miss your opportunity. The time has come.'[2] Clementine Churchill forwarded this letter to Lloyd George, together with an invitation to lunch. 'With Winston has departed the electric current of life which he gives to everything around him', she wrote.[3] By the time Lloyd George took up her invitation, on the 29th, the crisis was over. At the crucial Cabinet meeting, Asquith deftly came down in favour of conscription for unmarried men, the Derby scheme having failed. The only anti-conscriptionist minister to go through with resignation was John Simon, the Home Secretary. 'I asked Ll.G if he & the other die hards had tried to break the government', Clementine reported to her husband. However, 'he said there wasn't a chance as the P.M. had come right over on to their side'. She also wrote that Lloyd George had expressed 'great distress' at Churchill's not being in the government, and had said repeatedly, 'We must get Winston back'. But, she added, 'Ll.G. is a strange man. He was very polite & civil and most friendly, but for the moment the chance of working with you is gone & so his fire is gone and he is more detached than the other day'.[4] She divined correctly that Lloyd George's friendship was warmest when his friends were of greatest use to him.

Churchill at this time was similarly pragmatic. He believed that at any moment a situation might develop that would throw him together with Lloyd George again. 'Our relations are good – & should be kept so', he told his wife, praising her for showing hospitality to his ex-colleague and suggesting she do so again.[5] Moreover, as was seen at the end of the last chapter, when she wrote to him denouncing Lloyd George as treacherous, Churchill stressed that he foresaw conditions in which the two men would be able to work together. By contrast, he thought that his cooperation with Asquith was at an end. He put the position to her more than once, but did so most brutally in a letter of 10 January 1916. 'If I were killed he [Asquith] wd be sorry: but it wd suit his political hand. Ll.G. on the other hand wd not be sorry, but it wd not suit his political hand.'[6] Churchill did not always stick to this unsentimental view of affairs: at other times he insisted that, because of his interventions in the Marconi episode, Lloyd George owed him a personal debt.

He was still bitter. 'L.G. after all his activities is vy isolated and shut in', Churchill wrote to his mother. 'What a fool he was not to preserve his association with me.'[7] And to his cousin he wrote: 'L.G. seems after all his manoeuvres to be quite isolated & kept in control. He was foolish to throw me over for together we were a power.'[8] Certainly, Lloyd George could have done with more friends in the Cabinet. And his recent hostile reception by militant munitions workers, who resented his determination to do away with restrictive practices that slowed down production, showed that his popularity in the country was by no means universal. But Churchill, far from the centre of political events, was hardly the person to point to the isolation of others. He did, though, combine his resentment with reluctant praise, aimed at least in part at overcoming his wife's hostility towards a man upon whom he suspected his future career depended. Towards the end of January Clementine told him that 'Lloyd George expressed a great wish for a long talk with you'. She herself got on well with him, she said, 'but he is a sneak – I would never like you to be intimately connected'.[9] In reply Churchill wrote that Lloyd George had 'been vy faithless and is now friendless. Still he has been more on the true trail than anyone else in this war.'[10]

Churchill also made direct contact with Lloyd George. He wrote to him arguing that he, Lloyd George, appeared even more isolated than when he had seen him last, and that 'Asquith is stronger than ever.'[11] Lloyd George did not reply, but he did visit France in the company of Bonar Law, and the two men were able to meet up with Churchill and F. E. Smith, the latter also being in the country. There was 'full and complete agreement that Asquith had to be got rid of at all costs'. Lloyd George and Bonar Law also told Sir Douglas Haig, who had replaced John French as Commander-in-Chief, that there would be no objection from London were Churchill to receive the command of a brigade. As Martin Gilbert notes, this was a friendly gesture that probably strengthened Churchill's belief that he could work with Lloyd George. He saw his visitors as part of the nucleus of an alternative government.[12]

Lloyd George, back in Britain, lunched in company with Clementine Churchill, who continued to think him 'fair of speech, shifty of eye, treacherous of heart'.[13] She herself was involved in war work, helping to set up canteens to provide cheap meals for munitions workers. The day following their lunch, 3 February, Lloyd George formally opened one at Ponders End, in Middlesex. Asquith's daughter Violet also insisted on coming – and was viewed by Clementine as a Downing Street spy, there to see what was up between Churchill and Lloyd George. Clementine wrote to her husband: 'The great meeting is over and the whole thing went off brilliantly – Ll-G made a quite undistinguished speech and the shabby little tike altho' he said he had just returned from the Front never mentioned your name.' Lloyd George had also antagonized her over the question of who might become Air Minister, were such a post to be established. 'On the way home he said quite casually "I'm so surprised, Curzon wants the 'Air', I thought perhaps Winston might have done it – Do you think he would have liked it?"' Loyally, she responded that her husband would have done it better than anyone, but received no reply.[14] Lloyd George made a better impression on Churchill's mother. Lady Randolph wrote to her son: 'L.G. told me he had seen you & that you were in "gt" spirits & that your men worshipped you'.[15] This was typical Lloyd George flattery that he must have known would get back to its subject; although why he failed to make a similar full-strength effort in Clementine's hearing is unclear.

Soon after this Lloyd George was contemplating resignation, and the possibility of collaborating with Churchill. On 18 February C. P. Scott recorded in his diary a lengthy breakfast meeting with Lloyd George, who 'looked worn and old'. The previous October Edward Carson had resigned his position as Attorney General in protest at the inefficient conduct of the war, although his action had proved a nine-days wonder. Lloyd George now said to Scott: 'Carson was ineffective as leader of an Opposition because of his constant ill health and absence, but he and Carson and Churchill (who would return) would together make an effective Opposition.'[16] After Churchill returned to London on leave in early March, he put the matter differently. 'He and Lloyd George and Carson were the only men in the front rank with the instinct for action and capacity for carrying on a great war', he in turn told Scott. 'Carson was ill, George was for the time being under a cloud and Churchill alone remained.'[17] Churchill was itching to get back into the fray, and he now scented an opportunity.

At the start of his leave he discovered that Balfour was to present the naval estimates on 7 March 1916. He determined to speak, and was encouraged to do so by, among others, three MPs who were friends of Lloyd George.[18] The day before the debate he lunched with the man himself. Lloyd George wrote to his brother afterwards: 'He is anxious to come back. Sick of the trenches. He ought never to have gone there'.[19] Churchill delivered to the Commons a strong warning about the administration of the Admiralty, which, he suggested, was in danger of relaxing its efforts, if only unconsciously. He suggested that the building programme was inadequate, and warned of future dangers, such as might be presented by the German submarine campaign. 'Not very patriotic of Churchill, but he said a lot of true things', noted Maurice Hankey. Churchill's exhortations made a considerable impact on the House. However, at the end of the speech, he threw everything away. He made the incredible suggestion that Fisher – with whom he had recently been reconciled, and who was watching from the gallery 'with a face like an Indian Buddha' – should be recalled.[20] MPs were astonished, and in his reply the following day Balfour tore Churchill apart by contrasting his previous statements about Fisher's failure to support him with his current praise for his gifts. Churchill spoke again in response, but to little effect.

Lloyd George himself had observed to Riddell the previous month that Fisher had a genius for war and should be brought into the government in some capacity or other.[21] It is quite possible that he and Churchill discussed the issue at their lunch on 6 March. The Asquith set certainly suspected Lloyd George had provided the inside information on which the speech was based. And immediately after Churchill's démarche, Lloyd wrote to his brother William: 'Have just heard Winston's powerful speech. Well produced. Great effect.'[22] It seems that he started to show doubts only after he heard Balfour's reply. He wrote again to William on 8 March of the 'very sharp duel between Winston and Balfour. Winston had much the worst of it.' He added: 'W. wants to come back from the Army. He is a brilliant but most unreliable fellow.'[23] He wrote to William on 13 March: 'Poor Winston had to return to his dreary trenches. Sorry for him. A brilliant fellow without judgement which is adequate to his fiery impulse. His steering gear is too weak for his horse-power.'[24]

This trenchant comment contained much truth. It should not, however, be allowed to distract attention from Lloyd George's own lack of judgement during this episode. He was the government's most powerful critic from within, and Churchill its most powerful critic from without. They were surely right to suggest that the conduct of the war left much to be desired. But Lloyd George's willingness to countenance the recall of Fisher, and Churchill's direct advocacy of it, suggest that both were casting around fairly wildly in their search for constructive alternatives. This helps to explain a comment made by Curzon not long afterwards. Churchill, he wrote, 'is impetuous with or in spite of knowledge. Lloyd George is impetuous *without* it.'[25]

Churchill remained desperate to return to political life. Yet another Cabinet crisis was developing, over whether conscription should be extended. A split might give him another chance to bid for office. He wrote to F. E. Smith on 8 April:

> Generally speaking L.G. is the key to my position at the moment. However a new system might be formed, it seems to me that L.G. and I shd be together. If he came in to what must be in substance a Tory Administration, he wd need above all Liberal associates. I think you shd get hold of Rufus betimes and put to him vy plainly the personal obligation wh exists. He has always recognised it, and wd have gt weight on that point in that quarter.[26]

The last two sentences were, of course, a reference to Lord Reading, who, along with Lloyd George, had been caught up in the Marconi scandal. Here we see strongly Churchill's sense that Lloyd George owed him a substantial favour in return for his support during that affair. However, he used a different line when he wrote to him directly two days later. 'You have let several good chances go by in hope of a better', he told him bluntly. 'I cannot judge events & forces vy thoroughly from here, but I am inclined to think that this is the best opportunity that has yet offered: & that unless a decision to adopt universal compulsion is taken forthwith, you ought to resign.'[27]

Churchill returned once more to London, in order to take part in the Secret Session of parliament that had been called to debate the situation. He heard from C. P. Scott, to whom he had also written, that Lloyd George had indeed decided to leave the government. On 18 April Churchill and Lloyd George lunched with Arthur Lee MP, parliamentary military secretary at the Ministry of Munitions. Lee later told his wife 'that Winston and he had been wrestling for L.G.'s soul'.[28] Churchill wrote to his friend Archie Sinclair later the same day, 'I am just off to dine with Carson & Lloyd George, and have been able to unite various powerful wires wh were *criss cross*.'[29] But, as Churchill had thought possible all along, Asquith was again able to save his own skin, by caving in over the next days and weeks to the pressures for full-scale conscription. 'Churchill is very sick at the idea of the thing going through quietly', wrote Frances Stevenson. 'He is all for a split, and for the forming of a vigorous opposition, in which he would take an active part.'[30]

Although Churchill had not achieved his object, he determined finally to leave the Army and return to Westminster politics. In May he left his battalion for the last time. Lloyd George's career also took a new turn. In April there had been a nationalist rebellion – the Easter Rising – in Dublin. The British military authorities defeated the rebels without difficulty, but mishandled the aftermath. The summary executions of fifteen rebel leaders were attended by some grotesque details. James Connolly, who had been badly wounded in the fighting, had to be carried by stretcher to the execution yard. Joseph Plunkett married his fiancée in the Kilmainham prison chapel at 1.30 a.m., shortly before being taken out and shot. On 12 May Asquith halted the executions, but the damage had been done. The creation of martyrs brought about a widespread sympathy for the extremists in Ireland that had previously been lacking. Lloyd George was delegated the near-impossible task of brokering an Irish settlement acceptable to all sides. During May and June he negotiated, separately, with Carson and Redmond. He achieved agreement between them on immediate Home Rule only through creative ambiguity on the question of whether Ulster's exclusion was to be permanent or temporary. Once published, the deal ran into Conservative opposition and fell apart. Redmond's moderate, parliamentary Nationalist movement was further undermined. Meanwhile, a new situation was created by the death of Kitchener. Sent abroad on a further mission, this time to Russia, on 5 June his ship hit a mine and he drowned. His post at the War Office was offered to Lloyd George.

It was a few weeks before he accepted. However, the possibility that, if he did go to the War Office, Churchill might replace him at the Ministry of Munitions was in both men's minds well before he made his final decision. When Northcliffe saw Churchill in Lloyd George's office on the day Kitchener's death was announced, he joked, 'I suppose you have come after Ll.G.'s job'.[31] Churchill was affronted – perhaps because he was indeed eager to press his claims. As has been seen, he viewed Lord Reading as someone who might be able lean on Lloyd George on his behalf. In mid-June Reading wrote to Churchill: 'LG was at No 10 when I got back from you. I saw him afterwards – in a word he thinks it is premature to press you for the post in question – but is very sympathetic and as you wish it, notwithstanding his own views he will push it.'[32] On 2 July Riddell wrote in his diary:

> Winston was with LG for five hours. He is evidently pushing hard to get back into the Cabinet. LG said he thought Winston would be the best man to succeed him at the Munitions Department, but that the PM would not appoint him. I said I thought the appointment would be most unpopular. LG was afraid it might be. I said 'Winston's mind is concentrated on the war.' 'Yes,' replied LG, smiling, 'but it is more concentrated on Winston.'[33]

Churchill did not get the job, which went to Edwin Montagu. He complained to his brother that Lloyd George had made only 'a half-hearted fight about Munitions'. The new Secretary of State for War was, he said, 'very much alone' and 'none too well qualified' for his new job. But he was 'very friendly' towards Churchill, according to the latter's private sources.[34] He put it more harshly to C. P. Scott: 'Lloyd George had not lifted a finger to get him appointed'.[35]

It was now clear to Churchill that his best hope of future office was to exonerate himself over the Dardanelles. A commission had been established to look into the evidence. Lloyd George took up his War Office appointment at the beginning of July. According to the diary of Maurice Hankey, 'His first visitor was Lord Northcliffe; his second Churchill with a big box of papers. Absit omen [May this not be an omen]. I fear that they are trying to get at him over the Dardanelles papers Churchill's object being to clear his own character, and Northcliffe's to get in a backhander at the Prime Minister.'[36]

'LG is very affable and I see a good deal of him', Churchill wrote at the end of the month.[37] Too much, indeed, for some people. Lord Derby, now Undersecretary of State at the War Office, wrote to Lloyd George in August on 'the subject of Winston'. He said: 'I know your feelings about him and I appreciate very much that feeling which makes you wish not to hit a man when he is down, but Winston is never down or rather will never allow that he is down and I assure you that his coming to the War Office as he does is – not to put it too strongly – most distasteful to everybody in that office.'[38] The reputation of the Lloyd George–Churchill combination was a powerful one and was feared for a variety of reasons. Those sympathetic to Asquith thought, not unreasonably, that they were trying to kick him out of office. Hankey recorded one episode in his diary. 'Gen Cowans, at dinner with Ll. George and Churchill had heard Ll.G say that "we must get rid of the old man".' Hankey – who later became an admirer of Lloyd George – added 'Blackguard!'[39] Yet some who despised Asquith for his inefficiency were nonetheless worried that his two most dynamic Liberal critics were themselves in danger of undermining the fighting forces by interfering too much with the army. Lord Esher thought, at least at first, that the 'ignorant' though 'teachable' Lloyd George might be prepared to stand up for the army against intriguers like Churchill and F. E. Smith.[40] But such confidence was not universal. 'The Chief is getting a bit restive about Lloyd George', noted one of Northcliffe's journalists in October. 'He thinks L.G. is getting too friendly with Winston Churchill, whom he will not forgive for what he calls the Antwerp and Gallipoli blunders, and he is telling us to drive into the public mind the fact that political interference means increasing the death-roll of our army.' He sent an emissary to Lloyd George to tell him 'that he (L.G.) was too much in the company of Winston'. After Lloyd George kept the man waiting for hours and then failed to see him, Northcliffe determined to keep his distance for a while.[41]

Lloyd George's months at the War Office were not the happiest of his career. He was unable to wrest back from General Sir William Robertson, the Chief of the Imperial General Staff (CIGS), the wide powers that Kitchener had conceded to him. His time in the job coincided closely with the notorious Somme offensive, which he considered 'a bloody and disastrous failure'.[42] Lloyd George had major doubts about his top commanders, including Haig, whom he managed to alienate without achieving any good effect. He did, however, make a notable public intervention in the autumn. In an interview with an American journalist he proclaimed that Britain would fight the war 'to a knock-out'. This helped squash the danger, as he saw it, of a US-sponsored compromise peace that would have left Germany in control of swathes of captured territory. In terms of his struggles with Asquith, he stayed his hand for the time being. 'He thinks a lot; but *so far* has done nothing,' Churchill wrote in mid-September.[43] Churchill, for his part, occupied himself with the Dardanelles Commission.

Unionist dissent in parliament, organized by Carson, was increasing. Bonar Law was under fire as well as Asquith. On 8 November, there was a major rebellion on the obscure question of the sale of enemy property in Nigeria, which the Conservative leader had insisted on making an issue of confidence. Churchill was among those who voted against the government, which survived only narrowly. According to Asquith, Lloyd George dined with Carson on the evening of the debate. Moreover, Lloyd George 'paired' for the division with Arthur Lee – i.e. both men abstained as their opposing votes would have cancelled out – which was rather improper because Lee, as his personal secretary at the ministry of munitions, should by rights have supported the government on the issue.[44] 'Meanwhile, people who thought they knew [what they were talking about] were beginning to get very seriously apprehensive about the war and were beginning to lose their confidence', wrote Edwin Montagu not long after. 'Hysteria, always noticeable in the Press, in Winston, and sometimes in Lloyd George himself, began to make people want to turn everything upside down.'[45] Bonar Law and Lloyd George now hoped to reconstruct the government in such a way as to restore confidence and take day-to-day control of the war out of Asquith's hands. Towards the end of the month they consulted with Carson and Sir Max Aitken MP (a Canadian-born adviser to Bonar Law who was in the process of taking over the *Daily Express*). The proposal they developed, the precise details of which varied over the coming days, was for a new, small war committee. They envisaged, however, that Asquith would remain Prime Minister.

When Churchill saw C. P. Scott on 20 November, he cast doubt on such an idea. 'Speaking of the possibility of a reconstructed Ministry he said no change would be material which did not involve a change in the Premiership. Lloyd George, "with all his faults", was the only possible alternative Prime Minister.' As events would prove, this was all true enough, although it could have been added that he was also the only alternative Prime Minister who would even have dreamed of appointing Churchill to the Cabinet. That this was much in Churchill's mind is suggested by his answer to Scott's next question. 'I asked if in case George formed a ministry he could count on being included. He said he thought so – that George would desire it and that it would be in his interest.'[46] Churchill's hopes were soon to be dashed.

The crisis came to a head at the beginning of December. On the first of the month Lloyd George wrote to Asquith proposing a three-man war committee from which the latter, though remaining Prime Minister, would be excluded. He met with Asquith the same day and appears to have threatened to resign if the plan was not implemented. Asquith acknowledged the need for a new committee, but insisted on being its chairman. On 3 December, however, amid further signs of Unionist discontent, he yielded to Bonar Law and Lloyd George. Lloyd George would be chairman and Asquith would not have a seat. But on 4 December Asquith again changed his mind. Accordingly, Lloyd George resigned the next day. The resignations of Lord Curzon, Lord Robert Cecil, and Austen Chamberlain (known as the 'Three Cs') followed, signalling Asquith's loss of support amongst key Unionists. At 7 o'clock the following evening Asquith resigned in turn. His motivation for doing so remains debatable. He might simply have concluded he was beaten or, more probably, had miscalculated the extent of his own support. He may have believed that neither Bonar Law nor Lloyd George would be able to form a government, and that he himself would be recalled in triumph. If so, it was to prove a manoeuvre too far.

On the evening of 5 December, although it seemed likely that there would be a new Prime Minister, no one was yet certain who it would be. Bonar Law, as the leader of the second largest party, was the first to be asked by the King to form an administration. He was summoned to the palace as soon as Asquith resigned. During the evening, Churchill dined with Max Aitken and F. E. Smith. According to the recollections of Lord Beaverbrook (as Aitken was soon to become), Lloyd George was there too, but there is some reason to doubt this. He may have remained at the War Office with Carson.[47] To add to the complications of evidence, Beaverbrook, a notorious embellisher, told the story of the dinner in more than one version. Yet although, in the 1920s, Churchill objected to the publication of the tale, he did not dispute its central point. Beaverbrook's initial version, which is probably the one to be preferred, told of a pleasant evening spent before Lloyd George left to meet Bonar Law and Carson. After he had gone (or if he was in fact never there, simply in his absence), Aitken, Smith, and Churchill fell to discussing the composition of the new government. Beaverbrook recalled:

> Winston . . . turned to me and said that on the principle of the spoils to the victors I ought to have the Post Office. Rather with the idea of returning the compliment than anything else I said I hoped he would get an offer. 'What,' said Winston, 'aren't I to be in the Government?' I replied faithfully enough that I did not know – the thing was absurd as we didn't know who was to be Prime Minister yet. 'Smith,' said Winston with great emphasis, 'This man *knows* that I am *not* to be in the Government.' An almost ludicrous scene followed – Churchill changing from complete optimism to violent anger and depression. He abused me most violently, and when I got tired of it and replied in kind he picked up his hat and coat and without even putting them on dashed into the street. Smith ran out after him and tried to calm him but in vain – a curious end to the day.

In Beaverbrook's later version, published in his book *Politicians and the War*, he claimed that he had been deputed by Lloyd George to convey a hint to Churchill that he would not be included in the new ministry. It seems more likely that he simply realized what was obvious to many – that Unionist hostility to Churchill would prevent the latter's inclusion, and that he betrayed this through his words and tone. (At the least, he surely knew of Bonar Law's dislike of Churchill.) Churchill's own recollection was that the provocative comment was as follows: 'The new Government will be very well disposed to you. All your friends will be there. You will have a great field of common action with them.'[48] Whether Lloyd George had inspired these words directly is perhaps not all that important. One way or another, Churchill deduced correctly that he would not be given office, even before Lloyd George had been asked to form a government. Years later, he described this as the 'toughest moment of his life'.[49]

The following day Bonar Law gave up his attempt to form a government, after Asquith refused to serve under him. 'Accordingly D. was sent for about 7.0 o'clock & was asked to form a Gov. & he said he would', Frances Stevenson wrote. 'I saw him directly he returned & he was very pale & said he would like to run away to the mountains. "I'm not at all sure that I can do it", he said. "It is a very big task." '[50] But he set about the job with energy and skill. Large numbers of Liberal MPs agreed to back Lloyd George. Loyal supporters such as Christopher Addison (who took over Munitions) were included, in spite of their relative lack of experience. Out of loyalty to Asquith, however, all the Liberal members of the government that had just fallen refused to serve. This was the beginning of the fatal split in the party that would see the 'Coalition' and 'Asquith' wings run separate organizations. Lloyd George therefore had to look outside his own party. He won over the Labour Party, including its leader, Arthur Henderson, who accepted a seat in the new five-man War Cabinet. He also had Bonar Law's support, and managed to persuade Balfour to become Foreign Secretary. By the evening of 7 December, things were well in hand, but he still needed further heavyweight Unionist support.

He met with four key Unionists who had been members of the late government. They were Walter Long and the 'Three Cs' – Curzon, Cecil, and Chamberlain. Winning over these erstwhile political opponents, who were suspicious of him to varying degrees, was a challenge. (Curzon, however, had by this time already accepted a place in the War Cabinet without consulting his colleagues.) Lloyd George told the ex-ministers of the extensive promises of support he had already received, and outlined his plans for the structure and composition of the government. There was a lengthy discussion followed by broad agreement. The record of the meeting notes: 'In response to other questions, Mr. Lloyd George stated that he had no intention of asking Mr. W. Churchill or Lord Northcliffe to join the Administration.' Lloyd George also gave assurances on other controversial points. 'After these explanations, the Unionist ex-members stated their willingness to accept office under Mr. Lloyd George, and the latter expressed his intention to inform the King without delay that he was now in a position definitely to accept the duty of forming an Administration.'[51] By 7 o'clock he was Prime Minister.

Clearly, at his meeting with Long and the 'three Cs', Lloyd George did not put up much of a fight to secure Churchill's services. According to his *War Memoirs* he did make an effort with Bonar Law, presumably some hours or days earlier. Law had a 'profound distrust' of Churchill, he recalled. 'I did my best to persuade him to withdraw his objection and I urged the argument which is usually advanced on these occasions, that Mr. Churchill would be more dangerous as a critic than as a member of the Government.' Lloyd George put the question: 'Is he more dangerous when he is FOR you than when he is AGAINST you?' Law's reply was 'I would rather have him against us every time.' If this account is even roughly correct, there would certainly have been no point in making the case for Churchill to the others, who themselves would have strongly disapproved anyway. The Bonar Law–Lloyd George axis was essential. As the *War Memoirs* put it, 'I could not risk a break up of the political combination which was an essential foundation of the Government, for the sake of an immediate inclusion of Mr. Churchill in the Ministry.'[52] This was pure common sense. Yet emotions do not always conform to logic and Churchill, perhaps naturally, felt profoundly resentful at being kept from power. He wrote to Sinclair on 10 December: 'Of course I have every right to complain of LG who weakly & faithlessly bowed to Northcliffe's malevolent press. But this is not the hour when personal resentments however justified must influence conduct or colour opinion. I shall remain absolutely silent!'[53]

For a man who intended to remain silent, Churchill protested remarkably noisily, if only in private. That same day, Lloyd George invited Riddell to dine. The new premier seemed engagingly modest and full of fun. 'Referring to Winston, LG said that he had found it impossible to include him in the Government', the visitor recorded.

'The Conservatives would not have it and had LG insisted he could not have formed the Ministry.' Lloyd George asked Riddell to see Churchill and explain this, 'and tell him that he (LG) would endeavour to find some position for him, such as Chairman of the Air Board', once the Dardanelles Commission had reported.[54] This was a friendly gesture, although one cannot exclude the possibility that he feared Churchill as a potential opponent of the government and was trying to placate him. That seems to have been the way Churchill interpreted the message when Riddell delivered it the following day. He lectured Riddell about how hard done by he was. He had stuck by Lloyd George for twelve years, he said, and in so doing 'had almost invariably subordinated his views to those of LG'. He had stuck by him during the Marconi affair. 'LG had repaid him by bringing about his downfall when the Coalition was established, and now he had passed him by.' Churchill went on to hint strongly that he might indeed offer opposition to Lloyd George unless he was given a job. He told Riddell:

> I don't reproach him. His conscience will tell him what he should do. Give him that message and tell him that I cannot allow what you have said to fetter my freedom of action. I am still a member of the Liberal Party, and an event may happen at any moment which may lead me irrevocably to alter my position. I will take any position which will enable me to serve my country, but I have had enough soft soap and can only judge by actions. Had he stood by me he would have had a loyal and capable colleague whom he could trust. Instead of that he allied himself with associates who are not really in sympathy with him, and who, when he has served their purpose, will desert him without compunction. However, my only purpose is to help defeat the Hun, and I will subordinate my own feelings so that I may be able to render some assistance.[55]

When Riddell reported this to Lloyd George, the Prime Minister 'seemed somewhat distressed at Winston's attitude and said he was unreasonable'.[56] Afterwards, however, Churchill thought better of his comments. He phoned Riddell to say that 'he feared his message might have seemed minatory, but that this was not his intention.' Riddell promised to pass this on.[57] All the same, in the absence of a firm offer of a post, Churchill declined an invitation to see Lloyd

George. 'I do not want to have a chatterbox talk', he wrote to Sinclair, adding 'I hang heavy on his conscience and on his calculations.'[58] At the same time – just before Christmas – Carson, the new First Lord, vetoed the Air Board idea. Churchill was destined to spend further months in the wilderness.

The military situation that Lloyd George faced at the start of 1917 was alarming. John Grigg has made a strong argument that his predicament was as serious as that faced by Churchill in 1940, if not worse. This may be counterbalanced by Lloyd George's own belief, in 1940, that the situation was then bleaker than during his World War I premiership. But things were unquestionably dire. America was not yet a combatant and President Woodrow Wilson's attitude was uncertain. Russia was shortly to collapse into revolution. The French were wearying of the war. Stalemate persisted on the Western Front. The escalating German U-boat campaign posed a potentially catastrophic threat to British food supplies. There was also a burgeoning manpower crisis. In addition, Grigg notes, Lloyd George was in a politically more precarious position than Churchill would be during World War II. After Neville Chamberlain's death at the end of 1940, Churchill became leader of the Conservative Party that dominated his 'grand coalition' from which no major party was excluded. Lloyd George, by contrast, led only a faction of the Liberal Party, and was heavily dependent on his Tory allies. The Asquithians and the Irish remained outside his coalition, posing a potential threat. Many people at the time doubted his government could survive.[59] That it did so is a testament to the quality of his leadership.

Some of his innovations were profoundly practical. Not only was the small War Cabinet less unwieldy than its predecessor, but it also gained a Secretariat under the hyper-efficient Maurice Hankey. For the first time minutes were kept of Cabinet meetings, and these formed an essential guide to ministerial action. Although Lloyd George probably did not deserve as much personal credit as he later tried to claim for novelties such as the highly successful convoy system for shipping, he did make the brilliant appointment of Sir Joseph Maclay as Shipping Controller. There was also now a gradual move towards an efficient system of food rationing. Some of these developments had been anticipated under the previous government, and did not all take place overnight. There were further crises before the country was maximally organized for war. Yet, as Churchill later wrote, the 'vehement, contriving, resourceful, nimble-leaping Lloyd George seemed to offer a brighter hope, or at any rate a more savage effort' than the staid Asquith regime.[60] The era of 'wait and see' was at an end.

Where the Prime Minister fell down was in his relationship with his generals. Although he had hoped to avoid another failure like the Somme, he ended up putting his weight behind a new offensive, under the French general Robert Nivelle. This was launched in April 1917, and it too failed. This put Lloyd George in a weak position in relation to Haig. He felt now obliged to permit him to go ahead with his project of an assault in Flanders in July. This became known as the Third Battle of Ypres, or Passchendaele, a name that has become synonymous with doomed British soldiers floundering in the mud. In truth, the generals' tactics were not as idiotic as the 'lions led by donkeys' stereotype – which Lloyd George's own memoirs did much to encourage – suggests. If the Germans were to be turned out of France and Belgium, they had to be defeated militarily there, using the tactics that the army was gradually developing, and which finally paid off in the summer of 1918. This is by no means to say that the methods were perfect, but if there was a better alternative, Lloyd George failed to articulate and impose it. Ironically, his later description of his generals as narrow, blinkered and ignorant, that was so influential in damaging their reputations, also did much, indirectly, to harm his own. If lives had indeed been squandered pointlessly, the image of the war itself as a noble conflict was in danger. The consequent picture of 1914–18 as a time of 'mindless slaughter' contrasts today with the popular perception of 1939–45 as 'a just war'. This helps to explain why, in spite of their comparable skills as war leaders, it is now only Churchill who maintains the iconic status once also enjoyed by Lloyd George.

Writing in the 1920s, Churchill wrote of the way in which Lloyd George 'with unquailing eye' faced the 'awful contingencies' that confronted him during the early months of his premiership. He managed to live in the present, Churchill said, without taking short views. 'He surveyed the problems of each morning with an eye unobstructed by preconceived opinions, past utterances, or previous disappointments and defeats.' Moreover, 'Mr. Lloyd George in this period seemed to have a peculiar power of drawing from misfortune itself the means of future success.'[61] The tribute was well deserved, but one looks in vain for evidence of Churchill issuing such praise during the first half of 1917. The tone of his private comments was sour and at times derisive.

Riddell continued to act as a go-between, and to record the two men's criticisms of each other. He noted on 11 February: 'LG thinks that Winston meditates becoming the Disraeli of the Liberal Party and hopes to recover his position by making eloquent speeches.'[62] A few days later he found Churchill 'Very bitter.' He did not intend, he said, 'to be put off with mealy mouthed promises'. He 'reserved full liberty of action'.[63] Perhaps in part as a means of appeasing Churchill, Lloyd George performed a favour by lending him a draft copy of the Dardanelles report, which was debated in the Commons in March. The report did not quite exonerate Churchill, but he came out of it considerably better than Asquith and Kitchener did. In advance of the debate he was again contemplating office, but, as he told C. P. Scott, 'only in one of the chief posts'.[64]

A couple of weeks later Churchill wrote to Wilfrid Scawen Blunt. The letter, which Blunt copied into his diary, has hitherto remained unpublished, but it offers an important insight into Churchill's mindset at this time. He wrote: 'I see all the politicians now (except those stupid Tories) and I am on quite good terms with both old Fogies and the Artful Dodger'. Blunt interpreted 'the Artful Dodger' to be Lloyd George, and he was surely correct. The 'old Fogies' may have been Asquithites. Churchill went on to say that, on the whole, he had benefited from the Dardanelles report. There followed a rather peculiar passage, in which he told Blunt (who opposed the war):

> Very much worse times are coming upon us. God has become a convert to your views and is bent on the destruction of mankind (except the niggers). That is why he would not let me take Constantinople and so unite the Balkan States against our enemies ... Deeper and deeper is Christendom to sink in the abyss of slaughter, ruin and famine, and no one can be sure of survival or of the endurance of any institution.[65]

Perhaps the remarks about God were intended ironically, although, given the war situation, a sense of impending doom was not unnatural. Blunt's diary for 29 April gives further new evidence of Churchill's attitude to Lloyd George:

Of his personal prospects he spoke hopefully but he should have to wait his opportunity. Lloyd George had been his intimate friend for years and would have given him a place in his new Government, but Winston would not serve in what was practically a Tory Cabinet and preferred to wait. He was amused at my calling George a miserable little dog . . .[66]

The idea that Churchill had stood out of his own accord was a blatant untruth, and only the fact that Blunt was far from the centre of political events allowed him to get away with it. He was of course intriguing hard to get back in.

His difficulty was that he needed to criticize the government enough to make sure that Lloyd George would want to neutralize him by offering him a job. Yet, at the same time, he did not want to overdo it and thus alienate the Prime Minister. His defence of the radical periodical *The Nation* showed him in the guise of reasonably friendly critic. The paper had been banned from circulation abroad because of articles giving depressing facts about the military situation. When Lloyd George justified the restriction on the grounds that the articles would encourage the Germans, Churchill raised cheers and laughter by recalling 'the contempt, the robust and manly contempt, with which he used to treat that argument when it was used about encouraging the Boers.'[67] When he dined with H. W. Massingham, editor of *The Nation*, the following week, he appeared to be 'immensely pleased' about an article published in the paper poking fun at Lloyd George. The export ban was finally rescinded in October.[68]

Churchill still seemed politically cut off, in spite of his effectiveness in the Commons. At the end of April he was present when Lloyd George received the freedom of the City of London at the Guildhall. Frances Stevenson thought he looked 'very sulky', and, when he was asked what he thought of the Prime Minister's speech, he merely said 'Events will show.'[69] On 3 May he talked at length with C. P. Scott. 'His tone was rather bitter in speaking of Lloyd George whom he had evidently come to consider as his destined antagonist.' However, when Scott suggested to him that he should join the government, he said that 'he had had no personal quarrel with Lloyd George and was evidently quite ready for that solution.' Scott noted Churchill's 'hungry look . . . he evidently feels his political isolation bitterly'.[70]

By this time Lloyd George was actively considering bringing

Churchill in to the government in some capacity. The political obstacles were considerable, though. Churchill helped Lloyd George prepare the ground. His cousin, Freddie Guest, was now Chief Whip for the Coalition Liberals. Churchill suggested to Guest that, in order to head off the increasing parliamentary discontent about the conduct of the war, the Prime Minister should call a special Secret Session of the House of Commons. This plan, which was accepted, had a twofold advantage. Not only would it help Lloyd George deal with his critics, but it would also give a showcase for Churchill's own rhetorical skills, and help pave the way for his return.

This much of the story is well known. However, a document written by Edwin Montagu on 10 May, a few hours before the Secret Session, casts new light on Churchill's manoeuvrings.[71] Out of loyalty to Asquith, Montagu had refused to join the new government in December, but had now decided he did want to serve after all. (Among the Conservatives, he was almost as controversial a figure as Churchill.) He now wrote of how Guest had asked to see him a few days beforehand. 'Much to my amusement he immediately began to explain to me what a brilliant, self-sacrificing, self-effacing, far-seeing, courageous statesman Winston was, and he told me that he knew that Winston proposed at the Secret Session to explain to the House the terrible condition the country was in, the critical state of the war, and end up by urging upon the Prime Minister the terrible import-ance of a reunion of all parties and the inclusion of Asquith in his Cabinet.' Montagu was reminded of Churchill's disastrous speech the previous year advocating the recall of Fisher, and expressed grave doubts. He soon heard that when Guest raised the idea of bringing Asquith back, Lloyd George received it unfavourably. Churchill, however, subsequently rehearsed a speech on these lines to Montagu on the terrace of the Commons. Montagu's memorandum continues: 'He [Churchill] is a man whom, with all his defects, I know George would be glad to have with him, and I tried my best to hint to him that what he required seemed to me doubtful of achievement . . . It immediately seemed to me to be obvious that Winston's efforts so far as Asquith is concerned would be as unwelcome to Asquith as they were to George.' Montagu thought that Churchill would 'make himself quite impossible' at the Secret Session, 'and George will begin to think his Government requires no alteration'.[72]

Churchill's own later recollection was that he had sent Lloyd

George, via Guest, a précis of what he was planning to say.[73] Although this claim cannot be verified directly, it is broadly compatible with Montagu's testimony. Whether the key ideas of the speech were conveyed in a document, or orally via Guest, it seems clear that there was some process of consultation; one might say collusion. Churchill surely heard from Guest of the Prime Minister's disapproval, and thus altered his plans, avoiding another embarrassing flop. Asquith, who had not sought the Secret Session himself, 'maintained a neutral and a passive attitude in regard to it'. It was therefore Churchill who opened the debate. He described the challenging circumstances Britain faced. The Russian armies had collapsed, and although the Americans had recently entered the war, it would be some time before their forces were marshalled in strength in France. He thus implored Lloyd George to throw his personal weight against a renewed offensive in the West. 'Master the U-Boat attack', he urged. 'Bring over the American millions. And meanwhile maintain an active defensive on the Western Front, so as to economize French and British lives, and so as to train, increase and perfect our armies and our methods for a decisive effort in a later year.'[74]

No official record was kept of the Secret Session, but Churchill gave the gist of Lloyd George's reply in his memoirs. 'He accepted in principle my general statement about the main factors. He expressed a great measure of agreement with the argument I had used. But he declined to commit himself against a renewed offensive.'[75] John Simon – now on the backbenches – put a slightly different slant on things in his diary account:

> Lloyd George's argument was directly opposed to Winston's. If we waited to strike until 1918, what would the Germans do in the mean time? Would they not turn on Russia, which Winston had described as quite unable to resist her, and rapidly accomplish such tremendous results on the Eastern Front as would drive Russia to peace? The continuance of our offensive on the West was the way that we saved Russia from this pressure now.

Simon added: 'Winston to my mind demonstrated that we could not win this year, and Lloyd George demonstrated that we must go on bleeding at every pore until next.'[76] The debate strengthened both men's positions considerably. Lloyd George had benefited from being tipped off as to the general line Churchill was going to take, just as

Churchill had successfully gauged Lloyd George's attitude by using Guest as a conduit. The idea of advocating Asquith's return to office had been quietly dropped. After the Secret Session Montagu scribbled: 'W.S.C. made a wonderfully good speech admirably answered by L.G. no mention of this plan Ha ha!'[77]

Churchill recalled that after the debate he ran into Lloyd George behind the Speaker's chair. Satisfied at the outcome, the Prime Minister assured him 'of his determination to have me at this side. From that day, although holding no office, I became to a large extent his colleague.' He claimed that Lloyd George repeatedly discussed with him 'every aspect of the war and many of his secret hopes and fears'.[78] Contemporary evidence, however, suggests that, even though the relationship did now enter a new and closer phase, elements of tension remained. Frances Stevenson's diary for 19 May noted that Lloyd George was contemplating a reconstruction of the government. 'He says he wants someone in who will cheer him up and help & encourage him', Stevenson wrote, adding, 'I think D. is thinking of getting Winston in in some capacity.' Moreover, 'He has an intense admiration for his cleverness, & at any rate he is energetic and forceful.' But she did not know if Lloyd George's intention was serious, as he realized, she said, Churchill's limitations and thought him consumed by conceit. 'He has spoilt himself by reading Napoleon', the Prime Minister commented.[79] Churchill, for his part, continued to speak bitterly of Lloyd George, who, he told Riddell, had fettered his freedom of action 'by illusory promises of office'. Although he realized the Prime Minister was constrained by the Conservatives, 'Winston remarked that fate might ordain that LG and he would be opposed in a life-long struggle.' He also spoke of how, when he was going to fight a government, he made himself 'hate' it. 'I refrain however from assailing the private lives of individuals', Churchill added – which may just possibly have been a veiled hint that although he knew of Lloyd George's sexual indiscretions he would not use them against him.[80] And as was now his habit, Churchill alternated statements of willingness to work with Lloyd George with vague portents of future opposition to him, were his desire for office not to be accommodated.

Even making allowances for Churchill's understandable frustration, his was an ungrateful attitude, although, if it increased Lloyd George's fear of him, it may have done him some good. The Prime

Minister, in spite of his slighting, although entirely comprehensible, remarks about Churchill's self-absorption, was working hard to overcome the barriers to his inclusion in the government. 'For days I discussed with one or other of my colleagues Churchill, his gifts, his shortcomings, his mistakes, especially the latter,' he recollected. 'It was interesting to observe in a concentrated form every phase of the distrust and trepidation with which mediocrity views genius at close quarters.'[81] (This remark in his memoirs was considerably more flattering to Churchill than those he was accustomed to make in private at the time. It doubtless reflected in part Lloyd George's own view of why he himself was so widely distrusted.) Some ministers 'felt stronger about Churchill than about the Kaiser', he recalled.[82] Yet he now canvassed the idea that Churchill should be appointed, either to the Air Board or to the Ministry of Munitions. Protests poured in, to Bonar Law as well as Lloyd George, from, among others, Lord Curzon (Lord President of the Council), Walter Long (Colonial Secretary), Lord Derby (War Secretary), Sir George Younger (Chairman of the Conservative Party) and Lord Cowdray (the Air Board's incumbent Chairman). Cowdray warned that Churchill, if appointed, might make a bid for the premiership. It should be added, though, that opinion was not unanimously hostile to Churchill: the press baron Lord Rothermere and the South African statesman J. C. Smuts were influential supporters of the idea of giving him a post.

In mid-June Churchill turned down a tentative proposal from Lloyd George that he return to the Duchy of Lancaster. At the end of the month the two men travelled to Dundee, where Lloyd George received the freedom of the city and Churchill made a speech in his praise. By mid-July Lloyd George at last felt able to act. He had recently dispatched Northcliffe, who might have raised a fuss, on a government mission to the USA. He offered Churchill a choice of Air or Munitions. Churchill chose the latter, and the announcement was published in the press two days later, on 18 July.[83] In another controversial move, Montagu also joined the government, as Secretary of State for India. Churchill was not, however, to be in the War Cabinet.

The news of Churchill's appointment was unwelcome to Bonar Law, who had not been consulted. Lloyd George did not even tell him himself, but deputed Beaverbrook to do it, the day before the story appeared in the papers. Law, in his indignation, let his pipe go out. 'Lloyd George's throne will shake', he said.[84] Yet although Conservative MPs sent a deputation to their leader, Law stood by the Prime Minister's right to make the appointment he chose. Similarly, Walter Long, who first learned of the appointment from the press, protested strongly to Lloyd George. And he wrote to a friend: 'People say W.C. knows some dark secret in P.M.'s past & this is the price of silence!'[85] But Long did not resign. Austen Chamberlain thought Long was right to stay on, telling him: 'Of Winston I can only say that I hope the P.M. is right in thinking that he has taken to heart his error & that he will not use his new position to meddle with the armies or with war policy.'[86] The attitude of senior Conservatives was therefore one of disgruntled acceptance, hence the fulminations of backbench Tories and of the right-wing press came to naught. The party was 'sullen and annoyed' rather than actively rebellious.[87] When Lloyd George left for France a few days after the appointment Churchill ventured a joke. 'Don't get torpedoed; for if I am left alone your colleagues will eat me,' he wrote.[88]

Why had Lloyd George taken the action he did? His son Richard later wrote that, just after the appointment was made, the Prime Minister and the new Minister of Munitions dined together at 10 Downing Street. After the meal Lloyd George took Churchill into another room and showed him a framed *Daily Express* placard from the time of the Marconi affair. It said: 'Churchill defends Lloyd George'. The implication was that Churchill's new job was a reward for previous personal loyalty. 'It must have been a great moment for the two battle-scarred friends', the younger Lloyd George wrote.[89] Perhaps the touching scene in question did take place. But, however convenient and enjoyable it might have been for both men to present their relationship in such romantic terms, the picture painted is unconvincing. As has been seen, Churchill had previously tried to play the Marconi card to little avail. And although Lloyd George had now genuinely gone out on a limb, the idea that he would have taken such risks with his government out of sentiment is unrealistic. The 'blackmail' theory mentioned by Long (although not apparently taken very seriously even by him) does not hold water either. Even assuming that by now he had guessed the nature of the Prime Minister's relationship with Frances Stevenson, and was sufficiently unscrupulous to make use of the knowledge, which seems doubtful, the weapon was unusable. To have brought down Lloyd George would have been to destroy the only person at all likely to bring him back to office.

This is not to say that cynical explanations should be eschewed altogether. H. A. Gwynne, editor of the *Morning Post*, was one of those who thought Churchill's appointment 'an appalling disaster', so much so that he was tempted to stand against him at the inevitable by-election at Dundee, which Churchill won handsomely. At first Gwynne thought Lloyd George's decision unaccountable. But he soon reflected that the 'main object of his appointment of Winston was to deprive the Asquithian lot of the advantages of a man of energy and authority.'[90] A few months later the Conservative junior minister William Bridgeman noted that the Prime Minister's 'reception of Winston Churchill into his Govt. looked as if he were afraid of losing hold of all his old Liberal colleagues & being absorbed by us'.[91] Beaverbrook's retrospective view was that Lloyd George had to choose 'between the danger of Conservative resistance over Churchill and the greater hazard of the rising forces of a powerful opposition'.[92] These comments, although speculative, all contain much truth. Yet, if Lloyd George was guided principally by realpolitik, his calculations included a genuine desire to benefit from Churchill's obvious talents. The human element was part of the calculation. Lloyd George's attitude was well captured by Lord Esher in a letter to Douglas Haig, written before the appointment was made. Churchill's temperament, Esher wrote, 'is of wax and quicksilver, and this strange toy amuses and fascinates L George, who likes and fears him'.[93] In later years Lloyd George felt occasional pangs of regret for the fact that he had, in effect, rescued Churchill's career. In early 1941 the Labour MP Emanuel Shinwell observed that 'Lloyd George is very severe about Winston: said he picked him out of the gutter, but wished now he had left him there.'[94]

Churchill's return did much to improve his state of mind, and to assuage his bitterness at Lloyd George. Clementine told Wilfrid Scawen Blunt that at first she had opposed the move because she disliked Lloyd George. 'But she saw now that Winston had been right. He is quite happy in his return to power'.[95] She told C. P. Scott that her husband 'no longer felt any sense of grievance against Lloyd George for having left him out in the cold so long. He had only discovered on now entering the Ministry how bitter had been the opposition to him and he felt that Lloyd George had done a courageous thing in braving it.' (Churchill himself added the comment that, all the same, the Prime Minister had benefited from asserting himself in doing so.)[96] At the same time, the fact that Lloyd George was now Churchill's boss put their relationship on a more formal footing than previously. Before, Churchill wrote 'My dear David'; now he wrote 'My dear Prime Minister'.

Lloyd George, had remarked before the war that he did not think it right for a Prime Minister to have one of his ministers as his chief friend. To do so would create jealousy, he believed, 'and may often occasion misapprehension' when the premier took a line known to be that of his friend but opposed by other colleagues.[97] The Earl of Swinton, who served in governments headed by both Lloyd George and Churchill, wrote that the former was the harder-hearted of the two, having less compunction and fewer regrets when he had to dismiss ministers. Moreover, 'Winston was a close friend of many of his colleagues, I do not think Lloyd George was; he worked well with many and was always agreeable and charming, but I think few of them were really close friends.'[98] All the same, Lloyd George quickly took Churchill into his confidence on military matters. Many people thought he had the ear of the Prime Minister, although it may be noted that access does not always lead to influence.

Churchill was not, of course, an easy man to have as a subordinate. Continuing Tory suspicions of him contributed to the difficulties. Soon after his appointment both Lord Derby and Sir Eric Geddes (First Lord of the Admiralty) concluded, on the basis of a few comments he made off-the-cuff, that he was trying to interfere with the work of their respective departments. They were probably being oversensitive, although given Churchill's track record their reaction is understandable. Lloyd George's first reaction was to back Churchill strongly. Hankey, however, told Lloyd George and Churchill that they must 'let the clutch in gently' if they wanted to avoid Geddes's resignation. 'I think they were rather annoyed', he noted.[99] But his advice was taken. In order to calm Geddes down the Prime Minister offered him assurances that he had told Churchill not to meddle.

Churchill initially faced hostility from Ministry of Munitions civil servants, but, at his first meeting with officials, he won them over by joking about his own unpopularity. This was a sign that he had learnt at least a degree of humility as a consequence of his earlier fall from grace. Walter Layton, one of the Ministry's most important statisticians, recalled in his unpublished autobiography:

> Lloyd George's flair and drive had brought the colossal Ministry of Munitions to life, and had for the first time awakened and harnessed Britain's industrial strength to an all-out war effort. Winston Churchill's special contribution was to bring discipline and organisation to the Ministry. Of course Winston had his fire as well . . . But while Ll.G.'s personality had inspired individuals to throw the rule book overboard in the quest for results, Winston harnessed men into a disciplined team which he then drove.

Churchill quickly launched an internal reorganization. He established a Munitions Council, modelled on similar lines to the Board of the Admiralty and the Army Council. 'Winston's Council was a great improvement on the chaotic improvisation of Lloyd George', Layton believed.[100]

Churchill thus carried out his departmental role effectively. But he was clearly rather more in his element when, at the end of October, the Prime Minister summoned him to discuss the Italian military collapse, or when, as he did with considerable – and arguably unnecessary – frequency, he found reasons to travel to France. He put some of his surplus energy into missives to Lloyd George, not all of which he sent. Some were complaints, others contained unsolicited strategic advice. He received few replies, although, as Roy Jenkins points out, this does not necessarily mean the letters had no effect.[101]

One key domestic issue, wage settlements for munitions workers, was a source of friction over the winter, but on the big questions the two men were not far apart. After Churchill visited the front in September Haig noted in his diary that 'Winston admitted that Lloyd George and he were doubtful about being able to beat the Germans on the Western front.' Haig also wrote: 'I have no doubt that Winston means to do his utmost (as Minister of Munitions) to provide the Army with all it requires, but at the same time he can hardly help meddling in the larger questions of strategy and tactics; for the solution of the latter he has had no real training, and his agile mind is a danger because he can persuade Lloyd George to adopt and carry out the most idiotic policy.'[102] As the Passchendaele offensive ground to a halt in November the two men may have felt their doubts over strategy were vindicated, although Lloyd George's implied criticisms of his generals in public speeches did harm rather than good. In February 1918 the Unionist War Committee – representative of Tory MPs – passed resolutions 'warmly condemning the attacks on the generals, and forbidding L.G. to take Winston into the War Cabinet'. There is no evidence Lloyd George had actually intended to do so, but he resented the interference. The Marquess of Salisbury, who had taken the resolutions to him, 'gently pointed out to L.G. that he owed his position to Unionist support'.[103] The Prime Minister did, however, manage to assert his authority over the army a few days later when he removed William Robertson as CIGS, although this caused further controversy.

On 20 March 1918 Churchill was once more in France, staying at the front-line HQ of General Henry Tudor. An attack was expected imminently. On the morning of the 21st he awoke at a few minutes past four o'clock. 'Suddenly, after what seemed about half an hour, the silence was broken by six or seven very loud and very heavy explosions several miles away', he later recalled. 'And then, exactly as a pianist runs his hands across the keyboard from treble to bass, there rose in less than one minute the most tremendous cannonade I shall ever hear.'[104] This was the start of the devastating Ludendorff offensive, which threatened disaster to the Allies. Within a few days Churchill was back in London, in conclave with Lloyd George and others, as bad news poured in from the front. This was Lloyd George's finest hour. Swinton (who at this time was known as Philip Lloyd-Greame, and held an administrative position at the War Office) recollected:

> I was with Lloyd George every day when the Germans broke through in March 1918 and nearly separated the British and French armies. I was with Churchill for hours on the first night of Dunkirk. Both were alike – courageous, imperturbable, unshakeable and never doubting victory, however hopeless the odds seemed. I remember both using almost the same language, expressing not just the belief but the certainty that we should win through.[105]

Maurice Hankey's diary for 24 March records him being summoned to Downing Street at 6.30 p.m. Finding that Lloyd George had gone to dinner with Churchill, he pursued them to them to the latter's house in Eccleston Square, and found General Sir Henry Wilson, the new CIGS, there also. 'The news was about as bad as it could be, for the right of the IIIrd army had been stove in, and a breach made between it and the Vth army . . . There was nothing to be done, but Churchill, supported by Wilson, was heavily bombarding the P.M. with demands for a "levée en masse".'[106] Churchill not only wanted to broaden the age range for conscription (as agreed by the Cabinet the next day) but also to extend it to Ireland, which had previously been excluded. In so doing, he made common cause with the Conservatives, but although Irish conscription was eventually agreed and made it to the statute book, it was never enforced. Both he and the Prime Minister appreciated that this unpalatable measure needed to be coupled with a new Home Rule initiative, but this too proved a dead letter. In the meantime, as the Germans continued to make progress, Lloyd George sent him again to France.

He crossed the Channel on the 28th. The initial intention had been for him to see General Foch, the French commander who had just been appointed 'co-ordinator' of the Allied armies in the West and who was determined to make a stand. General Wilson, when he heard of this plan, thought it improper: Churchill should talk to Georges Clemenceau, the Prime Minister, rather than direct to a soldier. Churchill, at the Ritz, thus received a telephone message from Lloyd George 'to stick to Paris and not go directing strategy at French HQ'. Leo Amery, the man who gave Churchill the message, recorded this in his diary. Later he added in the margin: 'Needless to say he paid no attention & careered about the front the whole time.'[107] Churchill kept Lloyd George in close touch with his doings by phone and by telegram. He reported on the progress of the battle, and on his meetings with Clemenceau (known as 'the Tiger') whom he found to be a tower of strength. He also helped coordinate British and French pressure on the Americans to send help in the form of 120,000 infantrymen a month.

On 1 April Churchill wired Lloyd George telling him of Clemenceau's desire to meet him. Two days later the Prime Minister arrived and took part in an Allied conference at Beauvais. This meeting agreed new powers for Foch – Lloyd George subsequently won the British Cabinet's backing for the Frenchman's appointment as Commander-in-Chief of the Allied forces. He later viewed this new 'unity of command' as one of the crucial steps on the road to victory. After the conference Churchill joined the British contingent, which returned to England on a 'P' boat, a new type of craft designed to hunt submarines. Within a few days the German offensive ran out of steam. It had been a stunning tactical success, but had not achieved its strategic aim of dividing the British and French armies. Lloyd George's decision to send Churchill to France during the crucial days suggested a high level of confidence in him. Moreover, in retrospect he praised Churchill's continuing efforts on munitions at this crucial time. 'We were overwhelmed in the great attack of the 21st March, and we lost a very considerable number of guns, machine guns, ammunition and all kinds of supplies', he said in 1936. 'It was entirely due to the tremendous energy of Mr. Winston Churchill that not only did we make up the deficiency, but that in a very short time the Army was better equipped than it was before that disaster took place.'[108]

Perhaps buoyed up by the signs of Lloyd George's trust in him, Churchill, after his return, took the opportunity to offer the Prime Minister some political advice. He advocated replacing the 'narrow and unrepresentative' War Cabinet system with a more inclusive body.[109] He objected to the fact that, as things stood, ministers outside (such as himself) were called in for discussion of specific issues, but did not have true collective responsibility for government policy as a whole. He argued that this would lead to political weakness in the face of controversial issues and, in mid-April, drafted a letter to Lloyd George on these lines. This remained unsent, but at the start of May the two men discussed the question. It is not known precisely what was said, but the next day Churchill wrote to clarify his position. He would not, he said, ever 'accept political responsibility without recognised regular power.' He did not seek this power, although he thought the existing system unsound, and was content as long as the war lasted to serve 'in an administrative capacity, without troubling myself about political or party combinations, & to offer you personally in your intense labours for the national safety every aid & encouragement that a sincere friend can give'.[110] In the middle of the month, after a further talk, he sent another letter giving detailed advice and disclaiming personal ambition. He would 'be very glad to facilitate the creation of a political Cabinet by remaining exactly as I am'.[111] Lloyd George ignored his suggestions, thus laying bare the reality of the two men's relations. Churchill was highly useful to the Prime

Minister in a subordinate capacity and even for important special missions, but he was not at this stage a trusted confidant in political matters. His protestations of disinterested friendship did not appear convincing. And his attempts to attract Lloyd George's attention merely highlighted, when his counsel was rejected, Churchill's ongoing dependence on his boss's patronage.

Lloyd George himself was on the up. During the so-called 'Maurice debate' 9 May Asquith bungled an attack on him over the allegation, made in the press by General Sir Frederick Maurice, that the government had misled the House about the number of troops in France during the late German offensive. Asquith's defeat widened the Liberal divisions and strengthened Lloyd George, who defended himself in a highly skilful speech, albeit through a rather selective use of figures. There did not seem much prospect of an early conclusion to the war although a successful allied counter-offensive launched in July in fact marked the beginning of the end. Churchill continued to bombard the Prime Minister with advice. For example, he objected to the War Cabinet's announcement (made in response to a request by the Vatican) that there would be no air attacks on Germany on Corpus Christi day. He wrote: 'Do put your foot down on this. It is *abject*.'[112]

Maintaining the war effort on the home front was not always easy. When unofficial strikes broke out among engineering workers in Coventry, Birmingham and Manchester Churchill suggested that the strikers should be threatened with conscription. With the concurrence of the War Cabinet, Lloyd George gave an ultimatum, and the workers abandoned their action.[113] Churchill, for his part, was not always willing to make the personal sacrifices he enjoined on others. When he and Clementine visited Wilfrid Scawen Blunt in May he 'chuckled over his abuse of Ministerial privilege of using petrol for his motor excursion here and how he had evaded the pressure of the War Agricultural Committee to plough up his land at Lullenden', his house in Sussex.[114] Lloyd George's personal moral lapses tended to be on a grander scale than this, but he was not nearly as addicted to luxury as Churchill was, and his wartime household was quite frugal.

The Ministry of Munitions faced continuing manpower problems. The War Office wanted to release significant numbers of men from the factories to the army. Churchill complained that this was damaging output, particularly of tanks. He and Lloyd George had both played important parts in the development of these highly important weapons, thus demonstrating their joint interest in promoting 'modern' – and deadly – mechanical warfare. The War Cabinet supported Lord Milner, who had replaced Derby as Secretary of State for War. On 22 July, Churchill wrote to Lloyd George:

Questions wh the Prime Minister's conscience shd be asking him:-

1. Am I not one of the original founders of Tanks?
2. What am I doing to push them forward now?
3. Am I doing enough?
4. Can I not do more with my great power?
5. Are they going to be frittered away in more incidental fighting next year 1919 – as in every other year?
6. Have I not still got time to get a real move on?[115]

This was bold, even cheeky. It did not get a reply. However, even if it did not get Churchill what he wanted, it shows him confident in his relationship with the Prime Minister. Lloyd George was no stickler for formality, but he might not have tolerated this kind of approach from anyone else. To some extent he indulged Churchill, even if he did not always take him seriously.

He did, however, know how to manage him and others, as an earlier episode, also relating to tanks, appears to illustrate. The story was told in 1942 by Sir Albert Stern, who had been a key figure in the development of mechanical warfare. He told Basil Liddell Hart, the military historian, how in October 1917 the Army Council had cut the tank-building programme radically. According to a note made by Liddell Hart, Stern went at once to Churchill to get him to take action. 'To his surprise, Winston showed reluctance to do so saying that he could not go against professional opinion, and that he had been "out in the wilderness" for over two years as the price of opposing professional opinion, and was not inclined to court such a risk again. Stern argued with him that as the foster-parent of the tank he surely could not stand aside while the infant was being suffocated, and that, if such was his attitude, he was a "dishonest politician".' The two then had a blazing row, and Churchill sacked Stern. Stern, though, went to Lloyd George and got him to overturn the Army

Council's decision. 'At the same time, L.-G. appealed to him not to break with Winston and brought about a reconciliation', saying that both men were too important to be spared. After the war, when Stern wrote his memoirs, Lloyd George summoned him 'and said that he understood that the book was damaging to Winston, and that he, L-G., could not afford to see such an effect, since Winston was one of the few strong members of his Government, and the situation of the country was very difficult.' Accordingly, passages that reflected badly on Churchill were excised.[116]

Those post-war problems were still some way off, but, in the autumn of 1918, the Prime Minister started to contemplate calling a general election, even before hostilities had ended. Churchill told Derby in September 'that Lloyd George is really quite determined about the Election and thinks he will have an enormous majority'.[117] The accelerating German military collapse further heightened the need to think about the post-war future. Discussions on the formation of a reconstructed government on coalition lines with the inclusion of Asquith failed in September. Failure to reunify the party increased the importance to Lloyd George of prominent Coalition Liberals like Churchill and Montagu. Accordingly, he lunched with both men on 6 November, a few days before the Armistice. Montagu afterwards wrote a long memorandum describing what happened. 'It became obvious that the Prime Minister was anxious to find out whether he could rely on our support', he recorded; 'the Prime Minister both from personal affection and, rightly, from the importance he attached to him, determined to devote his fishing expedition in the main to landing Winston Churchill'. The discussion and its aftermath proved a fascinating illustration of the way both men used the rhetoric of friendship to secure political objects. According to Montagu:

Winston began sulky, morose and unforthcoming. The Prime Minister put out all his weapons. He addressed him with affection as 'Old man'. He reminded him of their old campaigns. He said that so well did he know him that he knew before he said anything that there was something about which he was unhappy. (This showed great perspicacity on the part of the Prime Minister, partly because Winston's face had all along been as sullen as you could possibly see it, and partly because for the last six months to my knowledge Winston has been speaking, if not open treason, open disgruntlement, which must have reached the Prime Minister's ears.)

Churchill then launched into an analysis of whether or not a general election should be held, in the end advising that it should. 'Finally, in a torrent of turgid eloquence, Winston exposed his hand.' He said that never would he allow any personal consideration to weigh with him. He was prepared to serve the state in any capacity, including opposition. Although opposition to Lloyd George would be 'very distasteful', he would 'accept it cheerfully if it were forced upon him'. And then, Montagu wrote, he began 'his usual arguments' against the War Cabinet system, 'the degradation of being a Minister without responsibility for policy, and so on'. Lloyd George cheerfully waved these arguments aside. The existing set-up, he said, would come to an end with the war. He had determined on a Cabinet of between ten and twelve, containing all the important ministers. Montagu noted the effect on Churchill: 'The sullen look disappeared, smiles wreathed the hungry face, the fish was landed.'

Montagu talked further with Churchill, who was 'in the seventh heaven of delight', after Prime Minister left. Mischievously he reminded him of what he, Churchill, had said previously, i.e. that he would stick with Lloyd George only for the duration of the war, and thereafter 'revert to his old friends'. 'I only did this for my own amusement', Montagu wrote; 'he has a new theory now, that once he joined Lloyd George, he joined him for ever, that he had always been Lloyd George's man and that he owed nothing to anybody else'. Churchill thus used the myth that the friendship had been constant and unbroken as a justification for his essentially opportunistic stand. That evening he and Montagu dined with Lloyd George, this time with other Liberal coalitionists present, and a post-war programme was discussed. Montagu noted that the Prime Minister 'said at one moment rather sharply to Winston, but intending it for all of us, that in the course of a few days he was entitled to know who were going with him and who were not'.[118] According to Christopher Addison, 'Churchill made some difficulties and lectured the community generally, as usual'. However, it was quite obvious 'that as he thought there would be a place for himself' in the Cabinet 'he would cooperate in his own way'.[119]

Churchill now pushed his luck a bit too far. Although he was ecstatic at the prospect of a Cabinet post, this had not been definitely offered, as Montagu rather cruelly pointed out to him after the lunch on 6 November. Lloyd George had said that the Cabinet would be expanded – but had not said who would be in it. Churchill therefore sent him a letter the next day. After some opening pleasantries, he wrote: 'It is not possible for me however to take the very serious & far-reaching political decision you have suggested to me without knowing definitely the character & main composition of the new Govt you propose to form for the period of reconstruction.' He added: 'I feel I cannot choose my own course without knowing who yr chief colleagues wd be.' He concluded by saying he did not wish to embarrass Lloyd George, and that if need be he would quit his government without complaint, feelings of friendship towards him intact.[120] But the purpose of the letter was almost impertinently transparent.

Lloyd George had a great talent for producing synthetic anger, so it is hard to gauge, merely from his reply, exactly how he felt. All the same, what he wrote was so vitriolic that Bonar Law – who presumably now saw the benefits of keeping Churchill in the government – toned it down before it was sent. The Prime Minister began by saying that, after the evening conversation at which agreement had been reached on policy, Churchill's letter 'came upon me as an unpleasant surprise. Frankly it perplexes me.' At this point, in the first draft, there followed a devastating pair of sentences. 'You will one day discover that the state of mind revealed in that letter is the reason why you do not win trust even where you command admiration. In every line of it national interests are completely overshadowed by towering personal concern.' These comments did not make it into the final version, which continued, nonetheless, in an almost equally harsh vein. Lloyd George's letter suggested 'that you contemplate the possibility of leaving the Government, and you give no reason for it except an apparent dissatisfaction with your personal prospects'. The problems of reconstruction would be as great as those of the war, Lloyd George continued. 'If you decide to desert me just as I am entering upon this great national task – although you have been good enough repeatedly to assure me that no one else could in your judgement do it as well – the responsibility must be yours.' Moreover, the choice of the government must be left to the Prime Minister, and Churchill's demand to know how it would be constituted was unprecedented. If he did not trust Lloyd George, he could look elsewhere for leadership. 'I should deeply and sincerely regret if anything came to sever a political and personal friendship which has now extended over fourteen years, but this is no time for half-hearted support.'[121]

To Lloyd George's reprimand, which was substantially deserved, Churchill wrote a somewhat wheedling response. 'You have certainly misconceived the spirit in wh my letter was written', he claimed. He did however make it clear that once the war and the immediate reconstruction period were over, 'I shd not feel able to take a part in political responsibilities no matter how interesting or important the office I held without a seat at the council table at wh we have sat together for so many years.'[122] This brought the crisis in relations to an end. If Lloyd George really had been genuinely upset – rather than merely wanting to put his argument on paper in case Churchill should choose to resign – he got over it soon enough. On 10 November he invited him to a special meeting of the War Cabinet to consider Germany's imminent capitulation. The peace came into effect at 11 a.m. the following day. After they heard the bells ring out, Churchill and his wife decided to go and offer their congratulations to Lloyd George. 'But no sooner had we entered our car than twenty people mounted upon it, and in the midst of a wildly cheering multitude we were impelled slowly forward through Whitehall.'[123]

That night, Churchill dined at Downing Street with Lloyd George, F. E. Smith and General Wilson. In his memoirs he recalled that they discussed the German fighting spirit, the future of Europe, and the spread of Bolshevism. He proposed, he said, that Britain should rush ships loaded with provisions to the starving Germans, a project which the Prime Minister favoured.[124] As far as they went, his recollections were probably accurate, but Wilson's diary for that day puts a different complexion on things. 'We discussed many things but principally the coming General Election! LG wants to shoot the Kaiser. FE agrees. Winston does not'.[125]

The discrepancy between the two accounts illustrates the selectivity of memory. This phenomenon had been much in evidence in the relationship between Lloyd George and Churchill during the tumultuous wartime years. The latter's end-of-war declaration 'that he had always been Lloyd George's man', overlooking his 1915 comment that 'Between me & Ll G tout est fini', is a key example. But Lloyd George himself was not immune. In the draft of his 8 November letter the PM contrasted his own treatment of Churchill with that meted out by Asquith, who had appointed him to the Duchy of Lancaster. 'I have never inflicted that insult upon you.'[126] This last phrase was removed from the letter as sent at Bonar Law's instigation – for in fact Lloyd George had offered Churchill that very post in the summer of 1917. When Churchill protested his undying friendship, or when Lloyd George resurrected the memory of the 'old campaigns', they were perpetuating a myth of permanent mutual loyalty that, as we have seen, had little foundation in reality. (In fairness, it should also be noted that their mutual criticism may at times have been as much about getting a point of view on record as about genuine personal resentment.) They constructed this myth, building up the reputation of their relationship, in large part for reasons of political convenience. This does not mean they were cynics. They appear to have meant what they said at the point when they said it, even when it was apparently accompanied by sudden amnesia regarding their own recent comments. Therefore, although the myth of the relationship cannot be accepted at face value, we need to be aware that the making of the myth was itself part of the relationship. The ongoing pattern of recrimination and reconciliation required, during each phase, a kind of denial of what had gone before. The myth was emotionally as well as politically useful. When they were getting on well, it helped them to erase the genuine bitterness of their previous disagreements. When they were getting on badly, the story of continuous devotion now betrayed by the other provided a grievance that justified current hostility. It was a scenario that would be played out time and again during the tense and troubled years of Lloyd George's post-war premiership.

Chapter Six

MASTER AND SERVANT

IN THE LATE 1920s, when Churchill was writing *The World Crisis*, his history-cum-memoir of the Great War, he arrived at some questions about events that he believed Lloyd George alone could answer. At this time Churchill was Chancellor of the Exchequer and Lloyd George was out of office, and the two were not as close as they had been before. He asked Bob Boothby, his parliamentary private secretary, to ask the former Prime Minister if he would see him. Lloyd George agreed readily, and arrived punctually at the appointed time. According to Boothby's later account, the two men were alone for about an hour, after which he heard Lloyd George leave:

> I sat alone in the Secretary's room. Nothing happened. No bell rang. After about ten minutes curiosity overcame me and I went in to find the Chancellor sitting in an armchair, gazing into the fire, in a kind of brown study. I said to him: 'How did it go?' He looked up and replied: 'You will be glad to hear that it could not have gone better. He answered all my questions.' Then a hard look came into his face and he went on: 'Within five minutes the old relationship between us was completely re-established. The relationship between Master and Servant. And I was the Servant.'[1]

Making some allowance for hyperbole, it seems reasonable to say that this was a fair depiction of the Lloyd George–Churchill relationship not only in 1917–18, but during the four years of the post-war coalition government too. It was not the case, of course, that Churchill merely did the Prime Minister's bidding. The war's aftermath saw one of their most prolonged and substantive disputes, over how to deal with the Russian Bolsheviks, as well close cooperation over issues such as Ireland. Churchill frequently chafed at Lloyd

George's authority. He was not, in any narrow sense, the ideal servant, nor was Lloyd George always the ideal master. The crucial point is that, in the face of behaviour that at times verged on insubordination, that authority remained intact. 'Ll George can *walk round Winston in astuteness!*' noted Margot Asquith in November 1918. She wrote of Churchill: 'Everyone he works with likes him & dislikes LlG – but the latter has made an amazing success of his life – charming and camouflaging & taking in quite remarkable men, the other takes in *no* one!' She added: 'Winston is like the bull & LlG (indeed much less dextrous men than LlG!) need not take either a very quick or a very long step to escape his charge.'[2] Arthur Lee, who became a Cabinet minister in August 1919, told his wife, after he had been in office for some time, that 'L.G.'s domination of the Cabinet is complete and wonderful. Winston, who talks a great deal, and usually in a stimulating and interesting way, is the only Minister who even tries to measure swords with him, but if it comes to a serious contest L.G. never has any difficulty downing him in argument.'[3]

Lloyd George's dominance was in part attributable to his personal prestige with the public as 'The Man Who Won the War'. This prestige was at its height just after the Armistice, and contributed much to his huge victory in the general election that followed. This was the 'coupon' election – so called following a derisive reference by Asquith to the letter of endorsement that approved coalition candidates received from Lloyd George and Bonar Law. The Labour Party withdrew from the coalition on 14 November. They and the Asquithites were therefore ranged against the Coalition Liberals, including Churchill of course, and the Tories. (Twenty-eight candidates also received the coupon under the banner 'National Democratic and Labour Party', a short-lived body led by Labour minister George Barnes, who refused to obey his party and resign from the government.) It was a heavily unequal battle. Labour won 63 seats, and the Asquith Liberals were reduced to a rump of 28. Asquith himself was defeated in his constituency of East Fife. The coalition ended up with 526 supporters in the Commons. Of these, only 133 were Liberals, and the Tories were thus heavily predominant within the government. Bonar Law is said to have said of Lloyd George, 'He can be Prime Minister for life if he likes.'[4] But the longer-term realities of power were reflected in a remark made by Walter Long.

'George thinks he won the election', Frances Stevenson reported him as having said. 'Well he didn't. *It was the Tories that won the election, and he will soon begin to find that out.*'[5] In spite of the Prime Minister's continued mastery of political tactics, and the personal loyalty he was to command from some key Conservatives such as Austen Chamberlain, he could not overcome the parliamentary arithmetic. As his own reputation began to decline, and as the bulk of the Tories ceased to regard him as an electoral asset, he would be more and more at the mercy of his allies.

The tensions in the government were inherent from the beginning, although they were masked by the public acclaim accorded to Lloyd George. Before the election Churchill did his best to make the coalition manifesto more radical. He wrote to the Prime Minister passing on to him the complaint of Lord Rothermere 'that your programme is not sufficiently advanced & that you are being held back by reactionary Tories.' Churchill suggested an enquiry into financial fortunes made during the war, many of which were thought to be the product of profiteering.[6] This was not the sort of plan to command enthusiasm from Conservatives, and it did not become part of the election platform. But Lloyd George clearly liked Churchill's political style, even if it was not always practical for him to accept his ideas. 'You and I must run this election' he had remarked to him (with more than a hint of flattery) a few days before receiving his letter. 'We are the only people who know anything about electioneering. Dear old Bonar has no more idea of it than an old hen.'[7]

Polling was on 14 December, although the results were not declared for another fortnight, as the time was needed to count the votes of those serving overseas. On 29 December Churchill met with Lloyd George, who offered him a choice of ministries: the War Office or the Admiralty. In either case he would have responsibility for Air, which was not to be maintained as a separate department. Later the same day Churchill sent him a letter stating unequivocally: 'My heart is in the Admy.'[8] However, on 9 January Lloyd George wrote to him saying that he had submitted his name to the King as Secretary of State for War and Air, and would he accept the post? (He added jokingly: 'Of course there will be but one salary!')[9] Churchill did so. The reason for the switch is not entirely clear. Churchill later suggested that Lloyd George had become concerned at discontent within the army about the way in which demobilization was being handled, and wanted him to take charge.[10] It may be, however, that the Prime Minister thought it too risky to put Churchill back into a job at which he had so conspicuously failed. Putting him at the War Office was nevertheless a bold move, especially for a Prime Minister who professed to believe that 'Winston has a very excitable brain' and that Churchill, though able, 'may go off at a tangent at any moment'.[11]

For the bulk of the next six months Lloyd George was absent at the peace conference in Paris that resulted in the highly controversial Treaty of Versailles. During the election he had given a number of hostages to fortune concerning the future treatment of Germany and the extent to which the Allies might extract financial reparation from her. Yet, as Kenneth O. Morgan has argued, he cannot be convicted of pure and sustained rabble-rousing jingoism.[12] During his speech in Bristol on 11 December, when dealing with the question of a war indemnity, he said that 'Germany must pay to the utmost limit of her capacity', but also stressed that there *were* limits to that capacity and that he did not want 'to raise any false hopes' and that it was unlikely in practice that Britain could expect to receive every penny. All the same, he did say on the same occasion that those who had started the war 'must pay to the uttermost farthing, and we shall search their pockets for it'.[13] Churchill's later verdict, which was eminently justified, was that 'In the hot squalid rush of the event he [Lloyd George] endeavoured to give satisfaction to mob-feeling and press chorus by using language which was in harmony with the prevailing sentiment, but which contained in every passage some guarding phrase, some qualification, which afterwards would leave statesmanship unchained.'[14] Churchill, for his part, placed much greater emphasis during the campaign on the impossibility of Germany paying the full cost of the war (as opposed to more limited reparation for the damage inflicted directly) and that a treaty that attempted to get her to do so would be valueless. He told the Cabinet, significantly, that 'it was important to get Germany on her legs again for fear of the spread of Bolshevism'.[15]

In part as a consequence of the mixed messages he himself had given out, Lloyd George arrived in Paris backed by the public expectation that the peace would be a harsh one. Georges Clemenceau, the French Prime Minister, was even more committed than

Lloyd George to the tough treatment of Germany. Woodrow Wilson, the US President, however, had set his face against inclusion of war costs in the reparations demanded. He was also the exponent of a well-meaning if frequently vague form of liberal internationalism. Yet his insistence on the right of national self-determination was not only often difficult to translate into practice, but also had the potential to conflict with the interests of Britain, France and Italy. Moreover, the conference did not have to deal only with Germany, but had also to consider the future of the other defeated powers, draw up new borders in Europe and the Middle East, deal with colonial questions, and design a new League of Nations to help guarantee the peace. Whilst Lloyd George was wrapped up in these vexing questions his engagement with Churchill and his concerns was necessarily intermittent. But although Churchill was involved only to a limited extent in the work of the peace conference, the two did clash over some significant issues.

Churchill had still not, as yet, been included in the full Cabinet. This rankled with him; he thought that the Prime Minister had gone back on a 'definite undertaking' that there would be an end to the five-man War Cabinet system, which in fact continued until October 1919.[16] All the same, he did sometimes speak highly of Lloyd George. (George Riddell noted sardonically 'It was not always thus, but one could hardly expect it.')[17] Lloyd George, though, was concerned about what Churchill was up to in his absence. The first source of contention was the latter's demobilization plan. This involved retaining compulsory military service for 1,150,000 soldiers, and releasing 2,200,000 longer-serving men back to civilian life, at the same time giving those who remained enlisted more leave and pay. Some such scheme was vital, not only to boost troop morale by putting an end to uncertainty, but also to ensure that Britain actually had an army to enforce the peace that Lloyd George was negotiating. But when the Prime Minister, who feared the political consequences, heard that Churchill had discussed the proposal with the War Cabinet he protested that he should have been consulted first. 'It is hardly treating the head of the Government fairly', he wrote.[18] Churchill responded, very reasonably, that the purpose had simply been to thrash out a provisional scheme before presenting it to him for his approval. A few days later he travelled to Paris and won Lloyd George's assent to the plan, which was then announced to the press, who 'took it all like lambs'.[19] However, this did not put an end to the Prime Minister's general suspicions of Churchill, which were probably reinforced by his civil servants. In May 1919, for example, Thomas Jones, of the Cabinet Secretariat, reported to Hankey (who was in Paris): 'One has the strong impression that Churchill is persistently pushing forward his policy in various directions, and, with the Prime Minister away, it is not easy to resist him.'[20]

Churchill's most contentious policy, which rightly gave Lloyd George cause for concern, was his support for aggressive intervention against the Bolsheviks in Russia. The diaries and memoirs of contemporaries are dotted with the Prime Minister's remarks on this theme. He described Churchill as 'a dangerous man' who had 'Bolshevism on the brain'.[21] He also compared him to Trotsky – although this may have been intended as a compliment – and said that 'Winston's anti-Bolshevik obsession had done great harm.' Churchill, he claimed, saw himself riding into Moscow on a white charger 'in a triumphal procession after the defeat of the Bolsheviks, and being acclaimed as the saviour of Russia!'[22] Frances Stevenson, doubtless reflecting Lloyd George's views at least in part, noted in mid-April 1919 that the 'disloyal & ambitious' Churchill was 'giving D. great trouble just at present, as being Secretary of State for War, he is anxious that the world should not be at peace, & is therefore planning a great war in Russia'.[23] In his memoirs Lloyd George blamed Churchill's attitude on his aristocratic lineage: 'His ducal blood revolted against the wholesale elimination of Grand Dukes in Russia.'[24]

In Churchill's view, the revolution of 1917 had been a disaster. He described in *The World Crisis* how Lenin had returned from Switzerland to Russia 'in a sealed truck like a plague bacillus'.[25] In 1919, in one of many powerful, even lurid, speeches on the question, he argued that 'Of all tyrannies in history the Bolshevist tyranny is the worst, the most destructive, and the most degrading.' The Soviet regime, he said, consisted of 'a foul combination of criminality and animalism'.[26] Lloyd George was scarcely pro-Bolshevik, but he thought that large-scale British military intervention to overthrow the Soviet regime would stimulate left-wing extremism at home. Churchill, he claimed to Riddell, wanted to conduct a war against the Bolsheviks: 'That *would* cause a revolution!'[27]

It should be emphasized that Britain's direct involvement in Russian affairs pre-dated Churchill's appointment as War Secretary.

For months prior to the Armistice money, men and materiel had been supplied to various anti-Bolshevik forces (the 'Whites') within the borders of the former Russian Empire. At the close of 1918 the troops of many other nations, including France and the USA, were there as well. Where Lloyd George differed from Churchill was not on the desirability of a White victory but over the amount of effort that should be expended by the British in order to bring it about. If Russia were genuinely anti-Bolshevik, he reasoned, then relatively limited support would be enough to ensure a White triumph. But if the Whites lacked the popular backing that would help them win more or less under their own steam, then for the Allies to try to impose a new government through force of arms would simply bolster the Reds, and at enormous expense. As he put it, 'Our principle ought to be "Russia must save herself". Nothing else would be of the slightest use to her.'[28] Churchill, though, was uncompromising. On 20 January Sir Henry Wilson (now, as CIGS, his key military adviser), wrote in his diary: 'Winston all against Bolshevism, & therefore, in this against LG.'[29] A few days later Churchill told the Prime Minister 'one might as well legalize sodomy as recognize the Bolsheviks'.[30]

In February Lloyd George returned to Britain temporarily. He decided to allow Churchill to go to Paris to make a presentation to the Allied leaders in favour of a coordinated anti-Bolshevik policy. He may have calculated that Woodrow Wilson, who was just about to leave for a sojourn in the USA, would squash the proposal. In fact the President was non-committal, and Churchill took this as sufficient excuse to start devising a scheme for an Allied Russian Council with a military commission that would draw up a war plan and assess whether it was likely to succeed. This drew an angry response from the Prime Minister in London: 'Am very alarmed at your second telegram about planning war against the Bolsheviks. The Cabinet have never authorised such a proposal.'[31] Churchill responded that in practice Britain was already at war with them, and that any assistance to the Whites would be limited, in accordance with Lloyd George's own views. Lloyd George, though, effectively crushed Churchill's plans by instructing that copies of the exchange of telegrams should be given to President Wilson's close adviser, Colonel House. As Henry Wilson noted, 'This was a low down trick, as this general tenor showed that LG did not trust Winston.'[32] The Council of Ten – the supreme decision-making body of the peace conference

– rejected the idea of the military commission. An indignant Churchill returned home.

Churchill saw Lloyd George as soon as he got back. There followed an exchange of letters between the two in which Lloyd George accused the War Office of failing to provide the Cabinet with sufficient information to reach a coherent Russian policy, and Churchill accused Lloyd George of 'altogether failing to address your mind to the real dangers that are before us'.[33] On 4 March the War Cabinet reached a clear decision: to withdraw over the coming months British troops from Murmansk and Archangel in northern Russia and also from the Caucasus in the south. The Whites were to be compensated, however, by the continued supply of arms and munitions to their own armies, and by the provision of military advisers. Lloyd George returned to the peace conference the next day, and a few days after that, following further discussions in London, Churchill followed him to Paris. After they talked there on the morning of 8 March Churchill agreed to implement the new policy. He did so only with extreme reluctance, and complained of 'the steady degeneration of so many resources and powers which, vigorously used, might entirely have altered the course of events' in Russia.[34] At the end of the month, Henry Wilson wrote in his diary: 'He is in a very critical mood about LG & I am sure is watching an opportunity to knife him.'[35]

The anti-Bolshevik forces at this time appeared to be doing well. Churchill was determined to interpret the Cabinet's decisions so as to obtain maximum leeway for aggressive action in their support. He successfully pressed Lloyd George to permit more British soldiers to be sent to northern Russia to provide protection for the evacuation of the existing troops. He subsequently proposed using these troops in a forward movement in an effort to link up with the forces of Admiral Kolchak, the leader of the Whites in the east, in order to make sure that as little territory as possible was in the hands of the Reds at the point the British withdrew. (By the end of May, though, Kolchak had experienced serious setbacks, and in July the plan was abandoned.) Churchill's almost fanatical attitude on the issue of Russia helps to explain his attitude to the German peace terms that Lloyd George had by now negotiated. The Germans should not be weakened too much, because their army might be needed to serve as a bulwark against the Soviets. He characterized his own policy as 'Kill the Bolshie, Kiss the Hun.'[36]

The terms were presented to the German delegates in Paris – who were treated almost as pariahs – on 7 May. The proposed treaty was a harsh one. Germany was not only to be deprived of much territory, and of her colonies, but also, among other things, her army and navy were to be limited and she was to be denied an air force. She was expected to pay reparations, although the sum – which turned out to be enormous – was not to be fixed until a later date. Furthermore, the Germans were to admit liability for starting the conflict in the first place – the much-resented 'War Guilt' clause. At the end of the month the Germans submitted their counter-proposals. Their case was impressive, exposing contradictions between the Allied terms and President Wilson's 'Fourteen Points', his war-time statement of principles for a just peace. Lloyd George was shaken. He summoned to Paris all the ministers who were able to come, and on 31 May they dined with him at his flat. 'The whole drift of the conversation was unanimous, Winston being the ring-leader.'[37] The consensus was that the terms were too severe, and should be amended. Lloyd George therefore went back to Clemenceau and Wilson and argued for moderation.

Clemenceau was obstinate. Wilson was exasperated by Lloyd George's abrupt change of tack. He pointed out that the British themselves had originally insisted on many of the points they now claimed to find objectionable. Equally ironically he himself now turned down the chance to bring the peace more into line with his own initial principles. 'Mr. Prime Minister,' he said after Lloyd George announced his change of heart, 'you make me sick!'[38] Only minor modifications to the treaty were agreed. It was unclear whether or not the Germans would sign; if they did not, the Allies would be forced to resume the war. As the tension built the day before the 23 June deadline, Churchill shared a hasty meal with Lloyd George, Henry Wilson and Maurice and Adeline Hankey.[39] Only at the very last minute did the Germans agree; and the formal signing ceremony took place in the Hall of Mirrors at the Palace of Versailles on 28 June. Lloyd George returned to London in triumph, although he had been expecting his reception to 'be rather a wash-out, as he knew that Winston had turned down the idea of getting troops to line the streets'.[40] It would not be long, though, before British opinion began to turn against the Versailles Treaty. John Maynard Keynes's seminal work *The Economic Consequences of the Peace*, published at the end of 1919, helped to catalyse this change. In March 1920 Churchill reproached his chief: 'Since the armistice my policy wd have been "Peace with the German people, war on the Bolshevik tyranny". Willingly or unavoidably, you have followed something vy near the reverse.'[41]

At the same time the Prime Minister was not without domestic enemies. Lord Northcliffe, whose megalomania had achieved extraordinary proportions, had turned against him. H. W. Wilson, chief leader writer of the *Daily Mail*, advised his boss at the start of April 1919 that 'It is a question whether Winston would not make a better Prime Minister than Lloyd George ... slippery though he is, he is less slippery than Lloyd George whom no one trusts.'[42] In the middle of the same month Lloyd George retaliated for the attacks on him by denouncing Northcliffe in the Commons. In a speech that was a parliamentary triumph, he referred to his adversary's 'diseased vanity', and as he said these words tapped his head to imply mental illness.[43] Two months later Walter Long warned him that Northcliffe was promoting a movement to supplant him with Churchill: 'He is undoubtedly trying to run Winston as your successor. I am quite sure the latter knows nothing of this and is in no way responsible for the use of his name, but I think it is also true that some of his more immediate friends give currency to the idea, and I know that from time to time they state quite openly that he is to become Prime Minister at a very early date.'[44] By this time, though, much of Northcliffe's power had already ebbed away, in part because of Lloyd George's attack. In August 1922 the great press baron died from a blood infection, which, in his last months, affected the balance of his mind. In his last ravings, he informed his staff that God was homosexual.[45]

In the summer of 1919 Lloyd George turned his attention to domestic policy, although the connection between this and international affairs was inescapable. Industrial unrest was on the upsurge – hence both Lloyd George and Churchill's (probably exaggerated fears) of revolution at home. In terms of its own agenda, the government had conflicting ambitions, as befitted its coalition character. The Prime Minister wanted both to follow in the footsteps of the New Liberalism, conducting social reform and thus taking the sting out of the unrest, and to cut public expenditure to help restore economic stability. At the same time events in Russia continued to cast a shadow. In July Lloyd George retreated to Criccieth, where he participated in policy discussions with a number of advisers and ministers, including a gloomy Churchill. Kolchak's military failure was now apparent – although the White forces under General Denikin in southern Russia were faring much better – and Lloyd George was inclined to withdraw support from him and from other anti-Bolshevik groupings. (Lloyd George feared the reactionary tendencies of Denikin, whom Churchill defended.) Hankey noted: 'The P.M. was always opposed to Winston's operations from Archangel and was only persuaded with great difficulty to assent to them, so he was in rather a "I told you so" kind of mood & twitted Winston a good deal, as he had previously done in Paris.' Churchill angled unsuccessfully for the creation of a new post of Minister of Defence, in the hope that he himself would be appointed to it.[46]

If Lloyd George was frustrated with the direction of his own government, Churchill at times managed to draw the Prime Minister's irritation onto his own head. Walter Long was now First Lord of the Admiralty. On 16 August, his son-in-law, George Gibb, wrote to the Conservative MP William Bull that, the previous day in Cabinet, 'the PM without the slightest warning attacked the Admiralty and the War Office on the grounds of their extravagance.' Long, for his part,

> felt very much inclined to resign at once: but he did not do so and answered all the questions literally flung at him with as much restraint as possible. WC lost his temper and I believe things were quite lively. He threatened to resign ... WL smiled when he told me that 'luckily he attacked the Admiralty first'. I daresay WC getting angry rather transferred the attention of all present to the War Office.[47]

A few days later Gibb sent Bull a further letter reporting that Lloyd George had realized his behaviour had been tactless 'and sent round a Cabinet minute almost directly afterwards putting everything right'. Gibb had also heard that Bonar Law 'had not noticed anything unusual in what had occurred at that Cabinet!!'[48] At the end of the month Lloyd George reprimanded Churchill for failing to turn his mind to economy. 'You will I am sure forgive me for saying that I think Russia has cost us more than the hundred millions odd we have spent on it,' he wrote, 'for an impression is left on my mind that the best thoughts of the War Office have been given to these military ventures in Russia, & that the important administrative questions upon which so many scores if not hundreds of millions depend have not received the same intense study.'[49]

Churchill, for his part, was increasingly isolated. The government did commit itself to providing Denikin with a final 'packet' of aid, with a view to helping his forces stand on their own feet within a few months, but other ministers lacked the appetite for further Russian enterprises. Churchill was attacked on the issue not only in the left-wing press but also in the papers owned by Lord Beaverbrook, with whom he had fallen out. The Prime Minister could hardly be pleased at the suggestion that he was unable to restrain one of his chief subordinates. Churchill, for his own part, could not rein in his delight at the advances of Denikin's troops. During a visit to Paris in September, Hankey sat up with Churchill and Jack Seely (now Undersecretary of State for Air) until after 1 a.m. He noted: 'the former (who had drunk a good deal) lectured us at enormous length & great brilliancy about Russia, spreading maps all over the floor. He is quite balmy [sic] in his enthusiasm for the anti-bolshevists.'[50] 'I don't know what to do with the boy', observed Lloyd George a few days later.[51] On the twentieth of the same month Churchill sent him a memorandum on Russia. He claimed in his accompanying letter that the Bolshevik regime was doomed, and urged that the Russian people should not be abandoned 'in the crisis of their fate'. He also described himself as Lloyd George's 'faithful lieutenant', a remark that could almost have been calculated to annoy a man who felt that his wishes were being consistently ignored.[52]

Hence, in part, the wounded tone of the reply. The Prime Minister protested again that his appeals to Churchill to concentrate on cutting spending had fallen on deaf ears. He claimed that the previous Friday he had entreated Churchill 'to let Russia be for at least 48 hours' and to spend the weekend preparing for the Cabinet's Finance Committee. In spite of a promise to do so, 'Your reply is to send me a four-page letter on Russia, and a closely printed memor-andum of several pages – all on Russia. I am frankly in despair.' He went on to cast doubt on Churchill's assertions: 'You confidently predict in your memorandum that Denikin is on the eve of some great and striking success. I looked up some of your memoranda made earlier in the year about Kolchak, and I find that you use exactly the same language in reference to Kolchak's successes.' Kolchak, of course, had gone on to fail. Later in the same letter Lloyd George wrote: 'I wonder if it is any use my making one last effort to induce you to throw off this obsession which, if you will forgive me for saying so, is upsetting your balance.'[53] Although the letter concluded on an emollient note, Churchill wrote back that he found it 'vy unkind & I think also unjust'. He wound up, after long paragraphs of self-justification, by deploying once more the rhetoric of companionship: 'surely I am not wrong in writing earnestly and sincerely to my chief & oldest political friend to let him know that things are not all right . . . Surely I was bound to do this.'[54]

Just after this exchange, H. A. L. Fisher, the President of the Board of Education, recorded Lloyd George as saying that Churchill was 'a greater source of weakness than of strength' to the government, and that he was 'like the Counsel that a solicitor employs not because he is the best man but because he would be dangerous on the other side.'[55] (This was a harsher variant of his 1916 comment to Bonar Law, which was referred to in the previous chapter.) On 8 October Lord Milner noted of a meeting of the Cabinet's Finance Committee: 'Proceedings chiefly remarkable for a vehement & rather unreasonable onslaught on Churchill by the P.M., wh. Churchill took with remarkable good humour.'[56] 'The P.M. and I have plenty of chaff on serious matters, especially when we differ', Churchill wrote on a later occasion, after Lloyd George pointedly asked for the Russian national anthem to be played in Churchill's presence. 'But it never offends.'[57] Churchill was so thin skinned that the last part of this claim does not seem totally convincing. But he had, at any rate, learnt that affecting not to care was the best way to deal Lloyd George's jibes.

The issue of Russia was not, in fact, all-consuming. A file in the Royal Archives reveals an episode that took place during the autumn of 1919, which is illuminating of other aspects of the men's relationship. The Army Council had mooted that the Prime Minister be awarded the Distinguished Service Order (DSO) and Churchill, in his capacity as Secretary of State for War, suggested this idea to George V. The King, however, appears to have been doubtful about it, as Churchill, having discussed the question with him, modified the proposal. In a letter of 16 October he formally suggested that Lloyd George should receive the medals of the kind granted to servicemen who had participated in the war.[58] The King, however, was doubtful about this idea too, as he made clear when he granted Churchill a further audience at the beginning of November. On this occasion, according to Clive Wigram, the King's assistant private secretary, 'H.M. said that he thought it would be difficult to give L.G. the medals and ignore the other ministers', i.e. those who had also served in government during the war. 'In any case H.M. felt that Asquith should be on the same footing as L.G.'.[59] Following this meeting, Churchill wrote to the King, telling him that he had consulted with Sir Henry Wilson who, as CIGS, had agreed with him that 'it is not desirable to extend this exceptional grant to other Cabinet Ministers'. Churchill emphasized to the King that 'The feeling that the award was desirable arose spontaneously among the Military Members of the Army Council' and that, furthermore there was 'no doubt that the purely military work done by Mr Lloyd George stands on an entirely different plane to that done by other Cabinet Ministers'.[60] After the receipt of this letter, Wigram recorded:

> The King says that he does not wish to quarrel with Winston as they both see eye to eye on so many questions . . .
>
> Winston [in his letter] says nothing about Asquith and very cleverly puts the onus on the Army Council . . .
>
> I think it is H.W. [Henry Wilson] sucking up to the P.M.
>
> The King is awkwardly placed because Winston & H.W. have probably already told L.G. all that has passed.[61]

The King replied to Churchill's letter on 25 November. He hinted that he was sceptical of the account he had been given: 'The proposal to confer War Medals upon civilians is so contrary to the military instinct and to the tradition of our Army that I could not help being surprised to learn that the suggested award to the Prime Minister arose spontaneously among the Military Members of the Army Council.' Moreover, 'In this instance I feel strongly that were I to approve of your Submission to confer War Medals for the first time upon a civilian, who, by my own Army Regulations, is not eligible to receive them, I could not refuse to make similar exceptions in favour of others, who had rendered services of a like character, even though of a lesser degree.'[62] In response, Churchill wrote again some days later, revealing that Wigram's surmise had been correct: he had indeed already told Lloyd George of the plan.

> When the Military Members of the Army Council first made this proposal to Mr. Churchill, he thought it necessary to ask the Prime Minister what his own wishes were. Mr. Lloyd George expressed great pleasure at the news. In fact, if Your Majesty will permit Mr Churchill to quote his actual words, he said 'he would rather have them than an Earldom'.

Churchill also pointed out that the Army Council had wide discretionary power in the grant of medals and that the King's formal assent was generally taken for granted. Churchill apologized for the unintentional embarrassment he had caused, and asked for another audience.[63] On this occasion, the King reiterated his objections to Lloyd George receiving the medals:

> At the same time, the King recognised the fact that as Mr. Churchill had approached the Prime Minister on the subject and had learnt from him how delighted he would be to receive the Medals, if they were not now given to him it would be obvious that they were withheld owing to His Majesty refusing his permission – thus placing the King in a very awkward position.

Accordingly, the King agreed – without, it seems, very much enthusiasm – that the medals should be given to Lloyd George, on the understanding that Asquith would be granted them too.[64] Churchill's energetic pursuit of the project could be seen either as an attempt to curry favour with the Prime Minister at a time when their relations were under strain, or as a genuine indicator of his regard for him.

The Russian war, of course, continued simultaneous with these developments. In late October Denikin's forces had suffered their first major setbacks. Soon the anti-Bolsheviks were being driven back on the other fronts too. 'Lunch with the PM', noted Fisher on 3 November, '[He] Launches out against Winston's misrepresentations of Russian situation. LG does not want Denikin to win.'[65] In the Commons, Churchill, with typical gusto, gave the clear impression that the government thought the Whites would triumph in the end and that Britain would support them as long as necessary.

All the more astonishment, then, when Lloyd George publicly announced an about-turn in policy. This was at London's Guildhall on 8 November. 'We cannot, of course, afford to continue so costly an intervention in an interminable civil war', he said. 'Our troops are out of Russia. Frankly I am glad. Russia is a quicksand.'[66] Churchill, who was present, was visibly surprised.

This pronouncement may have accelerated the collapse of the morale of the Whites, who were now in chaotic retreat. Churchill's dawning realization that the anti-Bolsheviks were doomed did not improve his relations with the Prime Minister. In mid-January 1920 Henry Wilson wrote in his diary that Lloyd George 'thinks Winston has gone mad'.[67] To Riddell, Lloyd George said that Churchill had tried to shout him down: 'To secure his own ends he becomes quite reckless.'[68] According to Thomas Jones, the Prime Minister, in Cabinet on 9 February, 'gave Winston a dressing down about Russia. Winston had been complaining that we had no policy. This the P.M. described as ridiculous. Our policy was to try to escape the results of the evil policy which Winston had persuaded the Cabinet to adopt.'[69]

Lloyd George now sought, with typical pragmatism, to establish relations with the Soviet government. On 31 May he had a meeting with Leonid Krassin, the head of a Russian trade delegation – a very significant mark of recognition for the new regime at a time when it was still on shaky foundations. The USSR was at war with Poland, and the Whites, under Denikin's successor General Wrangel, were about to launch a final offensive. In August, as the Soviets advanced with alarming rapidity against the Poles, it seemed briefly that there was a new risk of Britain herself being dragged into war. 'Winston is in despair and nearly off his head,' wrote Earl Beatty, the First Sea Lord. 'The only optimist is the Prime Minister, and he is too much so.'[70] In fact, optimism was justified. A successful Polish counter-offensive averted the need for action, for which it is doubtful that the government as a whole had any taste.

Lenin, however, scented a conspiracy: 'It is quite clear that LLOYD GEORGE and CHURCHILL have apportioned the rôles ... LLOYD GEORGE has deceived us with pacifism and has helped CHURCHILL to lend assistance to the Poles.' The Soviet representatives in Britain should, he said, use all their powers to explain this to the British workers.[71] Churchill made it his special mission to get the leaders of the trade delegation expelled, on account of such subversive activities. When, in November, the Cabinet decided to continue the negotiations, he 'was so upset that he declared himself unequal to discussing other items on the Agenda'.[72] Churchill's anti-Bolshevik obsession was by no means at an end, and, as will be seen, it would again become a significant factor in his relations with Lloyd George. But the Prime Minister's policy of learning to live with the Soviets was now firmly established.

Margaret MacMillan, in her recent prize-winning book *Peacemakers*, has noted that the Russian people paid a terrible price for the Bolshevik triumph in the civil war. Lenin established a tyrannical system that, she points out, Stalin subsequently exploited to horrible effect. On this basis, she declares baldly that Churchill was 'right' about the Bolsheviks and Lloyd George was 'wrong'.[73] But – if we are to use such black and white terms – the opposite was true. Although Lloyd George may have admired Lenin and Trotsky as men of action, he did not suffer from any illusion that they were nice people or that their methods of rule were beneficent. In August 1920, for example, he cited in the Commons the views of the philosopher Bertrand Russell, who had returned from a trip to Russia heavily disillusioned with the Bolsheviks. Communist rule, the Prime Minister said, involved an attempt by a tiny minority to 'tyrannize' the workers.[74] (Russell, who had been imprisoned in 1918 for agitating against the war, resented the fact that publication of his 'Bolshie book' had led to him being 'praised by people I hate – e.g. Winston and Lloyd George.')[75] Lloyd George was, though, well aware that the anti-Bolsheviks were not in all respects to be preferred. He was concerned by the lethal anti-Semitic pogroms that often accompanied their victories, despite Churchill's urgings of restraint upon the White forces.

Lloyd George, furthermore, took a broader view of the Russian question than Churchill was capable of. He had to consider not only whether the end of the Soviet regime was objectively desirable, but also whether the public were prepared to tolerate intervention and, indeed, to bear the financial burden. The flowering of the 'Hands Off Russia' campaign, sponsored by the TUC and the Labour Party at the time of the Russo-Polish war, provided strong evidence that they were not. Moreover, however unpleasant the Soviet regime was for the peoples who suffered under it, it did not, in the immediate post-war years, pose much of a direct threat to Britain. Diplomatic engagement with it was an intelligent realpolitik response, as Churchill belatedly recognized in the 1930s when arguing for an anti-Nazi 'Grand Alliance' to include the USSR. According to Lloyd George, speaking privately at the time of the White collapse in southern Russia, Churchill 'thinks that I have destroyed his policy. He admits that Denikin has failed as I prophesied he would, but he says that if I had used my power I could have made his campaign a success.'[76] This represented wishful thinking on Churchill's part. In fact, if Lloyd George made an error on the issue, it was in not acting to restrain Churchill and 'destroy' his policy earlier and more effectively than he did.

This leads back to the nature of the two men's relationship. In June 1920 Churchill told Riddell that Lloyd George was 'a wonderful man': 'It is extraordinary that we have been able to work together on such terms of personal friendship, notwithstanding the divergence of our views regarding Russia . . .'[77] This comment, which fits so neatly into the mythology of 'David and Winston', must be treated with caution. They did make protestations of regard for one another among their heated exchanges. There is a certain amount of evidence of genuine conviviality, including their joint enjoyment of the hospitality of the wealthy Unionist MP Sir Philip Sassoon. Nonetheless, we may suspect that Churchill, lacking allies, liked to advertise his (real or imagined) closeness to the Prime Minister as a means to bolster his own position. If he chose not to resign from the government – and he certainly considered the idea, most seriously over the Russian trade negotiations – it was not from personal loyalty but because he realized he would gain little support from others.

The fact remains that, in spite of Lloyd George's bitter criticisms of Churchill, he did not get rid of him, even though it might have been advantageous to do so. In the words of one historian who examined the 'Hands Off Russia' campaign, 'Lloyd George failed to take the one step which would have convinced the Labour movement of his sincerity – the dismissal of the man who epitomized the crusading spirit of anti-Bolshevism, Winston Churchill'.[78] It is true that the Prime Minister claimed that Churchill would be more dangerous outside the government than in, but, perhaps, this was a mere rationalization. All the same, if Churchill had some kind of emotional hold on him, Lloyd George did not necessarily always enjoy his company. In May 1920 Hankey noted that Lloyd George looked 'old and ill, but he had just had 24 hours of Winston Churchill which is enough to make anyone look old and ill'.[79] One exchange between the two, recorded by Frances Stevenson, a few months before this, captures the ambiguity of their relationship:

> 'Winston', said the P.M., 'is the only remaining specimen of a real Tory.' 'Never mind', laughed Winston, 'if you are going to include all parties, you will have to include me in your new National Party.' 'Oh no!' was D.'s retort, 'To be a party you must have at least one follower. *You* have none.'[80]

Churchill liked to imagine, rather arrogantly, that he was indispensable to Lloyd George; Lloyd George enjoyed belittling him by pointing out the sound reasons this was not so, whilst, at the same time, seeming unable to actually dispense with him.

Churchill's reference to a 'new National Party' relates to Lloyd George's proposal for 'fusion' of the parties within the coalition, under a new name. This would, he believed, secure the long-term future of the Coalition Liberals now that reunion with Asquith's so-called 'Wee Frees'[81] seemed impossible. Merger with the Unionists would, he hoped, give the government a clearer political identity, and improve its organization in the constituencies, thus making easier the battle against the Labour and Asquithite resurgence. For the coalition, in spite of its huge majority, had already run into political difficulties. Discontent with the government was compounded by Churchill's policy of intervention in Russia and by Lloyd George's neglect of the House of Commons. From March 1919 the coalition experienced a string of by-election losses. In January 1920, when Asquith was trying to get back into parliament at Paisley, Churchill thought Lloyd George obsessed with the contest – just as Lloyd George thought Churchill was obsessed by the Bolsheviks. Asquith won the seat, massively increasing the Independent Liberal majority; the coalition candidate, a Unionist, lost his deposit.[82]

Lloyd George seems to have broached 'fusion' privately as early as July 1919. Riddell wrote: 'Evidently he and Winston must have decided upon some joint action, as W, after his return to London from Criccieth, made a carefully prepared speech, proposing the formation of a Central Party, so called.'[83] (In this speech, made to a gathering of coalition MPs, Churchill praised 'my friend, Mr. Lloyd George, who really is the most necessary man this country has had for many years.')[84] It was, however, difficult to find a new name, let alone a platform, that would satisfy everyone. A policy document drafted by H. A. L. Fisher as a basis for fusion was criticized by Balfour. Lloyd George agreed with him that it had 'too many challenging details' – Home Rule for Scotland and Wales, proportional representation, and proposed new labour legislation were too radical to appeal to Unionists. Churchill – who had a growing reputation as a covert Tory sympathizer – was also dissatisfied with it.[85] On 16 March 1920 Lloyd George and Churchill tried to pressure Liberal ministers into accepting fusion.[86] But the ministers – including Fisher – were 'frightened at the idea of losing their identity as Liberals'.[87] Two days later Lloyd George made a speech to the 'Coaly Lib' MPs as a whole. Even though he now urged only closer cooperation with the Unionists, rather than fusion with them, his arguments fell completely flat. As Kenneth Morgan puts it, 'The Prime Minister simply banged the anti-socialist drum as crudely as Churchill and with as little effect.'[88] The fusion project died; and the Conservative leaders were not a little relieved that it was Lloyd George's own Liberal supporters who nailed down the coffin lid.

The New Year's festivities of 1920–1 found Lloyd George and Churchill as guests of Philip Sassoon at Lympne. They were both, Riddell noted, 'in great form'. The guests sat and listened to recordings of Warren G. Harding, the President-elect, and other US politicians, as Lloyd George and Churchill shouted humorous remarks into the gramophone horn. When the Prime Minister sang 'Cockles and Mussels' and other songs, Churchill looked on admiringly. 'What a wonderful man he is!' he said. 'What an actor he would have made!'[89] On New Year's Day Lloyd George proposed to Churchill that he move from the War Office to the Colonial Office. After a few days' reflection, Churchill accepted. Although he was not sorry to leave his existing department, he had misgivings about the political consequences for himself. 'I am afraid this venture is going to break me', he told Hankey despondently.[90] Henry Wilson noted in his diary on 23 January: 'Winston told me he took the Colonies because he would not have lasted much longer in the WO owing to differences with LG.'[91] Churchill had some difficulty getting the Prime Minister to make up his mind about the junior ministerial appointments that flowed from the Cabinet changes. A letter to his wife from Chequers is indicative of the frustrations of working with

Lloyd George: 'The PM has been as agreeable, evasive, elusive & indefinite as usual.'[92]

Churchill did not receive his seals of office until 7 February, but news of the appointment soon leaked out. Lord Hardinge, British ambassador to Paris, wrote to Curzon (now Foreign Secretary): 'what Winston Churchill and you told me as a great secret about his going to the Colonial Office, was to my great surprise telegraphed out here also by Reuter about the same time as I received your letter. What is the meaning of it all?'[93] Churchill, in accepting the post, had written to Lloyd George that he was 'deeply sensible' of the honour he was receiving and 'of the many acts of personal kindness by which you have marked our long friendship & political association'.[94] Yet his gratitude knew some bounds. One of his first major duties as Colonial Secretary was to preside over a conference of British officials in Cairo, which did much to determine the future of the Middle East. While he was there, during March, it was announced that Bonar Law was to retire from the government owing to ill health. (Lloyd George felt genuine affection for Law and was so moved that he broke down in the Commons when breaking the news.) Austen Chamberlain replaced Law not only as leader of the Conservative Party but also as Leader of the Commons and Lord Privy seal, creating a vacancy at the Exchequer. Churchill desperately hoped to receive the Chancellorship, but he was passed over in favour of Robert Horne, a Conservative of no great political weight. Laming Worthington-Evans, Churchill's successor as War Secretary, thought that the proposal to appoint Horne (or failing him, the Financial Secretary to the Treasury, Stanley Baldwin) was 'meant to keep out Winston!'[95]

Churchill was furious at Lloyd George's decision. This appears to have led him, together with Lord Birkenhead (the Lord Chancellor; formerly F. E. Smith), into an intrigue against the Prime Minister. Press rumours about his manoeuvres were nothing new, and tales of political conspiracy are, by their very nature, often difficult to verify. There is plenty of evidence in relation to this episode, however, albeit only of an indirect kind. In May Lloyd George remarked privately that he knew of Churchill's anger over Horne's appointment, and that 'he should not be surprised if Winston resigned, with a section of Conservatives who are tired of the LG régime because they think it too democratic'. He thought Churchill might try to lead this group and form an alliance with Birkenhead.[96] At the end of May Frances Stevenson recorded that 'D. is so sick with C. I don't think he cares if he does go.'[97] She suspected that Beaverbrook was involved in the conspiracy, and that he was also manipulating Bonar Law, who still lurked in the background of politics, although at this stage he showed no inclination to displace Lloyd George. By 22 June Lloyd George believed he had headed off the possibility of a crisis. The next day an article appeared in the *Manchester Guardian* claiming that an incipient revolt led by Birkenhead had been abandoned 'mainly on account of Mr. Churchill's refusal to go on ... He retired because he was convinced that the time was not yet, and that the revolt would have no chance of success.'[98] Frances Stevenson wrote in her diary

> We don't know who wrote it, or how he got the information, but it is all correct. Last night D. had an emphatic letter from F. E. denying the whole thing – but 'protesting too much'. But no word from Winston, who is openly accused of treachery in the article. D. says that Winston does not tell actual lies, & that is why he will not deny it.[99]

She also alleged, to Riddell, that

> The plot was to prevail upon LG to resign on the grounds of his health and to appoint Winston PM. This, however, resolved itself into a scheme to appoint Birkenhead. This change led to the defection of Winston and the break-up of the cabal.[100]

Austen Chamberlain, for his part, was unsure if the rumours were true, but, like Stevenson, noted that they had been 'passed in silence by Winston who is sulky ever since Horne was made Chancellor'.[101] This was indeed telling, given that Churchill was accustomed to leap to his own defence whenever he thought himself the victim of injustice. It is not, of course, entirely conclusive, but the balance of probabilities must be that Churchill did plot against Lloyd George. If so, so much for his public claims that the Prime Minister was 'the most necessary man' and his private ones (made to Riddell) 'that although he had had many disagreements with LG' he 'would always be prepared to stand by him in a pinch'.[102]

Indeed, even if the rumours were false, the fact that Lloyd George believed them shows how little trust he had in Churchill's loyalty. This was unsurprising given that, throughout these events, Churchill's hostility to him was fairly openly displayed. After his return from Cairo he did not make an effort to brief him. Stevenson noted: 'D. has only seen him in Cabinets & meetings of the kind, & Winston writes him "Dear Prime Minister", whereas it used to be "Dear Ll.G. or "My dear David" even.'[103] Austen Chamberlain urged Churchill not to 'hold aloof' from the Prime Minister, but without success.[104] Beaverbrook believed the Colonial Secretary to be 'the bitter enemy' of Lloyd George, who, he predicted, would attempt to placate him, although he had so far 'left Churchill to himself' since his return from Cairo.[105] Following a lunch with Churchill, Thomas Marlowe, the editor of the *Daily Mail*, told Northcliffe that 'Winston is fed up with Lloyd George . . . Winston holds it is not compatible with his seniority – as a Minister of several years' standing – to have to go to Horne – a Minister of two years – when he wants a little money.' Marlowe also reported that Churchill was 'very sore' that Lloyd George, who intended to take the limelight himself, would not let him take the chair at the forthcoming conference of Dominion prime ministers.[106]

It should be remembered that, although concern for his own position played, as ever, a strong part in Churchill's calculations, he also had some substantive differences with Lloyd George over policy. As his comment to Henry Wilson indicates, these had emerged during his period as War Secretary; and they were not restricted to the Russian issue. Churchill felt that the Prime Minister's Eastern policy was far too anti-Turk and pro-Greek. At the close of the war British troops controlled major parts of the former Ottoman Empire, including Palestine, Mesopotamia (modern Iraq) and Constantinople itself. In May 1919, with Allied consent, Greek troops occupied Smyrna, a Turkish port in Asia Minor which had a substantial Greek population. In August the Sultan's government – virtually powerless, given the presence of Allied forces in its capital – signed the Treaty of Sèvres, thus renouncing all its claims to territory outside Turkey, and allowing Smyrna and the surrounding area to be administered by the Greeks for five years in advance of a plebiscite. But Turkish nationalist forces under the army officer Mustafa Kemal disclaimed allegiance to the Sultan and opposed the Treaty. Lloyd George encouraged Greece's ambitions and indulged in chauvinistic rhetoric against the Turks, whom he regarded as a curse.[107] But Kemal's men were to prove more than a match for the Greeks, who, by 1922, were to be militarily humiliated.

Churchill sent Lloyd George a long letter about these issues at the start of December 1920, not long before his transition to the Colonial Office. 'I am vy sorry to see how far we are drifting apart on foreign policy', he began. He went on to argue that it was dangerous for Britain to be identified as the world's principal anti-Turk power, given that it had so many Muslims living within the boundaries of its own empire. British control of its new territories in other parts of the Middle East was made more difficult by the anti-Turk 'vendetta', he claimed. 'We seem to be becoming the most Anti Turk & the most pro-Bolshevik power in the world: whereas in my judgement we ought to be the exact opposite.' (He believed that a friendly Turkey could act as a bulwark against the Soviet Union.) His criticisms of Lloyd George included the accusation that 'one of the main causes of the trouble throughout the Middle East is *your* quarrel with the remnants of Turkey'. He concluded his letter with a threat of resignation coded in the language of candid friendship:

> Well there I have written what I have on my mind – & if you resent it so much the worse for all of us. I can never forget the service you did me in bringing me a fresh horse when I was dismounted in the war, & intensely longing to take a real part in the struggle. Office has not now the same attraction for me, & I have other new interests on wh I cd fall back. Therefore the counsels I offer are those of a friend & of a sincere friend – but of a friend who cannot part with his independence.[108]

Given that Churchill had recently failed to resign over the question of the Russian trade negotiations, Lloyd George might not have taken this terribly seriously. Some days later Churchill circulated a memorandum to the Cabinet arguing for a policy of friendship with Turkey, but this had little effect. When, in February 1921, he opposed the idea that Smyrna should become an independent province, on the grounds that this would worsen the problems of the Middle East, the Prime Minister slapped him down.[109] Churchill continued, fruitlessly, to advocate reaching an accommodation with Kemal. He would, though, later adopt a hard-line stance against the Turks during the crisis that led to Lloyd George's downfall.

Nevertheless Lloyd George was by no means wholly unresponsive to all of Churchill's concerns about the region as a whole. One thing that Churchill resented when at the War Office was that although he was expected to find the troops necessary to keep order there – and to ask parliament for money to pay for them – he had little say over how they were used. The Foreign Office administered Palestine; India Office administered Mesopotamia; and other territories were run by the Colonial Office. On the last day of 1920, the Cabinet agreed to Churchill's proposal to concentrate all these responsibilities within a new Middle East Department to be located within the Colonial Office. (This decision was reached before he himself accepted the Colonial Secretaryship, although he made its implementation on the lines he desired a condition of his acceptance.) This held out the possibility of substantial economies, one of Churchill's key aims in his new job. In particular, he was determined that either Mesopotamia should be governed more cheaply or that Britain should withdraw. The new arrangement represented a victory for Churchill, backed by Lloyd George, over Lord Curzon, who wanted the new department to be based in the Foreign Office.[110]

This provided the background to the March 1921 Cairo conference mentioned above. The key outcome of the meeting was the decision to install Feisal Ibn Hussein, third son of Sherif Hussein of Mecca, as first King of the newly renamed Iraq. His brother, Abdullah, was to rule the area known as Transjordan (which was to become modern-day Jordan). Once Churchill had informed London of these recommendations, Lloyd George sent him a telegram assuring him of the Cabinet's broad support for his plans. In June Churchill made a Commons statement on the Middle East. In what may have been an attempt to mend fences with him after the contretemps over Horne's appointment, the Prime Minister wrote offering his 'Hearty congratulations on its conspicuous success.'[111]

The two men were also in general agreement over another question discussed at Cairo: the future of Palestine. They shared the view that the Jews were highly influential, and that, therefore, their support should be secured through British backing for Zionism.[112] (There was some ambiguity in Churchill's position, however. One of his aides during his Middle Eastern trip thought it curious to hear him give 'a tremendously pro-Zionist speech . . . when one knows he is really not in sympathy with the Zionist cause'.)[113] The two were therefore keen to uphold the 1917 Balfour declaration, which had announced that the British government favoured the establishment of a 'national home' for the Jewish people in Palestine. They interpreted this as meaning that a Jewish state should be established in due course. They were not blind to all the difficulties that their policy might involve, and some of what they did provoked Zionist hostility, especially when they agreed to limits on Jewish immigration to Palestine. But they can, perhaps, be legitimately accused of paying insufficient attention to the rights of the Arabs. During a meeting with the prominent Zionist leader Chaim Weizmann in July 1921, Lloyd George said to Churchill: 'You mustn't give representative government to Palestine.'[114] As the Arabs formed the majority of the population, to do so would have been a terrible blow to the Zionist dream.

An equally problematic post-war issue was that of Ireland, Churchill's detailed involvement with which also dated back to his time as Secretary of State for War. The 1916 Easter Rising – or rather, the clumsy British response to it – had radicalized nationalist opinion. During 1917 the previously obscure party Sinn Féin won by-election victories, a prelude to its sweeping success in the 1918 general election. Completely eclipsing the moderate Home Rulers (who won only six seats), it triumphed in 73 out of the 105 Irish constituencies. The victorious Sinn Féin candidates refused to take up their seats at Westminster, instead establishing their own illegal parliament in Dublin, known as the Dáil Éireann, on 21 January 1919. The same day, two members of the Royal Irish Constabulary (RIC) were murdered during an ambush. This was the beginning of the bloody and brutal Anglo-Irish War (or War of Independence) that lasted until the middle of 1921. The Irish Republican Army (IRA), led by the young and dynamic Michael Collins, used highly effective guerrilla tactics against the British forces. Lloyd George and Churchill were among the prominent British figures who were targets for IRA kidnap.

In May 1920, as the situation deteriorated, Lloyd George asked for Churchill's help in providing reinforcements. Their joint determination to take a harsh line with the rebels can be seen from the records of a meeting that took place at the end of the month. Churchill argued for the establishment of a special tribunal to try murderers. 'It is monstrous that we have had some 200 murders and no one hung', he said. Ironical as it may seem, he went on to contrast the 'feebleness' of the existing system with the lightning efficiency of Bolshevik justice: 'After a person is caught he should pay the penalty within a week. Look at the tribunals which the Russian Government have devised.' At one point he turned to Lloyd George and said, 'You agreed six or seven months ago that there should be hanging.' The answer from Lloyd George was 'I feel certain you must hang.'[115] Both men also put considerable faith in the RIC's reserve force, which included many ex-servicemen, and was nicknamed the 'Black and Tans' on account of the colours in the uniforms they wore. This ill-disciplined body carried out wild and indiscriminate reprisals for IRA attacks. Houses were burnt down and people were shot without trial, but Churchill, who defended the 'loyal and gallant' Black and Tan officers, appeared to see little harm in this.[116] Likewise, Lloyd George argued 'that you cannot in the exciting state of Ireland punish a policeman who shoots a man whom he has every reason to suspect is connected with the police murders. This kind of thing *can* only be met by reprisals.'[117] Both defended this position in public, and both, by the autumn of 1920, still appeared confident the IRA would be defeated. 'We are going to break up this murder gang', Churchill declared at Dundee in October.[118] 'Unless I am mistaken, by the steps we have taken we have murder by the throat,' Lloyd George announced boldly in November. This was at the Guildhall. He went on to say (as reported by *The Times*): 'when the government were ready, we struck the terror [*sic*], and the terrorists are now complaining of terror. (Laughter and cheers.)'[119]

Nevertheless, by the end of the year they had moved to a more emollient stance. In June 1920, when Austen Chamberlain had suggested the government should negotiate with Sinn Féin, Lloyd George rejected the idea, as did Churchill, who said 'it was symptomatic that such a rotten proposal could be made'.[120] The plan was turned down. But at Cabinet on 29 December – two days after the government had declared martial law in four Irish counties – they took a different view. According to Henry Wilson, 'LG advanced the proposal of 1 or 2 months truce! He was backed by Winston who, to my disgust, was all in favour of it.'[121] However, the opposition of Wilson and the other generals was on this occasion decisive; martial law was extended further.

After Churchill's move to the Colonial Office there was a few months' hiatus in his close personal involvement with Irish affairs. In Cabinet in April, though, he argued in favour of going ahead with elections under the Government of Ireland Act, which had been

passed in December 1920. The act came into operation in May. It
created two parliaments that would operate on a Home Rule basis,
one for six counties in Northern Ireland and another for the remaining twenty-six counties of Southern Ireland. At the elections to the
Northern assembly, the Unionists won the bulk of the seats and
turned the parliament into a going concern. But in the South, Sinn
Féin were victorious and its elected members of course refused to
attend a body they considered illegitimate. By this stage Churchill
had emerged as one of a minority within the Cabinet who favoured
a truce; whereas Lloyd George now hesitated, Churchill 'frankly
acknowledged the failure of the policy of force'.[122] After informal
contacts had established that the Republican leaders were willing
to negotiate, Lloyd George decided to invite them to explore the
terms of a settlement. Both sides agreed a truce, which took effect on
11 July.

Although Lloyd George met Eamon De Valera, President of the
Dáil, for the first time at Downing Street three days later, substantive
talks did not start until the autumn. The difficulty was that Sinn Féin
was determined to achieve full independence for Ireland, whereas
the British were prepared only to grant Dominion status within the
Empire. But neither side was eager to renew the war, and, after
much to-ing and fro-ing, the Irish accepted an invitation to a
conference to ascertain 'how the association of Ireland with the
community of nations known as the British Empire can best be
reconciled with Irish national aspirations'.[123]

Negotiations started in October, and lasted eight weeks. Churchill
was chosen as one of the ministerial team of negotiators that was to
be headed by Lloyd George himself. The decision to include him
may have been an attempt on the Prime Minister's part to keep
him loyal; a few weeks later Frances Stevenson wrote that he had
'successfully wangled Churchill & Birkenhead' (the latter was also a
member of the team) into supporting his policy.[124] The Irish delegation was headed by Michael Collins and by Arthur Griffith, the
founder of Sinn Féin. Ominously, De Valera stayed away. Collins's
private notes of his impressions of the British negotiators make
fascinating reading and are worth reproducing at length:

> [On Lloyd George:] Born poor is therefore shrewd. Was lawyer
> therefore crafty. Nicknamed the 'Welsh Wizard' and for good

reason. Has a great deal of craft in his political methods, in his diplomatic approaches. Trusts that his fatherly air and benevolence will overcome all obstacles – craft again. 'Now Michael . . .' he says; or 'Now Mick . . .' On formal occasions it's 'Now Mr. Collins . . .' [He is] Not sure how far he can go with me . . . Would sell his nearest and dearest for political prestige. '14–'18 war good and bad for him. Hopes this affair will win him political prestige – which apparently he definitely needs.

[On Churchill:] Don't quite know whether he would be a crafty enemy in friendship. Outlook: political gain, nothing else. Will sacrifice all for political gain. Studies, I imagine, the detail carefully – thinks about his constituents, effect of so and so on them. Inclined to be bombastic. Full of ex-officer jingo or similar outlook. Don't actually trust him.[125]

He may, though, have been unfair to both. The negotiation of a settlement was unlikely to bring either man great political dividends. Rather, it was likely to alienate Unionists from the coalition. 'I have made up my mind that I will not coerce Southern Ireland', said Lloyd George privately, with a keen awareness of the risks he was taking. 'I may lose everything, but I shall have saved my soul anyway.'[126] And, in practice, Collins seems to have established a basis of trust with Lloyd George. He appears to have remained wary towards Churchill during the negotiations themselves, but he later expressed gratitude for his efforts.

Agreement was never going to be easy. The British were prepared to allow the creation of an Irish Free State, to consist of the twenty-six Southern counties, provided it remained within the British Commonwealth. They insisted on safeguards for the position of Northern Ireland, which would be able to continue as part of the United Kingdom if it wished. The Sinn Féiners objected to partition. They also fought against a solution that would leave the new state (at least nominally) under the sovereignty of the British Crown. By early November, Churchill later recalled, his colleagues were contemplating the break-up of the government: 'I urged that Ministers could not escape from their miseries by resignation.'[127] He wrote to Lloyd George: 'The criticism will certainly be made that the Government in resigning have abdicated their responsibility.'[128] The talks continued, although Churchill himself was not much involved in the latter stages. He was, however, present on the afternoon of 5 December, when Lloyd George gave the Irish delegates a powerful ultimatum. They must sign the treaty in its existing form – including the provisos for partition and allegiance to the Crown – or else quit and face a new war. After a few hours' consideration they agreed to sign, accepting the deal as the best available in the circumstances, and did so in the early hours of the next day. In January 1922, against the opposition of De Valera, the Dáil ratified the treaty by a narrow margin and a formal handover of power from Britain to the Irish followed. But radical republicans viewed the treaty as a sell-out, and in June Ireland descended into a ten-month civil war. Although the pro-treaty forces emerged victorious, a notable victim of the struggle was Michael Collins, who was shot dead by anti-treaty republicans in an ambush in August 1922. He had said, famously, that in signing the treaty he was signing his own death warrant.

Churchill later judged that the Irish treaty was fatal to Lloyd George's career. 'Within a year he had been driven from power', he wrote. 'Many other causes, some at least of which could have been avoided, contributed to his fall; but the Irish Treaty and its circumstances were unforgivable by the most tenacious elements in the Conservative Party.'[129] The same passage in his memoirs praised Lloyd George's political sacrifice, and suggests, tentatively, that it had led to a solution to the Irish problem. Churchill was not always so generous. Early in 1925 he dined with Lord Beaverbrook, who recorded: 'he criticises George very freely for the wicked Irish Treaty and declares that the Coalition Government ought to have continued to prosecute the war against Sinn Féin for another winter. I tried to shame him into acknowledgement of his leading part in making the Treaty. It is not easy to succeed.'[130] The disparity between Churchill's public and private statements should not necessarily be viewed as evidence of hypocrisy. Rather, it demonstrates the mercurial nature of his feelings about Lloyd George. He could move from bitter denunciations to protestations of faithful friendship with remarkable rapidity, and he was apparently equally sincere in both. One should not, however, leap from such an observation to the doubtful claim that, in spite of quarrels, his affection for Lloyd George never wavered. It did waver; and it not only wavered, it frequently collapsed.

As we have seen, Lloyd George's failure to appoint Churchill to the Exchequer triggered one of these collapses, and relations remained difficult for a few months afterwards. When Curzon protested to Lloyd George about Churchill's attempts to interfere with foreign policy, the Prime Minister wrote that he agreed: 'I have done my best to stopper his fizzing ... It is intolerable.'[131] And if the Colonial Secretary's behaviour left something to be desired, so did that of Lloyd George, who was 'in the habit of taunting' Churchill about Gallipoli.[132] There were also disagreements on domestic policy. In July 1921 Christopher Addison resigned his position as Minister Without Portfolio, in protest at cutbacks in the housing programme he had inaugurated when Minister of Health. (Lloyd George had moved Addison from the latter position in the spring, in reaction to Conservative 'anti-waste' sentiment, after the cost of the programme had spiralled. This showed how little scruple Lloyd George had about abandoning an ally who had ceased to be useful to him.) Churchill was one of those in Cabinet who opposed the cuts. On the day he resigned, Addison told his wife: 'Winston and co. think that L.G. is up against the biggest proposition of his life this time.'[133] The resignation – although it marked the death of radicalism in the coalition's social policy – proved a nine-days wonder. Churchill remained keen to show his independence, though. On 5 August, in Cabinet, the government whips requested that ministers cooperate on a political campaign in support of the coalition in the autumn. 'Winston says Doubtful if he can cooperate' noted H. A. L. Fisher in his diary. 'A significant hint. PM and AC [Austen Chamberlain] look with consternation. PM makes an appeal to Cabinet. Asks me later on what Winston is after.' According to Fisher, Churchill was dissatisfied with the state of the public finances – he felt there should have been a capital levy on war fortunes – and with the conduct of government business.[134]

At this time Churchill was struck by personal tragedy. At the end of June his mother had died, following a fall. Now his three-year-old daughter Marigold fell ill, and on 22 August she died. Both of these events brought him condolences from the Prime Minister, who had, of course, lost a child himself years before. The telegram to him on the death of Marigold read:

Deeply grieved so gallant a fight should have ended so sadly – You both have the consolation you did everything that could be

done to save the brave little life. I have the deepest sympathy for
you both in your sorrow – for I know what your anguish must
be.

    L.G.[135]

Days later, Edwin Montagu gave some of his friends 'a very
graphic account of Winston's agony over the death of his little girl
who died last week and of how Lloyd George had taken advantage
of it to make up all his differences with Winston'.[136] It needs to be
borne in mind, when considering this shocking claim, that Montagu
by this stage was a rather embittered man.

Whether as a consequence of cynical manipulation or not, the
Prime Minister's relations with Churchill do seem to have been
patched up to a degree. Disagreements continued, though. At the
end of September Churchill wrote a Cabinet memorandum on
unemployment, which, after a brief post-war economic boom, had
emerged as a serious problem. As he had told Lloyd George a few
days beforehand, he had been shocked to see in his constituency
'some men in bare feet & some children in a savage & starving
condition'.[137] In his memorandum he cast doubt on the wisdom of
continuing the government's policy of deflation. In response, Lloyd
George wrote to Churchill accusing him of 'an attempt to lay the
blame on your colleagues for present unemployment conditions' and
reproached him for having earlier supported Addison's 'very fatuous
policy with considerable vehemence and passion'. He concluded: 'I
am anxious to get the full benefit of your resourceful brain without
embarking upon discussions which will be not only fruitless but
exasperating, and divert our energies into channels which are neither
fertilizing nor navigable.'[138] According to Beaverbrook, Lloyd George
thought that the memorandum was a piece of mischief-making.
'Churchill only does it to annoy', he said.[139]

The seriousness of such disputes should not be exaggerated. Lloyd
George's decision to involve Churchill in the Irish talks was a sign
of confidence in him as well as a manoeuvre to keep him on side.
On 4 January 1922 Churchill wrote to Clementine from the South
of France, where both men were staying:

> The PM is singularly tame. I have never seen him quite like
> this. Vy pleased to have me with him again. He is piling a gt
> deal on to me now . . . He seems to me to have much less vitality

than formerly. But his manner is vy sprightly & his conversation
most amusing.[140]

Well might Lloyd George lack vitality, for his difficulties were
multiplying. He planned to dissolve parliament and renew his mandate, but, shortly after Churchill wrote his letter to Clementine, Sir
George Younger, the Chairman of the Conservative Party, made
public his opposition to this. Younger's threat that he and other
Tories would secede from the coalition scuppered Lloyd George's
hopes of an early election. This, in turn, was a serious dent to his
authority. The Prime Minister began to consider resignation. His
confidants differed about whether or not, if he did so, Churchill
would benefit. On 3 February Frances Stevenson wrote in her diary:
'Winston and F. E. will be furious when they learn of D.'s plan to go
out and leave the field to the Conservatives. That will not suit their
book at all.'[141] Philip Sassoon, though, warned Lloyd George: 'In
your resignation he [Churchill] would probably find his opportunity
– all the more willingly because he realises that so long as he is
associated with you he cannot hope to take the leading place.'[142] The
Prime Minister told Stevenson the following month that he agreed
'entirely' with Sassoon's 'estimate of Winston'.[143] Having consulted
Churchill, he offered, at the end of February, to resign in Austen
Chamberlain's favour. Although this provided Chamberlain with the
chance to form a homogeneous Conservative government, he
declined the opportunity. Contributing to this superficially surprising
decision were his genuine admiration for Lloyd George and his belief
in the importance of coalition as well as his own lack of confidence
and ambition. Therefore, the coalition staggered on for the time
being. In March, Sassoon, who had apparently changed his mind
about the nature of Churchill's calculations, opined to Lord Esher
that Lloyd George would be well advised to resign at once: 'But
Winston (whose views are always personal) advises him to hang on
because Winston does not want to give up his job & I am sure he
means to join the Tories at the earliest possible moment.'[144]
Given the uncertainty about the government's future, it is not
surprising that Lloyd George and Churchill's differences resurfaced.
In August 1921, in response to pressure from the press, a committee
was formed under Sir Eric Geddes (who was no longer a minister),
with the aim of achieving swingeing retrenchment in government

expenditure. Churchill objected to the procedure, and when, at the end of the year, he complained at Geddes's recommendations for major cuts to the budgets of the armed forces, he himself was given charge of a Cabinet committee on defence estimates. Its purpose was to establish what economies were possible without imperilling the country's security. It first met in January 1922. At the end of that month Churchill wrote to his wife that he did not 'feel the slightest confidence in L.G.'s judgement' on this issue. He added: 'Anything that serves the mood of the moment & the chatter of the ignorant & pliable newspapers is good enough for him.'[145] A few days later Frances Stevenson wrote in her diary that 'Winston is still nursing his ambition.' (This was the same entry in which she suggested that Lloyd George's plan to retire would not suit Churchill.) Her assessment, doubtless reflecting views held by Lloyd George, was that 'He [Churchill] is determined to oust Horne from the Exchequer, if he can, & is trying to defeat the Geddes recommendations & then to blame Horne for not economising.'[146] On 20 February, at a Cabinet meeting called to discuss the Geddes proposals, Churchill spoke to Lloyd George in a manner that appeared to show want of respect. He wrote the same day to apologize: 'The word "ungrateful" ought not to have been used, & I hope you will efface it from your memory.'[147] Yet the Prime Minister does not appear to have been in a forgiving mood: Churchill almost at once found himself excluded from a meeting of the Cabinet's Finance Committee.

Nevertheless, compromise was soon reached on the issue at hand. Churchill agreed to substantial, albeit modified, cuts. At the same time he defeated the Geddes Committee's recommendation that the air force should be carved up into army and navy branches. No sooner had this matter been settled, however, than the issue of the Bolsheviks raised its head again. Russia was experiencing a terrible famine. Lloyd George was inclined not only to grant humanitarian aid but also to countenance official British recognition of the Soviet government. He believed that bringing Russia back into the community of nations was essential in order to restore European peace and prosperity. Churchill, predictably, was opposed to him on this question. The forthcoming conference of European nations at Genoa was to discuss how relations with the USSR might be regularized. Lloyd George's attitude to Genoa thus became a key point of contention between him and Churchill.

The way the Prime Minister dealt with the issue was, it seems safe to say, influenced by new allegations of plots. Rumours were rife that he was about to relinquish office, and that Churchill might join the Unionists. In mid-March Lloyd George received two letters from Beaverbrook on this theme. The press lord had been vehemently anti-Lloyd George the previous year; but he was a man who changed his allegiances almost as often as he changed his socks. Beaverbrook suggested that Churchill had no intention of following Lloyd George were the latter to resign, but would rather join a new coalition under Austen Chamberlain. 'I put the probability of Conservative opposition to Winston's retention of office to him the other day', Beaverbrook said in his second letter. 'He was obviously immensely surprised and had not thought of it. However he soon persuaded himself that the danger was negligible.'[148] Lloyd George also heard of Churchill's alleged activities from Charles McCurdy, who was shortly to replace Guest as Coalition Liberal Chief Whip: 'Churchill having made his position absolutely clear – that in certain events he will join the Conservatives – has given a clear lead to Co. Libs who are prepared to follow him, & lobbying is going on'.[149] Perhaps less important than whether the claims were true is the impression they created in Lloyd George's mind.

One can well understand his suspicions when Austen Chamberlain wrote to him about Genoa, pointing out that Churchill formed an obstacle to agreement there. Churchill had, Chamberlain said, threatened to resign if the government granted *de jure* recognition to the Soviet government, thus presenting the Conservative leaders with a dilemma. '[O]ur position would be impossible if Winston retired because he was more Tory than the Tory Ministers', he wrote, before suggesting 'that you yourself should see Winston and have a quiet personal talk with him' before the Cabinet discussed the question.[150] Chamberlain, clearly, was doing his best to be helpful, but it would not have been surprising if Lloyd George had interpreted the letter as evidence that Churchill was hoping to engineer a Conservative revolt. Certainly, his response was an angry one. He told Chamberlain that he was bent on negotiating recognition at Genoa, and that if Churchill was determined to resign rather than assent to it, 'the Cabinet must choose between Winston and me'.[151] He sent a copy of the correspondence to Robert Horne, observing: 'I told you I thought Winston would be a real wrecker.'[152]

There was a frenzy of activity over the next few days. On the morning of 24 March the *Daily Chronicle* carried a report that stated that 'Mr. Lloyd George will part from his dearest political friend rather than abandon this great fundamental issue of politics', i.e. recognition of the Soviet Union. The article was based, apparently, on a briefing by Lloyd George, and Chamberlain, who thought it provocative, warned the Prime Minister that Churchill would view it as a direct challenge.[153] The same day Sassoon told Lloyd George that Beaverbrook thought Churchill was 'determined to resign over the Recognition question & join the Die Hards', i.e. the right wing of the Tories. Sassoon also reported Bonar Law's view that 'Winston will only go if he can rely on a very serious revolt in the Conservative Party' and that this was in fact unlikely to arise. The letter further noted the risk that Churchill would 'burn his boats' in a speech he was due to make the following night at Northampton, although Sassoon himself thought he would not 'do more than stage the pyre'.[154]

Lloyd George at this point was in Wales. He seems either to have received Sassoon's letter the day it was sent, or to have had some other equivalent form of information. At any rate, he phoned Chamberlain that evening in order to get him to put pressure on Churchill not to say anything too extreme in his speech. Chamberlain did so, and got Birkenhead to do the same. This appears to have worked: at any rate, Churchill did not 'burn his boats' at Northampton. Yet, evidently, Lloyd George did not think an appeal seen as coming from himself would be of much value. Chamberlain wrote to him, 'I did not use your name in making my appeal to him, for I understood that you would prefer that my intervention should appear as a spontaneous act of my own.'[155] Birkenhead's urgings may have been decisive. According to political gossip a few months later, he dominated Churchill at this time: 'he and he alone had kept him from resigning over [the] Bolshevists at Genoa'.[156]

On 27 March Churchill received a telegram from Lord Rothermere: 'YOU REMEMBER MY TELEGRAM FROM PARIS IN NOVEMBER HOPE YOU WILL NOT BE SO FOOLISH AS TO MISS ANOTHER OPPORTUNITY'.[157] The message was clear – he should resign. According to Thomas Jones, Churchill also received a message from Northcliffe, Rothermere's brother, similarly 'urging him to come out as the leader of the Tory Party'. (Northcliffe's message, like Rothermere's Novem-

ber one, does not appear to have survived.) Churchill thus entered a
ministerial meeting on the issue that evening, and a Cabinet the next
day, fortified by implied promises of press support should he break
with Lloyd George. The outcome was an agreement that the Soviet
government should be recognized only if it fulfilled important conditions, such as payment of the Tsarist government's debts and the
cessation of revolutionary propaganda. As these conditions were
unlikely to be met, it was clear that Lloyd George had, as Jones put
it, 'in substance . . . capitulated to Churchill.'[158]

The Genoa conference met in April. The Prime Minister,
removed from the domestic sphere, was not much inclined to work
within the constraints that had been imposed upon him by his
colleagues. Churchill, therefore, observed proceedings from a distance
with considerable alarm. However, the Soviets revealed during the
conference that they had been engaged in separate, secret negotiations with Germany. This produced an atmosphere of mistrust,
and the conference achieved little before it broke up in late May.
Two months later Churchill offered a further warning to Lloyd
George that should the issue of recognition arise again he should
have to resign. He wrote in this way, he said, simply to prevent
misunderstanding. He recalled a comment that Lloyd George had
made about him before – 'that I was a branch that cracked before it
broke'.[159] That is to say, he always gave due warning of issues on
which he might be compelled to leave the government. It might be
fair to say of Churchill during the 1919–22 period that he cracked a
great deal but never did break.

At the end of May another crisis started to develop in relation
to Ireland. A small body of men from the Free State crossed the
border with the North and occupied two villages, Pettigo and Belleek.
Collins and the other Irish leaders disclaimed any responsibility
for the incursion. In early June Churchill, with Cabinet approval,
ordered British troops to recapture Pettigo, an operation that involved
crossing into Free State territory. This was done successfully, but
Lloyd George nonetheless became nervous about further action to
take back Belleek. This, he thought, would be seen as a provocation
to the Free State and might lead to war, which he was desperate to
avoid. He sent Churchill a letter rebuking him for his alleged
recklessness. In spite of his concerns, Belleek was retaken with little
bloodshed. At one point during the crisis Lloyd George 'compared

Winston to a chauffeur who apparently is perfectly sane and drives with great skill for months, then suddenly he takes you over a precipice. He thought that there was a strain of lunacy.'[160] Thomas Jones, who recorded these comments, subsequently observed of Churchill: 'I have seen him lose his head at critical moments in the Irish business, and but for L.G.'s intervention we would have had bloodshed on the Border more than once.'[161] With regard to the Middle East, by contrast, Lloyd George took a tougher line than Churchill did, now deprecating the idea floated by the latter that Britain might withdraw from Iraq. Difficult as these issues were, though, neither of them precipitated a real breach between the two men.

During the summer a further problem emerged for the Prime Minister: the honours scandal. The practice of granting of honours in exchange for contributions to party funds was a long-established one. The Conservatives as well as the Liberals had done it in the past. Under Lloyd George it was done more blatantly, and on a bigger scale; but then, he had a particular need to build up his own political fund, as the Asquithians had control of the Liberal Party finances. Most historians are agreed, therefore, that the Unionist outcry at the government's June honours list involved a double standard. There were indeed some controversial names on the list – notably the peerage proposed for the South African mining entrepreneur Sir Joseph Robinson, whose methods of doing business were open to question. But the Tory critics were not really upset at the sale of honours per se. They simply wanted a bigger share of the proceeds for their own party. Nevertheless, the affair was a damaging blow to Lloyd George's reputation. 'It is indeed a decline', Churchill wrote to his wife. 'All this year we have suffered from his personal contradictions . . . & now lastly the Honours Gaffe.'[162]

Lloyd George continued to contemplate resignation – although in practice he did not stand down until forced. He had recently had a new house, named Bron-y-de, built for him in Churt, Surrey. It was designed by Philip Tilden. (Churchill was to hire the same architect to remodel Chartwell, the house that he was about to buy in Kent. When Thomas Jones stayed there in 1926, he noted: 'Tilden forgot to put a scullery at Churt: what he forgot at Chartwell I did not discover because he was a subject to be avoided.')[163] On 8 September Lloyd George sent Clementine Churchill a gift of apples. 'I am sending you samples of the produce of the Churt wilderness to which the Die Hards intend to relegate me soon!' he wrote. 'It is an exile which has no terror for me since I discovered its hidden treasures'.[164] The next day Turkish troops occupied Smyrna, after Greek forces had been routed. This was a key moment in the crisis that was to throw Lloyd George and Churchill together once more and to trigger for them both the political exile the Prime Minister had predicted for himself. He may not have appreciated, though, that in his own case it was to be permanent.

The Greeks had been in headlong retreat since late August; and Kemal's advance now seemed to pose a direct threat to British troops at Chanak, on the Asian side of the Dardanelles. On 15 September the Cabinet took a clear decision to defend, by force if need be, the neutral 'Zone of the Straits' (as laid out in the Treaty of Sèvres). Churchill was deputed to draw up a telegram to be sent to each of the Dominions informing them of this and seeking their active support. Lloyd George approved his draft, and the messages were sent out late the same evening. On the 16th, the two men worked together on a press communiqué, declaring it to be the duty of the wartime allies to defend 'the deep-water line between Europe and Asia against a violent and hostile Turkish aggression'.[165] The Dominion governments felt that this was an attempt to bounce them into war, and the majority of them declined to send troops. Alarm also grew in Britain at the prospect of a new conflict.

On 22 September Lloyd George gave Churchill charge of a Cabinet committee to oversee the detail of military movements. A few days later Churchill wrote to Archibald Sinclair, justifying his own shift to a more anti-Turk position. By this point, Lloyd George had reluctantly agreed that any future peace deal would have to involve the return of eastern Thrace from Greece to Turkey. Churchill told Sinclair:

> Thank God that awful pro-Greek policy against which we have so long inveighed has come to an end. We have paid an enormously heavy price for nothing. However, at the very end I have had to throw in my lot with LG in order to try to make some sort of front against what would otherwise have been a complete Turkish walk-over and the total loss of all the fruits of the Great War in this quarter.[166]

In private conversation, his views appeared less nuanced. Hankey recorded a dinner with him, Lloyd George, and Philip Sassoon, at which the men talked late into the night. 'Winston, hitherto a strong Turko-phile had swung round to the threat to his beloved Dardanelles and become Violently Turko-phobe and even Phil-Hellene.'[167] Hankey's perception was shared by Curzon. The latter told Chamberlain that he was 'very much alarmed at the idea put forward by Winston and the P.M. that we should once again seek the precarious and as I think worthless alliance of the Greeks, and very likely find ourselves once more at war with Turkey – with Greece alone on our side.'[168] Coming, as it did, from the Foreign Secretary, such dissent was very problematic for Lloyd George; indeed Curzon predicted that war would bring about the fall of the government.

In fact, the government could not be saved even though war was averted. At the end of September, the Cabinet, fearing an imminent attack on Chanak, drew up a powerful ultimatum to the Turks. If they did not withdraw their forces, the British would open fire. However, General Harington, commander of the Allied forces in Turkey, held back from delivering the message, fearing that it would be provocative. In the event, Kemal decided not to attack, and agreed to negotiate with Harington at Mudania. On 11 October a convention was signed, pending negotiation of a new peace treaty between the Allies and Turkey. (Under the 1923 Treaty of Lausanne Turkey recovered eastern Thrace, the Zone of the Straits and other territory.) Lloyd George and Churchill seemed to regret that the crisis had not developed into war. Hankey wrote in his diary: 'I walked across the Park with Churchill one evening towards the end of the crisis and he quite frankly regretted that the Turks had not attacked us at Chanak, as he felt that the surrender of Eastern Thrace was humiliating, and that the return of the Turks to Europe meant an infinity of trouble.' Hankey added: 'I don't think the Prime Minister felt very differently.'[169]

As the Chanak crisis receded, the political crisis in Britain grew. Asquithites singled out not only Lloyd George but also Churchill for public criticism. Francis Acland MP argued that 'Mr. Lloyd George and Mr. Winston Churchill and mere hangers-on of Mr. Lloyd George like the War Minister [Worthington-Evans] should go.'[170] Herbert Gladstone (Lord Gladstone as he now was) said it was unclear what was in 'the excitable heads of Mr. Lloyd George and

Mr. Winston Churchill'.[171] Asquith himself, in an attack on Lloyd George's overall style of government, spoke of 'amateurs in Downing-street'.[172] More troublingly for the proponents of coalition, heavy-weight Unionist dissent now emerged as well. On 7 October *The Times* published a letter from Bonar Law, in which he argued that 'We cannot alone act as the policeman of the world'.[173] The implied criticism of Lloyd George's policy seemed to show that Law was prepared to give an independent lead to Conservatives in a way that Chamberlain, the party's official leader, would not. As Law's health had now recovered, he was a potential alternative premier. By 13 October Lloyd George had concluded, as he told C. P. Scott, that 'a breakup is inevitable'. He did not, he said, know whether it would come before or after the general election that he hoped to hold. He said that when the coalition did end, 'I hope to carry some of the other Ministers with me – Chamberlain and Birkenhead who are both really Liberals and Horne. And Churchill, who is really a Tory, will be bound to follow.'[174]

In an unpublished draft of the first volume of *The Second World War*, Churchill made a remarkable claim, hitherto unnoticed by scholars. 'As Mr. Lloyd-George[']s principal lieutenant, I persuaded him to declare or to allow me to declare that he would in no circumstances continue to be Prime Minister after the election was over', he wrote. 'I still hoped that this might prove a solution and with his full agreement I planned to announce it at Cardiff where I was due to speak in a few days.' However, he wrote, events moved too quickly for this plan to be put into effect.[175] It is true that Churchill planned to make a speech (in fact at Bristol), and that this had to be cancelled because he fell ill. Nevertheless, although Churchill may have thought that he had convinced Lloyd George to take the course of action proposed, there is no independent evidence that he tried to do so, let alone that he succeeded. 'Vote for me and I will resign at once' is not, after all, much of an election cry; would Lloyd George have really taken it up? The passage is probably an example of Churchill's memory playing him false as, subconsciously, he exaggerated the extent of his own past influence.

What is certain is that, on 15 October, Lloyd George and other ministers dined with Churchill at his house on Sussex Square. A meeting of Conservative MPs was due to take place at the Carlton Club four days later. Austen Chamberlain promised to argue that the upcoming election should be fought on a coalition basis, with Lloyd George as leader. The Carlton Club meeting had been called by the Tory leaders in an attempt to seize the initiative from the rebels. Yet when the meeting took place, Chamberlain's high-handed demand for unquestioning loyalty turned the party against him. His speech was trumped by Stanley Baldwin, the Conservative President of the Board of Trade. Baldwin had decided to resign from the Cabinet because he had concluded, as he told his wife, that Churchill and Lloyd George were planning, for their own electoral advantage, to launch a 'Christian' war against Muslim Turkey.[176] He now attacked Lloyd George as 'a dynamic force', a phenomenon which he described as 'a very terrible thing; it may crush you but it is not necessarily right'.[177] The MPs voted by a heavy majority to withdraw from the coalition, and in so doing showed their lack of confidence in their own official leaders.

In the light of this Lloyd George had no alternative but to resign at once. He did so with a surprising degree of levity. On 23 October, as he prepared to leave Downing Street, Hankey found him 'in great form – absolutely hilarious'. For his private secretaries he performed an amusing mimicry of Bonar Law, who was to be the new Prime Minister, receiving a deputation.[178] Baldwin, who had imagined that by attacking the coalition he was committing career suicide, now became Law's Chancellor of the Exchequer. He was to dominate British politics for the next fifteen years. Lloyd George had drastically underrated him. Reputedly, when he first heard of Baldwin's opposition, a few days before the Carlton Club meeting, he said to Churchill: 'Does little Baldwin think he can turn us out?'[179]

Churchill, for his part, had missed the key events. On 16 October he had fallen ill, and two days later he was operated on for appendicitis. In his draft memoirs, he made the unrealistic conjecture that, in the absence of his own advice, Lloyd George had resigned precipitately.

> He could certainly have awaited further developments. He could have gone to the country with his Liberal and personal following ... we could at least have gone down fighting as a so-called National administration. I should have counselled this. But at the crucial moment I was prostrated . . .[180]

When preparing his book for publication in the 1940s, Churchill was persuaded by his advisers to slim down his account of the 1920s as a whole.[181] This suggestion that his illness made a material difference to the outcome (together with the claim that he had earlier persuaded Lloyd George to announce he would not stay on as Prime Minister) was therefore lost. In the published version, Churchill confined himself to noting that he had been out of action at the key moment, and that 'when I recovered consciousness I learned that the Lloyd George Government had resigned, and that I had lost not only my appendix but my Office as Secretary of State for the Dominions and Colonies'.[182]

The collapse of the coalition marked the end of an important phase, indeed the most constructive one, in the relationship between Churchill and Lloyd George. Their collaboration, problematic though it often was, had produced much of value, from pre-war welfare reform to the negotiation of the Irish treaty. There were to be no more joint achievements of this kind. For the time being, Churchill remained one of the ex-Prime Minister's main lieutenants, in opposition to the new Conservative government. However – in spite of some leading politicians' fears to the contrary – they would never hold office in the same government again. Lloyd George, of course, never returned to office at all, whereas Churchill still had his best (and some of his worst) years in front of him. As 1922 drew to a close, therefore, the 'Master and Servant' era was all but over. All the same, the two men could not have known that with any certainty at the time.

Chapter Seven

TWO WAYS OF LIBERALISM

AFTER THE FALL OF the coalition, Lloyd George and Churchill continued to work together, but only for a short time. The latter, by a series of crab-like stages, moved back towards the Conservatives, emerging in 1924 as Chancellor of the Exchequer in the newly elected Tory government. This not only divided him from Lloyd George but also shocked many of his new comrades. He had not lost his reputation as 'a bad colleague, trouble all round', not to mention as a political highwayman and blackmailer.[1] Lloyd George also remained a major political player, but in spite (and to some extent because) of the fears of other major figures, was never able to claw his way back into power. In an article written in the late 1920s, but apparently never published, Lord Beaverbrook contrasted the men's respective careers during the decade. He wrote that although Lloyd George had failed to rescue the Liberal Party, he had made 'a wonderful effort' to do so. The same compliment could not, he wrote, be paid to Churchill, who had 'left Liberalism to consummate its own suicide, and turned towards the rising sun of Toryism', and who, in spite of his promises to 'shake up the old gang', had simply joined the gang himself. The article concluded that

> Mr. Lloyd George has no Bishopric. He has faced failure and disaster in the middle of a great and glorious career. But there has been no office or emolument connected with his final effort to save the Liberal party. There are two ways of Liberalism – one selected by Mr. Lloyd George and the other by Mr. Winston Churchill.[2]

This paean to political constancy and selflessness was a bit rich, coming as it did from one of the most capricious and power-hungry individuals in public life at the time. Nevertheless, considered strictly on their own terms, Beaverbrook's comments are a good starting point for considering our protagonists' actions during this period.

There is a case that Lloyd George remained the country's most clearsighted and imaginative politician, putting forward convincing remedies that duller folk rejected, to the nation's detriment. Churchill, meanwhile, in part because of his love of office, threw in his lot with those same dull folk and made himself complicit in their errors, which contributed to depression and eventually war. That case is at least plausible. But did Churchill's parting from Lloyd George constitute a betrayal, either in personal terms or in those of principle?

To establish this we must return to our narrative. Churchill was unable to participate fully in the election campaign that followed the fall of the coalition because he was still recuperating from his appendectomy. On 23 October 1922 Lloyd George visited him as he convalesced, and found him bitter against Lord Curzon, one of the few heavyweight Tories who had accepted office from Bonar Law. The same day Lloyd George and Churchill were unanimously endorsed, as President and Vice-president respectively, of the organization of the ex-coalition Liberals.[3] Three days later parliament was dissolved. Churchill explained his attitude to recent developments in a message to the President of the Dundee Liberal Association. It contained an account of his relationship with Lloyd George that was carefully modulated to his own political purposes:

> In the political confusion that reigns, and with causes so precious to defend, I take my stand by Mr. Lloyd George. I was his friend before he was famous. I was with him when all were at his feet. And now to-day when men who fawned upon him, who praised even his errors, who climbed into place and Parliament upon his shoulders, have cast him aside ... I am still his friend and lieutenant.[4]

Churchill's claim of unbroken fidelity to Lloyd George was as doubtful as his assertion that he had been his friend before he was famous. What he was doing, of course, was using a motif of constancy as a symbolic contrast to the supposedly treacherous and scoresettling behaviour of those who had either now deserted the coalition or had refused to join it in the first place.

Although Churchill was genuinely convinced of his own righteousness, he was in reality no less calculating than many of those he attacked. He stood by Lloyd George not out of sentiment but because he considered it advantageous to do so. He believed, as he wrote to the former Prime Minister himself, that 'the Lloyd George wave' would 'grow stronger every month' as a result of the short period of 'ultra-Tory rule' that he believed the country was in for.[5] When it became clear that this was not true, Churchill made a transition, by degrees, to the Conservatives, thus allying himself with men he had previously denounced. Some of his colleagues at times suspected him of wanting to renew his alliance with his erstwhile leader, but no genuine opportunity to do so presented itself, and the matter was never put to the test. Lloyd George, for his part, never ruled out the possibility of a new collaboration, but he seemed just as happy attacking Churchill as he had been working with him. This was not hypocrisy; it was politics.

At the start of the 1922 campaign Lloyd George was in good spirits. At the end of October he, Birkenhead and Horne visited Whittinghame, Balfour's house in Scotland. Joan Lascelles, Balfour's niece, noted that the men were 'nearly as funny' when talking about Churchill as they were when mocking Curzon. She told her husband: 'Ll.G. had toned down Winston's manifesto from a Tory point of view, and had struck out sentences like – "Lord Curzon's idea of the H. of L. is a House of superior people like himself." . . . Winston had lately read the ethics of Aristotle, and confided to Ll.G. that he had already thought of so much of it before for himself.'[6]

The reference to toning down Churchill's manifesto was indicative of Lloyd George's difficulties in the election. It seemed possible that Law's supporters would not win with a majority big enough to allow him to carry on his government without assistance from some other group. The problem of the ex-coalition, or 'National', Liberals was this. They needed, on the one hand, to contest and win enough seats to hold the balance of power in parliament. In order to appear distinct from the Tories they needed to make some appeal to radicalism. On the other hand, they did not want to provoke the Conservatives into putting candidates up against them, or say anything that would rule out the possibility of future cooperation in government. Lloyd George, therefore, tried in his speeches to emphasize both his 'constitutional' and 'radical' credentials, and the effect was not a very happy one. Polling was on 15 November. The Conservatives won 345 seats, the National Liberals 62, the Asquithian

Liberals 54 and Labour 142, thus becoming the main opposition party for the first time.

Churchill – whatever he may have written about Curzon – was one of those who had opposed 'spreading the war' with the Conservatives. They did not oppose him at Dundee.[7] He lost his seat all the same. Edwin Scrymgeour, an independent socialist, headed the poll. (Scrymgeour had first fought the seat in 1908, when Churchill was contesting the by-election, receiving only 655 votes.) There was some qualified regret at this outcome among those now somewhat semi-detached Tories who deprecated the demise of the coalition. Horne and Balfour were both sorry that Churchill had lost, but agreed it might in one respect be good not to have him in the Commons for the time being 'as he wd never be able to help attacking the Govt.'. Balfour's view was that Churchill 'was really an almost reactionary Tory . . . but hanging on to Free Trade by the skin of his teeth to be able to be classed as a liberal'. The two 'agreed that Winston had no idea how unpopular he was',[8] and believed that 'Winston is longing to be taken over by the Conservative Party.'[9]

The loss of his seat was, of course, a terrific setback for Churchill. Lloyd George's prestige had fallen a fair way from the heights of 1918. But there was no doubt, even on the most optimistic analysis of Churchill's position, of the relative position of the respective reputations of the two. T. E. Lawrence ('Lawrence of Arabia') was a great admirer of Churchill, and wrote to console him after his defeat: 'in guts and power and speech you can roll over anyone bar Lloyd George: so that you can (or should) really not be in any hurry'.[10] But could Churchill continue to work with Lloyd George, and, if not, what should he do instead?

The coalition's supporters made some efforts to stay in touch with each other in the aftermath of the election. For example there was a 'Coalition repast' at Sassoon's house in Park Lane, at which Chamberlain, Lloyd George, Churchill and Birkenhead outlined their opinions on the political situation.[11] However, Churchill spent much of 1923 working on *The World Crisis* and on private business interests. As he was out of the Commons, his contacts with Lloyd George were necessarily fewer than when they had been members of the same government. At the end of January he told his wife of an approach by Edward Hilton Young, the new Chief Whip of Lloyd George's National Liberals, who wanted to find him a new seat. Churchill seemed open to this suggestion, although sceptical of success: 'He [Young] will no doubt look about, but it is what Asquith called "A dark and difficult adventure".'[12] There even appeared to be some hope that, stimulated by the growing Labour threat, the two parts of the Liberal Party might be reunited. For example, Beatrice Webb noted (with disdain) the attitude of Clifford Sharp, the editor of the *New Statesman*. 'The measure of his partisanship for the Liberal as against the Labour Party is his willingness, if not eagerness, to welcome back into the Liberal fold Lloyd George and Winston Churchill, both statesmen that he has virulently criticized and condemned, because he thinks their inclusion will strengthen the Liberal against the Labour Party.'[13] Lord Gladstone, a leading Asquithian, perceived Churchill (among others) as a brake on Lloyd George's natural inclination to come to terms.[14]

In May 1923 Law's brief period at 10 Downing Street ended. He resigned because he was terminally ill with throat cancer. Baldwin, the hero of the Carlton Club meeting, completed his meteoric ascent by beating Lord Curzon to the premiership. He was eager to reunite the Conservative Party by including erstwhile supporters of the coalition in his government. Churchill, of course, was not a Tory, but, in conversation with Horne, he mooted the possibility he might become one. 'I am what I have always been – a Tory Democrat,' he said. 'Force of circumstances has compelled me to serve with another party, but my views have never changed, and I should be glad to give effect to them by rejoining the Conservatives.'[15] However, he had not yet finally settled on doing so.

Lloyd George was unclear about his own future. As Churchill put it to Baldwin the following year, 'For L.G. . . . there were only three courses open: to become Prime Minister, to smash a Party, or to settle down as an Elder Statesman.'[16] During 1923 the former premier waited on events. He made a number of public calls for Liberal reunion, and occupied himself with journalism. In the autumn he embarked on a highly successful speaking tour of the USA and Canada. Then Baldwin made a mistake which offered his opponents an opportunity. At the Conservative Party conference in October he dramatically declared that unemployment could be ameliorated only by the introduction of protectionism. In his memoirs, Churchill alleged that the Prime Minister did this because he was 'disquieted by the fear that Mr. Lloyd George would rally, upon the cry of

Protection, the numerous dissentient Conservative leaders who had
gone out of office with the War Cabinet, and thus split the Government majority and even challenge the Party leadership'.[17] In fact,
Baldwin's motivation was probably not so cynical. At any rate, Bonar
Law had promised at the previous election that the Tories would not
introduce tariffs during the life of the next parliament. Therefore, if
Baldwin wanted to implement the policy he needed a new electoral
mandate. By putting free trade under threat, he had raised the one
issue that was guaranteed to unite the Liberals and rally Labour
against him.

On 9 November Lloyd George landed at Southampton, amid
great press excitement. Churchill, anticipating the election that was
to be called a few days later, sent him a message, by the hand of
Archibald Sinclair. It was addressed to 'My dear L.G.' and was
signed 'Yours always, W'. It read, in part: 'We are in for a big fight
– and I am glad to think *together*'.[18] Three days later, they met
Chamberlain and Birkenhead at Beaverbrook's house. Clementine
Churchill, who was firmly Liberal, had urged her husband not to
attend. She believed that to do so would be to risk jeopardizing the
goodwill of the Asquithians, by implanting in their minds the idea
that he wanted a new alliance with the Tories.[19] Beaverbrook may
have had some notion of reviving the coalition. The novelist Arnold
Bennett, who was another of his guests, wrote to his nephew of how
the politicians present were 'a self-seeking crowd who were plotting
& conspiring against the govt under the benign influence of Max',
how none of them had mentioned principles or the welfare of the
country, and how Churchill had had too much to drink and quar-
relled with Birkenhead. 'Arnold', Beaverbrook told Bennett afterwards, 'you've seen hell with the lid off.' And so, he felt, he had.[20]

There was no realistic chance of re-establishing the coalition, if
that, indeed, had been the purpose of the plotting. Almost immediately, on 13 November, Asquith and Lloyd George agreed to reunify
the Liberal Party. Within a week Churchill had accepted the Liberal
nomination for West Leicester. Beatrice Webb noted that although
the party was now 'under the ostensible leadership of Asquith', it was
'really under the leadership of Lloyd George and Winston'.[21] The
(Asquithian) National Liberal Club's portraits of the latter pair had
been taken down in 1921 and consigned to the cellar. Now they were
brought up again and restored to their former glory. The Club's

General Committee decided this 'unanimously and without discussion'. With heavy irony, *The Times* commented: 'It was better so, for there is always danger in recalling the past at the moment of reconciliation.'[22] This remark could have served as an epitaph, not only on Liberal reunion, but also on the many previous patch-ups between Lloyd George and Churchill themselves.

Election day was 6 December. During the campaign – the last he fought as a Liberal – Churchill did not shy away from his association with Lloyd George. Clementine Churchill was actively involved in the electioneering, and said in one of her speeches that 'with the single exception of Lloyd George my husband has been responsible for the passing of more legislation for the benefit of the working class than any other living statesman'.[23] However, Churchill was unable to overturn the existing Labour majority in West Leicester. He was beaten by over 4,000 votes. Ten days later Beaverbrook wrote to Robert Borden, the former Canadian Prime Minister, commenting on his friend's relationship with Lloyd George:

Churchill has definitely separated himself from George – and wishes this to be understood in the Inner Tabernacles of Liberalism. His idea is that the reversion of Asquith's leadership will fall to him, because George has against him certain powerful irreconcilables, who will never trust him again as leader. All this seems to me highly speculative.[24]

So it was; but if Churchill had told Beaverbrook that within a year he would be appointed as a Conservative Chancellor of the Exchequer, the incredulity would have been yet greater.

The national outcome of the election presented a complex picture. The Conservatives were still the largest party, winning 258 constituencies. Labour came second, with 191, and the Liberals followed with 159. This meant that the Tories could be forced from office if the other parties voted together. If they did so, Labour, as the second largest party, would be called on to form a government. Asquith quickly made plain that the Liberals would not prop up Baldwin's administration, and on this Lloyd George agreed with him. Their attitude made it inevitable that Ramsay MacDonald, the Labour leader, would become Prime Minister of a minority government. Lloyd George was more inclined than Asquith to offer Mac-

Donald active support, but both envisaged that he could in due course be turned out of power at some moment that would allow the Liberals to seize an advantage. Churchill profoundly disagreed with their strategy, believing that the advent of a Labour government would be a grave national misfortune. Years later, Baldwin recalled Churchill's view that it would have been better for the Liberals to have kept the existing government in office: 'he saw the political opportunity right enough but Ll.G saw red and wanted at all costs to get the Tories out'.[25] On 21 January 1924 the Conservative government was defeated in the Commons, and MacDonald became Prime Minister the next day.

A few days beforehand Lloyd George had observed privately that, 'for three years or more', he and Churchill had been 'at direct variance on vital questions'.[26] As if to prove the point, Churchill now broke definitively with the Liberals. At the start of February he declined the offer to fight Bristol West for the party. Later the same month, the Conservative MP for the Abbey Division of Westminster died. There was a possibility Churchill might be chosen by the local Conservative Association to fight the resultant by-election, but he declined to attend an interview with the Executive because he was unwilling to accept its decision as final.[27] An inexperienced candidate, Otho Nicholson, was chosen instead. Churchill nevertheless determined to contest the seat as an independent anti-socialist candidate. He had high hopes of attracting significant Tory (as well as Liberal) support, including that of many of the MPs who lived in the constituency. This was because, he told his wife, there were thirty Liberal MPs in the Commons who wanted to cooperate with the Conservatives '& who the Cons are anxious to win as allies'. If Churchill won the seat, he would provide the focus for this group.[28] One example of such reasoning was offered by Gideon Murray, a former Unionist MP who was an elector in the Division:

> I observe that L.G. is daily making himself more felt in the H of C. and is being highly successful in splitting in his own interests the ranks of the Government & the Labour & Socialist Party. – If Winston were in the House & on our side and sitting as an Independent member (not on the front opposition bench) he could counter this movement on L.G.'s part and would do so in his own as well as our interests. I know of no-one in the H of C.

on our side today who is capable of competing with L.G. in debate – *Winston could do it.*[29]

The Conservatives were, however, bitterly divided over Churchill's candidacy. 'I am afraid that turbulent, pushing busybody Winston is going to split our party', complained former Home Secretary William Bridgeman. 'I can't understand how anyone can want him or put any faith in a man who changes sides just when he thinks it is to his own personal advantage to do so.'[30] In mid-March Leo Amery publicly criticized Churchill, thus breaking the informal agreement among Shadow Cabinet members not to intervene. This allowed Churchill to extract a letter of support from Balfour, who 'would have given anything to be kept out of it all'.[31] Baldwin's private attitude was ambiguous, but in public he supported the official Conservative candidate. Austen Chamberlain wrote to his wife: 'If I can vote, I shall vote quietly for Winston saying nothing about it but it is amazing how unpopular he is ... I scarcely think that he will win & Ll G expects that the socialists will creep in between him and Nicholson.'[32] Lloyd George, for his part, wrote to Birkenhead: 'I hope Winston has not marched into a morass'.[33] Churchill was, in fact, beaten narrowly by Nicholson. But he had done well enough to show that he was a potential asset to the Tory Party. His return to its ranks was now in prospect.

His relations with Lloyd George do not seem to have been damaged by his ongoing political transition. If anything, they were more cordial than at many points when the two had been in the same party. In February Churchill enjoyed a pleasant evening with Lloyd George, Beaverbrook and Rothermere. During the by-election he sent Lloyd George a jokey telegram: 'Please inform me whether you desire to be personally canvassed or whether you feel able to elucidate the problem unaided'.[34] But the recipient did not live in the constituency, and responded: 'Sorry have no vote in this exciting and highly significant contest.'[35] Earlier, when Churchill told Lloyd George that he had resolved to stand, 'He said I was only acting in accordance with my convictions & made no reproaches of any kind.'[36]

In the aftermath of the election, Lloyd George wrote in the *Daily Chronicle* that Churchill's campaign had been overly defensive and insufficiently radical.[37] 'I read your article with great interest & pleasure', Churchill wrote to him. 'I was not strong enough to unfold a programme – nor was there time.'[38] This was in March. Early in April Churchill reported to Balfour that he had had 'a long talk with LG'. He claimed that Lloyd George 'has greatly altered his point of view, and seems inclined to lean towards those National Liberal elements which he somewhat precipitately dispersed after the last General Election'. (Churchill clearly felt that Liberal ex-coalitionists like himself had been frozen out.) Moreover, 'I think that if things are steered and driven in the right direction, he might well be a buttress of a future "Conservative and Liberal Union" Administration in which the colleagues who stood by him in 1922 were influential.'[39] It is true that Lloyd George was now becoming increasingly assertive against the Labour government, but whether or not this account accurately reflected his position is unclear. Churchill may well have been too hopeful. And his own apparent willingness to consort with Lloyd George was bound to raise Tory suspicions.

In the meantime, Baldwin was not proving very effective as Leader of the Opposition. He had had some successes. In February, he secured Conservative reunion, with Austen Chamberlain, Birkenhead and Horne agreeing to accept his leadership. For him, taking Birkenhead into the fold was the disagreeable part of the bargain with Chamberlain. In May Baldwin spoke unguardedly and at length to a journalist from the *People*, and vented some of his frustrations. He recalled his motivation for his intervention at the 1922 Carlton Club meeting: 'I spoke because I was determined that never again should the sinister and cynical combination of the chief three of the Coalition – Mr Lloyd George, Mr Churchill and Lord Birkenhead – come together again. But to-day you can see the signs of the times.' Later in the interview he added: 'all this intrigue – this Churchill plotting – is bad for the Party ... What do these intriguers want? Simply to go back to the old dirty kinds of politics!'[40] When the article was published Baldwin flatly, and unconvincingly, denied having uttered these indiscretions. Churchill should, though, perhaps have picked up a clue that praising Lloyd George was not the best way to ingratiate himself with the Conservatives and their leader.

In June, nevertheless, Churchill published an article in the *Weekly Despatch* entitled 'The Future of Mr Lloyd George'. It praised his wartime record in glowing terms, but criticized many of his actions since the Armistice as inconsistent with his great and glorious past. The conclusion of the piece made plain one of Churchill's intentions in writing as he did: to cajole Lloyd George into contemplating a new alliance with the Conservatives. It suggested that the Liberals might at some stage be forced to make common cause with the Tories against socialism. 'In such circumstances', Churchill wrote 'the nation and the Empire can certainly count on Mr Lloyd George.' Moreover, 'if a crisis of the first magnitude arose, the gravity and emergency of which dominated all minor considerations, the British people would surely turn for help, whether against internal or external foes, to the dauntless, tireless, resourceful, and commanding statesman to whom they resorted in the terrible times of war; and we may be sure that in the future as in the past they would not turn for help in vain'.[41]

The article caused Gideon Murray, who had so recently supported Churchill, to write to its author expressing his misgivings. He concluded from it that Churchill was prepared to work with Lloyd George as well as with the Unionists 'in the future reassortment of parties'. However, Murray said, such an arrangement would be unacceptable to Unionists: 'Many of us wish to see you definitely with us and when the time comes you can have our support if you want it; but if Lloyd George is with you anything may happen & it will create a discord which will most certainly affect your own position.'[42] Churchill wrote back: 'You need not draw any inferences of the kind you apprehend from my article.'[43] Yet it is very difficult to see what other inferences can be drawn from it – especially given Churchill's earlier private hope that Lloyd George could be the buttress of a future 'Conservative and Liberal Union' government.

The idea of such a government was not exclusive to Churchill. After the Abbey by-election there was talk in the press that his Liberal supporters, whilst holding back from a formal alliance with the Tories, might form a 'Liberal-Unionist' wing of the Conservative Party, on the lines of that which resulted from the 1886 Home Rule split.[44] Freddie Guest (who, it will be remembered, was Churchill's cousin and Lloyd George's ex-Chief Whip) actively tried to create some grouping like this at this time. Baldwin – his comments to the *People* notwithstanding – wanted to bring Churchill into the Conservative Party, as he had both talent and powerful supporters. But he was against any such halfway-house solution, especially if it threatened the future prospect of him being forced to collaborate with Lloyd George.

Early in July Baldwin and Austen Chamberlain agreed to reach out publicly to those Liberals who were in sympathy with the Tories but were not yet willing to join them formally. On the 17th of the month the two men made what were supposed to be coordinated speeches, but they gave radically different slants on this theme. Chamberlain, having referred explicitly to Churchill, said that it 'was a time for union among friends'. The Conservatives should welcome 'in no ungrudging spirit' those potential recruits who 'without joining our party see eye to eye with us'. Baldwin, after a strong attack on Lloyd George, said only that 'All those who feel that they can unconditionally adopt our policy' were welcome, and 'if any man is prepared to adopt our platform, let him come forward on it and say so like a man'.[45]

Chamberlain, who felt he had been double-crossed, was furious. He complained privately that Baldwin's speech was 'throughout an attack on Liberals *as such* without one word to distinguish between Lloyd George & Winston, & the only invitation he extended to any Liberal is to leave his party and join ours "like a man"'.[46] Baldwin, however, denied that he had departed from what had been agreed. 'I followed exactly the line I indicated to Winston after dinner at Sam Hoare's', he told Chamberlain, adding, 'Winston, in private, accepts our policy. It is up to him now to address a meeting and say so.'[47] He did now agree that Churchill could stand as a 'Constitutionalist' candidate, nominally retaining a fig leaf of independence but in fact receiving full Conservative support. (Churchill was eventually selected under this arrangement for the safe Tory seat of Epping.) But he also secured Churchill's unequivocal support for Conservatism. In a speech in Edinburgh on 25 September, Churchill declared: 'The King's Speech of the late Conservative Government unquestionably afforded a good and fair basis for the cooperation of reasonable men of all parties.'[48] By failing to distinguish publicly between Liberals of the Lloyd George and the Churchill stripe, Baldwin had in effect helped confirm the fact of the political divide between the two men.

Contacts between Lloyd George and Churchill had not, of course, come to an end. On 19 August the latter reported to his wife that he had 'had a long and very satisfactory talk with Ll.G., and we were closer together politically than we have been since he took part in putting in the Socialists'.[49] When Churchill visited Churt at the end of the month, Lloyd George spoke of supporting a future

Conservative government in the way that the Liberal Unionists had aided Lord Salisbury in the 1880s and 1890s. Churchill may have been attracted by such thoughts, but this was fantasy politics, because Lloyd George vastly overrated the likely extent of his own influence, he himself holding much of the blame for its decline. John Campbell, in his seminal study *The Goat in the Wilderness*, notes that Liberal reunion had quickly turned sour: 'In 1924 Lloyd George undid most of the good he had done himself in 1923.' Part of the problem was that, whereas he controlled most of the party's financial resources, through the Lloyd George fund, the Asquithites kept a grip on its national organization. And, while Lloyd George's personal relations with Asquith were better than might have been expected, the former was reluctant to disperse his stock of money to help followers of the latter. In Campbell's analysis, he came to favour a general election, in which the Liberals would probably do badly, because if Asquith and some of his colleagues lost their seats, the path would be cleared for Lloyd George's own, more energetic, leadership, and the money would be saved for a more promising opportunity. He underestimated, though, the probable scale of Liberal defeat.[50] Therefore, in plotting to cause an election by defeating the government in the Commons – manoeuvres of which he kept Churchill informed in detail – he was digging in his own political graveyard.

The issue he selected as a means to bring down MacDonald was one close to Churchill's heart: relations with the Bolsheviks. The Labour government's most notable successes had been in the field of foreign affairs. One of its first acts had been to give diplomatic recognition to the Soviet Union. Negotiations to settle remaining differences between the two governments started soon afterwards, and in August two treaties were concluded. One of these provided for further talks to settle the claims on Russia of British owners of bonds issued by the Tsarist government. If these new negotiations were concluded satisfactorily, the British government would guarantee a loan to the USSR. This was all perfectly sensible; indeed it was in line with Lloyd George's own past policy of trying to bring Russia back into the community of nations. His opposition to it – which focused on the loan in particular – was opportunistic.

After his 30 August visit to Churt, Churchill reported to Balfour and Carson: 'He [Lloyd George] is quite ready to try to turn the government out on the Russian Treaty, and to bring matters to a head as soon as Parliament reassembles.' Moreover, 'LG fully contemplated that an Election would follow the defeat of the Government, and the vote would be given with that prospect clearly in view.'[51] Lloyd George succeeded in converting Asquith and other leading Liberals to this course of action, although some members of the party were more doubtful. Churchill's old friend Archibald Sinclair (who had become an MP in 1922) wrote to Churchill in late September that he wished 'LG had not been quite so downright' in his hostility to the Russian agreement. 'Of course I am delighted that Asquith and Grey have come up to his support, but a good many of the rank and file seem to think he has been trying to snatch the lead, and would be inclined to resort to any expedient to avoid a general election, with which they think that LG is threatening them.'[52]

The Liberals put down a motion in the Commons declining to approve the treaties, but, in fact, the government was defeated over another question before it could be put to a vote. This other issue was the Campbell case. The government had reversed its decision to prosecute J. R. Campbell, the editor of the communist *Workers' Weekly*, for incitement to mutiny. This was presented by the government's opponents as an instance of it being soft on extremism. On 8 October the Conservatives decided to back a Liberal amendment to the Tories' own motion of censure, thus dooming the government, which had decided to treat the issue as a matter of confidence. In the ensuing election 'Red Scare' tactics were used against Labour. Most notoriously, the *Daily Mail* published the forged Zinoviev Letter, purporting to show that Moscow had given secret instructions to British Communists to stir up civil strife. Neither Churchill nor Lloyd George did anything to counter this atmosphere. The former described MacDonald as 'this futile Kerensky' – a reference to the leading figure in the Russian provisional government toppled by the Bolsheviks in 1917.[53] Lloyd George criticized the government for committing British tax revenue 'to a gigantic loan to a number of fanatical visionaries who are ruining the great land of Russia'.[54] This sort of rhetoric was more advantageous to the Conservatives, who swept back with 419 seats, than to the Liberals, who were reduced to a mere 40. Labour, though its tally fell to 151, was at least confirmed in its status as the second largest party.

The triumphant Baldwin made the shock decision to appoint Churchill, who had been elected with a handsome majority, as

Chancellor of the Exchequer. In his draft memoirs Churchill recalled that the Conservative Party was 'dumbfounded' by this. He noted: 'A quarter of a century before I had left them with bitterness and rancour. I had for ten years been with Lloyd George, the spear-point of Radicalism and their principal bugbear.'[55] According to the Prime Minister's own account, Churchill was as taken aback as anyone: 'He was greatly surprised, and showed it in his emotion. He pledged his loyalty and added "You have done more for me than Lloyd George ever did." '[56] This, of course, was grossly unfair to Lloyd George, who had resurrected Churchill's career in 1917 in the teeth of considerable opposition. Churchill, in his excitement, can perhaps be excused his ingratitude.

But what prompted the appointment? As told by Baldwin, it was the suggestion of Neville Chamberlain, who had served as Chancellor in 1923–4, and before that, briefly, as Minister of Health. (Neville was the half-brother of Austen, who became Foreign Secretary.) Chamberlain's diary account is rather different. It relates how he saw Baldwin on 5 November, prior to the Prime Minister's meeting with Churchill. Baldwin 'said he had decided to take Winston in at once – "He would be more under control inside than out" – and he thought of putting him at Health'. Chamberlain then expressed his own desire to return to the Ministry of Health, and Baldwin asked him who, in that case, should be Chancellor. Chamberlain's suggestion was Samuel Hoare, but the Prime Minister was not enthusiastic. According to Chamberlain, Baldwin then 'mentioned Winston but said he supposed there wd be a howl from the party. I said I thought there wd but that wd be so if he came in at all & I did not know that it wd be much louder if he went to the Treasury than to the Admiralty. On the whole I was inclined to say that W. for the Treasury was worth further consideration.' Writing in his diary that same day, Chamberlain concluded Baldwin 'had postponed his final decision till he had seen me but that he offered me the Exchequer expecting that I should decline & that he had determined in that case to offer it to Winston'.[57] Churchill, for his part, believed that his appointment came about as part of a subtle and complex manoeuvre to keep Neville Chamberlain out of 11 Downing Street, the success of which led the Chamberlains to feel aggrieved. 'When we all drew up at Buckingham Palace to receive our Seals, Patents and Offices from the King, the Chamberlain brothers would hardly speak to me.'[58]

Austen Chamberlain, certainly, was 'alarmed' at Baldwin's decision, 'not because I do not wish Winston well but because I fear that this particular appointment will be a great shock to the Party.'[59] Neville, though, had a genuine preference for the Ministry of Health, and did not resent Churchill being Chancellor instead of him. He thought, nevertheless, that the appointment was rushed and mismanaged, and felt 'thoroughly depressed' by Baldwin's 'incredible bungling.'[60] This may help to explain his stand-offish attitude towards Churchill at the Palace; however, a few weeks' reflection decided him that Baldwin's behaviour had been essentially honourable.[61]

The question of the Prime Minister's overall motivation is perhaps more important than that of who said what to whom and when. In 1951 one ex-minister – possibly Leo Amery – gave a retrospective explanation of the actions of Baldwin: 'The one dominant motive all through with him was fear of Lloyd George and his influence. It was fear of L.G.'s influence, combined with Winston's, over Austen and F. E. that led him to the amazing offer of the Exchequer to Winston.'[62] This sounds plausible, given Baldwin's undoubted loathing of 'the Goat', but it may be too glib an argument. Even if there was a Machiavellian aspect to his actions, Baldwin should surely be given some credit for making a good choice. He recognized that the new appointee had in him the makings of a successful Chancellor, as well as perceiving that the offer of such a key post would remove any justification for personal grievance on Churchill's part. As the Prime Minister put it to his confidant Thomas Jones, shortly after making his Cabinet, it would now be up to Churchill to be loyal, 'if he is capable of loyalty'.[63]

Of course, if Baldwin's intention was to bind Churchill to him, this was perfectly consistent with wanting to separate him from Lloyd George. If this was the Prime Minister's aim, then he was successful, at least for the time being. This was not immediately apparent. Lloyd George offered Churchill his 'Warm congratulations on your appointment to a great office', as indeed was only polite.[64] Churchill's response was effusive:

It gave me great pleasure to get your telegram.

I remember well the night when you dined with me on first assuming this office now 16 years ago.

What an extraordinary thing life is! I had not the slightest expectation, and fully prepared myself to return here having refused some unattractive office.

We must meet soon. I shall claim your advice – and I am sure you will give it me – on lots of things.

We have a wonderful opportunity, if we know how to use it.

Your many friends in this Cabinet will never forget the fearful days through which you led us to safety; and I shall never forget our many years of comradeship.[65]

Churchill did make some initial effort to consult in the manner promised. Early in December 1924 A. J. Sylvester, Lloyd George's private secretary, recorded that his boss had been asked to meet with the new Chancellor in the latter's room in the Commons. Churchill then gave him advance notice of a statement he was about to make on repayment of war debts.[66] But, although this may not have been merely a one-off occurrence, such contacts did not become frequent. Bob Boothby, who as Churchill's PPS at this time was in a good position to observe, recollected: 'When Churchill joined the Conservative Party and Baldwin's Government, he and Lloyd George inevitably drifted apart.'[67] (In strict accuracy, Churchill didn't formally rejoin the Conservative Party and the Carlton Club until 1925, but the point stands.) It was, in fact, impossible for them to retain much intimacy when pitched on opposite sides of the political debate.

This did not prevent Churchill from praising Lloyd George in private. Diana Mosley recalled Edward Stanley, one of Churchill's guests at Chartwell, remarking that he could not belong to a party led by Lloyd George. 'Thereupon' Churchill 'launched into such a paean glorifying his old friend and former leader as completely to convert at least one of his listeners.'[68] But when he made direct overtures, Lloyd George suspected an ulterior motive. In 1923 the oil companies Royal Dutch Shell and Burmah were seeking a merger with the Anglo-Persian Oil Company. They offered Churchill £5,000 to put their case to the government. Out of office and strapped for cash, he accepted, and saw Baldwin, who seemed sympathetic. The November general election put paid to the merger, and Churchill withdrew from the affair. But it was arguably very improper for him not to have revealed to Baldwin that he was acting as a paid lobbyist for the deal, rather than as a disinterested advocate. This explains Frances Stevenson's comments in March 1925: 'Winston is very friendly. D. thinks it may be something to do with an alleged oil deal that W was supposed to be in – and which might, if it got out, be unpleasant.' As Stevenson's granddaughter comments, it is hard to know whether Lloyd George's suspicions say more about him or about Churchill.[69]

There were not, for the time being, any major political confrontations between the two. Just as Churchill was eager to have Lloyd George's support for the government's extensions of social insurance, so Lloyd George seems at first to have been inclined to go easy on Churchill. At the end of April 1925 Churchill presented his first Budget. He took sixpence off income tax, compensated for a reduction in Super Tax with an increase in death duties, and announced that Britain would return to the gold standard (a fixed exchange-rate mechanism whereby the value of the pound was tied to the value of gold). He also declared that a duty was to be imposed on imported silk, and the government would soon introduce a Bill to establish an insurance-based pension scheme for the aged and for widows. This was a significant extension of social welfare reform. 'The old *laissez-faire* or *laissez-aller* ideas of mid-Victorian radicalism have been superseded, and no one has done more to supersede them than the right. Hon. Member for Caernarvon Boroughs', Churchill said in his speech. 'I am proud to have been associated with him from the very beginning of those large insurance ideas.'[70] Lloyd George, in his initial response to the Budget, offered the traditional congratulations, albeit in perhaps unusually fulsome terms. Churchill's had been 'an exceedingly masterly performance', and 'The whole of his scheme betrays, as we should have expected, an ingenious, resourceful and exceedingly ambitious mind.' Lloyd George was 'delighted' that he had undertaken to complete the scheme of insurance that the pre-war Liberal government had been able to establish in only limited form.[71] However, he grew more and more critical as the Finance Bill went through its various Commons stages.[72]

His various grounds of complaint included the silk duty, which Churchill intended simply as a revenue-raising measure but which was easily portrayed as a departure from free trade. More significant was the gold standard issue. The return to gold was in conformity with established economic orthodoxy and with the advice of Churchill's officials, whose views, to his great credit, he had accepted only after much probing and testing. There was, however, dissent, notably from John Maynard Keynes. In July Keynes published three articles, later put out as a pamphlet under the title *The Economic Consequences of Mr. Churchill*. He argued not against the return to gold on principle but against a return at the pre-war rate (equivalent to $4.86 to the pound). Sterling, he argued, was now seriously overvalued against the dollar, which would have damaging effects on the competitiveness of Britain's export industries, and cause unemployment. There is room for debate about how damaging the return to gold really was in practice, but Churchill came to regret it. In an unpublished draft of his memoirs, he complained that he had been 'misled by the Governor of the Bank of England, by the experts of the Treasury and by the Committee appointed by my Socialist predecessor'. He also admitted: 'I had no special comprehension of the currency problem, and therefore fell into the hands of the experts, as I never did later where military matters were concerned.'[73] In July Lloyd George dropped his initially cautious approach, and described the return to gold as 'this deed of egregious recklessness by the Chancellor of the Exchequer.'[74] As Campbell notes, 'By this time he was developing a full-scale attack on the Government's mishandling of the economy on every front, and the return to gold figured henceforward prominently among its crimes.'[75]

Lloyd George and Churchill were the dominating figures of the parliament, 'the only men who can fill the House of Commons', as H. A. L Fisher noted.[76] Thomas Jones observed that 'Winston . . . is the only one in the Cabinet who seems to have, what L.G. had, a sense of the dramatic in making proposals to the nation.'[77] Lloyd George, for his part, was able to enthral his listeners. (He told Churchill he felt 'he ought not to come to the House – but it was like not being able to keep away from the "pub"'.)[78] Churchill, though, was sometimes able to get the better of him. After one of the 1925 Finance Bill debates, Baldwin reported gleefully to the King on the 'rout' of Lloyd George. Churchill had begun his attack on a Liberal amendment 'by challenging Mr Lloyd George to say whether he had taken any part in drafting that amendment, whether he had approved of it, or whether he had even read it. Mr. Lloyd George's spontaneous action in endeavouring to obtain a copy of the Order Paper from the friends around him, and the look of guilt on his face were quite sufficient to convince the House that Mr. Churchill had made a very accurate guess.'[79] The boot, however, was sometimes on the other foot, as when, the following year, Lloyd George made a series of powerful attacks on Churchill's Economy Bill, aimed at reducing public expenditure. The cuts came at the expense of the social services, and Lloyd George called the Bill 'a gipsy stew-pot. What does a gipsy put in his stew-pot? A rabbit snared in a spinney, a hare trapped in a field. A chicken or two purloined from somebody's farm; and probably one or two hedgehogs.'[80] It should be emphasized that there is no evidence that these slanging matches led to any personal bitterness. For example when Lloyd George fell ill in 1927, the Churchills sent flowers, and he responded with a note of thanks giving details of his health.[81] At the very least, the niceties were preserved.

If Lloyd George had not lost his oratorical brilliance he was increasingly distrusted. 'He alone probably of the Opposition states-men could fill the Albert Hall', noted Fisher. 'Wherever he goes he is attended by huge crowds . . . And yet he can only command 17 votes in his own party'.[82] Whether or not this estimate of the number of his Commons followers was precisely correct, the remark captures the paradox of his situation. The aged Asquith, now in the House of Lords, was still the nominal leader of the Liberals but had ceased to be a constructive force. However, Lloyd George's attempts to reinvig-orate the party attracted the hostility of those who thought he was trying to grab the leadership for himself. Perhaps not all such criticisms were fair, but some of his moves, including his attempts to court opinion within the Labour Party, did show signs of opportunism (especially given his attitude in 1924). 'It is perfectly certain that LG will move steadily to the left', Churchill predicted early in 1926.[83] As he reported to Clementine a few days later, after dining with Lloyd George alone, there were some signs of loss of grip. 'I found him rather bothered, & quite astonishingly empty of knowledge & ideas, but vy genial and plucky', Churchill wrote. 'It surprised me to see how far adrift he was from the actual detailed prospect of Govern-ment business.'[84] The General Strike that took place in May 1926, however, gave Lloyd George the chance to be rid of Asquith, and also brought him further into conflict with Churchill.

The General Strike had its origins in the problems of the coal industry. British coal exports were doing badly, a problem exacer-bated, or so Lloyd George and others argued, by the return to gold. The mine-owners' reaction was to call for a lowering of wages and for longer hours from their workforce. The miners' leaders adamantly refused to comply. In July 1925 the government averted a showdown by announcing a nine-month subsidy, to maintain existing wages while a Royal Commission investigated the problems of the industry. This was a blatant attempt by the government to buy time while it constructed the emergency framework necessary to keep the country running in the event of strikes. Lloyd George, however, presented it as retreat in the face of a threat from sectional interests. 'Quite frankly, the Government were afraid of facing cold steel', he told the Commons. At the end of his speech he rubbed salt into the wound with a quotation from Lord Randolph Churchill: 'You call yourself a Government. Whom do you govern?'[85] Baldwin, showing the trust he now placed in Churchill's powers, remarked that 'L.G.'s speech was poisonous and Winston will deal with it.'[86] Churchill did so in the Commons, making the case – unusually for him – for patience, restraint and delay. In October, moreover, he made a speech at Chingford, at which he criticized Lloyd George's general habit of doom-mongering. 'Although there are many causes for anxiety, there is absolutely no justification for these panic-stricken and methodically exploited cries of pessimism and alarm.'[87]

The breathing space bought by the coal subsidy lasted until the spring of 1926. Intensive negotiations between the government and the TUC came to nothing. After they broke down, at midnight on 3 May, there began a general strike in support of the miners. Churchill and Lloyd George now found their respective positions somewhat reversed. The former became editor-in-chief of the *British Gazette*, a government newspaper with, unsurprisingly, a heavily biased news agenda. He asked Lloyd George for a contribution 'of a helpful nature' – Asquith, Grey and Balfour had all sent messages condemning the strike – but none was forthcoming.[88] Indeed, Lloyd George was forthright in his condemnation of the paper, which he described in public as 'a first-class indiscretion, clothed in the tawdry garb of third-rate journalism'. (Churchill's response was that 'the duty of the *British Gazette* was not to publish a lot of defeatist trash').[89] In a notorious episode, the *Gazette* at first refused to print a message from the Archbishop of Canterbury written in a spirit of conciliation; it was eventually buried on the back page.[90] Lloyd George criticized the original omission strongly in the Commons. After the strike was over, he commented that if Jesus Christ had come to London, his remarks would also have been excluded: 'The editorial blue pencil of Mr. Winston Churchill would certainly have cut right through the Sermon on the Mount.'[91]

Later, Churchill jeered about Lloyd George's attitude: 'When the General Strike was let loose upon us the Public had uncommonly little help from him!'[92] Lloyd George had in fact condemned the strike, but had criticized the government as well as the unions. He thought there should be negotiations, rather than demands for unequivocal surrender. In a 1928 speech Churchill alleged he had thought the strikers might succeed, 'and instead of choosing which side he was on and standing by with firmness he took up an attitude which, if they had succeeded and the constitutional government of this country had broken down, would have enabled him to come forward as the necessary man to pour oil on the troubled waters and restore the situation'.[93]

After the strike was over, it was often portrayed as an example of the peculiarly good-natured British way of conducting politics; stories of football matches between strikers and police were considered exemplary. However, in addition to the genuine cases of fraternization, there were also instances of violence. For example, on 5 May, strikers lobbed pieces of coal at trams, smashing their windows and injuring some passengers. The next day at Elephant and Castle in London a bus, driven by a strike-breaking volunteer, was set on fire (the mob first having ejected the driver). Similar episodes took place elsewhere, perhaps encouraging a belief among the innately cautious TUC leadership that things might get out of hand.[94] This may help to explain why, even though the strike remained solid, it was called off on 12 May, even though no meaningful assurances had been received from the government about the future of the coal industry; in effect a complete climb-down. These essentially moderate men, many of whom had had reservations about the use of the general strike weapon in the first place, may have feared that things would get out of hand. The miners, who felt themselves betrayed, were left to battle on alone. At last, in November, the coal strike collapsed, and the miners returned to work on the owners' terms. It was a bitter and humiliating defeat.

In the meantime, Lloyd George's attitude during the general strike was heavily criticized by the Asquithians. Asquith himself reprimanded him in a letter that seemed clearly intended to provoke

Lloyd George's departure from the Liberals. Lloyd George's reply – after the draft was heavily toned down with the help of C. P. Scott – was moderate in its tone. 'If there is another schism in the party', he wrote, 'one would like to know what it is about.'[95] His emollience appeared to put Asquith in the wrong; and in October the older man at last stood down as leader. He died in February 1928. Lloyd George now had a free hand to lead the Liberals as he saw fit. He was to take them on a more radical path, presenting a serious challenge to Churchill's policy at the Exchequer.

One of Lloyd George's greatest assets during this period was his partnership with Keynes, Churchill's critic regarding the gold standard. Keynes, the finest economist of the twentieth century, was a committed if somewhat unorthodox Liberal. He supported Lloyd George rather than Asquith during the general strike, leading to a breach with the latter. He was to be a key member of the Liberal Industrial Inquiry, established in late 1926, financed by £10,000 from the Lloyd George Fund. He chaired the subcommittee on Industrial and Financial Organisation. It should be noted, though, that he was only one of a range of experts who took part in the Inquiry. Lloyd George himself took an active role. Deliberations continued throughout 1927, addressing the problem of how to tackle Britain's persistent high unemployment. The figure never fell below 1 million between 1921 and 1938. The outcome was the publication, in February 1928, of *Britain's Industrial Future*, also known as the 'Liberal Yellow Book' because of the colour of its cover. It followed on from the 'Green' and 'Brown' books of 1925 that had dealt with land issues, and by which Lloyd George had set great store. Churchill declared his distrust in the virtues of a 'yellow dawn'.[96]

To a great extent the Yellow Book was simply a compendium of existing proposals. One of its most striking suggestions, following on from ideas Lloyd George had put forward in 1924, was the establishment of a National Investment Board (NIB). The NIB would borrow in order to carry out an expansionary programme, including road building, slum clearance and electrification. The report's faith in the power of the state to shorten dole queues contrasted with free market orthodoxy, and indeed with the course Lloyd George had followed when in power. Churchill subsequently noted that when the Cabinet had met in Scotland in September 1921, 'we toyed with these big schemes of artificial employment, but L.G. came down after a few days' reflection solidly against them'.[97] The irony was that, in the aftermath of those discussions, it was Churchill who had pressed Lloyd George, fruitlessly, for the government to do more.

Even now, Lloyd George took a strangely ambiguous attitude towards the report. Throughout the rest of the year, he made little use of the Yellow Book in his speeches.[98] Indeed, in the immediate aftermath of its publication, rather than arguing for expansion, he appeared to criticize the government for *excess* public expenditure. This was during a by-election campaign, and Churchill, in a message to the voters, was quick to exploit the contradiction. 'Mr. Lloyd George, in the teeth of facts and his own Yellow Book, does not hesitate to say that "the expenditure has increased by 40 millions", hoping, I suppose, that the Ilford electors will be taken in by this gross misstatement.'[99] In April, when Churchill launched his annual budget, Lloyd George focused not on unemployment, but on the proposal to reduce the burden of local government taxation on industry. He approved of the principle, which had been put forward in the Yellow Book, but strongly attacked the method proposed as inequitable between industries. Churchill argued in the Commons that Lloyd George had 'endeavoured by every resource at his disposal and all the knowledge and wide experience which he has accumulated in his career, to darken counsel and put a spoke in the wheel of reform, and to baffle and confuse the public mind.'[100] In September another by-election led to a further notable spat, in which Lloyd George described Churchill as 'the man who has imposed more fresh taxes than any Chancellor for over a century in time of peace' and Churchill said that Lloyd George's conduct during the General Strike was 'unworthy of one who had held the position of First Minister of the Crown'.[101]

Urged on by Seebohm Rowntree, one of the Inquiry's experts, Lloyd George determined to make a public works programme the cornerstone of the next Liberal general election campaign. The result, after further expert discussions at Churt, was the manifesto *We Can Conquer Unemployment*, which included a set of Keynesian (or proto-Keynesian) proposals, building on those of the Yellow Book. It was published in March 1929. Lloyd George had by now concluded that 'the Conservative leaders were the biggest collection of political duds that English History had ever known'. He claimed privately to have expressed this sentiment in the pamphlet, albeit 'in more parliamentary language' and with 'a footnote exempting Winston from the stigma'.[102] As published, the pamphlet contained no such footnote. More significant, though, was the substance. The public works plans were now costed, and the pamphlet included the dramatic pledge that work could be found for 596,000 men in the first year. Peter Clarke, in his authoritative work *The Keynesian Revolution in the Making*, finds this to have been somewhat over-optimistic; but the implication remains that, if put into effect, the proposals that were outlined in the pamphlet could still have reduced unemployment substantially.[103]

The 'Orange Book', as the pamphlet was also known, represented a brilliant attempt to seize the political initiative. As such it caused alarm in the Conservative camp. Within days of its publication there happened to be five by-elections in seats formerly held by Tories. Two were lost to the Liberals, one to Labour, and in the other two constituencies the Conservative majorities were slashed. How to react? One option was to try and outdo the Liberals. In February the Home Secretary, William Joynson-Hicks, wrote to Churchill in anticipation of the proposals. He enclosed a memorandum putting forward a scheme of public works to be financed by a government-backed loan. 'I have thought over this matter for some little time,' he explained, 'and have stolen L.G.'s thunder and have prepared the Memorandum because I am seriously worried as to the effect of the present position on the General Election.'[104] Churchill, however, was dismissive, pointing out that it would be inadvisable to overturn the established canons of the government's financial policy in the closing months of the parliament. 'We should not try to compete with L.G.', he remarked in March, 'but take our stand on sound finance.'[105] His doubts about the 'soundness' of the Liberal plans were influenced by the threat that spending money to create jobs would drive up prices. Churchill wrote to one of his civil servants of his belief 'that Mr Lloyd George has at the back of his mind a definite inflationary purpose in accordance with the general Keynes view'.[106]

This did not mean that Churchill underestimated the threat posed by Lloyd George. In fact, he put considerable effort into developing the anti-expansionary theories of his Treasury officials into a coherent argument that he could put before parliament. This formed the origin of his reference, in his April Budget statement, to 'the orthodox Treasury doctrine which has steadfastly held, that whatever might be the political or social advantages, very little additional employment and no permanent additional employment can in fact and as a general rule be created by State borrowing and State expenditure'.[107] The reasoning was that if the state spent money, it would simply prevent an equivalent amount of private investment from taking place. This was the clearest articulation yet of the notorious 'Treasury View', mocked by Keynes and Hubert Henderson in their pamphlet *Can Lloyd George Do It?*: 'You must not do anything, because this will only mean that you can't do something else.'[108] Churchill, however, had his own line in raillery. In an earlier part of his Budget speech he said that Lloyd George planned 'to borrow £200,000,000 and to spend it upon paying the unemployed to make racing tracks for well-to-do motorists to make the ordinary pedestrian skip'. He also noted the irony of Lord Rothermere's support for the Liberal proposals. The 'chief author of the anti-waste campaign' had 'enlisted under the Happy Warrior of Squandermania'.[109]

Churchill made further efforts to attack Lloyd George's plans. At the end of April J. C. C. Davidson, the Chairman of the Conservative Party, wrote to the Chancellor. He advised him that he had received reports from various parts of the country indicating that *We Can Conquer Unemployment* 'with all its defects, has made some headway'. The best way to counter this, Davidson argued, was for each of the ministers chiefly concerned to supply him with a signed letter of approximately 800 words, 'dealing destructively with Lloyd George's proposals, from the point of view of their particular Department'.[110] Churchill did not think much of this idea. A series of such letters from various Ministers 'would not attract attention as an answer to the Lloyd George pamphlet, and would confess a completely disconnected treatment of the problem'. In his opinion, the report on the Liberal plan that had been drawn up by an inter-departmental committee of civil servants should be published, first as a government White Paper 'and secondly by Central Office in a cheap form'. This procedure would have been a questionable use of the work of the civil service for party propaganda purposes, but Churchill thought the report 'perfectly proper to be published by a Government, provided the *names* of all officials are excluded. I understood nearly a month ago that this was going to be done, and was much surprised at the delay.'[111] In mid-May a White Paper was published, albeit on

somewhat different lines from those proposed by Churchill, further
reinforcing the Treasury View. *The Times* – which approved of the
arguments contained in the White Paper – admitted that it was
simply a presentation of the Conservative Party case.[112]

What should we conclude from this ideological battle as a whole?
The Treasury View was based on a fallacy, and Lloyd George's
proposals, had they been put into effect, might have mitigated
unemployment, although it is doubtful they could have 'conquered'
it. (Many of Britain's economic problems derived from a fall in
overseas demand, and were therefore not susceptible to a purely
internal stimulus.) Lloyd George himself therefore deserves much
credit for his approach, even if he was at first a little slow to grasp
the Yellow Book's political potential. It was not enough to secure a
full-scale Liberal revival, but it did at least demonstrate that the party
retained intellectual vitality. By contrast, the Conservative approach,
which stressed stability, proved not even to have the advantage of
being an election winner. We should not, however, rush to condemn
Churchill. He certainly cared about the unemployed, and repeatedly
pressed his civil servants to explain and justify their opposition to an
expansionary programme. Once they had done so, he accepted what
he believed to be the best expert advice available. Indeed, had he
taken the opposite view, it is very unlikely that, with a couple of
exceptions, he could have persuaded his colleagues to support public
works. Moreover, he must be given credit for other, more positive
aspects of his Chancellorship, including his derating scheme and his
significant contributions to pension and tax reform. He had not
abandoned all parts of the Liberal agenda that he had pioneered
with Lloyd George before 1914. As Martin Daunton has argued,
Churchill 'consciously seized the mantle of David Lloyd George' and
aimed 'to appropriate the ideology of "new Liberalism" which had,
to a large extent, migrated into the Labour party'.[113] In so doing he
did his best to exploit the reputation of his association with Lloyd
George for political purposes.

There is, of course, no doubt that in 1929 the two men did have
major and irreconcilable differences over economic policy. This is
what makes it so remarkable that, at practically the same time as
Churchill was denouncing Lloyd George as an inflationist and squan-
dermaniac, they should have engaged in discussions about potential
future collaboration. Rumours to this effect had been in the air for

some time. In March 1928 Baldwin observed Lloyd George, Churchill and Birkenhead standing together at a state dinner. 'The future Coalition', he remarked, in apparent seriousness.[114] (Birkenhead, however, was to leave the Cabinet a few months later, claiming he could not afford to live on the salary, and died in 1930, his health weakened by years of excessive drinking. Churchill was distraught.) In July of the same year William Bridgeman, now First Lord of the Admiralty, noted that 'There was very nearly a big row amongst the more protectionist part of our party against Winston, as they thought he had preached too rigid a free-trade doctrine' in a Commons speech. He added that 'People were rather afraid he was playing up to Lloyd George & a middle party again, but I think that was an unproved suspicion – though he is naturally very changeable.'[115] Those particular suspicions may well have been unfounded. However, on 18 February 1929 Lloyd George met with Churchill in the latter's room at the House of Commons. The former made what was for him the rare step of making a substantial record of what transpired. This suggests that he took the conversation seriously, although, in some ways, this seems hard to credit.

Lloyd George began by warning Churchill that Conservative prospects at the forthcoming general election were not good. It was likely, he said, that they would no longer be the largest party – an accurate prediction, as it turned out. He urged Churchill to persuade Baldwin 'in a case of that kind not to resign in a hurry before giving an opportunity for consultation with the Liberal Leaders; that we were just as anti-socialist as they were and had no anxiety to see a socialist government in control of the affairs of this country'. He then laid down several conditions for Liberal support for a minority Tory government. These included electoral reform, no introduction of tariffs and a reconstruction of the ministry. On all these points Churchill made emollient noises. According to Lloyd George, 'I then made it quite clear that we could support no Ministry which would not tackle the problems of Unemployment – more or less on the lines of our programme . . . this would involve raising a very considerable sum of money by a loan.' Churchill does not appear to have offered any comment on this, although any such insistence would surely have been a total bar to cooperation.

The two men nonetheless got into an involved, hypothetical discussion of what procedure might be followed when the new parliament met to ensure that Baldwin remained Prime Minister even if defeated in a vote of confidence. Churchill went on to say that if Lloyd George's terms were accepted 'the Government would have to be kept in power for two years'; Lloyd George said that this seemed reasonable. Churchill was also anxious for an electoral understanding to prevent Liberals fighting Conservatives in seats where the result would be to split the anti-socialist vote and let Labour win. Lloyd George, however, said 'that any arrangement of that kind was quite impossible' as the Liberals were already pledged to run 500 candidates. Churchill asked if there was any objection to him reporting the conversation to Baldwin. Lloyd George said that there was not, 'but that it would be quite impossible to enter into any arrangement at this stage – so much depended upon the result of the election and the attitude of our supporters'.[116] If so, the entire conversation – which had an air of unreality about it – would appear to have been rather pointless. It was another case of Lloyd George and Churchill playing fantasy politics. That they did so may be evidence of the powerful hold they still had on each other's imaginations, even if the prospects for practical collaboration were low. Shortly after their discussion Lloyd George claimed privately to believe that Churchill was in the wrong party. When this remark was reported to him, Churchill 'replied with a wry smile: "They only put me here to keep me safe"'.[117]

From Lloyd George's point of view, talk about working with the Conservatives was probably fairly harmless. It was possibly even mildly beneficial insofar as, via Churchill, he succeeded in sowing gloom within Tory ranks about the party's prospects. In a letter to his sister, Neville Chamberlain wrote of Churchill: 'A little while ago he dined with the Goat and came away in deep depression, having been filled up with confident prophecies of our complete discomfiture at the election.'[118] (Chamberlain should perhaps have taken the warnings a bit more seriously himself.) From Churchill's point of view, even the most tentative discussions with Lloyd George could only do him damage. In early March, J. C. C. Davidson lunched with Sir William Berry (soon to become Lord Camrose), an influential newspaper owner whose titles included the *Daily Telegraph* and the *Sunday Times*. Davidson found Berry 'very anti-Lloyd George and I also suspect very anti Winston . . . In a little monologue on Winston he put the position exactly as I understand it myself, the main point being that he is not trusted in the Party because he is always out for office and never prepared for opposition, and therefore people suspect he is already in negotiations with Lloyd George to secure a post as second man on the new ship if it is ever launched.'[119] In late March Beaverbrook noted that 'Churchill has no intention whatever of allying himself with Lloyd George, although rumours to this effect are doing him a great deal of harm.'[120]

In some respects the suspicions about Churchill were, as Beaverbrook suggested, unfair. Lloyd George and Churchill had not negotiated in the way Berry described – they had not discussed their respective future personal positions. Furthermore, Churchill does not appear to have kept the talk a secret from his colleagues, which he surely would have done had he been intending to jump ship from the Conservatives. On the other hand, he clearly did at least contemplate an alliance with Lloyd George, albeit an alliance that was to include not only himself but the rest of the Tory Party too. Berry's remarks about his thirst for office were at the general level accurate. His eagerness to ensure that the Conservatives stayed in power led him to ignore the strong feelings of many of his colleagues. Baldwin and Neville Chamberlain were determined that they would never serve in the same government as Lloyd George. Raising with them the possibility that they might do so was simply a way of causing unnecessary irritation. Baldwin appears to have told Ramsay MacDonald of what Churchill was up to, which was a good way of helping ensure nothing came of it.[121] He contemplated moving Churchill from the Exchequer, even in advance of the election. He did not do so, but it seems likely Churchill would have been replaced by Neville Chamberlain had the Tories won. Such mistrust of him was very much more than the tribute that mediocrity paid to genius. Churchill did allow his ambition – combined with his misplaced obsession with Lloyd George, who he seems to have thought could somehow help him attain it – to cloud his judgement. These errors help explain why, after 1929, he did not hold office for another ten years.

There was, it should be noted, yet a further complication in Lloyd George's relationship with Churchill around this time. This factor was the latter's book *The World Crisis*. The issue of Churchill's treatment of Lloyd George in this work, and of Lloyd George's treatment of Churchill in his own later *War Memoirs*, will be dealt with in detail in the next chapter. What is really interesting for our purposes here is that at almost the same time that Churchill was launching a full-scale assault on the Liberal unemployment plans, and meeting with Lloyd George to discuss possible post-election cooperation, he was also working on *The Aftermath*. This final part of *The World Crisis* dealt with, among other issues, the British intervention in the Russian civil war, a matter that threatened to reopen wounds in its author's relationship with Lloyd George. As will be seen later, Churchill's initial instinct was to pursue the old controversy wholeheartedly, but in the end he toned down his comments and edited out some rather explosive contemporary documents that he had at first planned to include. This rather suggests that Churchill was divided within himself about how to deal with his ex-colleague.

There was, of course, no place for ambiguity on the campaign trail. The election was to take place on 30 May. In the weeks before polling day, Churchill made repeated criticisms of Lloyd George and his policies – so many that not all of them can be mentioned here. In a 30 April broadcast he described his proposals to create jobs by building roads as 'very unsuitable and indeed, vicious' because this rough work would physically spoil skilled men's hands. He also paraphrased Lloyd George's economic views as 'Borrow money freely and splash it about well, and all will come right – as long as I [Lloyd George] do the splashing.'[122] In a speech a few days later, Churchill again attacked the road-building plans. Britain, he said, would in time be reduced to 'a few little strips of vegetation and enormous well-tarred motor racing tracks, occupied entirely by the profiteering contractors who have made the roads'.[123] (Perhaps he should be given credit as an environmentalist and early critic of Private-Public Partnerships.) On 7 May he accused Lloyd George of misunderstanding the nature of unemployment. There was, he claimed, no great standing army of unemployed, merely a constantly shifting population of four or five millions who at different times came onto the unemployment register.[124] The next day he criticized the Liberals for running so many candidates, the majority of whom could not win, which would have the effect of delivering seats to Labour. 'More especially is their conduct unjustifiable when we consider that the great bulk of these five hundred candidates will be supported by the Lloyd George fund which was raised for the express and avowed

purpose of enabling both Liberals and Conservatives to make common cause against Socialism.' It was, he argued, a breach of moral
faith.[125] On 13 May he returned to unemployment. The Liberals, he
said, were abandoning the traditions of Gladstonian finance. If they
succumbed 'to the temptations Mr. Lloyd George is now offering
them for party purposes it will not be because they are Liberals, but
only because they are electioneering politicians'.[126]

As might be expected, Lloyd George responded in kind. After
Churchill's broadcast he ridiculed the suggestion in it that the cure
for trade depression and unemployment was steady, stable government. Here is an excerpt from *The Times* report of this particular
speech: 'Mr. Churchill steady (laughter), stable (laughter)! Quite
enough of that. (Laughter.) He says that there are no unemployed
. . . That is how Mr. Churchill justifies the torpor and apathy of the
Government.'[127] A few days later, he mocked Churchill's suggestion
that the Liberals were planning to build race-tracks for the benefit of
profiteers: 'I wonder how many Liberal profiteers there are . . . What
nonsense he talks!'[128] In another speech, he criticized the government
White Paper that had dealt with the Liberal plans: 'I have no
objection to Mr. Churchill replying to me or anybody else, so long as
I can reply back, but I do object to a State document being published
with the seal of the Crown which is a purely political pamphlet
replying to a political opponent.'[129] He made more attacks on
Churchill besides.

The fact that they featured prominently in each other's speeches
should not be taken to mean that the election should be viewed as a
Lloyd George–Churchill duel. Both criticized other people in the
other's party too, as well, of course, as directing fire at Labour (which
Churchill claimed was unfit to govern). It should also be noted that,
notwithstanding their genuine differences over economics, there was
a slightly ersatz quality to their mutual denunciations. On 7 May
Ramsay MacDonald predicted to Baldwin that in the new parliament
'between Winston & LlG we should have a renewal of the old noisy
political sham fights'.[130] This remark might equally have applied to
the election campaign itself, during which both, naturally, also came
in for Labour criticism. For example Philip Snowden, the former
Labour Chancellor, accused Churchill of being like a nursemaid,
trying to frighten the children by using socialism as a bogeyman.
Lloyd George, Snowden said in the same broadcast, had 'made the

same pledges he was now making in 1918, and was given unlimited power to redeem them, but at the end of four years unemployment had risen sevenfold'.[131]

The electorate, it would seem, took Labour's own pledges to deal with unemployment seriously. The party was helped by Liberal and Conservative efforts that, the exchanges quoted above notwithstanding, were somewhat lacklustre. The Tory slogan 'Safety First' is generally considered an almost classically poor choice; and Lloyd George did not help his own party as much as he might have done, spending most of the campaign in Wales. The Liberals won only 59 seats – though they got 23.4 per cent of the popular vote – and the Conservatives 260. Labour won 288. Theoretically, Baldwin could have hung on and met parliament, perhaps doing some sort of deal with the Liberals to keep himself in power, as Churchill and Lloyd George had discussed in February. Churchill still, initially, favoured this course, although he did start to have doubts. Among those close to the Prime Minister the fear was, as Thomas Jones noted, 'that Ll.G. might keep S.B. in office for a week or a month, and humiliate him and his Party in every conceivable way. S.B.'s own instinct was to go out at once.'[132] Accordingly, Baldwin resigned on 4 June and MacDonald formed his second government, although he could not command a majority in the House of Commons.

What light, then, do the years between the fall of the coalition and the 1929 election cast on Lloyd George and Churchill's 'two paths of Liberalism'? The former clearly does deserve recognition not merely for his continuing dynamism but for his willingness to embrace creative solutions, most notably those advanced by Keynes. (This is not to say that those solutions were necessarily complete or unproblematic.) One should not, however, ignore his inconsistencies, for example his attitude to the Labour Party, which at times he denounced and at others seemed to want to lead. His critics' allegations of opportunism had some merit. Churchill, too, can easily be convicted on this score, if one has the inclination. Beaverbrook, in the article quoted at the start of this chapter (p. 238), noted that, during the Abbey by-election, he had presented himself as a 'reforming evangelist', critical of Baldwin's leadership. Yet, as Chancellor of the Exchequer, he became 'a prosperous Bishop contented under the old Pope'.[133] Nevertheless, he cannot be convicted of an outright betrayal. Lloyd George recognized that Churchill's move to the

Tories was a product of conviction, and did not resent it. Indeed, if his Chancellorship was not free of error, he did achieve modest but significant reforms, somewhat in the spirit of Edwardian Liberalism. These were also quite in line with the mildly progressive Conservatism of Pope Baldwin and Cardinal Neville Chamberlain. If the evangelist reached accommodation with them, this was not necessarily proof of his corruptibility, but was perhaps a sign that things were not quite as rotten in the Vatican as he had at first imagined.

Ultimately, one's verdict on Lloyd George and Churchill's respective actions in the 1920s must depend on one's own political proclivities. Advocates of state intervention to cure social ills will incline to favour the former; advocates of quietism and stability the latter. Greens, for their part, may find themselves in sympathy with Churchill's criticisms of 'roadmaking gone mad' – 'We shall not only run short of money, we shall run short of grass', he said.[134] In terms of their personal relationship, though, the conclusion is, for once, straightforward. As they were not in close touch after 1924 there was little scope for private acrimony – in spite of the fact that, in public, they were attacking each other with a new and considerable vehemence. The myth of their eternal friendship again proves unsustainable, not because there was actual hostility between them, but simply because of the infrequency of their contacts at this time. (This is not to say that they did not enjoy each other's company when they met.) Certainly, their mutual fascination continued, but from a distance. And the reputation of their relationship was still powerful. Other senior politicians took seriously the idea that their partnership might revive, and considered it a threat. The next years were to prove, however, that, in spite of Churchill's initial inclinations, this was a mirage. Their paths had diverged too far.

Chapter Eight

POLITICS AND MEMORY

WITHIN MONTHS OF the Labour government taking office, the Wall Street Crash plunged the world further into economic crisis and political turmoil. In Britain unemployment rocketed, and in 1931 there was a major realignment of the parties, in which the Conservatives emerged as the dominant force in a cross-party National Government headed by Ramsay MacDonald. In the United States, the economic consequences were yet more serious, although in 1932 the election of Franklin D. Roosevelt heralded an ambitious 'New Deal' that aimed at the revival of prosperity through government action. In Germany, economic devastation combined with chronic political instability to give Hitler his chance at power, which he seized with alacrity in 1933. He immediately posed a threat to the peace of Europe. It must be remembered, though, that he was not the sole danger. Japan invaded Manchuria in 1931, Mussolini's Italy attacked Abyssinia (modern Ethiopia) in 1935, and in 1936 the outbreak of the Spanish Civil War further exacerbated European tensions. It may well seem regrettable that Lloyd George and Churchill, with all their brilliant qualities, were out of power during this terrible time, for, if they could not have averted war, perhaps they could have ensured that Britain was better prepared for it when it came. Indeed, even before Churchill became Prime Minister in 1940, there had developed a powerful legend that 'the elderly mediocrities in British politics' had deliberately conspired 'to exclude from the Government of this country – permanently it was hoped – the only two men of authentic genius in our public life'.[1]

This legend cannot be accepted without challenge. It is true that a number of senior politicians continued to fear a renewed Lloyd George–Churchill alliance, did their best to prevent it coming about, and were mightily relieved that it did not do so. Some other – rather fewer and less influential – people continued to hope that the two men would combine, in order to tackle the national crisis. But these fears and hopes, although they may have affected key political calculations, were unrealistic. Lloyd George and Churchill would themselves, at various times and for different reasons, have welcomed a restoration of the partnership. But although they achieved temporary, tactical agreement on certain important issues, and continued to build up the myth of their friendship, they no longer had enough in common politically to make sustained cooperation viable. In addition, throughout the 1930s they each made some fundamental mistakes. In Lloyd George's case, these were to contribute to the eventual eclipse of his reputation by Churchill's. In Churchill's case, his errors cast serious doubt on his judgement, and made his warnings about Germany – a question on which, at the most basic level, he was right – appear to many as a typical example of his habit of exaggeration. It may have been a tragedy that their respective talents went unused, but if so it was a tragedy for which they themselves must shoulder a substantial amount of blame.

After the 1929 election Lloyd George and Churchill were expected, in the words of the Liberal MP Ernest Evans, to be 'the two dominating figures in the Parliament'.[2] They certainly provided many of the pyrotechnics, but that is not quite the same thing as domination. At an early stage, Churchill began to find himself isolated. Shortly after the election the Labour government recalled Lord Lloyd, Britain's High Commissioner in Cairo, and subsequently compelled him to resign. Egypt was nominally independent, but was dominated by Britain. Lloyd was a die-hard imperialist, whereas the new government wanted to make concessions to nationalist opinion, including restricting troop deployments in the country to the Suez Canal Zone. Churchill thought that the new policy showed weakness and that Lloyd had been treated badly. There is a letter in the Lloyd George papers that appears to relate to this episode and which, perhaps because it is undated, has had its significance overlooked. 'This is another of those turning points wh we have sometimes noted in our long tho varied association', Churchill wrote. 'All I suggest is that you shd join with us in asking that no irrevocable step shd be taken about Egypt until we come back' – that is, until parliament met. He added: 'Surely *you* can do this.'[3] However, Lloyd George appears not to have been disposed to help. Nor was the Conservative

Party leadership inclined to turn the issue into a point of contention with the government, and when, at the end of July, Churchill defended Lloyd in the Commons, he found little support. This was a harbinger of the situation he would later find himself in over the question of India.

There was another, potentially more fruitful, line of cooperation with Lloyd George open to him, however. In late June, a few days before the opening of parliament, the two men met and talked over the political situation. Having won more than a quarter of the vote, but less than a tenth of Commons seats, the Liberals had a clear interest in reform of the electoral system in the direction of proportional representation. Churchill, having informed Baldwin of his initial discussion with Lloyd George, made clear his view that the Conservatives should support an inquiry into reform. This was important, he thought, in order to help build up an understanding with the Liberals, with a view to keeping Labour in check. 'On the whole I agree with you in wishing the Government to have a fairly long run', he wrote to Baldwin. 'But the important thing is to build up such a relationship on the Oppn benches as will gradually give us control of events.'⁴ At a further meeting with Lloyd George, Churchill told him of Baldwin's reaction, which in essence was that the Conservatives would join in any enquiry in a constructive spirit and not with the deliberate aim of joining with Labour to do down the Liberals.⁵

In allowing these conversations to go on, Baldwin was probably concerned mainly to keep his options open. He certainly cannot have liked the idea of cooperation with Lloyd George, to which other important members of his team were also strongly opposed. Leo Amery strongly deprecated the idea, and noted in his diary: 'I was glad to find Neville in complete agreement, though he thought that several of our colleagues, more particularly Winston would wish to play the Lloyd George game.'⁶ Two weeks later, at a 'sort of Shadow Cabinet of Commons members to discuss policy', Amery found his worst fears realized. Churchill 'was definitely for cooperation with the Liberals on the basis of first agreeing with them on the electoral reform committee which is to be set up. It is quite evident that he has been colloguing vigorously with Lloyd George since the election and is heading straight for a coalition in which no doubt everything I have ever worked for is definitely to be thrown over.'⁷

The following week Amery recorded a further meeting of ex-ministers, at which 'Winston told us very confidentially of L.G.'s schemes'. Lloyd George had devised a scenario that involved defeating the government before it could introduce a Budget, after which the Tories would take office with Liberal support and then enact electoral reform before calling an election. This convoluted and perhaps discreditable plan had little hope of success, not least because many Liberal and Tory MPs would have refused to play up. It did not find a warm welcome from Churchill's colleagues, and although he was given a vague mandate to 'reconnoitre further to see exactly what L.G. meant and what guarantees he could give us', nothing came of it.[8] If Baldwin had been a more effective Leader of the Opposition he might have put an end to these manoeuvres at an earlier stage. 'Politics are disgusting', Neville Chamberlain wrote to his sister on 21 July. 'Winston is shoving very hard, with an eye to the leadership it is said, and S.B. remains obstinately in the background.'[9]

In the first weeks of the new ministry, Labour members alleged that Lloyd George and Churchill were coordinating their parliamentary tactics purely for the purposes of embarrassing the government.[10] They may have done so, although they did not necessarily engage in pre-planning. Donald Maclean, who had been a leading Asquithian, wrote that 'Ll.G. is, I think, in much closer touch with Winston, Worthington Evans, and Robert Horne than he is with any member of the Government.'[11] The last two named were, of course, Conservative former coalitionists.

During the debate on the King's Speech, Churchill described the government's plans for tackling unemployment as 'very moderate and sensible'.[12] By the same token, Lloyd George thought them inadequate: it was unlikely, he said, that the unemployed would be quite as pleased as Churchill was.[13] In mid-July, however, when a government resolution on the issue came up for debate, he claimed that it might commit the Commons to allowing potentially limitless expenditure. Whilst all the Treasury ministers were temporarily away from the chamber, he and Churchill used their absence as an excuse for holding up progress until the Financial Secretary returned to clarify the matter.

This gave Aneurin Bevan, newly elected member for Ebbw Vale and a rising Labour star, the chance to accuse them of colluding to obstruct efforts to help the workless. He also ridiculed their divergent approaches to the government scheme. Churchill 'found no ambition at all' in the government proposals, Bevan noted, but Lloyd George 'found most immense powers in them . . . Whereas we are accused from the Conservative Benches of not having sufficient ambition, indeed of being comparatively pedestrian, on the other benches we are accused of being enormously adventurous.'[14] In a further debate on unemployment the following year, James Maxton, another prominent socialist, observed that Lloyd George and Churchill had said that the problem was a serious one and not 'a matter of jests and for hurling gibes from one party to the other'. But, Maxton continued, 'each one of them spent the major portion of his speech in doing just exactly that thing that he deprecated'.[15] The 1929 parliament enhanced neither man's reputation for seriousness and responsibility.

At the start of August, Churchill left for a three-month trip to Canada and the USA. On 10 October he sent a telegram to Lloyd George, asking for his advice on the British political situation. Lloyd George responded with what, for him, was an unusually long letter. He thought that the position was 'perplexing' and that unless it was 'skilfully and boldly handled' it might 'become distinctly menacing'. He wrote that the government was popular, and predicted that, unless the Liberals and the Conservatives could reach a working agreement, 'the socialists will be in for at least 7 years'. He was eager to exchange views with Churchill upon the latter's return, and suggested that, at the least, the opposition parties should reach a common policy with regard to Labour's plans for the coal industry.[16] In spite of Lloyd George's predictions, the government soon ran into difficulties with which it struggled to cope. 24 October was Black Thursday, a seminal moment in the Wall Street Crash. Worse days followed, and the repercussions were felt around the world. In Britain, by March 1930, nearly half a million more people were unemployed than had been the case a year earlier.[17] Lengthening dole queues put pressure on the government's finances, and this was in due course to provide the trigger for its calamitous downfall.

Churchill confessed to Clementine immediately on his return from America that he had lost more than £10,000 in the crash. Lloyd George was experiencing a rather different complication in his personal life. In October Frances Stevenson gave birth to a daughter,

Jennifer. He may or may not have been the father: Stevenson had had an affair with Colonel Thomas Tweed, the Liberal party's chief organizer. But unlike Tweed – who died in 1940 – he did take an interest in Jennifer as she grew up. (She always called Lloyd George 'taid', the Welsh for 'grandfather', and was unaware, during his lifetime, that she might in fact be his daughter.)[18] It seems profoundly unlikely that Lloyd George and Churchill exchanged confidences on their respective problems. They do, however, seem to have perceived some potential for continued political cooperation.

There had been important developments over Indian policy while Churchill had been away. In an effort to meet the demands of the nationalists, the government had decided to make clear that India would eventually receive Dominion status, i.e. a substantial measure of self-government. On 31 October the Viceroy, Lord Irwin (later Lord Halifax), made a formal announcement to this effect. Baldwin – in Churchill's absence – secured the support of the Shadow Cabinet for the Irwin Declaration. However, many Conservatives (including Churchill) and some Liberals were unhappy with it. On 8 November, a few days after parliament had reassembled, Lloyd George criticized it. He did so on somewhat restricted grounds, arguing that it should not have been made prior to the report of the Royal Commission on India, chaired by Sir John Simon. The next day J. C. C. Davidson reported to Irwin that Churchill had sat forward during Baldwin's speech 'glowering and unhappy', and had then 'sat forward during the "Goat"'s speech cheering every mischievous passage in it'.[19]

Baldwin luckily managed to avoid a vote, which could have seen the bulk of the Tories joining Labour in one lobby and the party's right-wingers joining with Lloyd George and other ex-coalitionists in the other. Baldwin thought he saw a conspiracy between Lloyd George and some of his own 'disloyal colleagues' – whom could he have meant? – 'to try & drive him out of the leadership'.[20] Although Baldwin had escaped the worst, the debate made him 'very depressed' since 'it made him feel the hopelessness of trying to liberalize the Tory Party'. He complained that 'While he had been speaking there had been no word of approval from his own colleagues and as soon as Lloyd George got up Winston and Worthington-Evans on each side of him leant forward and punctuated every sentence with emphatic "hear hears"!'[21] The alliance between Lloyd George and Churchill over India was only temporary, however. The latter was soon to become disenchanted with the attitude of the former. In 1934 Frances Stevenson summed up Lloyd George's view as follows: '[U]nless you can come to terms with [the Indian National] Congress (& he does not seem to think this so out of the question as is supposed) the only thing to do is to govern India with a strong hand.'[22] Such sentiments fell a long way short of radical anti-imperialism, but the very idea of 'coming to terms' with the nationalists reflected a pragmatism on the issue that Churchill did not share.

Another, apparently promising, line of cooperation also came to little. As noted, Lloyd George had suggested that the Liberals and the Conservatives might develop a common policy with regard to the mining industry. The government's Coal Bill, as published in December, proposed a reduction in the miners' working day and protection for wages, combined with measures that would allow the mine owners to restrict output and maintain prices. In addition, there would be export subsidies. In the middle of the month, Amery noted in his diary that Churchill could gain no backing within the Shadow Cabinet for the idea that the Tories should support a proposed Liberal amendment to the Bill.[23] In the Commons, Lloyd George denounced the Bill as containing 'the worst features of Socialism and individualism without the redeeming features of either'.[24] This was one of a number of effective speeches on different issues at this time that helped restore his credibility. According to the *Nation*, 'with the doubtful exception of Mr. Churchill, there is no-one now in the House to touch him for all-round efficiency at the job of debating'.[25] Thomas Jones noted that Lloyd George had gained 'a new lease of life', and added: 'Winston is restive and would much prefer to be running in double harness with L.G. than with the cautious S.B.'[26] The Liberals achieved some important changes to the Bill (including the compulsory amalgamation of inefficient mines) but the Commons votes revealed divisions within the party. A few MPs voted with the government or abstained.

It may have been to secure unity that Lloyd George changed his attitude. At the end of February 1930, Nye Bevan commented on Lloyd George and Churchill's 'temporary re-alliance' over the Bill, 'which may be carried right through to the Division Lobby in their capacity as joint executioners'.[27] But it was already clear that the alliance was breaking down. In March it was announced that the Liberals would abstain on the remaining amendments, on the uncon-

vincing grounds that they did not wish to embarrass the government
during the ongoing Washington conference on naval disarmament.
'Mr. Lloyd George, who had declared it to be an incredibly bad Bill,
is now to stultify himself in the most cynical manner by becoming
responsible for its passage', complained Churchill.[28] Cooperation
between the two having borne little fruit – partly because other
members of both men's parties were hostile to the idea – Lloyd
George now inclined to try to work with Labour.

By this stage the government was floundering, and felt itself
increasingly in need of Liberal support. In May 1930 MacDonald
invited the opposition parties into consultation, in order to reach
consensus on how to deal with unemployment. Lloyd George
accepted. In the Commons, Churchill suggested that the Prime
Minister was taking a risk:

> I should be very careful, if I were he, before I invited the right
> hon. Member for Carnarvon Boroughs to come over and take
> charge of the Labour Government. I am sure that, once he were
> there, with his great knowledge, his immense drive and his grip
> of every aspect of the administrative machinery of Government,
> the best course thereafter for the Prime Minister to adopt would
> be to make a bargain that he should be permitted that he should
> go and sit among the Liberal party, and no doubt he would find
> himself quite happy.[29]

In fact, Lloyd George did not manage to impose any dramatic
new policy on the government, which continued to drift. He himself,
moreover, presided over an increasingly split party. In January 1930
he came under attack public from Lord Grey. In the autumn the
Conservatives put down an amendment to the King's Speech, regretting the government's failure 'to take any measures adequate' to
combat the economic crisis.[30] As Baldwin had, under pressure from
Neville Chamberlain, recently given a public pledge to pursue protectionism at the next election, this could easily be interpreted as a call
for tariffs. Chamberlain, indeed, backed tariffs when arguing for the
amendment, and this was the reason given for the abstention of
the majority of Liberal members when it came to a division. But a
few Liberals, including John Simon and Sir Robert Hutchison (the
Chief Whip), voted with the Conservatives. Indeed, the following
March Simon committed Liberal heresy by openly calling free trade

into question. In June 1931 he, Hutchison and Ernest Brown gave up the party whip.[31]

In former times, the fiscal question might have provided an issue on which Lloyd George and Churchill could unite. Amery, one of the most enthusiastic Tory advocates of tariffs, appeared to hope that the issue would drive the latter out of the Shadow Cabinet and even out of the party: 'It would be an immense accession of strength to us to get rid of Winston ... Winston will no doubt gravitate back to L.G. but what prospect there is for him is not easy to see.'[32] It was, however, unlikely that free trade could any longer provide a popular rallying cry, as protectionists could argue that the existing system had long been tried, but that unemployment persisted nonetheless. Churchill may well have sensed this, which could account for his decision not to resign from the Shadow Cabinet. His personal position was also weak. As Austen Chamberlain wrote, 'he cuts no ice with the Party & I really don't see how he can switch sides again though Ll.G. would no doubt be glad enough to get him'.[33]

For the time being, therefore, Churchill remained in a semi-detached position. He had told Baldwin that he would not fight an election on a policy of food taxes, but there had been no formal breach. He maintained his public criticisms of Lloyd George, who, he said, rested himself on three propositions. The first was that 'unemployment is a great, vital, urgent, evil and danger'. The second was that he had a cure, viz. to borrow money and spend it on public works. The third was 'that the government will not look at his scheme or carry it out in any effectual manner'. Yet, Churchill claimed, Lloyd George had decided to keep the government in office until the Liberals could extract from it electoral reform. 'Certainly this is not a very helpful contribution to the difficulties in which we all find ourselves involved.'[34] In some respects, these points were well made. However, the other course open to Lloyd George was to try to bring down the government, which would probably have led to the return of a protectionist Tory administration. If the consequences of protectionism were as disastrous as Churchill himself claimed, it is hard to see that this would have been a very helpful contribution to solving the nation's difficulties either.

It was not trade but Churchill's growing obsession with India that led to his final break with the Tory leadership. This also put a substantial obstacle in the way of future cooperation with Lloyd

George. In January 1931 an announcement by Lord Reading – who had served as Viceroy from 1921 to 1926 – provoked Churchill's wrath. This took place during a Round-Table Conference, called by the government at which Labour, Liberal and Conservative representatives discussed reform with Indian leaders. In a change from his previous position, Reading, with Lloyd George's support, declared that he was in favour of a federal structure for India. The proponents of this idea hoped that it would appeal to the Indian National Congress, which had refused to send delegates to the conference. To Churchill, the whole thing smacked of appeasement. On 8 January he wrote to his son Randolph: 'LlG has gone definitely to the left and his henchman, Reading, was put up to make a thoroughly defeatist speech on India at the Conference.'[35] The same day, he developed the point at greater length in a letter to Archie Sinclair, who had become an MP in 1922, and who had replaced Hutchison as Liberal Chief Whip after the latter's rebellion.

> I am deeply distressed by Reading's speech on India. It clearly shows that my last despairing hope that we should see again the great Lloyd George come to the aid of our country in its perils, must now die. India and its fortunes must be flung in to the political stewpan. The Tories have definitely accepted the view that he has fixed up with the left and is adjusting his views on every other topic. I cannot gainsay them. I fear the days when you and I will find ourselves together will never come.

Churchill also told Sinclair that he had hoped 'that India would be a bond of unity between the strong war-time forces' and thus provide a basis for 'joint action leading to a satisfactory adjustment in electoral law'. This supports the idea that he had, as many suspected at the time, been looking for an opportunity to revive the coalition. He continued: 'Good-bye to all that! I shall fight my corner on India to the end and have very powerful support guaranteed; but the great support I look for will be events.'[36]

This, undoubtedly, was a seminal moment in Churchill's political relations with Lloyd George. As will be seen, it was not true that he had given up hope for all time that Lloyd George would again be prepared to work with him. One could, indeed, see the old pattern still at work. During the Great War Churchill had declared the relationship over – 'tout est fini' – and yet then came back into the other man's orbit very quickly. This time, though, the gravitational pull was weaker. Lloyd George's importance on the political scene, although still considerable, had now fallen from its peak, and was soon to decline still further. At various times before the outbreak of World War II Churchill did look to him as a potential ally, but more in hope than in expectation. As public affairs revolved around Lloyd George less and less, so his attraction for Churchill declined, although he remained, still, an influence on his ex-colleague's increasingly independent if erratic trajectory.

It was ironic that, having alienated many of his colleagues by his apparent willingness to work with the 'left-wing' Lloyd George, Churchill should have chosen to break with them over India; for this issue threw him into the arms of the Tory right wing, which had previously been hostile to him. The crucial moment came at the end of January. In a Commons speech, Churchill attacked the proposals for an Indian constitution, including an All-India Federal Parliament, which had come out of the Round-Table Conference. Baldwin, in his reply, made an open defence of the plans, and said that a future Conservative government would have a duty to implement them. The next day, 27 January, Churchill resigned from the Shadow Cabinet.

He then embarked on a campaign of speeches designed to whip up opposition to the government's India policy, and to that of his own party. It would be mistaken to caricature his attitude as simply one of reaction in the manner of Colonel Blimp. He denied being an advocate of violent repression, and was genuinely concerned that the government's approach would encourage the extremists, leading to violence and unrest that would harm the Indian masses. Yet some of his comments were indefensible. Most notoriously, after Gandhi, who had recently been released from prison, met Irwin for talks in Delhi, Churchill observed: 'It is alarming and also nauseating to see Mr. Gandhi, a seditious Middle Temple lawyer, now posing as a fakir of the type well-known in the East, striding half-naked up the steps of the Vice-regal palace, while he is still organising and conducting a defiant campaign of civil disobedience, to parley on equal terms with the representative of the King-Emperor. Such a spectacle can only increase the unrest in India and the danger to which white people there are exposed.'[37]

It was therefore easy for Churchill's opponents to present him as an extremist, and, given his past history, as an opportunist. At first, his campaign seemed to go well, but Baldwin, who came almost to the point of resigning the leadership, managed to regain the initiative. In March the latter publicly denounced Beaverbrook and Rothermere, who had been working to undermine him, saying they sought 'power without responsibility – the prerogative of the harlot throughout the ages'. Churchill may have won sympathy for his position from many ordinary Conservatives, but his challenge was not powerful enough to overturn the front bench consensus between the main parties over Indian policy. And by pursuing it, he had ensured that there would be no place for him in the new cross-party administration formed in August 1931, in the wake of the Labour government's collapse.

The government's fall was brought about by a financial crisis. The crisis was created, or at least exacerbated, by the publication on 1 August of the report of the May Committee, which had been established some months earlier to consider savings in public spending. The report implied that the government was following an inflationary policy, and that radical cutbacks were needed. For some while the government failed to make clear its attitude to the report, and there was a run on sterling while the markets waited to see if cuts would be implemented. When the Cabinet at last met to discuss the situation there was no fundamental disagreement on the need for economies to restore financial confidence. However, a substantial minority of ministers refused to accept the cut in the rate of unemployment benefit upon which the majority, led by MacDonald and Philip Snowden (the Chancellor), were resolved. On 23 August the Cabinet agreed that it had no alternative but to resign. But, having handed in the Labour government's resignation, MacDonald immediately accepted the King's invitation to form a new administration in collaboration with Conservatives and Liberals. The majority of the Labour Party was excluded from this new 'National Government'. So were Lloyd George and Churchill.

Both men had previously had an inkling that some such government was to be formed. On 21 July the former diplomat Harold Nicolson recorded in his diary a dinner that took place at the house of Archie Sinclair. In addition to Lloyd George and Churchill, the guests included Brendan Bracken – who was a young Conservative MP and a friend of Churchill – and Oswald Mosley. Mosley, known to his friends as 'Tom', had begun his parliamentary career in 1918 as a Conservative. (In his memoirs he recalled that, as a young member, both Churchill and Lloyd George gave him the same advice: 'always to sleep some time between the midday and the evening meal.')[38] In 1920 he became an independent, later joined the Labour Party, and in 1929 achieved office under MacDonald, as Chancellor of the Duchy of Lancaster. He became frustrated by the government's failure to take bold measures to tackle unemployment, and in May 1930 he resigned. In March 1931 he left Labour to form the New Party, together with a handful of other MPs. According to Nicolson (himself a New Party supporter), Mosley had thought, in advance of the conclave at Sinclair's, 'it is quite possible that Winston and Lloyd George tomorrow will approach us for a promise of support in the event of a National Government being formed'. Mosley thought that Lloyd George might head such a government himself.

In fact, on the evening of the dinner, it quickly became clear that this was not exactly what was on Lloyd George's mind. After the meal the women present retired. (They were following a convention made all the more absurd by the fact that two of them, Cynthia Mosley and Megan Lloyd George, were serving MPs, both having been elected in 1929.) Lloyd George then launched the political conversation. Nicolson recounted:

> When left alone, Ll.G. begins at once: 'Now, what about this National Government? We here must form a National Opposition. I have every reason to believe that Baldwin and Ramsay at the slightest drop in the pound will come together in a Coalition. That moment must find us all united on the front opposition bench, and' (this very significantly, tapping on the table) 'we shall not be there long . . .' . . . The impression was that of a master-at-drawing sketching in a fig-leaf, not in outline, but by means of the shadows around it. Winston is very brilliant and amusing but not constructive. We all part on the assumption that although nothing has been said, the Great Coalition has been formed.[39]

It seems unlikely, in fact, that Churchill shared that assumption. It was not, apparently, that he was unwilling to work with Mosley but that, at this point, he saw little future in cooperation with Lloyd

George. Indeed, it is not clear how serious Lloyd George himself was about the idea. The matter was never put to the test fully, because on 26 July he fell seriously ill with prostate problems, and was operated on three days later. When the National Government was formed he was still convalescing. Churchill was on holiday in the South of France.

Herbert Samuel, who acted as Liberal leader in Lloyd George's absence, joined the government, as did John Simon and others, including Gwilym Lloyd George (who, like Megan, had followed his father into parliament). But Lloyd George's own attitude was ambiguous. He told A. J. Sylvester, his private secretary, that, unlike Samuel, he did not agree with the May Report.[40] However, he wrote in reply to a letter from MacDonald that 'The attitude you have taken is a truly heroic one'. Moreover, 'I am sorry I have not been able to give you any real help, but if the promise of the Doctors is redeemed I may be of some use later on.'[41] It seems probable that his genuine ill health provided him with a convenient excuse not to join the government, much to the relief of its key architects. As Sir Samuel Hoare, an influential Conservative and the new Secretary of State for India, wrote to Neville Chamberlain, who returned to the Ministry of Health, on 31 August: 'As we have said several times in the last few days, we had some great good luck in the absence of Winston and LlG.'[42]

This last remark should not be seen as proof of an active conspiracy against Lloyd George and Churchill by those who controlled the party machines. The belief that there had been such a plot was popularized by the famous polemic *Guilty Men*, published in the febrile atmosphere of the summer of 1940. It was shared by at least one Tory ex-minister, who wrote in 1951 that Baldwin had consented to coalition with MacDonald 'largely to keep out Winston and L.G.'.[43] But the exclusion of these 'brilliant old men', as Mosley called them in his memoirs, cannot be blamed entirely on 'their mediocre contemporaries'.[44] They themselves bore much of the responsibility. Churchill had left the Shadow Cabinet of his own free will, and thus more or less put himself out of the running, and there is little sign that Lloyd George even wished to be in the running. In addition, over the previous years they had both done much to provoke, through their apparent opportunism, the hostility of many influential people. It would be idle to deny that jealousy may have

contributed to that hostility, which can of course be read as mediocrity's backhanded tribute to genius, if one is so inclined. But one
might equally conclude that if Baldwin, Neville Chamberlain, Hoare
and MacDonald really did come up with a successful scheme to
baffle and keep down this superlatively talented pair, perhaps they
themselves were not quite so mediocre as is sometimes supposed.

We should also note that, even if Lloyd George had been well, it
is doubtful that a new collaboration with Churchill, of the kind
floated at the Sinclair dinner, would have been viable. Admittedly,
there is evidence Churchill hoped Lloyd George would return to
active politics. At the end of July, he wrote to the editor of the *Daily
Mail*, saying that he would like to write 'an article on Lloyd George's
services in the War, in the friendly atmosphere created by his illness,
and in the expectation of his resuming controversial politics in the
near future'. He stressed that the piece would not be 'of an obituary
character', as he expected him to make a full recovery, and as 'I
could not put myself in that mental position in regard to an old
friend of mine'.[45] The article itself, published on 12 August, described
Lloyd George's services to the nation as 'unique, majestic, and
impregnable', and blamed his political decline on his identification
'with the petty political exigencies of a small and dwindling party'.
Churchill wrote: 'Let us hope that when he is restored to full health,
he will stand squarely on his own feet and, untrammelled by party
ties and weak, discordant associates, give his own true counsel upon
National and Imperial questions to Parliament and the nation as a
whole.'[46]

The article doubtless reinforced the contemporary perception
that Churchill wanted to renew the old alliance. It should probably
be read, though, as a straightforward tribute, written without much
genuine expectation that Lloyd George would again be a major
political player. Once more, Nicolson's diary is illuminating. A week
after the National Government was formed he lunched with Mosley,
who told him that he had had a visit from Churchill's son
Randolph.

> It was clear that he had been sent on a mission by Winston. The
> latter asked whether Tom would join him and the Tory toughs
> in opposition . . . Tom asked Randolph why his father did not
> combine with Lloyd George and Horne to form an Opposition

of his own. Randolph replied, 'Oh, because without you, he will not be able to get hold of the young men.'[47]

Churchill may well have concluded that Lloyd George was somewhat past it, especially given the state of his health. But it also seems likely, given his comments of January, that he saw the question of India, and perhaps not that alone, as a substantive barrier to cooperation.

Moreover, both men's attitudes to the government now changed. Lloyd George became openly hostile. Churchill, by contrast, abandoned any thoughts of going into opposition. The National Government was at first supposed to be a strictly temporary expedient designed to deal with the immediate crisis. During September, though, MacDonald came under increasing Conservative pressure to call an election with the intention of winning the government a long-term mandate. The likely consequence would be a Tory-dominated administration with a free hand to impose tariffs. Churchill himself, in a Commons speech on 8 September, came out in favour of both tariffs and an election: 'there will be no revival of British industry in the circumstances to which we have come until a tariff is proclaimed. I go further and say that there will be no restoration of confidence at home or abroad until the Socialist party has again been defeated at the poll.'[48] (Twelve days later Britain was forced off the gold standard following speculation against the pound on the international currency markets, which certainly suggested financial confidence had not been restored.) Both the election and the tariff issue divided Churchill from Lloyd George, whose attitude was that 'the Liberals should oppose a General Election and refuse to co-operate therein even if there were no question of a tariff'.[49]

When, in early October, MacDonald agreed to an election, the Liberals divided anew. John Simon formed a new 'Liberal National' organization, and was joined by twenty-three MPs. Samuel's followers, although still dedicated to free trade, also remained within the government for the time being. Gwilym Lloyd George, however, resigned his position as parliamentary Secretary at the Board of Trade. (He insisted in his unpublished memoirs that he did so without consulting his father.)[50] This situation allowed Churchill to have a little fun in his election speeches. At Epping on 12 October he observed: 'There are the Simonites, who have thrown in their lot

boldly with the national cause; the Samuelites, about whom I am
unable to give any correct information; and the Lloyd Georgeites,
the most united party in this country – small but united by bonds far
above the ordinary connexions and associations of political life.
(Laugher.)'[51] (This was a reference to the fact that Lloyd George's
most prominent supporters were members of his own family.) On the
23rd, at Forest Gate, a heckler called out to him 'What about Lloyd
George?' 'I am sorry that we have not got Mr. Lloyd George with
us', Churchill responded, 'I did my best to bring him along.'[52]
Churchill's press articles may provide justification for this second
assertion, although there is no evidence that he had tried to persuade
him in person.

Polling took place on the 27th. The electorate was clearly persuaded by the rhetoric of the National Government's leaders, who
emphasized the need to sink partisan differences in the interests of
solving the economic crisis. The sense of national emergency contributed to the government's stunning victory. It won 554 seats; 473 of
these were held by Conservatives and the remainder of the National
Government contingent was made up of 13 'National Labour'
MPs (including of course MacDonald), 35 Liberal Nationals, and
33 Samuelite Liberals. On the opposition benches were a mere 52
Labour members and the four-strong Lloyd George 'family group'.
This last consisted of Lloyd George himself, Megan, Gwilym, and
Goronwy Owen (who was married to Gwilym's wife's sister). The
New Party won no seats at all; Mosley, its founder, formed the British
Union of Fascists the following year. Churchill increased his own
majority substantially, but was not offered a government post in the
reshuffle that followed the election.

An insight into his strategic thinking can be gained from a letter
to Archie Sinclair which, although undated, must have been sent
around the time of the election. Marked '*Serious* & Secret', it was a
reply to a letter from Sinclair, now lost, but which, it is clear,
expressed the hope that its author would one day work again with
Churchill. Sinclair, who had become Secretary of State for Scotland
when the National Government was formed, was a Samuelite.
Churchill's letter was later damaged by fire, and is partly illegible,
but the gist can be gathered: 'If you are ever to realize the extremely
kind wishes you express in yr letter, you must carefully but ruthlessly
detach yourself from the Samuelite group and establish solid Tory or

Simonite connexions. The Samuelites are wilderness-bound [?] & there they will only [?] find the fierce L.G. lies [?]. Be warned in good [word missing] by yr sincere friend.'[53]

In a further missive at the end of December, Churchill referred back to this letter: 'I hope you are enjoying your office and taking great pains with your work, and that you will always bear in mind the advice I gave you in the "ruthless letter" I wrote you some time ago, so that when the sheep are parted from the goats you may gambol safely with the righteous.'[54] As he had predicted, the free trade Samuelites could not last long in a government dominated by protectionists. In the summer of 1932, the Ottawa conference confirmed, via a series of bilateral accords with Dominion countries, the system of imperial preference that Britain had introduced that February. In September Sinclair resigned, together with the other Samuelite ministers, although Churchill urged him not to. As Churchill did not want Sinclair to join the Lloyd Georgeite 'goats' in the wilderness, he must have regarded them as uncongenial company for himself also. Indeed, he said in his December 1931 letter that his general political hopes were centred on the National Government.

That letter was sent from New York, where Churchill was recovering from a serious accident. He had been knocked down by a car whilst attempting to cross Fifth Avenue. (Lloyd George, always on the look out for a metaphor, claimed that Churchill had ignored traffic lights: 'It is not the only time he has paid no heed to signals.'[55] In fact, he had simply looked in the wrong direction.) For this reason, he postponed his planned lecture series and headed for the Bahamas. From there he wrote to his friend Brendan Bracken, on 8 January, asking for news of the political situation: 'Try above all things to make Lloyd George take a decent line over India. If he took the wrong line now it would be irreparable for him.'[56] This suggests that Churchill had not entirely given up on the idea that Lloyd George might take a 'decent line', in spite of his assertion a year before that his 'last despairing hope' that he would do so 'must now die'. On the other hand, there was now no more talk of 'the great Lloyd George' coming to the aid of the country in its perils, or even of his failure to do so. If Lloyd George took the wrong line it would bad *for him*, but he no longer, apparently, held the future of the nation in his hands.

On 17 January, Lloyd George's sixty-ninth birthday, Bracken and Randolph Churchill motored to Churt for Sunday lunch. Bracken reported to Churchill Senior that the former premier 'was amazingly healthy and looks about ten years younger'. Lloyd George's health had indeed improved considerably, although, in spite of his highly successful attempts to maintain his image as an extremely alert and energetic old man, he was never again quite as he had been before his illness. Bracken continued:

> His policy is to take no active part in politics until the summer. He believes that there is still much bloom on the National Government which, although fading rapidly, makes it unadvisable to create opposition at the present time. He spoke much of you and reiterated the feeling of comradeship, not to say affection, which he holds with all his strength. All the best experiences and achievements of his life were shared with you.[57]

Randolph gave a similar report, adding that Lloyd George was now 'a convinced food taxer, but I don't know whether he will come out with this publicly or not'.[58] Perhaps one should not be too cynical about the protestations of affection, but Lloyd George must have known that his flattering words would be repeated to their subject. He was certainly not close to Churchill politically at this time. 'I agree with you I cannot work with him', he told Frances Stevenson a few months later. 'On India & Russia – & now on disarmament he is on the extreme reactionary tack.'[59]

A. J. Sylvester had recently started keeping a diary systematically, creating an important source for the study of this period of Lloyd George's life. Sylvester recorded his boss, throughout the 1930s, making numerous references to Churchill's obstinacy, impulsiveness, conceit and lack of judgement. Of course, Lloyd George's attitude varied, but perhaps it was summed up best in a letter he wrote to Beaverbrook after a meal with him and Churchill in 1934. 'I enjoyed the dinner last week and especially the talk I had with you', he said. 'Winston is always interesting, but apt to take violent and extravagant views which make cooperation a little difficult.'[60] Admittedly he may on this occasion have been trying to flatter Beaverbrook, who was no less inclined to extravagant views than Churchill, or indeed Lloyd George himself. But he can hardly be blamed if he found Churchill's company wearing as well as fascinating. The irritation it produced in Lloyd George found its outlet in his disparaging private comments; the genuine admiration that it also stimulated was reflected in tributes such as that made in the presence of Bracken and Randolph Churchill.

Lloyd George made good on his commitment to stay out of active politics for the time being. In June 1932 Sylvester noted that 'L.G. comes to the House so seldom these days that a number of new M.P.s have not even seen him, let alone heard him speak.'[61] Instead, he was preparing for the epic task of writing his *War Memoirs*. This process can only be understood in relation to Churchill's experiences writing *The World Crisis*. The interrelated origins of the two works are worth examining at length. As George W. Egerton has observed, the two men's autobiographical contributions made 'an indelible mark on the historiography and social memory of their era'.[62] Moreover, the story of the creation of the books reveals much about the frequently problematic relationship between Lloyd George and Churchill themselves.

Lloyd George had first contracted to publish his memoirs in 1922, when still Prime Minister. The record-breaking £90,000 deal provoked a media storm. 'The Man Who Won the War' appeared to be profiting from the conflict. He promised to give the proceeds to charity, but the project lapsed. The contract was cancelled the following year and he returned the advances.[63] The 'irritation' this episode produced contributed to Churchill's difficulties in finding a publisher for his own book, on which he had already been working for some time.[64] As early as December 1921 – when he was still Lloyd George's Colonial Secretary – he had shown two chapters to the Prime Minister. The latter was 'well content with the references to himself'. (This may have been because Churchill had eliminated comments that were unflattering to him.) He also praised the style and 'made several pregnant suggestions' of which Churchill took account.[65] After the fall of the coalition, Churchill was able to wrap up work on the first volume. Serialization began in *The Times* in February 1923, and it was published by Thornton Butterworth in April. Given that so many key figures of the 1911–22 period, with which the several volumes of the book dealt, were still in active politics, it had great potential to generate controversy.

Churchill had quoted extensively from official documents, and this raised the issue of whether he had breached his duty of confidence as a former minister. The concept of 'freedom of information' was not a familiar one at the time. Questions were asked in the

Commons, and Bonar Law implied that Churchill had breached his Privy Councillor's oath.[66] A Cabinet committee – which in fact never met – was established to 'consider the whole question of the use of official material in personal memoirs and other publications'. Writing from the South of France, Churchill asked Lloyd George 'to consider whether anything can be done to safeguard our interests in laying our respective cases on war matters before the public at the proper time'.[67] Those interests related, of course, to the two men's ability to use official material to defend their respective reputations, but there was also a financial angle. Books based on previously secret documents were likely to be worth more than reminiscences of the traditionally anodyne variety.

Lloyd George, who was now 'keener than ever on defending himself', naturally sympathized with Churchill's position.[68] In a newspaper article entitled 'Should War Secrets Be Disclosed?' he took his cue from his former colleague's arguments: 'It is rather late in the day to make all this fuss about the publication of war documents, for Generals, Admirals, and Ministers in all lands, including ours, have during the last three years been inundating the European and American public with a flood of reminiscences, explanations, criticisms, attacks and defences on the conduct of the operations, either with the Great War or the Great Peace in which they were engaged.'[69] The government was, indeed, trying to shut the stable door after the horse had bolted. Churchill gained significant support from Maurice Hankey, who, as Cabinet Secretary, had much influence in these matters, and he was able to go ahead and publish his remaining volumes.[70] In 1938 Hankey observed that 'it was impossible to refuse statesmen like Mr Churchill or Mr Lloyd George, who had been attacked both at home and abroad, the right to use official documents in their replies – though it must be admitted that in some cases they have abused the privilege'.[71] Hankey may have had in mind the fact that the two men, after consulting one another, had successfully resisted official attempts in the 1930s to tighten secrecy by getting former ministers to return Cabinet papers in their possession.[72]

Churchill also received occasional assistance from Lloyd George. The key example is the 'Master and Servant' episode, referred to in Chapter 6, when the latter visited the Treasury to assist with questions that only he could answer. Another of the host of people

Churchill consulted was Lord Beaverbrook, who, after reading a draft of volume III, thought it insufficiently generous to Lloyd George. Hankey felt the same way, and Churchill appears to have added a passage that echoed closely his arguments in favour of Lloyd George.[73] Churchill, although he did not cut out the criticisms, responded to Beaverbrook by including a new passage paying homage to Lloyd George's ability to face 'awful contingencies' with 'unquailing eye'.[74] He also wrote to Beaverbrook in an attempt to rebut the impression that he was hostile to Lloyd George:

> In the upshot he [Lloyd George] was always wrong. He encouraged the Nivelle offensive which ended in disaster. He discouraged the final advance in 1918 which ended in success. He gave way about the prolongation of Passchendaele against a true conviction. Still there is no doubt he was much better as No 1 than any body else . . . The truth is that Armageddon was quite beyond the compass of anybody, even including you and me.[75]

There was of course an element of truth in Churchill's criticisms. He was not, though, nearly as eager to draw attention to the defects in his own record. There is an interesting commentary on his literary technique in a contemporary, multi-authored volume that aimed to debunk *The World Crisis*. In this book, Lord Sydenham of Combe observed that Churchill now condemned the original Allied occupation of Salonika.

> While, however, Mr. Churchill is thus quick to note the gross defects of Mr. Lloyd George's first contribution to war strategy, he asks us to 'Suppose, for instance, the war power represented by the 450,000 French and British casualties in the Champagne-Loos battle of 1915 had been used to force the Dardanelles and combine the Balkan States'!
> Such profitless imaginings could be multiplied – and parodied – indefinitely. In all we employed nearly 470,000 troops at Gallipoli and lost about 120,000 killed and wounded, while 74,000 tons of war shipping were sunk, and the drain upon our resources was very great.[76]

The fact that Sydenham, as well as being a defence specialist, was also a right-wing extremist who believed that the League of Nations was part of a worldwide Jewish conspiracy, does not detract from the

astuteness of these particular observations. Furthermore, Robin
Prior's brilliant critique, *Churchill's 'World Crisis' as History*, has shown
how Churchill obscured his own role in the origins of the Salonika
expedition.[77] Prior also casts light on the many other sleights of hand
that Churchill used to defend the dubious aspects of his record,
including Gallipoli. It is, of course, a general tendency of memoirists
to be more tender to their own failings than to those of others, and
Lloyd George would later prove himself no exception in this respect.

By 1928–9 Churchill was dealing not with the war, but with the
period of the coalition, as he put his final touches to the volume
entitled *The Aftermath*. In terms of his relationship with Lloyd George,
this was perhaps the most difficult part, because the two had clashed
so strongly over intervention in the Russian civil war. If Churchill
wanted to hold open the door to collaboration with Lloyd George in
the wake of the forthcoming general election (see Chapter 7), it would
be a mistake to reopen old wounds. And even if he in general wanted
to attack him, in order to maximize votes for the Conservatives, it
might be a mistake to do so on this particular issue, on which, as he
acknowledged in a letter to Lloyd George, 'most people will agree
with you'.[78] Churchill sent Lloyd George a number of draft passages
and chapters, relating to Versailles, Greece and Ireland as well as
Russia. Lloyd George read them quickly, with, he said, great interest.
But there were, he thought, 'very considerable gaps in your story
which must affect the judgement of those who read it on the general
attitude I took'. He therefore gave Churchill detailed notes on a
range of issues dealt with in the book. In particular, he was insistent
that it should include two telegrams from him on the Russian issue,
both of 16 February 1919, that Churchill, who had included them in
the original draft, was now proposing to discard. He wrote: 'If these
are omitted there will be nothing to show how I stood as Prime
Minister in reference to the Kolchak and Denikin enterprise.'[79]
Churchill took account of points Lloyd George raised about Ireland
and Greece, and over Russia he compromised. He printed the first
telegram, in which Lloyd George had given him a fairly mild warning
not to commit Britain to over-costly anti-Bolshevik operations. But
he left out the second, stronger one, which accused him of 'planning
war against the Bolsheviks'.

The case for discretion was advanced by Beaverbrook, who
warned Churchill that 'a general unpleasantness would ensue' if the

chapter was published in its original form, and also by Sinclair.[80] In mid-January 1929 the latter, in a long and tactful letter, pointed out a number of inconsistencies in the chapter, and raised the question of whether the telegrams should be published. Sinclair told Churchill that, 'whereas your telegrams are obviously unstudied in their phraseology and solely concerned with the practical conduct of affairs, Lloyd George's telegrams might have been written with a view to publication, so full are they of unimpeachable aphorisms of statesmanship. I am afraid, however, that these aphorisms will catch the eye and command the ready assent of many a general reader who is perplexed by the intricacies of the situation both in Russia and at the Peace Conference.'[81] In fact, by the time he received these warnings, Churchill had already decided to print the first telegram only; so the advice of Beaverbrook and Sinclair was not decisive on this point, although he may have been influenced to tone down the language of the chapter in general.[82] But he had, we may speculate, reached similar conclusions independently, although unsurprisingly he gave a different justification to Lloyd George. 'I have omitted from my account my second telegram to you and your scolding reply', he wrote. 'If I had published it I should have had to explain at length why I thought it unfair ... This would take up more space in my narrative than the importance of the incident warrants.'[83]

After the book was published in March, Churchill received a letter of praise from T. E. Lawrence (who now went under the name T. E. Shaw). 'I particularly like your fairness towards Ll George', it read. Moreover, 'You give him, not full marks, but more than's the fashion: and so you do yourself great credit.'[84] Churchill had indeed made efforts to be fair to Lloyd George, although, as has been seen, this had not been achieved entirely without prompting. Lloyd George, who read the book when convalescing from his 1931 operation, felt (predictably enough) that it did not do him justice. 'He said how tremendously conceited Winston was regarding his own efforts in the war', Sylvester recorded. 'He gave the book the title *The World Crisis* and, under this heading, he simply and solely explained his own case and defended himself.' (This was a rather prosaic echo of Balfour's celebrated comment on 'Winston's brilliant autobiography disguised as a history of the universe'.) Furthermore, Lloyd George complained, Churchill 'devoted two pages to showing what great efforts the Russians made to make munitions, yet he dismissed the whole of the British effort – which was, of course, [made by] L.G. – in two lines'.[85]

It would be absurd to claim that Lloyd George embarked on the massive enterprise of writing his own book simply out of jealously of Churchill's literary success. It would be equally wrong to portray the *War Memoirs* as a simple riposte to *The World Crisis*, an attempt to settle scores with Churchill. Lloyd George was more interested in vendettas with others, and in particular used his book to launch an assault on the memory of Haig, who had died in 1928. However, resentment against his former colleague may have formed some part of his motivation for writing. In 1930 Tom Clarke, the editor of the *News Chronicle*, attempted to exploit the men's presumed rivalry when he bought up the serial rights of Churchill's new book, *My Early Life*. Clarke wrote: 'I think it should make Lloyd George jealous and help bring him to heel in the matter of those *Memoirs* which I so badly want to scoop.'[86] (The ploy did not work: the *War Memoirs* were in due course serialized elsewhere.) After considerable preparation, Lloyd George started dictating his book in September 1932, and by June the following year he had completed 275,000 words.[87] The first two volumes were published that autumn, two more in 1934, and the two final ones in 1936. He confessed that, as he only started writing in his seventieth year, he found the task 'more burdensome' than did Churchill, 'who has wielded his pen from his very early years and is one of the most brilliant and dazzling writers we have today'.[88]

Praise of Churchill, though, was not much in evidence in the draft of the book itself. Lloyd George had to submit his manuscript to the official vetting process that had been established to deal with, in particular, *The World Crisis*.[89] Hankey therefore read it and, in April 1934, told Lloyd George that, 'Frankly, I do not like the passage about Mr Churchill, in spite of its dazzling brilliancy and truth'. He added that, although he himself was friends with Churchill, he was not putting in his plea for that reason. 'At the present time he [Churchill] is rather down on his luck and this passage will hit him dreadfully.'[90] Lloyd George responded: 'I will do my best to tone down the acerbities of truth. I am sending you a refurbished Winston.'[91] The published version still contained some harsh strictures on Churchill. But the strongest criticisms of him were attributed to Churchill's wartime enemies, who believed, Lloyd George wrote, that although his mind was 'a powerful machine' it had 'some obscure defect which prevented it from always running true'. Moreover, Churchill 'had in their opinion revealed some tragic flaw in the metal'. Lloyd George emphasized that 'I took a different view of his possibilities'. He thus succeeded in drawing the reader's attention to Churchill's alleged weaknesses whilst distancing himself from the charges he highlighted. 'As to Churchill's future,' the crucial passage concluded, 'it will depend on whether he can establish a reputation for prudence without losing audacity.'[92]

At the end of October 1936 Lloyd George's publishers gave a private dinner at the Reform Club in his honour, to mark the completion of the *War Memoirs*. (*The Truth about the Peace Treaties* was published in two volumes in 1938.) During the speeches, as noted elsewhere, he and Churchill paid each other extravagant praise, claiming that their mutual affection had never been disrupted by political disagreements. Churchill protested undying gratitude for the appointment to the Ministry of Munitions that had resurrected his career during the Great War. 'I remember being myself down and out and all the herd of Gadarene swine running over me which they are ever ready to do', he said. 'I had a friend who came along and gave me another horse at the closing stages of the great drama. It was "L.G.". I can never forget that.' Lloyd George, in turn, praised Churchill's efforts to produce weapons and ammunition in the wake of the German offensive of March 1918. Moreover, he related this point to the current government's recent failure, in the wake of Hitler's remilitarization of the Rhineland, to appoint Churchill to a defence post. Lloyd George said: 'The energy and skill which he displayed on that occasion seems to have disqualified him for a similar post in a similar emergency (Hear, hear).' Furthermore: 'you will hardly believe it but he and I have fought against each other and said some extraordinary nasty things – the nastiest things we could think of – but I think on the whole it is the longest friendship in British politics'.[93]

This was now an increasingly familiar theme on such occasions. At a lunch party on Lloyd George's golden wedding anniversary in 1938, the two again paid each other compliments. In the evening Lloyd George observed to Sylvester that 'throughout all the vicissitudes and quarrels between them their friendship had survived'.[94] But the marriage being celebrated that day was a sham. The public tributes led Sylvester to wonder what the world would have thought if it had known that the former Prime Minister spent the greater part of each year living not with his wife but with another woman. Lloyd George and Churchill's repeated protestations of regard for one another were also an exercise in image-making. The benign picture that they painted was at odds with their true feelings. Or rather, those feelings, incorporating jealousies and resentments as well as admiration, were naturally far more complicated than they made out. This is scarcely surprising. Even had they been capable of it, a greater level of emotional honesty would hardly have been appropriate in the contexts in which they were speaking. Some things are, perhaps, really better left unsaid.

As we have seen, Lloyd George's praise of Churchill on semi-public occasions was matched by frequent denigration of him in private; and even the *War Memoirs* delivered a very ambivalent message about him. He did sometimes speak up for him, but the messages were often rather mixed. On one occasion, for example, Thomas Jones suggested to him that Churchill's 'continuous drinking' was one of the things that helped disqualify him from a place in the government. Jones recorded Lloyd George's response:

> *L.G.* It hasn't clouded his intellect the least bit. Winston's got the constitution of a nigger. You look at him – that thick lower lip and bulging face and hunched shoulders and outstretched gorilla arms (all this illustrated) – you've only got to blacken his face to have a Moore and Burgess Minstrel. He is very tough.[95]

There was a similar ambiguity in Churchill's attitude to Lloyd George – albeit one that was not perhaps quite as pronounced. His reviews of various volumes of the *War Memoirs* were an attempt at balanced criticism. He found fault with the structure, and, more significantly, argued that, although Lloyd George had undoubtedly been the best man for the job of wartime Prime Minister, he had made several important misjudgements. But he described the work as a document of great historical significance, and made links to current politics, wondering why 'this doer of things and getter of things done' had in recent years been denied 'all opportunity to serve the State'.[96] In 1936, he turned down the opportunity to write a biography of Lloyd George, because he was too busy.[97] But in a review of a biography of Asquith, he noted how Lloyd George had had all the qualities his predecessor lacked: 'The nation, by some

instinctive, almost occult process, had found this out.'[98] When Margot
Asquith read this she wrote to Churchill. 'Dearest Winston I had no
idea that you thought so highly of Ll.G! – Your almost hysterical
panegyric of him in the News of the World (wh. my servants take in)
amazed me.'[99]

The following year the piece was republished in Churchill's *Great
Contemporaries*, a collection of essays in which, notably, there was no
chapter devoted to Lloyd George in his own right. Cecil King, a
nephew of Lords Northcliffe and Rothermere, and a significant press
figure himself, read the book in 1942. 'The essays are not good, but
give a good many sidelights on Churchill's own attitude', he wrote in
his diary. King added: 'He is obviously very anti-Lloyd George
(which I did not realize), not even including him among the "great"
contemporaries . . . To him Rosebery, Balfour, Asquith, and F. E.
Smith were great men, while Marx, De Valera, Hitler, and even
Lloyd George are vulgar upstarts who would be ignored if only
people were more sensible.'[100] Of course both of the readers in
question had their own biases, and it is not obvious that Churchill
was straightforwardly either 'pro-' or 'anti-Lloyd George' at this time.
Margot Asquith's and Cecil King's differing reactions to Churchill's
comments on Lloyd George show simply that his views could be read
in very different ways – which may to some extent reflect his own
mixed feelings towards a man who still had some apparent potential
to rival him as an alternative national leader.

There were, therefore, limits to the two men's attempts to
establish the reputation of their relationship. In their roles as 'memory
entrepreneurs', just as in current politics, each was keen to promote
his individual reputation, even if it had to be at the expense of the
other man's. At the same time, their joint myth was not fully within
their own control, and, when manipulated by political opponents,
could be dangerous to their immediate ambitions. As war drew
nearer, the Lloyd George–Churchill legend was as much a source of
weakness to the two men as of strength.

Chapter Nine

THESE TWO PIRATES

IT WAS PROBABLY UNREALISTIC to think that Lloyd George could still return to office. As the decade went on he seemed more and more interested in his farm at Churt, and in spending time with little Jennifer, than in politics. And when he did in engage with public affairs he appeared more interested in stirring up trouble than in making a serious bid for power. But in spite of his small parliamentary support base, he, like Churchill, was still feared. Ironically, though, on those occasions that they acted together, they may have undermined themselves through the very fact of their cooperation. For example in 1938 Victor Cazalet MP expressed the belief that any joint action by them was bound to fail. By virtue of them both being involved, 'a combination of Lloyd George and Winston was fatal to any attack on the government'.[1] At times they seemed to be the National Government's joint bogeymen, distrusted not only because of what they said but also because of their association with one another. If that was so, when they combined they did not so much team up as tie their respective shoelaces together.

The extent of establishment distrust seems clear from the efforts made to restrict their ability to broadcast. In 1932 a new system was inaugurated whereby an inter-party committee advised the BBC on political broadcasts. Asa Briggs, the historian of the Corporation, has written that 'The existence of this committee made it difficult for speakers, like Churchill, who were not on good terms with their parties, to broadcast on major political questions.'[2] In 1933 Churchill, Lloyd George and Austen Chamberlain (who was also now out of office) protested to J. H. Whitley, the Chairman of the BBC, at the exclusion of independent voices from the programme of political broadcasts scheduled for the autumn. It did no good (although in the years that followed Churchill was not kept off the air completely). In

fairness to the BBC, its next Chairman, R. C. Norman, did come to
appreciate that the exclusion of 'controversy' from the airwaves was
absurd and, at the very end of his tenure, came out and said so.
In April 1939, as the crisis in Europe deepened, he wrote to G. C.
Tryon, who as Postmaster General was the minister responsible. 'I
gravely doubt whether we are doing our duty ... It cannot be right
that their fellow countrymen should have no opportunity at such a
time of hearing statesmen of the standing and quality of Mr. Lloyd
George, Mr. Churchill and Mr. [Anthony] Eden – to name only a
few.'[3] Tryon thought that 'it would be most dangerous to allow the
B.B.C. greater latitude'.[4] A civil servant's note in the file makes
the reason clear. The question, it was noted, 'boils down to the fairly
simple one whether or not it is desirable for speeches to be made on
Foreign Policy in opposition to the views of the Government, and as
Mr. Lloyd George was specially mentioned, it must be realised that
the Opposition would be irresponsible and mischievous. The answer
must surely be that whatever is said in Parliament and in the Press,
it is definitely undesirable that at time like the present issues of
Foreign Policy should be discussed on the air.'[5] So much for the
BBC's supposed independence from political control. A little later the
government rejected the BBC's plans for a special programme to
boost recruiting to the armed services. The Lord Privy Seal, Sir John
Anderson, 'objected to having in all the big guns: Churchill, Lloyd
George etc., because he said that it would make people think that the
Government was in a hole and must have mismanaged its recruiting
in the past'. Anderson also 'objected to the proposed "crisis" programme as being likely to give people the idea that they might be
involved in a war in a few months time, say September'.[6] This,
remember, was 1939. You really couldn't make it up.

The threat of war was, of course, the defining issue of the decade.
Churchill had been concerned about the rise of Nazism a significant
time before Hitler seized power in Germany. His repeated warnings
about the need for British rearmament make a powerful contrast with
Lloyd George's notorious 1936 visit to Hitler and the fawning remarks
he made about him. That episode, perhaps more than anything else,
has cast a shadow over Lloyd George's reputation; his comments were
indeed inexcusable. Yet it would be wrong to dismiss him as a straightforward advocate of appeasement. Insofar as that policy was encapsulated in the actions of the National Government, he was strongly

opposed to it. Indeed, opposition to Baldwin and Neville Chamberlain may have been the sole consistent thread in his approach. Crucially, his attitude was never such as to lead Churchill, who repeatedly tried to enlist his support, to abandon all thoughts of future cooperation. A proper understanding of Lloyd George's position is unlikely to lead to a rehabilitation of his views. It is, however, essential in order to make sense of the two men's relationship at this time. Equally, it will help illuminate Churchill's own path during these years; he was not the utterly consistent visionary of popular legend.

In one respect, Lloyd George had a claim to greater far-sightedness than Churchill did. In 1925, three years after Mussolini came to power, he strongly condemned the Fascist regime in Italy. 'Repression, intimidation, arson, murder, were the instruments of government', he declared.[7] This was in contrast to Churchill's attitude. In 1923 he described Mussolini to Clementine as 'a swine', but three years later he spoke publicly of his 'commanding leadership'.[8] In 1927, during a visit to Italy, he met Il Duce, and, as he told journalists afterwards: 'Like so many others, I could not but be charmed with the friendly and simple attitude of Signor Mussolini, and by his calm & serene manner despite so many burdens and dangers.' The Italian Fascist movement, he went on, had 'rendered service to the whole world'.[9] In February 1933 he publicly praised Mussolini's 'Roman genius' and described the dictator as 'the greatest lawgiver among living men'. In this speech, he also expressed sympathy for Japan, which was behaving aggressively in the Far East.[10]

Germany, of course, was a different matter. In November 1932 Churchill warned the Commons – this was shortly before Hitler became Chancellor – that the community of nations should not allow Germany to rearm. The 'bands of sturdy Teutonic youths' marching through the Fatherland were not seeking mere 'equal status' but weapons, with which they would then demand the return of lost territories and colonies.[11] Initially, it seemed that Lloyd George shared the concerns expressed in this speech. A month earlier he had written to Henry Wickham Steed, the owner and editor-in-chief of the *Review of Reviews*. Steed, who was to become a powerful critic of Hitler and of appeasement, had long believed that another war with Germany was inevitable.[12] 'May I say how much I approve of the line you are taking on foreign policy', Lloyd George told him. 'The optimistic attitude taken officially by the Press on both foreign affairs and the economic position is entirely unjustified by the disturbing nature of the facts, and the public ought to be educated to an understanding before it is too late.'[13] A year later, though, when the Nazis had been in power for some months and the nature of the threat was yet more apparent, he took a different line.

In mid-October 1933 Germany withdrew from the international disarmament conference in Geneva, and from the League of Nations a week later. In the Commons Lloyd George was inclined to make excuses for her actions, taking the view that she had long laboured under genuine grievances. This, indeed, was the conventional wisdom at the time. The Versailles settlement was widely perceived as having been too harsh towards her, not only in terms of reparations and frontiers, but also in terms of arms limitations that had been imposed but then not followed up, as originally intended, by a general scheme of European disarmament. Lloyd George's view was that Germany 'could not manufacture armaments' other than rifles and perhaps machine guns.[14]

Churchill, in his own speech, challenged Lloyd George's supposition that he had some special claim to interpret the Treaty of Versailles, and rejected the view that Germany was under threat from its neighbours. Lloyd George, he said, had 'represented that Germany might have a few thousand more rifles than was allowed by the Treaty, a few more Boy Scouts, and then he pictured the enormous armies of Czechoslovakia and Poland and France, with their thousands of cannon, and so forth . . . The great dominant fact is that Germany has already begun to rearm.' Interestingly, though, Churchill explicitly presented himself as an enthusiast for the League of Nations, and criticized Lloyd George for having 'mocked and scolded the League' in a recent speech in the country. It was, he believed, vital to use the League as a means of cooperation with other European powers, 'in an attempt to address Germany collectively, so that there may be some redress of the grievances of the German nation' before her rearmament threatened the peace of the world.[15] Churchill did not, therefore, dissent from the common view that Germany had legitimate claims. He believed, though, that these could be addressed successfully only from a position of strength.

He continued to sound the alarm throughout 1934. In November he initiated a Commons debate on German air power. Lloyd George was not impressed by his views on the subject. About ten days before the debate he read a transcript of a Churchill broadcast in which he argued for a strong British air force. He told Sylvester he had a good mind to say in the House 'that had he not known the Rt Hon. Gentleman he would have said it was the speech of an unbalanced mind. Winston had talked as if Germany would come over here with her aeroplanes and blow us to pieces and as if France, Italy and everybody would meantime just wait and do nothing.'[16] They met at a dinner a few days later. 'They always enjoy a talk, even if they don't agree about anything', noted Frances Stevenson, who a few days beforehand had recorded Churchill's belief that the government might soon break up.[17] Churchill had obtained inside information about the growth of the German air force. On 24 November he sent Lloyd George a précis of what he planned to say in the debate – he also sent it to Baldwin, who as Conservative Party leader and Lord President of the Council was the real power in the government – and invited him to lunch. 'It appears that my amendment has caused much disturbance in Government circles', he wrote. 'The facts set out in the precis cannot I think be controverted and the Cabinet have woken up to the fact that they are "caught short" in this very grave matter.'[18]

The government were indeed worried. Lord Londonderry, the Secretary of State for Air, predicted in a letter to Ramsay MacDonald that Churchill's warnings would be followed by a speech by Lloyd George proclaiming 'that the solution of the problem is to grant equality to Germany, that we should have done this a long time ago, and that really Germany has been in the right and we have been in the wrong'. Londonderry advocated answering Churchill and pre-empting Lloyd George by announcing that the government knew of Germany's rearmament and was prepared to consider her claims to equality favourably.[19] Instead, Baldwin replied to Churchill's speech with a straightforward denial of his assertion that Germany was rapidly approaching air parity with Britain. (In fact, as early as March 1935, Hitler was to state that he had achieved parity, a debatable claim which nonetheless made it appear that the British government had been shockingly complacent.) Baldwin also found unconvincing the argument that Germany's civil aircraft could easily be converted for military use. Comparing a civil aircraft to a military one was like comparing Oxford and Cambridge, Eton and Winchester, or Lloyd George and Churchill, whom, he joked, were 'both perfect but not comparable'.[20]

Lloyd George, for his part, accepted Baldwin's assurances that Churchill's figures were exaggerated. He acknowledged that 'It is difficult to put the German case at the moment', as the Nazi regime seemed determined to 'exasperate and outrage' all varieties of opinion. Germany, however, was in 'a revolutionary temper', and 'a revolutionary country is a very dangerous country to treat as a pariah'. Although he thought the government was 'travelling blindly' he had little constructive to suggest, other than that there should be an attempt to persuade other European powers to offer to disarm if Germany did so too.[21] (Such apparent naivety was not uncommon. A few months later, Churchill himself reportedly said in private that 'he would be willing to support the abolition of aeroplanes altogether – civil as well as military'.)[22] Gwilym Lloyd George told Frances Stevenson in the debate's aftermath that some Tories were speaking of a new government. This would include the improbable combination of Baldwin, Lloyd George and Churchill.[23]

In spite of the apparent incompatibility of their respective positions, Churchill continued his efforts to win over Lloyd George. In April 1935 he urged him to read disclosures about air strength in the *Daily Telegraph*.[24] A few weeks later he sent him (and many other influential people) a memorandum on the same subject.[25] These overtures did not cost Churchill much effort, of course, and it would be wrong to read into them an exceptional commitment to securing the support of Lloyd George. Yet they appear to indicate that he did not so far despair of getting him to take a tougher line.

Churchill, of course, had to look for help even in apparently unpromising quarters. In his isolation he could not afford to be choosy. His difficulties were in part of his own making. His campaign against the government's India Bill contributed to the distrust with which many people viewed him. As David Reynolds has noted, the Indian issue was barely mentioned in his post-war memoirs, which presented his 1930s career as a plain tale of how his prescient warnings about the ambitions of the dictators were ignored.[26] As was the case over rearmament, so with India: the perception that he was intriguing for office may have hampered his efforts to be taken seriously. As the Tory MP Harold Macmillan observed, 'Where Lloyd George or Winston would fail, men with a tenth of their ability may win because they are disinterested.'[27]

Straightforward miscalculation also played a part in Churchill's

problems. In 1933, when the government established a Select Committee to examine its proposals for Indian constitutional reform, he,
together with Lloyd George and the Tory die-hard Henry Page
Croft, refused to serve on it. In 1934 he accused two members of the
committee, Samuel Hoare (the Secretary of State for India) and Lord
Derby, of putting improper pressure on witnesses to change their
evidence. He raised Hoare's ire by discussing the matter with, among
others, Lloyd George, who thought he had a strong case. Government supporters feared and suspected collusion between the two,
with the aim of causing a political upset. After Churchill made his
charges in the Commons in April, R. A. Butler, Hoare's parliamentary private secretary, wrote to Lord Brabourne, the governor of
Bombay, of how

> Winston developed his case with considerable force, having had
> time in which to consider it; Ll.G. had come in and kept bobbing
> up talking to the Speaker. On Sunday the Daily Mail had
> reopened its attack with a broadside on the Indian policy by
> Rothermere, and we consider that this is a resurrection of the
> intrigues against the Government which were so prevalent in the
> late Autumn. The combination of Rothermere, Ll.G. and
> Churchill is well known and I think Ll.G. thinks there is every
> chance of a first class crisis on this question.

Later in the same letter, Butler wrote:

> The whole upset will certainly make Winston's name stink more
> than it does at present with the reputable members of our party.
> I am inclined to think that it will do Winston down, whatever
> the effect it has on Sam [Hoare]. It is interesting to know that
> he approached [Clement] Attlee, the Leader of the Opposition
> [in the absence through illness of George Lansbury], against a
> member of his own party, over the weekend, and he was with
> Ll. G. on Saturday. This should settle our party's opinion of
> him.[28]

This is but one of many instances of Churchill's perceived
relationship with Lloyd George harming his own reputation. When
the House of Commons Committee of Privileges concluded that
Hoare and Derby had done nothing wrong, Churchill compounded
his problems by meeting defeat with ill grace. The episode as a whole

led Baldwin to conclude that 'Winston is fundamentally a blackguard. It's the dirtiest business I've ever encountered in politics. There are die-hards who'll stop at nothing to bring the Government down.' Understandably, the 'blackguard' remark, recorded by Thomas Jones, was omitted from the edition of his diary published in 1954.[29] Even after the debacle Hoare continued to fear that 'the Churchill–Lloyd George movement' would be able to damage the Indian reform programme; although he also recognized that Lloyd George was more of an unfriendly neutral than an active opponent of the government's plans.[30]

Although he was not averse to mischief-making over India, Lloyd George's true interests lay elsewhere. In January 1935, in a speech in Bangor, he launched his 'New Deal' programme in order to cure unemployment and other social evils. He urged the creation of a National Development Council and a small Cabinet on the War Cabinet model, and the raising of a Prosperity Loan in order to make use of idle capital. He emphasized that he was not a party leader and did not want to become one. Over the coming weeks and months he repeatedly stressed that he was chiefly concerned to get the government to adopt his proposals, and that if this involved him taking office, so be it; but that this was not his chief aim. His attitude was, in fact, ambivalent. In late February, according to Jones, he was 'reported as saying that he would like a small Cabinet of S.B., himself, Winston, Kingsley Wood and Hore-Belisha!'[31] (Wood was the Conservative Postmaster General; Leslie Hore-Belisha was the Liberal National Minister of Transport.) In May, however, he told Walter Layton, Chairman of the *News Chronicle*, that 'He definitely does not want to join the Government just now'. He did not wish to place himself in a position in which he would have to defend MacDonald or Simon. He said to Layton that if he attempted to speak in support of their diplomacy 'the words would choke me'.[32] Baldwin's comment on the New Deal launch was predictable, but it may have contained a grain of truth: 'It's nothing but a game to him and to Winston.'[33]

This remark had more justice in relation to Lloyd George than to Churchill. Yet Churchill's attitude to the proposals demonstrated a lack of consistency. Even in the eyes of some Liberals, the New Deal was not much more than 'the Yellow Book with trimmings'.[34] Churchill had of course denounced those previous proposals as inflationary and irresponsible. But after the Bangor Speech, he put out a press statement, as follows:

> Mr Lloyd George's proposals deserve the closest attention. They are at once virile and sober. They outline the kind of policy which any Government, calling itself 'National' ought to have thought of for itself. He is a little hard on Mr. Neville Chamberlain who has done most of the collar work of this administration. No doubt all the Chancellors of the Exchequer are the targets of criticism. But quite apart from Mr. Lloyd George's actual proposals, it is heartening to find a great public man showing so much resolute and vigorous desire to grapple with the grave evils and dangers of these times, and ready to make insistent mental exertion to come to the rescue of the weak and the poor, and those who are declared 'redundant' to our social system. It is all the more refreshing to read such a speech in contrast with the deplorable politician who now maunders at the head of the Government.[35]

Paul Addison's comment on this is that 'Churchill's tactic, like that of the Government, was to humour Lloyd George while keeping his proposals at a distance.'[36] Arguably, the statement went rather beyond what was required for those purposes – although it is indeed unlikely that Churchill was a genuine convert to Lloyd George's plans. At any rate, a striking element of it is the combination of the assault on MacDonald with the attempt to curry favour with Chamberlain.

Whatever construction is put upon his praise of Lloyd George, Churchill does not appear to have been enormously enthusiastic to work with him again at this point. In early March he wrote to his wife that Lloyd George 'of course' wanted to join the government and to 'reconstitute a kind of War Cabinet Government, in which I dare say I should be offered a place'. He added, though, that he himself would be disinclined to associate himself with any administration prior to a general election.[37] Meanwhile, the government went through the motions of considering the plans of Lloyd George, who does not appear to have been terribly keen to get them accepted. After a conversation with Lloyd George Layton concluded that 'he would prefer that the Government should give such an answer that he can break off the discussion'.[38]

While the negotiations went on, the prospect of Lloyd George and Churchill returning to government continued to be canvassed. In late February MacDonald was said to have accepted the idea of including Lloyd George. The majority of the Cabinet, though, apparently supported Chamberlain 'against a combination of L.G. and S.B.'.[39] (By mid-April, even Chamberlain was reported to be 'reconciled to the idea of George's entry', but this does not seem wholly convincing.)[40] Baldwin, for his part, seems to have been more hostile to Churchill than to Lloyd George. According to Geoffrey Dawson, the editor of *The Times*, he thought Churchill would be 'a disruptive force' but had 'a perfectly open mind' about Lloyd George. 'He thinks that L.G. and Winston *together* would be impossible.'[41] J. L. Garvin, veteran editor of the *Observer* and a founder member of the Other Club, pressed for that combination, however. He lay out his thinking in a letter to Viscount Astor, his paper's proprietor:

> Baldwin, with one of his curious kinks of unwisdom in personal matters, is stubborn against Winston. So says Ll.G.
> Now, while Winston is out, Conservative cohesion and enthusiasm cannot be restored; and Neville will remain what Ll.G. now discovers him to be – the arbiter in the Cabinet and Baldwin's master. Neville of course, in himself, is necessary and unshiftable. But Baldwin, to have his former command as leader of a re-united party, should in his own interest bring back Winston as a counter-weight when the India Bill is through.[42]

By now MacDonald, suffering from mental decline, was on the verge of retiring as Prime Minister. Shortly before formally replacing him on 7 June, Baldwin met alone with Garvin, who argued the case for taking Lloyd George and Churchill into the Cabinet. According to Jones, 'S.B. replied that it could not be now; this would be an attempt to preserve 1931; but he would keep an open mind for what might happen when the election came.'[43] ('Preserving 1931', of course, meant maintaining the National Government's increasingly worn cross-party veneer.) Jones, presumably, based this on what Baldwin told him. A few weeks later, though, the new Prime Minister gave R. A. Butler a rather different account. He had, he said, told Garvin that 'a great National Government' including Lloyd George and Churchill 'would make a very good Press Government, but that to rule the country a homogenous team with as much uniformity of ideas as possible was essential'.[44]

It is doubtful, then, that Baldwin had been serious about getting Lloyd George or Churchill into the government. Had he attempted such a thing he would probably have faced a serious revolt against his leadership of the Conservative Party. Five days after Baldwin resumed the premiership, Lloyd George launched a new initiative, the 'Council of Action for Peace and Reconstruction'. This was to be an organization aimed at gaining cross-party support for his proposals, although it appeared to many as an instrument of opposition to the National Government. In a letter written on the day of the launch, Baldwin wrote, 'Ll.G. *is* out for mischief – dirty and unholy.' A postscript to the same letter noted that – the India Bill having just passed its Third Reading – 'Winston is rapidly transferring his interest from India to Air!'[45] A week later he called off the Cabinet's discussions with Lloyd George, whose proposals were rejected. By the following year, if not earlier, Baldwin had reversed his preferences, as they had appeared in the spring of 1935. He contrasted Lloyd George and his amoralism unfavourably 'with Winston who, he said, could not tell a lie without growing pink in the face as he said it'.[46]

Not only was there little hope of Lloyd George and Churchill working together again inside the government – whatever Baldwin might have said about keeping an open mind for the future – but there was also little hope of them cooperating outside it either. At the Council of Action convention in July, Lloyd George attacked expenditure on arms, saying that the money should be spent on social improvement, an argument Churchill cannot have cared for much. Yet the reputation of their relationship had a hold on people's minds; the idea that they might collaborate was remarkably persistent. For instance Robert Bernays, a Liberal (and later Liberal National) MP, wrote in his diary in July 1935 that 'It is clear that Winston and Lloyd George attacking the government from different sides might provide a formidable combination in the next House when the government majority will be so infinitely smaller.'[47] Churchill's friend and adviser, the financier Abe Bailey, viewed the possibility of their cooperation more positively. 'You might drop Ll.G a hint in these times and with the hope of working together which is so necessary he should stop going for Neville or any member of the Govt.', he wrote to him in September. 'I would like to see you both in the team.'[48]

(Garvin's earlier advocacy was, of course, another example of this kind of thinking.) Yet although Churchill might have been prepared to butter up Baldwin and Chamberlain if he thought it the price of achieving office, it was not in Lloyd George's nature to 'stop going for' ministers. Such talk, however, was a testament to the power of the myth that Lloyd George and Churchill had built up about their relationship. They were still perceived in some quarters not only to be inseparable but also indispensable. The reality, though, was that Lloyd George was even more isolated than Churchill, and even the members of his entourage were becoming frustrated. Frances Stevenson wrote to a friend that she was 'profoundly unhappy' about Lloyd George's Council of Action campaign, which she thought lacked the necessary roots of popular support: 'But it's hopeless trying to influence him. He has had his own way for so long that it would take a far stronger person than myself to attempt the job, and even then they would probably be broken in the process.' She added: 'I've been bruised enough'.[49]

The late summer and autumn of 1935 were dominated by the crisis over Abyssinia. In August, with Mussolini's intention to invade the country clear, Hoare (now Foreign Secretary) and Anthony Eden (Minister for League of Nations Affairs) consulted Lloyd George, Churchill, and other senior figures. Lloyd George made clear that he did not favour unilateral action by Britain to restrain Italy, but 'The League procedure must in his view be tried out, and at a suitable moment we must make it clear that in the event of collective action we are prepared to take our part.'[50] He subsequently told the Italian ambassador that although he sympathized with Italian colonial claims, 'If he were in command in this country, he would with the assistance if necessary of only a relatively small number of League powers, close the Suez Canal while allowing sufficient supplies to reach the Italian forces in East Africa to keep them supplied, and so force Mussolini to open discussion.'[51] Churchill emphasized to Hoare and Eden that only collective action would be justified, and assured them he would support the government on those lines.

On 11 September Hoare spoke in Geneva in exactly this sense – that Britain would act against an Italian invasion, but only if other powers did too. As France, the other key force in the League, was reluctant, this was in practice a recipe for doing nothing. The speech was, however, widely interpreted as giving a strong British lead, with war as a conceivable outcome. Churchill was unhappy about this. On 26 September he gave a speech emphasizing that the quarrel lay not between Italy and Britain but between Italy and the League. 'I am surprised that so great a man, so wise a ruler, as Signor Mussolini should be willing, and even eager, to put his gallant nation in such an uncomfortable military and financial position.'[52] An exchange of letters in the Leo Chiozza Money Papers is revealing. Money, who had long ceased to be an MP, was sympathetic to Italy, and thought British hostility towards her inexplicable. He told Churchill: 'I deeply appreciate the tone and temper of your remarks, and especially I note that you deleted the Suez reference from the reports. A happy contrast to L.G.'s "cut the communications!" '[53] (It is not clear what 'the Suez reference' was, although Churchill's ability to suppress it says something about the pliability of journalists at the time.)[54] Churchill replied: 'Although I support the Government in the line they are taking, I am sure you will believe that I do it with most profound regret.'[55] This could be read as an indication of his willingness to trim his foreign policy line in the interests of getting back into government, of which he still held out hopes. The episode also suggests that, in this instance, Lloyd George took a slightly tougher line against fascist aggression than Churchill did. Similarly, during the Spanish Civil War, Churchill showed private pro-Franco sympathies, whereas Lloyd George spoke out clearly in favour of the Republican regime. In other words, where countries other than Germany were concerned, it was Lloyd George who was the more hawkish of the pair.

At the start of October 1935 Mussolini launched his invasion. Later that month Baldwin called an election, to be held on 14 November. The campaign was fought on the premise that the government would support collective security. Soon after the election it became clear that the government was in actuality prepared to abandon Abyssinia to the brutality of its Italian conquerors. In December it was revealed that Hoare and his French opposite number, Pierre Laval, had agreed a 'compromise' solution, whereby the Abyssinians would cede a significant part of their territory. Upon being faced with this embarrassment, the British government repudiated the plan, Hoare resigned, and Italy continued with its war, unimpeded by the ineffective sanctions imposed by the League.

In the meantime, the National Government had again triumphed at the polls. Labour increased its representation to 154, and the Liberals outside the government were further reduced in number. Samuel lost his seat and was replaced as leader by Archie Sinclair, with the support of Lloyd George, who together with the 'family group' now accepted the party whip again. Lloyd George's Council of Action had endorsed 362 candidates across the party spectrum. The exercise was of little value: sixty-seven of them won seats, but they did not afterwards behave as a group. Churchill also faced disappointment. It was widely expected that he would get a Cabinet post after the election. For example, at the end of October, the US ambassador attended a dinner given by him at Claridge's, and noted that 'as it is reported that he is likely to be in the next Government, probably as First Lord of the Admiralty, I was glad of an opportunity to talk with him'.[56] But the call never came, Baldwin claiming privately that 'If I consulted the Cabinet he [Churchill] would not get a single vote in his support.'[57]

Christmas found Churchill at Tangier, where he did some work on his biography of his ancestor the first Duke of Marlborough. He then moved on to Marrakesh, where he stayed at the same hotel as Lloyd George, who was working on his memoirs. Churchill found him 'very splendid and patriarchal', he told Clementine. He added, in the context of the government's foreign policy problems: 'What a fool Baldwin is, with this terrible situation on his hands, not to gather his [i.e. Lloyd George's] resources & experience to the public service.'[58]

The two men stimulated and amused one another, as A. J. Sylvester's diary records. When Churchill, in the room above Lloyd George, gave repeated yells in an attempt to silence another guest who insisted on practising the ukulele, 'L.G. said that the irritation caused by the noise of the ukulele was quite wiped out by Winston's performance.' They were received at two banquets, one given by the Pasha of Marrakesh and the other by his son. Frances Stevenson having departed and his wife having arrived, Lloyd George celebrated his seventy-third birthday. This provided him and Churchill with an opportunity to make brief speeches about their friendship, in line with the myth that they sought to promote. They had fought politically, Lloyd George claimed, 'without for one moment impairing the good feeling and the warmth' between them. There was, however, more than an edge of rivalry to the relationship. On 20 January 1936

George V died. This necessitated the presence of both men in London. Sylvester took the initiative and ordered a wreath to be sent to Windsor on Lloyd George's behalf. On hearing this, the former Prime Minister turned 'peculiar'. Sylvester noted:

> He said he would not pay for a wreath. Who else was sending one? I said: 'I have just spoken to Winston personally. He and his wife have already sent one.' That did it. I told him it would cost £10 and produced a black-edged card. This he inscribed: 'Deep grief from loyal servants, D. Lloyd George: Margaret Lloyd George.'[59]

Clearly, the depths of Lloyd George's grief were unfathomable.

During 1936 Lloyd George and Churchill's paths continued to intersect. On 7 March Germany sent troops into the demilitarized Rhineland. The British and French did nothing to stop them. Three days later the Commons debated the government's new defence White Paper. Churchill gave it qualified praise, and emphasized the need to prepare the economy for war, although he made little mention of the immediate crisis. Lloyd George listened to Churchill 'with very great admiration . . . and with a good deal of agreement'. However, he explicitly dissented from Churchill's estimate of the power of Germany. That country, he said, was 'Great, gigantic, the most formidable enemy the British Empire has fought but we fought her. We must not run away and work ourselves into a panic.' Moreover, 'You cannot proceed on the assumption that we are going to stand alone.'[60] Lord Lloyd wrote to Churchill after the debate: 'All but you and LG seemed like Pygmies.'[61] Another admirer, Sir Henry Strakosch, wrote that 'It was rather a tragic debate in some ways. Your speech and Ll G's sounded like voices from the past in the days when there were really great men to serve the Government of our country.'[62]

Randolph Churchill had recently fought a Scottish by-election as a Conservative against the official National Government candidate, Ramsay MacDonald's son Malcolm. He had lost. Churchill had been annoyed with his son, fearing that Baldwin might assume he himself had played some part in the challenge, although 'with Rothermere, Beaverbrook and Lloyd George all goading him [i.e. Randolph] on, I really cannot blame him'.[63] Randolph now wrote to Lloyd George praising his speech, although, he said, he 'didn't entirely agree with the conclusions about Germany'. In reply, Lloyd George hoped that the government would 'have the wisdom to choose your father for Defence Minister. It would be a very popular appointment in the House of Commons.'[64] Churchill, having bounced back again, was now a plausible candidate for such a position. *The Times*, for example, thought that whereas Lloyd George had allowed an element of partisanship to mar an otherwise admirable speech, Churchill's contribution had been, in spite of some exaggerations and omissions, 'deeply impressive and vital'.[65] But Baldwin announced, to the incredulity of many, that his new Minister of Defence Coordination would be not Churchill but Sir Thomas Inskip, the Attorney General. Lloyd George is said to have turned to Churchill and remarked: 'My Rt. Hon. Friend will realize it is more important to be good than clever.'[66]

In late May Thomas Jones wrote to a friend that 'On foreign policy L.G. is nearer to S.B. than he is to Winston.'[67] Yet in June Lloyd George made a remarkably powerful Commons speech in which he lambasted the government's foreign policy vacillations and its decision to drop economic sanctions against Italy, now that the conquest of Abyssinia was complete. He accused the government of 'cowardly surrender'.[68] Frances Stevenson wrote in her diary that the House was 'almost hysterical' and that the government front bench was 'literally cowed before his onslaught'. Furthermore: 'After the speech a young Tory Member went up to Winston & said he had never heard anything like it in the House. "Young man", replied W., "you have been listening to one of the greatest Parliamentary performances of all time." '[69] However, there was a flaw in the speech. Lloyd George's remark that Britain would never again (as in 1914) go to war for an 'Austrian quarrel' undermined the principle of collective security – for if Britain could opt out of involvement in an Austrian dispute, why shouldn't other countries also opt out of disputes when they saw fit? Furthermore, he and Churchill were not in accord on the details of foreign affairs. As Grigg has noted, they both held the government in contempt, yet rarely made a joint stand over a specific policy.[70] In July Churchill, Austen Chamberlain and Lord Salisbury led a parliamentary deputation to Baldwin on defence questions. Churchill had hoped that it would be an all-party delegation. Neville Chamberlain had feared that he and Lloyd George 'would work together and would accuse the Government of not taking Defence sufficiently seriously'.[71] But Lloyd George declined to take part, as did Sinclair and Clement Attlee, who was now the leader of the Labour Party.[72]

In many respects Lloyd George's tirades were unconvincing. As the veteran journalist J. A. Spender noted, 'No one really believes that he would have gone to war with Japan and Italy single-handed if he had been in power, as he seems to say, but saying it makes a great many people thank God for Baldwin and Safety First.'[73] Moreover, he misunderstood Hitler, underrated the power of Germany, and veered towards apologism for her aggression. 'I admire the new Germany, which interests me more than any other country in the world today', the *Berliner Tageblatt* reported him as saying in January 1935.[74] Shortly after the remilitarization of the Rhineland, he said that Hitler had not been to blame for 'the breach of a treaty, because there was provocation'. Rather 'his greatest offence was that in the inflammable conditions of Europe' he should commit that breach 'in so reckless a manner'.[75] In July 1936 he said in a speech at Nottingham that Hitler was unlikely to attack Belgium or France: 'I don't think Hitler is a fool. He is not going to challenge the British Empire again by that act of folly.'[76]

This last quotation points to the genuine difficulties of assessing Hitler's intentions. As launching a world war appeared to be, and indeed ultimately was, contrary to his long-term self-interest, it was easy enough to conclude that he wouldn't do so. We therefore have to be careful when evaluating contemporary statements. For example Lloyd George's praise, in May 1935, of Hitler's latest 'peace offer' as 'courageous and statesmanlike' may appear to be an example of his gullibility.[77] But, before judging, consider Churchill's own reaction: 'all must welcome the friendly tone of Herr Hitler, his friendly references to this country, and the several important points which he brought forward and which form a good basis upon which conversations could be opened and negotiations, perhaps, be founded'.[78] In November the same year Churchill published an article in *Strand Magazine* in which he wrote: 'We cannot tell whether Hitler will be the man who will once again let loose upon the world another war in which civilization will irretrievably succumb, or whether he will go down in history as the man who restored honour and peace of mind to the great Germanic nation and brought them back serene, helpful and strong, to the European family circle.'[79]

None of this excuses Lloyd George but it does show the importance of context. This point is illustrated by the fact that Churchill's
magazine article, as a whole, was thought by the German Foreign
Ministry to constitute an appalling insult to Hitler. Churchill was
prepared to pay occasional lip service to the possibility of Hitler's
sincerity, but these rhetorical concessions in the direction of the
conventional wisdom were necessary in the interests of persuading his
audience. Lloyd George's praise of Hitler was more forthright and all
the less justifiable. His trip to Germany in 1936 was the high – or
low – point. He travelled in company with Megan, Gwilym, Sylvester,
Thomas Jones, and T. P. Conwell Evans, who acted as translator.
On 3 September the party arrived at Berchtesgaden, where they were
joined by Lord Dawson of Penn, who had been George V's physician,
and had also advised Lloyd George. That evening the company dined
with Joachim von Ribbentrop, the German ambassador to Britain,
together with his wife and others. Lloyd George spared no efforts to
suck up to the regime. According to Sylvester, 'L.G. said there was
no doubt that Hitler, as far as Germany was concerned, was the
resurrection and the life.' After Ribbentrop outlined the religious
situation in Germany, 'L.G. suggested that Ribbentrop should try to
get Winston. The trouble with Winston was that he was fighting
everyone in turn: one day it was Russia, now it was Germany. L.G.
added: "If you could get him into your new church, it would be
worth while."' [80]

The next day Lloyd George and Ribbentrop were taken to an
interview with Hitler at his villa. Most unusually, they were transported using the Führer's own car and escort. Lloyd George and
Hitler discussed the importance of Anglo-German understanding, the
situation in Spain – Lloyd George denounced Franco's forces as
'military reactionaries' – and public works schemes. Hitler rehearsed
some of his favourite themes: Germany's shortage of raw materials
and her need for colonies. At the close of their talk, the two men
engaged in mutual flattery. Hitler said that during the war Lloyd
George had 'galvanized the people of Britain into the will for victory'.
Lloyd George said he was glad to receive this compliment from the
greatest German of the age and the greatest since Bismarck's day.
The British ambassador, Eric Phipps, wrote drily: 'whether Hitler
appreciated this last limitation I have not been able to ascertain'. On
the 5th there was a further interview, and on the 6th Lloyd George

saw Rudolf Hess, Hitler's deputy, in Munich. Lloyd George criticized Churchill to Hess, and later the same day once more to Ribbentrop. 'L.G. said he [Churchill] had no judgement.'[81] In an article in the *Daily Express* after his return from Germany, Lloyd George wrote that Hitler had achieved 'a marvellous transformation in the spirit of the people'.[82] He did stress that he himself deplored the persecution of the Jews, although he might have done better to tell this to Hitler when he met him, rather than to the correspondent of the *News Chronicle* when he got back.[83]

Lloyd George and Churchill's respective attitudes towards the Jews are worth examining in depth. In April 1937 the former published an article entitled 'What Has the Jew Done?' in *Strand Magazine*. In it, he wrote that the Jews were 'the most remarkable race that ever dwelt on this earth' and praised 'their inherent vitality and indomitable spirit'. The praise was by no means unqualified, though. Noting that 'the most unaccountable mystery in the history of the Jews is the persistence, the source, and the intensity of their persecution throughout the ages', he argued that the 'root of the trouble' was to be found in 'the determination of the Jews throughout the centuries not to lose their identity as a separate and distinct people in any land where they dwell'. In other words, 'They refuse to be good mixers.' Moreover, their insistence on maintaining their own rites and customs 'has been at the bottom of many a pogrom'. Lloyd George did accept that the Jews were not 'exclusively responsible for this isolationism', given that they had been so often subject to enforced ghettoization. 'No country is entitled to claim loyalty unto death from a people to whom it denied the elementary rights of humanity', he argued further, adding: 'A Jew fairly treated is a loyal citizen in all lands.'[84] Overall, his attitude was rather paradoxical. He condemned anti-Semitism, whilst at the same time suggesting that (to some extent voluntary) Jewish 'separateness' was in part to blame for it.

Churchill shared this ambivalent approach to the Jews. An article he wrote in or around June 1937 – but which he did not publish – is remarkable evidence of this. It was called 'How the Jews Can Combat Persecution', and pondered the causes of anti-Semitism. It may have been influenced by Lloyd George's piece, but there is no direct evidence of this. It is worth quoting at length. 'Whence comes this malignant fate that has dogged the Jewish people down the centuries,

with hardly a pause or respite?' Churchill asked. 'It would be easy to
ascribe it to the wickedness of the persecutors, but that does not fit
all the facts.' He went on to suggest that the Jews had perhaps been
inviting persecution unwittingly, in other words 'that they have been
partly responsible for the antagonism from which they suffer'. He
went on to say that this was not necessarily to the Jews' discredit, as
'Men are hated as often for their virtues as for their vices.' However,
he also went on to criticize them, via a roundabout route:

> In fact, the Jew is, as a rule, a good citizen. He is sober,
> industrious, law-abiding. He identifies himself – up to a point –
> with the country in which he lives. He is ready, if need be, to
> fight and to die for it . . .
>
> Yet there are times when one feels instinctively that all this
> is only another manifestation of the difference, the separateness
> of the Jew. He is acknowledging hospitality, a square deal given
> to himself and his people. But while he is prepared to pay for
> these things even with his life, he remains aloof.

It was this that gave rise to prejudice, Churchill thought. He
argued that the Jews themselves could counteract such hostility by
conducting themselves as citizens in such a way 'that the difference
will seem unimportant.' But, he added, this was not enough:

> It is not sufficient to meet all the obligations, obey all the behests
> of the law. It is not sufficient that individual Jews should be
> generous and public-spirited. There are others of whom the
> reverse may truthfully be said . . . The Jew in England is a
> representative of his race. Every Jewish moneylender recalls
> Shylock and the idea of the Jews as usurers. And you cannot
> reasonably expect a struggling clerk or shopkeeper, paying forty
> or fifty per cent interest on borrowed money to a 'Hebrew
> bloodsucker' to reflect that, throughout long centuries, almost
> every other way of life was closed to the Jewish people; or that
> there are native English moneylenders who insist, just as implac-
> ably, upon their 'pound of flesh'.

Churchill went on to suggest that 'the clothing trade is very
largely in the hands of Jews', and that the Jewish employers were
guilty of using sweated labour. He acknowledged that the direct
victims of this were often Jewish themselves, but also argued that the

willingness of these workers to accept low wages was problematic too: 'they are taking employment from English people – "taking the bread out of our mouths," as anti-Semitic orators will phrase it'. Later in the article, he wrote:

> Refugee Jews from Germany may be willing to work for lower wages and under worse conditions than English [people] would look at. If they are allowed to do so, and their numbers are sufficiently large, they may depress the standards of all workers, of whatever nationality, in the trades which they practise. That, I suggest, is bad citizenship. It is also bad policy. It creates an atmosphere in which anti-Semitism thrives.

Churchill suggested that Jews could counter anti-Semitism by widening the range of their personal contacts. 'I believe that Jews would be wise to avoid too exclusive an association in ordinary matters of business and daily life and that they should, as much as possible, avoid living in little groups and colonies of their own', he argued. 'Above all, they should be wary of exhibiting, in any position of authority, too marked a preference for fellow-Jews.' Another potential solution was intermarriage with Christians. 'The children of these marriages are frequently indistinguishable from the rest of us. But here we have, in effect, a process of absorption. That would solve the Jewish problem – but it is a solution which would mean the extinction of the Jews.' That, Churchill believed was unnecessary: 'No Jew needs to turn his back on the synagogue to win our good will.' He also thought it legitimate for Jews to use their economic resources to pressure governments that encouraged or condoned anti-Semitic persecution. 'There is in this no sinister conspiracy . . . when the victim of oppression is a brother in blood and faith, to attempt his succour becomes a sacred duty.'[85]

What is clear from the article is that Churchill's attitude to the Jews was very divided. On the one hand, his disapproval of anti-Semitic persecution – which is also clear from his other writings – was made plain. On the other, so was his belief that the Jews bore a significant degree of responsibility for that persecution because of the way that they conducted themselves, and that much of the solution to it lay in their own hands. The logical contortions are evident. It was perverse to argue that low-paid Jewish workers were the victims of their Jewish bosses, and, at the same time, that they were acting unfairly by taking employment from 'English people'. (Note the assumption that Jews were not English.) And to suggest that German Jewish refugees were guilty of 'bad policy' when they accepted low wages – as though they were acting collectively, rather than struggling to survive as families and individuals – was an equally twisted piece of reasoning. Arguably, he went further in his criticisms of the Jews than did Lloyd George – who did not use the term 'Hebrew bloodsucker' even in quotation marks. But the basic argument was the same.

Churchill's article was originally offered to the US publication *Liberty*. However, it was not published there as *Collier's*, for which he also wrote, objected to any of his articles appearing in a rival magazine. It then seems to have been offered to *Strand Magazine* in Britain, but they did not use it – because they had already accepted Lloyd George's piece on the same theme.[86] Two points about the episode are worth noting. First, if Churchill had felt really strongly about what he had written, he could have found some opportunity to express the same views elsewhere, perhaps in a speech. This he did not do. Second, unenlightened though his views may in many respects have been, they were not wildly exceptional for the time. This would appear to be shown by the fact that Lloyd George's (admittedly more moderately phrased) article did not provoke any especial fuss, even though it expressed a similar point of view.

There was a fascinating sequel to the tale. In the early part of 1940 Charles Eade, the editor of the *Sunday Dispatch*, came across the unpublished article. (The *Dispatch* was republishing some of Churchill's old journalism, and Eade had been given permission to search through old material looking for pieces that were usable.) On 7 March, he wrote to Churchill's Secretary, Kathleen Hill: 'I enclose a typescript of what I consider to be one of the most interesting articles Mr. Churchill has ever written. It is, as you see, about the Jews. I should very much like to publish this article in the "Sunday Dispatch" and I see no reason why Mr. Churchill should not agree to my doing so, but the question of Jews is a rather provocative one, and I thought I should ask his permission before going ahead with this particular contribution.'[87] A few days later Hill wrote back that she was sorry to disappoint, 'but Mr. Churchill thinks it would be inadvisable to publish the article "How the Jews can combat Persecution" at the present time'.[88] It is not entirely clear if Churchill had changed his views on the Jewish question, or whether he merely thought that it was impolitic to publish them in the circumstances of 1940. It is interesting to speculate, though, as to what the impact might have been on his career, and on his subsequent reputation, had he decided to proceed with publication at that moment, just weeks before the crisis that was to propel him to the premiership. In terms of the potential impact on political opinion, it might have been one thing to express the views he did in 1937, and quite another to have done so when Britain was actually at war with Nazi Germany.

Lloyd George's own indiscretions were used against him, even prior to the outbreak of war. In April 1939 Randolph Churchill, as a budding journalist, gained revenge for having been denied an interview with him by reprinting a number of compromising quotations in praise of Hitler in the diary column of the *Evening Standard*. Lloyd George appears to have had the decency to be embarrassed, although he showed this by venting his fury on Sylvester, accusing him, quite unreasonably, of having supplied the material.[89] After World War II, Churchill enjoyed reading Sylvester's published account of the 1936 German trip. According to his doctor, 'the way Lloyd George had been completely taken in and bamboozled by Hitler interested and pleased him. He, Winston, had not fallen into the trap which Hitler had contrived.'[90] Interestingly, although he had surely disapproved of Lloyd George's actions, there is no evidence that he told him or anyone else so at the time. In this case it was indeed true that political disagreement did not cause bad feeling in their personal relationship. A month after his return from Germany, Lloyd George was thanking Churchill in fulsome terms for the gift of one of his pictures, and looking forward to his attendance at the dinner for the completion of the *War Memoirs*.

The two men were also brought together by the abdication crisis. Both had known the new King, Edward VIII, for over two decades. In 1911, Lloyd George had coached him for his formal investiture as Prince of Wales; Churchill had read the proclamation. Edward's relations with his father, George V, had not been happy, and he had taken an offhand attitude towards his royal duties. During this new crisis, Lloyd George recalled how he and Churchill had taken 'the boy's part in the past when he had been in difficulties with the late King'.[91] Edward now wanted to marry Wallis Simpson, an American socialite who was about to be divorced for the second time. The government opposed him wedding a divorcee. Those in high political circles had known about the problem for some time, and there had been plenty of hints in the American media, but the matter only became public in Britain on 3 December, after the King had made plain to Baldwin that he would not renounce Mrs Simpson. Churchill took the King's side, and urged the government not to take any irrevocable steps. Lloyd George, on holiday in Jamaica, thought that 'this is Winston's chance to become Premier and he will back him, but it was like Winston to want to try to do it alone'.[92]

In the Commons on 7 December Churchill made one of the silliest mistakes of his career. Baldwin stated that the King was still considering the situation and that nothing had been decided. This in effect gave Churchill the delay for which he had asked; but because, apparently, he was not paying proper attention, he again demanded that 'no irrevocable step would be taken before the House had received a full statement'. He was howled down by MPs, many of whom suspected that he was simply trying to work up hostility to Baldwin. Amery recorded: 'He was completely staggered by the unanimous hostility of the House'.[93] A few days later it was announced that the King was determined to give up the throne. Baldwin's skilful handling of the situation won him cross-party sympathy. Lloyd George was still in the Caribbean. 'Winston is the only one who stood up in the synagogue of the Pharisees, but in spite of all his genius he is not a strategist, and he had no backing', he wrote to Gwilym. 'If the Labour Party had played up, Winston would have been very formidable.'[94] Churchill wrote to Lloyd George on Christmas Day that he was 'profoundly grieved' at what had happened, adding 'You have done well to be out of it'.[95]

By the time Lloyd George received the letter, he had already sent the ex-King a telegram – taking care also to inform the Press Association of its contents – deploring 'the shabby and stupid treatment' he had received and regretting 'the loss sustained by the British Empire of a monarch who sympathised with the lowliest of his subjects.'[96] Churchill sent Lloyd George a telegram in turn: 'Bravo All good wishes Winston'.[97] 'Lloyd George's telegram stirred the pulse of millions', Churchill commented in a letter to a friend. That was a classic piece of hyperbole.[98] The telegram, of course, stirred up Tory hostility, some of which reflected on Churchill too. Cuthbert Headlam, a once and future MP, wrote: 'like Winston, L.G. had no thought but for himself'. It seems that Baldwin felt roughly the same way. Nor was the negative reaction confined to Britain. The Governor General of Canada, Lord Tweedsmuir (the former John Buchan), reported that 'Winston has pretty well taken the place of Beaverbrook as Public Enemy No. 1, with Lloyd George a good second.'[99]

During the spring of 1937 the men set themselves up as the joint champions of the former King, now the Duke of Windsor. Both were members of the parliamentary Civil List Committee, which oversaw the royal family's finances, and were eager to ensure that the Duke received a generous allowance from the new King, his brother, George VI. There was in fact little reason to think that the Duke would be hard up, but any public discussion of the matter threatened embarrassment to the monarchy, if by any chance the considerable scale of the sums he had put by over the years was revealed. Chamberlain, the Chancellor, was deeply concerned, as he reported to his sister:

> The Civil List Committee has now been set up and I dont [sic] believe that I should have any serious trouble with the Labour Party were it not for Lloyd George and Winston – These two pirates have (for their own purposes) constituted themselves the champions of the Duke versus the King and they are trying to blackmail the latter into a regular swindling arrangement by threats of making trouble in Committee . . . I dont mean to let these bandits get away with it . . .[100]

Two days later in his diary he noted that 'we are always liable to trouble in the Com.ee from Winston and Ll.G. who are hunting together'.[101] After meeting with them separately, he managed to get them to agree to avoid public discussion, and the Civil List was approved without mention of provision for the Duke.[102] They received assurances that the King would provide for him.[103]

An episode that took place the following winter casts interesting light on the men's relations with the Duke, and with each other. All three, and the Duchess, attended a dinner party given by Maxine Elliott, an American former actress and society hostess, in the South of France. The Windsors had recently toured Germany, and the Duke now praised the Nazis' social achievements to the assembled company. He spoke of the impressive pithead baths at German mines. The scene was witnessed by the US journalist Vincent Sheean, who was Elliott's nephew by marriage. In his memoirs, published in 1943, he wrote: 'Mr. Churchill did not particularly enjoy praise of the Nazi régime, and although he had been remarkably silent throughout the meal (deferring like a schoolboy to the authority of Mr. Lloyd George and the Duke) he now spoke up to say that he had proposed compulsory shower-baths at the pithead long ago.'[104] Intriguingly, this passage was absent from the account of the party in the British edition of Sheean's book, in which there is no mention of Churchill's deference or of the Duke's admiration for the Nazis.[105] Possibly the publishers were concerned about the possibility of being sued for libel.

After the Coronation in May 1937 Baldwin retired, his reputation at an all-time high. He was succeeded by Neville Chamberlain. In his recent Budget, his last as Chancellor, Chamberlain had promised to introduce a form of profits tax to be known as the National Defence Contribution (NDC). He had not, however, thought out the details of the tax very well. The idea was unpopular in the City and with Tory backbenchers, and was attacked from the Labour side as 'a mere political device designed to meet the criticisms of the Labour Party against armament profiteering.'[106] Churchill exploited the discontent, delivering a witty speech in which he expressed the hope that 'we shall not have a draggle-tailed, tattered tax forced through the sulky lobbies'. Subsequently, Chamberlain stood up to concede that the NDC in its current form would be withdrawn, and that a simpler tax should be adopted in its place.[107] 'Winston's speech on the Profits Tax was a bid for office', Lloyd George remarked in private, 'but every day lost made his return now more difficult. Every member would vote to keep him out because of his dominating intellectual force and his experience.'[108] Although Chamberlain was briefly shaken, his overall position of command remained unassailable.

The story of Lloyd George and Churchill's relationship during the period prior to the outbreak of war – during which, and beyond, Chamberlain remained politically dominant – was one of both promise and frustration. It may seem strange that Churchill thought there was scope to cooperate on foreign policy with a man who had spoken so fulsomely about Hitler, even if they agreed on matters such as the abdication. Yet, after his return from Germany, Lloyd George was more interested in attacking the National Government on whatever basis was available than he was in offering further praise to the Nazis. Therefore, if Chamberlain advocated concessions to Germany (and Italy) he would attack him for it. Soon enough, then – although still believing that war could be avoided[109] – he was denouncing the British government for not taking a sufficiently tough line. This is not to say that he now expounded a totally coherent anti-appeasement policy, but he did use strong words. In December 1937, for example, he argued that the serious international situation was attributable 'to the sinister, powerful and resolute way in which foreign affairs had been handled by mighty militarist states which were the open and avowed enemies of freedom and democratic government' and, on the other hand, to 'the feeble, hesitant and pusillanimous way in which they had been mishandled by States which adhered to the principle of a free democracy'.[110] Although Churchill, for his part, was now emphasizing publicly how much he agreed with the government – he said that it was making 'a great effort for rearmament' and that the time was therefore ripe to negotiate from strength[111] – this was a point of view with which he was fundamentally in sympathy.

Prospects for cooperation between the two men may therefore have seemed good. In September 1937 Churchill wrote to Anthony Eden, who had replaced Hoare at the Foreign Office. He told him that Lloyd George was keen to dine with Eden, Churchill and a few others, 'to discuss the danger in which we stand, and the enormous deterioration in our position all over the world'.[112] Eden was unable to make it on this occasion, although he was happy to remain in touch. Lloyd George and Churchill jointly urged him to take a firm line with the Italians, and he seemed to be responsive.

In January 1938 the three all happened to be in the South of France at the same time, and met one day for lunch. A particularly important current issue was that of potential *de jure* recognition by Britain of Italy's conquest of Abyssinia. Chamberlain wanted to use this as a bargaining counter to establish good relations with Mussolini, whom he hoped could act as a counterweight against Hitler. Eden wrote in his diary that both Lloyd George and Churchill were 'strongly opposed' to recognition, and that 'both seemed impressed' by what he told them of his efforts to ensure foreign policy cooperation with the United States.[113] After he got back to London, his private secretary noted: 'A.E. has returned from his holiday much

fortified in his instinct against giving Italy *de jure* recognition.'[114]
Churchill stayed on in France a while longer, and was thus able to
attend the celebrations for Lloyd George's birthday and his golden
wedding.

In February Chamberlain insisted on starting talks with Italy
immediately. This provoked Eden's resignation. In the Commons
debate that followed, Churchill spoke in support of Eden's position.
Amery recorded that he did so 'with pretty hostile intent but great
restraint of diction, evidently sensing the feeling of the House and
realising that there was no hope of any cave [i.e. rebellion] worth
mentioning'. Lloyd George, 'who had come home racing across
Europe for the fray, shook his locks and went for Neville'.[115] But he
muffed his attack. He made some lapses of speech – a sign of his age
– and got the worst of an exchange with Chamberlain in which he,
Lloyd George, alleged that a crucial document had been concealed
from Eden. This helped the Prime Minister off the hook, and also
helped dent Lloyd George's confidence. The next day at dinner,
when reminded of what had happened, he said 'When I came into
the House tonight I felt just like a man, who has had a row in a pub,
going back to be thrown out.'[116] Sylvester's diary for this period
depicts a man who, on the surface, was full of energy and health but
who behaved increasingly badly to his family and staff and found it
ever more difficult to make political decisions.

In March 1938 the Germans sent troops into Austria, forcibly
unifying it with Germany. In the wake of this new crisis, the
Conservative MP 'Chips' Channon wrote in his diary that the
Commons was 'humming with intrigue'. The 'so-called "Insurgents"
are rushing about, very over-excited. They want to bring back
Anthony Eden and their Shadow Cabinet is alleged to include Lloyd
George, Winston and Eden.'[117] Such titbits of Westminster gossip are
not proof that Lloyd George and Churchill were involved in any
active conspiracy, but they are evidence of the continuing suspicion
with which government loyalists such as Channon viewed them.
Establishment nervousness was also provoked by the men's (separate)
visits to Paris the same month. They both met leading French
politicians. Eric Phipps, now ambassador to France, kept a watchful
eye on their respective activities, and reported on them to London.

Phipps told Lord Halifax, the new Foreign Secretary, that he had
impressed on Alexis Léger, the influential Secretary General of the

French Foreign Ministry, 'that he should let all the French parties know that Mr. Lloyd George represents very little more than himself in the England of to-day, and that they would do well to realise that they should take what he said with a considerable amount of salt.'[118] He later wrote that Lloyd George had indulged in 'mischievous pro-war propaganda' and had 'urged the French to go to war against the dictators and assured them of full British support'.[119] Lloyd George had indeed urged the French to intervene in the Spanish Civil War to the same extent that Germany and Italy were already doing. He felt that if help was given to the Republicans without announcement, this would find favour with some important parts of Conservative opinion. He said that 'Several of the more intelligent members of the Party, like Winston Churchill, were pro-Franco at first. But he now begins to see the danger, and is anti-Mussolini now.'[120]

Churchill, during his own conversations with the French, urged the creation of 'a close Anglo-French block against Germany in the first instance, with a kind of Central European and Balkan Grand Alliance joined thereto as the next step'. Reporting this, Phipps emphasized that 'Churchill's French interlocutors naturally realise that he only speaks for himself and a very small section of British public opinion, and I lay great stress on this, and urge liberal sprinklings of salt on what he says.'[121] Halifax read out one of Phipps's letters to his Cabinet colleagues, who were amused by the description of Churchill's attempts to speak French. On taking his leave from Léon Blum (the Prime Minister) and Joseph-Paul Boncour (the Foreign Minister) he had 'shouted out a literal translation of "We must make good", by "Nous devons faire bonne" (not even "bon"). This clearly stumped Boncour, who may even have attributed some improper meaning to it.'[122]

If the reaction of *Le Matin* was anything to go by, the French did not need much urging from Phipps in order to persuade them to take Lloyd George's comments with a substantial pinch of salt. Commenting on his symbolically charged visit to the tomb of Foch, the paper dismissed this as 'one of those monkey tricks at which the celebrated wizard excels'. It argued: 'There is nothing to guarantee that in three months' time Mr. David Lloyd George will not go and have tea at Berchtesgaden, and if Hitler asks him about his visit to the tomb of Foch, he will slap the Führer on the back and say "what, you who are so intuitive, you didn't understand? It was an electoral visit, my dear fellow. I only wanted to annoy Chamberlain" and the Führer will understand perfectly.'[123] Such suspicions had some basis. A few days before this article was published, Lloyd George had commented privately that Hitler was 'ascetic, very simple and is a very remarkable man with none of the vanities of Mussolini'.[124]

But although Phipps may have been right to claim that Lloyd George represented few people apart from himself, his similar assertion about Churchill was more questionable. Some sections of Liberal and left-wing opinion appear to have been shifting gradually towards his point of view – in part because of his rhetorical concessions in their direction. For example, in January 1938 the *News Chronicle* editorial team had debated whether or not to lend support to Churchill's admission to the Cabinet, which was once again being rumoured. The meeting 'generally agreed that since re-armament was now a necessity, it would be an immense advantage' to have him brought in. The editor, Gerald Barry, observed that 'it showed what a state public affairs had got into' when the *Chronicle* was 'prepared to welcome to the Cabinet a man who had had the name of a war-monger'. One of his journalists, Ivor Thomas, responded that 'since then Churchill's attitude had changed, that he was now a supporter of collective security, and was the President of the New Commonwealth'.[125] (The New Commonwealth Society was an international movement that aimed to strengthen the machinery of the League of Nations 'by the creation of an International Police Force to make aggressive war impossible'.)[126] Churchill's increasing emphasis on the place of the USSR in his proposed international alliance against fascism doubtless helped win over 'progressive opinion' too. The events of the autumn would show, however, that Chamberlain's command was under no real threat from such developments.

Some, though not all, of Churchill's foreign policy inconsistencies can be explained by his need to show that he was not a warmonger, in order to help him build a coalition of support. Hence, perhaps, some of his public optimism, during the late spring and summer of 1938, that things in Europe were on the upturn. A crisis was now developing over the Sudetenland – a part of Czechoslovakia, with a high concentration of ethnic Germans, that Hitler demanded should be incorporated into the Reich. Churchill for some time believed that the German population's grievances could be resolved in a reasonable and amicable fashion. As the Nazis became more and more aggressive, this seemed increasingly improbable, and Churchill's position stiffened accordingly.

At the same time he continued to try to collect allies, including Lloyd George. In August, the two men met, in company with 'Lloyd', probably Lord Lloyd.[127] Churchill was clearly doing his best to woo this individual. Lloyd George wrote to Churchill the following day that he had found Lloyd 'hesitant, and altogether a doubtful asset . . . A man in that frame of mind is a bad fighter, and is more likely to give you away than to help you.'[128] Churchill responded that he was surprised at this view of his guest: 'I thought him fairly receptive.' He continued:

> Let us make a plan to meet before you go to Wales. Everything
> is overshadowed by the impending trial of will-power which is
> developing in Europe. I think we shall have to choose in the
> next few weeks between war and shame, and I have very little
> doubt what the decision will be.[129]

Whether or not they did meet before Lloyd George's departure is unclear.

During September Chamberlain engaged in frantic shuttle diplomacy in an attempt to reach a deal with Hitler. He hoped to prevent him attacking Czechoslovakia, which would bring France to her assistance in accordance with her treaty obligations, forcing Britain to become involved too. However, such a deal could only be achieved by forcing Czechoslovakia to make concessions – in effect giving Hitler everything he wanted except for the satisfaction of achieving it by force. (The French, it should be stressed, were as reluctant to help the Czechs as Chamberlain was.) Up until almost the last moment, war seemed horribly imminent. Gas masks were issued, trenches were dug in public parks, and plans were made for the evacuation of children. Hence the ecstatic relief that met Chamberlain's dramatic air trip to Munich at the end of the month, and the signature of an agreement that ceded the Sudetenland to Germany.

To Churchill, of course, the agreement represented the choice of 'shame' over war. On the evening of 29 September, the day Chamberlain arrived in Munich, he attended an Other Club dinner at the Savoy. Lloyd George was also present. Churchill was in 'a towering rage and deepening gloom', having earlier failed to secure the signatures of Attlee and Eden on a telegram urging that onerous

terms should not be imposed upon the Czechs.[130] He does not seem
to have asked for Lloyd George's signature, perhaps appreciating that
its presence would simply irritate Chamberlain. On 5 October,
during the debate on the agreement, he declared that Britain had
'sustained a total and unmitigated defeat'.[131] He did not, however,
actually vote against the agreement but merely abstained, together
with twenty-nine other Conservatives. Lloyd George, for his part, did
not even attend the debate on the day of Churchill's speech, but did
vote against the agreement, as did the rest of the Liberal Party, and
Labour. His failure to speak may have been a sign of his general loss
of nerve about performing in the Commons. It was also explained by
his hatred of the Czech leader, Eduard Beneš ('that little swine'),
dating from the days of the Paris peace conference.[132] The link with
those days seemed a living one. Later in October Churchill wrote to
thank Lloyd George for the gift of his book on the peace treaties: 'All
now thrown away – not even by traitors – only muffs and boobies!'[133]

There was, clearly, a fair amount of overlap between the two men's
positions, but, during the remaining months of peace, cooperation
remained elusive. In mid-March 1939 German troops seized Prague,
demonstrating that Hitler's promises given at Munich had been valueless. The British government responded, at the end of the month, by
offering a guarantee to Poland that, 'in the event of any action which
clearly threatened Polish independence . . . His Majesty's Government would feel themselves bound at once to lend the Polish
Government all support in their power'.[134] Churchill and Lloyd
George reacted rather differently. In the Commons, on 3 April, the
former stressed his agreement with the government. Moreover, whilst
he emphasized that there was an identity of interest between the
USSR and the democracies, he did not press for an immediate formal
alliance: 'The Government have been wise in not forcing matters.'[135]
Lloyd George – who knew from Ivan Maisky, the Soviet ambassador
in London, that the Russians had not been consulted about the
guarantee – was more sceptical. He said that he agreed with much
of what Churchill had said, but thought he had underestimated the
importance of securing 'the pledged support' of the USSR. 'I cannot
understand why, before committing ourselves to this tremendous
enterprise, we did not secure beforehand the adhesion of Russia.'[136]
It was a good question.

That evening, after the House rose, both men went to see Maisky, together with Harold Nicolson. Churchill forcibly pointed out to the ambassador that, if the government's new policy was to work – that is, if it were to deter Germany – Russian cooperation was essential. The Poles, however, would be naturally suspicious, fearing Soviet designs on their country. 'Although they might be prepared at a pinch to let you in,' in the event of a German invasion, 'they would certainly want some assurances that you would eventually get out.' He demanded: 'Can you give us such assurances?' Nicolson's account of the meeting continues:

> Lloyd George, I fear, is not really in favour of the new policy and he draws Maisky on to describe some of the deficiencies of the Polish Army. Apparently many of their guns are pre-Revolution guns of the Russian Army. Maisky contends that the Polish soldiers are excellent fighters and that the officers are well-trained. Winston rather objects to this and attacks Lloyd George. 'You must not do this sort of thing, my dear. You are putting spokes in the wheel of history.'[137]

It is not entirely clear from this passage what Churchill objected to. Lloyd George was surely right to point out that the Poles – however brave they might be – were unlikely to be much of a match for the Germans. Presumably Churchill disapproved of him drawing attention to this inconvenient fact, because the Russians would feel less inclined to join an alliance if the Poles were likely to cave in quickly and leave them to face the weight of an attack. Perhaps he suspected him of mere contrariness and mischief making. A few days later, in private conversation, Churchill talked to him 'about our "smashing through" in case of war'. Lloyd George asked, pertinently, 'with what?'[138]

On 20 April Lloyd George told Sylvester that he was 'very sick with Winston'. This was because 'At one time he was in favour of an arrangement with Russia; then he stopped short; then he was in favour of national service, but he said, "When war comes". So he hedged on every question, thinking that by that means he would get into the Government.'[139] There were elements of truth in these comments, which were provoked by one of Churchill's speeches the previous week, but they were not wholly fair. Churchill, who did still entertain hopes of joining the Cabinet, had told Chamberlain that he would try to ensure that the speech in question was 'not unhelpful'.

But, the Prime Minister noted, it had, as delivered, 'an acid under-tone', provoked, he thought, by his failure to offer Churchill the position of Minister of Supply.[140] Churchill did hedge, and he was ambitious, but he was not a natural toady.

Churchill's own sense of disappointment with Lloyd George must have heightened at the end of the month during the debate over conscription. In reaction to events in Europe, the government planned to introduce compulsory military service. Opening the debate on the Military Training Bill, Chamberlain launched a direct attack on Lloyd George. He said that, if he were to speak in the debate, 'it will be interesting to know whether he is in favour of a larger measure of conscription, or whether he is against conscription altogether. I am sure he is ag'in the Government whatever they propose.' This was, perhaps, fair comment but it was not the sort of thing that, in days past, Lloyd George would have taken lying down. Yet now, as Sylvester recorded, he did not react: 'Attlee followed the P.M., then Sinclair and then Winston. L.G. sat through the lot. Winston made a great speech, much on the lines L.G. had decided on.' After Churchill finished his speech, in which he strongly wel-comed conscription, Lloyd George left the Commons chamber. He claimed to have an attack of neuralgia. Sylvester wrote:

> From 8 o'clock until 11 L.G. never stopped talking, which was not a bad effort for a fellow with neuralgia. Yet I had witnessed the mortifying spectacle of L.G. being flagrantly attacked by Neville Chamberlain, seeing Winston become the mouthpiece of L.G., and then the bitter disappointment of L.G. not speaking at the very last moment. Winston himself was amazed L.G. did not speak. He said to me in the Lobby: 'He *must* speak; why not, is it because he is just being naughty?'[141]

Lloyd George did speak in favour of the Bill some days later. He combined this with a stinging attack on the government's foreign policy as a whole. This provided evidence that his powers had by no means atrophied completely – but they could no longer be relied upon. In his private conversation he still sparkled but preferred reminiscence to current politics. As will be seen, Churchill had still not finally given up on the idea that the two might work together in government, but the hope was increasingly forlorn. This should perhaps, have been clear to Churchill from a lunch that he had with

Lloyd George and Brendan Bracken, just under a month before the outbreak of war. By his own account afterwards, Lloyd George advised Churchill not to join the government. (There was now a campaign in some parts of the press to bring him in.) 'They would only sit on his head', Lloyd George told Sylvester. 'If he went in now and there was an election, Neville would claim that it was his victory.' Lloyd George also said to Sylvester – although it is not clear whether he had told Churchill the same thing – that he himself 'had no hankering after office'. The idea of ministerial rank, he claimed, did not appeal to him in the least.[142] There does not therefore seem to have been much truth in Chamberlain's belief that 'the Winston Eden Lloyd George group' were conspiring to get into the Cabinet with a view to displacing him as Prime Minister in due course.[143]

Churchill was not offered a government job during the remaining weeks of peace, so he did not have to make up his mind about whether or not to take Lloyd George's advice. He would surely have jumped at the chance, though. It would have been unwise, at his age, to hold out for a better opportunity in the future. Lloyd George's comments were probably more a reflection of his own desire to avoid the burdens of office than they were the product of deep thinking about what would be good for Churchill's career. (There is, however, scope to debate whether Lloyd George wanted office or not, as will be seen in the next chapter.) Indeed, many of his remarks about Churchill, made over the previous decade, seem just as apt as comments on himself. Consider, for example, his dismissal of *The World Crisis*: 'Brilliantly written – but too much of an apologia to be of general value.'[144] Perhaps so – but the same could be said of *The War Memoirs*. Or his dinner table remark in 1936, that Churchill's 'whole attitude was summed up in a remark he had once made: "Success in politics depends on whether you can control your conscience."'[145] Didn't that sum up Lloyd George's own attitude equally well, if not better? And didn't his description that same year of Churchill as 'a stunter' now apply just as much, if not more, to himself?[146] Churchill made plenty of mistakes in the 1930s, but his biggest one, the Indian campaign, cannot easily be dismissed as a 'stunt'. It represented rather the remorseless pursuit of a wrong-headed idea in which he deeply and genuinely believed.

Lloyd George had, of course, persistently belittled Churchill for decades. Churchill had often repaid him in kind, but this habit seems to have faded away during the 1930s. Perhaps this was because these were the years in which he at last began to emerge from the older man's shadow. He was, at long last, maturing. Although there is much to criticize in Churchill's record during this period, it appears on the whole considerably more constructive than the efforts of Lloyd George. These were often brilliant in form but had a certain moral emptiness. A diary comment of Robert Bernays in 1935 is not wholly unjust: 'The difference between the two is, I believe, that Winston for all his *farrago* and bombastic nonsense is really fundamentally out to help the country and I wonder whether in his old age Lloyd George really is.'[147]

Interestingly, though, these were also the years in which the men's joint myth became yet more firmly cemented. This had clearly been absorbed by, for example, Harold Nicolson: 'They have had bitter battles in the past and have emerged from these combats with great respect for each other's talents and an affectionate sharing of tremendous common memories.'[148] There may have been some truth in what Nicolson said, but this was very much the 'authorized version' of the story of a difficult relationship. That version had clearly also impressed supporters such as Sir Arthur Crosfield, an industrialist and former Liberal MP, who wrote to Churchill in 1936: 'I have been saying to myself these last weeks what a very great thing it would be for the old country if you and your old friend and colleague, L.G., were once more working shoulder to shoulder and giving incomparable leadership to the same party in politics.'[149] There was an undoubted self-serving element to the myth of the relationship. It kept Lloyd George, as his own star waned, linked with the reputation of the other most interesting man in British politics. It kept Churchill in the same frame as a former Prime Minister and war leader, and kept alive memories of his historic past at a time when his future was uncertain. But it also held dangers for him, connecting him with a man who, in the present, had a not wholly undeserved image of irresponsibility. Though myth it may have been, it had not been constructed purely for cynical convenience. That it still had a real resonance, for Churchill at least, would be shown during the first year of war. But the hopes that he placed on it were to prove illusory.

Chapter Ten

I SHALL WAIT UNTIL WINSTON IS BUST

IN HIS 1952 NOVEL *Men at Arms*, Evelyn Waugh recounts the reaction of Guy Crouchback, the book's upper-class hero, to Churchill becoming Prime Minister. 'Guy knew of Mr Churchill only as a professional politician, a master of sham Augustan prose, a Zionist, an advocate of the Popular Front in Europe, an associate of the press-lords and of Lloyd George.'[1] Although Waugh never lost his personal distaste for Churchill, there was clearly some deliberate irony here.[2] But the remark is nonetheless a valuable reminder that, even in 1940, Churchill was still viewed in some quarters with scepticism and distrust – and that the reputation of his relationship with Lloyd George still played a part in this. In due course he was to conquer this problem with spectacular success. Dingle Foot, a Liberal MP during the period in question, observed in 1970 that Lloyd George had always been the centre of violent controversy. 'The same was true of Winston Churchill', he wrote. 'But Churchill has been canonised.'[3]

The change in the fortunes of their reputations owed much to the experience of World War II, and to the way in which it was subsequently interpreted, not least by Churchill himself. Lloyd George's part in bringing down the Chamberlain government, and thus assisting Churchill's path to No. 10, and Churchill's subsequent efforts to bring Lloyd George into his own administration, contributed to their ongoing joint myth. However, Lloyd George's advocacy of a compromise peace with Germany appeared to form an unheroic counterpoint to Churchill's determination that Britain would 'never surrender'. And by refusing his old colleague's offers of a place in his government during the crisis of 1940, he appeared to renege on the positive aspects of the Lloyd George–Churchill legend. It had been the long-standing hope of many of their supporters that, when the reign of the 'political pygmies' was at an end, the two would work

together in fulfilment of their joint destiny, and the nation's. Lloyd
George's failure to live up to the romance seemed almost a breach of
promise.

It was proof, in fact, of the messiness of reality. Over the years
the two men had themselves done their best to promote an image of
an idealized political friendship, but the war demonstrated, once
again, the complexity and ambiguity of their relationship. Contemporaries differed as to whether it was based on mutual hostility or
genuine affection. 'Churchill's predestined opponent was Lloyd
George', Hitler remarked in 1942, adding 'Unfortunately, he's twenty
years too old.'[4] This picture of them as fated antagonists was perhaps
no less 'romantic' than that, say, painted by Harold Nicolson after a
Commons debate a few months earlier. Nicolson wrote of Lloyd
George: 'When he criticised the Prime Minister he gazed across at
him with a firm aggressive chin of combat and opposition, but his
little eyes twinkled with admiration and (I am not in the least
exaggerating) with love.' To an extent, people saw in the relationship
what they wanted to see. Hitler – who, it must be remembered, had
never met Churchill and had met Lloyd George only briefly –
obviously liked the idea of Churchill meeting his match. Nicolson
– who did at least know both fairly well – liked the idea of frank
criticism being vented without personal animosity, and relished the
thought that the scene he described could be found nowhere 'except
in our own beloved House of Commons'.[5] The wildly varying nature
of opinions about them can in part be explained by the fact that
Churchill and Lloyd George themselves played up different aspects
of their joint myth at different times and to different audiences.

In the days before the outbreak of war in September 1939, the
two men consulted one another. They were also both in the mind of
the Prime Minister, Neville Chamberlain. The crisis that led to war
came over Danzig (modern day Gdansk). This city had a predominantly German population but was economically vital to Poland.
It had been created a Free City under League of Nations auspices
under the Treaty of Versailles. Hitler coveted it. In January 1940
Lloyd George claimed privately that 'Churchill telephoned me three
weeks before the war and told me Hitler's latest terms for a Danzig
settlement. Winston said, "I think they are not unreasonable," and I
agreed with him.'[6] The point cannot be verified. In any event, the
very slim chance of a peaceful solution vanished on 23 August, when

Germany and the USSR signed a non-aggression pact. This meant
that the Nazis would be able to attack Poland without the risk that
the Russians would come to its defence. Churchill observed, of the
Soviet Union's action in signing the pact, that, in the circumstances,
'it was the way he would expect that particular crocodile to behave'.[7]

The day the pact was signed, Lord Hankey (as Maurice Hankey,
who had retired as Cabinet Secretary the previous year, now was)
was summoned to see Chamberlain. He wrote in his diary that the
Prime Minister 'told me he had come to the conclusion that the time
had arrived to consider the question of establishing a War Cabinet,
and he wanted my advice'. Hankey gave him 'a pretty full description
of Lloyd George's War Cabinet', which had by now achieved an
almost mythical status as an ideal type. Chamberlain then asked him
about who was to be included in the new body:

> Q. Should Winston Churchill be in?
>
> A. I agreed with him that public opinion would expect it.
>
> Q. Should Ll.G. be in?
>
> A. A difficult question for me, as he was my old Chief and we
>   had always been good friends. He had a good war mind:
>   but I had heard he was very much aged (he is 76). I did not
>   trust his loyalty.[8]

When it came to the point, Churchill was included – doubtless
inevitably, given the press support he now commanded – and Lloyd
George was not. (His son Gwilym, however, was to join the government as a junior minister at the Board of Trade, and later held posts
under Churchill.) Perhaps the most remarkable thing about Hankey's
talk with Chamberlain was that the latter even raised the question of
including Lloyd George, to whom he had a strong aversion. On
25 August – as the government reaffirmed the British commitment to
Poland – Harold Nicolson wrote to his wife of a long talk he had had
with Lloyd George and Churchill. 'They said that it was hopeless to
expect Parliament to speak out except in a secret session. We should
have such a session at once and tell the P.M. what a hopeless old
crow he was.'[9]

On 1 September Germany invaded Poland. Two days later
Britain declared war on Germany and Chamberlain set about creating his War Cabinet. A document in the Walter Layton Papers casts

interesting new light on the appointments he made. Admittedly, the source is third-hand, but it rings true, and parts of it can be corroborated. It is a message from Archie Sinclair, reporting what Percy Harris, the Liberal Chief Whip, had been told by David Margesson, his government counterpart. Margesson told Harris at 2 p.m. on Sunday 3 September that the War Cabinet would consist of six members: Chamberlain, Churchill, Lord Chatfield, Hankey, Simon and Halifax. 'It was intended as far as possible for Ministers in the War Cabinet to be free of Departmental duties', Sinclair reported. However, 'Two hours later the War Cabinet was set up as at present with nine members and Churchill appointed to the Admiralty. The Cabinet had feared that as one among six and with no departmental ties, Winston would quickly dominate them; with the Admiralty to contend with, they hope his influence will be reduced to a manageable proportion.'[10] (The additional three members were Samuel Hoare, Kingsley Wood and Leslie Hore-Belisha.) Sinclair's message tallies with the fact that, two days before he made him First Lord, Chamberlain told Churchill that he would be appointed to a six-man War Cabinet as Minister without Portfolio. Moreover, the suggestion of continuing suspicion of Churchill accords with Hankey's remark on his own appointment: 'As far as I can make out my main job is to keep an eye on Winston!'[11]

Very shortly, Churchill was himself deputed to try and restrain Lloyd George. In an article published in the *Sunday Express* on 10 September the latter touched on the military weakness of Italy, which had not, as yet, entered the war. He alluded to the Italian rout at Caporetto in 1917. This upset the government, which was still eager to avoid offending the Italians, and which had warned the press 'to exercise particular discretion in their references to Italy'.[12] The Cabinet minutes for 11 September record Halifax's observation that Lloyd George's article 'contained references to the military value of the Italian army of a nature to embarrass our position with Italy'. Halifax thought that, although it would be possible to take action against the *Sunday Express*, this would be inadvisable. 'He understood that the First Lord of the Admiralty might be in a position to explain the position privately to Mr. Lloyd George'. Churchill agreed to help.[13] He wrote to Lloyd George, telling him that he had been asked 'to point out to you the very bad effect on our interests at the present moment which would be produced by sneers at Caporetto, about which the Italian army is so naturally sensitive.' He added: 'I quite agree with you that we should not show fear of Italian hostility, but we certainly do not want it.'[14] It may seem strange to find Churchill urging caution in this way, and equally strange that the government should have felt it necessary to offer an apology for the article to the Italians, upon whom, at any rate, it probably had little impact. (The British ambassador to Rome was given a brief to express the government's regret. This emphasized that 'Mr. Lloyd George, who has aged considerably in recent years, speaks for no one but himself and his views carry no weight in this country.')[15] He may well, though, have felt constrained by the views of his colleagues. Churchill's reward for his letter was 'a snorter of a reply' from Lloyd George.[16] 'When the Cabinet show that they have any understanding of the tragic mess into which they have plunged this country, or how to get us out of it, then I shall begin to pay some respect to any rebukes they may pass upon my articles', he wrote, with understandable irritation.[17] 'Thank you so much for your letter', answered Churchill, who does not appear to have taken offence. 'Please always let me know if there is anything I can do. When I get ahead of my Admiralty work I shall have more time, and should greatly value a talk.'[18]

As this suggests, Churchill was throwing himself into his new tasks with his customary enthusiasm. He was, moreover, now increasingly canvassed as a successor to Chamberlain who, like Asquith before him, had seemed more effective as a peacetime leader than as a wartime one. Not everyone, though, thought it would be a good appointment. John Colville was a young Foreign Office official who was soon to be appointed as one of Chamberlain's private secretaries, and afterwards served Churchill. On 28 September he wrote in his diary that it would probably be a good idea if Chamberlain made way for some more forceful successor. But, 'Unfortunately I can see no Lloyd George on the horizon at present: Winston is a national figure, but is rather too old; and the younger politicians do not seem to include any outstanding personality.'[19] Others thought that Churchill *was* a Lloyd George figure – but not in a good way. Sir Ernest Benn, who was a publisher and a prominent Conservative libertarian, thought that a Churchill premiership would be 'a catastrophe', and that the man himself would succeed, as Lloyd George had in his day, only 'in rousing the lower instincts of the nation'.[20]

Sadly, Lloyd George's actions in the autumn of 1939 rather

conformed to this stereotypical image of him as irresponsible and opportunistic. He does not appear to have sought power so much as the emotional satisfaction of creating a stir. He achieved this by advocating a peace deal with Hitler, tapping into a strong vein of public feeling. In the Commons, on the day the war broke out, he had appeared resolute. Churchill, following Chamberlain, had spoken of the need to 'save the whole world from the pestilence of Nazi tyranny'.[21] Later, after a speech by the former Labour leader George Lansbury, Lloyd George rose. He had apparently required a fair amount of encouragement in order to do so, but his speech was effective, and he closed by making the obvious comparison with the Great War: 'after 4½ years, terrible years, we won a victory for right. We will do it again.'[22] He was, however, pessimistic in private. As he told Churchill, in the letter in which he responded to his protest about the *Sunday Express* article, he did not voice his doubts in public 'because I am anxious not to do anything to add to the moral as well as physical gloom which seems to oppress the people at this moment'.[23] He did not hold his tongue for long.

The rapid defeat of the Poles at German hands contributed to his willingness to speak out. (The Russians also moved into Polish territory, as agreed in a secret protocol in the Nazi–Soviet pact.) Lloyd George caused a storm by criticizing, in newspaper articles, the Polish government's conduct during the invasion. After the Polish ambassador published a reply, he hit back in turn, arguing that the British people would not be prepared to make huge sacrifices to restore to Poland areas that were not ethnically Polish, or to re-establish a discredited regime. As Paul Addison has noted, this opened the possibility of a peace settlement which created an 'ethnic' Poland, with Germany and Russia retaining some of the territory they had won. It was not hard to present the continuation of the war as futile. At the end of September Hitler and Stalin made a joint call on Britain and France to accept the new status quo and bring hostilities to an end.[24] Some days earlier Lloyd George had met with a group of MPs of various different persuasions. 'He says he is frankly terrified and does not see how we can possibly win the war', Harold Nicolson wrote. Lloyd George urged a Secret Session, in which the government should be forced to reveal the prospects of victory. 'If our chances are 50/50, then it might be worthwhile organising the whole resources of the country for a desperate struggle. But if the chances are really against us, then we should certainly make peace at the earliest opportunity, possibly with Roosevelt's assistance.'[25]

On 3 October Chamberlain made clear in the Commons that Britain would not abandon the struggle. Lloyd George, however, now broached in public the idea of a negotiated peace. He told the House that Britain should 'seriously consider any proposals for peace which were specific, detailed, broad, which excluded nothing, but reviewed all the subjects that had been the cause of all the troubles of the last few years'.[26] His words suggested merely that any proposals the Germans put forward should receive careful consideration. Sylvester noted, however, that the speech was remarkable less for its actual content than for what it did not say. Lloyd George 'created, by his personality, the impression that we had damned well lost and that we should come to terms', he wrote. 'But he damned well did not say so. L.G. has that great gift. In private he is doing it every day of his life on some poor devil, but I have never seen him do it in public with such success.'[27] The speech was criticized by Alfred Duff Cooper, who had resigned as First Lord of the Admiralty in 1938 in protest at the Munich Agreement. He said that he deplored and regretted Lloyd George's words, which were bound to be misrepresented: 'If they had been spoken in a secret Session, they might have been valuable and helpful words, but being spoken in full and public Session of the House of Commons, they will go out to the world, with his name at the head of them, as a suggestion of surrender.'[28] Sylvester recorded that 'During the whole of Duff Cooper's speech, Winston was applauding him.'[29]

In private, Churchill tried to rein Lloyd George in. On 6 October Hitler made a speech in the Reichstag, proposing a peace conference and claiming that he had no demands on France. This was, he said, his 'last offer' to the Allies.[30] That same day Churchill sent Lloyd George a copy of a secret telegram from the eminent South African statesman J. C. Smuts, which gave his opinion that any German peace offer would be insincere. Lloyd George told Churchill that Smuts 'may be right in his conjecture that Hitler's peace offer has no other purpose than "simply that of a peace offensive to weaken us". That is why I would have a peace counter-offensive which would baffle him and strengthen us.'[31] The problem was that the Germans seemed cheered rather than baffled by Lloyd George's attempts to stimulate a 'peace counter-offensive'. 'Things no longer look quite so bad', wrote Joseph Goebbels, Hitler's Minister of Propaganda, after Lloyd George published an article arguing that the conference idea should receive serious consideration. Goebbels added, 'He [Lloyd George] would not be able to do this if the right mood did not exist in England.'[32] Certainly, Lloyd George, to his immense glee, received an enormous number of letters showing that many British people had a strong desire for peace. Sylvester believed that 'these bags of letters have literally turned L.G.'s head ... Every day he is crazy about the letters – not what is in them but "How many are there?"'[33] Lloyd George did, however, come in for press criticism, notably from the *Sunday Pictorial* and later from the *Daily Sketch*. On 21 October he made a further speech, this time in his constituency. He denied that he was in favour of peace at any price. However, 'We could be firm at a conference as well as on the battlefield.'[34] Churchill, by contrast, was emphatic that any conference that was to be accompanied by a truce would be disastrous. In conversation with W. P. Crozier, the editor of the *Manchester Guardian*, he referred to Lloyd George's interventions. 'I do not know what George is thinking about', he said. 'For God sake no weakness now; it would mean our total absolute defeat.'[35]

Nonetheless, there is some evidence that he was still eager to court Lloyd George politically. In mid-December the two men lunched together, and afterwards Lloyd George 'said he had thought Winston would never let him leave'. Churchill, with typical boyishness, 'had wanted to show L.G. everything' at the Admiralty. Sylvester did his best to find out if anything of substance had passed between them. He heard from Thomas Tweed, who had heard it from Frances Stevenson, 'that nothing definite was said but that "It is all right", meaning that Winston intends to get L.G. into the government when the chance arrives'.[36]

Lloyd George had not given up criticizing Churchill. This was the period of the 'phoney war', when the military situation appeared to have reached stalemate. At the same time, there were not many major domestic political developments. One of the few episodes of interest was the resignation of Hore-Belisha from the War Office in January 1940. Hore-Belisha was an energetic but abrasive man, and had succeeded in alienating Lord Gort, the head of the British Expeditionary Force in France. It is possible that his position was also harmed by anti-Semitic prejudice against him. Chamberlain told him he must be moved, and offered him another office as President of the Board of Trade, but he opted instead to return to the backbenches. According to Samuel Hoare, Churchill – who did not like Hore-Belisha much – knew about and approved of the decision to get rid of him, even though he himself was out of the country at the time. 'Latterly W.S.C. has been falling foul of H.B. over supply matters and has been disposed to talk him down in the Cabinet.'[37] Lloyd George, by contrast, thought that the constructive dismissal of Hore-Belisha was 'contemptible' and believed that Churchill was partly to blame for it. 'But why', said Hore-Belisha, on hearing him say this, 'should Churchill have done anything against me, if he did?' 'Oh, well', replied Lloyd George, 'he would not be sorry to see you out of his way, would he, on his road to the Premiership?'[38] Lloyd George seems to have been pleased by the thought that Hore-Belisha might emerge as a critic of the government and also as a potential threat to Churchill. 'I think he would be very much stronger as an independent and I think Winston will find that', he said.[39]

Chips Channon left a powerful word-portrait of our two protagonists at this time. Channon had been elected as a Tory MP in 1935, and was a National Government loyalist with an almost sickening dedication to the Prime Minister, with whom, on one occasion, he claimed to have fallen in love. Many people found him charming and generous, but he was also snobbish and vain, vices to which, to his credit, he did at least realize he was prone. He would probably not have minded the fact that he is now remembered for his brilliant, gossipy diaries rather than for his political achievements, which were frankly non-existent. The entry for 13 February 1940 is revealing:

In the House I had chats with both Winston Churchill and Lloyd George. Tweedle Dum and Tweedle Dee have rooms on our corridor: indeed we are sandwiched in between them. L.G. seems the more alert and hale of the two, in his too-blue suits, blue tie, and flowing mane of hair: he does not really know me: Winston, on the other hand, does, and dislikes me intensely, and shows it, though he tries not to: he talks to me as he does to all that are not his fervent followers – i.e. he sidles away from me, and looks down as he talks; he knows that I am a devoted Chamberlain man.[40]

One gets the impression from this that meeting Lloyd George must have been like coming across an early colour photograph made flesh – brightly coloured, but not quite convincing. The depiction of Churchill is equally compelling. We see him struggling to do that which he did worst – that is, contain himself. The Tweedle Dum and Tweedle Dee comparison, moreover, can be read as an amusing take on the myth of the Lloyd George–Churchill relationship, that they had never had a serious personal disagreement. It will be remembered that in *Alice Through the Looking Glass* these identical brothers, who 'looked so exactly like a couple of great schoolboys', agreed to have a battle: 'For Tweedledum said Tweedledee / Had spoiled his nice new rattle'. However, they were so frightened by a monstrous crow that 'They quite forgot their quarrel'. What was it in the book that so reminded Channon of Churchill? Perhaps it was the line ' "Let's fight till six, and then have dinner," said Tweedledum.'

Doubtless aware that his association with Lloyd George had the capacity to do him harm with Chamberlain loyalists, Churchill took some care not to reinforce their perceptions. Since the start of the war the *Sunday Dispatch* had been republishing Churchill's old articles. Charles Eade, the paper's editor, took personal charge of the details, 'because I realised that some of the old articles written years ago might have unfortunate implications if published now', and thus 'doubtful passages were eliminated by me'.[41] On a few occasions Eade ran into difficulties. One of these episodes occurred when he wanted to publish a piece in Churchill's name to celebrate Lloyd George's fiftieth anniversary as an MP, which was to take place in April. He cobbled together an article from two first published in 1931 plus a passage from Churchill's 1932 collection *Thoughts and Adventures*. Churchill's secretary, Kathleen Hill, wrote to Eade about it: 'Mr. Churchill has read this through carefully, but he fears the publication of this article at the present time would make difficulties for him, which he thinks you will readily understand.'[42] Eade did not give up, and adjusted the article further, and then sent it to Hill who showed it to Churchill. The new version did not stint in its praise of Lloyd George. '[H]istory will re-turn the pages back to Chatham to find his parallel in achievement', readers were told.[43] But it is notable that, in contrast with the 1931 originals, there was no suggestion that Lloyd George might 'come back' and play an active part in national politics. It was presumably because of this omission that Churchill felt able to pass the new draft for publication. He was happy to remind the public of Lloyd George's past glories, it appears; but he did not wish to be seen to imply that the former Prime Minister still had current potential. Given that later events seem to demonstrate that Churchill in fact thought Lloyd George was worthy of office, this must have been because he thought that mooting the idea in public would harm his own credibility.

Lloyd George, for his own part, remained firmly in the media eye. He was still producing press articles, and he carefully cultivated his image as the 'Welsh Wizard'. For example, in the popular magazine *Picture Post*, a photograph of him wearing a black cape was accompanied by the caption 'The Seer Whom Many would Welcome as Minister of Agriculture'. In the article alongside, Lloyd George argued for intensified arable cultivation to meet the shortage of food he anticipated. 'As yet we still have an ample supply', he wrote. 'But where shall we be if the war lasts, as Mr. Churchill says it may, "for many long years"?'[44] The following month, to coincide with his fiftieth anniversary as an MP, the same journal published a piece by Bob Boothby which predicted that 'A hundred years hence the historians will write that the greatest man produced by this country in our time was unquestionably David Lloyd George.'[45] A lot of people would naturally have disagreed, but the remark forms a useful reminder that Lloyd George still had his champions, and that some people still rated him above Churchill – whose 'finest hour' was of course yet to come.

Chamberlain found both men's reputations irksome to him. On 6 April he wrote to his sister Hilda that it was absurd for writers in the press 'to ascribe the winning of the last war to the particular way in which Ll.G. composed his cabinet, and no one can prove that we should not have won it more quickly if the Cabinet had been constructed like mine.'[46] In another letter, dated 4 May, he told her that Churchill's frequent changes of mind over military matters were at odds with his public image. 'I don't blame W.C. for these very natural alterations', he wrote. 'Only they don't square with the picture the gutter press & W.C.'s "friends" try to paint of the supreme War Lord.'[47] The context for these latter comments was the British military campaign in Norway. Its failure was to bring about Chamberlain's downfall, and his replacement by Churchill. The irony was that Churchill himself bore a heavy responsibility for the disaster.

Lloyd George's last great contribution to British public life was to help him avoid suffering the political consequences – or rather, to transcend them.

It was on 8 April that the Germans invaded Norway and Denmark. Churchill, like everyone else, was taken by surprise. When he learnt that German warships were on the move, he seems to have expected a naval battle rather than an amphibious landing, and reacted accordingly. The Cabinet, after disagreements and delays, sent troops for operations against Narvik (in the north of Norway) and Trondheim (on a more central part of the country's coast). The Trondheim operation was unsuccessful, and on 2 and 3 May the troops were withdrawn from the central region. Narvik was eventually taken, but soon had to be abandoned. Churchill, who had been appointed Chairman of the government's Military Co-ordination Committee a few days before the fiasco began, was an obvious candidate for blame. In an unpublished draft of his memoirs he confessed that, given all the muddle and confusion, 'it was a marvel – I really do not know how – [that] I survived and maintained my position in public esteem while all the blame was thrown on poor Mr. Chamberlain'.[48]

Given the part that he had played in the episode, it was not so surprising that, when parliamentarians began to consider the possibility that the military catastrophe would bring about the fall of the government, many of them predicted that Lloyd George, rather than Churchill, would be the new Prime Minister. On 30 April Harold Nicolson reported rumours on these lines, and noted that 'The Whips are putting it about that it is all the fault of Winston who has made another forlorn failure.'[49] Over the next few days he recorded comments to similar effect. 'People are so distressed by the whole thing that they are talking of Lloyd George as a possible P.M.', he wrote on 4 May. 'Eden is out of it. Churchill is undermined by the Conservative caucus.'[50] Interestingly, Sylvester later claimed to have 'had confirmation' that, at around this time, Churchill asked Lloyd George 'Will you serve under me if I form a government?' and that the reply was 'Of course I will.'[51] However, this cannot be corroborated from other sources.

Of those who advocated Lloyd George as a candidate for No. 10, some were people of demonstrably poor judgement, and others were lukewarm in their support, or indecisive. Boothby – a talented but somewhat doubtful character, who was rather too convinced of his own importance – 'used big words and built new Cabinets with Lloyd George as P.M.'.[52] That was at the start of May. Five days later, though, Boothby stated emphatically 'that there would be no change of Government, that Lloyd George and the Labour leaders were determined not to take charge of affairs at this juncture'.[53] Sir Stafford Cripps was a Labour left-winger who had been expelled from the party the previous year. Although he was to become a famously austere Chancellor of the Exchequer in the Attlee government after he was readmitted to the Labour fold in 1945, he had been best known in the 1930s for his excitable and extreme opinions. Now he was planning to publicize 'a draft alternative cabinet' in order to demonstrate that there was an alternative to Chamberlain. On 2 May he discussed the idea with Lloyd George 'who had just come from Winston'. Cripps wrote in his diary: 'Rather to my surprise he agreed Winston could not be P.M. and that it would have to be Halifax.'[54] Cripps's proposal was published anonymously on 6 May in the *Daily Mail*. In the original version, Lloyd George was to be Prime Minister, but in the published plan Lord Halifax was to take first place, with Lloyd George and Churchill as members of his Cabinet.[55]

Lloyd George also had a degree of support in press circles. J. L. Garvin's view was that 'L.G. was still good for six hours a day and it would be six hours of radium.'[56] On 9 May, at the *News Chronicle*'s editorial conference, Walter Layton, the paper's Chairman, said he thought it was necessary to decide which of the possible Prime Ministers it would support. 'Although he had originally thought Halifax was a possibility, he now felt that the only two names which would command support were Lloyd George and Churchill.' The political journalist A. J. Cummings 'definitely preferred Churchill as Premier, since he considered Lloyd George far too old for the job; though if Lloyd George had been ten years younger there would have been no question who was the right man'. In response to this, Layton gave his own opinion 'that an announcement that Lloyd George had taken over the Premiership would have a terrifically heartening effect here, and a correspondingly depressing effect in Germany'. He added that 'He personally was not sure that Churchill was up to his last-war standard of efficiency'.[57] It is not clear whether a firm decision was actually reached, and by this point

events had at any rate moved too far for the *News Chronicle* to have
an impact. What is really significant though is that even within this
remaining bastion of Liberalism, the support for Lloyd George was
far from rock solid. Some prominent Liberals – including, predictably, Archie Sinclair and Violet Bonham Carter (as Violet Asquith
now was) – undoubtedly preferred Churchill or even Halifax to
Lloyd George.[58]

The purpose of rehearsing the support that Lloyd George did
have, therefore, is not to make the romantic suggestion that he was a
serious rival to Churchill for the premiership in 1940. The point is,
rather, that Churchill's eventual triumph did not, in the run-up to
the Commons debate on Norway, appear a foregone conclusion.
Because of his role in the Norwegian expedition there was a threat
hanging over him. In these circumstances, a number of people who
were casting around for an alternative to Chamberlain lighted on
Lloyd George; some of them not, perhaps, without a sense of their
own desperation. We may even speculate that the government whips
were happy to see the rumour-mill producing that idea – at the same
time as they themselves sought to undermine Churchill – because
they thought it would frighten a fair few Conservatives from pressing
for a change of leader.

Lloyd George did not in fact do much to encourage those who
would have had him take office, whether as Prime Minister or in
another post. At a luncheon party held to sound him out, just in
advance of the crucial debate, Nancy Astor 'told him in her blunt
way that he had been produced for inspection and to be tested for
his fitness to return to the helm of the ship of state'. According to
Thomas Jones, who was also there, Lloyd George 'betrayed affection
for Winston springing out of a forty-year-old friendship'. Moreover,
'It was this which made him hesitate to speak tomorrow as it would
be difficult to do so without castigating Winston' for the navy's errors.
This was indeed a genuine dilemma, but it also seems possible that
Lloyd George was using his 'affection' for Churchill as an excuse for
not speaking, for fear of losing his nerve in the Chamber, as had
happened increasingly in the recent past. When asked what he would
do if offered a place in the Cabinet, he 'fenced', Jones noted. 'We
were left to infer that L.G. preferred to await his country's summons
a little longer, but that he expected to receive it as the peril grew.'[59]
It is hard to know what his intentions really were. He seems to have

been extremely adept at encouraging his admirers to think that he would do what they wanted and take office – at some point, just around the corner, when the moment was really right. The idea of doing so doubtless fed his ego, but he seems to have had hunger less for power itself than for the adulation of his hangers-on.

On the first day of the debate, 7 May, there were notable attacks on the government from Sir Roger Keyes (a Conservative MP and former admiral) and from Leo Amery. Amery quoted Oliver Cromwell at the Prime Minister: 'You have sat too long here for any good you have been doing. Depart, I say, and let us have done with you. In the name of God, go.'[60] On the second day Herbert Morrison announced that the Labour Party would press a vote of censure on the government. This provoked Chamberlain, in his response to Morrison's speech, into an ill-judged remark. Accepting the challenge of a division, he appealed to his 'friends in the House'. This comment, which brought him roars of support from the government benches, was innocuous; but it could easily be portrayed by his enemies as an improper appeal to personal loyalty at a time of great national crisis.[61] It was this that provided Lloyd George with an opportunity, not only to overcome his indecision about speaking, but also to produce one of the greatest parliamentary performances of all time.

Dingle Foot recalled that Lloyd George was not in the chamber when Chamberlain made the comment: 'I was sitting next to Megan on the Liberal bench and remember saying to her "there is the opening – your father must speak now". But she did not need telling and I do not think she heard me. She shot out of the House and went straight to her father's room.' Another Liberal MP, Clement Davies, seems also to have urged Lloyd George to speak – but he did not need much encouragement. In Foot's words, 'A little later he came in to destroy Chamberlain in a speech which lasted only 10 minutes but which contained all the dislike and contempt of 30 years.'[62]

The speech was in fact longer than Foot remembered; it lasted from 5.37 p.m. to 6.10 p.m. Churchill later recalled that this 'last decisive intervention of Mr. Lloyd George in the House of Commons' delivered 'a deeply-wounding blow' at Chamberlain.[63] Violet Bonham Carter recorded that Lloyd George 'made the best & most deadly speech I have ever heard from him – voice – gesture – everything was brought into play to drive home his indictment'.[64]

Lloyd George's wife and his daughter Olwen were in the gallery. Years later, Olwen wrote: 'I can still see poor Mrs. Neville sitting next to us looking so unhappy.'[65]

Lloyd George alleged that the Trondheim expedition had been 'half-prepared' and 'half-baked'. He painted a serious picture of Britain's strategic position. He wanted, he said, to tell the country the facts, even at the cost of unpleasantness. He did this not with a view to 'spreading dismay and consternation, but with a view to rousing real action and not sham action such as we have had'. When he said that British 'promissory notes are now rubbish in the market place', there were cries of 'Shame' from the government benches. But he hit back strongly: 'What is the use of not facing facts?' One of the most brilliant parts of the speech was an improvisation. Commenting on the failure of the navy to do more with regard to Norway, he said 'I do not think that the First Lord was entirely responsible for all the things that happened there.' At that point he was interrupted by Churchill, who said that he took complete responsibility for everything that had been done by the Admiralty, and that he took his full share of the burden of any blame. To this came Lloyd George's brilliant riposte, which brought loud laughter from MPs: 'The right hon. Gentleman must not allow himself to be converted into an air raid shelter to keep the splinters from hitting his colleagues.' This in effect suggested that Churchill was not really to blame for what had gone wrong, and that the true responsibility lay elsewhere, but that he was pretending otherwise out of loyalty towards Chamberlain. All these things were, in the circumstances, very helpful to Churchill. The other well-known part of the speech is the peroration. Speaking of Chamberlain, Lloyd George said:

> He has appealed for sacrifice. The nation is prepared for it so long as it has leadership ... I say solemnly that the Prime Minister should give an example of sacrifice, because there is nothing which can contribute more to victory in this war than that he should sacrifice the seals of office.[66]

Churchill had the difficult job of making a speech to wind up the debate, urging MPs to support the government when in actuality he cannot have been too sorry at the idea that it might fall. However, after Lloyd George's 'air raid shelter' remark, he was to some extent off the hook. His best option was to make a vigorous speech in the government's defence, hoping that he would be seen to be acting as a good colleague, but that his words themselves would not be taken too seriously. And, although he made a virtuoso performance, it was not enough, happily for him, to prevent a major rebellion. When the House divided, the government majority was 81 – a drastic drop from what was usual.

The psychological impact of this made it inevitable that the government would be reconstructed in some way. It was not yet clear, though, if Chamberlain would remain Prime Minister or, if not, who would replace him. Lloyd George even thought it possible that, if he resigned, he might advise the King to send for Clement Attlee, the Labour leader.[67] As Attlee himself appreciated, it was in fact quite impossible for Labour, given its weakness in the Commons, to form a government in its own right. Cripps saw Lloyd George on 9 May. 'I told him I had gathered from the labour people I had talked to that they did not want Halifax and that many of them were frightened of Winston with the result that suggestions were being made that he might take the job on', he wrote in his diary. Cripps added: 'He was as fearful as I was of Winston's lack of judgement if he should become P.M. but he was not anxious to take the job on himself as he foresaw fresh disaster within a very short period of time which he thought would make the position for a new government impossible as all the circumstances for that disaster had already been created by the old one.'[68]

In spite of what Cripps said, it is unlikely that there was any serious Labour support for Lloyd George. The party was, though, willing to serve in a coalition, under either Halifax or Churchill – but not under Chamberlain. On the day of Cripps's talk with Lloyd George, those three men met at 10 Downing Street. The Prime Minister said he was willing to resign if Labour would not serve under him. At this point, Halifax – who, as a member of the House of Lords, would have faced a serious disability in terms of leadership – ruled himself out as a candidate. Early the next day the news came through that Germany had invaded Belgium and Holland. During a meeting of the War Cabinet that afternoon, Chamberlain received confirmation that Labour would not serve under him, but were prepared to join a new government under a Prime Minister who would command the nation's confidence. Accordingly, he told the assembled ministers that he proposed to resign. After he had been to see the King in order to do so, Churchill was summoned to the Palace and asked to form a government.

In his memoirs, Churchill wrote of how, that day, when he at last went to bed at 3 a.m., he experienced 'a profound sense of relief. At last I had the authority to give directions over the whole scene. I felt as if I were walking with destiny, and that all my past life had been but a preparation for this hour and for this trial.'[69] This famous passage forms a marked contrast with Lloyd George's *War Memoirs*, in which the author's account of achieving the premiership, and any sense of what he might have felt about it, is quite overwhelmed by the detail of the political intrigues surrounding the event. We may be certain, furthermore, that – in contrast to what, in 1916, Lloyd George had claimed about his own experience[70] – Churchill felt no sense of embarrassment when, at his first Cabinet, his colleagues addressed him as 'Prime Minister'.

At the point that Churchill set about constructing his government, and for some time beyond, there was still considerable suspicion and resentment of him in Tory circles. Some MPs may have voted against the government or abstained in the crucial division in the hope of sending it a strong message, but without actually wishing to see the administration fall. For this reason it was essential for him to appoint Chamberlain – who remained leader of the Conservative Party – to a key position, knowing that he could not survive without his support. Chamberlain served Churchill loyally in the post of Lord President of the Council, although his feelings towards him were understandably mixed. The day after his resignation, the ex-premier wrote to his sister Ida that Churchill had been warm in his expressions of friendship. 'But he is surrounded by a very different crowd from what I am accustomed to and the stories that come to me of the method of government making which is going on now are disagreeably reminiscent of Lloyd Georgian ways.'[71] According to a diary entry made by Chamberlain a few weeks later, Churchill had proposed bringing Lloyd George himself into the government, possibly as Minister of Agriculture:

When W.C. was forming his Govt he did ask me about Ll.G. I said I would not work with him. W.C. then asked whether I should object to his being M/Agriculture. I said it might be that that would not bring us into association but I knew we couldn't

work together. At that he dropped the subject only saying . . .
that he didn't trust him not to be a defeatist. I was therefore
never asked to agree to his being M/Agriculture & therefore the
question of my agreement did not arise.[72]

As will be seen below, however, Churchill either thought that he
did have Chamberlain's consent, or was prepared to continue explor-
ing his proposal without it.

Chamberlain's suspicions of Lloyd George were increased (if that
were possible) in the aftermath of the Norway debate, when the latter
made an ill-judged contribution in the Commons. This was during
an adjournment debate on the afternoon of 9 May. Lloyd George
had been 'full of fire and beans' – according to Chips Channon –
and had said that the problems in Europe had been caused by the
failures of the Great War victors to live up to the promises they had
made at Versailles.[73] Chamberlain thought it likely that this attempt
'to justify Hitler on the ground that we had broken faith with
Germany' had been made by Lloyd George deliberately 'to separate
himself from the new Government and stake out a position from
which ultimately he might be called to make the peace'.[74] In fact, it
seems doubtful that Lloyd George had been so calculating – he
appears to have been stung into speaking by the remark of Beverley
Baxter MP that his earlier comments had, at various crucial
moments, encouraged Hitler. But it was not at all surprising that
Chamberlain took the view he did. As has been seen, his and Lloyd
George's mutual antipathy was long-standing. It dated back to
Chamberlain's experience as Director General of National Service
– a post in which he was neither happy nor a success – in 1916–17.
It was reinforced by Lloyd George's conviction (he was a believer
in phrenology) that Chamberlain's head was too small. Their dislike
and distrust of one another was to complicate their respective
relations with Churchill over the coming weeks.

On 13 May Churchill made his first speech in the Commons as
Prime Minister. His words were stirring ones: 'I would say to the
House, as I said to those who have joined this Government: "I have
nothing to offer but blood, toil, tears and sweat." '[75] Chamberlain,
though, received a warmer reception from Tory MPs than he did,
and this emphasized that the ex-premier remained a political force to
be reckoned with. Lloyd George, for his part, made a pretty speech,

'As one of the oldest friends of the Prime Minister in the House', congratulating Churchill on his elevation. He praised his 'glittering intellectual gifts, his dauntless courage, his profound study of war, and his experience in its operation and direction.'[76] 'Winston's eyes filled with tears', Sylvester recorded; 'he buried his face quickly in his left hand and wiped his face.' The two men's sentimental demonstration was moving and doubtless sincere. But there was also a sharpness in their relationship that was concealed from those who did not see them interacting at close hand. Sylvester noted: 'L.G. told Winston privately in the lobby that if he could not fight Neville Chamberlain how could he hope successfully to tackle Hitler?'[77]

That comment was a reference to Chamberlain's continuing influence within the government. By this time Lloyd George knew that he himself was not to be in the War Cabinet. The previous day he had told Sylvester that he did not think Churchill would approach him, and he claimed not to mind, saying that he would do no good in the government in the form it was constituted. 'Neville would have infinitely more authority than I would have, and he would oppose everything I proposed,' he said. Frances Stevenson, however, told Sylvester later the same day that Lloyd George 'was very much upset when he realised that the War Cabinet was fixed – and he had an idea he would be a member'. She added: 'Since then he has fortified himself with the idea that he will be given Agriculture or Food.'[78] Did he want to take office or not? Arguably – in the light of his refusal of the invitations Churchill made later – he wanted to be *offered* a job, but did not want the effort or responsibility of actually taking one up. Certainly, this interpretation is consistent with the monstrous, raging egotism that, by this stage in his life, was the dominant aspect of his personality. And it would certainly explain the difficulties he put in the path of Churchill's repeated attempts to bring him on board.

The first of these efforts appears to have been made shortly after the 'blood, toil, tears and sweat' speech. The evidence of what was said, and when, conflicts to a degree. John Colville, who was now private secretary to Churchill, wrote that same day (the 13th) that Lloyd George 'was afterwards invited into the P.M.'s room and offered the Ministry of Agriculture (for which the cheap press has always tipped him). He refused it because he thinks the country is in a hopeless position and he is generally despondent.'[79] However, it is not clear that a firm offer was made at this meeting. In a letter to Lloyd George at the end of the month, Churchill recalled that (at some unspecified point) 'The Ministry of Agriculture was discussed and one of my friends made representations to you.'[80] According to Lloyd George's reply, the friend was Beaverbrook – whom Churchill had made Minister of Aircraft Production – and the representations were made over the phone. He told Churchill:

> The offer did not come from you – in fact it was not an offer. Max, in the course of a conversation on the telephone suddenly asked me whether I would take the Ministry of Agriculture. He did not suggest that it was an offer or that he had even discussed it with you. In reply I told him exactly what I afterwards repeated to you – that I could not be responsible for the management of a Department with all its infinitude of control and supervision of detail which are not vital to the most urgent problems with which they have to deal. I was only concerned with the urgent need for food production on an extensive scale.[81]

In other words, Lloyd George refused to take office unless he was made into a food production supremo, without having to undertake many of the normal ministerial duties. The idea was not absolutely unprecedented. During World War I Sir Joseph Maclay had been in charge of the Ministry of Shipping, without being a member of either the House of Lords or the House of Commons, and so escaped the wearing job of justifying himself at the dispatch box. It was an inspired appointment on Lloyd George's part. But the unusual arrangement had succeeded only because Maclay was an essentially apolitical figure, and he did involve himself in the detailed running of his department. Overall, one cannot escape the sense that, in saying that he would not accept the Ministry of Agriculture unless he were excused the routine tasks, Lloyd George was laying down conditions that he knew it would be difficult for Churchill to accept. Or perhaps rather, as Sylvester put it damningly, he simply wanted 'to keep his cake and eat it. He wants a job, but he does not want the bother of it.'[82]

Undoubtedly Lloyd George was right to imagine that, at his advanced age, he would have found difficulty coping with a normal ministerial post. Yet his acolytes persisted in the view – presumably shared by Churchill to some extent – that if he accepted a post he would find a new lease of life. Along with that, they thought, his whole attitude to the war would change. 'If you were in the Government, you would not be talking peace,' Frances Stevenson claimed to have told him. She also told Sylvester that 'he [Lloyd George] talks about giving in without fighting because he thinks we are beaten. The whole point is that he hates Neville and the Government so much he would like to see them beaten, and he would like to see the English beaten.'[83] Both she and Sylvester were completely aware of Lloyd George's defeatism, then. Neither of them shared it. Yet, paradoxically, both continued to think that he should join the government.[84] It appears that, although by no means blind to his faults, they had so much emotional investment in his career, they needed to believe that he was still capable of being invigorated, physically and morally. They persuaded themselves that if only he could somehow be got into the government, he would be his old fighting self again, and that this in turn would be of great benefit to the war effort.

On 16 May Lloyd George lunched with Churchill at Admiralty House, as the latter had not yet moved to 10 Downing Street. General Ironside, the CIGS, found them together. 'L.G. looked very pink in the face with his long white hair', he wrote in his diary. 'Railing against Baldwin, who he said ought to be hanged. Chamberlain quite unfit to be P.M. He said he was sorry for Winston, who bore none of the responsibility for our condition.'[85] At this point – although adamant that he would neither join the War Cabinet nor accept the Ministry of Agriculture on normal terms – he still seems to have thought that he might yet become minister in charge of a new Food Council. Nevertheless, he returned from the lunch 'looking very grim', a natural reaction to the terrible war news, of which, it seems likely, Churchill had given him the latest details.[86]

France was in a state of military collapse. On 14 May the British War Cabinet learned that German forces had broken through at Sedan. On the morning of the 15th Churchill was awoken by a phone call from Paul Reynaud, the French Premier. Reynaud told him that the French counter-attack had failed. The road to Paris was open, he said, and the battle was lost. The next afternoon – after his lunch with Lloyd George – Churchill flew to Paris for a brief visit, and found Reynaud and his colleagues in a state of dejection. Over the coming days the news continued to worsen. On 25 May it was decided to evacuate the British Expeditionary Force (BEF) from France. The evacuation from Dunkirk began on the 26th. The next day, Belgium asked the Germans for an armistice, making the BEF's position yet more desperate. During five War Cabinet meetings on 26, 27 and 28 May, Churchill (with the help of other ministers including Chamberlain and Attlee) successfully resisted pressure from Halifax to put out peace feelers towards Germany.

It is hard to conceive of the mental agony that Churchill and his colleagues must have endured. It is unsurprising that, during this terrible time, he made some rash judgements. He might have been better off forgetting about Lloyd George entirely. Given the pressures he himself was under, he could have been more than forgiven for doing so. Yet, given the stress he was suffering, it is not hard to understand why, in fact, he spent a disproportionate amount of time and political capital in further efforts to get him to join the government. He treated this as a matter of some urgency. On 28 May, immediately after making a Commons statement on the capitulation of Belgium, he sent for Lloyd George. According to Sylvester, 'The P.M. then offered him a position in the War Cabinet, subject to the approval of Neville Chamberlain.'[87] Later that day Churchill sounded out Chamberlain on the issue. The latter was strongly opposed, as he recorded in his diary: 'I replied that it was best to be frank. If he thought Ll.G. would be more useful to him than I he had only to say so & I would gladly retire, but I could not work with him . . . It was for the P.M. to choose between us.' Churchill immediately replied that there was no question of Chamberlain resigning, and that he was far more helpful to him than Lloyd George could be. He said, moreover, that he himself 'did not trust Ll.G. He did not know his mind or whether he were not a defeatist. He would think no more of it. He had only toyed with the idea.'[88] Churchill did not reveal to Chamberlain the fact that he had already approached Lloyd George, and had thus much more than 'toyed' with the notion.

In the meantime, Lloyd George had determined not to accept the offer. He was insulted by his appointment being made conditional on Chamberlain's approval. He wrote to Churchill the next day:

It is the first time you have approached me personally on the subject and I can well understand the reason for your hesitancy for, in the course of our interview, you made it quite clear that if Chamberlain interposed his veto on the ground of personal resentment over past differences you could not proceed with the offer. This is not a firm offer. Until it is definite I cannot consider it.

He complained that his proposals for the reorganization of food supplies had been ignored, and was critical of Chamberlain and Halifax. 'Like millions of my fellow country-men I say to you that, if in any way you think I can help, I am at your call', he claimed. 'But if that call is tentative and qualified I shall not know what answer to give.'[89] The initial draft of the letter was even harsher about Chamberlain and Halifax, who were, Lloyd George said, 'directly responsible for the terrible mess in which we have been landed.' Chamberlain, he told Churchill, 'is so indispensable to you that you cannot invite to your counsels a man who had the greatest and most successful experience in the conduct of the last war without first of all obtaining his doubtful assent.'[90] But this self-serving passage did not make it into the letter as sent, which Sylvester delivered by hand.

On 30 May Churchill's reply arrived at Lloyd George's London office. Sylvester rang his boss – who proved incredibly impatient to know the contents – at home in Churt. 'I cannot complain in any way of what you say in your letter', Churchill wrote. However, he laid stress on the kindness and courtesy that he himself had received from Chamberlain since becoming Prime Minister: 'I have joined hands with him, and must act with perfect loyalty. As you say the enquiry I made of you yesterday can only be indeterminate, and I could not ask you to go further than you have done in your letter.' He assured Lloyd George that consideration of his proposals about food supplies had not been frustrated by 'personal or party difficulties' but had simply been put on hold 'after you had taken the decision that you did not at that time contemplate sharing responsibilities involved in joining the Administration'. He added: 'I trust that we shall keep in personal contact so that I may acquaint you with the situation as it deepens.'[91] To this Lloyd George replied in turn, denying that Churchill had ever made him a clear offer of the Ministry of Agriculture, but emphasizing that 'I certainly have no complaint to make as far as you are concerned.' Moreover, 'I am always at your disposal if you think I can do anything to help.'[92]

In spite of having previously told Chamberlain that he would not

carry the idea further, Churchill pressed ahead with trying to get
Lloyd George into the government. At this time, there was a growing
clamour in the press and the Labour Party for Chamberlain, Halifax
and other pre-war appeasers to be driven from office. This was not
something Churchill wanted. It was contrary to the spirit of true
national unity, and would at any rate have destabilized the government that he had only recently finished making. But it did give him
a lever over Chamberlain. On 5 June – the day after the Dunkirk
evacuation was completed, with almost miraculous success – the latter
went to see him and offered to resign. Churchill insisted that he
should not, as Chamberlain 'was giving him splendid help and he
wasn't going to have the Government which he had only just formed
knocked about'. Chamberlain then asked for the Prime Minister's
help in restraining the press attacks on him, and extracted a promise
from him to act. In Chamberlain's account, 'This was quite satisfactory but W. then reverted to L.G.' Churchill said that if forced to
choose between Lloyd George and Chamberlain he would opt for
the latter, but Chamberlain 'ought to consider whether it was right
to force such a choice on him'. He 'developed this proposition with
great earnestness saying that personal differences ought not to count
now & he was quite sure that L.G. would work loyally with me'.
Chamberlain promised to think it over, and the two men parted
amicably.[93]

Chamberlain also discussed the question with Halifax, who 'did
not think we need fear Ll.G. – who would perhaps be a useful brake
on Winston, but did not see how otherwise he would strengthen the
Govt.'.[94] Halifax, furthermore, talked to Churchill directly. 'Winston
told me', he wrote, 'that he meant to put him [Lloyd George]
through an inquisition . . . as to whether he had the root of the
matter in him. By this he means, so he explained to me, adopting a
formula I suggested to him, that any Peace terms now or hereafter
offered must not be destructive of our independence.'[95] The opposition to Lloyd George joining the government seemed to be
weakening.

On 6 June Churchill wrote to Chamberlain that he was 'much
encouraged by the line you took yesterday about LG'. He also
outlined his (apparently somewhat double-edged) reasons for wanting
Lloyd George. 'I am sure he would bring added strength to the
Government, and that otherwise, being treated as an outcast, he will

20. *Above.* With F. E. Smith in January 1922.

21. *Right.* Churchill and Lloyd George leaving Downing Street for the House of Commons in February 1922.

22. *Below.* Megan Lloyd George in 1923.

23. The cartoonist Bernard Partidge pokes some fun in 1927.

24. The clash between Lloyd George and Churchill over unemployment policy was a major feature of the 1929 election.

25. Political icons: dolls of Ramsay MacDonald, Lloyd George, Churchill and Stanley Baldwin in 1929.

26. *Above left*. Churchill with his daughter Diana at her wedding in 1932.

27. *Above right*. Lloyd George passes through the crowd at Diana Churchill's wedding.

28. *Left*. Lloyd George, cultivating his 'Welsh Wizard' image, March 1932.

29. Different hymn sheets: the two men, pictured here in 1934, both attacked the National Government, but took no consistent common line.

30. The War Cabinet, November 1939. Standing: Kingsley Wood, Churchill, Leslie Hore-Belisha and Lord Hankey. Front row: Lord Halifax, John Simon, Neville Chamberlain, Samuel Hoare and Lord Chatfield.

31. Faces of power. Clockwise, from top left: Balfour, Asquith, Lloyd George, Bonar Law, Chamberlain, Baldwin and MacDonald.

32. *Left*. Churchill with the Duke of Windsor in 1953. Did the Duke dream of returning as King and replacing Churchill with Lloyd George in 1940?

33. *Below*. Churchill in September 1940. Lloyd George criticised him for spending too much time touring bombed areas.

34. Lloyd George and Churchill seated behind J. C. Smuts, October 1942. Chips Channon wrote that 'of the three only the bronzed South African looked fit.'

35. Churchill, followed by Anthony Eden and J.C. Smuts (in uniform), leaving Lloyd George's memorial service in Westminster Abbey in April 1945.

36. After Victory in Europe, the ghosts of Pitt and Lloyd George assist Churchill to his rightful place.

BRITAIN'S GREATEST WAR PRIME MINIS

37. Megan Lloyd George with a statue of her father in 1955.

38. Churchill speaking in Biggleswade during the 1955 election. He attacked Megan Lloyd George for betraying her father's principles.

39. The Cabinet in 1955. Gwilym Lloyd George stands immediately behind Churchill.

become the focus for regathering discontents.' He did his best to reassure Chamberlain: 'Whatever happens you and I will continue to work together, but I should be very grateful to you if you felt able to work officially with him, and not make your assistance, which I value so highly, dependent upon his exclusion.' He stressed that he saw the question as 'very important for the general cohesion of the Government'. He even offered a 'guarantee' that Lloyd George 'will work fairly and honourably with you'.[96] Chamberlain received the letter the same morning that it was written, as he was digesting further attacks made on him in the press that day. He wrote back straight away. 'I think you realise how much you are asking of me but I cannot resist the appeal you make', he said. However, he laid down two conditions. The first was that Churchill should obtain from Lloyd George 'his personal assurance that on coming into the War Cabinet he will drop his personal feud and prejudice against me'. The second was that 'the campaign now being carried on against me and some of my Conservative colleagues by the Daily Herald, the News Chronicle and some Members of Parliament be stopped *before* any announcement is made about Lloyd George'. His reason for the second condition was that 'I cannot allow it to be said that his inclusion in the Govt is part of a bargain between you & me in return for which you have agreed to protect me.'[97] Quite clearly, though, that was the kind of bargain he was actually trying to strike.

It was, moreover, a deal that Churchill was willing to make. During that morning's Cabinet he passed Chamberlain a note saying that his conditions were accepted. After the main business of the meeting was over, ministers discussed the issue of the press. Chamberlain, by his own account, pointed out that while he had nothing to complain of in the behaviour to him personally of his Labour and Liberal colleagues, 'I was bound to ask myself what they were doing to allow these venomous attacks by members of their parties to go on while we were all supposed to be working harmoniously to win the war.'[98] Churchill too urged Attlee, Arthur Greenwood (another Labour member of the War Cabinet) and Archibald Sinclair (now Secretary of State for Air, but outside the War Cabinet) to stop the attacks. Chamberlain received assurances that the campaign against him would end. Churchill took a direct hand in making sure that the promises were fulfilled. Within hours he sent a message to Cecil King, the editorial director of the *Sunday Pictorial*. Its gist was 'that if the newspapers continue their attacks on the Chamberlain gang, they will get the Government out and on Wednesday morning there will be no Government'. King received the message the following morning, and in response made some enquiries. He wrote in his diary: 'Churchill has apparently fixed the [Daily] Herald through [Ernest] Bevin and the News Chronicle through Layton and probably Lloyd George direct.'[99] (Bevin had been leader of the powerful Transport and General Workers Union (TGWU) and was now Minister of Labour and National Service. He was a key figure in the Labour movement, and wielded major influence over the Herald which, being part-owned by the TUC, was seen as Labour's 'official' newspaper.) Churchill's interventions were effective. Chamberlain wrote on 8 June that the press campaign had stopped with great suddenness, 'like turning off a tap'.[100] It is notable that, although Churchill emphasized to King the threat that the attacks posed to the life of the government – which implied that it was the press's patriotic duty to desist – he had not previously acted to stop them. He did so only when the opportunity arose to extract from the situation, as he thought, something to his advantage, that is, Lloyd George's entry to the government.

Ironically, though, it was Chamberlain who got the best of the bargain, because Lloyd George did not fulfil the part assigned to him. On the morning of 6 June – the same day he accepted Chamberlain's conditions – the Prime Minister summoned Lloyd George to Downing Street. The message was conveyed by Churchill's secretary, Mrs Hill, to Sylvester by phone. Lloyd George was not in London, but he travelled up. Before the meeting, Lloyd George, fussing over his choice of suit and tie, 'got terribly het up'. Sylvester recorded that, as the car approached No. 10, 'L.G. said: "I won't go in with Neville."' As it drew up, Sylvester moved to help his boss get out, but Lloyd George stopped him. He wanted, it seemed, to make sure that he was the sole object of the press photographers' attention. The meeting with Churchill lasted an hour and a quarter. At last, Lloyd George appeared at the famous black front door, smoking a cigar. On the journey back, he told Sylvester 'that Winston had made him a firm offer this time to go in. He had never known him more friendly.' However, 'L.G. had told Winston that he must give him time to think it over.'[101] Lloyd George was in no hurry to make his intentions clear. Two days later Churchill passed Chamberlain a note in Cabinet. It read: 'The Wizard remains silent.'[102]

The lack of a clear answer naturally raised Churchill's suspicions. On the evening of 7 June he had a talk with Cecil King, at the latter's request. The previous day – before Lloyd George's meeting with Churchill – King had lunched at Churt. Lloyd George did not look fully his age, although he ate messily, whilst his false teeth clicked and rattled. 'From his eyes you can see he is really past it,' King wrote in his diary, 'though every now and then you catch a glimpse of his glance as it must have been.' Lloyd George spoke of Hitler 'as the greatest figure in Europe since Napoleon, and possibly greater than him'. In spite of these indications of decline and poor judgement, King thought that 'Of all the political figures I have talked politics with, Lloyd George seemed to me the most realistic.' This was because 'He sums the situation up as it is, without any trace of wishful thinking.'[103] When King mentioned the meeting to the Prime Minister, 'Churchill looked thoughtful and asked himself if Lloyd George was trying to get the Government out – not that Churchill thought he could possibly succeed.'[104]

Churchill's concerns about Lloyd George's intentions may well have increased over the course of the next fortnight. The war was going from bad to worse. On 10 June Italy declared war on Britain. This led the planned Secret Session of the Commons to be postponed. Chamberlain noted: 'L.G. had given no sign of life up to this morning & W.C. thought he must be waiting to see whether the debate wd bring about my resignation before committing himself.' He added: 'If so the postponement will upset his plans'.[105] Of more immediate concern than the Italian declaration was the French collapse, which was in its final stages. The Prime Minister made further flying visits to France, where he made desperate but fruitless attempts to stir the politicians and soldiers to continued resistance. On 14 June the Germans entered Paris. Two days later Paul Reynaud resigned as premier. His place was taken by Marshall Philippe Pétain, the octogenarian hero of the 1916 Battle of Verdun. Within hours Pétain's new government asked the Germans for an armistice, which was signed on 22 June. From this point on his regime and his name were indelibly associated in British minds with collaborationism and defeatism. Almost inevitably people began to draw comparisons between Pétain and Lloyd George, another symbolic figure from a bygone age who, in his dotage, was suspected of wanting to take power in order to make peace with Hitler. Churchill did not see him in that light – yet.

He kept a close eye, though, on his activities. He did not, it seems, view them with approval. Churchill soon came to believe that some of his colleagues were planning, not to displace him, but to get him to reorganize his government, remove the Chamberlainite 'Old Gang', and bring in Lloyd George. This was the so-called 'Under-secretaries' Plot'. It involved ministers (predominantly junior ones), most of whom Churchill himself had brought in from the cold when constructing his administration. One of these was Boothby, Undersecretary at the Ministry of Food. During the first part of June he lunched with Lloyd George, who wanted to talk to him about food production. They did so at White's, a well-known London club. According to Boothby's recollection, 'this caused a tremendous stir. Within the hour it had been reported to Churchill that I was plotting to make Lloyd George Prime Minister instead of himself. He may have believed it.'[106] Actually, Boothby had something different in mind. He followed up the lunch with a letter to Lloyd George some days later. 'I cannot help thinking that the moment has now come when you should go into the Government at all costs,' he wrote, and added: 'In my view the only Government now capable of saving us is a dictatorial triumvirate consisting of Winston, yourself, and a representative of the Labour Movement – be it Attlee or another.'[107]

These ideas soon took a more concrete form. On the morning of 17 June Leo Amery, now Secretary of State for India, met with Harold Macmillan, a progressive Tory anti-appeaser and future Prime Minister, who had been appointed by Churchill to a junior post at the Ministry of Supply. They discussed, according to Amery's diary, 'what were the practical changes needed in our system of government'. These, they concluded, should involve 'a different personnel of the War Cabinet which at present contains only one live man viz. Winston'. The two men met later the same morning with Lloyd George, Boothby, Clement Davies, J. L. Horabin (a Liberal MP) and Arthur Salter (independent MP for Oxford University and Parliamentary Secretary at the Ministry of Shipping). While they talked 'news came in that [the] French Army had given up'. Amery drafted a letter to Churchill summarizing the group's recommendations and asking him to see a deputation. After lunch the group adjourned to White's and afterwards to Lloyd George's office overlooking the Thames. According to Davies's later account, Lloyd George was not asked to sign the letter, nor did he express his views on its contents: 'All that he had said was that if member[s] of the Government felt that way then it was only right that they should put it into writing and put it before the Prime Minister.'[108] (Years later, Amery recalled another detail of the meeting – that Lloyd George was still angry that Churchill had asked Chamberlain's approval for bringing him into the War Cabinet. He fumed as he strode up and down, Amery claimed, and said, 'to think that I who saved the country should be allowed into the Cabinet by the gracious permission of that pinhead'. The story is not implausible, but it should be emphasized that it does not appear in Amery's contemporary diary.) Later in the day Amery heard from Boothby, Macmillan and Davies that 'Bevin shared their general point of view but could take no step without consulting his party leaders'. Amery, who saw himself as the leader of the cabal, persuaded them that, rather than send the letter, he should approach Churchill directly the following day.[109] News of the group's activities spread like wildfire – indeed they themselves had talked to Tories who were hostile to their plan, such as Lord Salisbury and Duff Cooper. After the Conservative MP Charles Waterhouse heard of the idea for a triumvirate of Churchill, Lloyd George and Bevin he commented: 'in spite of our peril the rats are gnawing at the bung-hole of the Ship of State'.[110]

On 18 June, Churchill made one of his most famous speeches in the House of Commons. He repeated it the same evening in a radio broadcast. The peroration is, justly, the most famous part: 'Let us . . . brace ourselves to our duties, and so bear ourselves that, if the British Empire and its Commonwealth last for a thousand years, men will still say, "This was their finest hour."' An earlier passage was also highly significant. It demanded an end to recriminations against the Chamberlainites:

> Of this I am quite sure, that if we open a quarrel between the past and the present, we shall find that we have lost the future. Therefore, I cannot accept the drawing of any distinctions between Members of the present Government . . . It is absolutely necessary at a time like this that every Minister who tries each

day to do his duty shall be respected; and their subordinates must know that their chiefs are not threatened men, men who are here today and gone tomorrow, but that their directions must be punctually and faithfully obeyed.[111]

It is not clear whether Churchill knew specifically of the 'Under-secretaries' Plot' at the time of this Commons speech, but, if not, he learnt of it immediately afterwards. The Prime Minister therefore knew what was afoot when he agreed to see Amery, who had been pressing for an audience. He told him firmly that it was the task of junior ministers 'to stick to the job he had given them. If any one of the Government wished to criticise its working or its composition they should resign and criticise from outside.'[112] Churchill was even more brutal with Boothby, who wrote to him the following day, 'telling him how to run the war', and appearing to suggest that Lloyd George should be given a government post. Boothby admitted the folly of this in his memoirs, in which he recalled how the Prime Minister summoned him to Downing Street and 'went through my letter sentence by sentence, and scorched it'.[113] Five years later Churchill still had a vivid recollection of how 'a number of Tories had tried to break up the Government and to engineer the formation of a kind of dictatorial triumvirate consisting of L.G., himself and Bevin'.[114]

But although Churchill slapped the junior ministers down, he himself seems still to have wanted to recruit Lloyd George to his side. That is, he wanted him provided that getting him did not mean jettisoning Chamberlain. In her autobiography, Frances Stevenson claimed to have received an important phone call from Brendan Bracken on the night of 19–20 June. (Bracken, an influential figure with Churchill, was now his parliamentary private secretary.) She wrote:

> I was roused from a deep sleep by the ringing of the telephone by my bedside and the voice of Brendan Bracken speaking from the Cabinet Room at Downing Street and asking to speak to L.G. I said that L.G. was in bed and that I could not disturb him. Bracken went on to say that Churchill wishes to offer him a post in his Cabinet, and I gathered that L.G. could have anything he liked to ask for, provided he would lend his name to Churchill's team, and his policies. L.G.'s friends, so said Bracken,

all thought he should come in. But I knew by this time that L.G.
would not, and there was no point in waking him.

There is no reason to doubt that some such call took place, but
there is a question mark over the date, because she appears to have
conflated the events she described with others that took place the
following year.[115] All the same, we may note that a Secret Session of
the House of Commons, which had earlier been postponed, was due
to take place on the 20th. If Stevenson was right about the timing,
this would help to explain the urgency of the late-night appeal.
Churchill may have wanted to forestall the possibility that Lloyd
George would use the occasion to attack Chamberlain's continuing
presence in the government.

In fact the debate was uneventful. 'The secret session passed off
all right & I think the heresy hunt has been at least scotched',
Chamberlain noted with some satisfaction the next day. 'L.G. came
down to speak but put his notes in his pocket. I guess he found the
atmosphere unsympathetic. He has not replied to Winston's offer to
come in & I suspect plans to be the Marshal Pétain of Britain. W.C.
is fed up with him.'[116] If Churchill did feel that way it would have
been understandable. There is some evidence, however, that he
was not yet completely disillusioned. Bracken was again part of the
channel of communication. 'I lunched with Brendan today, and
gathered that Winston increasingly feels the need of you', Boothby
wrote to Lloyd George on 6 July. 'He thinks you spurned his last
invitation. If another reaches you in the course of the next few days,
I beg of you to give it serious and – if possible – favourable
consideration.'[117]

Lloyd George was delighted to receive this letter, but it did not
persuade him to change his mind. Instead, he asked to see Boothby,
who then wrote to Churchill explaining why Lloyd George had never
replied to his invitation to join the War Cabinet. His reasons,
Boothby said, were twofold. First, Lloyd George 'did not wish to
commit himself in writing to opinions which would put him in the
position of having tried to force Mr Chamberlain out of the Government against his will, and thus to a breach with the Conservative
Party and perhaps also with yourself which might prove irreconcilable'. Second, Beaverbrook had 'strongly urged him not to answer for
the time being'. Lloyd George had understood from him 'that Mr

Chamberlain contemplated resigning in the near future; and that premature action on his part would therefore do no good, and might do harm'. None of this was terribly convincing. Lloyd George could surely have found some way of communicating his thoughts to Churchill at a much earlier stage. He seems, in fact, to have been simply unwilling to give a straight answer to the invitation, and indeed did not do so now. Boothby got the impression, he told Churchill, 'that *au fond* he is not only willing but anxious to serve'.[118] But if so he had a funny way of showing it.

Why had Churchill gone to such lengths to get Lloyd George into the War Cabinet? There were, undoubtedly, some positive reasons. It seems fair to assume that Churchill would not have gone to such lengths in order to appoint someone he thought would be an actual liability. To Chamberlain, after all, he said he would value Lloyd George as a counsellor, and that he would bring strength to the government. Yet he also said that he distrusted him, and that he feared he would act as a focal point of opposition to the government if he were not brought in. It was natural for Churchill to emphasize these negative reasons to Chamberlain, who was unlikely to be persuaded that Lloyd George would be a definite asset. It seems reasonable to think, though, that the longer Lloyd George failed to commit himself the more Churchill's fear and mistrust grew. The desire to buy off trouble by giving him a job may have come to outweigh, in the Prime Minister's mind, his likely actual contribution to the war effort.

Aside from these general considerations, however, there was another possible motivation for Churchill's repeated, even frenzied, efforts to get Lloyd George on board. In 1971 the historian Paul Addison advanced an ingenious theory. He noted that Churchill in 1940 was not nearly as confident of eventual British victory as his public rhetoric implied, and as is popularly assumed. 'His attitude towards compromise peace seems to have been that while *he* would never agree to it, he recognized that others might negotiate an untreasonable peace.' Churchill thus foresaw the possibility, Addison suggested, that a Halifax or Lloyd George government might be able to secure 'reasonable' terms. 'Churchill appreciated Lloyd George's position and did not regard it as dishonourable.' Moreover, 'It was a mark of Churchill's brilliance that he could foresee a role for others should he fail.'[119] Others, such as Bernd Martin, have followed this account of Churchill's reasoning: 'The future British Pétain was first to be sworn to the cause of national integrity, and then taken into the Cabinet to prepare for a smooth transfer of power should worse come to worst.'[120]

The theory, though intriguing, is problematic. It is perfectly true that Churchill did not rule out a peace deal by some future successor. As he told President Roosevelt, 'If members of the present administration were finished and others came in to parley amid the ruins . . . no one would have the right to blame those then responsible if they made the best terms they could for the surviving inhabitants.'[121] But there is little if any direct evidence that Churchill planned for Lloyd George to be that successor. His 6 June comment to Halifax quoted above – that he wanted to be sure that Lloyd George agreed that any future peace deal should maintain British independence – may seem compelling. But that, surely, is what he would have wanted from anyone he was considering appointing to the War Cabinet. It does not by any means prove that he had thought out a plan for a transition of power in the event of military defeat, or that he envisaged Lloyd George in particular becoming Prime Minister in those circumstances. And one should not overstate the degree to which his public image was at odds with his private attitude. On 18 June Chamberlain commented to Churchill on Lloyd George's failure to respond to his offer. He thought that the older man might be 'waiting to be the Marshal Pétain of Britain'. Churchill replied, 'Yes, he might, but there won't be any opportunity.'[122] This remark appears to undermine the Addison thesis quite severely.

Lloyd George's reasons for not accepting a government post were if anything more complicated than the reasons for Churchill's offers. At one level they appear straightforward, and discreditable. To his private circle he certainly gave the impression that he was biding his time before, in due course, he was inevitably called upon to perform a Pétain-type role. 'L.G. has some idea he is coming in on the peace settlement, that he will be able to make peace where Winston won't,' Frances Stevenson told Sylvester in September. In October Lloyd George himself told Sylvester, 'I shall wait until Winston is bust.' In November Stevenson again reported that 'He feels that when the crash comes he will have to come in and make peace.'[123]

The Nazis do appear to have hoped that he would play the Pétain part. On 22 July German agents in London reported to von

Ribbentrop that the Duke of Windsor (who was in Portugal, having fled France as it fell) had urged George VI to replace Churchill's government with a new pro-German Cabinet. They also reported that Lloyd George too had advised the King to appoint a new Cabinet. The same day an Italian newspaper claimed that the Duke wanted Lloyd George to become Prime Minster of a fascist regime in Britain.[124] The details of these claims were almost certainly incorrect. There appears to be no evidence in the Royal Archives that either Lloyd George or the Duke had any direct contact with George VI at this time, as was alleged. But the Duke was certainly sympathetic to the idea of peace with Germany, and possibly to the idea of Lloyd George returning as Prime Minister in order to help achieve this. The question is whether he was simply naive, or whether he was guilty of something worse.

There is some intriguing, if rather ambiguous, evidence of his role. After the war the journalist Geoffrey Bocca was commissioned by Beaverbrook to write a biography of the Duchess of Windsor. He travelled to Lisbon and interviewed Ricardo do Espírito Santo Silva, the Portuguese banker who played host to the Windsors after they had left France in 1940. Santo Silva claimed that Baron von Hoyningen-Hühne, the German Minister in Portugal, acting on instructions from Berlin, had at that time proposed to the Duke that, once a Nazi invasion of Britain had succeeded, he should return to Britain as King, with Lloyd George as his Prime Minister. (It should be noted that he did not make any explicit claim that the Duke had met the ambassador face to face.) He also showed Bocca a letter, in what appeared to be the Duke's handwriting. According to Bocca's later recollection, it read, 'Dear Espirito Santo, I enjoyed our meeting last night and hope you will stay in touch with the baron.' However, some months after the original interview, Santo Silva requested that Bocca meet him urgently, and they dined together in Paris. Bocca recalled, 'He was very nervous, kept cracking his knuckles and said that the letter was a fake, and would I please not use it . . .'[125]

What are we to make of this? Contemporary German documents confirm that German emissaries were in touch with the Duke, and did their utmost to persuade him not to leave Europe. (Churchill had appointed him Governor of the Bahamas, doubtless as a means of getting him out of the way.) On 31 August von Ribbentrop sent to the German legation in Lisbon a message that was to be conveyed to the Duke orally. Its substance was that the 'Churchill clique' stood in the way of Britain making peace with Germany, and that Germany was determined to force her to make peace. 'It would be a good thing if the Duke were to keep himself prepared for further developments. In such case Germany would be willing to cooperate most closely with the Duke and to clear the way for any desire expressed by the Duke and Duchess. The direction in which these wishes tend is quite obvious and meets with our complete understanding.'[126] This was a clear hint that the couple could become King and Queen of a new British regime, if they were prepared to play the part assigned them. Hühne's reply to von Ribbentrop shows that this message was given to the Duke via Santo Silva. So a key part of the latter's later claims – which he then mysteriously withdrew – are borne out. The exchange of telegrams makes no explicit mention of Lloyd George's putative role, but this may nonetheless have been raised in Santo Silva's conversation with the Duke. According to Hühne,

> In his reply, which was given orally to the confidant [Santo Silva], the Duke paid tribute to the Führer's desire for peace, which was in complete agreement with his own point of view . . . To the appeal made to him to cooperate at a suitable time in the establishment of peace, he agreed gladly. However, he requested that it be understood that at the present time he must follow the official orders of his Government. Disobedience would disclose his intentions prematurely, bring about a scandal, and deprive him of his prestige in England. He was also convinced that the present moment was too early to come forward, since there was as yet no inclination in England for an approach to Germany. However, as soon as this frame of mind changed he would be ready to return immediately.[127]

Accordingly, the Duke departed for the Bahamas at the start of August, although he does not appear to have given up entirely on the idea of acting to help end the war. Apparently, in the middle of the month he sent a cable to Santo Silva, 'asking him to send a communication as soon as action was advisable'.[128] There seems never to have been a reply; presumably the Germans had given up on the idea that he could be useful to them.

The Duke may have stopped short of outright treachery, but his actions certainly reflected badly on him. Lloyd George was less culpable: he cannot be directly blamed for the role he possibly played in the ex-King's fantasies of a comeback, nor, indeed, for the hopes that the Nazis themselves seem to have vested in him. In all, comparisons with Pétain are doubtful, even in spite of the apparently damning evidence that came from Lloyd George's own mouth. It was not the case, it should be stressed, that Lloyd George wanted Britain simply to give up fighting, or that he contemplated Nazi occupation with equanimity. He did doubt that Britain could win the war fighting alone but, as Addison rightly argues, he still wanted it to be fought as vigorously as it could be in order that the terms of the subsequent peace might be as advantageous as possible.[129]

Lloyd George not only differed from Churchill on strategy, but was also highly critical of his style of war leadership. These points were, of course, related. A few days after the fall of France he commented to Sylvester that, although Churchill himself had brains, the War Cabinet consisted of 'duds and mutts'. This, he suggested, was because Churchill could not cope with being surrounded by men of genuine ability. 'Winston is an able man, but he is not a leader. He does not want men around him with understanding minds. He would rather not have them. He is intolerant of them.'[130] This, of course, reflected Lloyd George's animus against Halifax and Chamberlain. In mid-July, he lunched with Thomas Jones, who urged him to join the government. Lloyd George was 'adamant' against doing so: 'It was like calling a specialist in when the patient's case was nigh hopeless. Winston was at the mercy of Neville with his party majority.' He argued that if he took office, 'Whatever I put up would be suspect and would be opposed.' Churchill, he said, was not prepared to 'smash the Tory Party to save the country, as I smashed the Liberal Party. Winston has intellectual and rhetorical power, but he has no psychological insight.' Lloyd George claimed that he did not seek the premiership, and was ready to 'serve under Winston and with Bevin but not with the present crowd'.[131] At the beginning of October he wrote to Frances Stevenson that 'I am glad I am not in.' Churchill's 'stubborn mind', he said, was 'blind to every essential fact which does not fit in with his ambitions'.[132] Later the same month he told her that 'Winston now feels that he is God & the only God.'[133] On 11 November he explained to Frances Stevenson's daughter Jennifer that 'If I entered the Cabinet I should soon have to resign because of total disagreement with the plans and methods of this lot and that would do no good.'[134] Lloyd George also insisted repeatedly that one of his reasons for not working with Churchill was that he feared a quarrel that would damage their friendship – another way of saying, perhaps, that he could not cope with being someone else's subordinate.

But strategic and personal differences were not the whole story behind Lloyd George's refusal to enter the government. He was increasingly obsessed by the threat of air raids – he had an expensive and elaborate underground shelter built at Churt – and was often reluctant to come to London for that reason. At times he became a nervous wreck. He must therefore have found the pressure to take a leading part in affairs once more to some degree unwelcome. This pressure came from, among others, Stevenson, Sylvester, Jones, Garvin and Beaverbrook. These individuals had different motivations. Beaverbrook, of course, was a congenital intriguer. The ageing Garvin, by this stage, may simply have been living in the past. Many of Lloyd George's closest associates, though, were trying to save his reputation. Taking office, or at least making some great patriotic speech, were essential, they thought, in order to prove he was no Pétain. Taking 'a proper job of work', moreover, would help him conquer his fear of bombing, which he would no longer have time to think about.[135] They also tried to convince him that the existing composition of the War Cabinet was no reason for him not to join it, and that Churchill would be amenable to his advice. Jones told him that 'once he (L.G.) was inside the situation would at once be changed, [and] that he was an explosive force and nothing would long remain as it was'.[136] Some of his advisers may also have believed that there was genuine popular disappointment at his failure to take office. The novelist Francis Brett Young wrote to Stevenson, who was a friend of his, of his 'great grief' that Lloyd George had 'not thought fit to join Winston in an advisory if not an executive capacity. Wherever I go I hear this disappointment expressed. You would be astonished (or would you?) to hear how often he is called for by the man in the street.'[137]

Perhaps ashamed at his lack of courage, Lloyd George rationalized his inaction along the lines previously stated. The more he came up with excuses, the more his friends harassed him, and the more they harassed him the more he came up with excuses. (On one occasion Stevenson told him openly 'that he had done absolutely nothing to help his country in this war . . . he had been very annoyed with her and had said it was a damned lie'.)[138] Arguably, then, it was not the case that either personal antipathy towards Churchill or opposition to his policies were the fundamental causes of his decision not to join the government. Rather, he said harsh things about Churchill and denounced his leadership in an attempt to justify his determination not to do so. This is not to say that the resentment he expressed against him was not genuine, but merely that the emotions had a complicated origin.

Throughout the summer and autumn of 1940 the military situation remained extremely serious. The Battle of Britain raged as the German Luftwaffe attempted to cripple the RAF as a prelude to invasion. In early September the Germans began bombing British cities by night – which in fact proved a major strategic error, because it distracted resources from the attempt to achieve air superiority during daylight hours. By the end of that month, after the Luftwaffe experienced heavy losses, Hitler called off his invasion plan. But for as long as British survival rested on a knife-edge, so Churchill's position and newfound public popularity remained inevitably fragile. On 24 July Chips Channon noted in his diary that 'Lloyd George, whose affection for Winston has noticeably cooled of late, predicts that after the PM's first blunder, the country, now admittedly hysterically infatuated with him, will turn against him and only remember his mistakes.'[139]

If Churchill had a similar sense of the precariousness of his position, that might explain why (if the rumours to this effect were correct) he continued to entertain the idea of giving Lloyd George a job. In early August Hugh Dalton, a senior Labour Party figure and Minister of Economic Warfare, warned Attlee about 'movements further to increase the size of the War Cabinet by addition of Lloyd George'. Dalton had heard 'that both P.M. and the Beaver wanted this'. A few weeks later, though, he was pleased to note that the idea had 'faded out a bit'. At the end of September Chamberlain, who was suffering from cancer, resigned. He died on 9 November and Churchill succeeded him as leader of the Conservative Party. The *Tribune*, the left-wing weekly founded by Stafford Cripps, observed that in doing this Churchill had given up a unique and prestigious position as a national leader above party. It explained to its readers, though, that Churchill was 'a skilled politician and he thinks about Mr. Lloyd George' – that is to say, he remembered how in 1922

Tory MPs had ejected a successful war leader from Downing Street once he ceased to serve their party purposes.[140]

Chamberlain's resignation thus allowed Churchill to get hold of the Tory machine, in order to prevent history repeating itself. It also removed one of Lloyd George's excuses for not joining the government. Lady Astor tried to persuade Dalton – and also, Dalton suspected, everybody else – that Lloyd George would be a valuable addition to the Cabinet as he would be able to 'hold Winston'.[141] But although there were changes – Bevin was one of those who joined the enlarged War Cabinet – no offer went to Lloyd George. Churchill may by this point have appreciated that the opposition of Dalton, Attlee and others to the idea outweighed any advantages the appointment would have brought.

For Beaverbrook (himself a member of the War Cabinet since August) intrigue sprang eternal, however. In late October he sent an emissary to Lloyd George at Churt. The man was F. W. Farey-Jones, one of Beaverbrook's underlings at the Ministry of Aircraft Production. He reported that Churchill was 'entirely in the hands of sycophants who feed and fan his illusions', and warned of impending military disasters in Egypt and Greece. Lloyd George told Frances Stevenson that Farey-Jones suggested that 'I should put myself in touch with B. without loss of time & that I should concoct some plan for saving this country from the doom into which it is heading with its accustomed blind fury'. When Beaverbrook himself rang up, Lloyd George said he was unwilling to join the government or take any other action. Moreover, 'it was no use my talking in the House without saying what I really thought & that if I did so they would say I was nagging and defeatist . . . it was still less use talking to Winston as he would not listen'.[142] Nevertheless, he agreed, without apparent enthusiasm, to see Beaverbrook at his Ministry a few days later. The particular disasters that Beaverbrook was predicting were averted, though, and therefore there was no accompanying political crisis to exploit. Lloyd George, we may speculate, was probably rather relieved.

On 12 December Lord Lothian died. Years before, as Philip Kerr, he had been Lloyd George's private secretary; in 1939 he had been appointed ambassador to the USA. That evening at Chequers Churchill began to muse about how to replace him. Given the urgent necessity of bringing America into the war, the appointment was an important one. 'He would like to try L.G. if he could trust him', John Colville wrote in his diary. Colville suggested alternative candidates, but, as the evening went on, the Prime Minister, in his own words, 'sweetened to the idea of L.G.', suggesting that 'his knowledge of munitions problems and his fiery personality marked him out'. He believed, he said, that Lloyd George would be willing to serve – a triumph of hope over experience, if there ever was one. Ambassadors were responsible to the Foreign Secretary, and Colville pointed out that Lloyd George might object to serving under Halifax. Churchill responded to this objection by proposing to make Lloyd George a member of the War Cabinet, in order to 'sweeten the pill'. Moreover, 'He believed L.G would be loyal to him; if not he could always sack him.' Colville's tactful attempts to deflect his boss from the course he had determined on were brushed aside. To the suggestion that Stafford Cripps, now ambassador to Moscow, could be transferred to Washington, Churchill replied that Cripps 'was a lunatic in a country of lunatics and it would be a pity to move him'. In an expansive, brandy-fuelled mood he acted, as so often, on impulse and telephoned Gwilym Lloyd George 'to sound him out about his father', without, as yet, having even consulted Halifax.[143] Many people, of course, were likely to be appalled by the plan. Dalton, having heard the 'awful rumours', recorded his view that Lloyd George was suffering from 'senility, pessimism and ambition, a fatal combination'. That phrase had originally been used to him by Charles de Gaulle, the Free French leader, about Pétain.[144]

Halifax did, in fact, prove amenable, and on 14 December Churchill cabled President Roosevelt. He said that he was thinking of proposing to Lloyd George that he should take Lothian's place, 'and I should be very glad to know quite informally that this would be agreeable to you'. He added, 'I have reason to hope that he would not be unwilling to face the arduous responsibilities' – presumably he had deduced this from his conversation with Gwilym – and asked for a quick reply. Roosevelt responded the next day: 'Choice will be entirely agreeable. I knew him in world war.' However, there was also perhaps a hint that the President was not too keen on the idea, possibly because of the fear that Lloyd George might make terms with Germany: 'I assume that over here he will in no way play into the hands of the appeasers.'[145] Lloyd George was determined not to accept, however. In mid-December he had two long talks with

Churchill at 10 Downing Street on successive days. According to the latter's recollection, 'He showed genuine pleasure at having been invited' but 'was sure that at the age of seventy-seven he ought not to undertake so exacting a task'.[146] Churchill afterwards told Attlee that Lloyd George had given the impression of great age: 'His nose was sharp as a pen and he babbled of pigs.'[147]

Why was the offer made? Churchill acknowledged later that Lloyd George had not been 'happily circumstanced in British politics' at this time, and that the two men's views on the war had differed. 'There could be no doubt, however that he was our foremost citizen, and that his incomparable gifts and experience would be devoted to the success of his mission.'[148] But given the obvious problems with appointing him to the post – Churchill acknowledged shortly after he made the offer that he 'would naturally not have been able to do the bulk of the work because of his great age' – suspicions of course arise about the motives for proposing him.[149] Was Churchill, perhaps, trying to remove an unwanted political rival from the scene?

People assumed he was attempting such a manoeuvre when, after Lloyd George's refusal, he appointed a reluctant Halifax to the Washington job instead. On 20 December Colville recorded that 'The P.M. lunched with Beaverbrook and L.G. and upset everybody very much by appearing to listen to the former's wild remarks about the proposed Cabinet reshuffle (consequent on Halifax's appointment) and to a suggestion that L.G. should enter the Government in some agricultural capacity.'[150] Victor Cazalet concluded 'that Winston wanted H. out of the country so that L.G. might join the Government'. (He added: 'What a gang! W.C., Ll.G. and Beaverbrook.')[151] Of course, if that had been the plan all along, it seems unlikely that Churchill would have tried to appoint Lloyd George to Washington first. In all, the possibility that there had been some Machiavellian intent behind the offer to Lloyd George cannot be fully discounted. Yet it seems more likely that Churchill had a sincere but misguided hope that Lloyd George would be able to make himself useful in what was, after all, a very important job. This was wishful thinking. In Churchill's defence, he seems to have been unaware when the idea first struck him of the degree to which Lloyd George had aged even since the summer.

Lloyd George's age, poor health and lack of a conventionally diplomatic disposition were perfectly good reasons for turning down the posting. Inevitably, though, observers read more into it than this, and, in fact, he seems to have encouraged them to do so. 'Lloyd George is obviously keeping himself for the succession if needed', reflected Cecil King at the end of the year. A few months later Lloyd George told King that he had not taken the Washington embassy 'as he considers the result of the war will be decided here, not in America'.[152] The implication of that remark was that he still wanted to take some significant role in domestic politics. And yet, the idea that he was biding his time, waiting for some opportune moment to re-emerge into the limelight, must have seemed increasingly implausible even to him. He had, after all, snubbed all the concrete chances presented to him, and the waiting game was not one that could be played convincingly by a man in his late seventies. Gladstone, admittedly, had been 82 when he became Prime Minister for the last time, and Churchill would start his second and final premiership in 1951 at the age of 76, but Lloyd George's actions, as opposed to his private words, suggest that he no longer possessed such an insatiable appetite for power. Lloyd George claimed to Sylvester that, in the closing days of 1940, Churchill had made him yet a further offer of a government post: 'Winston himself telephoned me at Christmas and asked me to join him, but I said "No".'[153] During January 1941 rumours about Lloyd George continued, although Eden reassured Dalton that 'Beaverbrook is the only person who would wish to work him in.' Dalton in turn assured Eden that 'I could easily get all my [Labour] colleagues standing on their hind legs and waving their tails in fury at any such suggestion.'[154]

Lloyd George now suffered a demoralizing blow. In December, his wife Margaret – who had been rightly convinced that he would never take office again – was severely injured in a fall. In January, her condition worsened. Snowdrifts delayed him as he travelled from Churt to North Wales to be with her – feeling, perhaps, some degree of remorse for his behaviour towards her over the years – and she died before he arrived. It had been no one's idea of a perfect marriage, but Lloyd George was grief-stricken nonetheless. He received a message of consolation from Churchill, who once again addressed him as 'My dear David', as in the pre-World War I years, rather than, as latterly, 'My dear L.G.'. He spoke of Margaret Lloyd George as 'that great woman, who embodied all that is most strong and true in the British race'. Lloyd George was touched by the letter, observing, 'Winston always says so much in so little.'[155] He wrote back, in a very shaky hand: 'She was a great pal in a stormy life. For you her admiration was unswerving in good and evil fortune.'[156]

Yet, in spite of this sentimental exchange, there is other evidence that Lloyd George's private bitterness towards Churchill was growing. Bob Boothby's memoirs give a powerful flavour of this, in relation to his own downfall as a minister. In October 1940 he had been suspended from his post at the Ministry of Food because of allegations of financial impropriety. He was accused of failing, when making pre-war efforts to persuade the Treasury to compensate British holders of Czech assets lost when the Germans seized Prague, to disclose that he had a direct financial interest in the outcome. Boothby had certainly been unwise, but Churchill – whom he had alienated with the presumptuous letter of advice he had sent him in June – could doubtless have saved him had he wanted. Instead, a Select Committee was established, and in January it produced a report hostile to Boothby, who immediately resigned. Soon after, Lloyd George summoned him to Churt and greeted him by saying, 'Churchill has behaved to you like the cad he is.' This, Boothby claimed, was the only time he had seen the former Prime Minister in anger, and 'although I knew the anger was on my behalf, I was pretty frightened'. There was no obvious reason for Lloyd George to feel so strongly about the matter – unless the anger was feigned and he was trying to recruit Boothby to his own standard. The episode had no important consequences. What is significant is not the detail but the impression left on Boothby: 'Driving back to London, I reached the conclusion that the relationship between these two titans was based on mutual admiration and mutual fear, but not on mutual affection.'[157]

In accounting for Lloyd George's strength of feeling against Churchill, it is worth reflecting that not all of the former's criticisms of the latter's war leadership were misplaced. Churchill conceded that Lloyd George may have had 'more imagination and more depth as PM than I have', but argued that 'I have more experience, and know more, of war.'[158] He certainly did have much direct war experience but this, perhaps, was what deluded him into thinking that he was a master strategist. He had a commendable desire to maintain the principle of civilian control of the armed services. In his attempts to enforce it, however, he drove his military advisers to distraction. He held meetings late at night, and – not always being entirely sober – conducted them with considerable inefficiency. He had a 'something must be done' mentality, unable to tolerate inevitable and necessary periods of inaction, and appearing to cherish military operations almost more for their own sake than for any broader purpose. Hence his preference for dramatic, 'showy' schemes that the military men thought hare-brained. Most notably, General Sir Alan Brooke, CIGS from 1941 onwards, repeatedly denounced Churchill's behaviour in his diary, describing him, towards the end of the war, as 'a public menace': 'Without him England was lost for a certainty, with him England has been on the verge of disaster time and again.' The diary, it should be stressed, was written in the heat of the moment, and after the war Brooke conceded that he had made insufficient allowance for Churchill's difficulties. 'I thank God I was given an opportunity of working alongside such a man,' he wrote.[159] The more appalling aspects of Churchill's behaviour, therefore, should not distract us from his genuine contribution. Nor should we conclude that he was weaker as a war leader than Lloyd George had been in World War I, and certainly not that Lloyd George himself would have done better in World War II. But, as Attlee later observed, there was some truth in Lloyd George's comment on Churchill: 'he's got ten ideas and one of them is right, but he never knows which it is'.[160]

Certainly, in the first half of 1941, there appeared significant reasons to cast doubt on Churchill's effectiveness. British forces were sent to Greece in March. (Lloyd George later claimed to have advised the Prime Minister against this in person.)[161] They had to be withdrawn in April, in the face of a German invasion; 11,000 troops were lost. Also in April the British army in North Africa, which had performed well against the Italians, had to retreat swiftly in the face of newly arrived German forces headed by Erwin Rommel. Public criticism grew, although Churchill himself, of course, was by no means exclusively responsible for all the problems. On the 16th of the month, Cecil King lunched at Churt, where he found that Lloyd George had been mulling the political prospects. 'If we definitely defeat the Germans in Libya, Lloyd George thought Churchill could survive the evacuation of Greece; but if we did badly there would be considerable political repercussions', King wrote. He added: 'He considers Winston would remain as premier, but would have to accept the guidance of a Cabinet of five or so members without portfolio.' It was clear, in King's view, that Lloyd George expected to be a member of such a Cabinet.[162] Ten days later Lloyd George saw Robert Menzies, the Australian Prime Minister and, to the now familiar criticisms of the existing War Cabinet system, he added the contention that 'Winston should be at the helm, instead of touring the bombed areas'.[163] Guy Liddell, MI5's Director of Counter-Espionage, noted on 6 May that Lloyd George was surrounded by a small group of MPs (including Hore-Belisha) who intended to attack the government. (It is not clear what Liddell's sources of information were.) 'No personal attack on Winston is contemplated and Lloyd George's ultimate object is to get into the Cabinet on his own terms', he wrote.[164] But if Lloyd George really did contemplate entering the Cabinet, he can only have done so as one contemplates certain kinds of agreeable fantasy, that one would in practice be unwilling to fulfil. He would have found some reason or other for rejecting any terms that Churchill might have realistically offered.

In fact, the time for that was now past. The Prime Minister, who had previously pursued Lloyd George with an ardour that may well seem excessive, now appears to have taken a deliberate decision to make sure that he could never return. At the beginning of May Leo Amery noted in his diary that he had heard that Beaverbrook 'had had a row with Winston over the question of whether L.G. should be invited into the Government'.[165] If the intelligence was correct, the only credible explanation is that Beaverbrook was still pressing for this, but that Churchill was now opposed. The Prime Minister's attitude became plain during the debate on the progress of the war that took place on 6–7 May 1941. The government had called for a vote of confidence – and the sense of occasion was heightened by the fact that this was almost the exact anniversary of the Norway debate that had brought down Chamberlain the previous year.

On the second day Lloyd George spoke from the opposition front bench. He pointed out the seriousness of the situation, but it was not an overtly defeatist speech: 'we have suffered severe wounds, painful and serious wounds, none fatal, in my judgement, but grave if neglected'. He concluded with a call for a 'real War Council'. Churchill, he said, was 'a man with a very brilliant mind – but for that very reason he wanted a few more ordinary persons to look after him', independent people who would stand up to him.[166] This was the occasion of which Harold Nicolson wrote fancifully of Lloyd

George gazing at Churchill 'with love'. Chips Channon painted a rather more plausible picture. 'Lloyd George fulminated for a full hour: he was weak at times, at others sly and shrewd, and often vindicative [*sic*] as he attacked the Government.' Channon observed that Churchill 'was obviously shaken, for he shook, twitched, and his hands were never still'. When the Prime Minister rose, however, he was in brilliant form, 'pungent, amusing, cruel, [and] hard-hitting'.[167] The cruelty was evident in his treatment of Lloyd George:

> I must ... say that I did not think Mr. Lloyd George's speech was particularly helpful at a period of what he himself called discouragement and disheartenment. It was not the sort of speech which one would have expected from the great war leader of former days, who was accustomed to brush aside despondency and alarm, and push on irresistibly towards the final goal. It was the sort of speech with which, I imagine, the illustrious and venerable Marshal Pétain might well have enlivened the closing days of M. Reynaud's Cabinet.[168]

Lloyd George stayed, as convention obliged, to hear Churchill's speech, but as soon as it was over he was out of the Commons 'like a shot out of a gun'.[169] He abstained in the vote of confidence, which the government won by a crushing 477 votes to 3. 'Churchill's speech to the House of Commons: excuses and very little information', noted Goebbels in his diary. 'But no sign of weakness ... Lloyd George's criticisms were harsh but will not meet with general approval. England's will to resist is still intact.'[170] Interestingly, though, Lloyd George's criticisms did meet approval from P. J. Grigg, the Permanent Secretary at the War Office (not to be confused with Edward Grigg, Lloyd George's former private secretary). Grigg was trusted by Churchill, so much so that in due course he appointed him Secretary of State for War, which was a most unusual career progression for a civil servant. After the debate Grigg wrote to his father: 'I agreed with nearly all L-G said & in some ways it is a pity that Winston's immense dialectical skill should have enabled him to get away with it so easily – for unless more drive at the top is shown there is trouble coming.'[171]

Churchill's wounding comparison of Lloyd George to Pétain – which drew loud, appreciative laughter – had surely not been made spontaneously. We may guess that, as with many of Churchill's 'impromptu witticisms', there had been careful preparation. As the Prime Minister was well aware, other people had been drawing the same parallel ever since the fall of France. It is unlikely to have been just a stray remark that slipped off his tongue in the heat of the moment. Presumably he calculated that it was necessary in order to undermine support for Lloyd George (the strength of which he may have overestimated). He must also have known that, once he had given the insult his imprimatur, it would 'stick', as Dalton noted with glee.[172] The comment marked, therefore, Churchill's final and public acceptance that he could never again ally himself with Lloyd George. The two men had had, of course, supposedly irrevocable bust-ups before, which had been followed by further bouts of political cooperation. But although Churchill had clung to the idea of renewed collaboration with incredible tenacity until only a few months before, this was the end of the road. He had ceased to draw political strength from the relationship – although not, as will be seen in the final section of this book, from its reputation.

How did Lloyd George react to Churchill's damaging verbal assault on him? John Grigg writes that 'Despite the "Pétain" gibe, there was no personal breach between the two men.'[173] By contrast, some authors assert, in identical terms, that 'Lloyd George never forgave the insult'.[174] The former view is an example of the prevalent, romantic interpretation of the men's relationship; the latter forms an interesting exception to it. There is, undoubtedly, evidence to support both opinions. Grigg notes that, for example, in September 1941 the men had a three-hour lunch at 10 Downing Street – hardly a sign of estrangement. Moreover, on one occasion, Beaverbrook, in yet a further attempt to get Lloyd George into the government, sent Michael Foot, one of his journalists, to try to persuade him to take office. The response was 'Who? Me? Old Papa Pétain?'– but Lloyd George laughed as he said it.[175] On the other hand, two months after the debate, Frank Owen, the editor of the *Evening Standard*, found that 'Old Lloyd George was very bitter about being called Pétain by Churchill in the House of Commons.' (Lloyd George also complained to him that Churchill spent too much time 'looking down the barrels of guns'.)[176] Sylvester's diary confirms that, at the very least, Lloyd George found the remark highly disconcerting: 'There is no doubt that it went right home.'[177] It seems, then, that the idea that Churchill and Lloyd George continued in undimmed mutual regard is not wholly plausible – but, by the same token, it was not true that there was now a sharp rupture in what had previously been a harmonious relationship. The negative elements of Lloyd George's view of Churchill were, as we have seen, long established. The Pétain remark may have intensified the existing bitterness. At the same time affection – or the tropes of behaviour that had, in their relationship, often passed for signs of it – had not entirely disappeared.

One thing about the episode is indisputable: in its aftermath, Lloyd George entered the final phase of his political marginalization. Churchill was not yet out of the woods. Crete fell to the Germans at the end of May, leading to renewed criticism of the government. But Lloyd George did not renew his Commons attack: he was, in fact, never to make another major speech there. There were still those who wanted to get him into the government. Among these were the usual suspects, such as Lady Astor, who assured him he would only need to do three hours' work a day.[178] There were also some new figures involved. Hankey, who had made efforts to keep Lloyd George out in 1939, now wanted him in. The change is doubtless explained by his own increasing disaffection with Churchill, who had demoted him from the War Cabinet in 1940, and who was to sack him altogether in 1942. Hankey's efforts – which also involved Edward Grigg – unsurprisingly bore no fruit. The message that eventually came back to Hankey, via Grigg, was that 'Ll.G. thinks that nothing short of unseating Winston will do any good.'[179] (Lloyd George had not argued before that Churchill should actually be dispensed with.) Another man who tried to persuade Lloyd George was P. J. Grigg.[180] He was a fairly heavyweight figure, but support for Lloyd George was mainly the preserve of a disaffected and somewhat eccentric minority. 'An Opposition is being formed out of the left-outs of all Parties, – LG, Hore-Belisha, [Emanuel] Shinwell [a Labour MP], [Earl] Winterton [a Conservative MP], and some small fry, mostly National Liberals', Churchill wrote to his son in June. 'They do their best to abuse us whenever the war news gives us an opportunity, but there is not the slightest sign that the House as a whole, or still less the country, will swerve from their purpose.'[181]

Lloyd George, although isolated, had not changed his opinions. He revealed to Hankey in May 1941 that he had recently impressed upon Churchill that he was 'dead against his constant reiteration that he would never make peace with Hitler or any of his gang'. That attitude, he thought, would merely prolong the war. 'When Ll.G. had said this kind of thing to Winston the latter had replied "Nothing would induce me to treat with these fellows". Whereat Mrs. Churchill had piped in with 'Well, Mr. Lloyd George, we can all change our minds can't we?'[182] (That, perhaps, was a hint that even she agreed that her husband was being too stubborn.) After the two men's lunch in September, Lloyd George commented that 'Churchill had clearly shown his unsuitability for the premiership'.[183] He declined to take political action, though. 'I am afraid it would be in vain for my voice to be lifted in protest or criticism as long as Winston has the unchallenged control of war direction', he wrote to Lady Milner. 'He is displaying all the qualities of brilliant, but erratic judgement, pursued with blind stubbornness which characterised his actions in the last war.'[184]

In spite of the entry of Russia into the war in June 1941, and of the USA in December, bad war news did not dry up. In February 1942, after the fall of Singapore to the Japanese, Cecil King's secretary saw Lloyd George at the House of Commons. 'He was stamping up and down and calling Churchill "the old fool", and saying that he had burnt all the bridges behind him and stopped up all possible ways of escape.'[185] After the fall of Tobruk to the Germans in June of the same year, Lloyd George encouraged parliamentary rebels to press a vote of censure to a division – which in the event the government won handsomely – although he was not present in the Commons himself when it took place. King heard that 'Lloyd George won't take any strong line himself, because he does not want to damage Gwilym's political career'.[186] On another occasion, Lloyd George gave Shinwell a somewhat more edifying reason for declining to participate in active opposition. 'This is Winnie's war. I have had mine.'[187] By this stage – mid-1942 – even Beaverbrook had written off his hopes of Lloyd George returning to office.[188]

The disasters of 1942 put Churchill under continued pressure. His key rival was not Lloyd George, but Stafford Cripps. After his return from Russia in January, Cripps won considerable popularity, because of his perceived role in bringing the Soviets into the war. On the back of this he entered the War Cabinet in February, although Churchill did not much care for his austere ways and somewhat haughty manner. In March, Basil Liddell Hart recorded a conversation with Lloyd George:

Talking of Winston, L.G. reflected that he was 'so much of a child'. Now, according to reports of many who are in close contact with him, he seems to have lost confidence in himself, and, feeling troubled, was wanting to find someone he could lean on – as, in similar circumstances, he had turned to L.G. in the past. That was why his action in taking Cripps into the Cabinet was not so unwilling as was popularly believed – part of him was quite eager to have Cripps to take a share of the responsibility.[189]

These comments are intriguing because they suggest a plausible motivation for Churchill's earlier, rather desperate, attempts to bring Lloyd George himself into the government. Cripps soon differed with Churchill over the conduct of the war. Nonetheless, a clash between them in the autumn of 1942 did not provoke a crisis, because Cripps agreed to postpone his resignation until the outcome of General Montgomery's campaign in the North African desert was known. 'You are an honest man', Churchill told him. 'If you had been Ll.G. you would have resigned on the issue of a "second front".'[190] This was a reference to the public campaign in favour of Russia's demand that Britain and America launch an attack in Europe, to which Lloyd George did indeed show signs of sympathy. In November, after Montgomery's victory at El Alamein, Cripps accepted demotion to the Ministry of Aircraft Production. After this, Churchill's political position was secure.

For the remainder of the war Churchill no longer had much cause to think of Lloyd George. The latter did occasionally creep into the Prime Minister's conversational recollections. During one lengthy Cabinet monologue, for example, he gave 'great praise to Lloyd George', saying that his insight and judgement at the end of the previous war had been 'quite wonderful'.[191] There were still occasional direct contacts between the two. In May 1942 they discussed the problem of the Soviet Union's claim to the Baltic States, and Lloyd George may have succeeded in influencing government policy on this question.[192] In July he and Churchill lunched together once more. In October, J. C. Smuts, the South African Premier, addressed both Houses of Parliament. Lloyd George, acting as chairman, introduced him. Dalton, for one, was not impressed by Lloyd George's reference to 'this terrible war': 'He said nothing to show which side he was on.'[193] Afterwards, Chips Channon came across Churchill, Smuts and Lloyd George sitting together. He noted that 'Of the three only the bronzed South African looked fit.'[194] A few days later Randolph Churchill sent his father a letter, in which he passed on the substance of a conversation he had had with Henry Fildes, a Liberal National MP who was in touch with Lloyd George. 'He confirms his inherent Pétainism', Randolph wrote. 'Fildes says that even at Churt Ll.G. sleeps every night in a deep shelter!'[195] This was bitchy, but not completely off the mark. A few weeks earlier Liddell Hart found that Lloyd George, having earlier briefly taken a more positive and aggressive line on the war, was again 'as pessimistic as ever, and also showing signs of age'.[196]

Lloyd George was certainly in serious decline now. In January 1943 he managed only a halting reply to Eden's tribute to him on his eightieth birthday. In February he recorded a vote in favour of a rebel Labour amendment, which pressed for the immediate adoption of Sir William Beveridge's recently published social security plan, which was to form the cornerstone of the post-war welfare state. (Churchill thought Beveridge 'an awful windbag and a dreamer', which is some indication of the distance he had travelled, in terms of his attitude to social reform, since his pre-World War I Liberal days.)[197] In June Churchill, after making a parliamentary statement, spoke briefly to Lloyd George, and in September they talked at the bar of the House of Commons. 'It was strange to see those two fathers of victory standing there together', Harold Nicolson observed. 'The eyes of the House were upon them.'[198] He had earlier written a striking and slightly cruel description of Lloyd George's advancing decrepitude: 'for an instant the old charm and vigour reappeared, but then once again there fell on his face that mask of extreme and inarticulate old age. He is now a yellow old man with a mane of dead-white hair, and uncertain movements of his feet and hands.'[199]

In October Lloyd George at last married Frances Stevenson. The wedding, in Guildford Register Office, took place in spite of the vociferous and even hysterical opposition of his daughter Megan. The rest of his family were not best pleased either. Among the flood of congratulations from other quarters was a message from Winston and Clementine Churchill. Presumably, at some point during the previous thirty years, Churchill had cottoned on to the nature of Stevenson's relationship with Lloyd George, and therefore the news of the wedding cannot have been any great shock. At any rate, when he met the couple in the Commons the following year he acted graciously to Frances Lloyd George, as she now was.

In January 1944 Churchill sent a telegram of congratulations to Lloyd George on his birthday, and received a message of thanks in reply. There was a further exchange in May, after a meeting of the Other Club. Smuts and Churchill telegraphed: 'The Other Club send you their affectionate greetings. We missed you very much last night but we hope you will take the chair at our victory dinner.' Lloyd George responded to Churchill: 'Many thanks for yours and Smuts telegram. Looking forward to victory dinner, but you must take the chair. Best luck to you.'[200] On 24 May he went to the Commons to hear Churchill make a speech on foreign affairs, and did so once more on 6 June for the latter's statement on the successful Allied landings in Normandy. After that, he never went again. Frances Lloyd George sent a telegram to Churchill upon his birthday in November and, the following month, the Prime Minister replied to Lloyd George direct. 'Forgive me for being so long in replying to your message on my birthday. I learnt a lot from you and shall always be grateful for your great kindness and friendship to me. I hope to see you soon – Winston Churchill'.[201] Churchill, of course, had often felt bitter resentment towards Lloyd George in the past, but he glossed this over. Given that Lloyd George clearly did not have long to live, this was, undoubtedly, the proper thing to do. By issuing warm compliments to a man who had now ceased to be a rival, Churchill gave proof of his own greatest virtue – magnanimity.

By now Lloyd George was suffering from cancer, although he was not informed of the diagnosis. In September he travelled to North Wales. He stayed at Tŷ Newydd, a farm at Llanystumdwy that he had bought in 1940. The visit was supposed to be a brief one, but in fact he never returned to Churt. It was clear that the war in Europe could not now last long, and its end was likely to bring an election. Lloyd George was clearly in no condition to fight his seat, and the other parties locally were unwilling to allow him a walkover. Yet he still hoped to be able to contribute to discussions on the eventual peace settlement. The obvious solution, much as he might regret severing his connection with the Commons, was for him to go to the House of Lords, which in earlier days he had so vigorously denounced. On 18 December, at Tŷ Newydd, he received an urgent message that had been couriered from London. 'L.G. opened it', Sylvester recorded. 'I watched his face. The contents seemed to give him pleasure. He said not a word, but his eyes showed that he was reading it again. Then he handed it to Frances, with the remark: "That is very nice." '202 The letter read:

> My dear David,
>   Some of your friends have been to me expressing the desire to spare you the labours of a contested election at Criccieth. It has occurred to me that perhaps you might be willing to allow me to submit your name to the King for an Earldom. I have reason to believe that this would be agreeable to His Majesty, and I am sure it would give the greatest pleasure to all those who worked with you and under you in the old days, and to none more than to
>   Your old friend,
>   Winston S. Churchill

The next day Lloyd George sent a telegram to Downing Street: 'Gratefully accept'. The day after that he sent a follow-up letter, expressing his gratitude to Churchill 'for suggesting such a high honour for an old friend'.203 The announcement was made in the 1945 New Year honours list, and he took the title Earl Lloyd-George of Dwyfor. But he did not live to see the peace. By February his health had taken a severe turn for the worse. He showed considerable resilience. At the end of the month one of his doctors wrote: 'At one moment he is too weak to talk, and the next he is walking across the room and back, and even jokingly refers to going out.'204 He struggled on until 26 March, when he died in bed, attended by his wife, his daughters, Sylvester, and others.

There are two pathos-ridden final entries in Frances Lloyd George's diary, which she had not kept consistently for some years. One is from 24 May 1944, and records Lloyd George's last conversation with Churchill:

> D. decided on Wednesday to go to hear Winston's speech, and we are both glad, for the House gave him (D.) a touching welcome. I wonder if they realize how near it may be to his last appearances [sic]. Winston, whom we met in the corridor afterwards, was nice to us both. D. was rather inclined to be critical of the Government's policy, but I thought Winston very patient & I finally managed to turn the conversation to his pictures: we

parted very happily. It was a perfect spring day, but as we drove through the smiling countryside there was a heavy sadness in my heart.

The other entry is dated 27 May but, coming first in the original diary, is perhaps from an earlier year:

D. & I today discussed Lord Acton and his phrase 'I have no contemporaries'. I said the same thing might apply to D. He agreed, & said, 'I regard Winston as my only contemporary. We have always been friends. That is the reason that I have preferred to adopt an attitude of indifference to his policy and his Government – instead of openly quarrelling.'[205]

It is a telling comment on their relationship that Lloyd George was able to acknowledge Churchill as his contemporary – that is, as his equal – only once the latter had, after so many years in his shadow, at last eclipsed him in reputation.

Chapter Eleven

EPILOGUE

CHURCHILL WAS TOLD OF Lloyd George's death the evening of the day it happened, after he returned to London from a short visit to the Western Front. The following day, 27 March, both Houses of Parliament adjourned out of respect, and on the 28th tributes were paid in the Lords and Commons. Churchill's speech was effective, but not spectacularly so. His most quotable line was that Lloyd George 'was the greatest Welshman which that unconquerable race has produced since the age of the Tudors'.[1] Clementine Churchill approved. 'I loved your speech about Ll.G.', she wrote to her husband after she read it. 'It recalled forgotten blessings which he showered upon the meek & lowly.'[2] John Colville, by contrast, considered his tribute 'eloquent in parts and well delivered but not, I thought, as good as that he paid to Neville Chamberlain in 1940'.[3]

Other speakers inevitably drew parallels between Lloyd George and Churchill. Aneurin Bevan, for example, observed that the deceased 'was, like the Prime Minister, a formidable and even terrifying debater, but he possessed what the Prime Minister also possesses, and that is the generosity of greatness'. He also made the comment, quoted in the introduction to this book, that there was a lesson to be learned from the two men's exclusion from office between the wars. It demonstrated that even the most powerful personalities could only be politically effective if allied with 'great mass machines'.[4] Some people were also moved to make private comparisons between the two. When he heard of Lloyd George's death, Leo Amery noted in his diary: 'The essence of the difference lies in the fact that Ll.G. was purely external and receptive, the result of intercourse with his fellow men, and non-existent in their absence, while Winston is literary and expressive of himself with hardly any contact with other minds.'[5]

Lloyd George was buried on 30 March, not in Westminster Abbey, as Churchill had anticipated, but on the banks of the River Dwyfor, as he himself had desired.[6] The coffin was transported to the spot on a farm cart, with the mourners following on foot. Churchill made efforts to ensure that those of Lloyd George's grandsons who were in the armed forces were able to attend. It was not an occasion at which public figures were expected to be present, and so Churchill himself was not there; he went instead to the memorial service held in Westminster Abbey in April. Churchill later spoke 'with scorn' of Lloyd George's 'farm-cart funeral', according to his doctor, Lord Moran. He said that he, for his own part, wanted to be buried like a soldier. ' "Very well, dear," Clemmie interposed soothingly, "you shall be buried like a soldier." '[7] Both men, clearly, were concerned that their deaths should be attended by the appropriate symbolism. Lloyd George wanted to reaffirm the simplicity of his roots, and his commitment to Wales, which in truth had at times been somewhat ambivalent; Churchill wanted to be remembered as a man of military as much as of political action.

During the war Churchill had assured Anthony Eden, his designated successor, that he would 'not make Lloyd George's mistake of carrying on after the war'.[8] In fact, at the time of Lloyd George's death he had another ten years of active political life ahead of him – much to Eden's frustration. As long as he remained in politics, he did his best to extract kudos from Lloyd George's political legacy, and from his own former association with him. There were compelling reasons for him to do so. First, it was a means to win over Liberal voters to the Tory colours. Second, he hoped to prevent those in other parties from making their own claims to the Lloyd George mantle. Nor was it insignificant that both Gwilym and Megan Lloyd George were still in politics.

In May 1945, after the Allies had achieved victory in Europe, the Labour and Liberal parties withdrew from Churchill's coalition. He therefore formed a caretaker government, to rule until an election could be held. Although the new administration was bound to be predominantly Conservative, he wanted it to have as broad a base as possible, so that it might maintain at least some vestigial claims to 'National' above-party status. Gwilym Lloyd-George[9] was to form a convenient Liberal fig-leaf to protect the modesty of the government's ample and largely naked Tory flesh. He was an able but not a driven man, and had entered parliament only because of paternal pressure. In his unpublished memoirs he made the paradoxical admission that 'I thoroughly enjoyed over thirty years in the House of Commons, but, in a sense, I can truthfully say that I was bored by politics.'[10] He was popular with MPs, and was an admirer of Churchill who, in turn, supported his failed 1942 bid to become Speaker. In March 1945, just a few days before his father's death, he made a public statement of his intention to fight the next election 'as a Liberal candidate supporting the National Government'.[11] Therefore, when the other Liberals left office, he continued in post as Minister of Fuel and Power. There were a few other non-Tories in the government as well, including the remnants of the National Liberals. The sixth Earl of Rosebery, son of Lord Rosebery, the former Liberal Prime Minister, became Secretary of State for Scotland, which fractionally strengthened the government's Liberal credentials.

During the election campaign Churchill stressed his own liberalism. 'I am a Liberal as much as a Tory', he claimed in a speech in Oldham, one of his former stamping grounds, not long before polling day. 'I do not understand why Liberals pretend they are different from us. We fight and stand for freedom and we have succeeded in bringing forward a programme that any Liberal government led by Mr. Lloyd George or Mr. Asquith would have been proud to carry through in a Parliament.'[12] This was also one theme of the notorious election broadcast in which he claimed that a socialist government 'would have to fall back on some form of *Gestapo*, no doubt very humanely directed in the first instance'. He emphasized that the government still had 'a Rosebery and a Lloyd-George to carry forward the flags of their fathers'.[13] His claim to the tradition was, of course, contested. Megan Lloyd George claimed that she, as an opponent of the government, was upholding her father's beliefs: 'I am a David Lloyd-George Liberal.'[14] One Labour tactic was to claim that there was indeed an analogy between Lloyd George and Churchill. 'If Mr. Churchill were to win this election the consequences would be exactly what they were after the Tory victory of 1918', argued Harold Laski, Chairman of Labour's National Executive Committee. 'They would use Mr. Churchill for their purposes and would then throw him over in the same way as the Tory party threw over Lloyd George when they had squeezed out of him the last drop of utility they could get.'[15]

Laski's comments were part of a wider strategy. Churchill was undoubtedly popular as an individual. Labour's best hope, therefore, was to acknowledge his strengths as a war leader, and avoid personal attacks on him, whilst suggesting that if returned to power he would be in hock to a reactionary Tory Party and no good as a peacetime premier. This approach seems to have worked. When the results were announced on 26 July it turned out that Labour, with 393 seats, had won a landslide victory. Attlee became Prime Minister; the war with Japan ended shortly afterwards.

Churchill, understandably, took his defeat hard. Clement Davies had replaced Sinclair as Liberal leader, because the latter had lost his seat in the election. 'I want to tell you that we are deeply concerned about Winston', Davies told Sinclair a few months later. 'He is a great man, a great figure and an outstanding personality, but something is going amiss. Sometimes he behaves like an ill-mannered gamin, making faces and putting out his tongue and so on. To me and a great number of us this is more than sad. It is a tragedy and we wish to heaven someone could persuade him to keep away and do the task that he and he alone can worthily perform, namely, writing the history of the wonderful part played by this old country in the war.'[16] Churchill was in fact, at that very time, preparing for the epic task of writing his memoirs. They were published in six volumes between 1948 and 1954. Yet he showed no inclination to abandon front-line politics. Major international speeches, notably at Fulton, Missouri and at Zurich in 1946, helped cement his reputation. This may in turn have helped him recover some of his lost equilibrium.

As Leader of the Opposition Churchill demonstrated a powerful interest in the Liberal Party. He was eager to work with it in order to build a broad anti-socialist front as a means of regaining office, or, failing that, to establish the Tories' claims to be the true heirs of Liberalism. The Liberals themselves – reduced to a mere dozen MPs – recognized early in the new parliament that Churchill would continue to try exploit the Lloyd George name. Sinclair wrote to Davies in December 1945: 'Gwilym is behaving badly. What are we to do about him? – leave him to smoulder on the Tory bonfire, or try to snatch him from the burning?' Sinclair favoured trying to win him back – which in fact was a lost cause. One of his arguments for doing so was that otherwise 'The Tories will boast, at the next

Election – as Winston boasted in the last Election – of having a Lloyd
George in their ranks.'[17]

Churchill, for his part, took the view that 'A Party is not a club,
becoming more and more eclectic. It ought to be a "snowball starting
an avalanche".'[18] He therefore stressed in public that Conservatives
and Liberals should work together as 'co-belligerents' against the
Labour government.[19] He achieved mixed success. In May 1947,
under the so-called Woolton–Teviot pact, the residuum of the
National Liberals agreed to form joint constituency associations with
the Conservatives. However, many in the Liberal Party proper were
enraged when parliamentary candidates were selected by those associations to run under the label 'Liberal and Conservative' or some
such variant thereof. (There were around fifty such candidates,
including Gwilym Lloyd-George, in the 1950 election, although even
in his case a large section of the local Conservative Association would
have much preferred a genuine Tory.)[20] They thought their party
name was being misappropriated. The resultant bad feeling did
nothing to assist Churchill's hopes of cooperation with the independent Liberals.

There were some within the Liberal Party, such as Violet Bonham
Carter, who were sympathetic to the idea of cooperation, but there
was considerable hostility from others, including Clement Davies. In
August 1947 Lord Woolton, the Conservative Party Chairman, sent
Churchill some extracts from recent Liberal speeches. 'They are as
violently partisan and anti-Tory as anything the Socialists have ever
perpetrated,' he wrote, 'and I think we delude ourselves if we imagine
that such people will enter into any agreement with us.'[21] Churchill
responded robustly, urging Woolton to do everything in his power 'to
promote unity of action with the Liberals on the basis of an Independent Liberal Party. On this being achieved depends the future revival
of Britain.'[22] Moreover, in 1948, he expressed to his Shadow Cabinet
'the wish that Liberals who wished to join the Conservative Party
should be given every facility to get seats.'[23] In the general election of
February 1950, the Liberals put forward 475 candidates. This threatened to split the anti-Labour vote. There was an extremely limited
number of local pacts with the Conservatives – but the idea did not
spread, rather, we may imagine, to Churchill's chagrin.

During the election campaign itself Churchill went so far as to
offer one of the Conservative Party's broadcast slots to Bonham

Carter, who had not been one of the Liberal Party's own chosen broadcasters. She turned it down, seemingly at the behest of Davies, and with apparent regret. In his speeches, Churchill had to spend efforts rebutting the allegation that, when Home Secretary in 1910, 'he had sent troops to shoot down Welsh miners' in the Tonypandy riots.[24] (In fact, no one had been killed.) He also sought to make more positive use of the memory of the past, in order to claim some credit himself for Labour's popular reforms:

> I was the friend and comrade of the most famous Welshman of our time, David Lloyd George ... He it was who launched the Liberal forces of this country effectively into the broad stream of social betterment and social security along which all modern parties now steer. Nowadays this is called 'the welfare State'. We did not christen it, but it was our child.

At the same time he made oblique reference to Bevan who, as Attlee's Minister of Health, had pioneered the National Health Service. Labour liked to portray Bevan as 'a second Lloyd George'; but, Churchill emphasized, 'There can be no greater insult to his memory'.[25]

The result of the election was disappointing to all sides. Labour won – which was naturally displeasing to the Conservatives – but its majority was reduced to a mere five seats, meaning that another election was likely soon. (Labour could take a small amount of comfort from its candidate's narrow defeat of Gwilym Lloyd-George at Pembroke.) The Liberals lost three seats – a quarter of their total representation – and 319 deposits. Yet Churchill's enthusiasm for cooperation with the Liberals remained undimmed. 'I am having a very difficult time with Churchill', wrote Woolton that September. 'He is determined to bring about some arrangement with the Liberals ... A month ago he asked me to see him, and I told him that I saw no prospect of the Party finding his views acceptable. It was a difficult meeting, in which he told me that of course he would resign if he could not have his way: I told him that I thought perhaps we had better both resign, and then there need not be any further conversation about it.'[26] Neither man did so, but stalemate had been achieved.

It seems unlikely that the Tories could in fact have gained much from a pact or alliance. When the next election came, in October

1951, the Liberals could muster only 109 candidates. Churchill, seeking to sweep up as many ex-Liberal voters as possible, continued to play the Lloyd George card. (Not exclusively so, however; he also emphasized the Asquith connection by speaking for Bonham Carter, who had no Conservative opponent, at Colne Valley. She lost anyway.) He lent strong support to Gwilym Lloyd-George, who, despite deep divisions in the local party association, stood and won as a Conservative at Newcastle. Elsewhere, Conservative leaflets quoted a 1925 denunciation of socialism by David Lloyd George – he had described it as 'the very negation of liberty' – and also included a picture of him. Megan Lloyd George protested against this attempt by the Tories to claim her father's endorsement from beyond the grave.[27] She herself was narrowly defeated at Anglesey.

The Conservatives won the general election with a majority of seventeen. Although the Liberals won only six seats, Churchill offered a Cabinet post to Clement Davies, who, in refusing, helped to safeguard the future of the Liberals as an independent political force. Churchill made Gwilym Lloyd-George Minister of Food and then, in 1954, Home Secretary. We should not imagine that he was motivated in these appointments exclusively by the belief that the Lloyd George name won votes. He also discerned other qualities in Gwilym. One of the Home Secretary's duties was to review the cases of prisoners who had been sentenced to death by the courts and decide whether or not to grant clemency. Churchill remarked privately that Gwilym 'would hang them all right if he had to'.[28]

Churchill's final term in office formed a rather sad coda to his career. His refusal to give up the reins of power, even after he suffered a stroke in June 1953, has long been a stick in the hands of those who wish to demythologize him. He was not a completely spent force. His public speeches often showed the old brilliance, and his private remarks the familiar wit. There were some policy achievements – in terms of housing, for example, and in foreign affairs – but these were mainly the responsibility of his subordinates. The Prime Minister's own doomed pursuit of a rapprochement with the Soviet Union was an embarrassment, if not positively risky to the Anglo-American alliance. His behaviour was increasingly erratic. He had, however, long since been a national institution, and as such was very hard to dislodge. In July 1954 Harold Macmillan suggested to Eden that Churchill's 'almost child-like determination to get his way at all costs and regardless of other results must be, partly at any rate, a result of his mental illness'.[29] This was a bit unfair – but only a bit. It is hard to say whether Churchill's barnacle-like clinging to office was more or less appealing than Lloyd George's comparable determination, in 1940, to devise ingenious excuses for remaining in retirement. At last his position became unsustainable and in April 1955, at the age of 80, he finally retired as Prime Minister. Eden, who succeeded him, called an election, which took place in May.

During the campaign Churchill – who remained an MP – made a number of speeches in support of the government. On 17 May he spoke at Biggleswade, where there was no Liberal candidate standing. Gwilym Lloyd-George had been booked to speak for the Conservatives; Megan Lloyd George, who had recently joined the Labour Party, was planning to campaign for the other side. In his speech Churchill ridiculed Megan's decision to become a 'convert to Socialism'. 'This is a big jump for anyone, especially for her father's daughter, to take', he said.[30] The next day she hit back, criticizing Churchill's habit of quoting her father's 1925 attack on socialism, which had been made, she pointed out, at a time when circumstances had been rather different. 'But no one knows better than Sir Winston Churchill how embarrassing it is to be confronted with speeches from the past', she went on. 'I hesitate in this mild election to recall some of the gloriously vituperative things he said about the Conservatives.'[31] The day after, the Conservatives announced that Frances Lloyd George intended to vote Conservative.[32]

It is doubtful that any of this had a significant impact on the outcome of the election, which the Conservatives won handsomely. It is clear, nevertheless, that, a decade after the death of the man himself, Lloyd George's name retained some of its symbolism. Gwilym continued as Home Secretary during Eden's brief premiership, but lost office when Harold Macmillan became Prime Minister, and was 'kicked upstairs' to the House of Lords. The following month – February 1957 – Megan won a by-election for Labour at Carmarthen. Although her new party considered her enough of an asset to include her in its general election broadcasts, she was never given a front-bench role, nor was she given office when Labour won in 1964. For as long as Churchill had remained leader of the Conservatives, there had still been a 'Lloyd George factor' in British politics; but after he stood down it withered away.

Ironically, Churchill's post-1945 efforts to use his past connection
with Lloyd George to his political advantage were made at a time
when the latter's historical reputation was in the doldrums, if not in
actual decline. Of course, his prestige had long since fallen from the
heights of 1918. Churchill himself, writing in 1931, had blamed this
on Lloyd George's obsession with the minutiae of post-World War I
Liberal Party politics. Lloyd George's manipulations, he argued with
perception, had continued 'ceaselessly and perennially until the
British public and the world at large have not only lost all interest in
the game, but have almost forgotten, nay doubted and disputed, the
glorious days which went before'.[33] Lloyd George's 1936 visit to
Hitler does not appear to have done him, at the time, as much harm
as, with the benefit of hindsight, one might expect. But his advocacy
of a compromise peace in 1939 dealt another blow to his stature.
Even sympathetic biographers were subsequently forced to concede
that his attitude 'at this stage bewildered and pained many of his
friends, and seemed very much out of keeping with his known
character'.[34] When Churchill compared him to Pétain in 1941, it
appeared merely to confirm what was already being widely said.
Lloyd George's subsequent acceptance of a peerage – which was
disliked even by members of his own family – drew further criticism,
from those who thought he had undermined such radical credentials
as he retained. It seemed, by the time of his death, that he could no
longer do anything right. It was not, of course, that everyone had
forgotten his achievements, but the new generation did not hold him
in great esteem. In 1946 Robert Bruce Lockhart commented to
Anthony Eden and Toby Low, a young Conservative MP, that 'the
question of the relative greatness of Winston and Lloyd George'
would be worthy of study. Lockhart noted in his diary that 'Toby
Low, who was a little boy in the last war, was surprised that anyone
would put L.G. on the same level. Anthony after some consideration
gave the verdict in favour of W.S.C. but pointed out that in wartime
every leader was, to some extent, built up artificially.'[35] Subsequently,
the fate of Lloyd George's reputation was entangled in rivalries
between biographers and other would-be custodians of his memory.

Lloyd George left his papers not to his children but to his widow.
The reason for this, according to Gwilym, was his opinion that no
son should ever write his father's life. 'There is only one exception',
Lloyd George apparently said: 'that is W.S.C. in the life of his

father'.[36] He may have made a comparatively wise choice. Gwilym did not have a biographer's disposition or the time to complete the job and when, in 1960, Richard Lloyd George produced a ghost-written volume, which made allegations about his father's sexual infidelities, it was considered by many to be a hatchet-job. Frances Lloyd George, for her part, wanted an 'official' life of her late husband, and was eager to discourage anyone other than her nominated biographer from writing about him. She failed. She denied cooperation to Thomas Jones for his biography but Gwilym and Megan – who of course disliked her intensely – offered him access to material they controlled (Jones's book was published in 1950). She also made the mistake of getting on the wrong side of A. J. Sylvester, who claimed she had gone back on a promise to involve him in the preparation of the official biography. His book *The Real Lloyd George*, based to a great extent on his own diaries, was published in 1947. 'The Dowager is mad, for the reason that I am in first', Sylvester wrote privately. 'Well, she should not have double-crossed me.'[37]

Sylvester's volume did not show his late chief in a good light. He had kept copious shorthand notes during his years with Lloyd George and after the book was published nobody successfully challenged his versions of conversations. The account of the visit to Hitler, and the revelation of details of the negotiations about Lloyd George joining the government in 1940, added greatly to the interest of the work. Undoubtedly, though, Sylvester's lengthy time in the demanding but essentially dead-end job of looking after an ex-Prime Minister had made him a rather a bitter man. He had long nursed the vain hope of getting a knighthood; he later claimed that Lloyd George had asked this for him from Churchill in 1944 as a last request, but 'Winston never acknowledged that letter and took no action'.[38] His general sense of resentment may have contributed to the somewhat carping tone of the book, which seemed to revel in the details of Lloyd George's egocentric childishness. The *Manchester Guardian*'s review was probably fair: 'Greatly interesting and important as the book is, you put it down feeling that the man you have met in its pages falls below the stature of the real Lloyd George – the greatest British peace Minister of this century and hardly second to Mr. Churchill as a War Minister.'[39] Churchill, on the basis of the book's reputation, cut Sylvester when he met him in the House of Commons; but then, having read it, changed his attitude. According to Lord Moran, who discussed it with him in December 1947, this was because it revealed the 'outrageous' things Lloyd George had said about him in private. These included the comment that Churchill 'was lacking in judgement' and was 'no leader'. Moran surmised Churchill's train of thought was: 'Perhaps, after all, Lloyd George deserved what Sylvester had given him.'[40]

The official biography, by the journalist Malcolm Thomson, appeared in 1948, and was competent but unexciting. The most interesting thing about it was the introduction by Frances Lloyd George, in which she reflected on, among other things, her husband's relationship with Churchill. The passage is fascinatingly ambivalent. She clearly relished referring to a comment by the late T. E. Lawrence to the effect that Lloyd George had dominated Churchill, and she made plain that Lloyd George had distrusted the latter. Yet she also emphasized the men's delight in each other's company, in spite of their different outlooks and lack of complete mutual understanding. And she promoted the established myth of 'Winston and David', which was to become a historical cliché: 'When they fell out in politics they did not hesitate to express their feelings, but underneath the friendship stood firm.'[41] We may suspect that she sensed that the best way to protect her husband's reputation from continuing assaults was to link it to the still-growing Churchill legend. At the same time, though, she wanted to make absolutely clear who, in her view, had been the senior partner.

After Thomson's book appeared, and needing money, she sold the Lloyd George Papers and her own diary to Beaverbrook. Churchill was concerned about this, and telephoned Beaverbrook, who later recounted the conversation as follows:

> *W.S.C.* 'Am I in the L.G. papers?'
>
> *Max* 'Yes.'
>
> *W.S.C.* 'How do I come out?'
>
> *Max* 'Bloodily.'
>
> *W.S.C.* 'Are you in?'
>
> *Max* 'Yes.'
>
> *W.S.C.* 'How do you come out?'
>
> *Max* 'Bloody awful.'

Churchill, it appears, was relieved.[42] Beaverbrook commissioned a new life of Lloyd George, by Frank Owen, which appeared in 1954. Although marred by a rather melodramatic style – its title, *Tempestuous Journey*, gives the flavour – it was not a bad book. Beaverbrook also made use of the papers in his own works of contemporary history-cum-reminiscence; interestingly, he was one of the few writers on the topic who did not promote the established myth of the Lloyd George–Churchill relationship. Overall, he deserves considerable credit for promoting interest in Lloyd George and facilitating the work of historians. After his death in 1964, the Beaverbrook Library was established to house the papers of Lloyd George and key contemporaries such as Bonar Law. It was closed down in the mid-1970s – Beaverbrook's heirs lacked his imagination and interest in history – but during its brief existence, under the directorship of A. J. P. Taylor, it was a haven for scholars of twentieth-century politics. This coincided with a flowering of historical interest in Lloyd George, reflected in the work of John Grigg, John Campbell and many others. This was not enough, though, to resurrect the fortunes of his popular reputation. The publication of Frances Lloyd George's memoirs in 1967, and her diaries and letters in the 1970s, was invaluable from the historical point of view, as it confirmed the long-standing and intimate nature of her relationship with Lloyd George. (Frances herself died in 1972, having outlived both Gwilym and Megan; when she sent a wreath to the latter's funeral, a friend of the family commented that they would have tossed it into the sea if they hadn't feared that 'it would poison the fish'.)[43] Yet this documentary confirmation of Lloyd George's long-standing unfaithfulness to his first wife was bound to take a toll on his good name, particularly as it spurred Sylvester in turn to publish a much fuller and franker version of his own diary. This helps to explain why it was Churchill, not Lloyd George, who was by now confirmed as the stereotype of the great war leader.

That was also due in part to Churchill's own efforts as an historian-cum-autobiographer. It was not that, in his account of the interwar and World War II period, he unfairly denigrated Lloyd George. His criticisms of him did not go much beyond fair comment. For example, of Hitler's power of fascination, he wrote that 'No one was more completely misled than Mr. Lloyd George, whose rapturous accounts of his conversations make odd reading today.'[44] Of the two men, though, it was Churchill who in general proved the more successful 'memory entrepreneur'. David Reynolds, in his superlative study of Churchill's six volumes, attributes this in part to his sheer talent at writing. He notes that Lloyd George's own war memoirs had been rapturously received at the time they were published, and their author's achievements compared to those of Pitt the Younger. 'But in the 1950s the man and his memoirs were rarely mentioned in the same breath as Churchill. LG had written as an embittered old man whose political career was over. His partisanship was transparent, whereas Churchill's was coloured by literary skill, varnished by current diplomacy and illuminated by a philosophy of history.'[45]

Moreover, Churchill successfully secured for himself an official biography that dominated subsequent historiography. In 1960 he gave his son Randolph permission to write a *Life*, to be published after his death. Randolph's relations with his father had never been easy, but he was keen to demonstrate filial devotion. He completed two volumes before his own death in 1968. The final six volumes, written by Martin Gilbert, appeared over the next twenty years. This invaluable work, although admiring of Churchill, is no mere hagiography; and it is certainly not the case that the 'official' account, in Churchill's memoirs or in the biography, went unchallenged either in his lifetime or afterwards. In particular, the publication of extracts from the diaries of Alan Brooke and Lord Moran was potentially damaging to his reputation, but there were plenty of Churchill partisans ready to rush to the defence. In all, there is a significant contrast with the rivalries, the drip-feed of salacious revelations, and the sheer bitchiness that attended much that was published about Lloyd George.

Once Churchill had been established in the popular mind as the very acme of leadership, in part through these processes of biography and memoir, it was hard to dislodge him, however hard professional historians might work to show that the picture was in fact more complicated. Politicians on both sides of the Atlantic sought to make use of his iconic status in support of their own agendas; and the more they did so, the more they reinforced that status, at the expense of Lloyd George among others. (Senator John F. Kennedy, in his speech accepting the Democratic nomination for the presidency of the USA in July 1960, was unusual in quoting Lloyd George as well as Churchill.) Churchill became a symbol of an idealized form of inspirational 'toughness', against which opponents were measured and found wanting. President George W. Bush has become an arch-exponent of this self-validating approach. In July 2001 he said of Churchill: 'He was a man of great courage. He knew what he believed. And he really kind of went after it in a way that seemed like a Texan to me ... He charged ahead, and the world is better for it.'[46] If it is not easy to imagine him saying the same thing about Lloyd George that is not necessarily a reflection of the latter's intrinsic merits relative to those of Churchill.

The main aspects of the Churchill legend were well established by the time that the man himself left 10 Downing Street. His years of retirement, though, were ridden with pathos. They were not, it is true, entirely devoid of interest or pleasure. Together with his researchers, he completed his massive *History of the English-Speaking Peoples*, work on which had been suspended by the outbreak of war in 1939. He continued to travel, and spent much time in the South of France. As his faculties deteriorated, though, he became increasingly withdrawn and depressed. He could occasionally be prompted to reminisce, and showed glimmers of his old self. In August 1961 Piers Dixon, son of the British ambassador to France, recorded some of his comments: 'Balfour had been the best leader we had had in this century. Lloyd George had not been as good. Chamberlain had been better than Baldwin, in fact quite good.' With a twinkle in his eye, Churchill added: 'But then you see I am prejudiced. The first thing he did when the war started was to ask me to join his government.'[47] One of his last public statements – albeit a rather anodyne one that was probably prepared for him by his private secretary – was a message sent for the celebrations of Lloyd George's centenary in 1963. 'It is most fitting that the Centenary of the birth of the great David Lloyd George should thus be marked', it read. 'His renown and his vast services to our country, in particular during the First World War, will always be remembered.'[48] In 1964 Churchill at last gave up his seat in the House of Commons. That December, shortly after his ninetieth birthday, he attended a dinner of the Other Club, which he and Lloyd George had played a key role in founding over fifty years before. Sir Colin Coote, former editor of the *Daily Telegraph*, observed Churchill on this occasion: 'It had become increasingly difficult to awake the spark, formerly so vital; and all that could be said was that he knew where he was and was happy to be there. With that his colleagues had to be, and were, content.'[49] On 10 January 1965 Churchill had a major stroke and went into a coma. Two weeks later he died, seven decades to the day after his father. During the eloquent tributes paid to him next day in the House of Commons, none of the speakers thought to compare him to Lloyd George.

Could it be, though, that Churchill's reputation now overshadowed that of Lloyd George because the latter was in fact the lesser man? Those who had known both differed on the issue. Contemporaries who at one time or another took the minority line that Lloyd George was superior included Bob Boothby, Aneurin Bevan, Kingsley Martin (editor of the left-wing *New Statesman and Nation*), Cecil King and P. J. Grigg. Not all of these men were of excellent judgement, and perhaps should not be considered too great a loss to the pro-Churchill team. The more orthodox view came to be encapsulated in the phrase, 'Lloyd George was the abler politician, Churchill the greater statesman.'[50] This may seem superficially persuasive. The scientist and writer C. P. Snow, who knew both men, cast doubt on the idea's sufficiency, however. 'It would be perverse not to agree that Churchill had the more rigid and upright character: but I should have thought that it was equally perverse not to agree that L.G. had by far the deeper social insight', he wrote in 1967. 'A progressive-minded man will blind himself to some of L.G.'s faults: a romantic reactionary will do the same for Churchill.'[51] It is worth remembering, too, that – at least in so far as their respective performances as war leaders is concerned – the two men operated in different circumstances. 'Lloyd George was finding his way through an untried field', noted Walter Layton. 'Winston Churchill was applying the lessons of the first war and adapting a highly developed apparatus of government.'[52] Given the potential pitfalls it is perhaps unsurprising that several of the historians who have compared Lloyd George and Churchill have in the end declined to adjudicate between them.

The question, though, is easier to answer if it is reformulated. It may not be very meaningful to ask if Churchill proved himself 'greater' in 1940–45 than Lloyd George did in the rather different conditions of 1916–18. But it seems perfectly sensible to ask about their respective performances *in parallel* during the lengthy period when their careers overlapped. By this measure, from the time of their first meeting in 1901 to the fall of the coalition in 1922, Lloyd

George consistently outclassed Churchill. That is not to say that, when they differed on policy, it was he who was always right. There were some issues, such as the 1914 naval estimates crisis, where Churchill could claim greater foresight; although arguably, as suggested in Chapter 3 of this book, there was more to that controversy than first meets the eye. Lloyd George was, however, more adroit and subtle than Churchill during this period. He was able to attract and maintain a personal following. When he made speeches he did not merely impress his hearers; he often moved them too. He knew how to handle delegations. He tried to get his way through charm rather – on the whole – than by bullying. He was capable of restraint. And most crucially he also had judgement – that elusive thing that Churchill, in spite of his many obvious talents, transparently seemed to lack.

Between 1922 and 1929 the case becomes more difficult, although it is tempting to make it out in favour of Lloyd George, still a genuinely dynamic figure, and his innovative unemployment proposals, over Churchill's economic orthodoxy and his lurid denunciations of socialism. Neither man did much to impress during the short-lived Labour government that followed; but then, neither did anyone else. For the period after 1931, though, Churchill undoubtedly comes out on top. The ill-judged India campaign notwithstanding, he began to show a maturity and constructiveness that now eluded Lloyd George. His warnings about the power of Germany may not have demonstrated total consistency, and his praise of Mussolini still seems shocking. Yet he, at least, carefully avoided visiting Hitler; and in the general tenor of his arguments on foreign policy he had a much greater claim to subsequent vindication than Lloyd George did. In relation to 1939–40, one hardly need draw attention to the contrast between Churchill's steadfastness and Lloyd George's defeatism; and by mid-1941 Lloyd George had ceased to count politically. In January 1944 Cecil King wrote in his diary that Churchill 'stands for our glorious past. That is why he, quite rightly, is seriously afraid only of Lloyd George, who also represents that past.'[53] But, if that had once been true, Churchill no longer had any reason to fear his old colleague. His own superior capacities were by this stage abundantly evident.

It remains only to ask how the two men's attitudes to one another can best be described. C. P. Snow noted how, in old age,

Lloyd George spoke often of Churchill, and 'always in the same tone':

> It was a tone curiously mixed of affection, quasi-respect, and a kind of mockery. He admired Churchill's strength, his power, his inventiveness, his undefeatable intransigence – but, with a kind of Welsh malice (which often made me feel that he was looking at Englishmen through a foreigner's eyes), he thought him a bit of an ass.[54]

This was quite near the mark. But did this attitude amount to friendship? Perhaps the furthest one can go in that direction is to endorse the restrained comment made by Thomas Jones, when trying to solicit from Churchill a foreword for his biography of Lloyd George: 'so far as he ever had a political friend you were that friend'.[55] Of course, if Jones had really wanted his foreword – Churchill claimed, perfectly plausibly, to be too busy to provide one – he should have laid it on a bit thicker than that. But what he said, qualification included, was accurate.

As for Churchill's attitude towards Lloyd George: he probably felt the importance of the relationship more deeply than the other man did. In the early years in particular, he relied on him quite heavily. When he felt positive about him, he felt very positive; but equally, whenever he did not get the support to which he felt himself entitled he became extremely resentful. Hence his rapid switches between praise of Lloyd George and equally lavish condemnation. This was a pattern in other of Churchill's relationships too. Archibald Rowlands, Permanent Secretary of the Ministry of Aircraft Production when Beaverbrook was in charge, once observed that his minister's relations with Churchill were like a troubled marriage: 'They quarrel, but cannot break away from each other. They feel a sense of repulsion, combined with an equally strong sense of attraction.'[56] This could also describe how Churchill felt about Lloyd George, although Lloyd George, unlike Beaverbrook, was capable of indifference in response. In all, Bob Boothby's comment, quoted in the previous chapter, may provide as good a summation as is possible of the Lloyd George–Churchill relationship. As he suggested, it was based on mutual admiration and mutual fear – although unlike him, we may perhaps allow that mutual affection did at times creep in.

This book has demonstrated that the idea that Lloyd George and Churchill were close friends whose affection for one another was never interrupted by political vicissitudes is a myth. It was, however, a myth which they themselves worked hard to create, and one in which, at times, they both believed. It was undoubtedly a self-serving myth, which allowed the men to portray themselves jointly as meeting an ideal, that of masculine politicians who were able to deal with the personal and the political in quite different compartments. As such, it had clear political functions. But it cannot be dismissed simply as a veneer under which cynical individuals, for their own purposes, disguised the truth of their feelings. The key point, which it is important to reiterate, is that *the myth-making was part of the relationship.* The construction of the myth involved a selectivity of memory. It was not that Lloyd George and Churchill forgot past arguments but, in reinterpreting them to fit with the myth, they denied their true intensity. Why was this? The philosopher Avishai Margalit suggests that 'Our inability to relive an emotion is one of the things that makes us reevaluate or revise our account of our past emotion.' If this model is accepted, Lloyd George and Churchill re-evaluated their previous emotions – and created their joint myth – because, in the intervals between their quarrels, the sense of bitterness really did fade. Therefore, although the myth may have been historically untrue, the processes by which it was born formed a route to the periodic healing of relations between the two men. If it is important for us to see beyond the myth, then, we should acknowledge its function as a means of emotional repair. Margalit stresses that forgetfulness is not the same as forgiveness, which is a *conscious* effort to overcome resentment. Nevertheless, 'Forgetfulness may in the last analysis be the most effective method of overcoming anger and vengefulness.'[57] Truth and reconciliation are not always compatible; and Lloyd George and Churchill should not be criticized too heavily for sometimes preferring the latter to the former.

On 28 March 1955 Churchill, during his last days as Prime Minister, made his final speech in the House of Commons. He moved a motion proposing that, now that the customary ten years had elapsed since his death, a monument be erected to Lloyd George. Striking a personal note, he reaffirmed the myth of the two men's relationship:

My friendship with this remarkable man covered more than forty years of House of Commons life ... Whether in or out of office, our intimate and agreeable companionship was never darkened, so far as I can recall, by any serious spell of even political hostility.

As a first-hand witness, I wish to reaffirm the tribute I paid to his memory on his death. I feel that what was said then has only grown and strengthened and mellowed in the intervening decade.[58]

After his retirement, one of Churchill's last public duties was to serve on the committee to advise on the memorial. There was some question of whether it should be erected in the Commons Lobby or the north side of Parliament Square. Churchill had made his own preference clear before leaving Downing Street: 'Of course it must be in the Commons Lobby.'[59] In 1957 the committee proposed that the memorial should take the form of a statue by Sir Jacob Epstein. It was to be located in the Members' Lobby, on one side of the Churchill Arch that leads into the Commons chamber. (The arch is so-called because after it was damaged by wartime bombing Churchill urged that it be rebuilt from the rubble as a reminder.) However, Epstein died in August 1959, having completed only a scale model. The committee was reconstituted – Churchill, who was by now very frail, did not feel able to serve – and a new sculptor, Uli Nimptsch, was selected. Nimptsch's statue, unveiled in 1963, depicted Lloyd George in morning dress, in Commons debating pose, forefinger raised. It was no masterpiece, and was later said to make its subject look 'like a provincial pettifogger raising a piddling point of order'.[60]

After Churchill's death, a statue of him too was commissioned – the ten-year rule was waived in his case – to stand on the vacant plinth on the other side of the arch. The sculptor was Oscar Nemon and it was completed in 1969. The problem was that it was significantly larger than that of Lloyd George, which it seemed likely to overwhelm visually. One suggestion was that the Lloyd George statue should therefore be moved. Hearing of this, Frances Lloyd George protested to the Prime Minister, Harold Wilson. She did not, she wrote, like the existing statue of her husband, but she thought the decision that Lloyd George and Churchill should occupy

opposite pedestals should be adhered to 'even if it means commission-
ing another statue of Winston'.[61] Wilson agreed to look into the issue,
and, in her letter of thanks, Frances invoked the Lloyd George–
Churchill myth: 'I am very glad you have taken the matter up and
will be prepared to arbitrate upon it, so that we can say: "David and
Winston were together in their lives, and in their death they were not
divided." '[62] A partial solution to the disparity between the statues
was found by adjusting both plinths and increasing the height of the
base of the Lloyd George statue, which remained in its original place.
However, when the Churchill statue was unveiled the discrepancy
was still obvious, and drew criticism. The Labour MP Charles
Pannell, a former Minister of Public Building and Works, wrote to
Wilson, asking him to agree to a new Lloyd George statue 'which
would symbolize historically his proper comparison with the late
Winston Churchill as a statesman and war leader of no less stature'.[63]
He also said in the Commons that the existing monuments had a
'man and boy' appearance.[64] But the criticisms did not lead to action,
and the two statues have remained unchanged in place ever since.

    That, though, is appropriately symbolic of the fate of the popular
reputations of their subjects. Lloyd George, though he still finds his
champions, is overborne by Churchill who, in his bold and familiar
contours, dominates the scene. This reverses what was for a long time
true in life, Churchill having only fully escaped Lloyd George's orbit
at a fairly late stage in his career. Yet if the pairing of the memorials
does not do both men full justice, it does capture something: the
uneasiness, as well as the closeness, of the relationship between them.
And if that assists the reappraisal of the relationship's reputation, so
much the better. The myth of 'David and Winston' represents how
we would like our politicians to behave – and allows us to comfort
ourselves in our present discontents by contrasting the idealized
image of these two iconic statesmen with the seemingly reprehensible
activities of their modern-day successors. Yet it does not help us to
understand either the past or the present. 'Statesmen are for history;'
Joseph Chamberlain once remarked, 'let us be content with politicians'.[65] In fact, historians should be content with them too.

Notes

Abbreviations used in the notes:

CSC   Clementine Spencer-Churchill
DLG   David Lloyd George
HLRO   House of Lords Records Office, London
MLG   Margaret Lloyd George
NA   The National Archives, Kew, London
RSC   Randolph Spencer Churchill
WG   William George
WSC   Winston Spencer Churchill
WSC CV Companion volume to Randolph Churchill and Martin Gilbert,
        Winston S. Churchill, 8 vols., 1966–88 (see bibliography for details)
WSC CW Churchill, Winston, *The Collected Works of Sir Winston Churchill*, 34
        vols., Library of Imperial History/Hamlyn, London, 1973–6

Unless otherwise stated, all Churchill's speeches cited are to be found in the 8-volume *Winston S. Churchill: His Complete Speeches, 1897–1963* (Chelsea House, New York, 1974), edited by Robert Rhodes James.

Introduction – A Relationship and its Reputation

1 Thomas Jones diary, 11 Jan. 1937, Thomas Jones Papers, National Library of Wales, Class Z.
2 C. P. Snow, *Variety of Men*, Macmillan, London, 1967, p. 94.
3 See Henk te Velde, 'Charismatic Leadership, c. 1870–1914', in Richard Toye and Julie Gottlieb (eds.), *Making Reputations: Power, Persuasion and the Individual in Modern British Politics*, I. B. Tauris, London, 2005, pp. 42–55.
4 Edwin Montagu to H. H. Asquith, 20 Jan. 1909, Edwin Montagu Papers, Trinity College, Cambridge, AS1/1/21.
5 Dingle Foot, 'Review of the Autobiography of Frances Lloyd George', Oct. 1967, Dingle Foot Papers, Churchill College, Cambridge, DGFT 7/12.

6 'Rough notes taken of speeches delivered on the occasion of a private dinner given by Messrs. Ivor Nicholson & Watson at the Reform Club on Thursday, October 29th 1936 in honour of the Rt. Hon. D. Lloyd George O.M. M.P., on the occasion of the completion of his "War Memoirs"', Lloyd George Papers, HLRO, LG/G/208/4.

7 Richard Lloyd George, *My Father, Lloyd George*, Crown, New York, 1961, p. 180.

8 Randolph Churchill, *Winston S. Churchill*, vol. II: *Young Statesman, 1901–1914*, Heinemann, London, 1967, p. 306.

9 Marvin Rintala, *Lloyd George and Churchill: How Friendship Changed Politics*, Madison Books, Lanham, MD, 1995; Robert Lloyd George, *David & Winston: How a Friendship Changed History*, John Murray, London, 2005. Robert Lloyd George is the great-grandson of David Lloyd George.

10 A. J. P. Taylor (ed.), *Lloyd George: A Diary by Frances Stevenson*, Harper & Row, New York, 1971, p. 253 (entry for 13 Feb. 1934).

11 WSC to CSC, 10 Jan. 1916, in Mary Soames (ed.), *Speaking for Themselves: The Personal Letters of Winston and Clementine Churchill*, Doubleday, London, 1998, p. 150.

12 Avishai Margalit refers to 'memory entrepreneurs' in his book *The Ethics of Memory*, Harvard University Press, Cambridge, MA, 2002. 'Reputational entrepreneurs' would also be appropriate. See Gary Alan Fine, 'Reputational Entrepreneurs and the Memory of Incompetence: Melting Supporters, Partisan Warriors, and Images of President Harding', *American Journal of Sociology*, vol. 101, no. 5. (March 1996), pp. 1159–93.

13 Quoted in A. P. Lentin, *Guilt at Versailles: Lloyd George and the Pre-History of Appeasement*, Methuen, London, 1985, p. 18.

14 'Call to Honour Lloyd George for Millennium', BBC News online, http://news.bbc.co.uk/1/hi/wales/539522.stm, 28 Nov. 1999 (consulted 18 May 2005).

15 Richard Toye, 'The Churchill Syndrome: The Uses of an Image Since 1945', unpublished manuscript.

16 'President Bush Discusses Importance of Democracy in Middle East', 4 Feb. 2004, http://www.whitehouse.gov/news/releases/2004/02/20040204-4.html.

17 Rory Carroll, 'Mbeki Attacks "Racist" Churchill', *Guardian*, 5 Jan. 2005.

18 Parliamentary Debates, House of Commons, 5th Series, vol. 409, 28 March 1945, cols. 1385–6.

One – PATHS TO POWER, 1863–1905

1 W. R. P. George, *The Making of Lloyd George*, Faber and Faber, London, 1976, p. 57.

2 William George, *My Brother and I*, Eyre and Spottiswoode, London, 1958, p. 4.

3 'Mr. Lloyd-George', *Manchester Guardian*, 22 April 1908.

4 See especially John Grigg, *The Young Lloyd George*, HarperCollins, London, 1990 (originally published 1973), and Bentley Brinkerhoff Gilbert, *David Lloyd George: A Political Life: The Architect of Change, 1863–1912*, Ohio State University Press, Columbus, 1987.

5 WSC to Lady Randolph Churchill, postmark 16 Feb. 1891, WSC CV I, Part 1, p. 227.

6 Roy Jenkins, *Churchill*, Macmillan, London, 2001, p. 10.

7 Winston S. Churchill, *My Early Life* [originally published by Thornton Butterworth, London, 1930], WSC CW, vol. I, p. 123.

8 George, *My Brother and I*, p. 43.

9 See, for example, John M. McEwen, *The Riddell Diaries, 1908–1923*, Athlone Press, London and Atlantic Highlands, NJ, 1986, p. 65 (entry for 21 May 1913).

10 Grigg, *Young Lloyd George*, p. 44.

11 Lord Esher diary, 8 September 1909, Esher Papers, Churchill College, Cambridge, 2/12.

12 Churchill, *My Early Life*, p. 16.

13 Gilbert, *Architect of Change*, p. 45.

14 Parliamentary Debates, House of Commons, 3rd Series, 28 April 1884, vol. 287, col. 771.

15 Herbert Du Parcq, *Life of David Lloyd George*, 4 vols., Caxton, London, 1912, vol. I, p. 43.

16 Churchill, *My Early Life*, p. 26.

17 Robert Rhodes James (ed.), *Memoirs of a Conservative: J. C. C. Davidson's Memoirs and Papers, 1910–37*, Weidenfeld and Nicolson, London, 1969, p. 55. Contemporaries commonly referred to Lloyd George as 'L.G.' or 'Ll.G.'

18 Churchill, *My Early Life*, p. 28.

19 Lord Randolph Churchill to Lord Salisbury, 20 Dec. 1886, quoted in Roy Foster, *Lord Randolph Churchill: A Political Life*, Clarendon Press, Oxford, 1981, p. 306.

20 Roland Quinault, 'Churchill, Lord Randolph Henry Spencer (1849–1895)', *Oxford Dictionary of National Biography*, Oxford University Press, Oxford, 2004; http://www.oxforddnb.com/view/article/5404, accessed 8 June 2005.

21 See Foster, *Lord Randolph Churchill*, pp. 382–403.

22 'New Books', *Manchester Guardian*, 2 Jan. 1906.

23 Du Parcq, *Life of David Lloyd George*, vol. I, p. 158.

24 David Lloyd George to Margaret Owen, n.d. [probably 1885], in Kenneth O. Morgan (ed.), *Lloyd George Family Letters, 1885–1936*, University of Wales Press and Oxford University Press, Cardiff and London, 1973, p. 14.

25 John Greenaway, *Drink and British Politics since 1830: A Study in Policy-Making*, Macmillan, London, 2003, pp. 1, 37, 45.

26 Parliamentary Debates, House of Commons, 4th Series, vol. 345, 13 June 1890, cols. 873–5.

27 Winston Churchill to the ninth Duke of Marlborough, 24 Jan. 1899, MSS Marlborough vol. 1, no. 52, Library of Congress.

28 Clive Ponting, *Churchill*, Sinclair-Stevenson, London, 1994, p. 30.

29 'Rough notes taken of speeches delivered on the occasion of a private dinner given by Messrs. Ivor Nicholson & Watson at the Reform Club on Thursday, October 29th 1936 in honour of the Rt. Hon. D. Lloyd George O.M. M.P., on the occasion of the completion of his "War Memoirs"', Lloyd George Papers, HLRO, LG/G/208/4.

30 Churchill, *My Early Life*, pp. 311, 313.

31 DLG to MLG, 2 Oct. 1899, Morgan, *Family Letters*, p. 123.

32 'Mr. Lloyd George at Bangor', *North Wales Observer*, 13 April 1900, typescript copy in Lloyd George Papers, HLRO, LG/A/9/2/13.

33 Gilbert, *Architect of Change*, p. 199.

34 Parliamentary Debates, House of Commons, 4th Series, vol. 89, 18 Feb. 1901, col. 406.

35 DLG to WG, 18 Feb. 1901, quoted in W. R. P. George, *Lloyd George: Backbencher*, Gower Press, Llandysul, 1983, p. 330.

36 Churchill, *My Early Life*, pp. 378–9.

37 Parliamentary Debates, House of Commons, 4th Series, vol. 89, 18 Feb. 1901, col. 407.

38 *Daily Telegraph*, 19 Feb. 1901 and *Daily News*, 19 Feb. 1901, both quoted in WSC CV II, Part 1, pp. 9, 11–12.

39 Gilbert, *Architect of Change*, p. 198; Grigg, *Young Lloyd George*, pp. 278–80.

40 H. H. Asquith to Margot Asquith, 20 Feb. 1901, Margot Asquith Papers, Bodleian Library, Oxford, MSS Eng. c.6689, f. 82.

41 Churchill, *My Early Life*, p. 380.

42 Colin Cross (ed.), *Life with Lloyd George: The Diary of A. J. Sylvester, 1931–45*, Macmillan, London, 1975, pp. 88, 191 and n. 7 (entries for 17 Dec. 1932 and 24 Jan. 1938).

43 Winston S. Churchill, *Great Contemporaries* [originally published by Thornton Butterworth in 1937, and in a revised, extended edition in 1938], WSC CW, vol. XVI, p. 187.

44 Du Parcq, *Life of David Lloyd George*, vol. II, p. 266.

45 Peter T. Marsh, *Joseph Chamberlain: Entrepreneur in Politics*, Yale University Press, New Haven and London, 1994, p. 175.

46 'Mr. Lloyd-George at Birmingham', *The Times*, 19 Dec. 1901.

47 WSC to J. Moore Bayley, 23 Dec. 1901, WSC CV II, Part 1, p. 104.

48 WSC to Lord Rosebery, 23 Oct. 1902, Rosebery Papers, National Library of Scotland, MS 10009, f. 126.

49 Alice Balfour diary, 18 Nov. 1922, Balfour Papers, National Archives of Scotland, GD433/2/136.

50 Paul Addison, *Churchill on the Home Front, 1900–1955*, Pimlico, London, 1993, p. 36.

51 DLG to Leo Chiozza Money, 29 Jan. 1912, Leo Chiozza Money Papers, Cambridge University Library, Add. 9259/IV/37.

52 WSC to Chiozza Money, 13 Jan. 1914, Chiozza Money Papers, Add. 9259/
    IV/22.

53 Martin Daunton, 'Money, Sir Leo George Chiozza (1870–1944)', *Oxford
    Dictionary of National Biography*, Oxford University Press, Oxford, 2004. See
    also 'Sir Leo Chiozza Money', *The Times*, 30 Sept. 1944; 'Hyde Park Case',
    The Times, 3 May, 1928; and the entry on Sir Patrick Gardner, by David
    Howell, in Keith Gildart, David Howell and Neville Kirk (eds.), *Dictionary of
    Labour Biography*, vol. XI, Macmillan, London, 2003, pp. 115–16.

54 Leone George Chiozza, *British Trade and the Zollverein Issue*, The Commercial
    Intelligence Publishing Co., London, 1902. Quotation at p. 65.

55 WSC to John St. Loe Strachey, 23 May 1902, John St. Loe Strachey
    Papers, HLRO, STR/4/10.

56 WSC to Chiozza Money, 13 Jan. 1914, Chiozza Money Papers, Add. 9259/
    IV/22.

57 WSC to J. H. Lawton, 1 July 1903, WSC CV II, Part 1, p. 206.

58 WSC to Rosebery, 10 Oct. 1902, ibid., p. 168.

59 WSC to Alfred Harmsworth, 1 Sept. 1903, Northcliffe Papers, British
    Library, Add. 62156.

60 WSC to Alfred Harmsworth, 18 Sept. 1903, ibid.

61 WSC to Hubert Carr-Gomm, 5 Dec. 1903 (copy), British Library of Political
    and Economic Science, Archives Division, Coll. Misc. 0472.

62 WSC to Alfred Harmsworth, 1 Sept. 1903, Northcliffe Papers, Add. 62156.

63 WSC to Alfred Harmsworth, 12 Oct. 1903, ibid. Lloyd George had
    described Chamberlain's policy as 'A perpetual feast for pigs'. Harmsworth
    assured Churchill that there had simply been an editorial error; 'A Feast for
    Pigs', *Daily Mail*, 12 Oct. 1903 and Harmsworth to WSC, 13 Oct. 1903,
    both in WSC CV II, Part 1, pp. 233–4.

64 WSC to Alfred Harmsworth, 26 Aug. 1903, Northcliffe Papers, Add. 62156.

65 WSC to Lord Hugh Cecil, 1 Jan. 1904, WSC CV II, Part 1, pp. 281–5.

66 DLG to WG, 31 Dec. 1903, quoted in George, *Backbencher*, p. 413.

67 Jenkins, *Churchill*, p. 88 & n.

68 Gilbert, *Architect*, p. 279.

69 'The Cobden Centenary', *The Times*, 6 June 1904.

70 DLG to WG, 20 July 1904, quoted in George, *Backbencher*, p. 391.

71 Lord Tweedmouth to WSC, 21 July 1904, WSC CV II, Part 1, p. 353.

72 'Mr. Churchill and Mr. Lloyd-George at Carnarvon', *The Times*, 19 Oct.
    1904.

73 DLG to WSC, Feb. 1905, Churchill Papers, Churchill College, Cambridge,
    CHAR 2/22/48–9.

74 DLG to WG, 8 Feb. 1905, William George Papers, National Library of
    Wales, 1530.

75 Viscount Tenby, unpublished draft autobiography, p. 27, Viscount Tenby
    Papers, National Library of Wales, 23671C.

76 DLG to WG, 31 July 1905, William George Papers, 1644.

77 WSC to Rosebery, 25 April 1905, Rosebery to WSC, 4 May 1905, and

WSC to Rosebery, 9 May 1905, all in WSC CV II, Part 1, pp. 390–1. See also p. 390 n. 1.

78 'Ready to Oblige', cartoon of 25 Jan. 1905, reproduced in *Lloyd George by Mr. Punch*, Cassell, London, 1922, p. 20.

79 DLG to WSC, 5 Dec. 1905 (telegram), WSC CV II, Part 1, p. 409.

80 Frances Lloyd George, *The Years that Are Past*, Hutchinson, London, 1967, pp. 59–60.

81 DLG to WG, 5 Dec. 1905, William George Papers, 1715.

82 DLG to WG, [7 Dec. 1905], William George Papers, 1717.

83 DLG to WG, 8 Dec. 1905, George, *My Brother and I*, p. 206.

84 Cross, *Life with Lloyd George*, pp. 91–2 (entry for 28 Feb. 1933). See also p. 92 n. 4.

Two – SUPPORTERS RAMPANT

1 Violet Bonham Carter, *Winston Churchill as I Knew Him*, Reprint Society, London, 1966 (originally published by Eyre and Spottiswoode, 1965), pp. 160–1.

2 H. G. Wells, *The New Machiavelli*, Penguin, Harmondsworth, 1946 (first published 1911), p. 192.

3 'Mr. Lloyd-George at Criccieth', *The Times*, 1 Jan. 1906.

4 'Mr. Lloyd-George', *Manchester Guardian*, 29 Dec. 1905.

5 'Mr. Lloyd-George at Criccieth', *The Times*, 1 Jan. 1906.

6 'Mr. Lloyd-George', *Manchester Guardian*, 30 Dec. 1905.

7 'Mr. Lloyd-George at Criccieth', *The Times*, 1 Jan. 1906.

8 'Mr. Lloyd-George at Croydon', *The Times*, 6 Jan. 1906.

9 'Mr. Lloyd-George at Carnarvon', *The Times*, 19 Jan. 1906.

10 'Mr. Joynson-Hicks', *Manchester Guardian*, 12 Jan. 1906.

11 'In Angel Meadow', *Manchester Guardian*, 8 Jan. 1906; reproduced in Randolph Churchill, *Winston S. Churchill*, vol. II: *Young Statesman, 1901–1914*, Heinemann, London, 1967, pp. 123–4.

12 Joynson-Hicks's election address, *Manchester Guardian*, 4 Jan. 1906.

13 'Manchester', *Manchester Guardian*, 2 Jan. 1906.

14 J. Lee Thompson, *Northcliffe: Press Baron in Politics, 1865–1922*, John Murray, London, 2000, p. 130.

15 WSC to William Royle, 28 Nov. 1905, William Royle Papers, Manchester Local Studies Unit.

16 Paul Addison, *Churchill on the Home Front, 1900–1955*, Pimlico, London, 1993, p. 49.

17 Speech of 22 Feb. 1906.

18 'Mr. Churchill', *Manchester Guardian*, 12 Jan. 1906; 'Mr. Churchill', *Manchester Guardian*, 16 April 1908.

19 DLG to WSC (telegram) 15 Jan. 1906, Churchill Papers, Churchill College, Cambridge, CHAR 4/9/44.

20 J. H. Lewis diary, 11 April 1908, J. H. Lewis Papers, D31, National Library of Wales.

21 Speech of 7 May 1907.

22 DLG to WG, 6 May 1907, William George Papers, National Library of Wales, 1896.

23 Speech of 18 May 1907.

24 'The Imperial Conference', *The Times*, 7 May 1907.

25 Editorial, *The Times*, 10 May 1907.

26 Herbert Du Parcq, *Life of David Lloyd George*, 4 vols., Caxton, London, 1912, vol. III, p. 498.

27 'Draft Interim Report of the Committee of the Cabinet appointed to consider the proposed All-British Route to Australasia via Canada', n.d., Churchill Papers, CHAR 10/52/115.

28 WSC, 'All Red Memo' (draft), Churchill Papers CHAR 10/52/111–114.

29 WSC to Lord Crewe, 15 May 1908, Crewe Papers, Cambridge University Library, C7.

30 Crewe to WSC, 16 May 1908, Crewe Papers, C7.

31 WSC to Francis Hopwood, 17 Oct. 1907, Lord Southborough (Francis Hopwood) Papers, Bodleian Library, Oxford, Box 5.

32 The comment was that of Lord Crewe, Elgin's replacement as Secretary of State for the Colonies. Crewe to DLG, 1 Aug. 1910, Crewe Papers C/31.

33 WSC to Lord Crewe, 14 June 1910, Crewe Papers, C7.

34 Cameron Hazlehurst and Christine Woodland (eds.), *A Liberal Chronicle: Journals and Papers of J. A. Pease, 1st Lord Gainford, 1908–1910*, Historians' Press, London, 1994, p. 178 (entry for 12 May 1910).

35 Edward David (ed.), *Inside Asquith's Cabinet: From the Diaries of Charles Hobhouse*, John Murray, London, 1977, p. 94 (entry for 30 June 1910).

36 DLG to WG, 24 May 1907, William George Papers, 1900. In William George, *My Brother and I*, Eyre and Spottiswoode, London, 1958, p. 210, this letter is quoted, but with the word 'unscrupulous' censored.

37 DLG to WG, 16 July 1907, George, *My Brother and I*, p. 211.

38 Frances Lloyd George, *The Years that Are Past*, Hutchinson, London, 1967, p. 49.

39 DLG to WG, n.d., George, *My Brother and I*, p. 218.

40 Adam Tooze, 'Marshallian Macroeconomics in Action: the Industrial Statistics of the Board of Trade, 1907–1935', unpublished manuscript.

41 Parliamentary Debates, House of Commons, 4th Series, vol. 196, 11 Nov. 1908, cols. 329, 335.

42 Esher diary, 9 March 1908, Esher Papers, Churchill College, Cambridge, 2/11.

43 Esher diary, 26 Jan. 1908, Esher Papers, ibid.

44 Esher diary, 9 March 1908, Esher Papers, 2/11.

45 WSC to H. H. Asquith, 14 March 1908, WSC CV II, Part 2, pp. 754–6.

46 Esher diary, 20 March 1908, Esher Papers, 2/11.

47 See Edwin Montagu to Asquith, 3 March 1908, Edwin Montagu Papers, Trinity College, Cambridge, Box 3 AS1/7/6.

48 Randolph Churchill, *Young Statesman*, p. 247.

49 Margot Asquith diary, 8 & 9 April 1908, quoted in Colin Clifford, *The Asquiths*, John Murray, London, 2002, pp. 136–7.

50 Margot Asquith to WSC, 10 April 1908, WSC CV II, Part 2, pp. 771–2.

51 WSC to Asquith, 10 April 1908, ibid., p. 772.

52 DLG to Asquith, 11 April 1908, Asquith Papers, Bodleian Library, Oxford, 11/77–8.

53 Bonham Carter, *Winston Churchill*, p. 165.

54 Arthur C. Murray, 'Churchillian Recollections', n.d. [1948 or after], Elibank Papers, National Library of Scotland, MS 8818, ff. 2–3.

55 'Mr. Lloyd-George and "Election Enthusiasm"', *Manchester Guardian*, 22 April 1908.

56 DLG to WG, 28 April 1908, William George Papers, 2054.

57 DLG to WSC, 23 Aug. 1908, WSC CV II, Part 2, p. 812.

58 Leo Amery to Alfred Deakin, 26 Aug. 1908, Leo Amery Papers, Churchill College, Cambridge, AMEL 2/2/8.

59 DLG to WG, 12 Sept. 1908, William George Papers, 2101.

60 WSC to DLG 29 Aug. 1908, quoted in John Grigg, *Lloyd George: The People's Champion, 1902–1911*, Eyre Methuen, London, 1978, p. 164.

61 J. M. McEwen (ed.), *The Riddell Diaries, 1908–1923*, Athlone Press, London and Atlantic Highlands, NJ, 1986, p. 20 (entry for 17 Oct. 1908).

62 Edwin Montagu to Asquith, Jan. 1907, Montagu Papers, Box 3, AS1/7/1.

63 Asquith to St. Loe Strachey, 9 May 1908, quoted in Bentley Brinkerhoff Gilbert, *David Lloyd George: A Political Life: The Architect of Change, 1863–1912*, Ohio State University Press, Columbus, 1987, p. 340.

64 DLG to WG, 6 May 1908, quoted in George, *My Brother and I*, p. 220.

65 Esher diary, 7 May 1908, Esher Papers, 2/11.

66 R. B. Haldane to Elizabeth Haldane, 14 May 1908, R. B. Haldane Papers, National Library of Scotland, MS 6011.

67 Norman and Jeanne MacKenzie (eds.), *The Diary of Beatrice Webb*, vol. III: *1905–1924: 'The Power to Alter Things'*, Virago, London, 1984, p. 94 (entry for 19 May 1908).

68 Addison, *Churchill on the Home Front*, p. 68.

69 'The Cabinet and the Army', *The Times*, 13 July 1908.

70 R. B. Haldane to Mary Haldane, 13, 14 and 18 July 1908, and to Elizabeth Haldane, 15 July 1908, Haldane Papers, MS 5980.

71 R. B. Haldane to Mary Haldane, 23 July 1908, ibid.

72 David, *Inside Asquith's Cabinet*, p. 73 (entry for 27 July 1908).

73 J. Hugh Edwards, *The Life of David Lloyd George with a Short History of the Welsh People*, vol. IV, Waverley, London, n.d. [1913], p. 101.

74 Speech of 14 Aug. 1908.

75 DLG to WSC, 23 Aug. 1908, WSC CV II, Part 2, p. 813.

76 'Two Cabinet Bounders', *Justice*, 22 Aug. 1908, copy in Hardinge of
   Penhurst Papers, Cambridge University Library, 14, f. 32.
77 'Mr. Churchill at Swansea' (editorial), *The Times*, 17 Aug. 1908.
78 Edward VII to Charles Hardinge, 25 Aug. 1908, quoted in Philip Magnus,
   King Edward the Seventh, John Murray, London, 1964, p. 411.
79 Esher diary, 23 Aug. 1908, Esher Papers, 2/11.
80 Text of telegram from DLG to Asquith, 21 Aug. 1908, Asquith Papers,
   11/176–7.
81 Esher diary, 23 Oct. 1908, Esher Papers, 2/11.
82 J. H. Lewis diary, 11 April 1908, J. H. Lewis Papers, D31.
83 J. H. Lewis diary, 8 Sept. 1908, ibid.
84 Hazlehurst and Woodland, *Liberal Chronicle*, p. 83 (entry for 30 Oct. 1908).
85 Ibid., p. 89 (entry for 17 Nov. 1908).
86 See DLG to WG, 17 July 1908, William George Papers, 2089, and Frances
   Lloyd George, introduction to Malcolm Thomson, *David Lloyd George: The
   Official Biography*, Hutchison, London, n.d. [1948], pp. 9–30, at p. 17.
87 Gilbert, *Architect of Change*, pp. 359–61.
88 Stephen Koss, *Asquith*, Allen Lane, London, 1976, p. 106.
89 See the exchanges of telegrams and letters in Reginald McKenna Papers,
   Churchill College, Cambridge, 3/20; WSC to McKenna, Sept. 1908, and
   McKenna to WSC, 24 Sept. 1908, WSC CV II, Part 2, pp. 934–7.
90 DLG to WSC, 21 Dec. 1908, ibid., p. 937.
91 H. H. Asquith to Margot Asquith, 21 Feb. 1909, Margot Asquith Papers,
   Bodleian Library, Oxford, MSS Eng. c.6690, f. 184.
92 Winston S. Churchill, *The World Crisis*, Part I: *1911–1914* [originally
   published by Thornton Butterworth, London, 1923], WSC CW, vol. VIII,
   pp. 37–8.
93 See, for example, Jon Sumida, 'Churchill and British Sea Power, 1908–29',
   in R. A. C. Parker (ed.), *Winston Churchill: Studies in Statesmanship*, Brassey's,
   London, 1995, pp. 5–21.
94 See Lord Fisher to Reginald McKenna, 22 Aug. 1910, Fisher Papers,
   Churchill College, Cambridge, 1/10/498; and Fisher to McKenna, 8 Nov.
   1911, Fisher Papers, 1/10/540: 'Lloyd George seems to be my special
   friend, which I don't understand'.
95 Esher diary, 27 Sept. 1908, Esher Papers, 2/11.
96 Lord Askwith, *Industrial Problems and Disputes*, John Murray, London, 1920,
   p. 272.
97 Beatrice Webb to Betty Balfour, 28 Dec. 1911, Balfour Papers, National
   Archives of Scotland, GD433/2/343/46–52.
98 See Lucy Masterman, *C. F. G. Masterman: A Biography*, Nicholson and
   Watson, London, 1939, p. 97.
99 Speech of 11 October 1906; Churchill to H. G. Wells, 9 Oct. 1906, H. G.
   Wells Papers, University of Illinois, C–238–2.
100 David C. Smith has provided a fascinating survey of Churchill's relationship
    with Wells, but he overlooks the the latter's influence on the former:

NOTES

'Winston Churchill and H.G. Wells: Edwardians in the Twentieth Century', *Cahiers Victoriens et Edouardiens*, no. 30 (1989), pp. 93–116. I am grateful to Patrick Parriander for this reference.

101 Lucy Masterman diary, 8 Dec. 1910, Masterman Papers, University of Birmingham, Special Collections, 29/2/2/2.

102 Winston Churchill, 'The Untrodden Field in Politics', *The Nation*, 7 March 1908.

103 'Mr. Lloyd-George', *Manchester Guardian*, 14 April 1908. Similarly, see Montagu to Asquith, 11 Feb. 1908, quoted in S. D. Waley, *Edwin Montagu: A Memoir and an Account of his Visits to India*, Asia Publishing House, London, 1964, p. 26.

104 J. A. Spender, *Life, Journalism and Politics*, 2 vols., Cassell, London, 1927, vol. I, p. 158.

105 Masterman, *C. F. G. Masterman*, p. 177.

106 Gilbert, *Architect of Change*, pp. 354–5.

107 Addison, *Churchill on the Home Front*, p. 73; José Harris, *William Beveridge: A Biography* (2nd edn), Clarendon Press, Oxford, 1997, p. 178.

108 Lucy Masterman diary, 19 Oct. 1908, Masterman Papers, 29/2/2/1.

109 WSC to Asquith, 26 Dec. 1908, WSC CV II, Part 2, p. 860.

110 DLG to the Master of Elibank, 17 April 1911, Elibank Papers, MS 8802, ff. 209–14.

111 DLG to the Master of Elibank, Easter Monday (17 April) 1911, Elibank Papers, MS 8802, f. 215.

112 WSC to CSC, 22 April 1911, WSC CV II, Part 2, p. 1069.

113 Lucy Masterman diary, 26 Nov. 1908, in Masterman, *C. F. G. Masterman*, p. 114.

114 DLG to WG, 9 Dec. 1908, George, *My Brother and I*, p. 222.

115 Montagu to Asquith, c. Dec. 1908, Montagu Papers, Box 3, AS1/7/21.

116 Wilfrid Scawen Blunt, *My Diaries: Being a Personal Narrative of Events 1888–1914: Part Two* [1900–1914], London, Martin Secker, n.d., p. 278 (entry for 3 Oct. 1909).

117 Undated typescript narrative, reproduced in Masterman, *C. F. G. Masterman*, p. 137.

118 DLG to WG, [22 April 1909], William George Papers, 2217.

119 WSC to H. W. Massingham, 22 Jan. 1909, WSC CV II, Part 2, p. 872.

120 Lucy Masterman diary, 31 May 1909, *C. F. G. Masterman*, p. 129.

121 Strachey to John Burns, 23 Oct. 1908, John St. Loe Strachey Papers, HLRO, STR 3/3/9.

122 *Punch*, 29 Dec. 1909.

123 This was a view shared by Leo Amery: 'What I hear is that Lloyd-George and Winston, who were for a bold Socialist policy, or even for a protectionist tariff, have been definitely squashed by Asquith who, with the help of Grey and Haldane, is now completely master in his own house.' It is doubtful that Lloyd George and Churchill advocated a socialist or a protectionist policy, but what is significant is that Asquith was seen by

Amery, a political opponent, as being fully in charge of affairs. Amery to
Deakin, 19 Jan. 1909, Amery Papers, AMEL 2/2/8.

124 D. R. Daniel [Memoir], reporting a talk on 21 May 1909, quoted in Grigg, *People's Champion*, p. 178.

125 David, *Inside Asquith's Cabinet*, p. 80 (entry for 31 Oct. 1909).

126 'Notes of the Week', *British Weekly*, 21 Jan. 1909.

127 Speech of 14 Jan. 1909, WSC CV II, Part 2, p. 900.

128 Scawen Blunt, *My Diaries, Part Two*, p. 275 (entry for 2 Oct. 1909).

129 WSC to Marlborough, 7 Dec. 1909 (cheque), Marlborough Papers, Library of Congress, Washington, DC, vol. I.

130 David, *Inside Asquith's Cabinet*, p. 78 (entry for 4 June 1909).

131 'The Budget League Bingley Hall Demonstration, Friday, September 17th, 1909', Montagu Papers, Box 4, AS/1/11/1.

132 Speech of 9 Oct. 1909, quoted in Gilbert, *Architect of Change*, pp. 394–6.

133 Speech of 4 Sept. 1909.

134 Quoted in Roy Douglas, 'The Mother of all Monopolies', reprinted from *Land & Liberty*, September–October 1983, http://www.cooperativeindividualism.org/douglas_churchill_on_land_monopoly.html (consulted May 2005).

135 Esher diary, 8 Sept. 1909, Esher Papers, 2/12.

136 Almeric Fitzroy diary, 1 September 1909, Almeric Fitzroy Papers, British Library, vol. XI, MS Add. 48380*, f. 199.

137 'Review of Parliament', *The Times*, 3 Sept. 1909.

138 Asquith observed, 'my observations don't seem to have been taken as a hint'. Hazlehurst and Woodland, *Liberal Chronicle*, p. 132 (entry for 6 Sept. 1909).

139 Ivor Guest to WSC, 12 Oct. 1909, Churchill Papers, CHAR 2/39/102–4.

140 WSC to CSC, 2 Nov. 1909, WSC CV II, Part 2, p. 917.

141 WSC to CSC, 3 Nov. 1909, Clementine Churchill Papers, Churchill College, Cambridge, CSCT 2/2, f. 32.

142 Michael Wolff (ed.), *The Collected Essays of Sir Winston Churchill*, Library of Imperial History, London, 1976, vol. II, p. 424.

143 Lewis Harcourt to Asquith, 26 Jan. 1910, Asquith Papers.

144 Margot Asquith diary, 1 Feb. 1910, quoted in Clifford, *The Asquiths*, pp. 164–5.

145 Margot Asquith to WSC, 10 Feb. 1910, WSC CV II, Part 2, p. 967.

146 Lucy Masterman diary, Feb. 1910, Masterman, *C. F. G. Masterman*, p. 154.

147 J. H. Lewis diary, 25 Feb. 1910, J. H. Lewis Papers, D31.

148 David, *Inside Asquith's Cabinet*, p. 89 (entry for 16 April 1910).

149 WSC to Edward VII, 6 April 1910, WSC CV II, Part 2, p. 1003.

150 Bonham Carter, *Winston Churchill*, p. 161.

151 David, *Inside Asquith's Cabinet*, p. 90 (entry for 30 April 1910).

152 Masterman, *C. F. G. Masterman*, p. 173.

153 WSC to Alexander Murray, 26 May 1910, Elibank Papers, MS 8802.

154 The memoranda can be found in Robert J. Scally, *The Origins of the Lloyd George Coalition: The Politics of Social-Imperialism, 1900–1918*, Princeton University Press, Princeton, NJ, 1975, pp. 375–86, quotation at p. 375.

155 DLG to Lord Crewe, 20 Oct. 1910, Crewe Papers, C/31.

156 Lucy Masterman diary, 11 Sept. 1911, Masterman Papers, 29/2/2/2.

157 DLG to WSC, 25 Sept. 1910, WSC CV II, Part 2, pp. 1023–4.

158 Lucy Masterman diary, 12 Oct. 1910, Masterman Papers, 29/2/2/2.

159 McEwen, *Riddell Diaries*, pp. 46–7 (entry for 2 July 1912).

160 WSC to DLG, 6 Oct. 1910, WSC CV II, Part 2, pp. 1024–5.

161 Lucy Masterman diary, 12 Oct. 1910, Masterman Papers, 29/2/2/2.

162 'Mr. Lloyd George at Mile-End', *The Times*, 22 Nov. 1910.

163 DLG to Charles Masterman 3 Feb. 1911, Masterman Papers, 4/1/3/4.

164 Charles Eade diary, 11 Sept. 1942, Charles Eade Papers, Churchill College, Cambridge. For the episode as a whole, see Randolph Churchill, *Young Statesman*, pp. 391–2.

165 DLG to MLG, 14 Dec. 1910, in Kenneth O. Morgan (ed.), *Lloyd George, Family Letters, 1885–1936*, University of Wales Press and Oxford University Press, Cardiff and London, 1973, p. 154.

166 MacKenzie and MacKenzie, *Diary of Beatrice Webb*, vol. III, p. 149 (entry for 30 Nov. 1910).

167 Esher diary, 27 Sept. 1908, Esher Papers, 2/11.

168 McEwen, *Riddell Diaries*, p. 25 (entry for Nov. 1911).

Three – ALLIANCE UNDER STRAIN

1 J. H. Lewis diary, 16 March 1912, J. H. Lewis Papers, National Library of Wales, D31.

2 Wilfrid Scawen Blunt, *My Diaries: Being a Personal Narrative of Events 1888–1914: Part Two* [1900–1914], Martin Secker, London, n.d., pp. 289, 300 (entries for 13 Feb. and 27 April 1910).

3 David Stafford, *Churchill and Secret Service*, Abacus, London, 2000 (first published 1997), pp. 34–5.

4 Walter Runciman to Reginald McKenna, 27 March 1910, cited in Stephen E. Koss, *Lord Haldane: Scapegoat for Liberalism*, Columbia University Press, New York and London, 1969, p. 56.

5 John Burns diary, 6 February 1912, John Burns Papers, British Library, MS 46334.

6 The Earl of Swinton, *Sixty Years of Power: Some Memories of the Men Who Wielded It*, Hutchinson, London, 1966, p. 40; Marvin Rintala, *Lloyd George and Churchill: How Friendship Changed Politics*, Madison Books, Lanham, MD, 1995, pp. ix–x.

7 F. E. Hamer (ed.), *The Personal Papers of Lord Rendel*, Ernest Benn, London, 1931, p. 236, quoting Rendel's diary entry for 27 Feb. 1910; John Grigg,

'Rendel, Stuart, Baron Rendel (1834–1913)', *Oxford Dictionary of National Biography*, Oxford University Press, Oxford, 2004.

8 Richard Burdon Haldane, *An Autobiography*, Hodder & Stoughton, London, 1929, p. 217.

9 Norman and Jeanne MacKenzie (eds.), *The Diary of Beatrice Webb*, vol. II: *1892–1905: 'All the Good Things of Life'*, Virago, London, 1983, p. 327 (entry for 10 June 1904).

10 Norman and Jeanne MacKenzie (eds.), *The Diary of Beatrice Webb*, vol. III: *1905–1924: 'The Power to Alter Things'*, Virago, London, 1984, p. 101 (entry for 16 Oct. 1908).

11 Bentley Brinkerhoff Gilbert, *David Lloyd George: A Political Life: The Architect of Change, 1863–1912*, Ohio State University Press, Columbus, 1987, pp. 83–4.

12 Lord Moran, *Winston Churchill: The Struggle for Survival, 1940–1965*, Constable, London, 1966, p. 368, (diary entry for 17 Jan. 1952).

13 Randolph Churchill, *Winston S. Churchill*, vol. II: *Young Statesman, 1901–1914*, Heinemann, London, 1967, p. 79.

14 J. A. Spender, *Life, Journalism and Politics*, 2 vols., Cassell, London, 1927, vol. I, p. 163.

15 Colin Cross (ed.), *Life with Lloyd George: The Diary of A. J. Sylvester, 1931–45*, Macmillan, London, 1975, p. 148 (entry for 4 Sept. 1936).

16 Cross, *Life with Lloyd George*, p. 92 (entry for 28 Feb. 1933).

17 John Grigg, *Lloyd George: The People's Champion, 1902–1911*, Eyre Methuen, London, 1978, pp. 66–7; Gilbert, *Architect of Change*, p. 16.

18 John M. McEwen (ed.), *The Riddell Diaries, 1908–1923*, Athlone Press, London and Atlantic Highlands, NJ, 1986, p. 46 (entry for 2 July 1912).

19 Violet Bonham Carter, *Winston Churchill as I Knew Him*, Reprint Society, London, 1966 (originally published by Eyre and Spottiswoode 1965), p. 163.

20 Martin Pugh, *The Pankhursts*, Penguin, London, 2002, p. 128.

21 WSC to H. N. Brailsford, 19 April 1910, WSC CV II, Part 3, p. 1434.

22 Paul Addison, *Churchill on the Home Front, 1900–1955*, Pimlico, London, 1993, p. 133.

23 H. N. Brailsford to WSC, 21 April 1910, WSC CV II, Part 3, pp. 1435–6.

24 Lucy Masterman, *C. F. G. Masterman: A Biography*, Nicholson and Watson, London, 1939, p. 166 (diary entry for 12 Oct. 1910).

25 This was the term used by Churchill; Lloyd George said 'this is not a democratic Bill': Parliamentary Debates, House of Commons, 5th Series, vol. 19, 12 July 1910, cols. 223, 309. See also F. M. Leventhal, *The Last Dissenter*, Clarendon Press, Oxford, 1985, p. 77.

26 H. N. Brailsford to WSC, 12 July 1910, WSC CV II, Part 3, p. 1436.

27 J. H. Lewis diary 16 July 1910, Lewis Papers, D31.

28 Leventhal, *Last Dissenter*, pp. 77–8; Addison, *Churchill on the Home Front*, p. 134.

29 DLG to WG, 13 July 1910, William George Papers, National Library of Wales, 2404.

30 Addison, *Churchill on the Home Front*, p. 135.
31 J. Graham Jones, 'Lloyd George and the Suffragettes', *National Library of Wales Journal*, vol. 33, no. 2 (Winter 2003), pp. 1–33, at p. 13.
32 Pugh, *The Pankhursts*, pp. 219, 227.
33 C. P. Scott diary, 15 June 1911, C. P. Scott Papers, British Library, Add. 50901, ff. 13–16.
34 DLG to the Master of Elibank, 5 Sept. 1911, Elibank Papers, National Library of Scotland, MS 8802, ff. 308–11.
35 DLG to William George, 8 Nov. 1911, William George Papers, 2524.
36 Leventhal, *Last Dissenter*, pp. 84–5.
37 H. N. Brailsford to DLG 18 March [1912], Earl Lloyd-George Papers, National Library of Wales, MS 22523E.
38 Riddell diary, 19 Dec. 1911, Riddell Papers, British Library, MS 62956, f. 73.
39 Riddell diary, 6 Feb. 1912, Riddell Papers, MS 62956, f. 79.
40 Trevor Wilson (ed.), *The Political Diaries of C. P. Scott, 1911–1928*, Collins, London, 1970, p. 59 (entry for 23 Jan. 1912). Churchill advocated somewhat different criteria from time to time. An undated set of notes passed in Cabinet between him, Lloyd George and Grey show that Lloyd George rejected one version as 'too much like the Disraeli "fancy" Franchise Bill which was laughed out by [John] Bright [in 1859]'. Grey agreed with Lloyd George. 'Notes in Cabinet', WSC CV II, Part 3, p. 1456.
41 WSC to DLG, 16 Dec. 1911, Lloyd George Papers, HLRO, LG/C/3/15/12.
42 F. E. Smith to Andrew Bonar Law, 27 Dec. 1911, WSC CV II, Part 3, p. 1478.
43 WSC to the Master of Elibank, 18 Dec. 1911, ibid., p. 1473.
44 WSC to Asquith, 21 Dec. 1911, ibid., pp. 1475–6.
45 Leventhal, *Last Dissenter*, p. 86.
46 H. N. Brailsford to DLG, 18 March [1912], Earl Lloyd-George Papers, MS 22523E.
47 DLG to Brailsford, 19 March 1912, ibid.
48 Pugh, *The Pankhursts*, p. 243.
49 DLG to WG, 29 March 1912, William George Papers, 2583.
50 Brailsford to WSC, 8 July 1910, WSC CV II, Part 3, p. 1436.
51 Victor Cazalet diary, 3 April 1927, quoted in Robert Rhodes James, *Victor Cazalet: A Portrait*, Hamish Hamilton, London, 1976, p. 118.
52 WSC to Lord Northcliffe, 9 May 1911, Churchill Papers, Churchill College, Cambridge, CHAR 28/117/65. See also WSC CV V, Part 3, p. 506 n. 1.
53 John Campbell, *F. E. Smith: First Earl of Birkenhead*, Cape, London, 1983, p. 270.
54 Speech of 6 July 1933, quoted in Colin R. Coote, *The Other Club*, Sidgwick & Jackson, London, 1971, p. 79.
55 WSC to DLG, 13 Nov. 1910, WSC CV II, Part 2, p. 1211.
56 WSC to DLG, 3 March 1911, ibid., pp. 1247–8.
57 WSC to George V, 14 March 1911, ibid., p. 1248.
58 McEwen, *Riddell Diaries*, p. 24 (entry for June 1911).

59 DLG to WG, 7 April 1911, William George Papers, 2465.

60 Riddell diary 10 Oct. 1914, Riddell Papers, MS 62958, ff. 94–5.

61 Masterman, *C.F.G. Masterman*, p. 208 (diary entry for 11 Sept. 1911).

62 Burns diary, 20 Aug. 1911, Burns Papers, MS 46333.

63 Esher diary, 5 May 1908, Esher Papers, Churchill College, Cambridge, 2/11.

64 Winston S. Churchill, *The World Crisis*, Part I: *1911–1914* [originally published by Thornton Butterworth, London, 1923], WSC CW, vol. VIII, pp. 46–50.

65 Wilson, *Diaries of C. P. Scott*, pp. 48–9 (entry for 22 July 1911).

66 Gilbert, *Architect of Change*, p. 454.

67 Quoted in C. E. Callwell, *Field-Marshall Sir Henry Wilson: His Life and Diaries*, vol. I, Cassell, London, 1927, p. 99.

68 Maurice Hankey to John Fisher, 24 Aug. 1911, Fisher Papers, Churchill College, Cambridge, 1/10.

69 DLG to WSC, 25 Aug. 1911, Lloyd George Papers, C/3/15/6.

70 Callwell, *Sir Henry Wilson*, vol. I, p. 103; Gilbert, *Architect of Change*, p. 457.

71 WSC to DLG, 14 Sept. 1911 and DLG to WSC, 15 Sept. 1911, WSC CV II, Part 2, pp. 1124–5.

72 Churchill, *World Crisis*, Part I, p. 67.

73 Thomas Jones diary, 3 June 1923, Thomas Jones Papers, National Library of Wales, Class Z.

74 Haldane, *Autobiography*, pp. 230–2.

75 Haldane to Edward Grey, 2 Oct. 1911, quoted in Dudley Sommer, *Haldane of Cloan: His Life and Times, 1856–1928*, George Allen and Unwin, London, 1960, pp. 246–7. According to this letter, Haldane's visit to Archerfield took place 'on Thursday', i.e. on 28 September.

76 Riddell diary, Nov. 1911, Riddell Papers, MS 62596.

77 See Almeric Fitzroy, *Memoirs*, 2 vols., London, Hutchinson, 1925, vol. I, p. 464 (diary entry for 17 Oct. 1911).

78 DLG to MLG, 10 Oct. 1911, in Kenneth O. Morgan, *Lloyd George, Family Letters, 1885–1936*, University of Wales Press and Oxford University Press, Cardiff and London, 1973, p. 160.

79 'Minute of conversation at Archerfield, Friday October 20th 1911', McKenna Papers, MCKN 4/2.

80 John Burns diary, 30 October 1911, Burns Papers, MS 46333.

81 Haldane to his mother (no date given), quoted in Sommer, *Haldane of Cloan*, pp. 248–9.

82 McEwen, *Riddell Diaries*, p. 24 (entry for November 1911).

83 Gilbert, *Architect of Change*, p. 460.

84 DLG to WG, 10 Feb. 1912, William George Papers, 2554.

85 DLG to WG, 4 July 1912, William George Papers, 2621.

86 J. A. Pease diary, 16 March 1912, Gainford Papers, Nuffield College, Oxford, MSS 33; Addison, *Churchill on the Home Front*, pp. 162–4.

87 McEwen, *Riddell Diaries*, p. 41 (entry for 27 April 1912).

88 Lucy Masterman diary, 26 June 1912, Masterman Papers, University of Birmingham, Special Collections, 29/2/2/2.

89 DLG to WG, 8 July 1912, William George Papers, 2623.

90 McEwen, *Riddell Diaries*, p. 48 (entries for 27 & 28 July 1912).

91 Margot Asquith diary, 1 Nov. 1912, quoted in Colin Clifford, *The Asquiths*, John Murray, London, 2002, p. 202.

92 Riddell diary, 24 Nov. 1912, Riddell Papers, MS 62956, f. 191.

93 Riddell diary, 26 Nov. 1912, Riddell Papers, MS 62956, f. 192.

94 McEwen, *Riddell Diaries*, p. 51 (entry for 28 Nov. 1912).

95 Riddell diary, 3 Dec. 1912, Riddell Papers, MS 62956, f. 197.

96 The story was first revealed by John Grigg in 1973: *The Young Lloyd George*, HarperCollins, London, 1990 (originally published 1973), chapter 7.

97 Cameron Hazlehurst and Christine Woodland (eds.), *A Liberal Chronicle: Journals and Papers of J. A. Pease, 1st Lord Gainford, 1908–1910*, Historians' Press, London, 1994, p. 145 (entry for 3 Dec. 1909).

98 Bentley Brinkerhoff Gilbert, *David Lloyd George, A Political Life: The Organizer of Victory, 1912–16*, Batsford, London, 1992, pp. 40–1.

99 DLG to CSC 8 Jan. 1913, Clementine Churchill Papers, Churchill College, Cambridge, CSCT 3/13/10.

100 CSC to DLG, 10 Jan. [1913], Earl Lloyd-George Papers, MS 22524E.

101 Frances Lloyd George, *The Years that Are Past*, Hutchinson, London, 1967, p. 54.

102 Churchill had earlier considered writing to the committee himself, but was discouraged from doing so by Herbert Samuel. See Edward Marsh to Sambrook (unidentified), 6 Jan. 1913, Herbert Samuel Papers, HLRO, A/38 Part 1.

103 Randolph Churchill, *Young Statesman*, p. 555.

104 Lord Northcliffe to WSC, 6 June 1913, WSC CV II, Part 3, p. 1747.

105 Lord Northcliffe to WSC, 11 April 1913, ibid., p. 1740.

106 WSC to Northcliffe, 12 April 1913, Northcliffe Papers, British Library, MS Add. 62156, f. 50.

107 *The Times*, 29 April 1913, reproduced in WSC CV II, Part 3, p. 1743.

108 WSC to Northcliffe, 5 June 1913, ibid., pp. 1746–7.

109 Esher diary, 13 June 1913, Esher Papers, 2/12.

110 Parliamentary Debates, House of Commons, 5th Series, vol. 54, 18 June 1913, cols. 448–9.

111 Masterman diary, 23 June 1913, Masterman Papers, 29/2/2/2.

112 Duff Cooper, *Old Men Forget*, Rupert Hart-Davis, London, 1954, p. 46.

113 Speech of 1 July 1913.

114 John Campbell has recently provided an authoritative account of the relationship in *If Love Were All . . . The Story of Frances Stevenson and David Lloyd George*, Cape, London, 2006.

115 Lucy Masterman diary, 18 June 1913, Masterman Papers, 29/2/2/2.

116 Eliot Crawshay-Williams, *Simple Story: An Accidental Autobiography*, John Long, London, 1935, pp. 131, 133; 'Lieut-Col. E. Crawshay-Williams', *The Times*, 12 May 1962. Correspondence on the case can be found in the Lloyd

George Papers, HLRO, LG/C/3/15/28–9 and in the Churchill Papers, CHAR 1/107, and CHAR 1/112.

117 Lucy Masterman diary, 18 June 1913, Masterman Papers, 29/2/2/2.
118 See Grigg, *People's Champion*, pp. 181–9.
119 DLG to MLG, 21 Aug. 1897, in Morgan, *Family Letters*, p. 112.
120 DLG to MLG, 24 July, 1924, ibid., p. 203.
121 Grigg, *People's Champion*, pp. 181–2.
122 DLG to WG, 11 March 1909, William George Papers, 2197.
123 Frances Lloyd George, *Years that Are Past*, pp. 42–3, 52–3.
124 Nancy Astor (1879–1964) in 1919 became the first woman MP to take her seat in the House of Commons.
125 A. J. P. Taylor (ed.), *Lloyd George: A Diary by Frances Stevenson*, Harper & Row, New York, 1971, pp. 110, 190, 186 (entries for 28 July 1916, 29 Nov. 1919 and 25 May 1919).
126 DLG to Frances Stevenson, 23 May 1923, in A. J. P. Taylor (ed.), *My Darling Pussy: The Letters of Lloyd George and Frances Stevenson, 1913–41*, Weidenfeld and Nicolson, London, 1975, p. 64.
127 Ruth Longford, *Frances, Countess Lloyd George: More than a Mistress*, Gracewing, Leominster, 1996, p. 54.
128 WSC to CSC, 17 Oct. 1909, WSC CV II, Part 2, p. 914.
129 Ian Packer, *Lloyd George, Liberalism and the Land: The Land Issue and Party Politics in England, 1906–1914*, Royal Historical Society, London, 2001, pp. 2, 83.
130 Duke of Marlborough, 'The Land Question', *Daily Mail*, 17, 18, 19, 20 & 25 March 1913.
131 Riddell diary, 24 March 1913, Riddell Papers MS 62957, f. 45.
132 DLG to Charles Masterman, 10 Sept. 1913 (copy), Masterman Papers, 4/1/3/8.
133 Packer, *Lloyd George, Liberalism and the Land*, pp. 119, 122 and n. 60.
134 DLG to CSC 24 Oct. 1913, Clementine Churchill Papers, CSCT 3/15/12.
135 DLG to WG, 13 Oct. 1913, William George Papers, 2773.
136 McEwen, *Riddell Diaries*, p. 71 (entries for 31 Oct. and 1 Nov. 1913). Emphasis in original.
137 Ibid. (entry for 2 Nov. 1913).
138 Margot Asquith to DLG, 17 Nov. 1913, quoted in Randolph Churchill, *Young Statesman*, pp. 655–6. Emphasis in original.
139 DLG to WG, 16 Dec. 1913, William George Papers, 2803.
140 Speech of 10 Nov. 1913.
141 Quoted in Arthur J. Marder, *From Dreadnought to Scapa Flow: The Royal Navy in the Fisher Era, 1904–1919*, vol. I: *The Road to War, 1904–1914*, Oxford University Press, London, 1961, p. 316.
142 McEwen, *Riddell Diaries*, p. 72 (entry for 14 Dec. 1913).
143 Edward David (ed.), *Inside Asquith's Cabinet: From the Diaries of Charles Hobhouse*, John Murray, London, 1977, p. 154 (entry for 20 Dec. 1913).
144 Cabinet notes, 16 Dec. 1913, WSC CV II, Part 3, p. 1833. Emphasis in original.

145 McEwen, *Riddell Diaries*, p. 73 (entries for 14 and 18 Dec. 1913).

146 'Arms and the Nations: Mr. Lloyd George's Bold Indictment', *Daily Chronicle*, 1 Jan. 1914.

147 WSC to J. Masterton-Smith, 3 Jan. 1914, WSC CV II, Part 3, p. 1841.

148 Asquith to Venetia Stanley, 6 Jan. 1914, in Michael Brock and Eleanor Brock (eds.), *H. H. Asquith: Letters to Venetia Stanley*, Oxford University Press, Oxford, 1982, pp. 40–1.

149 'Mr. Churchill's Reply', *Daily Mail*, 5 Jan. 1914.

150 WSC to Hopwood, 10 Jan. 1914, Lord Southborough (Francis Hopwood) Papers, Bodleian Library, Oxford, Box 5.

151 H. H. Asquith to Margot Asquith, 9 Jan. 1914, Margot Asquith Papers, Bodleian Library, Oxford, MSS Eng. c.6691, f. 116.

152 'Mr. Churchill's Reply', *Daily Mail*, 5 Jan. 1914.

153 WSC to Leo Chiozza Money, 13 Jan. 1914, Leo Chiozza Money Papers, Cambridge University Library, Add. 9259/IV/22.

154 James Masterton-Smith to Chiozza Money, 23 Jan. 1914, Chiozza Money Papers, Add. 9259/IV/23.

155 WSC to Chiozza Money, 24 Jan. 1914, Chiozza Money Papers, Add. 9259/IV/24.

156 Scott diary 16 Jan. 1914, C. P. Scott Papers, British Library, Add. 50901, f. 93.

157 McEwen, *Riddell Diaries*, p. 77 (entry for 17 Jan. 1914).

158 H. H. Asquith to Margot Asquith, 20 Jan. 1914, quoted in J. A. Spender and Cyril Asquith, *Life of Herbert Henry Asquith, Lord Oxford and Asquith*, 2 vols., Hutchinson, London, 1932, vol. II, p. 76.

159 Wilson, *Diaries of C. P. Scott*, p. 75 (entry for 21 Jan. 1914).

160 Ibid., p. 77 (entry for 21 Jan. 1914).

161 DLG to WG, 22 Jan. 1914, William George Papers, 2806.

162 DLG to WG, 26 Jan. 1914, William George Papers, 2807.

163 DLG to WG, 28 Jan. 1914, William George Papers, 2808.

164 McEwen, *Riddell Diaries*, p. 79 (entry for 25 Jan. 1914).

165 Draft letter from WSC to DLG, 26 Jan. 1914, WSC CV II, Part 3, pp. 1854–5. A note on the original indicates it was sent on 27 January: see Churchill Papers, CHAR 13/26/8.

166 David, *Inside Asquith's Cabinet*, p. 158 (entry for 27 Jan. 1914).

167 DLG to Asquith, 27 Jan. 1914, Asquith Papers, Bodleian Library, Oxford, 25/158–9. Partially reproduced in WSC CV II, Part 3, p. 1855.

168 DLG to WSC, 27 Jan. 1914, ibid., p. 1856.

169 WSC to DLG, 27 Jan. 1914, ibid., p. 1855.

170 Ibid., n. 2; David, *Inside Asquith's Cabinet*, pp. 158–60 (entries for 27, 28 and 29 Jan. 1914).

171 McEwen, *Riddell Diaries*, p. 80 (entry for 25 Jan. 1914).

172 David, *Inside Asquith's Cabinet*, p. 158 (entry for 27 Jan. 1914).

173 Beauchamp, C. Hobhouse, McKenna, Runciman and Simon to H. H. Asquith, 29 Jan. 1914, Asquith Papers, 25/170–7.

174 Wilson, *Diaries of C. P. Scott*, p. 80 (entry for 6 Feb. 1914). A bell-wether is the lead sheep of a flock. A bell is hung around its neck.

175 Lady Randolph Churchill to WSC, 29 Jan. 1914, Churchill Papers, CHAR 1/392/11–12.

176 Marder, *From Dreadnought to Scapa Flow*, vol. I, p. 325; Churchill, *World Crisis*, Part I, p. 178.

177 Randolph Churchill, *Young Statesman*, p. 681.

178 Riddell diary 25 Jan. 1914, Riddell Papers, MS 62958, f. 15.

179 'G.W.B.' [Gerald Balfour], 'Notes of a conversation with Sir F. Hopwood at the Admiralty, May 21/1914', 23 May 1914, Balfour Papers, National Archives of Scotland, GD433/2/118/42.

180 Wilson, *Diaries of C. P. Scott*, p. 76 (entry for 21 Jan. 1914).

181 Addison, *Churchill on the Home Front*, pp. 104–5.

182 WSC to Asquith, 17 Sept. 1913, Asquith Papers, 38, ff. 193–5.

183 'Mr. Law on Ulster's Resistance', *The Times*, 29 July 1912.

184 WSC to John Redmond, 31 Aug. 1912, John Redmond Papers, National Library of Ireland, Dublin.

185 Speech of 8 Oct. 1913.

186 Austen Chamberlain, 'Memo. of conversation with Winston Churchill. Nov. 27 1913', Austen Chamberlain Papers, University of Birmingham, Special Collections, AC 11/1/21.

187 Roy Jenkins, *Asquith*, Collins, London, 1986, p. 340.

188 Riddell diary, 14 March 1914, Riddell Papers, MS 62958, f. 24.

189 Leo Amery, 'The Curragh Crisis: Diary of Events', Leo Amery Papers, Churchill College, Cambridge, 1/2/29.

190 'Naval Policy', *The Times*, 18 March 1914.

191 Riddell diary, 14 March 1914, Riddell Papers, MS 62958, f. 24.

192 Speech of 14 March 1914.

193 DLG to WG, 16 March 1914, William George Papers, 2827.

194 'Mr. Lloyd George on the Crisis', *The Times*, 23 March 1914.

195 Stephen Koss, *Asquith*, Allen Lane, London, 1976, pp. 136–7.

196 Burns diary, 31 March 1914, Burns Papers, MS 46336.

197 W. A. S. Hewins diary, 26 March 1914, W. A. S. Hewins Papers, University of Sheffield, Special Collections, Box 122, section 179.

198 'G.W.B.' [Gerald Balfour], 'Notes of a conversation with Sir F. Hopwood ', 23 May 1914, Balfour Papers, GD433/2/118/42.

199 Fitzroy, *Memoirs*, vol. II, p. 542 (entry for 23 March 1914).

200 David, *Inside Asquith's Cabinet*, p. 176 (entry for 24 July 1914).

201 Churchill, *World Crisis*, Part I, p. 193.

202 Randolph Churchill, *Young Statesman*, p. 554.

203 Marder, *From Dreadnought to Scapa Flow*, vol. I, p. 319.

204 Riddell diary, 3 Dec. 1912, Riddell Papers, MS 62956, f. 197.

205 WSC to DLG, 1 Sept. 1912, WSC CV II, Part 3, pp. 1643–4.

206 DLG to WG, 12 June 1912, William George Papers, 2606.

207 Roy Jenkins, *Churchill*, Macmillan, London, 2001, p. 144 & n.

208 Quoted ibid.

209 Fitzroy, *Memoirs*, vol. II, p. 540 (entry for 7 March 1914).

210 DLG to WG, 11 Nov. 1910, William George Papers, 2429.

211 Masterman, *C. F. G. Masterman*, p. 234 (entry for 26 June 1912).

212 H. H. Asquith to Margot Asquith, 23 Jan. 1914, in Spender and Asquith, *Life of Herbert Henry Asquith*, vol. II, p. 76.

213 David, *Inside Asquith's Cabinet*, p. 121 (entry for 13 Aug. 1912).

Four – Tout est Fini

1 Marvin Rintala, *Lloyd George and Churchill: How Friendship Changed Politics*, Madison Books, Lanham, MD, 1995, p. 119.

2 Michael G. Fry, *Lloyd George and Foreign Policy*, vol. I: *The Education of a Statesman, 1890–1916*, McGill-Queen's University Press, Montreal and London, 1977, p. 147.

3 WSC to CSC, 24 Sept. 1911, in Mary Soames (ed.), *Speaking for Themselves: The Personal Letters of Winston and Clementine Churchill*, Doubleday, London, 1998, pp. 55–6.

4 Arthur C. Murray diary, 7 January 1912, Elibank Papers, National Library of Scotland, MS 8814.

5 John M. McEwen, *The Riddell Diaries, 1908–1923*, The Athlone Press, London and Atlantic Highlands, NJ, 1986, p. 32 (entry for 10 Feb. 1912).

6 Fry, *Education of a Statesman*, p. 159.

7 Martin Gilbert, *Winston S. Churchill*, vol. III: *1914–1916*, Heinemann, London, 1971, pp. 1–2.

8 WSC to DLG, 18 Oct. 1912, Lloyd George Papers, HLRO, LG/C/3/15/16.

9 Gilbert, *Winston S. Churchill*, vol. III, p. 475.

10 Lucy Masterman diary, 27 Nov. 1912, in Lucy Masterman, *C. F. G. Masterman: A Biography*, Nicholson and Watson, London, 1939, pp. 244–5.

11 WSC to Marlborough, 6 Nov. 1912, Marlborough Papers, Library of Congress, Washington, DC, vol. III.

12 Edward David (ed.), *Inside Asquith's Cabinet: From the Diaries of Charles Hobhouse*, John Murray, London, 1977, p. 179 (undated entry for August 1914).

13 Asquith to Venetia Stanley, 1 Aug. 1914, in Michael Brock and Eleanor Brock (eds.), *H. H. Asquith: Letters to Venetia Stanley*, Oxford University Press, Oxford, 1982, p. 140.

14 Gilbert, *Winston S. Churchill*, vol. III, p. 23.

15 DLG to MLG, 3 Aug. 1914, in Kenneth O. Morgan (ed.), *Lloyd George, Family Letters, 1885–1936*, University of Wales Press and Oxford University Press, Cardiff and London, 1973, p. 167.

16 WSC to CSC, 28 July 1914, WSC CV II, Part 3, p. 1989.

17 Francis Bertie, memorandum of a conversation with Lloyd George, 19 Feb. 1912, NA, PRO, FO 800/171.
18 Wilfred Scawen Blunt diary, 12 May 1918, Wilfred Scawen Blunt Papers, Fitzwilliam Museum, Cambridge, MS 18–1975.
19 Cabinet notes, 1 Aug. 1914, WSC CV II, Part 3, pp. 1914–15. Emphasis in original.
20 Gilbert, *Winston S. Churchill*, vol. III, p. 23–4, citing Wilson's diary entry for 1 Aug. 1914.
21 J. A. Pease, diary entry for 2 Aug. 1914, quoted in Cameron Hazlehurst, *Politicians at War: July 1914 to May 1915: A Prologue to the Triumph of Lloyd George*, New York, Alfred A. Knopf, 1971, p. 66.
22 Asquith to Venetia Stanley, 2 Aug. 1914, in Brock and Brock, *Letters*, p. 146.
23 Asquith to Venetia Stanley, 3 Aug. 1914, ibid., p. 148.
24 Asquith to Venetia Stanley, 4 Aug. 1914, ibid., p. 150.
25 Frances Lloyd George, *The Years that Are Past*, Hutchinson, London, 1967, pp. 73–4.
26 Margot Asquith diary, 8 May 1915, quoted in Colin Clifford, *The Asquiths*, John Murray, London, 2002, p. 229.
27 Margot Asquith to WSC, 17 July 1919, Churchill Papers, Churchill College, Cambridge, CHAR 2/106/16. Emphasis in original.
28 Mark Pottle (ed.), *Champion Redoubtable: The Diaries and Letters of Violet Bonham Carter, 1914–1945*, Weidenfeld and Nicolson, London, 1998, p. 25 (entry for 22 Feb. 1915, written 22–23 May 1915). Emphasis in original.
29 Riddell diary, 6 Aug. 1914, Riddell Papers, British Library, MS 62958, f. 71; Gilbert, *Winston S. Churchill*, vol. III, p. 35.
30 Peter Hennessy, *Whitehall*, Secker and Warburg, London, 1989, pp. 60–1. See also David French, 'The Rise and Fall of "Business as Usual"', in Kathleen Burk (ed.), *War and the State: The Transformation of British Government, 1914–1919*, Allen and Unwin, London, 1982, p. 19.
31 Riddell diary, 18 Aug. 1914, MS 62958, f. 83. Dogger Bank is a sandbank in the North Sea.
32 John Horne and Alan Kramer, *German Atrocities, 1914: A History of Denial*, Yale University Press, New Haven and London, 2001. For these figures and examples see pp. 74, 15, 32–5.
33 Winston S. Churchill, *The World Crisis*, Part I: *1911–1914* [originally published by Thornton Butterworth, London, 1923], WSC CW, vol. VIII, pp. 270–1.
34 David Lloyd George, *Through Terror to Triumph*, Hodder and Stoughton, London, 1915, pp. 1–15.
35 John Grigg, *Lloyd George: From Peace to War, 1912–1916*, Penguin, London, 2002 (originally published 1985), p. 171.
36 WSC to Richard and Gwilym Lloyd George, telegram, Criccieth 15 Sept. 1914, David Lloyd George Papers (Brynawelon Group), National Library of Wales, MS 20463C. The telegram may well refer to Lieutenant Colonel Oswald Fitzgerald, Lord Kitchener's Personal Military Secretary.

37 McEwen, *Riddell Diaries*, p. 91 (entry for 21 September 1914).

38 Asquith to Venetia Stanley, 5 Oct. 1914, in Brock and Brock, *Letters*, pp. 262–3.

39 Riddell diary, 6 Oct. 1914, Riddell Papers, MS 62958 f. 92.

40 DLG to WSC, 7 Oct. 1914, WSC CV III, Part 1, p. 178.

41 Riddell diary, 10 Oct. 1914, Riddell Papers, MS 62958, ff. 94–5.

42 A. J. P. Taylor (ed.), *Lloyd George: A Diary by Frances Stevenson*, Harper & Row, New York, 1971, p. 6 (entry for 23 Oct. 1914).

43 McEwen, *Riddell Diaries*, p. 93 (entry for 25 Oct. 1914).

44 Trevor Wilson (ed.), *The Political Diaries of C. P. Scott, 1911–1928*, Collins, London, 1970, p. 112 (entry for 27 Nov. 1914).

45 WSC to DLG, 22 Oct. 1914, WSC CV III, Part 1, p. 213.

46 John Pollock, *Kitchener*, Constable, London, 1998, p. 419; DLG to WSC, 28 Oct. 1914, ibid., p. 224.

47 McEwen, *Riddell Diaries*, p. 94 (entry for 6 Nov. 1914).

48 David, *Inside Asquith's Cabinet*, p. 207 (entry for 13 Nov. 1914).

49 Taylor, *A Diary by Frances Stevenson*, p. 19 (entry for 23 Dec. 1914).

50 J. Lee Thompson, *Northcliffe: Press Baron in Politics, 1865–1922*, John Murray, London, 2000, p. 241.

51 David Lloyd George, *War Memoirs*, 2 vols., Odhams Press, London, 1938 (originally published in 6 vols., 1933–6), vol. I, p. 450.

52 DLG to Asquith, 31 Dec. 1914, Asquith Papers, Bodleian Library, Oxford, 13/254–255.

53 Asquith to Venetia Stanley, 1 Jan. 1915, in Brock and Brock, *Letters*, pp. 357–8.

54 DLG, Memorandum, 'Suggestions as to the Military Position', 31 Dec. 1914, WSC CV III, Part 1, pp. 350–6.

55 WSC, Memorandum, 31 Dec. 1914, ibid., pp. 347–9.

56 Maurice Hankey, Memorandum, 28 Dec. 1914, ibid., pp. 336–43.

57 Lord Kitchener to WSC, 2 January 1915, ibid., p. 361.

58 WSC to Sackville Hamilton Carden (telegram), 3 Jan. 1915, ibid., p. 367.

59 Meeting of the War Council: extract from Secretary's notes, 13 Jan. 1915, ibid., pp. 409–10.

60 Wilson, *Diaries of C. P. Scott*, p. 193, n. 6.

61 Margot Asquith diary, 25 Jan. 1915, WSC CV III, Part 1, p. 454.

62 The first dated letter of the series was written on 11 January 1915, and was a continuation of a previous undated letter, possibly of the same day (Lloyd George Papers, HLRO, LG/4/11/1–2). These concerned Zeppelins. Air defence had been the issue over which Fisher had made his first resignation threat to Churchill a few days before. Lloyd George, although no stickler for procedure, would have been aware that Fisher's decision to broach such a matter with the minister of another department implied a want of confidence in Churchill.

63 J. H. Lewis diary, 12 Feb. 1915, J. H. Lewis Papers, National Library of Wales, D31.

64 Fisher to DLG, 29 Jan. 1915, Lloyd George Papers, HLRO, LG/C/4/11/3. Emphasis in original.

65 DLG to Fisher, 30 Jan. 1915, Fisher Papers, Churchill College, Cambridge, 1/18, 928.

66 Fisher to DLG, 10 Feb. 1915, Lloyd George Papers, HLRO, LG C/4/11/5. Emphasis in original.

67 Meeting of the War Council: extract from Secretary's notes, 19 Feb. 1915, WSC CV III, Part 1, p. 529.

68 WSC to Jack Churchill, 26 Feb. 1915, ibid., p. 580.

69 Gilbert, Winston S. Churchill, vol. III, p. 311.

70 Meeting of the War Council: extract from Secretary's notes, 24 Feb. 1915, WSC CV III, Part 1, pp. 558–9.

71 R. J. Q. Adams, Arms and the Wizard: Lloyd George and the Ministry of Munitions, 1915–1916, Cassell, London, 1978, p. 25.

72 DLG to WSC, 26 March 1915, Churchill Papers, CHAR 13/43/69–74.

73 Adams, Arms and the Wizard, p. 27.

74 Asquith to Venetia Stanley, 21 March 1915, Brock and Brock, Letters, p. 495.

75 Asquith to Venetia Stanley, 25 March 1915, ibid., p. 508; Margot Asquith to DLG, 24 March 1915, WSC CV III, Part 1, p. 739.

76 Asquith to Venetia Stanley, 29 March 1915, Brock and Brock, Letters, p. 517.

77 Asquith to Venetia Stanley, 29 March 1915 [ii], ibid., p. 519.

78 Asquith to Venetia Stanley, 30 March 1915 [ii], ibid., p. 522.

79 David Dilks (ed.), The Diaries of Sir Alexander Cadogan O.M., 1938–1945, Cassell, London, 1971, p. 395 (entry for 3 Aug. 1941).

80 Bentley Brinkerhoff Gilbert, David Lloyd George: A Political Life: The Organizer of Victory, 1912–16, Batsford, London, p. 161.

81 Taylor, A Diary by Frances Stevenson, pp. 41–2 (entry for 8 April 1915).

82 DLG to WSC, 5 April 1915, WSC CV III, Part 1, p. 769.

83 WSC to DLG, 5 April 1915, ibid., p. 770. Emphasis in original.

84 Taylor, A Diary by Frances Stevenson, p. 42 (entry for 8 April 1915).

85 McEwen, Riddell Diaries, p. 105 (entry for 11 April 1915).

86 See Margot Asquith diary, 8 May 1915, Margot Asquith Papers, Bodleian Library, Oxford, MSS Eng. c.6692, d.3211, ff. 261–5.

87 Lloyd George, War Memoirs, vol. I, p. 133.

88 'Need for Shells', The Times, 14 May 1915.

89 Lloyd George, War Memoirs, vol. I, pp. 134–5.

90 Taylor, A Diary by Frances Stevenson, p. 50 (entry for 15 May 1915).

91 Fisher to Bonar Law, 17 May 1915, Bonar Law Papers, HLRO, BL/37/2/34.

92 Lloyd George, War Memoirs, vol. I, pp. 135–6.

93 Winston S. Churchill, The World Crisis, Part II: 1915 [originally published by Thornton Butterworth, London, 1923], WSC CW, vol. IX, p. 365.

94 See Colin Cross (ed.), Life with Lloyd George: The Diary of A. J. Sylvester, 1931–45, Macmillan, London, 1975, p. 59 (entry for 28 Nov. 1931).

95 Margot Asquith to DLG, 17 May 1915, WSC CV III, Part 2, p. 898. Emphasis in original.
96 WSC to Asquith, 17 May 1915, ibid.
97 Taylor, *A Diary by Frances Stevenson*, p. 52 (entry for 19 May 1915).
98 McEwen, *Riddell Diaries*, p. 114 (entry for 19 May 1915).
99 WSC to Asquith, 21 May 1915, WSC CV III, Part 2, p. 926.
100 Lloyd George, *War Memoirs*, vol. I, p. 139.
101 McEwen, *Riddell Diaries*, p. 118 (entry for 23 May 1915).
102 Taylor, *A Diary by Frances Stevenson*, p. 60 (entry for 15 Sept. 1915).
103 ibid.
104 McEwen, *Riddell Diaries*, p. 119 (entry for 26 May 1915).
105 Lord Reading diary, 27 May 1915, Lord Reading Papers, India Office Library, MS Eur/F118/152.
106 Reading diary, 28 May 1915, Reading Papers, MS Eur/F118/152.
107 WSC to Archibald Sinclair, 9 June 1916, WSC CV IV, Part 1, pp. 5–6.
108 Margot Asquith diary, 9 June 1915, Margot Asquith Papers, d.3212; quotations reproduced in Clifford, *The Asquiths*, pp. 279–80.
109 McEwen, *Riddell Diaries*, p. 125 (entry for 4 July 1915).
110 Gilbert, *Winston S. Churchill*, vol. III, p. 473.
111 DLG to Asquith, 19 May 1915, Asquith Papers, 14/36–8.
112 Lloyd George, *War Memoirs*, vol. I, pp. 146, 360.
113 Adams, *Arms and the Wizard*, p. 172.
114 Winston S. Churchill, *The World Crisis*, Part III: *1916–1918* [originally published by Thornton Butterworth, London, 1927], WSC CW, vol. X, p. 301.
115 Walter Long to the Marquess of Lansdowne and Bonar Law, 13 June 1915, Walter Long Papers, British Library, Add. 62404.
116 Speech of 3 June 1915, Lloyd George, *Through Terror to Triumph*, pp. 97–110.
117 Speech of 5 June 1915.
118 Gilbert, *Organizer of Victory*, p. 253.
119 J. A. Pease diary, 3 June 1915, Gainford Papers, Nuffield College, Oxford, MS 34.
120 WSC to John Seely, 12 June 1915, WSC CV III, Part 2, pp. 1016–17.
121 Scawen Blunt diary, 14 Aug. 1915, Scawen Blunt Papers, MS 15–1975.
122 Reading diary, 13 July 1915, Reading Papers, MS Eur/F118/152.
123 WSC to Sinclair, 30 July 1915, WSC CV IV, Part 1, p. 7.
124 Taylor, *A Diary by Frances Stevenson*, p. 59 (entry for 15 Sept. 1915).
125 H. H. Asquith to Margot Asquith, 13 Aug. 1915, Margot Asquith Papers, MSS Eng. c.6691, ff. 200–2.
126 Taylor, *A Diary by Frances Stevenson*, p. 59 (entry for 15 Sept. 1915).
127 Christopher Addison diary, 19 Sept. 1915, Christopher Addison Papers, Bodleian Library, Oxford, MS Addison dep. c. 1., ff. 194–8.
128 Addison diary, 21 Oct. 1915, Addison Papers, MS Addison dep. c. 1., ff. 259–60.
129 Wilson, *Diaries of C. P. Scott*, pp. 139–40 (entry for 1 Oct. 1915).

130 Taylor, *A Diary by Frances Stevenson*, p. 65 (entry for 11 Oct. 1915).

131 WSC to Asquith, 6 Oct. 1915, WSC CV III, Part 2, p. 1203.

132 Oliver, Viscount Esher (ed.), *Journals and Letters of Reginald Viscount Esher*, vol. 3: *1910–1915*, Ivor Nicholson & Watson, London, 1938, p. 263 (entry for 12 Oct. 1915).

133 Lewis diary, 23 Oct. 1915, Lewis Papers, D31.

134 Margot Asquith to Hankey, 15 Oct. 1915, WSC CV III, Part 2, p. 1219.

135 Margot Asquith to Kitchener, 18 Oct. 1915, ibid., p. 1225.

136 Taylor, *A Diary by Frances Stevenson*, p. 69 (entry for 19 Oct. 1915).

137 Addison diary, 21 Oct. 1915, Addison Papers, MS Addison dep. c. 1.

138 See Christopher Addison, *Four and a Half Years: A Personal Diary from June 1914 to January 1919*, 2 vols., Hutchinson, London, 1934, vol. I, p. 139.

139 WSC to Asquith, 11 Nov. 1915, WSC CV III, Part 2, p. 1249.

140 Speech of 15 Nov. 1915.

141 Addison diary, 17 Nov. 1915, Addison Papers, MS Addison dep. c. 1, f. 283.

142 DLG to WSC, 16 Nov. 1915, WSC CV III, Part 2, p. 1271.

143 T. H. Buck to Ralph David Blumenfeld, 21 Nov. [1915], Ralph David Blumenfeld Papers, HLRO, BLU/1//4/BU.1.

144 McEwen, *Riddell Diaries*, p. 140 (entry for 18 Dec. 1915).

145 Esher diary, 1 Dec. 1915, reproduced in WSC CV III, Part 2, p. 1298.

146 CSC to WSC, 30 Dec. 1915, in Soames, *Speaking for Themselves*, p. 142.

147 WSC to CSC, 2 Jan. 1916, ibid., p. 145.

Five – Don't Get Torpedoed

1 Edward Louis Spiers diary, 28 Dec. 1915, WSC CV III, Part 2, p. 1345.

2 WSC to DLG, 27 Dec. 1915, ibid.

3 CSC to DLG, n.d. [28 Dec. 1915], Lloyd George Papers, HLRO, LG/D/16/8/4.

4 CSC to WSC, 29 Dec. 1915, in Mary Soames (ed.), *Speaking for Themselves: The Personal Letters of Winston and Clementine Churchill*, Doubleday, London, 1998, p. 141.

5 WSC to CSC, 1 Jan. 1916, ibid., p. 143.

6 WSC to CSC, 10 Jan. 1916, ibid., p. 150.

7 WSC to Lady Randolph Churchill, 16 Jan. 1916, Churchill Papers, Churchill College, Cambridge, CHAR 28/127.

8 WSC to the Duke of Marlborough, 22 Jan. 1916, WSC CV IV, Part 1, p. 15.

9 CSC to WSC, 24 Jan. 1916, in Soames, *Speaking for Themselves*, p. 160.

10 WSC to CSC, 26 Jan. 1916, ibid., p. 162.

11 WSC to DLG, 25 Jan. 1916, WSC CV III, Part 2, p. 1395.

12 Martin Gilbert, *Winston S. Churchill*, vol. III: *1914–1916*, Heinemann, London, 1971, p. 697. Quotation from Edmund Hakewill Smith, a member of Churchill's battalion, who was present at the meeting.

13 CSC to WSC, 2 Feb. 1916, quoted ibid., p. 698.

14 CSC to WSC, 4 Feb. 1916, in Soames, *Speaking for Themselves*, p. 167. See also WSC CV III, Part 2, p. 1411, n. 3.

15 Lady Randolph Churchill to WSC, ibid., p. 1411.

16 Trevor Wilson (ed.), *The Political Diaries of C. P. Scott, 1911–1928*, Collins, London, 1970, p. 182 (entry for 18 Feb. 1916).

17 Ibid., p. 187 (entry for 6–8 March 1916).

18 Gilbert, *Winston S. Churchill*, vol. III, p. 711.

19 DLG to WG, 6 March 1916, William George Papers, National Library of Wales, 3054.

20 Hankey diary, 7 March 1916, Maurice Hankey Papers, Churchill College, Cambridge, HNKY 1/1.

21 Riddell diary, 11 Feb. 1916, Riddell Papers, British Library, MS 62960 f. 19.

22 DLG to WG, 7 March 1916, in William George, *My Brother and I*, Eyre and Spottiswoode, London, 1958, p. 253.

23 DLG to WG, 8 March 1916, William George Papers, 3056.

24 DLG to WG, 13 March 1916, in George, *My Brother and I*, p. 253.

25 Lord Curzon to Lord Lansdowne, 7 June 1916, quoted in David Gilmour, *Curzon*, John Murray, London, 1994, p. 443.

26 WSC to F. E. Smith, 8 April 1916, WSC CV III, Part 2, p. 1482.

27 WSC to DLG, 10 April 1916, ibid., p. 1485.

28 Ruth Lee diary, in Alan Clark (ed.), *'A Good Innings': The Private Papers of Viscount Lee of Fareham*, John Murray, London, 1974, p. 149.

29 WSC to Sinclair, 18 April 1916, WSC CV IV, Part 1, p. 22. Emphasis in original.

30 A. J. P. Taylor (ed.), *Lloyd George: A Diary by Frances Stevenson*, Harper & Row, New York, 1971, p. 107 (entry for 19 April 1916).

31 Lord Northcliffe to LG, 7 June 1916, WSC CV III, Part 2, p. 1513.

32 Lord Reading to WSC, 14 June 1916, ibid., pp. 1517–18.

33 John M. McEwen, *The Riddell Diaries, 1908–1923*, Athlone Press, London and Atlantic Heights, NJ, 1986, p. 162 (entry for 2 July 1916).

34 WSC to John Churchill, 15 July 1916, WSC CV III, Part 2, p. 1530.

35 Wilson, *Diaries of C. P. Scott*, p. 224 (entry for 27 July 1916).

36 Hankey diary, 8 July 1916, Hankey Papers, HNKY 1/1.

37 WSC to Seely, 31 July 1916, WSC CV III, Part 2, p. 1532.

38 Lord Derby to DLG, 19 Aug. 1916, ibid., p. 1545.

39 Hankey diary, 3 Aug. 1916, ibid., p. 1540.

40 Esher diary, 11 Aug. 1916, Esher Papers, Churchill College, Cambridge, 2/16.

41 Tom Clarke, *My Northcliffe Diary*, Victor Gollancz, London, 1931, p. 102 (entry for 12 Oct. 1916).

42 Hankey diary, 1 Nov. 1916, in Stephen Roskill, *Hankey: Man of Secrets*, 3 vols., Collins, London, 1970–4, vol. I, p. 312.

43 WSC to Sinclair, 15 Sept. 1916, WSC CV IV, Part 1, p. 26.

44 Hankey diary, 10 Nov. 1916, Hankey Papers, HNKY 1/1.

45 Memorandum by Montagu, 9 Dec. 1916, Edwin Montagu Papers, Trinity College, Cambridge, Box 4, AS/1/10/1.

46 Wilson, *Diaries of C. P. Scott*, p. 235 (entry for 20–2 Nov. 1916).

47 Bentley Brinkerhoff Gilbert, *David Lloyd George, A Political Life: The Organizer of Victory, 1912–16*, Batsford, London, 1992, pp. 407–8.

48 The story of the different versions and Churchill's own comments is to be found in J. M. McEwen, 'A Churchill Story: Dinner at F. E. Smith's, 5 December 1916', *Queen's Quarterly*, vol. 83, no. 2 (Summer 1976), pp. 273–7.

49 Earl of Avon, *The Eden Memoirs: The Reckoning*, Cassell, London, 1965, p. 277.

50 Taylor, *A Diary by Frances Stevenson*, p. 133 (entry for 6 Dec. 1916).

51 'Memorandum of Conversation between Mr. Lloyd George and certain Unionist ex-Ministers, December 7, 1916', reproduced in Lord Beaverbrook, *Politicians and the War, 1914–1916*, single-volume edition, Oldbourne, London, 1960, pp. 520–7. Quotations at pp. 526, 527.

52 David Lloyd George, *War Memoirs*, 2 vols., Odhams Press, London, 1938 (originally published in 6 vols., 1933–6), vol. I, p. 636.

53 WSC to Sinclair, 10 Dec. 1916, WSC CV IV, Part 1, p. 36.

54 McEwen, *Riddell Diaries*, pp. 178–9 (entry for 10 Dec. 1916).

55 Ibid., p. 179 (entry for 11 Dec. 1916).

56 Ibid. (entry for 12 Dec. 1916).

57 Ibid., p. 180 (entry for 13 Dec. 1916).

58 WSC to Sinclair, 20 Dec. 1916, WSC CV IV, Part 1, p. 37.

59 John Grigg, *Lloyd George: War Leader, 1916–1918*, Allen Lane, London, 2002, pp. 1–10; David Reynolds, *In Command of History: Churchill Fighting and Writing the Second World War*, Allen Lane, London, 2004, pp. 174, 565, n. 27.

60 Winston S. Churchill, *Great Contemporaries* [originally published by Thornton Butterworth in 1937, and in a revised, extended edition in 1938], WSC CW, vol. XVI, p. 92.

61 Winston S. Churchill, *The World Crisis*, Part III: *1916–1918* [originally published by Thornton Butterworth, London, 1927], WSC CW, vol. X, p. 256.

62 McEwen, *Riddell Diaries*, p. 184 (entry for 11 Feb. 1917).

63 Ibid., p. 185 (entry for 14 Feb. 1917).

64 Wilson, *Diaries of C. P. Scott*, p. 268 (entry for 15–16 March 1917).

65 WSC to Wilfrid Scawen Blunt, April 1917, copied into the latter's diary, 5 April 1917, Scawen Blunt Papers, Fitzwilliam Museum, Cambridge, MS 17–1975.

66 Scawen Blunt diary, 29 April 1917, ibid.

67 Speech of 17 April 1917.

68 Henry Nevinson diary, 26 April 1917, Henry Nevinson Papers, Bodleian Library, Oxford, MS Eng. misc. e 620/2; Alfred F. Havighurst, *Radical Journalist: H. W. Massingham (1860–1924)*, Cambridge University Press, Cambridge, 1974, p. 255. The article in question, which was written by Nevinson, was 'Instans Tyrannus', *The Nation*, 21 April 1917.

69 Taylor, *A Diary by Frances Stevenson*, p. 157 (entry for 29 April 1917).

70 Wilson, *Diaries of C. P. Scott*, p. 285 (entry for 30 April–4 May 1917).

71 There is a brief summary of the document in S. D. Waley, *Edwin Montagu: A Memoir and an Account of His Visits to India*, Asia Publishing House, London, 1964, p. 123. Although this rightly states that Guest believed Churchill would urge Asquith's inclusion in the government, it fails to make clear that Montagu also heard from Churchill himself that this was his firm intention.

72 Montagu memorandum, 10 May 1917, Montagu Papers, Box 2, AS1/12/14.

73 Edward Marsh to A. J. Sylvester, 26 July 1926 and Sylvester to Marsh, 9 Aug. 1926, Lloyd George Papers, HLRO, LG/G/4/4/15; WSC to DLG, 24 Nov. 1934, Lloyd George Papers, HLRO, LG/G/4/5/8.

74 Churchill, *World Crisis*, Part III, pp. 253–4.

75 Ibid., p. 255.

76 John Simon diary, 10 May 1917, John Simon Papers, Bodleian Library, Oxford, MS Simon 2.

77 Montagu memorandum, 10 May 1917, Montagu Papers, Box 2, AS1/12/14.

78 Churchill, *World Crisis*, Part III, p. 255.

79 Taylor, *A Diary by Frances Stevenson*, p. 158 (entry for 19 May 1917).

80 Riddell diary, 'Sunday', Riddell Papers, MS 62961. A later pencil note adds 'about 27 July 1917', but this cannot be correct. McEwen suggests 29 June as an alternative (see *Riddell Diaries*, pp. 192–3 & p. 404, n. 18) but that was a Friday. A reference to Lloyd George and Churchill going to Dundee 'next week' makes 24 June 1917 the most likely date.

81 Lloyd George, *War Memoirs*, vol. I, p. 637.

82 Richard Lloyd George, *My Father, Lloyd George*, Crown, New York, 1961, p. 182.

83 One consequence of Churchill's appointment is little-known but striking. When out of office he had been approached by Ideal Films Ltd to write a film about the origins of the war. He agreed to this, but his return to power put an end to the project. Harry Rowson, Ideal's co-founder later recalled: 'after hearing what had happened to our Winston Churchill story, I suddenly got the idea that the life of Lloyd George, our Prime Minister, contained unlimited material for a film story'. The new film, *The Life Story of David Lloyd George*, was directed by Maurice Elvey and starred Norman Page as the Prime Minister. It was a hagiographical epic, which, in cinematic terms, was in some respects ahead of its time. It was complete by the autumn of 1918. But, it seems, Lloyd George took against the film, for reasons which are not wholly clear. The Ideal company's executives – already reeling from allegations in the periodical *John Bull* that they were German sympathizers – were induced to suppress the film. They handed over the only copy to solicitors Lewis and Lewis, who were apparently representing Lloyd George's interests in some way. In return they received £20,000 cash, to cover the costs of production. The negative did not turn

up until 1994, found amongst material owned by Lloyd George's grandson. Happily, it proved possible to restore it. Interestingly, the film shows the young Lloyd George watching a debate between Lord Randolph Churchill and Gladstone, and later shows him debating with Randolph Churchill himself, but the character of Winston Churchill does not appear in the film. All these details are related in David Berry and Simon Horrocks (eds.), *David Lloyd George: The Movie Mystery*, University of Wales Press, Cardiff, 1998, quotation at p. 35.

84 Lord Beaverbrook, *Men and Power, 1917–1918*, Hutchinson, London, 1956, pp. 136–7.

85 Walter Long to William Bull, 22 July 1917, William Bull Papers, Churchill College, Cambridge, 4/16.

86 Austen Chamberlain to Long, 24 July 1917, Walter Long Papers, British Library, Add. 62405, ff. 76–7.

87 John Ramsden (ed.), *Real Old Tory Politics: The Political Diaries of Sir Robert Sanders, Lord Bayford, 1910–35*, Historians' Press, London, 1984, p. 88 (entry for 20 July 1917).

88 WSC to DLG, 22 July 1917, in Churchill, *World Crisis*, Part III, p. 335.

89 Richard Lloyd George, *My Father*, p. 185.

90 H. A. Gwynne to Lady Bathurst, 20 July 1917, and Gwynne to Henry Rawlinson, 23 Aug. 1917, in Keith Wilson (ed.), *The Rasp of War: The Letters of H. A. Gwynne to the Countess Bathurst, 1914–1918*, Sidgwick & Jackson, London, 1988, pp. 221, 225.

91 Philip Williamson (ed.), *The Modernisation of Conservative Politics: The Diaries and Letters of William Bridgeman, 1904–1935*, Historians' Press, London, 1988, p. 128 (entry for Feb. 1918).

92 Beaverbrook, *Men and Power*, p. 127.

93 In July, Esher wrote to another correspondent: 'I hear that the appointments of Winston and Montagu are equally most unpopular, and that L.G. is supposed by his best friends to be off his head! His security is that no one will put him out to put Mr. A in!' Lord Esher to Douglas Haig, 30 May 1917, WSC CV IV, Part 1, p. 64; Esher to Alexander Murray, 22 July 1917, Elibank Papers, National Library of Scotland, MS 8804.

94 William Armstrong (ed.), *With Malice Toward None: A War Diary by Cecil H. King*, Sidgwick & Jackson, London, 1970, p. 107 (entry for 19 Feb. 1941). King heard the story not at first hand but from Stuart Campbell, editor of the *Sunday Pictorial*. However, Lloyd George's reported comments are in line with other harsh things he said about Churchill during this period.

95 Scawen Blunt diary, 16 Sept. 1917, Scawen Blunt Papers, MS 17–1975.

96 Wilson, *Diaries of C. P. Scott*, p. 300 (entry for 24 Aug. 1917).

97 Riddell diary, 8 Feb. 1913, Riddell Papers, MS 62957, f. 21.

98 The Earl of Swinton, *Sixty Years of Power: Some Memories of the Men Who Wielded It*, Hutchinson, London, 1966, p. 42.

99 Hankey diary, 17 Aug. 1917, in Roskill, *Man of Secrets*, vol. I, p. 425.

100 Walter Layton, 'Adventures in Peace and War' (unpublished memoir),

pp. 169, 169a, 170, 173, Walter Layton Papers, Trinity College, Cambridge, Box 147.

101 Roy Jenkins, *Churchill*, Macmillan, London, 2001, p. 327.

102 Robert Blake (ed.), *The Private Papers of Douglas Haig, 1914–1919*, Eyre and Spottiswoode, London, 1952, pp. 254–5 (entries for 13 and 14 Sept. 1917).

103 C. à Court Repington, *The First World War, 1914–1918*, Constable, London, 1920, p. 229 (entry for 12 Feb. 1918).

104 Churchill, *World Crisis*, Part III, p. 411.

105 Swinton, *Sixty Years*, p. 40.

106 Maurice Hankey diary, 24 March 1918, Hankey Papers, 1/4, partially reproduced in WSC CV IV, Part 1, p. 277.

107 Leo Amery diary, 28 March 1918, ibid., p. 282 & n. 2.

108 'Rough notes taken of speeches delivered on the occasion of a private dinner given by Messrs. Ivor Nicholson & Watson at the Reform Club on Thursday, October 29th 1936 in honour of the Rt. Hon. D. Lloyd George O.M. M.P., on the occasion of the completion of his "War Memoirs"', Lloyd George Papers, HLRO, LG G/208/4.

109 WSC to DLG, 15 April 1918 (unsent draft), WSC CV IV, Part 1, p. 302.

110 WSC to DLG, 4 May 1918, ibid., p. 310.

111 WSC to DLG, 15 May 1918, ibid., p. 316.

112 WSC to DLG, 17 June 1918, ibid., p. 327.

113 Paul Addison, *Churchill on the Home Front, 1900–1955*, Pimlico, London, 1993, p. 191.

114 Scawen Blunt diary, 13 May 1918, Scawen Blunt Papers, MS 18–1975.

115 Quoted in Martin Gilbert, *Winston S. Churchill*, vol. IV: *1916–1922*, Heinemann, London, 1975, p. 120.

116 Basil Liddell Hart, 'Talk with Sir Albert Stern', 22 Sept. 1942, Basil Liddell Hart Papers, Liddell Hart Centre for Military Archives, King's College, London, LH11/1942/77. Liddell Hart noted that Stern made certain errors of detail when relating the story, but the gist of it seems plausible.

117 David Dutton (ed.), *Paris 1918: The War Diary of the British Ambassador, the 17th Earl of Derby*, Liverpool University Press, Liverpool, 2001, p. 198 (entry for 12 Sept. 1918).

118 Edwin Montagu, memoranda of 6 & 7 Nov. 1918, in Waley, *Edwin Montagu*, pp. 182–90.

119 Christopher Addison diary, 6 Nov. 1918, Christopher Addison Papers, Bodleian Library, Oxford, MS Addison dep. c.4, f. 178.

120 WSC to DLG, 7 Nov. 1918, WSC CV IV, Part 1, p. 408.

121 DLG to WSC, 8 Nov. 1918, draft corrected in Bonar Law's hand in Lloyd George Papers, HLRO, LG/F/8/2/38, and version as sent in WSC CV IV, Part 1, pp. 408–10.

122 WSC to DLG, 9 Nov. 1918, ibid., p. 410.

123 Churchill, *World Crisis*, Part III, p. 543.

124 Winston S. Churchill, *The World Crisis*, Part IV: *The Aftermath* [originally

published by Thornton Butterworth, London, 1929], WSC CW, vol. XI, pp. 20–1.

125 Wilson diary, 11 Nov. 1918, WSC CV IV, Part 1, p. 412.

126 DLG to WSC, 8 Nov. 1918, draft, Lloyd George Papers, HLRO, LG/F/8/2/38.

Six – MASTER AND SERVANT

1 Lord Boothby, *Recollections of a Rebel*, Hutchinson, London, 1978, pp. 51–2.

2 Margot Asquith diary, 30 Nov. 1918, WSC CV IV, Part 1, p. 431. Emphasis in original.

3 Ruth Lee diary, 13 May 1921, in Alan Clark (ed.), *'A Good Innings': The Private Papers of Viscount Lee of Fareham*, John Murray, London, 1974, p. 209.

4 Lord Beaverbrook, *Men and Power, 1917–1918*, Hutchinson, London, 1956, p. 325.

5 A. J. P. Taylor (ed.), *Lloyd George: A Diary by Frances Stevenson*, Harper & Row, New York, 1971, p. 169 (entry for 5 March 1919). Emphasis in original.

6 WSC to DLG, 21 Nov. 1918, WSC CV IV, Part 1, p. 421.

7 John M. McEwen, *The Riddell Diaries, 1908–1923*, Athlone Press, London and Atlantic Highlands, NJ, 1986, p. 249 (entry for 17 Nov. 1918).

8 WSC to DLG, 29 Dec. 1919, WSC CV IV, Part 1, p. 448.

9 DLG to WSC, 9 Jan. 1919, ibid., p. 450.

10 Winston S. Churchill, *The World Crisis*, Part IV: *The Aftermath* [originally published by Thornton Butterworth, London, 1929], WSC CW, vol. XI, pp. 52–3.

11 McEwen, *Riddell Diaries*, p. 257 (entry for 16 Feb. 1919).

12 Kenneth O. Morgan, *Consensus and Disunity: The Lloyd George Coalition Government, 1918–1922*, Clarendon Press, Oxford, 1979, pp. 39–41.

13 'Prime Minister on Conscription', *The Times*, 12 Dec. 1918.

14 Churchill, *The Aftermath*, p. 49.

15 War Cabinet minutes, 10 Nov. 1918 (extract), WSC CV IV, Part 1, p. 412.

16 Keith Middlemas (ed.), *Thomas Jones: Whitehall Diary*, 3 vols., Oxford University Press, London, 1969–71, vol. I, p. 86 (entry for 14 May 1919).

17 McEwen, *Riddell Diaries*, p. 255 (entry for 26 Jan. 1919).

18 DLG to WSC, 18 Jan. 1919, WSC CV IV, Part 1, p. 461.

19 WSC to DLG, 29 Jan. 1919, ibid., p. 494.

20 Jones to Hankey, 8 May 1919, in Middlemas, *Whitehall Diary*, vol. I, p. 85.

21 McEwen, *Riddell Diaries*, p. 267 (entry for 11 April 1919).

22 Thelma Cazalet-Keir, *From the Wings*, Bodley Head, London, 1967, pp. 62, 64. The remark about the triumphal procession dates from mid-March 1922.

23 Taylor, *A Diary by Frances Stevenson*, p. 179 (entry for 13 April 1919).

24 David Lloyd George, *The Truth About the Peace Treaties*, 2 vols., Victor Gollancz, London, 1938, vol. I, p. 325.

25 Churchill, *The Aftermath*, p. 73.

26 Speech of 11 April 1919.

27 McEwen, *Riddell Diaries*, p. 257 (entry for 16 Feb. 1919). Emphasis in original.

28 DLG to Philip Kerr, 19 Feb. 1919, Papers of Philip Kerr, 11th Marquis of Lothian, Lothian Muniments, National Archives of Scotland, GD40/17/771.

29 Henry Wilson diary, 20 Jan. 1919, WSC CV IV, Part 1, p. 471.

30 Mary Spears diary, 24 Jan. 1919, ibid., p. 479.

31 DLG to WSC, 16 Feb. 1919, ibid., p. 538.

32 Wilson diary, 17 Feb. 1919, ibid., p. 541.

33 WSC to DLG, 21 Feb. 1919, ibid., p. 550.

34 WSC to DLG, 14 March 1919, ibid., p. 586.

35 Wilson diary, 26 March 1919, ibid., p. 594.

36 Martin Gilbert, *Winston S. Churchill*, vol. IV: *1916–1922*, Heinemann, London, 1975, p. 278, citing the recollections of Violet Bonham Carter.

37 Edwin Montagu, 'Note dictated Wednesday, 4th June 1919', in S. D. Waley, *Edwin Montagu: A Memoir and an Account of His Visits to India*, Asia Publishing House, London, 1964, p. 211.

38 A. Lentin, *Guilt at Versailles: Lloyd George and the Pre-History of Appeasement*, Methuen, London, 1985, p. 100.

39 Hankey diary, 2 July 1919 (reviewing previous three months), Maurice Hankey Papers, Churchill College, Cambridge, 1/5.

40 Taylor, *A Diary by Frances Stevenson*, p. 187 (entry for 29 June 1919).

41 WSC to DLG, 24 March 1920, WSC CV IV, Part 2, p. 1053.

42 H. W. Wilson to Lord Northcliffe, 3 April 1919, Northcliffe Papers, British Library, Add. 62201, f. 89.

43 J. Lee Thompson, *Northcliffe: Press Baron in Politics, 1865–1922*, John Murray, London, 2000, pp. 325–6.

44 Walter Long to DLG, 15 June 1919, Lloyd George Papers, HLRO, LG/F/33/2/54.

45 A. N. Wilson, *After the Victorians: The Decline of Britain in the World*, Farrar, Straus and Giroux, New York, 2005, p. 191, citing S. J. Taylor, *The Great Outsiders: Northcliffe, Rothermere and the 'Daily Mail'*, Weidenfeld and Nicolson, London, 1996, p. 218.

46 Hankey diary, 22 July 1919, Hankey Papers 1/5. This entry is misdated and mistranscribed in WSC CV IV, Part 2, pp. 741–2.

47 George A. Gibb to William Bull, 16 Aug. 1919, William Bull Papers, Churchill College, Cambridge, 4/20.

48 Gibb to Bull, 20 Aug. 1919, ibid., 4/20.

49 DLG to WSC, 30 Aug. 1919, WSC CV IV, Part 2, p. 827.

50 Hankey diary, 14 Sept. 1919, Hankey Papers 1/5.

51 McEwen, *Riddell Diaries*, p. 291 (entry for 20 Sept. 1919).

52 WSC to DLG, 20 Sept. 1919, WSC CV IV, Part 2, p. 865.

53 DLG to WSC, 22 Sept. 1919, ibid., p. 868.

54 WSC to DLG, 22 Sept. 1919, ibid., p. 870–2.

55 H. A. L. Fisher diary, 23 Sept. 1919, ibid., p. 874.

56 Alfred Milner diary, 5 Oct. 1919, Alfred Milner Papers, Bodleian Library, Oxford, dep. 90.

57 Edward Grigg, Military Secretary to the Prince of Wales, was asked by Lloyd George to play the anthem, but failed at first to detect that this was intended as a dig at Churchill. Grigg felt compelled to apologize to the latter: 'I felt indignant when I realised – it was a rotten thing to do.' Grigg to WSC, 19 Dec. 1919, and Churchill's reply of the same date, Churchill Papers, Churchill College, Cambridge, CHAR 2/106/159, 163.

58 Winston Churchill to George V, 16 Oct. 1919, Royal Archives, Windsor Castle, RA PS/GV/Q 1557/1.

59 Clive Wigram, memorandum of 18 Nov. 1919, Royal Archives, RA PS/GV/Q 1557/3.

60 Churchill to George V, 17 Nov. 1919, Royal Archives, RA PS/GV/Q 1557/2.

61 Clive Wigram, memorandum of 18 Nov. 1919, Royal Archives, RA PS/GVQ 1557/3.

62 George V to Churchill, 25 Nov. 1919, Royal Archives, RA PS/GV/Q 1557/5.

63 Churchill to George V, 7 Dec. 1919, Royal Archives, RA PS/GV/Q 1557/6.

64 Lord Stamfordham, memorandum of 16 Dec. 1919, Royal Archives, RA PS/GV/Q 1557/7.

65 Fisher diary, 3 Nov. 1919, WSC CV IV, Part 2, p. 945.

66 Quoted in W. P. Coates and Zelda K. Coates, *A History of Anglo-Soviet Relations*, Lawrence & Wishart, London, 1944, p. 2.

67 Wilson diary, 16 Jan. 1920, WSC CV IV, Part 2, p. 1004.

68 McEwen, *Riddell Diaries*, p. 303 (entry for 24 Jan. 1920).

69 Middlemas, *Whitehall Diary*, vol. I, p. 105 (entry for 9 Feb. 1920).

70 Earl Beatty to Lady Beatty, 4 Aug. 1920, in B. McL. Ranft (ed.), *The Beatty Papers: Selections from the Private and Official Correspondence and Papers of Admiral of the Fleet Earl Beatty*, vol. II: *1916–1927*, Scolar Press for the Navy Records Society, Aldershot, 1993, p. 96.

71 Decrypted telegram from G. V. Chicherin to L. B. Kamenev, 28 Aug. 1920, conveying a message from Lenin, Lloyd George Papers, HLRO, LG F/203/1/11 no. 14.

72 Hankey diary, 18 Nov. 1920, WSC CV IV, Part 2, p. 1246.

73 Margaret MacMillan, *Peacemakers: The Paris Conference of 1919 and Its Attempt to End War*, John Murray, London, 2001, p. 91.

74 Parliamentary Debates, House of Commons, 5th Series, 10 Aug. 1920, col. 268.

75 Bertrand Russell to Elizabeth Russell, 16 Feb. 1921, in Nicholas Griffin (ed.), *The Selected Letters of Bertrand Russell: The Public Years, 1914–1970*, Routledge, London, 2001, p. 223.

76 McEwen, *Riddell Diaries*, p. 306 (entry for 6 March 1920).

77 Ibid., p. 314 (entry for 12 June 1920).

78 L. J. Macfarlane, 'Hands off Russia: British Labour and the Russo-Polish War, 1920', *Past and Present*, no. 38 (Dec. 1967), pp. 126–52, quotation at p. 152.

79 Hankey diary, 23 May 1920, Hankey Papers 1/5.

80 Taylor, *A Diary by Frances Stevenson*, p. 197 (entry for 17 Jan. 1920). Emphasis in original.

81 A joking reference to a diminutive group of hardline Scottish Presbyterians, The Free Church of Scotland.

82 Lady Frances Balfour to 'G.W.B.' [Gerald Balfour], 27 Jan. 1920, Balfour Papers, National Archives of Scotland, GD433/2/287.

83 McEwen, *Riddell Diaries*, p. 285 (entry for 12–15 July 1919).

84 Speech of 15 July 1919.

85 DLG to Arthur Balfour, 18 Feb. 1920, Balfour Papers, GD433/2/1/32.

86 Morgan, *Consensus and Disunity*, p. 185.

87 Bonar Law to Arthur Balfour, 24 March 1920, Balfour Papers, GD433/2/1/36.

88 Morgan, *Consensus and Disunity*, p. 185.

89 Riddell diary, 1 Jan. 1921, Riddell Papers, British Library, MS 62966 f. 1.

90 Hankey diary, 8 Jan. 1921, Hankey Papers, 1/5.

91 Henry Wilson diary, 23 Jan. 1921, WSC CV IV, Part 2, p. 1319.

92 WSC to CSC, 6 Feb. 1921, ibid., p. 1333. Chequers is a country house retreat in Buckinghamshire, donated to a trust by Arthur and Ruth Lee, for the use of successive Prime Ministers in perpetuity. The trust came into effect in January 1921.

93 Lord Hardinge to Lord Curzon, 18 Jan. 1921, Hardinge of Penhurst Papers, Cambridge University Library, 44, f. 92.

94 WSC to DLG, 4 Jan. 1921, WSC CV IV, Part 2, pp. 1289–90.

95 Henry Wilson diary, 29 March 1921, ibid., p. 1418.

96 McEwen, *Riddell Diaries*, p. 343 (entry for 14 May 1921).

97 Taylor, *A Diary by Frances Stevenson*, p. 219 (entry for 31 May 1921).

98 'The Scheme that Failed', *Manchester Guardian*, 23 June 1921.

99 Taylor, *A Diary by Frances Stevenson*, p. 223 (entry for 24 June 1921).

100 McEwen, *Riddell Diaries*, p. 345 (entry for 24 June 1921).

101 Austen Chamberlain to Hilda Chamberlain, 26 June 1921, in Robert C. Self (ed.), *The Correspondence of Sir Austen Chamberlain with his Sisters Hilda and Ida, 1916–1937*, Cambridge University Press for the Royal Historical Society, Cambridge, 1995, p. 160.

102 McEwen, *Riddell Diaries*, p. 320 (entry for 23 July 1920).

103 Taylor, *A Diary by Frances Stevenson*, p. 210 (entry for 26 April 1921).

104 Notes exchanged in Cabinet, 8 May 1921, WSC CV IV, Part 3, p. 1464.

105 Lord Beaverbrook to Sir Robert Borden, 12 May 1921, ibid., p. 1466.

106 Memorandum from Thomas Marlowe to Lord Northcliffe, 30 May 1921, ibid., p. 1478.

107 Morgan, *Consensus and Disunity*, p. 319.

108 WSC to DLG, 4 Dec. 1920, WSC CV IV, Part 2, pp. 1260–2.

109 Morgan, *Consensus and Disunity*, citing NA, PRO, CAB 23/28, minutes of a conference of ministers, 18 Feb. 1921.

110 See Curzon to Lord Hardinge, 12 Jan. 1921, Hardinge Papers, 44, ff. 72–4.

111 DLG to WSC, 16 June 1921, WSC CV IV, Part 3, p. 1511.

112 Tom Segev, *One Palestine, Complete: Jews and Arabs under the British Mandate*, Little, Brown, London, 2000, pp. 38, 158; Norman Rose, 'Churchill and Zionism', in Robert Blake and Wm. Roger Louis (eds.), *Churchill*, Oxford University Press, Oxford, 1993, pp. 147–66, at pp. 150–1.

113 Maxwell Coote diary, 29 March 1921, Maxwell Henry Coote Papers, Liddell Hart Centre for Military Archives, King's College, London.

114 A record of the meeting, which took place on 22 July 1921, can be found in WSC CV IV, Part 3, pp. 1558–61.

115 Middlemas, *Whitehall Diary*, vol. III, p. 19 (entry for 31 May 1920).

116 Wilson diary, 30 Aug. 1920, WSC CV IV, Part 2, p. 1195.

117 H. A. L. Fisher diary, 24 Sept. 1920, ibid., p. 1215.

118 Speech of 16 Oct. 1920.

119 'The Guildhall Banquet', *The Times*, 10 Nov. 1920.

120 Wilson diary, 2 June 1920, quoted in Gilbert, *Winston S. Churchill*, vol. IV, p. 453.

121 Wilson diary, 29 Dec. 1920, WSC CV IV, Part 2, p. 1277.

122 Middlemas, *Whitehall Diary*, vol. III, p. 85 (entry for 6 July 1921).

123 'Draft Reply adopted at Gairloch', 21 Sept. 1921, ibid., p. 116.

124 Taylor, *A Diary by Frances Stevenson*, p. 234 (entry for 6 Nov. 1921).

125 Collins's notes, as quoted in Rex Taylor, *Michael Collins*, Hutchinson, London, 1958, pp. 154–5.

126 J. H. Lewis diary, 10 Nov. 1921, J. H. Lewis Papers, National Library of Wales, D31.

127 Churchill, *The Aftermath*, p. 303.

128 WSC to DLG, 9 Nov. 1921, WSC CV IV, Part 3, p. 1666.

129 Churchill, *The Aftermath*, p. 307.

130 Lord Beaverbrook to Lord Rothermere, WSC CV V, Part 1, p. 389.

131 Cabinet note, 4 July 1921, WSC CV IV, Part 3, p. 1542.

132 Middlemas, *Whitehall Diary*, vol. I, p. 179 (entry for 9 Nov. 1921).

133 Christopher Addison to Isobel Addison, 14 July 1921, quoted in Morgan, *Consensus and Disunity*, p. 103.

134 Fisher diary, 5 Aug. 1921, H. A. L. Fisher Papers, Bodleian Library, Oxford, Box 17.

135 Transcript of telegram from DLG to WSC, Aug. 1921, Churchill Papers, CHAR 1/141/74.

136 John Julius Norwich (ed.), *The Duff Cooper Diaries, 1915–1951*, Weidenfeld and Nicolson, London, 2005, p. 150 (entry for 21 Aug. 1921).

137 WSC to DLG, 23 Sept. 1921, Lloyd George Papers, HLRO, LG F/9/3/87.

138 DLG to WSC, 1 Oct. 1921, WSC CV IV, Part 3, pp. 1637–9.

139 Lord Beaverbrook, *The Decline and Fall of Lloyd George: And Great Was the Fall Thereof*, Collins, London, 1963, p. 94.

140 WSC to CSC, 4 Jan. 1922, WSC CV IV, Part 3, p. 1712.

141 Taylor, *A Diary by Frances Stevenson*, p. 241 (entry for 3 Feb. 1922).

142 Philip Sassoon to DLG, 13 Feb. 1922, WSC CV IV, Part 3, p. 1772.

143 DLG to Frances Stevenson, 15 March 1922, in A. J. P. Taylor (ed.), *My Darling Pussy: The Letters of Lloyd George and Frances Stevenson, 1913–41*, Weidenfeld and Nicolson, London, 1975, p. 36.

144 Sassoon to Esher, 6 March 1922, WSC CV IV, Part 3, p. 1794.

145 WSC to CSC, 27 Jan. 1922, in Mary Soames (ed.), *Speaking for Themselves: The Personal Letters of Winston and Clementine Churchill*, Doubleday, London, 1998, pp. 247–8.

146 Taylor, *A Diary by Frances Stevenson*, p. 241 (entry for 3 Feb. 1922).

147 WSC to DLG, 20 Feb. 1922, WSC CV IV, Part 3, p. 1783.

148 Beaverbrook to DLG, 15 March 1922, ibid., p. 1808.

149 Charles A. McCurdy to DLG, 17 March 1922, Lloyd George Papers, HLRO, LG/F/35/1/38.

150 Austen Chamberlain to DLG, 21 March 1922, WSC CV IV, Part 3, p. 1814.

151 DLG to Austen Chamberlain, 22 March 1922, ibid., p. 1818.

152 DLG to Robert Horne, 22 March 1922, ibid., p. 1816.

153 Gilbert, *Winston S. Churchill*, vol. IV, pp. 778–9.

154 Sassoon to DLG, 24 March 1922, WSC CV IV, Part 3, p. 1826.

155 Austen Chamberlain to DLG, 25 March 1922, ibid., p. 1827.

156 Joan Lascelles, 'Whittinghame. Nov. 19th 1922' (typed note included in Alice Balfour's diary), Balfour Papers, GD433/2/136.

157 Telegram from Lord Rothermere to WSC, 27 March 1922, Churchill Papers, CHAR 2/121/116.

158 Middlemas, *Whitehall Diary*, vol. I, pp. 197, 195.

159 WSC to DLG, 26 July 1922, WSC CV IV, Part 3, p. 1942.

160 Middlemas, *Whitehall Diary*, vol. III, p. 212 (entry for 8 June 1922).

161 Ibid., vol. I, p. 302 (entry for 4 Nov. 1924).

162 WSC to CSC, 18 July 1922, in Soames, *Speaking for Themselves*, p. 258.

163 Middlemas, *Whitehall Diary*, vol. II, p. 67 (entry for 25 Aug. 1926).

164 DLG to CSC, 8 Sept. 1922, WSC CV IV, Part 3, p. 1982.

165 Press communiqué, 16 Sept. 1922, ibid., p. 1994.

166 WSC to Sinclair, 25 Sept. 1922, ibid., p. 2029.

167 Hankey diary, 4 Oct. 1922, covering 23–27 Sept., in Stephen Roskill, *Hankey: Man of Secrets*, 3 vols., Collins, London, 1970–4, vol. II, p. 289. The dinner was on 27 September.

168 Curzon to Austen Chamberlain, 27 Sept. 1922, quoted in Gilbert, *Winston S. Churchill*, vol. IV, p. 840.

169 Hankey diary, 17 Oct. 1922, in Roskill, *Man of Secrets*, vol. II, p. 295.

170 'Liberal MP's Plea for Honesty', *The Times*, 3 Oct. 1922.

171 'Cabinet's "Vital Mistake"', *The Times*, 4 Oct. 1922.

172 'Mr. Asquith on the Crisis', *The Times*, 7 Oct. 1922. Asquith was particularly hostile to the Cabinet Secretariat, 'a new excrescence which the Coalition have grafted on to our administrative fabric'.

173 'The Near East: Pronouncement by Mr. Bonar Law', *The Times*, 7 Oct. 1922.

174 Trevor Wilson (ed.), *The Political Diaries of C. P. Scott, 1911–1928*, Collins, London, 1970, p. 427 (entry for 13 Oct. 1922).

175 Churchill draft memoirs, Churchill Papers, CHUR 4/76A, f. 38.

176 Lucy Baldwin memorandum, n.d. [late 1922], in Philip Williamson and Edward Baldwin (eds.), *Baldwin Papers: A Conservative Statesman, 1908–1947*, Cambridge University Press, Cambridge, 2004, p. 71.

177 Roy Jenkins, *Baldwin*, Collins, London, 1987, p. 52.

178 Hankey diary, 23 Oct. 1922, in Roskill, *Man of Secrets*, vol. II, pp. 299–300.

179 Gilbert, *Winston S. Churchill*, vol. IV, p. 864.

180 Churchill draft memoirs, Churchill Papers, CHUR 4/76A, f. 40.

181 David Reynolds, *In Command of History: Churchill Fighting and Writing the Second World War*, Allen Lane, London, 2004, pp. 84–5.

182 Winston S. Churchill, *The Gathering Storm* [originally published as vol. I of *The Second World War*, Cassell, London, 1948], WSC CW, vol. XXII, p. 14.

Seven – Two Ways of Liberalism

1 Violet Milner to William Bridgeman, 21 July 1925, quoting the reaction of Lord Milner (her late husband) to the appointment, William Bridgeman Papers, Shropshire Records and Research Centre, Shrewsbury, 4629/1/1925/64; F. S. Oliver to Bridgeman, 17 Nov. 1924, Bridgeman Papers, 4629/1/1924/92.

2 Lord Beaverbrook, 'Two Ways of Liberalism: Mr. Lloyd George and Mr. Churchill', n.d. [1924–9], Beaverbrook Papers, HLRO, BBKG/5/10.

3 'Liberals and Ex-Premier', *The Times*, 23 Oct. 1922.

4 WSC to J. C. Robertson, 27 Oct. 1922, WSC CV IV, Part 3, pp. 2095–6.

5 WSC to DLG, 2 Nov. 1922, ibid., p. 2115.

6 Joan Lascelles to Edward Lascelles, 28–30 Oct. 1922, Balfour Papers, National Archives of Scotland, GD433/2/76, f. 12.

7 H. A. L. Fisher diary, 2 Nov. 1922, WSC CV IV, Part 3, p. 2113.

8 Alice Balfour diary, 18 Nov. 1922, Balfour Papers, GD433/2/136.

9 Joan Lascelles,'Whittinghame. Nov. 19th 1922', ibid.

10 T. E. Lawrence to WSC, 18 Nov. 1922, WSC CV IV, Part 3, p. 2124.

11 John Vincent (ed.), *The Crawford Papers: The Journals of David Lindsay Twenty-seventh Earl of Crawford and Tenth of Earl of Balcarres, 1871–1940, during the Years 1892 to 1940*, Manchester University Press, Manchester, 1984, p. 466 (entry for 17 Nov. 1922).

12 WSC to CSC, 30 Jan. 1923, in Mary Soames (ed.), *Speaking for Themselves:*

The Personal Letters of Winston and Clementine Churchill, Doubleday, London, 1998, p. 268.

13 Norman MacKenzie and Jeanne MacKenzie (eds.), *The Diary of Beatrice Webb*, vol. III: *1905–1924, 'The Power to Alter Things'*, Virago, London, 1984, p. 409 (entry for 10 Dec. 1922).

14 Lord Gladstone to Donald Maclean, 23 Jan. 1923, Herbert Gladstone Papers, British Library, Add. MS 46474, ff. 29–30.

15 John M. McEwen, *The Riddell Diaries, 1908–1923*, Athlone Press, London and Atlantic Highlands, NJ, 1986, p. 388 (entry for 30 May 1923).

16 Keith Middlemas (ed.), *Thomas Jones: Whitehall Diary*, 3 vols., Oxford University Press, London, 1969–71, vol. I, p. 276 (entry for 9 April 1924).

17 Winston S. Churchill, *The Gathering Storm* [originally published as vol. I of *The Second World War*, Cassell, London, 1948], WSC CW, vol. XXII, p. 14.

18 WSC to DLG, 8 Nov. 1923, Lloyd George Papers, HLRO, LG/G/4/4/6.

19 CSC to WSC, n.d., in Soames, *Speaking for Themselves*, p. 269. Soames suggests that this letter dates from the summer of 1923. However, Martin Gilbert's belief that it relates to the November episode appears more convincing: *Winston S. Churchill*, vol. V: *1922–1939*, Heinemann, London, 1976, p. 18.

20 Arnold Bennett to Richard Bennett, 12 Nov. 1923, in James Hepburn (ed.), *Letters of Arnold Bennett*, vol. IV: *Family Letters*, Oxford University Press, Oxford, 1986, p. 406.

21 Mackenzie and Mackenzie, *Diary of Beatrice Webb*, vol. III, p. 428 (entry for 19 Nov. 1923).

22 'Out of the Tomb', *The Times*, 22 Nov. 1923.

23 Quoted in Dennis Bardens, *Churchill in Parliament*, Robert Hale, London, 1967, p. 157.

24 Beaverbrook to Robert Borden, 16 Dec. 1923, quoted in Kenneth Young, *Churchill and Beaverbrook: A Study in Friendship and Politics*, Eyre and Spottiswoode, London, 1966, p. 67.

25 Stanley Baldwin to Thomas Jones, 25 Nov. 1940, in Philip Williamson and Edward Baldwin (eds.), *Baldwin Papers: A Conservative Statesman, 1908–1947*, Cambridge University Press, Cambridge, 2004, p. 477.

26 Account by Donald Maclean of a conversation with Lloyd George, 17 Jan. 1924, Donald Maclean Papers, Bodleian Library, Oxford, Dep. c.467, ff. 69–72.

27 W. A. S. Hewins diary, 6 March 1924, W. A. S. Hewins Papers, University of Sheffield, Special Collections, Box 124, section 183.

28 WSC to CSC 24 Feb. 1924, WSC CV V, Part 1, p. 113.

29 Gideon Murray, Master of Elibank to Rupert (unidentified; but an MP), 8 March 1924, Papers of the Viscounts and Barons of Elibank, National Archives of Scotland, GD32/25/73. Emphasis in original. A letter of support for Churchill from Murray was published in *The Scotsman* on 10 March 1924.

30 William Bridgeman to Caroline Bridgeman, 9 March 1924, Bridgeman Papers, 4629/1/1924/8.
31 Alice Balfour diary, 15 March 1924, Balfour Papers, GD433/2/136.
32 Austen Chamberlain to Ivy Chamberlain, 12 March 1924, WSC CV V, Part 1, p. 120.
33 DLG to Birkenhead, 11 March 1924, quoted in John Campbell, *Lloyd George: The Goat in the Wilderness, 1922–1931*, Cape, London, 1977, p. 93.
34 WSC to DLG, 17 March 1924, Lloyd George Papers, HLRO, LG/G/4/4/7.
35 DLG to WSC, 18 March 1924, ibid., LG/G/4/4/8.
36 WSC to CSC, 24 Feb. 1924, WSC CV V, Part 1, p. 114.
37 *Daily Chronicle*, 22 March 1924, cited in Campbell, *Goat in the Wilderness*, p. 93.
38 WSC to DLG, 21 March 1924, Lloyd George Papers, HLRO, LG/G/4/4/9.
39 WSC to Arthur Balfour, 3 April 1924, WSC CV V, Part 1, p. 139.
40 'Baldwin Turns and Rends His Critics', *People*, 18 May 1924, reproduced in Williamson and Baldwin, *Baldwin Papers*, pp. 490–3.
41 'The Future of Mr Lloyd George', *Weekly Despatch*, 29 June 1924, in Michael Wolff (ed.), *The Collected Essays of Sir Winston Churchill*, 4 vols., Library of Imperial History, London, 1976, vol. II, p. 137.
42 Gideon Murray to WSC, 2 July 1924, WSC CV V, Part 1, p. 169.
43 WSC to Gideon Murray, 3 July 1924, ibid., p. 170.
44 'Political Notes', *The Times*, 27 March 1924.
45 'Labour Failures: Mr. A. Chamberlain's Indictment' and 'Labour Rifts: Mr. Baldwin on the Coming Fight', *The Times*, 18 July 1924.
46 Austen Chamberlain to Hilda Chamberlain, 19 July 1924, in Robert C. Self (ed.), *The Correspondence of Sir Austen Chamberlain with his Sisters Hilda and Ida, 1916–1937*, Cambridge University Press for the Royal Historical Society, Cambridge, 1995, p. 255 (emphasis in original).
47 Baldwin to Austen Chamberlain, 21 July 1924, Austen Chamberlain Papers, University of Birmingham, Special Collections, AC 35/5/2a.
48 Speech of 25 Sept. 1924.
49 WSC to CSC, 19 Aug. 1924, in Soames, *Speaking for Themselves*, p. 283.
50 Campbell, *Goat in the Wilderness*, pp. 79, 101–2.
51 WSC to Balfour and Edward Carson, 1 Sept. 1924, WSC CV V, Part 1, pp. 190–1.
52 Sinclair to WSC, 23 Sept. 1924, ibid., p. 199.
53 Speech of 25 Oct. 1924.
54 Speech of 27 Oct. 1924, quoted in Campbell, *Goat in the Wilderness*, p. 106.
55 Churchill draft memoirs, Churchill Papers, Churchill College, Cambridge, CHUR 4/76A, f. 56.
56 Middlemas, *Whitehall Diary*, vol. I, p. 303 (entry for 8 Nov. 1924).
57 Neville Chamberlain diary, 5 Nov. 1924, Neville Chamberlain Papers, University of Birmingham, Special Collections, NC 2/21.
58 Churchill draft memoirs, Churchill Papers, CHUR 4/76A, f. 148.

59 Austen Chamberlain to Stanley Baldwin, 6 1924, Austen Chamberlain
    Papers, AC 35/5/4.
60 Neville Chamberlain diary, 6 Nov. 1924, Neville Chamberlain Papers, NC
    2/21.
61 See Neville Chamberlain diary, 1 Dec. 1924, ibid.
62 An unidentified Conservative ex-Cabinet Minister to Thomas Jones, 12 Nov.
    1951, in Thomas Jones, *A Diary with Letters, 1931–1950*, Oxford University
    Press, London, 1954, p. xxxii. The view expressed by the ex-minister
    certainly corresponded with Amery's. See Amery diary, 27 March 1952, Leo
    Amery Papers, Churchill College, Cambridge.
63 Middlemas, *Whitehall Diary*, vol. I, p. 303 (entry for 8 Nov. 1924).
64 DLG to WSC, 7 Nov. 1924, WSC CV V, Part 1, p. 238.
65 WSC to DLG, 8 Nov. 1924, quoted in A. J. Sylvester diary, 8 Nov. 1924,
    A. J. Sylvester Papers, National Library of Wales, A1.
66 Sylvester diary, 10 Dec. 1924, ibid.
67 Lord Boothby, *Recollections of a Rebel*, Hutchinson, London, 1978, p. 51.
68 Diana Mosley, *A Life of Contrasts*, Hamish Hamilton, London, 1977, p. 40.
69 Ruth Longford, *Frances, Countess Lloyd George: More than a Mistress*, Gracewing,
    Leominster, 1996, p. 87.
70 Speech of 28 April 1925.
71 Parliamentary Debates, House of Commons, 5th Series, vol. 183, 28 April
    1925, cols. 94–5.
72 Campbell, *Goat in the Wilderness*, pp. 115–16.
73 Churchill draft memoirs, Churchill Papers, CHUR 4/76A, f. 13.
74 'Government Trade Policy. Mr. Lloyd George's Criticism', *The Times*,
    11 July 1925.
75 Campbell, *Goat in the Wilderness*, p. 116.
76 H. A. L. Fisher to J. H. Lewis, 16 Feb. 1926, J. H. Lewis Papers, National
    Library of Wales, A1/293.
77 Middlemas, *Whitehall Diary*, vol. I, p. 316 (entry for 17 May 1925).
78 WSC to CSC, 25 March 1925, WSC CV V, Part 1, pp. 449–50.
79 Baldwin to George V, 26 May 1925, ibid., p. 488.
80 Robert Rhodes James, *Churchill: A Study in Failure, 1900–1939*, Weidenfeld
    and Nicolson, London, 1970, p. 164.
81 DLG to WSC, 20 Jan. 1927, Churchill Papers, CHAR 1/194.
82 Fisher to Lewis, 16 Feb. 1926, Lewis Papers, A1/293.
83 WSC to Alfred Mond, 29 Jan. 1926, WSC CV V, Part 1, p. 635.
84 WSC to CSC, 4 Feb. 1926, ibid., p. 641.
85 Parliamentary Debates, House of Commons, 5th Series, vol. 187, 6 Aug.
    1925, cols. 1610, 1613.
86 Middlemas, *Whitehall Diary*, vol. I, p. 328 (entry for 6 Aug. 1925).
87 Speech of 19 Oct. 1925.
88 WSC to DLG, 7 May 1926, Lloyd George Papers, HLRO, LG/G/4/4/13.
89 Rhodes James, *Churchill*, p. 171.

90 Paul Addison, *Churchill on the Home Front, 1900–1955*, Pimlico, London, 1993, p. 263.
91 ' "If Christ Came to London" ', *Daily Mail*, 28 June 1926.
92 Draft press statement, 14 Nov. 1927, WSC CV V, Part 1, p. 1104.
93 Speech of 24 Sept. 1928.
94 Martin Pugh, *'Hurrah for the Blackshirts!' Facsists and Fascism in Britain Between the Wars*, Cape, London, 2005, pp. 100–1.
95 DLG to Asquith, 24 May 1926 (and reproduced in *The Times* 26 May), quoted in Campbell, *Goat in the Wilderness*, p. 142.
96 Speech of 14 Feb. 1928.
97 Middlemas, *Whitehall Diary*, vol. II, p. 176 (entry for 6 March 1929).
98 Alan Booth and Melvyn Pack, *Employment, Capital and Economic Policy: Great Britain, 1918–1939*, Basil Blackwell, Oxford, 1985, p. 48.
99 'Message for the Electors of Ilford', 21 Feb. 1928, WSC CV V, Part 1, p. 1212.
100 Speech of 27 July 1928.
101 'Mr. Lloyd George and the Government', *The Times*, 24 Sept. 1928; WSC, speech of 24 Sept. 1928. (This speech was also referred to earlier in this chapter.)
102 Kenneth Young (ed.), *The Diaries of Sir Robert Bruce Lockhart*, 2 vols., Macmillan, London, 1973, vol. I: *1915–1938*, p. 80 (entry for 1 March 1929).
103 Peter Clarke, *The Keynesian Revolution in the Making, 1924–1936*, Clarendon Press, Oxford, 1988, p. 97.
104 William Joynson-Hicks to WSC, 6 Feb. 1929, quoted in Clarke, *Keynesian Revolution*, p. 54.
105 Middlemas, *Whitehall Diary*, vol. II, pp. 175–6 (entry for 6 March 1929).
106 WSC to Frederick Leith-Ross, 2 March 1929, quoted in Clarke, *Keynesian Revolution*, p. 63.
107 Speech of 15 April 1929.
108 John Maynard Keynes, *The Collected Writings of John Maynard Keynes*, vol. IX: *Essays in Persuasion*, Macmillan/Cambridge University Press, for the Royal Economic Society, London, 1972, p. 124.
109 Speech of 15 April 1929.
110 J. C. C. Davidson to WSC, 25 April 1929, NA, PRO, T161/303.
111 WSC to Davidson, 28 April 1929, NA, PRO, T161/303.
112 *The Times*, 13 May 1929, cited in Clarke, *Keynesian Revolution*, p. 96.
113 Martin Daunton, *Just Taxes: The Politics of Taxation in Britain, 1914–1979*, Cambridge University Press, Cambridge, 2002, p. 135.
114 Margaret Cole (ed.), *Beatrice Webb's Diaries, 1924–1932*, Longman's, Green, London, 1956, p. 165 (entry for 14 March 1928).
115 William Bridgeman to M. C. Bridgeman, 29 July 1928, in Philip Williamson (ed.), *The Modernisation of Conservative Politics: The Diaries and Letters of William Bridgeman, 1904–1935*, Historians' Press, London, 1988, p. 215.
116 'Note of an interview with Mr. Winston Churchill W.C. at his room in the

House of Commons on the 18th February 1929', in Peter Rowland, *Lloyd George*, Barrie & Jenkins, London, 1975, pp. 649–51.

117 Young, *Diaries of Sir Robert Bruce Lockhart*, vol. I, p. 80 (entry for 1 March 1929).

118 Neville Chamberlain to Hilda Chamberlain, 2 March 1929, in Robert Self (ed.), *The Neville Chamberlain Diary Letters*, 4 vols., Ashgate, Aldershot, 2002–5, vol. III: *The Heir Apparent, 1928–33*, p. 126.

119 Robert Rhodes James (ed.), *Memoirs of a Conservative: J. C. C. Davidson's Memoirs and Papers, 1910–37*, Weidenfeld and Nicolson, London, 1969, pp. 296–7 (Davidson diary entry for 6 March 1929).

120 Beaverbrook to Borden, 26 March 1929, WSC CV V, Part 1, p. 1451.

121 Neville Chamberlain to Hilda Chamberlain, 4 July 1931, in Self, *Neville Chamberlain Diary Letters*, vol. III, p. 266.

122 Broadcast of 30 April 1929.

123 Speech of 6 May 1929, quoted in Gilbert, *Winston S. Churchill*, vol. V: *1922–1939*, p. 327.

124 Speech of 7 May 1929.

125 Speech of 8 May 1929.

126 Speech of 13 May 1929.

127 'Mr. Lloyd George in Scotland', *The Times*, 4 May 1929.

128 'Mr. Lloyd George on Liberalism', *The Times*, 10 May 1929.

129 'The White Paper', *The Times*, 16 May 1929.

130 J. R. MacDonald diary, 7 May 1929, in Williamson and Baldwin, *Baldwin Papers*, p. 217.

131 'Labour Financial Policy', *The Times*, 4 May 1929.

132 Middlemas, *Whitehall Diary*, vol. II, p. 192 (entry for 20 June 1929).

133 Beaverbrook, 'Two Ways of Liberalism', Beaverbrook Papers, BBKG/5/10.

134 Speech of 10 May 1929.

Eight – POLITICS AND MEMORY

1 Robert Boothby, 'At Home With Lloyd George', *Picture Post*, 20 April 1940.

2 Ernest Evans to J. H. Lewis, 18 July 1929, J. H. Lewis Papers, National Library of Wales, A1/374.

3 Winston Churchill to Lloyd George, n.d. [probably 1929], Lloyd George Papers, HLRO, LG/C/3/15/13. Emphasis in original.

4 WSC to Stanley Baldwin, 26 June 1929, WSC CV V, Part 2, p. 8.

5 WSC to Baldwin, 29 June 1929, ibid., p. 101.

6 John Barnes and David Nicholson (eds.), *The Empire at Bay: The Leo Amery Diaries, 1929–1945*, Hutchinson, London, 1988, p. 41 (entry for 27 June 1929).

7 Ibid., pp. 42–3 (entry for 11 July 1929).

8 Ibid., p. 45 (entry for 17 July 1929).

9 Neville Chamberlain to Hilda Chamberlain, 21 July 1929, in Robert Self

(ed.), *The Neville Chamberlain Diary Letters*, 4 vols., Ashgate, Aldershot, 2002–5, vol. III: *The Heir Apparent, 1928–33*, p. 150.

10 See, for example, the speech of J. H. Thomas, Parliamentary Debates, House of Commons, 5th Series, vol. 230, 19 July 1929, cols. 794–5.

11 Donald Maclean to Lord Gladstone, 30 July 1929, Herbert Gladstone Papers, British Library, 46474, f. 220.

12 Speech of 3 July 1929.

13 Parliamentary Debates, House of Commons, 5th Series, vol. 229, 3 July 1929, col. 141.

14 Parliamentary Debates, House of Commons, 5th Series, vol. 230, 16 July 1929, col. 341.

15 Parliamentary Debates, House of Commons, 5th Series, vol. 246, 16 Dec. 1930, col. 1187.

16 DLG to WSC, 16 Oct. 1929, WSC CV V, Part 2, pp. 103–5.

17 Robert Skidelsky, *Politicians and the Slump: The Labour Government of 1929–1931*, Papermac, London, 1994, p. 145.

18 Jennifer Longford, undated memo, Frances Stevenson Papers, National Library of Wales, X3/1.

19 J. C. C. Davidson to Lord Irwin, 9 Nov. 1929, Robert Rhodes James (ed.), *Memoirs of a Conservative: J. C. C. Davidson's Memoirs and Papers, 1910–37*, Weidenfeld and Nicolson, London, 1969, p. 309.

20 William Bridgeman to M. C. Bridgeman, 23 Nov. 1929, in Philip Williamson (ed.), *The Modernisation of Conservative Politics: The Diaries and Letters of William Bridgeman, 1904–1935*, Historians' Press, London, 1988, p. 235.

21 Earl of Lytton to Irwin, 9–10 Nov. 1929, in Philip Williamson and Edward Baldwin (eds.), *Baldwin Papers: A Conservative Statesman, 1908–1947*, Cambridge University Press, Cambridge, 2004, p. 224.

22 A. J. P. Taylor (ed.), *Lloyd George: A Diary by Frances Stevenson*, Harper & Row, New York, 1971, p. 273 (entry for 14 May 1934).

23 Barnes and Nicolson, *Empire at Bay*, p. 57 (entry for 16 Dec. 1929).

24 Parliamentary Debates, House of Commons, 5th Series, vol. 233, 19 Dec. 1929, col. 1672.

25 'Life and Politics', *The Nation and Athenaeum*, 28 Dec. 1929.

26 Jones to J. Burgon Bickersteth, 23 Dec. 1929, in Keith Middlemas (ed.), *Thomas Jones: Whitehall Diary*, 3 vols., Oxford University Press, London, 1969–71, vol. II, p. 229.

27 Parliamentary Debates, House of Commons, 5th Series, vol. 235, 27 Feb. 1930, col. 2465.

28 Speech of 26 March 1930.

29 Speech of 28 May 1930.

30 'Government's Record', *The Times*, 3 Nov. 1930.

31 John Campbell, *Lloyd George: The Goat in the Wilderness, 1922–1931*, Cape, London, 1977, pp. 274–5, 286, 292–3.

32 Barnes and Nicolson, *Empire at Bay*, p. 84 (entry for 14 Oct. 1930).

33 Austen Chamberlain to Hilda Chamberlain, 27 Oct. 1930, in Robert C. Self

(ed.), *The Correspondence of Sir Austen Chamberlain with His Sisters Hilda and Ida, 1916–1937*, Cambridge University Press for the Royal Historical Society, Cambridge, 1995, p. 357.

34 Speech of 16 Dec. 1930.

35 WSC to RSC, 8 Jan. 1931, WSC CV V, Part 2, p. 243.

36 WSC to Archibald Sinclair, 8 Jan. 1931, in Ian Hunter (ed.), *Winston and Archie: The Letters of Sir Archibald Sinclair and Winston S. Churchill, 1915–1960*, Politico's, London, 2005, p. 195.

37 Speech of 23 Sept. 1931.

38 Oswald Mosley, *My Life*, Nelson, London, 1968, p. 10.

39 Nigel Nicolson (ed.), *Harold Nicolson: Diaries & Letters, 1930–1939*, Collins, London, 1966, pp. 81–2 (entry for 21 July 1931).

40 Colin Cross (ed.), *Life with Lloyd George: The Diary of A. J. Sylvester, 1931–45*, Macmillan, London, 1975, p. 37 (entry for 23 Aug. 1931).

41 DLG to Ramsay MacDonald, 30 Aug. 1931, quoted in Campbell, *Goat in the Wilderness*, p. 298.

42 Samuel Hoare to Neville Chamberlain, 31 Aug. 1931, WSC CV V, Part 2, p. 354.

43 An unidentified Conservative ex-Cabinet Minister (possibly Amery: see Chapter 7 note 62) to Thomas Jones, 12 Nov. 1951, in Thomas Jones, *A Diary with Letters, 1931–1950*, Oxford University Press, London, 1954, p. xxxii.

44 Mosley, *My Life*, p. 277.

45 WSC to W. A. McWhirter, 31 July 1931, WSC CV V, Part 2, p. 336.

46 'Will Lloyd George "Come Back"?', in Michael Wolff (ed.), *The Collected Essays of Sir Winston Churchill*, 4 vols., Library of Imperial History, London, 1976, vol. II, pp. 225–7.

47 Nicolson, *Diaries, 1930–39*, p. 89 (entry for 31 Aug. 1931).

48 Speech of 8 Sept. 1931.

49 'Note of events during the week ended Saturday, October 3rd, 1931', Maurice Hankey Papers, Churchill College, Cambridge, HNKY 1/8.

50 Viscount Tenby, unpublished draft autobiography, Viscount Tenby Papers, National Library of Wales, 23671C, pp. 38–9.

51 Speech of 12 Oct. 1931.

52 Speech of 23 Oct. 1931.

53 WSC to Sinclair, n.d., Thurso Papers, Churchill College, Cambridge, THRS II, 85/3. My transcription differs slightly from that given in Hunter, *Winston and Archie*, pp. 196–7, but the sense is not affected.

54 WSC to Sinclair, 30 Dec. 1931, in Hunter, *Winston and Archie*, p. 199.

55 Cross, *Life with Lloyd George*, p. 66 (entry for 16 Dec. 1931).

56 WSC to Brendan Bracken, 8 Jan. 1932, Churchill Papers, Churchill College, Cambridge, CHAR 1/401A/23.

57 Bracken to WSC, 21 Jan. 1932, Churchill Papers, CHAR 1/398A/54. A few days later Bracken met Thomas Jones, who recorded: 'He had lunched with L.G. on the latter's birthday, and found him in tremendous form; he

drank nearly a bottle of champagne at lunch and walked eight miles. Winston on the other hand is ill with insomnia, and neuritis, and talked on the phone with Bracken that morning complaining of his poor condition.' Jones diary, 28 Jan. 1932, Thomas Jones Papers, National Library of Wales, Class Z.

58 RSC to WSC, 1 Feb. 1932, Churchill Papers, CHAR 1/231.
59 DLG to Frances Stevenson, 28 Sept. 1932, in A. J. P. Taylor (ed.), *My Darling Pussy: The Letters of Lloyd George and Frances Stevenson, 1913–41*, Weidenfeld and Nicolson, London, 1975, p. 192.
60 DLG to Beaverbrook, 13 Feb. 1934, Lloyd George Papers, HLRO, LG/G/3/6/28.
61 Cross, *Life with Lloyd George*, p. 77 (entry for 7 June 1932).
62 He was perhaps referring more to Churchill's World War II memoirs than to *The World Crisis*, but the point stands. George W. Egerton, 'The Lloyd George "War Memoirs": A Study in the Politics of Memory', *Journal of Modern History*, vol. 60, no. 1 (March 1988), pp. 55–94, at p. 92.
63 Ibid.
64 WSC to CSC, 27 Jan. 1923, WSC CV V, Part 1, p. 19.
65 WSC to CSC, 29 Dec. 1921, in Mary Soames (ed.), *Speaking for Themselves: The Personal Letters of Winston and Clementine Churchill*, Doubleday, London, 1998, p. 244; Robin Prior, *Churchill's 'World Crisis' as History*, Croom Helm, London, 1983, p. 260.
66 'Parliament', *The Times*, 20 Feb. 1923.
67 WSC to DLG, 28 Feb. 1923, Lloyd George Papers, HLRO, LG/G/4/4/4; David Reynolds, *In Command of History: Churchill Fighting and Writing the Second World War*, Allen Lane, London, 2004, p. 25.
68 Middlemas, *Whitehall Diary*, vol. I, p. 233 (entry for 9 March 1923).
69 David Lloyd George, 'Should War Secrets be Disclosed?', *Western Mail*, 17 March 1923.
70 Hankey to Bonar Law, 8 March 1923, Bonar Law Papers, HLRO, BL/112/1/3.
71 M. P. A. Hankey to Neville Chamberlain, 15 June 1938, 'Mr. Lloyd George's Book on the Peace Treaties', NA, PRO, FO 370/554.
72 Reynolds, *In Command*, p. 27; Violet Pearman (Churchill's principal secretary, 1929–38) to Frances Stevenson, 21 Sept. 1934, Lloyd George Papers, HLRO, LG/G/4/5/5.
73 Prior, *Churchill's 'World Crisis'*, p. 259; Hankey to Churchill, 8 Dec. 1926, Churchill Papers, CHAR 8/204/144–59.
74 Winston S. Churchill, *The World Crisis*, Part III: *1916–1918* [originally published by Thornton Butterworth, London, 1927], WSC CW, vol. X, p. 256.
75 WSC to Beaverbrook, 30 Nov. 1926, WSC CV V, Part 1, p. 890.
76 Lord Sydenham of Combe, 'Mr. Churchill as Historian', in Lord Sydenham et al., *The World Crisis: A Criticism*, 2nd edition, Hutchinson, London, n.d. [1928], pp. 9–39, at p. 15.

77 Prior, *Churchill's 'World Crisis'*, pp. 172–3.

78 WSC to DLG, 27 Dec. 1928, WSC CV V, Part 1, p. 1405.

79 DLG to WSC, 8 Jan. 1929, Lloyd George Papers, HLRO, LG/G/4/4/21.

80 Beaverbrook to WSC, 16 Jan. 1929, Churchill Papers, CHAR 8/222/79.

81 Sinclair to WSC, 16 Jan. 1929, in Hunter, *Winston and Archie*, p. 191. In an unsent draft of this letter, Sinclair asked: 'Why provoke this controversy? Let Lloyd George expose himself and take the offensive if he will.' Thurso Papers, THRS II, 85/3.

82 WSC to DLG, 9 Jan. 1929, Lloyd George Papers, HLRO, LG/G/4/4/22.

83 WSC to DLG, 16 Jan. 1929, Churchill Papers, CHAR 8/222 f. 67.

84 T. E. Shaw to WSC, 18 March 1929, WSC CV V, Part 1, p. 1447.

85 Cross, *Life with Lloyd George*, p. 60 (entry for 1 Dec. 1931); Max Egremont, *Balfour: A Life of Arthur James Balfour*, Collins, London, 1980, p. 321.

86 Tom Clarke, *My Lloyd George Diary*, Methuen, London, 1939, p. 8 (entry for 26 June 1930).

87 Cross, *Life with Lloyd George*, p. 81 (entry for 28 Sept. 1932); Egerton, 'The Lloyd George "War Memoirs"', p. 62.

88 'Rough notes taken of speeches on Thursday, October 29th 1936', Lloyd George Papers, HLRO, LG/G/208/4.

89 Egerton, 'The Lloyd George "War Memoirs"', p. 68.

90 Hankey to DLG, 16 April 1934, Lloyd George Papers, HLRO, LG/G/212.

91 DLG to Hankey, 18 April 1934, ibid.

92 David Lloyd George, *War Memoirs*, 2 vols., Odhams Press, London, 1938 (originally published in 6 vols., 1933–36), vol. I, p. 638.

93 'Rough notes taken of speeches on Thursday, October 29th 1936', Lloyd George Papers, HLRO, LG/G/208/4.

94 Cross, *Life with Lloyd George*, p. 191 (entry for 24 Jan. 1938).

95 Jones diary, 16 March 1935, Jones Papers, Class Z.

96 Review of volume III of Lloyd George's *War Memoirs*, *Daily Mail*, 21 Sept. 1934, in Wolff, *Collected Essays*, vol. III, p. 98.

97 See Ivor Nicolson to WSC, 30 Jan. 1936, Churchill Papers, CHAR 8/528A, f. 10.

98 Winston S. Churchill, *Great Contemporaries* [originally published by Thornton Butterworth in 1937, and in a revised, extended edition in 1938], WSC CW, vol. XVI, p. 94.

99 Margot Asquith to WSC, 22 Feb. 1936, Churchill Papers, CHAR 8/528A, f. 37.

100 William Armstrong (ed.), *With Malice Toward None: A War Diary by Cecil H. King*, Sidgwick & Jackson, London, 1970, p. 188 (entry for 24 Aug. 1942).

Nine – THESE TWO PIRATES

1   Victor Cazalet to Stanley Baldwin, 24 Feb. 1938, in Robert Rhodes James, *Victor Cazalet: A Portrait*, Hamish Hamilton, London, 1976, p. 200.

2   Asa Briggs, *The Golden Age of Wireless: The History of Broadcasting in the United Kingdom*, vol. II, Oxford University Press, London, 1965, p. 145.

3   R. C. Norman to G. C. Tryon, 5 April 1939, NA, PRO, PREM 1/301.

4   H. Napier to O. S. Cleverly, 6 April 1939, ibid.

5   O. S. Cleverly, note on the question of political broadcasts, 20 April 1939, ibid.

6   Remarks of S. H. Wood reporting the views of John Anderson, 'Report of Interview at Minister of Labour, 5 June 1939', quoted in Briggs, *The Golden Age of Wireless*, pp. 657–8.

7   'Mr. Lloyd George on Liberal Task', *The Times*, 6 Jan. 1925.

8   WSC to CSC, 5 Sept. 1923, in Mary Soames (ed.), *Speaking for Themselves: The Personal Letters of Winston and Clementine Churchill*, Doubleday, London, 1998, p. 275; Speech of 27 Jan. 1926.

9   Press statement of 20 Jan. 1927.

10 Martin Gilbert, *Winston S. Churchill*, vol. V: *1922–1939*, Heinemann, London, 1976, p. 457, quoting speech of 17 Feb. 1933.

11 Speech of 23 Nov. 1932.

12 'Steed, Henry Wickham (1871–1956)', *Oxford Dictionary of National Biography*, Oxford University Press, Oxford, 2004, http://www.oxforddnb.com/view/article/36260, accessed 19 Sept. 2005.

13 DLG to Wickham Steed, 27 Oct. 1932, Henry Wickham Steed Papers, British Library, ff. 274–6.

14 Parliamentary Debates, House of Commons, 5th Series, vol. 281, 7 Nov. 1933, col. 103.

15 Speech of 7 Nov. 1933.

16 Colin Cross (ed.), *Life with Lloyd George: The Diary of A. J. Sylvester, 1931–45*, Macmillan, London, 1975, p. 112 (entry for 17 Nov. 1934).

17 A. J. P. Taylor (ed.), *Lloyd George: A Diary by Frances Stevenson*, Harper & Row, New York, 1971, p. 292 (entry for 22 Nov. 1934).

18 WSC to DLG, 24 Nov. 1934, WSC CV V, Part 2, p. 936.

19 Lord Londonderry to Ramsay MacDonald, 26 Nov. 1934, WSC CVV, Part 2, pp. 942–3. Churchill had earlier described the Air Minister to Lloyd George as 'That half-wit Charlie Londonderry.' Taylor, *A Diary by Frances Stevenson*, p. 292 (entry for 22 Nov. 1934). After he lost office the following year, Londonderry became a leading apologist for Germany. See Ian Kershaw, *Making Friends With Hitler: Lord Londonderry and Britain's Road to War*, Allen Lane, London, 2004.

20 Parliamentary Debates, House of Commons, 5th Series, vol. 295, 28 Nov. 1934, col. 881.

21 Ibid., cols. 905–22.

22 Robert Bernays to Lucy Brereton, 6 June 1935, in Nick Smart (ed.), *The Diaries and Letters of Robert Bernays, 1932–1939*, Edwin Mellen, Lewiston/Queenston/Lampeter, 1996, p. 201.

23 Taylor, *A Diary by Frances Stevenson*, pp. 293–4 (entry for 30 Nov. 1934).

24 Telegram from WSC to DLG, 6 April 1935, Lloyd George Papers, HLRO, LG/G/4/5/11.

25 See Churchill Papers, Churchill College, Cambridge, CHAR 2/243/57. Lloyd George is, however, omitted from the list of recipients given in WSC CV V, Part 2, p. 1156, n. 1.

26 David Reynolds, *In Command of History: Churchill Fighting and Writing the Second World War*, Allen Lane, London, 2004, p. 105.

27 Smart, *Diaries and Letters of Robert Bernays*, p. 85 (entry for 4 Aug. 1933).

28 Rab Butler to Lord Brabourne, 19 April 1934, Lord Brabourne Papers, India Office Library, MS Eur/F97/20 c, ff. 198, 202.

29 Thomas Jones diary, 28 April 1934, Thomas Jones Papers, National Library of Wales, Class Z. Compare with Thomas Jones, *A Diary with Letters, 1931–1950*, Oxford University Press, London, 1954, pp. 126–7.

30 Samuel Hoare to Lord Willingdon, 23 Aug. 1934, Viscount Templewood Papers, India Office Library, MSS Eur/E240/4, f. 1110.

31 Jones to Lady Grigg, 24 Feb. 1935, Jones Papers, Class Z.

32 Walter Layton, 'Note of conversation with Mr. Lloyd George, Friday, May 17th, 1935', Walter Layton Papers, Trinity College, Cambridge, Box 104/34.

33 Jones to Lady Grigg, 26 Jan. 1935, in Philip Williamson and Edward Baldwin (eds.), *Baldwin Papers: A Conservative Statesman, 1908–1947*, Cambridge University Press, Cambridge, 2004, p. 328.

34 A. J. Cummings to Walter Layton, 21 Dec. 1934, Layton Papers, Box 7/13/1.

35 WSC, Statement to the Press Association, WSC CV V, Part 2, p. 989. In the original draft, MacDonald was referred to as a 'deplorable person'; 'politician' was substituted for 'person' by hand. Churchill Papers, CHAR 2/234/22.

36 Paul Addison, *Churchill on the Home Front, 1900–1955*, Pimlico, London, 1993, p. 309.

37 WSC to CSC, 2 March 1935, in Soames, *Speaking for Themselves*, p. 389.

38 Layton, 'Note of conversation with Mr. Lloyd George, May 17th, 1935', Layton Papers, Box 104/34.

39 Jones to Lady Grigg, 24 Feb. 1935, Jones Papers, Class Z.

40 N. J. Crowson, *Fleet Street, Press Barons and Politics: The Journals of Collin Brooks, 1932–1940*, Cambridge University Press for the Royal Historical Society, Cambridge, 1998, p. 101 (entry for 18 April 1935).

41 Dawson memorandum, 4 May 1935, in Williamson and Baldwin, *Baldwin Papers*, p. 331.

42 J. L. Garvin to Lord Astor, May 1935, Jones Papers, Class Z.

43 Jones to Lady Grigg, 1 June 1935, in Jones, *Diary with Letters*, pp. 151–2.

44 R. A. Butler [19–21] July 1935, in Williamson and Baldwin, *Baldwin Papers*, p. 342.

45 Baldwin to William Bridgeman, 12 June 1935, ibid., p. 333. Emphasis in original.

46 Smart, *Diaries and Letters of Robert Bernays*, p. 246 (entry for 3 March 1936).

47 Ibid., p. 213 (entry for 12 July 1935).

48 Abe Bailey to WSC, 29 Sept. 1935, Churchill Papers, CHAR 2/237/77.

49 Frances Stevenson to Francis Brett Young, 7 Aug. 1935, Francis Brett Young Papers, University of Birmingham, Special Collections, 2945. NB some other lines of this letter have been rendered illegible by a later hand, apparently deliberately.

50 Samuel Hoare, 'Italo-Abyssinian Dispute: Record of a conversation between Sir Samuel Hoare, Mr. Eden and Mr. Lloyd George, August 21st, 1935', Templewood Papers, Cambridge University Library, Part VIII, file 1.

51 Memorandum on Lloyd George's lunch with Dino Grandi, 27 September 1935, Papers of Philip Kerr, 11th Marquis of Lothian, Lothian Muniments, National Archives of Scotland, GD40/17/113, ff. 172–4.

52 Speech of 26 Sept. 1935.

53 Money to WSC, 27 Sept. 1935, Leo Chiozza Money Papers, Cambridge University Library, Add. 9259/IV/27.

54 Speech of 26 Sept. 1935.

55 WSC to Money, 1 Oct. 1935, Money Papers, Add. 9259/IV/28.

56 Robert Worth Bingham diary, 28 Oct. 1935, Robert Worth Bingham Papers, Library of Congress, Box 1, vol. III.

57 Jones to Lady Grigg, 16 Nov. 1935, in Williamson and Baldwin, *Baldwin Papers*, p. 354.

58 WSC to CSC, 30 Dec. 1935, in Soames, *Speaking for Themselves*, p. 404.

59 Cross, *Life with Lloyd George*, pp. 138–9, 141 (entries for 14, 17 and 27 Jan. 1936).

60 Parliamentary Debates, House of Commons, 5th Series, vol. 309, 10 March 1936, cols. 2027, 2034, 2035.

61 Lord Lloyd to WSC 11 March 1936, WSC CV V, Part 3, p. 67.

62 Henry Strakosch to WSC, 11 Marcch 1936, ibid.

63 WSC to CSC, 8 Jan. 1936, in Soames, *Speaking for Themselves*, p. 407.

64 Randolph Churchill to DLG, 11 March 1936 and DLG to Randolph Churchill, 13 March 1936, quoted in Winston S. Churchill, *His Father's Son: The Life of Randolph Churchill*, Weidenfeld and Nicolson, London, 1996, p. 134.

65 'After the Debate', *The Times*, 12 March 1936.

66 The Earl of Swinton, *Sixty Years of Power: Some Memories of the Men who Wielded It*, Hutchinson, London, 1966, p. 53.

67 Jones to Abraham Flexner, 23 May 1936, Jones, *Diary with Letters*, p. 209.

68 Parliamentary Debates, House of Commons, 5th Series, vol. 313, 18 June 1936, col. 1232.

69 Taylor, *A Diary by Frances Stevenson*, p. 324 (entry for 20 June 1936).

70 John Grigg, 'Churchill and Lloyd George', in Robert Blake and Wm. Roger Louis (eds.), *Churchill*, Oxford University Press, Oxford, 1993, p. 107.

71 Cabinet minutes, 6 July 1936, WSC CV V, Part 3, p. 234.

72 Gilbert, *Winston S. Churchill*, vol. V: *1922–1939*, p. 768.

73 J. A. Spender to Archibald Sinclair, July 1936, Thurso Papers, Churchill College, Cambridge, THRS III, 16/1.

74 *Berliner Tageblatt*, 29 Jan. 1935, interview with Lloyd George, quoted in 'Lloyd George on Hitler and Nazi Germany', (a collection of quotations apparently compiled in June 1940), Churchill Papers, CHUR 4/141 A, ff. 61–3.

75 Parliamentary Debates, House of Commons, 5th Series, vol. 310, 26 March 1936, col. 1481.

76 Speech of 15 July 1936, quoted in 'Lloyd George on Hitler and Nazi Germany', Churchill Papers, CHUR 4/141 A, ff. 61–3.

77 DLG, article in *Sunday Pictorial*, 26 May 1935, quoted ibid.

78 Speech of 22 May 1935.

79 Churchill, 'The Truth about Hitler', *Strand Magazine*, Nov. 1935.

80 Cross, *Life with Lloyd George*, pp. 146–7 (entry for 3 Sept. 1936).

81 Eric Phipps to Robert Vansittart, 14 Oct. 1936, NA, PRO, FO 954/10; Cross, *Life with Lloyd George*, p. 151 (entry for 6 Sept. 1936).

82 DLG, article in the *Daily Express*, 17 Sept. 1936, quoted in 'Lloyd George on Hitler and Nazi Germany', Churchill Papers, CHUR 4/141 A, ff. 61–3.

83 *News Chronicle*, 21 Sept. 1936, quoted in Peter Rowland, *Lloyd George*, Barrie & Jenkins, London, 1975, p. 736.

84 David Lloyd George, 'What Has the Jew Done?', *Strand Magazine*, April 1937.

85 Winston S. Churchill, 'How the Jews Can Combat Persecution', n.d. [c. June 1937], Churchill Papers, CHAR 8/573/17–32.

86 Kathleen Hill to WSC, 12 March 1940, Churchill Papers, CHAR 8/660/32.

87 Charles Eade to Hill, 7 March 1940, Churchill Papers, CHAR 8/660/33.

88 Hill to Eade, 13 March 1940, Churchill Papers, CHAR 8/660/31. On 12 March, Hill wrote a minute to Churchill outlining the article's history; at the bottom of this he wrote 'better *not*', i.e. better not publish (CHAR 8/660/32; emphasis in original). On 21 March – after she had sent the negative response to Eade – she wrote again to Churchill: 'This is the article on the Jews which Mr. Eade would like to publish, and which you said you would try to find time to read.' Hand- and type-written notes on this minute indicate that Churchill passed the article to Brendan Bracken on 23 March, asking him to look at it 'and see if it is harmless.' Churchill added: 'I have forgotten all about it.' Bracken wrote: 'Yes. It is harmless BB.' But an additional note, presumably by Churchill, reads 'Let me see it in its final form' (Hill to WSC, 21 March 1940, CHAR 8/660/27). It is not clear whether he did read the article or not, but, either way, he never gave the

go-ahead for publication. After Churchill became Prime Minister the *Dispatch* continued to publish his old articles, on the basis of a clear understanding. Eade wrote: 'I should . . . be careful not to use anything controversial [*sic*] such as the article about the Jews, which might be undesirable in the present circumstances' (Eade to Hill, 11 May 1940, CHAR 8/660/90). Its absence from Ronald I. Cohen's authoritative *Bibliography of the Writings of Sir Winston Churchill* (3 vols., Thoemmes Continuum, London, 2006) would appear to confirm that the article has never been published anywhere since.

89 A. J. Sylvester, *The Real Lloyd George*, Cassell, London, 1947, pp. 245–6 (entry for 26 April 1939).

90 Lord Moran, *Winston Churchill: The Struggle for Survival, 1940–1965*, Constable, London, 1966, p. 326.

91 Sylvester diary, 2 Dec. 1936, quoted in J. Graham Jones, 'Lloyd George and the Abdication of Edward VIII', *National Library of Wales Journal*, vol. 30, no. 1 (summer 1997), pp. 89–105, at p. 94.

92 Sylvester diary, 5 Dec. 1936, quoted ibid., p. 94.

93 John Barnes and David Nicholson (eds.), *The Empire at Bay: The Leo Amery Diaries, 1929–1945*, Hutchinson, London, 1988, p. 432 (entry for 7 Dec. 1936).

94 DLG to Gwilym Lloyd George, 11 Dec. 1936, reproduced in Jones, 'Lloyd George and the Abdication', p. 90.

95 WSC to DLG, 25 Dec. 1936, quoted in Gilbert, *Winston S. Churchill*, vol. V: *1922–1939*, p. 831.

96 Quoted in Sylvester, *Real Lloyd George*, p. 232.

97 WSC to DLG, 24 Dec. 1936, Churchill Papers, CHAR 1/286/133.

98 WSC to Bernard Baruch, 1 Jan. 1937, WSC CV V, Part 3, p. 521.

99 Lord Tweedsmuir to Baldwin, 3 Feb. 1937, Stanley Baldwin Papers, Cambridge University Library, Box 97, f. 183.

100 Neville Chamberlain to Hilda Chamberlain, 10 April 1937, in Robert Self (ed.), *The Neville Chamberlain Diary Letters*, Ashgate, Aldershot, 2002–5, vol. IV: *The Downing Street Years, 1934–1940*, p. 244.

101 Neville Chamberlain diary, 12 April 1937, quoted in Sarah Bradford, *King George VI*, Weidenfeld and Nicolson, London, 1989, p. 237.

102 Bradford, *King George VI*, pp. 237–8.

103 Charles Higham, *Wallis: Secret Lives of the Duchess of Windsor*, Sidgwick & Jackson, London, 1988, p. 177.

104 Vincent Sheean, *Between the Thunder and the Sun*, Random House, New York, 1943, p. 64.

105 Vincent Sheean, *Between the Thunder and the Sun*, London, Macmillan, 1943, pp. 49–50.

106 The words were those of Herbert Morrison: Parliamentary Debates, House of Commons, 5th Series, vol. 324, 31 May 1937, col. 802.

107 Ibid., cols. 897, 926–7.

108 Jones, *Diary with Letters* (entry for 12–14 June 1937).

109 'On the whole, I am optimistic as to the prospects of peace for another decade': David Lloyd George, 'Why War?', *Strand Magazine*, July 1937, vol. 93, pp. 256–65, at p. 265.

110 'Britain's Role in the World: Mr. Lloyd George's Appeal', *The Times*, 3 Dec. 1937.

111 Speech of 7 Oct. 1937; Clive Ponting, *Churchill*, Sinclair-Stevenson, London, 1994, p. 394.

112 WSC to Anthony Eden, 3 Sept. 1937, WSC CV V, Part 3, p. 759.

113 Anthony Eden diary, 5 Jan. 1938, Avon Papers, University of Birmingham, Special Collections, AP 20/1/18. In his memoirs, Churchill seems to have misdated the lunch as having taken place in August 1937: Winston S. Churchill, *The Gathering Storm* [originally published as vol. I of *The Second World War*, Cassell, London, 1948], WSC CW, vol. XXII, p. 154.

114 John Harvey (ed.), *The Diplomatic Diaries of Oliver Harvey, 1937–1940*, Collins, London, 1970, p. 70 (entry for 15 Jan. 1938).

115 Barnes and Nicholson, *Empire at Bay*, p. 458 (entry for 22 Feb. 1938).

116 Cross, *Life with Lloyd George*, p. 197 (entry for 24 Feb. 1938).

117 Robert Rhodes James (ed.), *'Chips': The Diaries of Sir Henry Channon*, Weidenfeld and Nicolson, London, 1967 (repr. 1993), pp. 151–2 (entry for 17 March 1938).

118 Phipps to Halifax, 18 March 1938, Eric Phipps Papers, Churchill College, Cambridge, PHPP1/20, f. 1.

119 John Herman, *The Paris Embassy of Sir Eric Phipps: Anglo-French Relations and the Foreign Office*, Sussex Academic Press, Brighton, 1998, pp. 85 and 207, n. 64, citing Phipps to Halifax 18 & 22 March 1938, FO 800/311, and Phipps's telegram of 16 July 1938.

120 Cross, *Life with Lloyd George*, p. 204 (entry for 18 March 1938).

121 Phipps to Halifax, 27 March 1938, Phipps Papers, PHPP1/20, f. 13.

122 Phipps to Halifax, 28 March 1938, WSC CV V, Part 3, p. 964.

123 *Le Matin*, 20 March 1938, quoted in Phipps to Foreign Office (telegram), 20 March 1938, NA, PRO, FO 371/21615.

124 Cross, *Life with Lloyd George*, p. 202 (entry for 17 March 1938).

125 'Agenda and Notes on Policy Conference', 21 Jan. 1938, Layton Papers, Box 89/8.

126 'Mr. Churchill and the New Commonwealth', *The Times*, 8 June 1936.

127 The only obvious alternative, G. W. Lloyd (MP for Birmingham Ladywood and a junior minister) does not seem plausible.

128 DLG to WSC, 10 Aug. 1938, Lloyd George Papers, HLRO, LG/G/4/5/28.

129 WSC to DLG, 13 Aug. 1938, Lloyd George Papers, HLRO, LG/G/4/5/29. Partially reproduced in WSC CV V, Part 3, p. 1117.

130 Colin Coote, cited in Gilbert, *Winston S. Churchill*, vol. V: *1922–1939*, p. 988.

131 Speech of 5 Oct. 1938.

132 Cross, *Life with Lloyd George*, p. 219 (entry for 5 Oct. 1938).

133 WSC to DLG, 17 Oct. 1938, Lloyd George Papers, HLRO, LG/G/4/5/33.

134 Parliamentary Debates, House of Commons, 5th Series, vol. 345, 31 March 1939, col. 2415.

135 Speech of 3 April 1939.

136 Parliamentary Debates, House of Commons, 5th Series, vol. 345, 3 April 1939, cols. 2506, 2510.

137 Nigel Nicolson (ed.), *Harold Nicolson: Diaries & Letters, 1930–1939*, Collins, London, 1966, p. 394 (entry for 3 April 1939).

138 Cross, *Life with Lloyd George*, p. 227 (entry for 6 April 1939).

139 Sylvester, *Real Lloyd George*, pp. 243–4 (entry for 20 April 1939).

140 Neville Chamberlain to Ida Chamberlain, 15 April 1939, Self, *Neville Chamberlain Diary Letters*, vol. IV, p. 406.

141 Sylvester, *Real Lloyd George*, pp. 246–8 (entry for 27 April 1939). Emphasis in original.

142 Ibid., p. 252 (entry for 4 Aug. 1939).

143 Neville Chamberlain to Ida Chamberlain, 10 June 1939, in Self, *Neville Chamberlain Diary Letters*, vol. IV, pp. 420–1.

144 DLG to Frances Stevenson, 26 Nov. 1931, in A. J. P. Taylor (ed.), *My Darling Pussy: The Letters of Lloyd George and Frances Stevenson, 1913–41*, Weidenfeld and Nicolson, London, 1975, p. 155.

145 Cross, *Life with Lloyd George*, p. 142 (entry for 5 May 1936).

146 Jones, *Diary with Letters*, p. 222 (entry for 14 June 1936).

147 Smart, *Diaries and Letters of Robert Bernays*, p. 213 (entry for 12 July 1935).

148 Nicolson, *Diaries, 1930–39*, p. 387 (entry for 3 April 1939).

149 Arthur Crosfield to WSC, 4 Dec. 1936, Churchill Papers, CHAR 2/261/22.

Ten – I Shall Wait Until Winston Is Bust

1 Evelyn Waugh, *Men at Arms*, Penguin, London, 1964 (originally published 1952).

2 For Waugh's later views, see his letter to Ann Fleming, 27 Jan. 1965, in Mark Amory (ed.), *The Letters of Evelyn Waugh*, Weidenfeld and Nicolson, London, 1980, p. 630.

3 Dingle Foot, 'Ll.G.: Statesman Who Played to Win', *Daily Telegraph*, 24 March 1970.

4 Hugh Trevor-Roper, *Hitler's Table Talk, 1941–44: His Private Conversations*, Weidenfeld and Nicolson, London, 1953 (repr. 1973), p. 184 (6 Jan. 1942).

5 Nigel Nicolson (ed.), *Harold Nicolson: Diaries and Letters, 1939–1945*, Collins, London, 1967, p. 164 (entry for 7 May 1941).

6 Hugh Cudlipp, *Walking on the Water*, Bodley Head, London, 1976, pp. 109–10.

7 Bob Boothby, Memorandum of a conversation with Ivan Maisky, 17 Sept. 1939, Lloyd George Papers, HLRO, LG/G/3/13/12.

8 Hankey diary, 23 Aug. 1939, in Stephen Roskill, *Hankey: Man of Secrets*, 3 vols., Collins, London, 1970–4, vol. III, p. 413.

9 Harold Nicolson to Vita Sackville-West, 25 Aug. 1939, in Nigel Nicolson (ed.), *Vita and Harold: The Letters of Vita Sackville-West and Harold Nicolson*, Weidenfeld and Nicolson, London, 1992, p. 314.

10 Message from Archibald Sinclair, 5 Sept. 1939, Walter Layton Papers, Trinity College, Cambridge, Box 11/208.

11 Hankey to Adeline Hankey, 3 Sept. 1939, in Roskill, *Man of Secrets*, vol. III, p. 419.

12 Foreign Office to Sir Percy Loraine (telegram), 10 Sept. 1939, Churchill Papers, Churchill College, Cambridge, CHAR 19/2A/34.

13 NA, PRO, CAB 65/1, W. M. (39) 12th Conclusions, 11 Sept. 1939.

14 WSC to DLG, 12 Sept. 1939, in Martin Gilbert (ed.), *The Churchill War Papers*, vol. I: *At the Admiralty: September 1939–May 1940*, Heinemann, London, 1993, p. 87.

15 Foreign Office, 10 Sept. 1939, Churchill Papers, CHAR 19/2A/34.

16 Colin Cross (ed.), *Life with Lloyd George: The Diary of A. J. Sylvester, 1931–45*, Macmillan, London, 1975, p. 236 (entry for 12 Sept. 1939).

17 DLG to WSC, 13 Sept. 1939, in Gilbert, *Churchill War Papers*, vol. I, p. 88.

18 WSC to DLG, 16 Sept. 1939, Lloyd George Papers, HLRO, LG/G/4/5/39.

19 John Colville, *The Fringes of Power: Downing Street Diaries, 1939–1955*, Hodder and Stoughton, London, 1985, p. 29 (entry for 28 Sept. 1939).

20 Ernest Benn to John Simon, 2 Oct. 1939, quoted in Martin Gilbert, *Winston S. Churchill*, vol. VI: *Finest Hour, 1939–1941*, Heinemann, London, 1983, p. 47.

21 Speech of 3 Sept. 1939.

22 A. J. Sylvester, *The Real Lloyd George*, Cassell, London, 1947, pp. 253–4 (entry for 3 Sept. 1939).

23 DLG to WSC, 13 Sept. 1939, in Gilbert, *Churchill War Papers*, vol. I, p. 88.

24 Paul Addison, 'Lloyd George and Compromise Peace in the Second World War', in A. J. P. Taylor (ed.), *Lloyd George: Twelve Essays*, Hamish Hamilton, London, 1971, pp. 361–84, at p. 367.

25 Nicolson, *Diaries and Letters, 1939–45*, p. 35 (entry for 20 Sept. 1939).

26 Parliamentary Debates, House of Commons, 5th Series, vol. 351, 3 Oct. 1939, col. 1873.

27 Cross, *Life with Lloyd George*, p. 238 (entry for 3 Oct. 1939).

28 Parliamentary Debates, House of Commons, 5th Series, vol. 351, 3 Oct. 1939, cols. 1878–9.

29 Cross, *Life with Lloyd George*, p. 238 (entry for 3 Oct. 1939). In a letter to his wife the same day, Sylvester wrote that 'Winston was angry with his [Lloyd George's] speech. Neville was not.' (Quoted in A. P. Lentin, *Lloyd George and the Lost Peace: from Versailles to Hitler, 1919–1940*, Palgrave, Basingstoke, 2001, p. 160, n. 84.) However, Chamberlain made clear in a letter to his sister Ida

of 8 October that he had no sympathy for Lloyd George, who 'has become nothing but a bundle of selfishness and malice', or for his position. See Robert Self (ed.), *The Neville Chamberlain Diary Letters*, Ashgate, Aldershot, 2002–5, vol. IV: *The Downing Street Years, 1934–1940*, p. 455.

30 'Hitler's Plan of Peace for Europe', *The Times*, 7 Oct. 1939.

31 DLG to WSC, 9 Oct. 1939, Lloyd George Papers, HLRO, LG/G/4/5/41.

32 Fred Taylor (ed.), *The Goebbels Diaries, 1939–1941*, Hamish Hamilton, London, 1982, p. 14 (entry for 9 Oct. 1939).

33 Cross, *Life with Lloyd George*, p. 239 (entry for 12 Oct. 1939).

34 'Mr. Lloyd George's Protest', *The Times*, 23 Oct. 1939.

35 A. J. P. Taylor (ed.), *W. P. Crozier: Off the Record: Political Interviews, 1933–1943*, Hutchinson, London, 1973, p. 105 (interview, 13 Oct. 1939).

36 Cross, *Life with Lloyd George*, pp. 244–5 (entries for 14 Dec. 1939 and 4 Jan. 1940).

37 Walter Layton, 'Note of Conversation with Sir Samuel Hoare on Jan. 5 1940', Layton Papers, Box 104/81.

38 Taylor, *Off the Record: Political Interviews*, pp. 130–1 (interview with Hore-Belisha, 20 Jan. 1940).

39 Cross, *Life with Lloyd George*, p. 246 (entry for 6 Jan. 1940).

40 Robert Rhodes James (ed.), *'Chips': The Diaries of Sir Henry Channon*, Weidenfeld and Nicolson, London, 1967 (repr. 1993), pp. 232–3 (entry for 13 Feb. 1940).

41 Charles Eade diary, 19 Nov. 1941, Charles Eade Papers, Churchill College, Cambridge.

42 Kathleen Hill to Charles Eade, 1 April 1940, Churchill Papers, CHAR 8/660, f. 25.

43 Churchill, 'Lloyd George', *Sunday Dispatch*, 14 April 1940.

44 Lloyd George, 'Use the Land!', *Picture Post*, 2 March 1940.

45 Robert Boothby, 'At Home with Lloyd George', *Picture Post*, 20 April 1940.

46 Neville Chamberlain to Hilda Chamberlain, 6 April 1940, in Self, *Neville Chamberlain Diary Letters*, vol. IV, p. 514.

47 Neville Chamberlain to Hilda Chamberlain, 4 May 1940, ibid., p. 527.

48 Quoted in David Reynolds, *In Command of History: Churchill Fighting and Writing the Second World War*, Allen Lane, London, 2004, p. 126.

49 Nicolson, *Diaries and Letters, 1939–45*, p. 74 (entry for 30 April 1940).

50 Ibid., p. 75 (entry for 4 May 1940).

51 Sylvester, *Real Lloyd George*, p. 263 (entry for 12 May 1940).

52 Kenneth Young (ed.), *The Diaries of Robert Bruce Lockhart*, 2 vols., vol. II: *1939–1965*, Macmillan, London, 1980, p. 52 (entry for 2 May 1940).

53 N. A. Rose (ed.), *Baffy: The Diaries of Blanche Dugdale, 1936–1947*, Valentine, Mitchell, London, 1973, p. 168 (entry for 7 May 1940).

54 Stafford Cripps diary, 2 May 1940, Stafford Cripps Papers, Bodleian Library, Oxford.

55 Simon Burgess, *Stafford Cripps: A Political Life*, Victor Gollancz, London, 1999, pp. 136–7; Peter Clarke, *The Cripps Version: The Life of Sir Stafford Cripps, 1889–1952*, Allen Lane, London, 2002, p. 171.

56 Thomas Jones, *A Diary with Letters, 1931–1950*, Oxford University Press, London, 1954, p. 457 (entry for 7 May 1940).

57 'Notes on Policy Conference no. 52', 9 May 1940, Layton Papers, Box 89/8.

58 Mark Pottle (ed.), *Champion Redoubtable: The Diaries and Letters of Violet Bonham Carter, 1914–1945*, Weidenfeld and Nicolson, London, 1998, p. 21 (entry for 2–14 May 1940).

59 Jones, *Diary with Letters*, p. 457 (entry for 7 May 1940).

60 Parliamentary Debates, House of Commons, 5th Series, vol. 360, 7 May 1940, col. 1150.

61 Parliamentary Debates, House of Commons, 5th Series, vol. 360, 8 May, 1940, col. 1266. The details in this section of MPs' reactions to this and other speeches in the debate are taken from the accounts printed in *The Times*.

62 Dingle Foot, 'Review of the autobiography of Frances Lloyd George', Oct. 1967, Dingle Foot Papers, Churchill College, Cambridge, DGFT 7/12. See also Dingle Foot to Olwen Carey Evans, 16 Jan. 1967 and Carey Evans to Foot, 29 Jan. 1967, ibid.

63 Winston S. Churchill, *The Gathering Storm* [originally published as vol. I of *The Second World War*, Cassell, London, 1948], WSC CW, vol. XXII, p. 424.

64 Pottle, *Champion Redoubtable*, p. 210 (entry for 2–14 May 1940).

65 Carey Evans to Foot, 29 Jan. 1967, Foot Papers, DGFT 7/12.

66 Parliamentary Debates, House of Commons, 5th Series, vol. 360, 8 May 1940, cols. 1277–83.

67 Hugh Dalton, *The Fateful Years: Memoirs, 1931–1945*, Frederick Muller, London, 1957, p. 309.

68 Cripps diary, 9 May 1940, Cripps Papers.

69 Churchill, *The Gathering Storm*, p. 428.

70 DLG to WG, 9 Dec. 1916, in William George, *My Brother and I*, Eyre and Spottiswoode, London, 1958, p. 257.

71 Neville Chamberlain to Ida Chamberlain, 11 May 1940, in Self, *Neville Chamberlain Diary Letters*, vol. IV, p. 530.

72 Neville Chamberlain diary, 31 May 1940, Neville Chamberlain Papers, University of Birmingham, Special Collections, NC 2/24.

73 Rhodes James, *'Chips'*, p. 248 (entry for 9 May 1940).

74 Neville Chamberlain to Ida Chamberlain, 11 May 1940, in Self, *Neville Chamberlain Diary Letters*, vol. IV, p. 530.

75 Speech of 13 May 1940.

76 Parliamentary Debates, House of Commons, 5th Series, vol. 360, 13 May 1940, col. 1510.

77 Cross, *Life with Lloyd George*, pp. 261–2 (entry for 13 May 1940).

78 Ibid., p. 261 (entry for 12 May 1940).

79 Colville, *Fringes of Power*, p. 129 (entry for 13 May 1940).

80 WSC to DLG, n.d. [29 May 1940], Lloyd George Papers, HLRO, LG/G/4/5/48.

81 DLG to WSC, 31 May 1940, Lloyd George Papers, HLRO, LG/G/4/5/49.

82 Sylvester, *Real Lloyd George*, p. 264 (entry for 16 May 1940).

83 Cross, *Life with Lloyd George*, p. 262 (entry for 15 May 1940).

84 Sylvester was not in fact completely consistent on this point. After the fall of France in June he wrote in his diary that he had previously been against Lloyd George joining the government 'but now the situation has deteriorated so much that it is vital that L.G. should be inside. He has such vision, and I have such faith in him still.' Ibid., p. 267 (entry for 14 June 1940).

85 Roderick Macleod and Denis Kelly (eds.), *The Ironside Diaries, 1937–1940*, Constable, London, 1962, pp. 310–11 (entry for 16 May 1940).

86 Sylvester, *Real Lloyd George*, p. 264 (entry for 16 May 1940).

87 Cross, *Life with Lloyd George*, p. 263 (entry for 28 May 1940).

88 Neville Chamberlain diary, 28 May 1940, Neville Chamberlain Papers, NC 2/24.

89 DLG to WSC, 29 May 1940, Lloyd George Papers, HLRO, LG/G/4/5/47.

90 Cross, *Life with Lloyd George*, p. 265 (entry for 29 May 1940).

91 WSC to DLG, n.d. [29 May 1940], Lloyd George Papers, HLRO, LG/G/4/5/48.

92 DLG to WSC, 31 May 1940, Lloyd George Papers, HLRO, LG/G/4/5/49.

93 Neville Chamberlain to Ida Chamberlain, 8 June 1940, in Self, *Neville Chamberlain Diary Letters*, vol. IV, p. 537.

94 Neville Chamberlain diary, 5 June 1940, Neville Chamberlain Papers, NC 2/24.

95 Halifax diary, 6 June 1940, quoted in The Earl of Birkenhead, *Halifax: The Life of Lord Halifax*, Hamish Hamilton, London, 1965, p. 459; see also Andrew Roberts, *'The Holy Fox': A Life of Lord Halifax*, Weidenfeld and Nicolson, London, 1991, p. 243.

96 WSC to Neville Chamberlain, 6 June 1940, in Martin Gilbert (ed.), *The Churchill War Papers*, vol. II: *Never Surrender: May 1940–December 1940*, Heinemann, London, 1994, p. 255.

97 Neville Chamberlain to WSC, 6 June 1940, Churchill Papers, CHAR 20/11/90–3.

98 Neville Chamberlain to Ida Chamberlain, 8 June 1940, in Self, *Neville Chamberlain Diary Letters*, vol. IV, p. 538.

99 William Armstrong (ed.), *With Malice Toward None: A War Diary by Cecil H. King*, Sidgwick & Jackson, London, 1970, p. 48 (entry for 7 June 1940).

100 Neville Chamberlain to Ida Chamberlain, 8 June 1940, in Self, *Neville Chamberlain Diary Letters*, vol. IV, p. 538.

101 Sylvester, *Real Lloyd George*, p. 269 (entry for 6 June 1940). A slightly fuller

version of the entry is reproduced in Cross, *Life with Lloyd George*, pp. 266–7, but misdated 4 June.

102 Neville Chamberlain to Ida Chamberlain, 8 June 1940, in Self, *Neville Chamberlain Diary Letters*, vol. IV, p. 538.

103 Armstrong, *With Malice Toward None*, pp. 44–6 (entry for 6 June 1940).

104 Ibid., p. 52 (entry for 7 June 1940).

105 Neville Chamberlain diary, 10 June 1940, Neville Chamberlain Papers, NC 2/24.

106 Lord Boothby, *Recollections of a Rebel*, Hutchinson, London, 1978, p. 148.

107 Boothby to DLG, 15 June 1940, Lloyd George Papers, HLRO, LG/G/3/13/12.

108 Clement Davies to Leo Amery, 21 June 1955, Leo Amery Papers, Churchill College, Cambridge, AMEL 8/83.

109 John Barnes and David Nicholson (eds.), *The Empire at Bay: The Leo Amery Diaries, 1929–1945*, Hutchinson, London, 1988, pp. 624–5 (entry for 17 June 1940) and p. 601, quoting Amery to Boothby, 18 June 1955.

110 Quoted in Andrew Roberts, *Eminent Churchillians*, Weidenfeld and Nicolson, London, 1994, p. 165.

111 Speech of 18 June 1940.

112 Barnes and Nicholson, *Empire at Bay*, pp. 625–6 (entry for 18 June 1940).

113 Boothby, *Recollections*, p. 166; Boothby to WSC, 19 June 1940, Churchill Papers, CHAR 20/1/3–5.

114 Churchill mistakenly recalled that the events in question had taken place in July rather than June. Colville, *Fringes of Power*, p. 587 (entry for 11 April 1945).

115 Her account quotes at length from *Times* articles which she claims appeared on 19 June 1940, and then says that the phone call took place 'That night'. But in fact the articles in question did not appear until 19 June 1941. Frances Lloyd George, *The Years that Are Past*, Hutchinson, London, 1967, pp. 262–4; 'Organizing Victory' and 'Organizing for Victory', *The Times*, 19 June 1941.

116 Neville Chamberlain to Hilda Chamberlain, 21 June 1940, in Self, *Neville Chamberlain Diary Letters*, vol. IV, p. 543.

117 Boothby to DLG, 6 July 1940, Lloyd George Papers, HLRO, LG/G/13/26.

118 Boothby to WSC, 9 July 1940, reproduced in Boothby, *Recollections*, pp. 148–50.

119 Addison, 'Lloyd George and Compromise Peace', pp. 382–3. Emphasis in original.

120 Bernd Martin, 'Churchill and Hitler, 1940: Peace or War?', in R. A. C. Parker (ed.), *Winston Churchill: Studies in Statesmanship*, Brassey's, London, 1995 (repr. 2002), pp. 83–96, at p. 93.

121 WSC to Franklin D. Roosevelt, 20 May 1940, in Warren F. Kimball (ed.), *Churchill & Roosevelt: The Complete Correspondence*, vol. I: *Alliance Emerging, October 1933–November 1942*, Princeton University Press, Princeton, NJ, 1984, p. 40.

122 Neville Chamberlain diary, 18 June 1940, quoted in John Charmley, *Churchill: The End of Glory: A Political Biography*, Hodder and Stoughton, London, 1993, p. 417.

123 Cross, *Life with Lloyd George*, pp. 279, 281 (entries for 23 Sept., 3 Oct. and 10 Nov. 1940).

124 Charles Higham, *Wallis: Secret Lives of the Duchess of Windsor*, Sidgwick & Jackson, London, 1988, p. 253.

125 Geoffrey Bocca, 'Mentor and Tormentor', in Logan Gourlay (ed.), *The Beaverbrook I Knew*, Quarter Books, London, 1984, pp. 169–77, at pp. 173–4.

126 Joachim Von Ribbentrop to the Legation in Portugal, 31 July 1940, in *Documents on German Foreign Policy, 1918–1945: Series D (1937–1945)*, vol. X: *The War Years, June 23–August 31, 1940*, HMSO, London, 1957, p. 378.

127 Oswald von Hoyningen-Hühne to Von Ribbentrop, 2 Aug. 1940, ibid., p. 398.

128 Telegram from Hühne, 15 Aug. 1940, quoted ibid., n. 5.

129 Addison, 'Lloyd George and Compromise Peace', p. 379.

130 Cross, *Life with Lloyd George*, p. 268 (entry for 25 June 1940).

131 Jones, *Diary with Letters*, pp. 464–5 (entry for 13 July 1940).

132 DLG to Frances Stevenson, 4 Oct. 1940, in A. J. P. Taylor (ed.), *My Darling Pussy: The Letters of Lloyd George and Frances Stevenson, 1913–41*, Weidenfeld and Nicolson, London, 1975, p. 239.

133 DLG to Frances Stevenson, 22 Oct. 1940, ibid., p. 245.

134 Quoted in Ruth Longford, *Frances, Countess Lloyd George: More than a Mistress*, Gracewing, Leominster, 1996, p. 146.

135 Cross, *Life with Lloyd George*, p. 278 (entry for 23 Sept. 1940).

136 Jones, *Diary with Letters*, p. 465 (entry for 13 July 1940).

137 Francis Brett Young to Francis Stevenson, 10 July 1940, Francis Brett Young Papers, University of Birmingham, Special Collections, 2970.

138 Cross, *Life with Lloyd George*, p. 269 (entry for 26 June 1940).

139 Rhodes James, *'Chips'*, p. 262 (entry for 24 July 1940).

140 'Churchill Is no Fool', *Tribune*, 17 Jan. 1941.

141 Ben Pimlott (ed.), *The Second World War Diary of Hugh Dalton, 1940–45*, Cape, London, 1986, pp. 72, 80, 88 (entries for 6 Aug., 1 Sept. and 3 Oct. 1940).

142 DLG to Frances Stevenson, 22 Oct. 1940, in Taylor, *My Darling Pussy*, pp. 244–5.

143 Colville, *Fringes of Power*, pp. 367–8 (entry for 12 Dec. 1940).

144 Pimlott, *Diary of Hugh Dalton*, p. 121 (entry for 14 Dec. 1940).

145 WSC to Roosevelt, 14 Dec. 1940, Roosevelt to WSC 15 Dec. 1940, in Kimball, *Churchill and Roosevelt*, p. 114. See also Robert Lloyd George, *David & Winston: How a Friendship Changed History*, John Murray, London, 2005, p. 235, and David Day, *Menzies & Churchill at War*, Angus & Robertson, London, 1986, p. 35.

146 Winston S. Churchill, *Their Finest Hour* [originally published as vol. II of *The Second World War*, Cassell, London, 1949], WSC CW, vol. XXIII, pp. 363–4.

147 Pimlott, *Diary of Hugh Dalton*, p. 130 (entry for 22 Dec. 1940).

148 Churchill, *Their Finest Hour*, p. 363.

149 WSC to Halifax, 26 Dec. 1940, Churchill Papers, CHAR 20/2B/174.

150 Colville, *Fringes of Power*, p. 381 (entry for 20 Dec. 1940).

151 Victor Cazalet diary, 23 Dec. 1940, quoted in Robert Rhodes James, *Victor Cazalet: A Portrait*, Hamish Hamilton, London, 1976, p. 248.

152 Armstrong, *With Malice Toward None*, pp. 87, 120 (entries for 26 Dec. 1940 and 16 April 1941).

153 Cross, *Life with Lloyd George*, p. 283 (entry for 15 Jan. 1941).

154 Pimlott, *Diary of Hugh Dalton*, p. 142 (entry for 15 Jan. 1941).

155 WSC to DLG, 22 Jan. 1941, Lloyd George Papers, HLRO, LG/G/4/5/52, and Cross, *Life with Lloyd George*, p. 288 (entry for 26 Jan. 1941), where the letter is reproduced.

156 DLG to WSC, 3 Feb. 1941, Churchill Papers, CHAR 2/418/31.

157 Boothby, *Recollections*, pp. 173–4. Boothby seems to have got some aspects of the story wrong. He wrote that the incident took place between the publication of the report on 21 January and his resignation speech a week later. In fact, Lloyd George was in Wales during that time.

158 Taylor, *Off the Record: Political Interviews*, p. 334 (entry for 29 May 1942).

159 Alex Danchev and Daniel Todman (ed.), *War Diaries, 1939–1945: Field Marshal Lord Alanbrooke*, Weidenfeld and Nicolson, London, 2001, pp. 590, 713 (entry for 10 Sept. 1944, and post-war comment).

160 Francis Williams, *A Prime Minister Remembers: The War and Post-War Memoirs of Rt. Hon Earl Attlee*, Heinemann, London, 1961, p. 46.

161 Hankey diary, 29 May 1941, in Roskill, *Man of Secrets*, vol. III, p. 511.

162 Armstrong, *With Malice Toward None*, p. 121 (entry for 16 April 1941).

163 Menzies diary, 26 April 1941, quoted in Day, *Menzies & Churchill at War*, p. 152.

164 Nigel West, *The Guy Liddell Diaries*, vol. I: *1939–1942: MI5's Director of Counter-Espionage in World War II*, Routledge, London, 2005, p. 145 (entry for 6 May 1941).

165 Barnes and Nicholson, *Empire at Bay*, pp. 685–6 (entry for 2 May 1941).

166 Parliamentary Debates, House of Commons, 5th Series, vol. 371, 7 May 1941, cols. 871, 880.

167 Rhodes James, *'Chips'*, p. 303 (entry for 7 May 1941).

168 Speech of 7 May 1941.

169 Cross, *Life with Lloyd George*, p. 291 (entry for 7 May 1941).

170 Taylor, *Goebbels Diaries*, p. 355 (entry for 9 May 1941).

171 P. J. Grigg to F. A. Grigg, 9 May 1941, P. J. Grigg Papers, Churchill College, Cambridge, PJGG 9/6/13.

172 Pimlott, *Diary of Hugh Dalton*, p. 199 (entry for 7 May 1941).

173 John Grigg, 'Churchill and Lloyd George', in Robert Blake and Wm. Roger Louis (eds.), *Churchill*, Oxford University Press, Oxford, 1993, p. 108. Similarly, see Robert Lloyd George, *David & Winston*, p. 236.

174 Dennis Bardens, *Churchill in Parliament*, Robert Hale, London, 1967, p. 244; Charmley, *End of Glory*, p. 449.

175 Mervyn Jones, *A Radical Life: The Biography of Megan Lloyd George, 1902–66*, Hutchinson, London, 1991, p. 159.

176 Armstrong, *With Malice Toward None*, p. 132 (entry for 7 July 1941).

177 Cross, *Life with Lloyd George*, p. 291 (entry for 8 May 1941).

178 Ibid. (entry for 16 May 1941).

179 Hankey diary, 9 June 1941, in Roskill, *Man of Secrets*, vol. III, p. 515.

180 Cross, *Life with Lloyd George*, p. 293 (entry for 4 Aug. 1941).

181 WSC to RSC, 8 June 1941, reproduced in Gilbert, *Finest Hour*, p. 1105.

182 Hankey diary, 29 May 1941, in Roskill, *Man of Secrets*, vol. III, p. 510. Lloyd George had also told a version of this story to Kingsley Martin in February 1941. See Kingsley Martin, *Editor: A Second Volume of Autobiography, 1931–45*, Hutchinson, London, 1968, pp. 289–90.

183 Armstrong, *With Malice Toward None*, p. 143 (entry for 3 Oct. 1941).

184 DLG to Lady Milner, 21 Jan. 1942 (copy), Violet Milner Papers, Bodleian Library, Oxford, MS 45, C422/2.

185 Armstrong, *With Malice Toward None*, p. 159 (entry for 18 Feb. 1942).

186 Ibid., pp. 183–4 (entry for 20 July 1942).

187 Emanuel Shinwell, *Conflict without Malice*, Odhams Press, London, 1955, p. 165.

188 Basil Liddell Hart, 'Talk with Beaverbrook, 11th June, 1942', Basil Liddell Hart Papers, Liddell Hart Centre for Military Archives, King's College, London, 11/1942/42.

189 Basil Liddell Hart, 'Talks with Lloyd George. 22nd–23rd March, 1942', ibid.

190 Robin Barrington-Ward diary, 2 Oct. 1942, quoted in Clarke, *Cripps Version*, p. 366.

191 Pimlott, *Diary of Hugh Dalton*, p. 583 (entry for 22 April 1943).

192 Basil Liddell Hart, 'Talk with Lloyd George, 14th June 1942', Liddell Hart Papers, 11/1942/48.

193 Pimlott, *Diary of Hugh Dalton*, p. 506 (entry for 21 Oct. 1942).

194 Rhodes James, *'Chips'*, p. 341 (entry for 21 Oct. 1942).

195 RSC to WSC, 25 Oct. 1942, Churchill Papers CHAR 1/369.

196 Basil Liddell Hart, 'Odd Notes for History', 26 Sept. 1942, Liddell Hart Papers, 11/1942/73.

197 G. S. Harvie-Watt, *Most of My Life* (1980), p. 117, quoted in Kevin Jefferys, *The Churchill Coalition and Wartime Politics, 1940–1945*, Manchester University Press, Manchester, 1991, p. 119.

198 Harold Nicolson to Nigel and Ben Nicolson, 21 Sept. 1943, in Nicolson, *Diaries and Letters, 1939–45*, p. 322.

199 Harold Nicolson to Nigel and Ben Nicolson, 23 June 1943, ibid., p. 302.

200 J. C. Smuts and WSC to DLG, 12 May 1944, and DLG to WSC, 14 May 1944, Lloyd George Papers, HLRO, LG/G/4/5/67–8.

201 Frances Lloyd George to WSC, 30 Nov. 1944, Churchill Papers, CHAR

2/513/67; WSC to DLG, 10 Dec. 1944, Lloyd George Papers, HLRO, LG/G/4/5/19.

202 Cross, *Life with Lloyd George*, p. 334 (entry for 18 Dec. 1944).

203 WSC to DLG 17 Dec. 1944, and DLG to WSC, 20 Dec. 1944, Frances Stevenson Papers, HLRO, FLS/6/25.

204 R. Rees Prytherch to Lord Dawson, 26 Feb. 1945, reproduced in Cross, *Life with Lloyd George*, p. 339.

205 A. J. P. Taylor (ed.), *Lloyd George: A Diary by Frances Stevenson*, Harper & Row, New York, 1971, p. 238 (entries for 24 May 1944 and 27 May, unspecified year).

Eleven – EPILOGUE

1 Speech of 18 March 1945.

2 CSC to WSC, 30 March 1945, in Mary Soames (ed.), *Speaking for Themselves: The Personal Letters of Winston and Clementine Churchill*, Doubleday, London, 1998, p. 520.

3 John Colville, *The Fringes of Power: Downing Street Diaries, 1939–1955*, Hodder and Stoughton, London, 1985, p. 222 (entry for 28 March 1945).

4 Parliamentary Debates, House of Commons, 5th Series, vol. 409, 28 March 1945, cols. 1385–6.

5 John Barnes and David Nicholson (eds.), *The Empire at Bay: The Leo Amery Diaries, 1929–1945*, Hutchinson, London, 1988, p. 1034 (entry for 26 March 1945).

6 Olwen Carey Evans, *Lloyd George Was My Father*, Gomer Press, Llandysul, 1985, p. 171.

7 Lord Moran, *Winston Churchill: The Struggle for Survival, 1940–1965*, Constable, London, 1966, p. 326 (diary entry for 7 Dec. 1947).

8 Anthony Eden diary, 30 Sept. 1940, in Earl of Avon, *The Eden Memoirs: The Reckoning*, Cassell, London, 1965, p. 145.

9 He now hyphenated his surname.

10 Viscount Tenby, unpublished draft autobiography, Viscount Tenby Papers, National Library of Wales, 23671C.

11 'Major Lloyd-George's Future', *The Times*, 20 March 1945.

12 'Mr. Churchill in the North', *The Times*, 27 June 1945.

13 '"Vote National, Not Party": Prime Minister's Broadcast Attack on Socialism', *The Times*, 5 June 1945.

14 'In West Riding Valleys', *The Times*, Wednesday, 4 July 1945.

15 'Government Hopes in Scotland', *The Times*, 5 July 1945.

16 Clement Davies to Archibald Sinclair, 30 May 1946, Thurso Papers, Churchill College, Cambridge, THRS IV, 1/10.

17 Sinclair to Davies, 3 Dec. 1945, ibid.

18 WSC to Lord Woolton, 3 Aug. 1946, Conservative Party Archive, Bodleian Library, Oxford, CCO 3/1/64.

19 Speech of 16 May 1947.

20 E. C. Bradbury to the General Director of the Conservative Party (Stephen Piersenne), 21 Jan. 1950, Appendix B, Conservative Party Archive, CCO 4/3/43.

21 Lord Woolton to WSC, 7 Aug. 1947, Churchill Papers, Churchill College, Cambridge, CHUR 2/64/21.

22 WSC to Woolton, 11 Aug. 1947, Churchill Papers, CHUR 2/64/19–20.

23 Conclusions of Consultative Committee, 14 July 1948, Conservative Party Archive, LCC 1/1/3.

24 H. G. Nicholas, *The British General Election of 1950*, London, Macmillan, 1951, p. 94.

25 Speech of 8 Feb. 1950.

26 Woolton to Lord Salisbury, 28 Sept. 1950, Woolton Papers, Bodleian Library, Oxford, MS Woolton 21, ff. 73–83.

27 D. E. Butler, *The British General Election of 1951*, London, Macmillan, 1952, p. 95.

28 Anthony Montague Browne, *Long Sunset: Memoirs of Winston Churchill's Last Private Secretary*, Cassell, London, 1995, p. 227.

29 Peter Catterall (ed.), *The Macmillan Diaries: The Cabinet Years, 1950–1957*, Macmillan, London, 2003, p. 338 (entry for 23 July 1954).

30 Speech of 17 May 1955.

31 'Nationalizing the Water Industry', *The Times*, 19 May 1955.

32 D. E. Butler, *The British General Election of 1955*, Macmillan, London, 1955, p. 72, n. 1.

33 'Lloyd George', *Sunday Pictorial*, 6 Sept. 1931, in Michael Wolff (ed.), *The Collected Essays of Sir Winston Churchill*, 4 vols., Library of Imperial History, London, 1976, vol. III, p. 56.

34 Malcolm Thomson, *David Lloyd George: The Official Biography*, Hutchison, London, n.d. [1948], p. 448.

35 Kenneth Young (ed.), *The Diaries of Sir Robert Bruce Lockhart*, 2 vols., vol. II: *1939–1965*, Macmillan, London, 1980, pp. 526–7 (entry for 16 Feb. 1946).

36 Viscount Tenby, unpublished draft autobiography (notes), Viscount Tenby Papers, 23671C.

37 A. J. Sylvester to Walter Belcher, 13 March 1947, A. J. Sylvester Papers, National Library of Wales, D6.

38 Sylvester to Gwilym Lloyd-George, 22 Jan. 1953, Viscount Tenby Papers, MS 23668E.

39 Review of *The Real Lloyd George*, *Manchester Guardian*, 2 Oct. 1947.

40 Moran, *Struggle for Survival*, p. 326 (diary entry for 7 Dec. 1947).

41 Frances Lloyd George, 'Introduction', in Thomson, *David Lloyd George*, pp. 9–30, at 16–17.

42 Young, *Diaries of Sir Robert Bruce Lockhart*, vol. II, pp. 718–19 (entry for 14 Oct. 1950).

43 Lord Boothby, *Recollections of a Rebel*, Hutchinson, London, 1978, p. 161.

474 NOTES

44 Winston S. Churchill, *The Gathering Storm* [originally published as vol. I of *The Second World War*, Cassell, London, 1948], WSC CW, vol. XXII, p. 158.

45 David Reynolds, *In Command of History: Churchill Fighting and Writing the Second World War*, Allen Lane, London, 2004, p. 497.

46 'President Discusses European Trip: Remarks by the President in Acceptance of Bust of Winston Churchill', 16 July 2001, http:// whitehouse.fed.us/ (consulted 29 Dec. 2005).

47 Piers Dixon diary, 13 Aug. 1961, quoted in Martin Gilbert, *Winston S. Churchill*, vol. VIII: *'Never Despair', 1945–1965*, Heinemann, London, 1988, p. 1327.

48 'Commemoration of the Centenary of the Birth of David Lloyd George, 17th January, 1863: Prichard-Jones Hall, University College of North Wales, Bangor, Saturday, 30th March, 1963', Walter Layton Papers, Trinity College, Cambridge, Box 7/39.

49 Colin R. Coote, *The Other Club*, Sidgwick & Jackson, London, 1971, p. 110.

50 The Earl of Swinton, *Sixty Years of Power: Some Memories of the Men who Wielded It*, Hutchinson, London, 1966, p. 38.

51 C. P. Snow, *Variety of Men*, Macmillan, London, p. 97.

52 'Commemoration of the Centenary of the Birth of David Lloyd George . . .', Layton Papers, Box 7/39.

53 William Armstrong (ed.), *With Malice Toward None: A War Diary by Cecil H. King*, Sidgwick & Jackson, London, 1970, p. 241 (entry for 2 Jan. 1944).

54 Snow, *Variety of Men*, p. 97.

55 Thomas Jones to WSC, 13 March 1950, Thomas Jones Papers, National Library of Wales, A1.

56 Basil Liddell Hart, 'Talk with Rowlands (dinner), 11th June 1942', Basil Liddell Hart Papers, Liddell Hart Centre for Military Archives, King's College, London, 11/1942/43.

57 Avishai Margalit, *The Ethics of Memory*, Harvard University Press, Cambridge, MA, 2002, pp. 140, 193.

58 Speech of 28 March 1955.

59 Handwritten note by WSC, 25 March 1955, in NA, PRO, PREM 11/4355.

60 'MPs want a new statue of LG', *The Times*, 4 Dec. 1969.

61 Frances Lloyd George to Harold Wilson, 20 July 1969, Frances Stevenson Papers, National Library of Wales, FA 1.

62 Frances Lloyd George to Wilson, n.d. [26 Oct. 1969], ibid.

63 'MPs want a new statue of LG', *The Times*, 4 Dec. 1969.

64 'Statue of Lloyd George Called "Caricature"', *Daily Telegraph*, 21 Jan. 1970.

65 Quoted by Austen Chamberlain: 'Rough notes taken of speeches . . . on Thursday, October 29th 1936', Lloyd George Papers, HLRO, LG/G/208/4.

Bibliography

ARCHIVAL SOURCES

Bodleian Library, Oxford
Christopher Addison Papers
H. H. Asquith Papers
Margot Asquith Papers
Conservative Party Archive
Stafford Cripps Papers
H. A. L. Fisher Papers
Donald Maclean Papers
Alfred Milner Papers
Violet Milner Papers
Henry Nevinson Papers
John Simon Papers
Lord Southborough Papers
Woolton Papers

British Library, London
John Burns Papers
Almeric Fitzroy Papers
Herbert Gladstone Papers
Walter Long Papers
Northcliffe Papers
Riddell Papers
C. P. Scott Papers
Henry Wickham Steed Papers

British Library of Political and Economic Science, London
Letters from Winston Churchill to Hubert Carr-Gomm (copies)

Cambridge University Library
Stanley Baldwin Papers
Crewe Papers
Hardinge of Penhurst Papers

Leo Chiozza Money Papers
Templewood Papers

Churchill College, Cambridge
Leo Amery Papers
William Bull Papers
Clementine Churchill Papers
Winston Churchill Papers
Charles Eade Papers
Esher Papers
Fisher Papers
Dingle Foot Papers
Maurice Hankey Papers
P. J. Grigg Papers
Reginald McKenna Papers
Eric Phipps Papers
Thurso Papers

Fitzwilliam Museum, Cambridge
Wilfrid Scawen Blunt Papers

House of Lords Record Office, London
Beaverbrook Papers
Ralph David Blumenfeld Papers
Andrew Bonar Law Papers
David Lloyd George Papers
Herbert Samuel Papers
Frances Stevenson Papers
John St Loe Strachey Papers

India Office Library, London
Lord Brabourne Papers
Lord Reading Papers
Viscount Templewood Papers

Library of Congress, Washington DC
Robert Worth Bingham Papers
Marlborough Papers

Liddell Hart Centre for Military Archives, King's College, London
Maxwell Henry Coote Papers
Basil Liddell Hart Papers

Manchester Local Studies Unit
William Royle Papers

The National Archives, Kew, London
NA, PRO, CAB 65/1
NA, PRO, FO 370/554
NA, PRO, FO 800/171
NA, PRO, PREM 1/301
NA, PRO, T161/303

National Library of Ireland, Dublin
John Redmond Papers

National Archives of Scotland, Edinburgh
Balfour Papers
Papers of the Viscounts and Barons of Elibank
Papers of Philip Kerr, 11th Marquis of Lothian, Lothian Muniments

National Library of Scotland, Edinburgh
Elibank Papers
R. B. Haldane Papers
Rosebery Papers

National Library of Wales, Aberystwyth
William George Papers
Thomas Jones Papers
J. H. Lewis Papers
David Lloyd George Papers (Brynawelon Group)
Earl Lloyd-George Papers
A. J. Sylvester Papers
Frances Stevenson Papers
Viscount Tenby Papers

Nuffield College, Oxford
Gainford Papers

The Royal Archives, Windsor
Royal Archives

Shropshire Records and Research Centre, Shrewsbury
William Bridgeman Papers

Trinity College, Cambridge
Walter Layton Papers
Edwin Montagu Papers

University of Birmingham, Special Collections
Avon Papers
Austen Chamberlain Papers
Neville Chamberlain Papers
Masterman Papers
Francis Brett Young Papers

University of Illinois
H. G. Wells Papers

University of Sheffield, Special Collections
W. A. S. Hewins Papers

OFFICIAL SOURCES

Parliamentary Debates (Hansard)

PUBLISHED DOCUMENT SERIES

Documents on German Foreign Policy, 1918–1945: Series D (1937–1945), vol. X: *The War Years, June 23–August 31, 1940*, HMSO, London, 1957

INTERNET RESOURCES

'Call to Honour Lloyd George for Millennium', BBC News online, http://news.bbc.co.uk/1/hi/wales/539522.stm, 28 Nov. 1999
Douglas, Roy, 'The Mother of all Monopolies', reprinted from *Land & Liberty*, September–October, 1983 http://www.cooperativeindividualism.org/douglas_churchill_on_land_monopoly.html
'President Bush Discusses Importance of Democracy in Middle East', 4 Feb. 2004, http://www.whitehouse.gov/
'President Discusses European Trip: Remarks by the President in Acceptance of Bust of Winston Churchill', 16 July 2001, http://whitehouse.fed.us/

NEWSPAPERS AND PERIODICALS

British Weekly
Daily Chronicle
Daily Mail
Daily Telegraph
Manchester Guardian / The Guardian
Nation / Nation and Athenaeum
Picture Post
The Scotsman
Strand Magazine
Sunday Dispatch
The Times
Tribune
Western Mail

BOOKS AND ARTICLES

Official Biography of Winston Churchill
Churchill, Randolph S., *Winston S. Churchill*, vol. I: *Youth, 1874–1900*, Heinemann, London, 1966
————, *Winston S. Churchill*, vol. II: *Young Statesman, 1901–1914*, Heinemann, London, 1967
Gilbert, Martin, *Winston S. Churchill*, vol. III: *1914–1916*, Heinemann, London, 1971
————, *Winston S. Churchill*, vol. IV: *1916–1922*, Heinemann, London, 1975
————, *Winston S. Churchill*, vol. V: *1922–1939*, Heinemann, London, 1976
————, *Winston S. Churchill*, vol. VI: *Finest Hour, 1939–1941*, Heinemann, London, 1983
————, *Winston S. Churchill*, vol. VII: *Road to Victory, 1941–1945*, Heinemann, London, 1986
————, *Winston S. Churchill*, vol. VIII: *'Never Despair', 1945–1965*, Heinemann, London, 1988

Companion Volumes to the Official Biography
Churchill, Randolph S. (ed.), *Companion Volume I, Part 1*, Heinemann, London, 1966
————, *Companion Volume II, Parts 1, 2 and 3*, Heinemann, London, 1969
Gilbert, Martin (ed.), *Companion Volume III, Parts 1 and 2*, Heinemann, London, 1972
————, *Companion Volume IV, Parts 1, 2 and 3*, Heinemann, London, 1977
————, *Companion Volume V, Parts 1, 2 and 3*, Heinemann, London, 1979
————, *The Churchill War Papers*, vol. I: *At the Admiralty: September 1939–May 1940*, Heinemann, London, 1993
————, *The Churchill War Papers*, vol. II: *Never Surrender: May 1940–December 1940*, Heinemann, London, 1994

Other Published Sources
Adams, R. J. Q., *Arms and the Wizard: Lloyd George and the Ministry of Munitions, 1915–1916*, Cassell, London, 1978
Addison, Christopher, *Four and a Half Years: A Personal Diary from June 1914 to January 1919*, Hutchinson, London, 1934
Addison, Paul, *Churchill on the Home Front, 1900–1955*, Pimlico, London, 1993
Amory, Mark (ed.), *The Letters of Evelyn Waugh*, Weidenfeld and Nicolson, London, 1980
Armstrong, William (ed.), *With Malice Toward None: A War Diary by Cecil H. King*, Sidgwick & Jackson, London, 1970
Askwith, Lord, *Industrial Problems and Disputes*, John Murray, London, 1920
Avon, Earl of, *The Eden Memoirs: The Reckoning*, Cassell, London, 1965
Ball, Stuart (ed.), *Parliament and Politics in the Age of Churchill and Attlee: The Headlam*

Diaries, 1935–1951, Cambridge University Press for the Royal Historical Society, Cambridge, 1999

Bardens, Dennis, *Churchill in Parliament*, Robert Hale, London, 1967

Barnes, John and Nicholson, David (eds.), *The Empire at Bay: The Leo Amery Diaries, 1929–1945*, Hutchinson, London, 1988

Beaverbrook, Lord, *Men and Power, 1917–1918*, Hutchinson, London, 1956

——, *Politicians and the War, 1914–1916*, single-volume edition, Oldbourne, London, 1960

——, *The Decline and Fall of Lloyd George: And Great Was the Fall Thereof*, Collins, London, 1963

Berry, David and Horrocks, Simon (eds), *David Lloyd George: The Movie Mystery*, University of Wales Press, Cardiff, 1998

Birkenhead, Earl of, *Halifax: The Life of Lord Halifax*, Hamish Hamilton, London, 1965

Blake, Robert (ed.), *The Private Papers of Douglas Haig, 1914–1919*, Eyre and Spottiswoode, London, 1952

Blake, Robert and Louis, Wm. Roger (eds.), *Churchill*, Oxford University Press, Oxford, 1993

Blunt, Wilfrid Scawen, *My Diaries: Being a Personal Narrative of Events 1888–1914: Part Two* [1900–1914], Martin Secker, London, n.d.

Bonham Carter, Violet, *Winston Churchill as I Knew Him*, Reprint Society, London, 1966 (originally published by Eyre and Spottiswoode, 1965)

Booth, Alan and Pack, Melvyn, *Employment, Capital and Economic Policy: Great Britain, 1918–1939*, Basil Blackwell, Oxford, 1985

Boothby, Lord, *Recollections of a Rebel*, Hutchinson, London, 1978

Bradford, Sarah, *King George VI*, Weidenfeld and Nicolson, London, 1989

Briggs, Asa, *The Golden Age of Wireless: The History of Broadcasting in the United Kingdom*, vol. II, Oxford University Press, London, 1965

Brock, Michael and Brock, Eleanor (eds.), *H. H. Asquith: Letters to Venetia Stanley*, Oxford University Press, Oxford, 1982

Burgess, Simon, *Stafford Cripps: A Political Life*, Victor Gollancz, London, 1999

Burk, Kathleen (ed.), *War and the State: The Transformation of British Government, 1914–1919*, Allen and Unwin, London, 1982

Butler, D. E., *The British General Election of 1951*, Macmillan, London, 1952

——, *The British General Election of 1955*, Macmillan, London, 1955

Callwell, C. E., *Field-Marshal Sir Henry Wilson: His Life and Diaries*, 2 vols., Cassell, London, 1927

Campbell, John, *Lloyd George: The Goat in the Wilderness, 1922–1931*, Cape, London, 1977

——, *F. E. Smith: First Earl of Birkenhead*, Cape, London, 1983

——, *If Love Were All . . . The Story of Frances Stevenson and David Lloyd George*, Cape, London, 2006.

Carey Evans, Olwen, *Lloyd George Was My Father*, Gomer Press, Llandysul, 1985

Catterall, Peter (ed.), *The Macmillan Diaries: The Cabinet Years, 1950–1957*, Macmillan, London, 2003

Cazalet-Keir, Thelma, *From the Wings*, Bodley Head, London, 1967

Charmley, John, *Churchill: The End of Glory: A Political Biography*, Hodder and Stoughton, London, 1993

Chiozza, Leone George, *British Trade and the Zollverein Issue*, The Commercial Intelligence Publishing Co., London, 1902

Churchill, Winston, *The Collected Works of Sir Winston Churchill*, 34 vols., Library of Imperial History/Hamlyn, London, 1973–6

Churchill, Winston S., *His Father's Son: The Life of Randolph Churchill*, Weidenfeld and Nicolson, London, 1996

Clark, Alan (ed.), *'A Good Innings': The Private Papers of Viscount Lee of Fareham*, John Murray, London, 1974

Clarke, Peter, *The Keynesian Revolution in the Making, 1924–1936*, Clarendon Press, Oxford, 1988

———, *The Cripps Version: The Life of Sir Stafford Cripps, 1889–1952*, Allen Lane, London, 2002

Clarke, Tom, *My Northcliffe Diary*, Victor Gollancz, London, 1931

———, *My Lloyd George Diary*, Methuen, London, 1939

Clifford, Colin, *The Asquiths*, John Murray, London, 2002

Coates, W. P. and Coates, Zelda K., *A History of Anglo-Soviet Relations*, Lawrence & Wishart, London, 1944

Cohen, Ronald I., *Bibliography of the Writings of Sir Winston Churchill*, 3 vols., Thoemmes Continuum, London, 2006

Cole, Margaret (ed.), *Beatrice Webb's Diaries, 1924–1932*, Longman's, Green, London, 1956

Colville, John, *The Fringes of Power: Downing Street Diaries, 1939–1955*, Hodder and Stoughton, London, 1985

Cooper, Duff, *Old Men Forget*, Rupert Hart-Davis, London, 1954

Coote, Colin R., *The Other Club*, Sidgwick & Jackson, London, 1971

Crawshay-Williams, Eliot, *Simple Story: An Accidental Autobiography*, John Long, London, 1935

Cross, Colin (ed.), *Life with Lloyd George: The Diary of A. J. Sylvester, 1931–45*, Macmillan, London, 1975

Crowson, N. J. (ed.), *Fleet Street, Press Barons and Politics: The Journals of Collin Brooks, 1932–1940*, Cambridge University Press for the Royal Historical Society, Cambridge, 1998

Cudlipp, Hugh, *Walking on the Water*, Bodley Head, London, 1976

Dalton, Hugh, *The Fateful Years: Memoirs, 1931–1945*, Frederick Muller, London, 1957

Danchev, Alex and Todman, Daniel (eds.), *War Diaries, 1939–1945: Field Marshal Lord Alanbrooke*, Weidenfeld and Nicolson, London, 2001

Daunton, Martin, 'Money, Sir Leo George Chiozza (1870–1944), *Oxford Dictionary of National Biography*, Oxford University Press, Oxford, 2004

———, *Just Taxes: The Politics of Taxation in Britain, 1914–1979*, Cambridge University Press, Cambridge, 2002

David, Edward (ed.), *Inside Asquith's Cabinet: From the Diaries of Charles Hobhouse*, John Murray, London, 1977

Day, David, *Menzies & Churchill at War*, Angus & Robertson, London, 1986

Dilks, David (ed.), *The Diaries of Sir Alexander Cadogan O.M., 1938–1945*, Cassell, London, 1971

Du Parcq, Herbert, *Life of David Lloyd George*, 4 vols., Caxton, London, 1912–13

Dutton, David (ed.), *Paris 1918: The War Diary of the British Ambassador, the 17th Earl of Derby*, Liverpool University Press, Liverpool, 2001

Edwards, J. Hugh, *The Life of David Lloyd George with a Short History of the Welsh People*, vol. IV, Waverley, London, n.d. [1913]

Egerton, George W., 'The Lloyd George "War Memoirs": A Study in the Politics of Memory', *Journal of Modern History*, vol. 60, no. 1 (March 1988), pp. 55–94

Egremont, Max, *Balfour: A Life of Arthur James Balfour*, Collins, London, 1980

Esher, Oliver, Viscount (ed.), *Journals and Letters of Reginald Viscount Esher*, vol. III: *1910–1915*, Ivor Nicholson & Watson, London, 1938

Fine, Gary Alan, 'Reputational Entrepreneurs and the Memory of Incompetence: Melting Supporters, Partisan Warriors, and Images of President Harding', *American Journal of Sociology*, vol. 101, no. 5 (March 1996), pp. 1159–93

Fitzroy, Almeric, *Memoirs*, 2 vols., Hutchinson, London, 1925

Foster, Roy, *Lord Randolph Churchill: A Political Life*, Clarendon Press, Oxford, 1981

Fry, Michael G., *Lloyd George and Foreign Policy*, vol. I: *The Education of a Statesman, 1890–1916*, McGill-Queen's University Press, Montreal and London, 1977

George, W. R. P., *The Making of Lloyd George*, Faber and Faber, London, 1976

——, *Lloyd George: Backbencher*, Gower Press, Llandysul, 1983

George, William, *My Brother and I*, Eyre and Spottiswoode, London, 1958

Gilbert, Bentley Brinkerhoff, *David Lloyd George: A Political Life: The Architect of Change, 1863–1912*, Ohio State University Press, Columbus, 1987

——, *David Lloyd George: A Political Life: The Organizer of Victory, 1912–16*, Batsford, London, 1992

Gildart, Keith, Howell, David and Kirk, Neville (eds.), *Dictionary of Labour Biography*, vol. XI, Macmillan, London, 2003

Gilmour David, *Curzon*, John Murray, London, 1994

Gourlay, Logan (ed.), *The Beaverbrook I Knew*, Quarter Books, London, 1984

Greenaway, John, *Drink and British Politics since 1830: A Study in Policy-Making*, Macmillan, London, 2003

Griffin, Nicholas (ed.), *The Selected Letters of Bertrand Russell: The Public Years, 1914–1970*, Routledge, London, 2001

Grigg, John, *The Young Lloyd George*, HarperCollins, London, 1990 (originally published 1973)

——, *Lloyd George: The People's Champion, 1902–1911*, Eyre Methuen, London, 1978

——, *Lloyd George: From Peace to War, 1912–1916*, Penguin, London, 2002 (originally published 1985)

——, *Lloyd George: War Leader, 1916–1918*, Allen Lane, London, 2002

——, 'Rendel, Stuart, Baron Rendel (1834–1913), *Oxford Dictionary of National Biography*, Oxford University Press, Oxford, 2004

Haldane, Richard Burdon, *An Autobiography*, Hodder and Stoughton, London, 1929

Hamer, F. E. (ed.), *The Personal Papers of Lord Rendel*, London, Ernest Benn, 1931

Harris, José, *William Beveridge: A Biography* (2nd edn), Clarendon Press, Oxford, 1997

Harvey, John (ed.), *The Diplomatic Diaries of Oliver Harvey, 1937–1940*, Collins, London, 1970

Havighurst, Alfred F., *Radical Journalist: H. W. Massingham (1860–1924)*, Cambridge University Press, Cambridge, 1974

Hazlehurst, Cameron, *Politicians At War: July 1914 to May 1915: A Prologue to the Triumph of Lloyd George*, New York, Alfred A. Knopf, 1971

Hazlehurst, Cameron and Woodland, Christine, *A Liberal Chronicle: Journals and Papers of J. A. Pease, 1st Lord Gainford, 1908–1910*, Historians' Press, London, 1994

Hennessy, Peter, *Whitehall*, Secker and Warburg, London, 1989

Hepburn, James (ed.), *Letters of Arnold Bennett*, vol. IV: *Family Letters*, Oxford University Press, Oxford, 1986

Herman, John, *The Paris Embassy of Sir Eric Phipps: Anglo-French Relations and the Foreign Office*, Sussex Academic Press, Brighton, 1998

Higham, Charles, *Wallis: Secret Lives of the Duchess of Windsor*, Sidgwick & Jackson, London, 1988

Horne, John and Kramer, Alan, *German Atrocities, 1914: A History of Denial*, Yale University Press, New Haven and London, 2001

Hunter, Ian (ed.), *Winston and Archie: The Letters of Sir Archibald Sinclair and Winston S. Churchill, 1915–1960*, Politico's, London, 2005

Jefferys, Kevin, *The Churchill Coalition and Wartime Politics, 1940–1945*, Manchester University Press, Manchester, 1991

Jenkins, Roy, *Asquith*, Collins, London, 1986

———, *Baldwin*, Collins, London, 1987

———, *Churchill*, Macmillan, London, 2001

Jones, J. Graham, 'Lloyd George and the Abdication of Edward VIII', *National Library of Wales Journal*, vol. 30, no. 1 (summer 1997), pp. 89–105

———, 'Lloyd George and the Suffragettes', *National Library of Wales Journal*, vol. 33, no. 2 (winter 2003), pp. 1–33

Jones, Mervyn, *A Radical Life: The Biography of Megan Lloyd George, 1902–66*, Hutchinson, London, 1991

Jones, Thomas, *A Diary with Letters, 1931–1950*, Oxford University Press, London, 1954

Kershaw, Ian, *Making Friends with Hitler: Lord Londonderry and Britain's Road to War*, Allen Lane, London, 2004

Keynes, John Maynard, *The Collected Writings of John Maynard Keynes*, vol. IX: *Essays in Persuasion*, Macmillan/Cambridge University Press, for the Royal Economic Society, London, 1972

Kimball, Warren F. (ed.), *Churchill and Roosevelt: The Complete Correspondence*, vol. I: *Alliance Emerging, October 1933–November 1942*, Princeton University Press, Princeton, NJ, 1984

Koss, Stephen E., *Lord Haldane: Scapegoat for Liberalism*, Columbia University Press, New York and London, 1969

————, *Asquith*, Allen Lane, London, 1976

Lentin, A., *Guilt at Versailles: Lloyd George and the Pre-History of Appeasement*, Methuen, London, 1985

————, *Lloyd George and the Lost Peace: From Versailles to Hitler, 1919–1940*, Palgrave, Basingstoke, 2001

Leventhal, F. M., *The Last Dissenter*, Clarendon Press, Oxford, 1985

Lloyd George, David, *Through Terror to Triumph*, Hodder and Stoughton, London, 1915

————, *War Memoirs*, 2 vols., Odhams Press, London, 1938 (originally published in 6 vols., 1933–6)

————, *The Truth About the Peace Treaties*, 2 vols., Victor Gollancz, London, 1938

Lloyd George, Frances, *The Years that Are Past*, Hutchinson, London, 1967

Lloyd George, Richard, *My Father, Lloyd George*, Crown, New York, 1961

Lloyd George, Robert, *David & Winston: How a Friendship Changed History*, John Murray, London, 2005

Lloyd George by Mr. Punch, Cassell, London, 1922

Longford, Ruth, *Frances, Countess Lloyd George: More than a Mistress*, Gracewing, Leominster, 1996

Macfarlane, L. J., 'Hands off Russia: British Labour and the Russo-Polish War, 1920', *Past and Present*, no. 38 (Dec. 1967), pp. 126–52

MacKenzie, Norman and Mackenzie, Jeanne (eds.), *The Diary of Beatrice Webb*, vol. II: *1892–1905: 'All the Good Things of Life'*, Virago, London, 1983

————, *The Diary of Beatrice Webb*, vol. III: *1905–1924: 'The Power to Alter Things'*, Virago, London, 1984

Macleod, Roderick and Kelly, Denis (eds.), *The Ironside Diaries, 1937–1940*, Constable, London, 1962

MacMillan, Margaret, *Peacemakers: The Paris Conference of 1919 and Its Attempt to End War*, John Murray, London, 2001

Magnus, Philip, *King Edward the Seventh*, John Murray, London, 1964

Marder, Arthur J., *From Dreadnought to Scapa Flow: The Royal Navy in the Fisher Era, 1904–1919*, vol. I: *The Road to War, 1904–1914*, Oxford University Press, London, 1961

Margalit, Avishai, *The Ethics of Memory*, Harvard University Press, Cambridge, MA, 2002

Marsh, Peter T., *Joseph Chamberlain: Entrepreneur in Politics*, Yale University Press, New Haven and London, 1994

Martin, Kingsley, *Editor: A Second Volume of Autobiography, 1931–45*, Hutchinson, London, 1968

Masterman, Lucy, *C. F. G. Masterman: A Biography*, Nicholson and Watson, London, 1939

McEwen, J. M., 'A Churchill Story: Dinner at F. E. Smith's, 5 December 1916', *Queen's Quarterly*, vol. 83, no. 2 (Summer 1976), pp. 273–7

————, *The Riddell Diaries, 1908–1923*, Athlone Press, London and Atlantic Highlands, NJ, 1986

Middlemas, Keith (ed.), *Thomas Jones: Whitehall Diary*, 3 vols., Oxford University Press, London, 1969–71

Montague Browne, Anthony, *Long Sunset: Memoirs of Winston Churchill's Last Private Secretary*, Cassell, London, 1995

Moran, Lord, *Winston Churchill: The Struggle for Survival, 1940–1965*, Constable, London, 1966

Morgan, Kenneth O., *Consensus and Disunity: The Lloyd George Coalition Government, 1918–1922*, Clarendon Press, Oxford, 1979

———, (ed.), *Lloyd George, Family Letters, 1885–1936*, University of Wales Press and Oxford University Press, Cardiff and London, 1973

Morris, A. J. A., 'Steed, Henry Wickham (1871–1956)', *Oxford Dictionary of National Biography*, Oxford University Press, Oxford, 2004

Mosley, Diana, *A Life of Contrasts*, Hamish Hamilton, London, 1977

Mosley, Oswald, *My Life*, Nelson, London, 1968

Nicholas, H. G., *The British General Election of 1950*, Macmillan, London, 1951

Nicolson, Nigel (ed.), *Harold Nicolson: Diaries & Letters, 1930–1939*, Collins, London, 1966

———, *Harold Nicolson: Diaries and Letters, 1939–1945*, Collins, London, 1967

———, *Vita and Harold: The Letters of Vita Sackville-West and Harold Nicolson*, Weidenfeld and Nicolson, London, 1992

Norwich, John Julius (ed.), *The Duff Cooper Diaries, 1915–1951*, Weidenfeld and Nicolson, London, 2005

Packer, Ian, *Lloyd George, Liberalism and the Land: The Land Issue and Party Politics in England, 1906–1914*, Royal Historical Society, London, 2001

Parker, R. A. C. (ed.), *Winston Churchill: Studies in Statesmanship*, Brassey's, London, 1995 (repr. 2002)

Pimlott, Ben (ed.), *The Second World War Diary of Hugh Dalton, 1940–45*, Cape, London, 1986

Pollock, John, *Kitchener*, Constable, London, 1998

Ponting, Clive, *Churchill*, Sinclair-Stevenson, London, 1994

Pottle, Mark (ed.), *Champion Redoubtable: The Diaries and Letters of Violet Bonham Carter, 1914–1945*, Weidenfeld and Nicolson, London, 1998

Prior, Robin, *Churchill's 'World Crisis' as History*, Croom Helm, London, 1983

Pugh, Martin, *The Pankhursts*, Penguin, London, 2002

———, *'Hurrah for the Blackshirts!' Fascists and Fascists in Britain Between the Wars*, Cape, London, 2005

Quinault, Roland, 'Churchill, Lord Randolph Henry Spencer (1849–1895)', *Oxford Dictionary of National Biography*, Oxford University Press, Oxford, 2004

Ramsden, John (ed.), *Real Old Tory Politics: The Political Diaries of Sir Robert Sanders, Lord Bayford, 1910–35*, Historians' Press, London, 1984

Ranft, B. McL. (ed.), *The Beatty Papers: Selections from the Private and Official Correspondence and Papers of Admiral of the Fleet Earl Beatty*, vol. II: *1916–1927*, Scolar Press for the Navy Records Society, Aldershot, 1993

Repington, C. à Court, *The First World War, 1914–1918*, Constable, London, 1920

Reynolds, David, *In Command of History: Churchill Fighting and Writing the Second World War*, Allen Lane, London, 2004

Rhodes James, Robert, *Churchill: A Study in Failure, 1900–1939*, Weidenfeld and Nicolson, London, 1970

———, *Victor Cazalet: A Portrait*, Hamish Hamilton, London, 1976

———, (ed.), *'Chips': The Diaries of Sir Henry Channon*, Weidenfeld and Nicolson, London, 1967 (repr. 1993)

———, *Memoirs of a Conservative: J. C. C. Davidson's Memoirs and Papers, 1910–37*, Weidenfeld and Nicolson, London, 1969

———, *Winston S. Churchill: His Complete Speeches, 1897–1963*, 8 vols., Chelsea House, New York, 1974

Rintala, Marvin, *Lloyd George and Churchill: How Friendship Changed Politics*, Madison Books, Lanham, MD, 1995

Roberts, Andrew, *'The Holy Fox': A Life of Lord Halifax*, Weidenfeld and Nicolson, London, 1991

———, *Eminent Churchillians*, Weidenfeld and Nicolson, London, 1994

Rose, N. A. (ed.), *Baffy: The Diaries of Blanche Dugdale, 1936–1947*, Valentine, Mitchell, London, 1973

Roskill, Stephen, *Hankey: Man of Secrets*, 3 vols., Collins, London, 1970–4

Rowland, Peter, *Lloyd George*, Barrie & Jenkins, London, 1975

Scally, Robert J., *The Origins of the Lloyd George Coalition: The Politics of Social-Imperialism, 1900–1918*, Princeton University Press, Princeton, NJ, 1975

Segev, Tom, *One Palestine, Complete: Jews and Arabs under the British Mandate*, Little, Brown, London, 2000

Self, Robert C. (ed.), *The Correspondence of Sir Austen Chamberlain with his Sisters Hilda and Ida, 1916–1937*, Cambridge University Press for the Royal Historical Society, Cambridge, 1995

———, *The Neville Chamberlain Diary Letters*, vol. III: *The Heir Apparent, 1928–33*, Ashgate, Aldershot, 2002

———, *The Neville Chamberlain Diary Letters*, vol. IV: *The Downing Street Years, 1934–1940*, Ashgate, Aldershot, 2005

Sheean, Vincent, *Between the Thunder and the Sun*, Random House, New York and, with a modified text, Macmillan, London, 1943

Shinwell, Emanuel, *Conflict without Malice*, Odhams Press, London, 1955

Skidelsky, Robert, *Politicians and the Slump: The Labour Government of 1929–1931*, Papermac, London, 1994 (originally published 1967)

Smart, Nick (ed.), *The Diaries and Letters of Robert Bernays, 1932–1939*, Edwin Mellen, Lewiston/Queenston/Lampeter, 1996

Smith, David C., 'Winston Churchill and H.G. Wells: Edwardians in the Twentieth Century', *Cahiers Victoriens et Edouardiens*, no. 30 (1989), pp. 93–116

Snow, C. P., *Variety of Men*, Macmillan, London, 1967

Soames, Mary (ed.), *Speaking for Themselves: The Personal Letters of Winston and Clementine Churchill*, Doubleday, London, 1998

Sommer, Dudley, *Haldane of Cloan: His Life and Times, 1856–1928*, George Allen and Unwin, London, 1960

Spender, J. A., *Life, Journalism and Politics*, 2 vols., Cassell, London, 1927

Spender, J. A. and Asquith, Cyril, *Life of Herbert Henry Asquith, Lord Oxford and Asquith*, 2 vols., Hutchinson, London, 1932

Stafford, David, *Churchill and Secret Service*, Abacus, London, 2000 (first published 1997)

Swinton, Earl of, *Sixty Years of Power: Some Memories of the Men who Wielded It*, Hutchinson, London, 1966

Sydenham, Lord, et al., *The World Crisis: A Criticism*, 2nd edn, Hutchinson, London, n.d, [1928]

Sylvester, A. J., *The Real Lloyd George*, Cassell, London, 1947

Taylor, A. J. P. (ed.), *Lloyd George: A Diary by Frances Stevenson*, Harper & Row, New York, 1971

———, *Lloyd George: Twelve Essays*, Hamish Hamilton, London, 1971

——— (ed.), *W. P. Crozier: Off the Record: Political Interviews, 1933–1943*, Hutchinson, London, 1973

——— (ed.), *My Darling Pussy: The Letters of Lloyd George and Frances Stevenson, 1913–41*, Weidenfeld and Nicolson, London, 1975

Taylor, Fred (ed.), *The Goebbels Diaries, 1939–1941*, Hamish Hamilton, London, 1982

Taylor, Rex, *Michael Collins*, Hutchinson, London, 1958

Thompson, J. Lee, *Northcliffe: Press Baron in Politics, 1865–1922*, John Murray, London, 2000

Thomson, Malcolm, *David Lloyd George: The Official Biography*, Hutchison, London, n.d. [1948]

Tooze, Adam, 'Marshallian Macroeconomics in Action: The Industrial Statistics of the Board of Trade, 1907–1935', unpublished manuscript

Toye, Richard, 'The Churchill Syndrome: The Uses of an Image since 1945', unpublished manuscript

Toye, Richard and Gottlieb, Julie (eds.), *Making Reputations: Power, Persuasion and the Individual in Modern British Politics*, I. B. Tauris, London, 2005

Trevor-Roper, Hugh (ed.), *Hitler's Table Talk, 1941–44: His Private Conversations*, Weidenfeld and Nicolson, London, 1953 (repr. 1973)

Vincent, John (ed.), *The Crawford Papers: The Journals of David Lindsay Twenty-seventh Earl of Crawford and Tenth of Earl of Balcarres 1871–1940 during the Years 1892 to 1940*, Manchester University Press, Manchester, 1984

Waley, S. D., *Edwin Montagu: A Memoir and an Account of his Visits to India*, Asia Publishing House, London, 1964

Waugh, Evelyn, *Men at Arms*, Penguin, Harmondsworth, 1964 (originally published 1952)

Wells, H. G, *The New Machiavelli*, Penguin, Harmondsworth, 1946 (originally published 1911)

West, Nigel (ed.), *The Guy Liddell Diaries*, vol. I: *1939–1942: MI5's Director of Counter-Espionage in World War II*, Routledge, London, 2005

Williams, Francis, *A Prime Minister Remembers: The War and Post-War Memoirs of Rt. Hon. Earl Attlee*, Heinemann, London, 1961

Williamson, Philip (ed.), *The Modernisation of Conservative Politics: The Diaries and Letters of William Bridgeman, 1904–1935*, Historians' Press, London, 1988

Williamson, Philip and Baldwin, Edward (eds.), *Baldwin Papers: A Conservative Statesman, 1908–1947*, Cambridge University Press, Cambridge, 2004

Wilson, A. N., *After the Victorians: The Decline of Britain in the World*, Farrar, Straus and Giroux, New York, 2005

Wilson, Keith (ed.), *The Rasp of War: The Letters of H. A. Gwynne to the Countess Bathurst, 1914–1918*, Sidgwick & Jackson, London, 1988

Wilson, Trevor (ed.), *The Political Diaries of C. P. Scott, 1911–1928*, Collins, London, 1970

Wolff, Michael (ed.), *The Collected Essays of Sir Winston Churchill*, 4 vols., Library of Imperial History, London, 1976

Young, Kenneth, *Churchill and Beaverbrook: A Study in Friendship and Politics*, Eyre and Spottiswoode, London, 1966

Young, Kenneth (ed.), *The Diaries of Sir Robert Bruce Lockhart*, 2 vols., Macmillan, London, 1973, 1980

Index

abdication crisis, 322–3

Abdullah, King of Transjordan, 219

Abyssinia, Italian invasion, 272, 311, 315, 326

Acland, Francis, 234

Addison, Christopher: on DLG's conscription policy, 155; DLG's criticism of, 226; diary, 8, 155; Munitions Ministry, 170; resignation, 225; on WSC's conversation style, 191; on WSC's Munitions meddling, 153; on WSC's resignation speech, 156

Addison, Paul, 308, 341, 368–9, 372

Agadir crisis, 86, 87–8, 122, 125

Aitken, Sir Max, see Beaverbrook, first Baron

Alexandra Palace meeting (1904), 32–3

'All Red' transport scheme, 43, 94

Allan, Maud, 49

Amery, Leo: on abdication, 323; on Asquith's social life, 49; attack on Chamberlain, 350; on Baldwin, 253; on Beaverbrook and DLG, 381; on Coal Bill, 278; criticisms of WSC, 246; on DLG's death, 391; on DLG's morals, 49; on Italy policy, 327; on relationship between DLG and WSC, 274–5, 391; tariff policy, 280; Undersecretaries' Plot, 364–5, 366; on WSC in France, 186; on WSC's naval estimates, 115

Anderson, Sir John, 301

Anglo-Persian Oil Company, 254

Anti-Tithe League, 17

Antwerp, defence of (1914), 131–2, 166

Army, British: proposed cuts, 51–2, 54; strategy against Germany, 88; 29th Division, 137, 139

Army Council, 207

Asquith, Elizabeth, 75–6

Asquith, H. H.: Archerfield visitors, 89–90; attack on DLG, 235; biography, 298; Budgets, 50–1; Cabinet shuffle, 89–91; Chancellor of Exchequer, 35, 50–1; coalition (1915), 145; Colonial Conference (1907), 42; conscription issue, 152, 155, 159; Curragh incident (1914), 116; Dardanelles campaign, 137, 154, 175; death, 260; dinner for key ministers (1912), 93; drink problem, 62; Easter Rising, 164; election (1923), 244; Fisher's resignation, 144; franchise policy, 80; General Strike, 258; Irish Home Rule policy, 73, 114, 115, 116, 164–5; Liberal leadership, 257, 260; Liberal reunification strategy, 243; Lords policy, 54, 58, 63, 66, 68; Marconi affair, 95, 97; Maurice debate (1918), 188; minimum wage issue, 92; munitions issue, 139, 143; naval estimates (1914), 104–5, 108, 109–10; old age, 257; Paisley election (1920), 213; premiership, 45–7, 53, 60, 167–8, 340; relationship with DLG and WSC, 59–60, 62–3, 100, 119–20, 140–1, 146–7, 166, 194, 259–60, 299–300; Relugas Compact, 35; resignation, 168–9; return mooted, 177, 179, 190; Russian policy, 251; social life, 49, 59; on speeches, 24; Venetia Stanley, letters to, 105, 131, 140, 145; War Committee, 156; war leadership, 167–8; war medals question, 208, 209; War Office, 155; Wee Frees, 213; women's suffrage issue, 77, 82–3; WWI outbreak, 124, 126–7

Asquith, Margot: advice to DLG, 104; Cabinet leak issue, 47; conversation with DLG, 142; conversation with Clementine Churchill, 148; conversation with WSC (1910), 64–5, 70; DLG defends Fisher to, 136; on fall of Liberal government, 145; husband's letters, 152; on relationship between DLG and WSC, 71, 93, 149, 154, 196, 299; on WSC's intriguing, 140; on WSC's speeches, 149, 151; on WWI outbreak, 127

Asquith, Violet, *see* Bonham-Carter, Violet

Astor, Nancy, Viscountess, 101, 349, 375, 384

Astor, Waldorf, second Viscount, 309

Attlee, Clement: conscription debate, 333; Czech policy, 330–1; defence policy, 316; DLG's old age, 377; German peace policy, 358; government, 396; Labour Party leadership, 316; premiership question (1940), 352; press influence, 361; Prime Minister (1945), 394; War Cabinet question, 374, 375; on WSC, 380

Aubers Ridge, battle of (1915), 143

Austria: German annexation of, 327; naval building plans, 123; ultimatum to Serbia, 117–18, 123; war with Serbia, 124

Aylesford, Edith, Countess of, 14

Aylesford, Heneage Finch, seventh Earl of, 14

Bailey, Abe, 310

Baldwin, Stanley: abdication crisis, 323–4; Chancellor of Exchequer, 236; Conservative leadership, 270–1, 304; defence issues, 315–16; DLG's view of, 236; Financial Secretary to Treasury, 215; general election (1923), 244–5; general election (1924), 251; German air power question, 304–5; India policy, 277, 282–3; Leader of Opposition, 247, 275; *People* interview, 247; Prime Minister, 242, 251–3, 309–10; protectionist policy, 242–3, 279–80; relationship with DLG, 286, 302, 309; relationship with Liberals, 248–9, 274; relationship with MacDonald, 269, 285; relationship with WSC, 258, 265–6, 267, 286, 304, 309; resignation (1929), 270; retirement, 325; view of DLG, 1, 6, 256, 274, 309–10; view of WSC, 1, 6, 246, 249, 307, 309–10, 313; appoints WSC as Chancellor, 251–3

Balfour, Arthur: constitutional conference, 68; Balfour declaration (1917), 219; Education Bill, 26; Foreign Secretary, 170; fusion issue, 214; General Strike, 258; munitions issue, 139; premiership, 26; relationship with Asquith, 63, 68, 140; relationship with DLG, 34, 140; relationship with WSC, 27, 30, 34, 140, 162–3, 241, 246, 247, 295, 299; resignation as Prime Minister, 35; successor as Unionist leader, 86; tariff policy, 29; War Council, 139–40; Whittinghame house, 240; women's suffrage policy, 77

Balfour, Gerald, 117

Balkan War, First (1912–13), 123

Barnes, George, 196

Barry, Gerald, 329

Bastiat, Claude Frederic, 27

Baxter, Beverley, 354

Bayley, J. Moore, 26

BBC, 300–1

Beatty, David, first Earl, 210

Beauchamp, William Lygon, seventh Earl, 110, 126

Beaufort, Henry Fitzroy Somerset, ninth Duke of, 62

Beauvais conference (1918), 186

Beaverbrook, Max Aitken, first Baron: account of dinner with WSC (1916), 169–70; Baldwin's denunciation, 283; biography of Duchess of Windsor, 370; coalition revival plan, 243; comparison of DLG's and WSC's careers, 238–9, 270; DLG's papers, 401–2; influence on WSC's writings, 293, 294–5; intriguer, 373, 375; *Politicians and the War*, 169; press attacks on WSC, 206; question of DLG's inclusion in WSC's wartime government, 356, 375, 377, 378, 381, 383, 385; relationship with DLG, 229, 290, 378; relationship with WSC, 206, 244, 246, 377, 407; rumours of intrigue against DLG, 216; War Cabinet issues, 367, 374, 376; war committee proposal, 168; on WSC's appointment in DLG's government, 180–1, 182; on WSC's relationship with DLG, 217, 224, 226, 229, 244, 267

Beaverbrook Library, 402

Belgium: German invasion of (1914), 121, 124, 125, 126–8; German invasion of (1940), 352; surrender (1940), 358

Bell, Alexander Graham, 2

Beneš, Eduard, 331

Benn, Sir Ernest, 340

Bennett, Arnold, 243

Berliner Tageblatt, 316

Bernays, Robert, 310, 335

Berry, William, *see* Camrose, first Baron

Bevan, Aneurin, 9, 275–6, 278, 391, 396, 405

Beveridge, Sir William, 387

Bevin, Ernest, 362, 365, 366, 375

Birkenhead, F. E. Smith, first Earl of: anti-Asquith movement, 161; 'Coalition repast', 241; Germany policy, 193; intriguer, 166, 215; Irish policy, 222; Lord Chancellor, 215; Marconi case, 95–6; Other Club, 85; relationship with Baldwin, 247; relationship with DLG, 215, 235, 246, 265; relationship with WSC, 163, 215–16, 230, 243, 246, 265; social life, 86, 152, 169, 240; WSC's

Exchequer position, 253; WSC's opinion of, 299
Birmingham, rioting, 25–6
Birrell, Augustine, 115, 119
Black and Tans, 221
Blandford, George Spencer-Churchill, Marquess of (WSC's uncle), 14
Blenheim Palace, 11, 53
Blum, Léon, 328
Blunt, Wilfrid Scawen, 151–2, 175–6, 182, 188
Bocca, Geoffrey, 370
Boer War: first (1880–1), 20; second (1899–1902), 20–1, 26, 40
Boncour, Joseph-Paul, 328
Bonham-Carter, Violet (née Asquith): on Cabinet leak, 47; at canteen opening, 161; on DLG's speeches, 350; general election (1951), 397; on relationship between DLG and WSC, 38, 66–7, 76; view of Conservative–Liberal cooperation, 395–6; view of DLG, 349; on WWII outbreak, 127
Boothby, Robert (Bob): DLG premiership question (1940), 347–8; financial improprieties, 379; memoirs, 366, 379; on relationship between DLG and WSC, 195, 254, 407; relationship with DLG, 367–8; relationship with WSC, 366, 379; resignation, 379; Undersecretaries' Plot, 364–5, 366; view of DLG, 346, 405; WSC's PPS, 195, 254
Borden, Robert, 244
Bouvet, French battleship, 138
Bowles, Thomas Gibson, 23
Brabourne, Michael Knatchbull, fifth Baron, 306
Bracken, Brendan, 283, 289–9, 291, 334, 366–7
Brailsford, Henry Noel, 77, 81, 82, 83, 84
Bridgeman, William, 182, 246, 265
Briggs, Asa, 300
Britain, Battle of (1940), 374
Britain's Industrial Future (Liberal Yellow Book), 260–1, 264
British Gazette, 258
British Union of Fascists, 288
British Weekly, 61
Brooke, Alan, 380, 403
Brown, Ernest, 280
Buckingham Palace, inter-party conference (1914), 117
Budget League, 61, 94
Bulgaria, 123
Bull, William, 205
Burns, John, 41, 60, 73, 91, 116, 126

Bush, George W., 7, 128, 404
Butler, R. A., 306

Caernarfon Boroughs, constituency, 17–18
Cairo conference (1921), 215, 219
Campbell, John, 250, 402
Campbell, J. R., 251
Campbell-Bannerman, Henry, 22, 32–3, 35, 36, 41, 45–6
Camrose, William Berry, first Baron, 266–7
Canada: communications, 43; Dreadnoughts, 107
Carden, Admiral Sir Sackville Hamilton, 135, 136, 138
Carlton Club meeting (1922), 235–6, 247
Carr-Gomm, Hubert, 99
Carr-Gomm, Kathleen, 99
Carson, Edward: ill health, 162; Irish policies, 115, 117, 164; Marconi case, 95–6; relationship with DLG, 167, 169, 250; resignation as Attorney General, 161–2; Unionist, 96, 115, 167; war committee plan, 168
Carysfort, HMS, 132
Cazalet, Victor, 84, 300, 377
Cecil, Lord Hugh, 30, 31–2
Cecil, Lord Robert, 168, 170
Chamberlain, Austen: BBC protest, 300; Carlton Club meeting (1922), 235–6; Chancellor of Exchequer, 33; Finance Bill speeches, 33–4; Foreign Secretary, 252; Irish policies, 114, 221; leadership of Conservative Party, 215; premiership question, 227, 229; relationship with Baldwin, 247, 248–9, 252–3, 315; relationship with DLG, 170, 197, 227, 235–6; resignation, 168; view of WSC, 181, 216, 225, 246, 253, 280
Chamberlain, Joseph: Birmingham rioting, 25–6; Boer War, 20; Colonial Secretary, 20, 36; comparison with DLG, 66; DLG on, 18; on politicians, 410; resignation (1903), 33, 36; tariff reform, 27, 29–30, 36; WSC's opposition to, 27, 30, 31
Chamberlain, Neville: Budget (1937), 325; Chancellorship question, 252–3; Commons speech (1940), 354; death, 173, 374; fall of government, 336, 346, 352, 381; German policy, 326; Health Minister, 253, 285; negotiations with Hitler, 330–1; Italy policy, 326–7; premiership, 325, 340, 346–7; press campaign against, 360, 361; progressive Conservatism, 271; protectionism, 279; relationship with DLG, 286, 302, 309,

Chamberlain, Neville (*cont.*)
315–16, 338, 353–4, 358–61, 365, 367–8, 372; relationship with WSC, 286, 302, 308, 315–16, 332–3, 353–5, 359–61; resignation, 374–5; view of DLG, 267, 274, 309, 338, 353–4, 358; War Cabinet, 338–9, 343–4; war policy, 342, 358; on WSC, 266, 275; WSC's tribute, 391

Chanak crisis, 233–4

Channon, Henry 'Chips', 327, 344–5, 354, 374, 382, 387

Chartwell, 232, 254

Chatfield, Alfred Chatfield, first Baron, 339

'Chinese Slavery', 39, 40–1

Chiozza Money, Leo, 27–9, 106–7, 312

Church of England, 26

Churchill, Clementine (née Hozier, WSC's wife): attitude to Frances Stevenson, 101–2; Blunt visit, 188; conversation with Margot Asquith, 148; dinner with Asquiths, 148–9; DLG's marriage, 387; election campaign (1923), 244; engagement, 49; finances, 276; Liberal views, 243; peace celebrations (1918), 193; relationship with DLG, 68, 95, 101, 148, 157, 159–61, 182, 232–3, 385; wedding, 49–50; women's suffrage issue, 78, 83; on WSC's funeral plans, 392; on WSC's tribute to DLG, 391

Churchill, Diana (WSC's daughter), 59, 81

Churchill, Jack (WSC's brother), 137

Churchill, Jennie, Lady Randolph (Jerome, WSC's mother), 13, 110–11, 161, 225

Churchill, Lord Randolph (WSC's father), 13–17, 18, 19, 25–6, 105, 258

Churchill, Marigold (WSC's daughter), 45, 225–6

Churchill, Randolph (WSC's son): biography of father, 118, 403; by-election defeat, 314; death, 403; on DLG, 387; journalism, 322; lunch with DLG, 289–90, 291; Mosley visit, 286–7; on naval estimates discussion, 111; on relationship between DLG and WSC, 4, 118; relationship with DLG, 289–90, 314–15, 322

CHURCHILL, WINSTON: birth, 2, 11, 13; childhood, 12; education, 12, 15–16, 19; military career, 19–20; elected to Commons (1900), 20; maiden speech, 22–4; first meeting with DLG, 24–5; joins Liberals, 27, 32; Undersecretary for the Colonies, 36; election campaign (1906), 39, 40–1; Colonial Conference (1907), 42–3; African tour, 43;

Cyprus commitment, 43–4; President of Board of Trade, 43, 45, 46–7, 50, 56, 73; by-elections (1907), 48–9; wedding, 49–50; Army cuts campaign, 51–2; behaviour in Cabinet, 52; Dreadnoughts campaign, 54–5; National Insurance Bill, 57–8; election campaign (Jan–Feb 1910), 64, 70; Home Secretary, 65–6, 77, 85–7, 89; Criccieth visit, 68–9; election campaign (Dec 1910), 70; women's suffrage issue, 77–84; Other Club, 85, 330, 404; miners' strike, 85–6; rail strike, 86–7; Agadir crisis, 87–8, 122; defence issues, 88–9; First Lord of the Admiralty, 85, 89–90, 93, 119, 127–8, 145–6; naval estimates (1912), 93; Marconi affair, 95–6, 97–8, 118, 160, 163–4, 172, 181; attitude to Frances Stevenson, 101–2, 387–8; land reform, 102–3; naval estimates (1914), 93, 104–13, 115, 406; Irish Home Rule, 112–17, 119; WWI policy, 121; German talks proposal, 122–3; WWI outbreak, 124–7; Antwerp, defence of, 131–2, 166; war strategy, 134, 153–4; Dardanelles campaign, 135–9, 142–4, 147, 154, 156; munitions issue, 139, 145; Fisher's resignation, 144, 146, 147; Chancellor of Duchy of Lancaster, 146–7, 157; conscription issue, 151, 152, 154–5, 332; resignation, 156; army service on Western Front, 156–7, 163, 164; Dardanelles Commission, 166, 167; hopes for place in new ministry, 169–70; Minister of Munitions, 150, 180–5, 297; in France, 185, 186; Secretary of State for War and Air, 197–8, 214, 217, 218–19; German peace terms policy, 198, 202–3; demobilization plan, 199–200; Russian policy, 200–3, 205–6, 209–13, 228, 230, 250, 294, 332; Turkish policy, 217–18, 233–4; Central Party proposal, 213–14; Colonial Secretary, 214–15, 219, 225, 237, 291; intrigue against DLG, 215–16; Middle East policy, 219–20, 232; Irish policy, 220–4, 231–2, 237, 294; daughter's death, 225–6; appendicitis operation, 236–7, 239; election defeat (1922), 240; Liberal nomination (West Leicester), 243; election defeat (1923), 244; break with Liberals, 245; Westminster (Abbey Division) election defeat, 245–6; Epping selection, 249; return to Conservative Party, 238, 240, 242, 246, 249, 251–2, 254, 270–1; election (1924), 251–2; Chancellor of Exchequer, 195, 238, 251–2,

270–1; first Budget (1925), 255–6; General Strike (1926), 258–9; meeting with Mussolini (1927), 302; Budget (1928), 261; Budget (1929), 263; Egyptian policy, 273–4; parliamentary tactics, 274–6; North American trip, 276; Wall Street Crash, 276; Indian policy, 277–8, 280–3, 287, 305–6, 334, 406; resignation from Shadow Cabinet, 282, 285; election campaign (1931), 287–8; traffic accident, 289; in Bahamas, 289; National Government, 300; Italian policy, 302, 326, 339–40, 406; German policy, 302–5, 314, 406; Spanish Civil War, 312, 328; in Marrakesh, 313; view of Hitler, 316–17; attitude to Jews, 318–22; abdication crisis, 322–4; French conversations, 328; WWII policy, 336, 341, 342; in Chamberlain's War Cabinet, 338; First Lord of the Admiralty, 339–40; Norway campaign, 346–7, 349–51; premiership, 173, 353; formation of government, 353–4; War Cabinet, 355, 364, 368, 374, 375; in France, 357, 363; Undersecretaries' Plot, 364–6; leader of Conservative Party, 173, 374–5; war strategy, 379–80; last conversation with DLG, 389–90; Earldom for DLG, 388–9; DLG's death, 391; tribute to DLG, 391; caretaker government, 392–3; general election (1945), 392–6; response to election defeat, 394; Leader of Opposition, 394–5; response to DLG biography, 400–1; election campaign (1950), 395–6; election (1951), 397; final term in office, 397–8; stroke (1953), 397; retirement, 398, 404–5; death, 2, 405; funeral, 392; statue in Commons, 409–10

PERSON: appearance, 298, 387; background, 12, 13–15, 38; character, 1–2; character compared to DLG, 1–2, 47, 75–6, 183, 222–3, 335, 391, 406; conversation style, 1–2, 75, 119; drinking, 141, 206, 298; faults, 120; finances, 19, 94, 276; home at Chartwell, 232; marriage, 49–50, 101; morals, 188; old age, 404; oratory, 3, 74–5; painting, 151; religion, 2, 16; reputation, 6–7, 238, 241, 340, 346, 348, 402–6; self-absorption, 123; skills, 57; volatility, 182, 232, 394

SPEECHES: Commons maiden speech, 22–4; Cyprus (1908), 43–4; (1906), 56; Leicester (1909), 62, 63; influence on 1910 election results, 64; election campaign (Dec 1910), 70; interrupted, 81; Manchester (1913), 103;

Guildhall (1913), 104; Dundee (1913), 114; Bradford (1914), 115–16; Dundee (1915), 151; resignation (1915), 156; Commons (1916), 162–3; Dundee (1920), 221; Chingford (1925), 258; (1940), 129; Commons (1940), 351–2, 354, 365–6; Commons (1941), 382; tribute to DLG, 391; Fulton, Missouri (1946), 394; Zurich (1946), 394; final Commons speech (1955), 408–9; Biggleswade (1955), 398

WRITINGS: biography of father, 17, 399–400; biography of Marlborough, 313; *Great Contemporaries*, 299; *History of the English-Speaking Peoples*, 404; journalism, 8, 19, 20, 247, 316–17, 318–22, 345–6; memoirs, 394, 402; *My Early Life*, 24, 296; *The River War*, 20; *The Second World War*, 235, 402; *The Story of the Malakand Field Force*, 19; *Thoughts and Adventures*, 345; 'The Untrodden Field in Politics', 56; *The World Crisis*, 55, 195, 200, 241, 267–8, 291–6, 334

Churt, DLG's home (Bron-y-de): air raid shelter, 373, 387; architecture, 232; Bracken and Randolph at, 289–90; Cecil King's visits, 363, 380; DLG's career, 300, 359; DLG's last days, 387, 388; farm, 233, 300; Liberal manifesto discussions, 261; WSC's visit, 249

Civil List Committee, 324

Clarke, Peter, 262

Clarke, Tom, 296

Clemenceau, Georges, 186, 198–9

Coal Bill (1929–30), 278–9

Collier's, 321

Collins, Michael, 220, 222–3, 224, 231

Colonial Conference (1907), 42–3

Colville, John, 340, 355, 376, 391

Commercial Intelligence, 28

Committee of Imperial Defence (CID), 88, 91

Conciliation Bill, 78–80, 83–4

Conciliation Committee, 77–8

Connolly, James, 164

conscription (National Service): Cabinet struggle over, 154–5; *Daily Mail* articles by Duke of Marlborough, 102–3; DLG's policy, 8, 150–1, 152, 154–5, 333; DLG's speech (1915), 150–1; Irish, 186; Military Training Bill, 333; resignation issue, 155, 159; WSC's approach, 152, 154–5, 332, 333

Conservative Party: caretaker government (1945), 392–3; franchise issues, 3; general election (1900), 21; general election (1918), 196–7; general election (1924), 238; honours

Conservative Party (*cont.*)
   scandal, 232; Irish Home Rule policy, 114;
   Liberal coalition, 2, 143, 144–6, 148, 227,
   241; National Government (1931), 272;
   relationship with Liberals after WWII, 395,
   396; votes for women, 77; WSC's departure,
   27, 32; WSC's leadership, 374; WSC's
   return, 238, 240
Cooper, Alfred Duff, 342, 365
Coote, Colin, 404
Coronation (1937), 325
Council of Action, 310, 311, 313
Cowdray, Weetman Pearson, first Viscount, 180
Crawshay-Williams, Eliot, 99
Crete, fall of (1941), 384
Crewe, Robert Crewe-Milnes, Marquess of, 47
Criccieth, 15, 68, 205
Cripps, Sir Stafford, 348, 352, 374, 376, 385–6
Croft, Henry Page, 306
Cromwell, Oliver, 350
Crosfield, Sir Arthur, 335
Crozier, W. P., 343
Cuba, 19
Cummings, A. J., 348
Curragh incident (1914), 116
Curzon of Kedleston, George Curzon, first
   Marquess of: Air Ministry question, 161;
   Chanak crisis, 234; comparison between
   DLG and WSC, 163; conscription question,
   152, 154–5; Foreign Secretary, 215, 219,
   234; Lord President of the Council, 180;
   place in Law government, 239; premiership
   question, 242; relationship with DLG, 170;
   relationship with WSC, 180, 219, 225, 239;
   resignation from Asquith government, 168;
   War Cabinet, 170
Cyprus, 43–4
Czechoslovakia, German threat, 330–1

Daily Chronicle, 47, 105–6, 131, 230, 246
Daily Express, 168, 181, 318
Daily Herald, 361, 362
Daily Mail, 30, 40, 96, 102, 106, 128, 133, 204,
   217, 251, 348
Daily News, 23
Daily Sketch, 343
Daily Telegraph, 23, 266, 305, 404
Dalton, Hugh, 374, 375, 378, 383, 386
Danzig (Gdansk) crisis, 337
Dardanelles, 135–9, 142–4, 147, 154, 156
Dardanelles Commission, 166, 167, 172, 175
Daunton, Martin, 264
Davidson, J. C. C., 263, 266, 277

Davidson, Randall, 258
Davies, Clement, 350, 364–5, 394, 395, 396,
   397
Davies, David, 70
Dawson, Geoffrey, 309
Dawson of Penn, Bertrand Dawson, first
   Viscount, 317
de Gaulle, Charles, 376
de Robeck, John, 138–9
De Valera, Eamon, 222, 224, 299
Denikin, Anton, 205, 206, 209, 212, 294
Derby, Edward Stanley, seventeenth Earl of:
   recruitment scheme, 155, 159; view of WSC,
   166, 180, 183; War Secretary, 180, 189;
   WSC's accusations, 306
Dillon, John, 73
Disraeli, Benjamin, 14
Dixon, Piers, 404
Donald, Robert, 131
Dreadnoughts, 54–5, 105
Dundee: by-election (1908), 49, 241; by-election
   (1917), 182; general election (1922), 241
Dunkirk, evacuation of (1940), 358, 360

Eade, Charles, 321, 345
Easter Rising (1916), 164
Economy Bill (1926), 257
Eden, Anthony: compares DLG and WSC, 399;
   Czech policy, 330–1; on DLG, 378, 387;
   Foreign Secretary, 326; Italy policy, 311,
   326, 327; Minister for League of Nations
   affairs, 311; premiership question, 347;
   reputation, 301; resignation, 327; successor
   to WSC, 392, 397–8
Education Bill (Balfour Act 1902), 26–7, 31–2,
   39
Edward VII: Asquith's premiership, 46;
   Aylesford scandal, 14; Balfour's resignation,
   35; death, 67; Lords reform issue, 63, 66; on
   WSC, 13; view of DLG and WSC, 52–3, 62
Edward VIII, *see* Windsor, Duke of
Egerton, George W., 291
Egypt, British policy, 273–4
El Alamein, Battle of, 385
elections, general: (1880), 15; (1886), 16; (1900),
   21; (1906), 17, 38–41, 56; (Jan-Feb 1910),
   63–4; (Dec 1910), 70–1; (1918), 196–7;
   (1922), 239–41; (1923), 241; (1924), 238,
   251–2; (1929), 268–9, 270, 273, 274; (1931),
   287–8; (1935), 312–13; (1945), 6, 392–6;
   (1950), 395–6; (1951), 396–7; (1955), 398
electoral reform, 274
Elgin, Victor Bruce, ninth Earl of, 36

Elibank, Alexander Murray, Baron Murray of (earlier Master of Elibank): Irish policy, 83; Marconi affair, 94, 96; relationship with DLG, 57, 80; relationship with WSC, 67, 82

Elliott, Maxine, 324–5

Enchantress, 118

Epping constituency, 249

Epstein, Jacob, 409

Esher, Reginald Brett, second Viscount: discussion with WSC on premiership, 45–6; on DLG and WSC, 53, 87, 96, 166, 182, 227; on King's attitude to DLG and WSC, 62; meeting with WSC at St Omer, 157

Evans, Ernest, 273

Evans, T. P. Conwell, 317

Evening Standard, 322, 383

Everest, Mrs (nurse), 14, 16

Ewart, John Spencer, 73

Farey-Jones, F. W., 375

Fawcett, Millicent, 76, 77

Feisal Ibn Hussein, King of Iraq, 219

Fildes, Henry, 387

Fisher, H. A. L.: on DLG, 257; on DLG and WSC, 207, 209, 256; policy document, 214; on WSC, 225

Fisher, John, first Baron: 'Big Navy' policy, 55; character, 135–6; Dardanelles strategy, 136–7, 143–4; reappointment as First Sea Lord, 135; recall question, 162, 163, 177; relationship with DLG, 55, 136–7, 144; relationship with WSC, 135–6, 143–4, 147, 162; resignation, 143–4

Fitzroy, Almeric, 62

Foch, Ferdinand, 186, 328

Foot, Dingle, 4, 336, 350

Foot, Michael, 383

Fourth Party, 14, 32

France: Abyssinia crisis, 311, 312; British troops, 90; Czech policy, 330; fall (1940), 363; German declaration of war (1914), 124; German invasion (1940), 357–8

franchise: Reform Bill (1884), 14–15; transition to full democracy, 3; women's suffrage issue, 40, 72, 76–84

Franchise Bill, 80–1, 82, 84

Franco, Francisco, 317

Franz Ferdinand, Archduke, 117, 123

free trade: British position, 27; election issue (1906), 39, 42, 50; imperial preference question, 42, 289; Liberal resignations, 279–80, 289; protectionism issue, 242–3,

279, 289; tariff reform policy, 27, 42; WSC's approach, 241

French, Sir John, 143, 161

Gallipoli campaign, 136–7, 142–3, 154, 157, 166, 225

Gandhi, Mahatma, 282

Garvin, J. L., 67, 309, 311, 348, 373

Gaulois, 139

Geddes, Sir Eric, 150, 183, 227–8

General Strike (1926), 257–9, 261

Geneva disarmament conference (1933), 303

Genoa, conference of European nations, 228–9, 231

George V: Baldwin's reports, 256; death, 314; DLG war medals, 8, 207–8; Irish policy, 114–15; Lords reform, 69; miners' safety issue, 86; political compromise initiative, 67; relationship with son Edward, 322; temperance pledge, 141; view of WSC, 122; WSC's War and Air post, 197

George VI, King, 324, 352–3, 370

George, Elizabeth (Lloyd, DLG's mother), 11–12

George, Mary (DLG's sister), 11

George, William (DLG's brother), 11–13, 30–1, 44, 163

George, William (DLG's father), 11

Germany: Agadir crisis, 87–8, 122, 125; air power, 303–4; annexation of Austria, 327; British declaration of war, 338; DLG's visit, 52, 57; DLG's visit to Hitler (1936), 301; Haldane mission (1912), 122; Hitler's rise to power, 272, 301, 302; invasion of Belgium (1914), 121, 124, 125, 126–8, (1940), 352; invasion of Czechoslovakia, 331; invasion of France, 357–8, 363; invasion of Poland, 338, 341; League of Nations withdrawal, 303; mobilization (1914), 124; naval spending, 106, 122–3; Rhineland invasion, 314; Soviet pact (1939), 338, 341; war with France, 124; war with Russia, 124; Windsors' tour, 324–5

Gibb, George, 205

Gilbert, Martin, 137, 161, 403

Gladstone, Herbert, first Viscount, 234, 242

Gladstone, William, 14–15, 16, 113, 378

Goebbels, Joseph, 343, 382

gold standard, 255–6, 260, 287

Gort, John Vereker, sixth Viscount, 343

Gough, Hubert, 116

Government of Ireland Act (1920), 221–2

Grand, Sarah, 73

Greece: campaign (1941), 380; First Balkan War, 123; Salonika expedition question, 137; Smyrna issue, 217, 233

Greenwood, Arthur, 361

Grey, Edward: Agadir crisis, 87; Balkan situation (1914), 117; defence issues, 88; General Strike, 258; German talks issue (1914), 123; Irish Home Rule policies, 73; Liberal leadership question, 45; on naval crisis, 55; relationship with Campbell-Bannerman, 35, 36; relationship with DLG, 53, 71, 251; relationship with WSC, 53, 64, 71, 140, 146, 151, 279; women's suffrage issue, 76, 80, 82, 83; WWI outbreak, 124, 126, 127, 132

Griffith, Arthur, 222

Grigg, Edward, 382, 384

Grigg, John, 130, 173, 315, 383, 402

Grigg, P. J., 382, 384, 405

Guest, Frederick, 148, 177–8, 179, 229, 248

Guest, Ivor, 63

Guilty Men, 285

Gwynne, H. A., 182

Haig, Douglas, 161, 167, 182, 184, 296

Haldane, R. B.: Asquith visit, 89–90; defence issues, 88, 89; German mission (1912), 122; Irish Home rule policies, 73; relationship with Campbell-Bannerman, 35, 36; relationship with DLG and WSC, 51–2, 53, 73–4, 91; Secretary of State for War, 46, 51, 90

Halifax, Edward Wood, third Viscount (earlier Lord Irwin): DLG's view of, 359, 372; Foreign Secretary, 327–8, 376; premiership question, 348–9, 352; press campaign against, 360; relationship with WSC, 360, 376; US ambassador, 377; Viceroy of India, 277, 282; War Cabinet, 339; war policy, 358, 368–9

Hankey, Adeline, 203

Hankey, Maurice Hankey, first Baron: advice to Chamberlain, 338; advice to DLG and WSC, 183; Chanak crisis, 234; Committee of Imperial Defence (CID), 89; comparison between DLG and WSC, 1–2; Dardanelles campaign, 137; on DLG at War Office, 166; on DLG's resignation, 236; DLG's *War Memoirs* publication, 296; efforts to persuade DLG to join government, 384; German breakthrough (1918), 185–6; on relationship between DLG and WSC, 205, 212–13; Versailles Treaty, 203; War Cabinet

(1939–40), 339, 384; War Cabinet Secretariat (1917), 173, 200; war strategy, 134–5; on WSC's Colonial Office appointment, 214; on WSC's Commons speech (1916), 162; on WSC's Russian policy, 206; WSC's *World Crisis* publication, 292–3

Harcourt, Lewis 'Lulu', 51, 64, 126

Harding, Warren G., 214

Hardinge, Charles Hardinge, first Baron, 215

Harington, Charles, 234

Harris, Percy, 339

Hawtrey, Ralph, 123

Headlam, Cuthbert, 323

Henderson, Arthur, 170

Henderson, Hubert, 263

Henry, Charles, 49

Henry, Julia, 49

Hess, Rudolf, 318

Hewins, W. A. S., 117

Hicks Beach, Michael, 29

Hill, Kathleen, 321, 345, 362

Hitler, Adolf: air power, 304; British appeasement policy, 7; British invasion plan, 374; Chamberlain's negotiations, 330–1; Danzig issue, 337; DLG's view of, 316–17, 322, 328–9, 363, 384–5; DLG's visit, 301, 317–18, 399, 400, 402; Jewish policies, 318; Munich agreement, 330; peace conference proposal (1939), 342; Polish position, 341; Rhineland remilitarization, 297; rise to power, 272, 301, 302; Sudetenland demands, 329, 330; view of WSC and DLG, 337; WSC's view of, 299, 316–17, 322

Hoare, Sir Samuel: Chancellor appointment question, 252; Foreign Secretary, 311, 312, 326; Italy policy, 311, 312; relationship with DLG and WSC, 285, 286; resignation, 312; Secretary of State for India, 285, 306–7; social life, 249; War Cabinet, 339; on WSC and Hore-Belisha, 344; WSC's attack on, 306–7

Hobhouse, Charles: on DLG and WSC, 52, 67, 120, 124, 132; naval expenditure policy, 104, 110

Holland, German invasion (1940), 352

Home Rule Bill, third (1912), 113–14

Hopwood, Sir Francis, 47–8, 112, 117

Horabin, J. L., 364

Hore-Belisha, Leslie, 307, 339, 343–4, 381, 384

Horne, Robert: appointment as Chancellor, 215, 216, 219; Baldwin's leadership, 247; relationship with DLG, 229, 275;

relationship with WSC, 242; view of WSC, 240, 241; WSC's intrigues against, 228
House, Edward M., 201
Hoyningen-Hühne, Baron von, 370–1
Hutchison, Robert, 279–80, 281

imperial preference, 42, 289
India: constitutional reform proposals, 306; Dominion status policy, 277; federal structure proposal, 281, 282; WSC's view, 280–3
India Bill, 305, 310
India Office, 219
Indian National Congress, 278, 281
industrial unrest, 72, 85–7, 90, 188, 257–9
Inflexible, HMS, 138
Inskip, Thomas, 315
Iraq, 219, 232
Ireland: civil war (1922–3), 224; civil war threat, 72; conscription (1918), 186; Easter Rising (1916), 164, 220; Home Rule issue, 65–6, 73, 83, 112–13; in 1918–22, 7, 195; Lord Lieutenancy, 14; Pettigo-Belleek incident (1922), 231–2; treaty (1921–2), 224, 237; War of Independence, 220–1
Irish Nationalists, 64, 73, 113, 115
Irish Republican Army (IRA), 220–1
Irish Unionists, 113–14, 115
Irish Volunteers, 114
Ironside, Edmund, 357
Irresistible, HMS, 138–9
Irwin, Lord, *see* Halifax, third Viscount
Isaacs, Godfrey, 94
Isaacs, Rufus, *see* Reading, first Marquess of
Italy: DLG on Caporetto, 339–40; invasion of Abyssinia, 272, 311–12, 315, 326; Mussolini's rise to power, 302; war with Britain (1940), 363

Japan: aggression, 302; end of war (1945), 394; invasion of Manchuria, 272; Singapore capture, 385
Jenkins, Roy, 119, 184
Jews, 8, 211, 219–20, 318–22
Johnson, Lyndon B., 7
Jones, Thomas: on Baldwin and DLG, 270, 309, 315; on Baldwin and WSC, 253, 307, 309; biography of DLG, 400, 407; Cabinet Secretariat, 200; on Churt and Chartwell, 232; on DLG's reluctance to join government, 372, 373; Hitler visit, 317; on relationship between DLG and WSC, 210,

278, 298, 315, 349; on WSC's influence, 200, 256; on WSC's press support, 230–1
Joynson-Hicks, William, 40, 41, 49, 262
Justice, 52

Kennedy, John F., 7, 403
Kenney, Annie, 76
Kerensky, Alexander, 251
Keyes, Sir Roger, 350
Keynes, John Maynard, 204, 256, 260, 263, 270
King, Cecil: comparison between DLG and WSC, 405, 406; on DLG, 363, 378, 380–1, 385; press attacks on Chamberlain, 361–2; on WSC's view of DLG, 299
Kitchener, Herbert Kitchener, first Earl: attitude to Welsh, 132; conscription issue, 152, 155; Dardanelles campaign, 135, 137, 139, 175; death, 165; fact-finding mission, 155; munitions issue, 139, 143, 150; relationship with DLG, 142; relationship with Robertson, 167; Salonika expedition plan, 154; Secretary of State for War, 128; Sudan campaign, 19–20; temperance pledge, 141; WSC's criticisms of, 19–20
Kolchak, Alexander, 202, 205, 207, 294
Krassin, Leonid, 210

Labour Party: DLG's War Cabinet, 170; election (1918), 196; election (1922), 241; election (1923), 244–5; election (1924), 251; election (1929), 270; election (1945), 394; government collapse (1931), 283; Hands Off Russia campaign, 211; Liberal attitudes to, 242; rise of, 3; Soviet Union recognition, 250
Ladysmith, siege of, 20
land: campaign, 92, 102–3, 112; Land Ministry proposal, 103; taxes, 60
Lansbury, George, 341
Lascelles, Joan, 240
Laski, Harold, 393–4
Laurier, Wilfrid, 43
Lausanne, Treaty of (1923), 234
Laval, Pierre, 312
Law, Andrew Bonar: attempt to form government (1916), 169–70; background, 114; coalition with Liberals, 144–5; health, 215, 235, 242; Irish policy, 114; papers, 402; premiership, 236, 239; relationship with DLG, 6, 167–8, 171, 196–7, 207, 215, 216, 235, 236; relationship with WSC, 161; resignation as PM (1923), 101, 242; retires temporarily (1921), 215; social life, 86; tariff

Law, Andrew Bonar (*cont.*)
  policy, 243; view of WSC, 16, 171, 180–1, 192, 230, 292
Lawrence, T. E., 241, 295, 401
Layton, Walter, 184, 307–8, 338–9, 348, 362, 405
Le Bas, Hedley, 131
Le Matin, 95, 328
League of Nations, 293, 303, 311–12, 337
Lee, Arthur, 164, 167, 196
Léger, Alexis, 327–8
Lenin, V. I., 200, 210, 211
Lewis, J. H., 41, 53, 66, 72, 136, 154
Liberal Industrial Inquiry, 260
Liberal National Association, 287
Liberal Party: Boer War split, 21, 26; caretaker government (1945), 392–3; conscription policy, 103; coalition, 2, 143, 144–6, 148, 173, 227, 241; Davies leadership, 394; DLG's achievements, 238–9; electoral reform policy, 274; finances, 232; free trade issue, 27, 279–80; honours scandal, 232; government (1905), 31, 36; general election (1906), 41; general election (1910), 64, 113; general election (1929), 270, 274; general election (1945), 394; Independent Liberals, 213; Lords reform, 93; National Liberals, 241, 243, 247, 384, 393, 395; postwar relationship with Conservatives, 395, 396; reunification, 243; Sinclair leadership, 313, 394; split (Asquith/Coalition), 170, 196, 213; split (1931), 287–8; votes for women, 77, 84; WSC's career, 27, 32, 238
Liberal Unionists, 18
Liberty, 321
Licensing Bill (1904), 33
Licensing Bill (1908), 53, 58–9
Liddell, Guy, 381
Liddell Hart, Basil, 189, 385–6, 387
Lindemann, F. A., 141
Lister, Joseph, 2
Llanfrothen burial case, 18
Llanystumdwy, 12
Lloyd, George, first Baron, 273–4, 330
Lloyd, Richard (DLG's uncle), 11–12

LLOYD GEORGE, DAVID, Earl Lloyd-George of Dwyfor: birth, 2, 11; childhood, 12–13; education, 12–13, 14, 16; legal career, 15; elected to Commons (1890), 18; maiden speech, 18–19; view of Boer War, 20, 21–3; first meeting with WSC, 24–5; Birmingham visit, 25–6; President of Board of Trade, 35–6, 41, 45, 56–7; election campaign (1906), 39–40, 41; Chancellor of Exchequer, 43, 44, 46–7, 56–7, 65; daughter's death, 44; Henry affair rumours, 49; at Churchill wedding, 49–50; Army cuts campaign, 51–2; German visit, 52, 57; Dreadnoughts campaign, 54–5; National Insurance scheme, 57–8, 86, 92; 'People's Budget' (1909–10), 58–9, 60–2, 65, 67; election campaign (1910), 64; coalition proposal, 68–9; Churchill visit, 68–9; election campaign (Dec 1910), 70; women's suffrage issue, 78–84; Other Club, 85, 388; rail strike, 87; Agadir crisis, 87–8, 122; defence issues, 88–9; land campaign, 92, 102–3, 112; naval estimates (1912), 93; Marconi affair, 85, 94–8, 118, 129, 160, 163–4, 172, 181; naval estimates (1914), 104–13, 115, 406; Irish Home Rule, 112–17, 119; Budget (1914), 129; WWI policy, 121–2; WWI outbreak, 124–7; munitions issue, 133–4, 139, 149; war strategy, 134, 153–4, 380; temperance campaign, 141; coalition issue, 145–6; WSC's fall from grace, 146–9; Minister of Munitions, 149–50; conscription issue, 8, 150–1, 152, 154–5, 332; WSC's resignation, 156–7; Irish negotiations (1916), 164–5; War Office, 165–7; Asquith's resignation, 168–9; Prime Minister, 158, 170–1; War Cabinet, 173, 338, 346; war strategy, 174, 184–5; WSC appointment, 180–3; in France, 181; Beauvais conference, 186; general election question (1918), 190–1; general election (1918), 196–8; Paris peace conference, 198–9, 203–4; Russia policy, 200–3, 205, 209–12, 228, 230, 250–1, 294, 332; Turkish policy, 217–18, 233–4; war medals, 8, 207–9; WSC's intrigues against, 215–16; Middle East policy, 219–20, 232; Irish policy, 220–4, 231–2, 237, 294; resignation question, 227–8, 235; honours scandal, 232; resignation, 4, 236–7; election campaign (1922), 240; North American speaking tour (1923), 242–3; General Strike, 258–9, 261; illness (1927), 257; Yellow Book, 260–1, 307; parliamentary tactics, 274–6; birth of Frances Stevenson's daughter, 276–7; India policy, 277–8, 287, 306; view of National Government, 287, 300; illness (1931), 285; sixty-ninth birthday, 289–90; farming at Churt, 300; Italy policy, 302, 315, 326, 339–40; Germany policy, 302–4,

312, 314; New Deal programme, 307–8; Council of Action campaign, 310, 311, 313; Spanish Civil War, 312, 328; in Marrakesh, 313; view of Hitler, 317–18, 322, 325; visit to Hitler, 301, 317–18, 322, 328–9, 399, 400, 402; attitude to Jews, 318, 321; abdication crisis, 322–4; golden wedding anniversary (1938), 297–8, 327; WWII policy, 336, 341, 342–3, 368–9; premiership question (1940), 347–50; 1940 government proposals, 353–4; refusal of place in 1940 government, 336–7, 355–9; continuing question of government place, 359–63, 366–70, 374–5, 400; Undersecretaries' Plot, 364–6; question of 'Pétain' role, 368–73, 382–4, 387, 399; criticized for failure to take office, 373–4; US ambassador question, 376–8; wife's death, 378–9; criticisms of WSC's war leadership, 379–81, 384–5; marriage to Frances Stevenson, 101, 387–8; last visit to Commons, 388; last illness, 388–9; last conversation with WSC, 389–90; Earldom, 388–9, 399; death, 2, 4, 389, 391; WSC's tribute, 391; funeral, 392; papers, 399–400, 401; biographies, 400–2; statue in Commons, 408–10; centenary celebrations, 404

PERSON: appearance, 344–5, 346, 357, 363, 377, 387; background, 11–12, 38; character, 1–2, 120, 355; character compared to that of WSC, 1–2, 47, 75–6, 183, 222–3, 335, 391, 406; conversation style, 1–2, 75; egotism, 355; finances, 46, 94; home at Churt, *see* Churt; influence, 4, 92; letters, 8, 30–1, 44, 95; marriage, 17, 44, 100–1, 297–8; morals, 99–100, 188; oratory, 3, 9, 18–19, 74–5, 97, 257; relationship with Frances Stevenson, 98–102, 181; religion, 2, 13, 18; reputation, 6, 92, 160, 232, 241, 257, 301, 340–1, 346, 348–9, 399, 402, 403, 406; sexual indiscretions, 99–100, 179, 400; skills, 57, 87

SPEECHES: Commons maiden speech (1890), 18–19; Bangor (1900), 8, 22; Commons (1901), 22–3; Limehouse (1909), 62; Newcastle (1909), 62; influence on 1910 election results, 64; Mansion House (1911), 88, 91; Commons speech (Marconi affair 1913), 96–7; Bedford (1913), 103; Swindon (1913), 103; Huddersfield (1914), 116, 117; Queen's Hall (1914), 129–30; on conscription (1915), 150–1; Bristol (1918), 198; Guildhall (1920), 221; Bangor (1935), 307–8; Commons (1936), 315; Commons

(1938), 327; Commons (1939), 341, 342; Commons (1940), 350–1, 354–5; Commons (1941), 381–2

WRITINGS: journalism, 242, 318, 339, 346; *War Memoirs*, 171, 267–8, 291, 296–8, 313, 322, 334, 353, 403

Lloyd George, Gwilym (DLG's son): death, 402; on defence debate, 305; on DLG biography, 399–400; election (1931), 288; election defeat (1950), 396; election (1951), 397; Hitler visit, 317; political career, 285, 338, 385, 392–3, 394–5, 397; on relationship between DLG and WSC, 33–4; relationship with WSC, 376, 398; resignation (1931), 287; war service, 130

Lloyd George, Mair (DLG's daughter), 44, 100

Lloyd George, Margaret (Owen, DLG's wife): at Commons, 78, 351; daughter's death, 44, 100; death, 101, 378–9; on DLG's ambitions, 17; on DLG's schooling, 16; golden wedding anniversary, 297–8; in Marrakesh, 313; relationship with DLG, 44, 100–2, 124, 378; view of WSC, 68, 111

Lloyd George, Megan (DLG's daughter): death, 402; DLG's biography, 400; DLG's second marriage, 387; election (1931), 288; election defeat (1951), 397; Hitler visit, 317; Labour Party membership, 398; naval estimates story, 111; political career, 284, 285, 392, 393, 398; relationship with DLG, 350, 393; relationship with Frances, 387, 400

Lloyd George, Olwen (DLG's daughter), 132, 351

Lloyd George, Richard (DLG's son), 4, 130, 181, 400

Lloyd George, Robert (DLG's great-grandson), 5

Lloyd George Fund, 260, 268–9

Lockhart, Robert Bruce, 399

Londonderry, Charles Vane-Tempest-Stewart, seventh Marquess of, 304

Long, Walter: Colonial Secretary, 180; First Lord of Admiralty, 205; on 1918 election, 196–7; relationship with DLG, 150, 170, 204; view of WSC, 181, 204

Lords, House of: Budget passed (1910), 67; Conservative dominance, 41, 51; DLG's peerage, 388–9; DLG's speech against, 62; government struggle with (1909–11), 58; Irish Home Rule issue, 65–6; King's position, 63, 66, 69–70; Licensing Bill veto, 53–4, 58; Parliament Act (1911), 113;

Lords, House of (*cont.*)
　　reform policy, 67–8, 69–70, 72; rejection of
　　Budget (1909), 60–1, 63
Loreburn, Robert Reid, first Earl, 63, 83, 114
Lothian, Philip Kerr, eleventh Marquess of, 375,
　　376
Low, Toby, 399
Ludendorff offensive (1918), 185
Lyttelton, Alfred, 36

McCurdy, Charles, 229
MacDonald, Malcolm, 314
MacDonald, Ramsay: National Government
　　(1931), 272, 283, 285; Prime Minister (1924),
　　244–5; Prime Minister (1929), 270, 284;
　　relationship with Baldwin, 267, 269, 285;
　　relationship with DLG and WSC, 286,
　　307–8, 309; retirement, 309; unemployment
　　policy, 279, 283, 284
McKenna, Reginald: character, 75–6, 136;
　　defence issues, 54, 87, 88–9; First Lord of the
　　Admiralty, 54, 90; Fisher's resignation, 144;
　　Home Secretary, 89, 90–1; Licensing Bill, 33;
　　naval estimates (1914) issue, 104, 110;
　　relationship with DLG, 35, 140; relationship
　　with WSC, 140; Treasury post, 36; War
　　Committee, 156; WWI outbreak, 127
Maclay, Sir Joseph, 173, 356
Maclean, Donald, 275
Macmillan, Harold, 305, 364–5, 397, 398
MacMillan, Margaret, 211
Maisky, Ivan, 331–2
Manchester, DLG's birth, 11
Manchester Guardian, 17, 36, 80, 88, 216, 343,
　　400
Manchester North-West: constituency, 32; by-
　　election (1908), 11; general election (1906),
　　40–1; by-election (1907), 48–9
Marconi affair, 94–8; effect on DLG's
　　reputation, 129; influence on relationship
　　between DLG and WSC, 118, 160, 163–4,
　　172, 181: Other Club, 85
Marder, Arthur, 118
Margalit, Avishai, 408
Margesson, David, 339
Marlborough, Charles Spencer-Churchill, ninth
　　Duke of (WSC's cousin), 53, 61, 102
Marlborough, Lady Frances Vane, Duchess of
　　(WSC's grandmother), 13
Marlborough, John Spencer-Churchill, seventh
　　Duke of (WSC's grandfather), 13
Marlowe, Thomas, 217
Marrakesh, 313

Martin, Bernd, 368–9
Martin, Kingsley, 405
Marx, Karl, 299
Mary, Queen, 122
Massingham, H. W., 23–4, 140, 176
Masterman, Charles, 57, 65, 92, 131
Masterman, Lucy: on Carr-Gomm divorce case,
　　8, 99; on DLG and WSC, 57, 59, 67, 69,
　　92; on DLG's oratory, 97; on Margaret LG's
　　dislike of WSC, 68; on rail strike, 87; social
　　life, 65
Masterton-Smith, James, 107
Maurice, Sir Frederick, 188
Maxse, Leo, 95
Maxton, James, 276
May Committee/Report, 283, 285
Mbeki, Thabo, 7
Menzies, Robert, 381
Merchant Shipping Act (1906), 45
Mesopotamia, 219
Middle East, 7, 219–20, 232
Military Training Bill, 333
Mill, John Stuart, 27
Milner, Alfred, first Viscount, 20, 189, 207
Milner, Lady, 385
miners: Coal Bill (1929–30), 278–9; General
　　Strike (1926), 257–8; strike (1910), 85–6;
　　strike (1912), 92
Miners Federation, 92
minimum wage, 92, 103
Montagu, Edwin: on Balfour's influence, 140;
　　on DLG and WSC, 190–2, 226; on DLG's
　　Budget, 59; on free trade policy, 50;
　　marriage, 145; munitions issue, 139;
　　Munitions Minister, 165; Secretary of State
　　for India, 180; temperance issue, 141; on
　　war anxieties, 167; on WSC's speeches, 3,
　　177–8, 179
Montenegro, First Balkan War, 123
Montgomery, Bernard, 386
Moran, Charles Wilson, first Baron, 392, 401,
　　403
Morgan, Kenneth O., 198, 214
Morley, John, 45–6, 117, 121, 124, 126
Morning Post, 20, 182
Morrison, Herbert, 350
Mosley, Cynthia, 284
Mosley, Diana, 254
Mosley, Oswald (Tom), 283–4, 285, 286–7, 288
Mowat, Sir Francis, 27
Munich Agreement (1938), 330, 331, 342
Munitions, Ministry of, 28, 149–50, 153, 170,
　　180, 183–4

Munitions Committee, 149
Munitions Council, 184
Murray, Alexander, *see* Elibank
Murray, Gideon, 245, 248
Mussolini, Benito, 7, 272, 302, 311–12, 406
Mustafa Kemal, 217–18, 233, 234

Narvik expedition (1940), 347
Nation, The, 140, 176, 278
National Defence Contribution (NDC), 325
National Government, 7, 272, 283–7, 288, 300, 312–13
National Health Service, 396
National Insurance, 28, 57–8, 86, 92
National Investment Board (NIB), 260–1
National Liberal Club, 97, 243–4
National Review, 95
National Union of Women's Suffrage Societies (NUWSS), 76, 77
Naylor, R. A., 39
Nemon, Oscar, 409
Neue Freie Presse, 52
New Commonwealth Society, 329
New Party, 284, 288
New Statesman, 242, 405
News Chronicle, 296, 307, 318, 329, 348–9, 361, 362
Nicholson, Otho, 245, 246
Nicolson, Harold: on DLG's attitude to WWII, 341; Maisky meeting, 332; on Mosley and WSC, 283–4, 286–7; on Norway campaign, 347; on relationship between DLG and WSC, 335, 337, 381–2, 387
Nimptsch, Uli, 409
Nivelle, Robert, 174
Norman, R. C., 301
Normandy landings (1944), 388
North Africa, 380
North Wales Observer, 22
Northcliffe, Alfred Harmsworth, first Viscount: death, 204; Marconi affair, 96; Other Club, 85; press campaign for DLG, 140, 154–5; relationship with DLG, 140, 148, 166–7, 171, 204; relationship with WSC, 30, 165, 230–1; report on DLG and WSC, 217; USA mission, 180
Northcote, Stafford, 25
Norwegian campaign (1940), 346–7, 349–51, 354, 381

Observer, 309
Ocean, HMS, 138–9

Oldham: by-election (1899), 20; constituency party, 30; general election (1900), 21
Ollivant, Alfred, 126
Omdurman, Battle of (1898), 19, 133
Other Club, 85, 127, 309, 330, 388, 404
Ottawa conference (1932), 289
Owen, Frank, 383, 402
Owen, Goronwy, 288

Packer, Ian, 102
Palestine, 219–20
Pall Mall Gazette, 34
Pankhurst, Christabel, 76, 79, 80
Pankhurst, Sylvia, 40, 79, 80
Pannell, Charles, 410
Panther, gunboat, 87
Paris Peace Conference (1919), 15–16, 101, 198–9, 203–4
Parliament Act (1911), 113
Patents and Designs Act (1907), 45
Pease, J. A., 53, 92, 94, 104, 126, 151
Peel, Robert, 62
pensions, 39–40, 50–1
People, 100, 247, 248
Pétain, Philippe, 363–4, 367, 369, 372–3, 376, 382–3
Phipps, Eric, 317, 327–9
Picture Post, 346
Pitt, William (the Younger), 403
Plunkett, Joseph, 164
Poland: British guarantee, 331–2; Danzig crisis, 337–8; German invasion, 338, 341
Pollard, A.F., 17
Port of London Authority, 45
Prior, Robin, 294
protectionism, 242–3, 279–80, 289
Punch, 34, 60

railways, 56–7; strike (1911), 86–7
Reading, Rufus Isaacs, first Marquess of: on Carr-Gomm divorce, 99; diary, 147–8; Marconi affair, 94–5, 97, 163; on naval estimates, 104; on relationship between DLG and WSC, 148, 152, 165; social life, 131; Viceroy of India, 281
Reagan, Ronald, 7
Redmond, John, 73, 114, 115, 117, 164–5
Reform Act (1884), 14–15
Relugas Compact, 35
Rendel, Stuart, first Baron, 73
Repington, Charles Court, 143, 148
Review of Reviews, 302
Reynaud, Paul, 357, 363, 382

Reynolds, David, 305, 403
Rhondda Valley, miners (1910), 85–6, 118, 396
Ribbentrop, Joachim von, 75, 317–18, 370–1
Riddell, George: conversations with DLG, 50, 71, 81, 146–7, 162, 165, 171–2, 200, 210; conversations with WSC, 147, 172, 199, 216; go-between role, 172, 175; on Irish policy, 115; knowledge of DLG–Frances relationship, 101; on naval estimates debate, 107; Other Club, 127; on relationship between DLG and WSC, 91, 104, 109, 115, 131–2, 213–14; on WSC, 90
Rintala, Marvin, 5
Robertson, William, 167, 185
Robinson, Joseph, 232
Rommel, Erwin, 380
Roosevelt, Franklin D., 9, 272, 342, 369, 376
Rosebery, Albert Edward Primrose, sixth Earl, 393
Rosebery, Archibald Primrose, fifth Earl, 29, 30, 34, 299
Rothermere, Harold Harmsworth, first Viscount: Baldwin's denunciation, 283; on coalition manifesto, 197; Randolph's career, 314; relationship with WSC, 180, 230, 246; support for Liberal proposals, 263
Rowlands, Archibald, 407
Rowntree, Seebohm, 261
Royal Irish Constabulary (RIC), 220–1
Royal Military Academy, Sandhurst, 19
Royal Navy: Belfast presence, 116; Committee of Imperial Defence presentation, 88–9; Dreadnoughts campaign (1908–9), 54–5; mobilization (1914), 126; naval estimates (1912), 93; naval estimates (1914), 17, 93, 104–13
Runciman, Walter, 104, 110, 126
Russell, Bertrand, 211
Russia: Bolsheviks, 195, 200–3, 206, 210–11, 250; civil war, 7; famine, 228; German declaration of war, 124; Whites, 201, 202, 205, 209–10; *see also* Soviet Union
Russo-Polish war, 211

Saddam Hussein, 7
Salisbury, James Gascoyne-Cecil, fourth Marquess of, 185, 315, 365
Salisbury, Robert Cecil, third Marquess of, 16, 19, 26, 250
Salonika: Allied occupation, 293, 294; expedition proposal, 134, 135, 137, 154
Salter, Arthur, 364

Samuel, Herbert, 95, 104, 141, 285, 287–9, 313
Sarajevo, 117
Sassoon, Philip, 212, 214, 227, 230, 241
Scott, C. P.: conversation with Clementine, 182; conversations with DLG, 80, 81, 107, 108, 161–2, 235; conversations with WSC, 165, 168, 175, 176; on naval estimates debate, 112; on relationship between DLG and WSC, 110, 132, 153; relationship with DLG, 88, 164, 260; relationship with WSC, 88, 164
Scrymgeour, Edwin, 241
Secret Sessions of Commons: (1917), 177–8; (1940), 363, 367
Seely, Jack, 116, 117, 151, 206
Serbia: Austrian ultimatum, 117–18, 123; Austro-Hungarian declaration of war, 124; First Balkan War, 123
Sèvres, Treaty of (1919), 217, 233
Sharp, Clifford, 242
Shaw, Thomas, 35
Sheean, Vincent, 325
Shinwell, Emanuel, 182, 384, 385
Silva, Ricardo do Espírito Santo, 370–1
Simon, Sir John: DLG's appeal to, 126; free trade issue, 279–80; Liberal Nationals, 287; National Government, 285; naval estimates issue, 110; relationship with DLG, 307; resignation, 159; Royal Commission on India, 277; on Secret Session, 178; War Cabinet, 339
Simpson, Wallis, *see* Windsor, Duchess of
Sinclair, Archibald: advice to WSC, 295; Air Secretary, 361; conscription issue, 333; defence issues, 316; dinner, 283–4; Liberal Chief Whip, 281; Liberal leadership, 313, 394; message to DLG, 243; MP, 251, 281; resignation, 289; Secretary of State for Scotland, 288; view of DLG, 349; on War Cabinet, 339; WSC's letters, 148, 152, 164, 171, 173, 233, 281, 288–9
Singapore, fall of (1942), 385
Sinn Féin, 220, 221, 222, 224
Smith, Adam, 27
Smith, F. E., *see* Birkenhead first Earl of
Smuts, J. C., 180, 342, 386–7, 388
Snow, C. P., 405, 406–7
Snowden, Philip, 269, 283
Somme offensive (1916), 167, 174
South Africa, 20–1, 39
Soviet Union: Baltic States claim, 386; invasion of Poland, 341; Nazi pact (1939), 338, 341; recognition issue, 230–1, 250; second front

demand, 386; treaties, 250; war with
Germany (1941), 385; WSC's postwar
policies, 397; *see also* Russia
Spanish civil war, 272, 312, 328
Spender, J. A., 75, 316
Spiers, Louis, 159
Stalin, Joseph, 211, 341
Stanley, Edward, 254
Stanley, Venetia, 105, 131, 140, 145
Steed, Henry Wickham, 302
Stern, Sir Albert, 189–90
Stevenson, Frances (later Lloyd George): affair
with Tweed, 277; on Antwerp, 132; birth of
daughter, 276–7; on conscription issue, 155,
164; on Council of Action campaign, 311;
on Dardanelles, 154; death, 402; diary, 98,
131–2, 389, 401; DLG's biographies, 400,
401; on DLG's Commons speech (1936),
315; DLG's death, 389; on DLG's defeatism,
357; DLG's papers, 399–400, 401; on
DLG's premiership, 170; DLG's statue,
409–10; on DLG's war policy, 126; on
Fisher resignation, 144; general election
(1918), 197; general election (1955), 398;
on India policy, 278; on Irish policy, 222;
in Marrakesh, 313; marriage to DLG, 101,
387–8; memoirs, 98, 126, 402; on question
of DLG's place in wartime government, 343,
355, 366–7, 369, 372, 373–4; on
relationship between DLG and WSC,
141–2, 152, 153, 179, 213, 216, 227, 254–5,
304; relationship with DLG, 98, 100–2; sale
of DLG papers, 401; on WSC's ambitions,
228; WSC's attitude to, 101–2; on WSC's
departure from Admiralty, 146; on WSC's
French relations, 132–3; on WSC's Russian
policy, 200
Stevenson, Jennifer, 276–7, 372
Strachey, John St Loe, 60
Strakosch, Sir Henry, 314
Strand Magazine, 316, 318, 321
Sudan, 19–20
Sudetenland, 329, 330
Suez Canal, 273, 311
suffragettes, 40, 76–84
Sunday Dispatch, 321, 345
Sunday Express, 339, 341
Sunday Pictorial, 343, 361
Sunday Times, 266
Swinton, Philip Cunliffe-Lister (earlier Lloyd-
Greame), first Earl of, 183
Sydenham of Combe, George Clarke, first
Baron, 293

Sylvester, A. J.: on air power, 304; diary, 290;
diary publication, 402; on DLG's advice to
WSC, 334; on DLG's behaviour, 327;
DLG's death, 389; on DLG's defeatism,
357; on DLG's marriage, 297–8; on DLG's
postbag, 343; on George V's death, 314;
Hitler visit, 317, 322; on May Report, 285;
on question of DLG's place in wartime
government, 347, 355, 356–7, 358, 359,
362, 369, 373, 378; *The Real Lloyd George*,
400–1; on relationship between DLG and
WSC, 254, 290, 313, 332–3, 372, 383;
relationship with DLG's widow, 400; on
The World Crisis, 295; on WSC in
Commons, 342

tanks, 2, 188–9
tariff reform, 27, 42
Taylor, A. J. P., 402
temperance, 18, 30, 141
Thatcher, Margaret, 7
Thomas, Ivor, 329
Thomson, Malcolm, 401
Thornton Butterworth, 291
Tilden, Philip, 232
Times, The, 26, 42, 51, 52, 96, 143, 148, 221,
235, 244, 264, 269, 291, 309, 315
Tirpitz, Alfred von, 135
Tobruk, fall of (1942), 385
Tonypandy, 85, 396
Trades Disputes Bill, 31–2
Trades Union Congress (TUC), 211, 362
Transjordan, 219
Tribune, 374
Trondheim expedition (1940), 347, 351
Trotsky, Leon, 200, 211
Tryon, G. C., 301
Tudor, Henry, 185
Turkey: Caucasus offensive, 135; Chanak crisis,
233–4; First Balkan War, 123; Smyrna issue,
217–18, 233; WWI entry, 132
Tweed, Thomas, 277, 343
Tweedsmuir, John Buchan, first Baron, 324

Ulster, 112, 113–14, 119, 165
Ulster Volunteer Force (UVF), 114
Undersecretaries' Plot, 364–6
unemployment: Baldwin's policy, 242; DLG's
policy, 7, 261–2, 265, 268, 270, 275–6, 279;
Liberal Industrial Inquiry, 260;
MacDonald's plan, 279; public works policy,
261–2; relief, 40; rise, 272; WSC's approach,
7, 268–9, 275–6

Unionist War Committee, 185
United States of America: New Deal, 272; Wall
    Street Crash, 272, 276; WWII entry (1941),
    385
USSR, *see* Soviet Union

Verdun, Battle of (1916), 363
Versailles, Treaty of (1919), 198, 203–4, 303,
    337, 354
Von Donop, Stanley, 139

Wall Street Crash, 272, 276
War Committee, 156, 157
War Council, 139–40, 156
War Office: DLG's position, 165–7; Hore-
    Belisha's resignation, 343–4; Kitchener's
    position, 128, 133, 155; munitions issue,
    133–4, 149, 188; Russian policy, 202;
    WSC's position, 197–8, 214, 217, 218–19
Waterhouse, Charles, 365
Waugh, Evelyn, 336
We Can Conquer Unemployment, 261–2, 263
Webb, Beatrice, 51, 56, 71, 74, 242, 243
Weekly Despatch, 247
Weizmann, Chaim, 220
welfare reforms, 21, 72
Wells, H. G., 38, 56, 102
West Leicester constituency, 243, 244
Westminster (Abbey Division) constituency,
    245–6
Whitley, J. H., 300
Wigram, Clive, 208
Wilhelm II, Kaiser, 87

Williams, W. Llewelyn, 78
Wilson, Arthur, 89
Wilson, Harold, 409–10
Wilson, Henry: Agadir crisis, 125; Committee of
    Imperial Defence, 88–9; on DLG and
    military situation, 126; Downing St dinner,
    193; Irish policy, 221; on relationship
    between DLG and WSC, 201, 210, 214,
    217; Versailles Treaty, 203; war medals
    issue, 208; WSC in France, 186
Wilson, H. W., 204
Wilson, Woodrow, 173, 199, 203
Windsor, Duchess of (earlier Wallis Simpson),
    322–4, 370–1
Windsor, Duke of (earlier Edward VIII), 322–5,
    370–2
Winterton, Edward Turnour, sixth Earl, 384
women, votes for, 40, 72, 76–84
Women's Social and Political Union (WSPU),
    76, 77, 79, 81
Wood, Kingsley, 307, 339
Woolton, Frederick Marquis, Baron, 395, 396
Woolton-Teviot pact (1947), 395
Workers' Weekly, 251
Worthington-Evans, Laming, 215, 234, 275, 277
Wrangel, Peter, 210

Young, Edward Hilton, 241–2
Young, Francis Brett, 373
Younger, Sir George, 180, 227
Ypres, Third Battle of (Passchendaele), 174, 184

Zinoviev letter, 251